Family Policy

GOVERNMENT AND FAMILIES
IN FOURTEEN COUNTRIES

Family Policy

GOVERNMENT AND FAMILIES IN FOURTEEN COUNTRIES

**Sheila B. Kamerman
and Alfred J. Kahn,
editors**

Columbia University Press • New York

Library of Congress Cataloging in Publication Data
Main entry under title:
Family policy.
Includes bibliographical references and index.
1. Family policy.   I. Kamerman, Sheila B., 1928–
II. Kahn, Alfred J., 1919–
HQ518.F34   301.42   78-18015
ISBN 0-231-04464-X

Columbia University Press
New York   Guildford, Surrey
Copyright © 1978 Columbia University Press
All rights reserved
Printed in the United States of America
10 9 8 7 6 5 4 3 2

From S.B.K.: to my husband, Morton Kamerman

From A.J.K.: to my sister, Lillian K. Cieciura

Each a unique model of family support

Preface

OUR EXPLORATION OF family policy in other countries was launched in order to stimulate discussion in the United States. Inevitably, there will be questions asked as to: the selection of countries included here and those omitted; the way in which countries are classified; the order in which the articles are presented; the authors and the perspectives they represent.

Our previous international research had convinced us that the experiences of relatively comparable countries are most useful for cross-national policy learning. Obviously, all contrasts stimulate and challenge, but in policy development the questions to be faced and the choices to be made are more demanding. If the objective is the sharing of experience about social policy, countries which are relatively similar (despite some range) in their industrialization–urbanization and their demographic patterns learn most directly and immediately from one another.

We visited sixteen countries in the process of identifying and recruiting authors. Nonetheless, other countries might have been included but for budget and time constraints. Since our particular focus was family policy, our first selections were those countries having an explicit family policy: countries where the term is widely used and there is some agreement as to its meaning. This group was supplemented by several countries with a growing interest in family policy, although there might be less clear implementation in the public policy arena, narrower scope to the action, or less definition and use. Finally, we decided to include a few countries in which the idea of "family policy" was not yet acceptable (and indeed often rejected) but where we were able to identify scholars who were interested in experimenting as we were with a policy analysis exercise by exploring family policy in their countries.

The final selection is, in part, serendipitous. Although there is no country we would eliminate, there are several we would have included but a variety of circumstances did not permit. Without question, it is an interesting group of countries and, we believe, a stimulating collection of papers.

The order of presentation is designed to underscore alternative perspectives on family policy as well as its different status among the countries. Thus the country papers are organized into three sections:

1. Countries with an explicit, comprehensive family policy: France, Czechoslovakia, Hungary, Norway, Sweden
2. Countries with an explicit but more narrowly focused family policy, where the term is usually used to describe a specific policy field: Austria, the Federal Republic of Germany, Poland, Finland, Denmark
3. Countries without any explicit family policy and where the notion of such a policy is rejected: the United Kingdom, Canada, Israel, the United States.

Each cluster of papers, however, includes very different perspectives because of country differences as well as the distinctive viewpoints of individual authors. Not only are there personal assessments involved but, by deliberate choice, a variety of disciplines is also represented. We doubt that any readers or all authors would classify each paper as we have. In any case, the ''section'' boundaries clearly are somewhat permeable.

When viewed as a whole, the collection offers an unusual multidisciplinary assessment of family policy, reflecting the perspectives of economics, sociology, psychology, medicine, social work, political science, public administration. Obviously, the conclusions of each paper are those of the individual authors; each country's experience might be assessed somewhat differently by someone else. Perhaps of equal importance, it should be stated that the interpretation and conclusions in the introductory essay and the U.S. chapter as well as in the concluding analysis are our own. We drew extensively on our interviews in each country, on our reading of the papers, and on the formal as well as informal comments of participants at the International Working Party on Family Policy, the conference we organized and directed, where these papers were first presented.[1] The final responsibility for the ideas and themes we highlight, the interpretations we make, and the conclusions we reach are our own.

None of these papers would have been written, nor could the conference at which they were originally discussed have been held, without support of our sponsors, the Carnegie Corporation, the Office of Child Development (Department of Health, Education, and Welfare, hereafter referred to as

---

[1] Arden House, Columbia University, Harriman, N.Y., April 17–21, 1977.

HEW), and the Social and Rehabilitation Service (HEW). We are particularly grateful to Mrs. Barbara Finberg, the program officer at Carnegie who was among the earliest to offer support for this endeavor, and to Saul Rosoff, Edith Grotberg, David Smith, Richard Shute, and Dorothy Lally, the responsible HEW officials and project officers, for their timely and enthusiastic backing. In addition, research centers and government agencies in several countries supported the conference participation and paper preparation by a number of the authors, thus permitting somewhat broader coverage than the grant resources permitted. We wish particularly to thank the Research Institute for Labor and Social Affairs (Prague), the Danish National Institute of Social Research (Copenhagen), Väestölitto (Helsinki), and the Institute for Social Research (Oslo), as well as the scientific bodies which provided travel resources for several European participants.

Our efforts to learn about family policy in these countries and to recruit authors were facilitated by the remarkable cooperation of government officials and research center scholars in all these, as well as in other, countries. We also had helpful guidance in Geneva from: the United Nations, Europe; the International Labor Office; and the International Social Security Association. The names of the particular individuals who assisted us are too numerous to mention; that does not mean that we do not recognize our debt and appreciate the help given.

The logistics of manuscript preparation would have been impossible without the responsible work of Susan Cantor assisted by Eleanor Mefford. Dorothy M. Swart was our exacting and indispensable editor.

Sheila B. Kamerman
Alfred J. Kahn
New York, 1978

Contents

Contents

Family Policy

GOVERNMENT AND FAMILIES IN FOURTEEN COUNTRIES

FAMILIES AND THE IDEA
OF FAMILY POLICY

RECENT DEVELOPMENTS in the United States, Canada, and Europe confirm that the family continues to be at center stage. Interest in family policy and its potential development as a field or as offering a criterion to guide public action also is clearly growing. Whether or not the two are directly related, and whether or not there is a natural progression from concern with the family to interest in family policy, is not yet clear. Nor is there consensus on exactly what is happening to the family in the industrialized world, how family change should be regarded, or what is meant by family policy. All this, then, is the focus of the present volume.

Despite an extensive history in Europe, the term "family policy" received only limited use in the U.S. until the Carter-Mondale administration began to popularize the expression as part of a general surge of interest in the family.[1] In 1973, Vice-President Walter Mondale, then Senator, chaired a series of hearings on the American family at which a number of experts in different fields testified to the importance of the family in American society and expressed concern about the social changes affecting the family or reflected in the family.[2] Several suggested the need for "a national family policy" as a more deliberate expression of society's acknowledgment of the importance of the family and of concern with what was happening to and in

---

[1] See, for example, the campaign speech by Jimmy Carter in New Hampshire, August 3, 1976, and the position paper on the family submitted at President Carter's request by Joseph Califano, Secretary of Health, Education, and Welfare.

[2] U.S. Senate, Subcommittee on Children and Youth, *American Families: Trends and Pressures* (Washington, D.C.: Government Printing Office, 1974).

the family.[3] Some also recommended development of something called a "family impact statement," implying something similar to the kind of statement and process mandated by federal legislation for proposed policies and programs affecting the environment.[4] None of these proposals provided specific details as to: (a) the content of a national family policy; (b) what a family impact statement would look like; (c) how either could be developed or implemented in a pluralistic society in which the ethic supports—and idealizes—individualism and denies any role to government vis-à-vis the family. Nor did any of the experts fully clarify just how "the family" was to be defined for these social purposes, although some did suggest "all types of families" without greater specificity.

At the same time, and in some instances even earlier, others, who had been exposed to the European experience and to the extensive use of the term as well as the variety of applications in different countries, were also writing about family policy.[5] The discussions ranged from clarifying why Americans rejected the concept to suggesting possible advantages in developing a family policy—or at least experimenting with its use as a criterion to be used in developing social policy, along with such other criteria as social justice, equality, environmental protection. Except for brief illustrations of what might be included or how the concept could be applied, none of these writers provided any comprehensive plan of action or policy focus. Some possible dangers inherent in the development of a family policy were pointed out, however; for example, reference was made to the hazards of a narrow and inflexible definition of "family" or a moralistic and rigid perspective on what is "good" or "bad" for the family.[6] Regardless, exploration and experimentation with use of the concept were urged.

[3] See, for example, the testimony of Urie Bronfenbrenner, Margaret Mead, Andrew Billingsley, Edward Zigler. *Ibid.*

[4] For discussion of this and some of the issues surrounding the development of a family impact statement, see Sheila B. Kamerman, *Developing a Family Impact Statement* (New York: Foundation for Child Development, 1976).

[5] See, for example, *Journal of Marriage and the Family,* Special Issue: "Government Programs and the Family," Vol. XXIX, No. 1 (1967); Daniel Patrick Moynihan, Foreword to Alva Myrdal, *Nation and Family* (Cambridge, Mass.: M.I.T. Press, 1968); Alvin Schorr, *Explorations in Social Policy* (New York: Basic Books, Inc., 1968), pp. 143–63; Ellen Winston, "A National Policy on the Family," *Public Welfare,* XXVII (1969), 54–55.

[6] Sheila B. Kamerman and Alfred J. Kahn, "Explorations in Family Policy," *Social Work,* XX (1976), 181–86; Sheila B. Kamerman, "Public Policy and the Family: a New Strategy for Women as Wives and Mothers," in Jane Roberts Chapman and Margaret Gates, eds., *Women into Wives* (Beverly Hills, Calif.: Sage Publications, 1977), pp. 195–214.

The Vocabulary of Family Policy

To facilitate discussion, we developed a preliminary conceptualization in which we reviewed and analyzed how the term "family policy" could be defined and how it was used in the literature and in reports and documents from several countries.[7] In effect, we tried to launch a discussion by suggesting a family policy "vocabulary."

We began by stating that family policy means everything that government does to and for the family. We suggested three distinctions within family policy:

1. *Explicit family policy* with its two subcategories:
   (*a*) specific programs and policies designed to achieve specified, explicit goals regarding the family; (*b*) programs and policies which deliberately do things to and for the family, but for which there are no agreed-upon over-all goals regarding the family[8]
2. *Implicit family policy:* governmental actions and policies not specifically or primarily addressed to the family, but which have indirect consequences.

More specifically, we defined family policy as referring to deliberate actions taken toward the family, such as day care, child welfare, family counseling, family planning, income maintenance, some tax benefits, and some housing policies. Here the family is clearly the object of such governmental policies. In contrast, implicit family policy includes the incidental, indirect, or unanticipated consequences of policies designed to accomplish very different objectives: for example, industrial locations, decisions about road building, trade and tariff regulations, immigration policy.

We pointed out that the purposes of family policy may be manifest ("to provide for optimum child development") or latent (to encourage women to enter the labor force). Consequences may be intended or unintended, direct or indirect, mutually consistent or inconsistent. Family policy is concerned both with the effects on the family of all types of activities and with the efforts to use "family well-being" as an objective or as a source of goals and

---

[7] Both articles (*ibid.*) provide illustrations of how the concept could be applied to existing U.S. policies.

[8] Definitions inevitably oversimplify. "Explicit" and "implicit" are relative terms as are "comprehensive" and "fragmented." France has an extensive explicit family policy which is not completely coherent, according to Questiaux and Fournier. Even where the actions on the family are clear, there may be differing views as to which objectives are being served.

standards in developing public policy. Thus family policy may be both a field of activity and a perspective.

In addition to these distinctions, we noted the importance in family policy analysis of differentiating the interests of the family as a unit from those of particular roles and statuses within the family (father, mother, child), and the complexity and tension inherent in implementing such distinctions.

We recognize that in defining the term "implicit family policy" this broadly, all government policies can be defined as "family policy," and a valid question arises as to the distinction between family policy and social policy broadly defined. We will return to this point when we discuss alternative definitions of family policy. However, it is our contention that raising the issue of implicit family policies in multiple-policy domains may serve to underscore the pervasiveness of government activity with regard to the family in those societies which deny having any family policy at all. It remains to be seen whether sensitizing discussants in such countries to the unanticipated effects of policies on families can generate more deliberate injection of family concerns into policy areas clearly directed at families and family members.

Varying with political and social systems, family policies may be uniform (even monolithic), or pluralistic and competing. Despite some fears to that effect, family policy does not per se preclude diversity.

Family policy is certainly not a new concept. It was employed, first, in Europe in the context of income redistribution policies favoring large families (e.g., family allowances or demogrants, income tax policies) and second, in relation to population policy and concerns about long-term demographic projections. Both of these orientations to family policy continue, as will be seen in the articles on France, Czechoslovakia, Finland, and Hungary. Of particular interest is the fact that extensive use of family policy measures for these purposes suggests that such policies may be effective in redistributing income but probably provide no incentive for increased fertility, other than a short-term calendar effect.[9]

A third use of the family policy concept has been to describe public policies providing supportive and substitute care for dependent and/or inadequate family members (orphans, the handicapped, the aged, the poor, and

[9] That is, couples may have a first child sooner and a second child more closely after, but do not seem impelled to have a third or subsequent child unless at the same time that incentives for having children are increased, rigid, antiabortion measures are also employed. Family spacing may be affected, but family size seems to be more a consequence of the general economy, unemployment, standard of living, broad cultural and social forces, than a response to simple incentives or disincentives.

the homeless). An extension of this practice is the broader use of the concept in recent years to cover the concern of industrialized societies with preventing dependency and other social problems, generally, and with providing supportive and helping services to average, ordinary families faced with the growing complexities and stresses of daily living.[10] Almost all the articles included here take account of this view of family policy, although it is more central to the discussion in some (United Kingdom, U.S., Canada) than in others.

More recently, the concept of family policy has been employed in two other contexts. Some experts, recognizing that helping the family may be the most effective way to improve the conditions of children's lives, have begun to use the concept as a way to think about public policies affecting children.[11] Vedel-Petersen, writing about Denmark, provides a particularly interesting example of this approach. Finally, in some countries and among some people, the whole field of social policy for women has come to be defined as a major component of family policy. This field encompasses, among others, such issues as: social insurance benefits for working mothers or housewives; child care programs and social welfare benefits for child care; a wide range of supportive services for working mothers; changes in income tax and Social Security treatment of women generally; part-time and flexitime employment. In one way or another, every paper in this volume underscores the centrality of women's policy to family policy. It is accented in the papers from Sweden, Norway, and Poland and employed as a major analytic perspective by the Israeli contributors.

In the sense discussed thus far, *family policy may be defined as a field* in which certain objectives regarding the family are established (e.g., large families, healthier children, less financial burden attached to raising children, more equality for women, well-cared-for children, and so forth), and various policies and measures are developed to achieve these goals. As a "field," family policy has parameters which include population policy and family planning, cash and in-kind transfer payments, employment, housing, nutrition, health policies. Personal social services, child care, child development, and the whole field of social policy for women have all been defined by some analysts, at least, as part of this field. Illustrating one such ap-

---

[10] See Alfred J. Kahn and Sheila B. Kamerman, *Not for the Poor Alone* (Philadelphia: Temple University Press, 1975).

[11] For some discussion of this in the U.S., see Kenneth Keniston and the Carnegie Council on Children, *All Our Children: the American Family under Pressure* (New York: Harcourt Brace Jovanovich, 1977).

proach for Denmark, Vedel-Petersen describes family policy as "measures in support of families with children."

An alternative definition of family policy is that it is *an instrument*. According to this definition, societies may identify goals which need not have direct relevance to the family but require some sort of behavior on the part of the family or family members for goal attainment. Family policy then becomes the rubric covering these policies promoting or influencing such behavior. Indeed, there are those who would claim that family policy is always an instrument, whether overt or covert—that it is, essentially, a means to implement social control. As such, *family policy may also be defined as a "rationale"* (or rationalization), providing an acceptable reason for achieving latent, perhaps even unacceptable, objectives.

There is no doubt that over the long run most countries have seen the family as a significant vehicle for achieving broader political or social goals ranging from political indoctrination to labor market behavior. The most important, long-standing, and familiar illustration is in the field of labor market policy.[12] Women have been recruited into the labor force in Eastern Europe, Cuba, and China through the establishment of child care facilities, maternity allowances, and so forth. Or they have been encouraged to withdraw from the labor market in times of growing unemployment through the establishment of child care leaves and cash maintenance grants. The more subtle and indigeneous incentives and disincentives are not as readily acknowledged or discerned and the debate continues as to whether the desire of women to work, or the decision to make work feasible and attractive, comes first in a given country at a given time. This use of family policy as an instrument of labor market policy is described extensively in the Swedish and Hungarian articles.

A second illustration of family policy as an instrument relates to the view of the family as the primary transmitter of societal values. Ferge, in the Hungarian paper, points out the inherently conservative nature of the family, and the importance of family policy measures in compensating children for the inequities inherent in the differential status of their families. Sokołowska, writing about Poland, makes a similar point, but from a different perspective. She stresses that the family is the most important intervening variable in affecting children, and that appropriate family policies can help the family to be an agent of social change rather than an obstacle to it. Al-

---

[12] For some discussion in the literature see Sidney and Beatrice Webb, *English Local Government: English Poor Law* (London: Longmans, Green, 1927); Frances Fox Piven and Richard A. Cloward, *Regulating the Poor* (New York: Pantheon Books, 1971).

though the concept of family policy may not be used in Israel, Honig and Shamai describe certain family-related policies which are clearly designed to influence family behavior and compensate children for deprivation suffered by and in their families, as well as to acculturate the children to new and preferred values. Indeed, the children are often seen as a vehicle for affecting their parents.

A less important and more recent use of family policy as instrument is mentioned in the U.K. and U.S. papers, which describe emerging interest in developing policies to support families in their social service roles, especially that of providing social care to the elderly and the handicapped. The assumption here is that family care is cheaper and may be more humane. Yet as discussed by Land and Parker in the U.K. paper, the changing role of women, the family members traditionally responsible for this task, raises major questions as to how and where responsibility for this function will fall.

Still another definition of family policy—probably the most recent—is its use *as perspective or criterion for social policy choice*. Such an approach could apply to all policy arenas—tax policy, transportation, military policy, land use, and so forth—and suggests the use of family well-being as one of the criteria for decision-making as well as an outcome for assessing the consequences of policies generally. Although it is this definition that we ourselves find most attractive, we recognize that it can be found more in some of the recent literature, or in general discussion, than as an operational aspect of existing policies in other countries. Liljeström, discussing the Swedish situation, and Ferge, in analyzing Hungary, both suggest the importance of this use and indicate its growing significance in policy discussions generally.

We would of course be remiss if we implied that any one of these definitions is clearly dominant in any country, or that our conceptualization is accepted and employed uniformly. However, using our vocabulary, as one reads these papers, it seems clear that family policy is a field in many countries. Moreover, in several it is employed also as an instrument, rationale, and occasionally as perspective. Indeed, Henriksen criticizes the field of family policy in Norway by employing family policy as an evaluative criterion. She concludes that family policy in Norway functions more as an instrument and rationale than anything else, since it does not contribute to or support "family well-being" per se.

We suggest that regardless of formal definitions, the critical issue may be the extent to which family well-being (whatever the components) is employed as an outcome criterion for assessing policies or as a source of decision rules for developing options and making choices. We would comment, further, that in no country is family policy viewed as a single policy but rather as a *cluster of policies,* measures, benefits, and so forth, which are directed at the family.

Now, having provided the vocabulary for discussion, suggested several alternative views on how family policy may be defined and used, and indicated how different authors view their own countries' experience, we turn to the complex and highly sensitive task of defining what is meant by "family" when we talk of family policy.

What Is a Family?

Family policy has the potential of conservative or regressive application and use to support what some people define as the traditional family exclusively and to acknowledge only traditional family roles. Nonetheless, it may be worth noting that all the countries described provide special benefits to single-parent, female-headed families. There seems to be uniform acceptance of the fact that any family that has only one person to provide economic support as well as nurture and care of a child needs and warrants special assistance. It remains for the reader to consider whether such benefits provide an incentive to take on such status, whether the status really matters, whether the incentive becomes important only if adequate benefits are not provided to two-parent families, or whether there should be any concern in any case if the objective is to benefit children.

Indeed, the traditional family (two parents, one breadwinner, one or more children) is more likely to be featured in the rhetoric of countries that reject a family policy (U.S., U.K., Canada) or in some specific policies that affect families in such countries (e.g., social security) than it is in countries that support an explicit family policy (France, Sweden, Hungary).

All countries that have an explicit family policy, regardless of how comprehensive it may be, include in their definition of a family the presence of at least one parent and one or more children. According to Liljeström, the occasion for family policy arises currently because parenthood and *other* male-female roles are in conflict. Only one country specifically includes a lone couple in its definition of family (France). Although several of the countries have outstanding programs and policies regarding the aged (Sweden, Denmark, Federal Republic of Germany [F.R.G.]), none specifically locates such activity under the rubric of family policy. Nor do they concern themselves with family networks as part of their family policies. In contrast, authors attempting to analyze implicit family policy in their countries do define "family" more broadly to take account of such phenomena as kinship networks and support for the aged (U.K. and U.S.).

Although the term "one-person family" has been employed in the U.S.,[13] we suggest that it has no real usefulness in any discussion of family policy which we and others would contend presumes at least a dyad. Clearly, social policy that affects individuals is important; however, it does not seem helpful to deal with such policies as part of family policy. Such an approach wipes out any distinctiveness in family policy, and underscores the identity with all social policy rather than any unique focus. If family policy is a useful idea, it requires a family definition that means something.

The question of using the household as the target rather than something called a family has also been raised. We agree that both individuals and households may be valid targets of social policy. However, we also suggest that it is worth exploring for *some* policy purposes a definition of family that involves a primary emotional commitment and relationship. Furthermore, we are inclined to think that any family type in which at least one minor child is present warrants special attention; in fact, concern with family units which include at least one minor child may represent the core of what is unique in the concept of family policy. We would note that in laying claim to having a family policy all of the countries described here employ such a definition: at least one adult and one minor child.

Considering the numerous types of families (two-parent, married; two-parent, contractual; one-parent, divorced; one-parent, separated; one-parent, widowed; one-parent, unmarried; a grandparent and a child; a guardian and a child), it would seem that family policy refers to many different types of families. We have already established that it also refers to many different types of policies. Thus "family policy" becomes a surrogate for "fami*lies* poli*cies.*"

Why the Interest in Family Policy Now?

We commented earlier that the term "family policy" has a long history in Europe and indeed was used in the U.S. in the 1960s, although never with the widespread interest and enthusiasm which have emerged recently. While

[13] As in the Congress of the United States, Congressional Budget Office, Background Paper No. 17, "Poverty Status of Families under Alternative Definitions of Poverty," January 13, 1977.

visiting sixteen countries in the process of selecting authors for the papers which appear in this volume, and in connection with our other research, we were struck by the pervasiveness of interest in the subject even in countries which reject the idea of a family policy, and regardless of the disparate meanings and interpretations attached to the term. In country after country we were told of new or renewed interest in family policy. In Sweden, France, and Norway the subject was central to the then current domestic political debate. We tried to discover why this seemed to be happening in so many places at the same time and we encouraged authors to provide their own explanations.

In the midst of a conference at which these papers were discussed, the American participants were galvanized when the Swedish member, Rita Liljeström, raised the same question publicly. She asked: "Why now in the U.S. are you raising the question of family policy? What is the current crisis that suggests the need for a family policy?" The Americans responded in a variety of ways, explaining what they thought was generating interest in this country. Subsequent discussions with several European participants and a careful reading of these papers confirm the international nature of some of the factors then listed, while suggesting the importance of still others. Surely, no discussion of family policy internationally would be complete without some analysis of the factors which may be contributing to this upsurge of interest.

We would begin by stating that all the countries discussed here continue to view the family as the central institution for the economic support, nurture, care, and socializing of children. All the authors would agree that the family is uniquely qualified for the production of children. No institution is viewed as a replacement for the family.

Indeed, it is this primary function of the family to produce children that underscores one major factor in the European discussion, the population issue. Growing concern about population—both the total size in a given country and the age composition—has played a significant role in stimulating new or renewed interest in family policy in many of these countries. We mentioned earlier that population objectives played such a role in earlier family policy developments; it seems clear that such concerns are contributing to similar policies in several countries which heretofore have ignored the issue.

"Demographic panic," as it has been termed, has two aspects. First and most basic is the recognition that a society can survive only if enough children are born and reared to adulthood. All of Europe except some of the

Mediterranean countries has experienced a gradual decline in the birth rate during this century. Except for a brief upsurge after World War II the decline has accelerated, especially during the past decade. Based on projections of current rates, several countries foresee a national population decline by the early twenty-first century, not just zero population growth. Regardless of whether or not one believes that population stability or a small decline per se should evoke concern, a second aspect provides reinforcement for this anxiety: the concomitant short-term[14] increase in the aged dependency ratio (the ratio of retirees to the population of productive adults). As birth rates fall, a smaller number of children will comprise, in time, a reduced work force which will have to continue supporting a large aged population. An immediate question in many countries that have recently increased entitlements is: how will the increased burden of pensions and other social insurance costs of the aged be borne?

It is in this context that many have suggested that the search for incentives for bearing and rearing children is what is motivating individuals and policy-makers in many countries to become interested in family policy. In Hungary, Czechoslovakia, and France population concerns are already reflected in national policies, while in the F.R.G. and Finland the search is a subject of growing discussion. As already noted, it is questionable that any single policy incentive or disincentive to have children has any lasting effect on long-term fertility rates.

Population objectives may be a potent factor in the resurgence of interest in family policy in Europe; however, it has not been, thus far, in the U.S. Indeed, the subject is anathema to many in this country—as it is to many Europeans to whom the history of the 1930s and 1940s is a strong deterrent.

In contrast, two other developments have had a major impact on the surge of family policy interest on both continents: (1) changes in family structure and composition; and (2) changes in family function and roles. How these changes are defined, the implications for society, and the nature of the public policy response may vary among countries, but in each and every country visited, in every paper included here, in all of our discussions, some aspect of family change is viewed as particularly important.

Among the changes discussed are: decreases in the marriage rate; increases in the rates of separation and divorce; increases in the number of

---

[14] Obviously, if the fertility rate stabilizes at a low figure the demographic pattern will stabilize also. Only a major breakthrough in certain diseases of the aged would then disrupt this pattern again.

cohabitating couples; increases in the number of children born out of wedlock; increases in the number of children exposed to serial parenting; increases in the number of female-headed, one-parent families; decreases in the birth rate and in the size of families.

Closely related to these structural changes are the changes in family roles, especially the changing role of women. It is generally agreed that by far the most significant change is the increased labor force participation rate of women in all industrialized countries. Inevitably, as more women work outside the home, either because two incomes are needed for an adequate or desired standard of living or because full and equal participation in society assumes the employment of women, there are concomitant changes in the roles of men. Parenting roles of men and women are affected, as are the ways in which children become socialized in the family. If both women and men are employed outside the home and are expected to rear children, the question of how children are cared for during the day becomes increasingly important.

Changes in labor market conditions have also led to an interest in family policy. Again, very different conditions may generate interest in the potential utility of this orientation. Thus, in countries with a large number of unskilled women and inadequate jobs for such women, family policy may be oriented toward providing an incentive for women to withdraw from the labor force (or toward providing a new job category—family day care mothers—to assure such women of employment). On the other hand, in countries with full or near full employment, family policy may seek to facilitate female participation in the labor force. From still another perspective, a country's policy in selecting from among such options as use of immigrant or foreign "guest workers," increased technology, and expanded use of female labor also has obvious family implications. If the choice is to expand the labor supply through greater female participation in the labor force, then obviously child care arrangements and related measures become essential. Indeed, all these aspects of recent and current labor market conditions in Europe have been mentioned as stimulating interest in family policy, and generating specific policy options.

Regardless of the relative influence of labor market needs on the one hand, or equality goals on the other, these changes have played an enormously important role in stimulating the discussion of family policy in all countries. As was pointed out during some of our exploratory visits and confirmed even more strongly in conference discussions, changes in family structure, increased female labor, and the drive for greater equality for women constitute together the most important influences on the growth of interest in family policy everywhere.

This much said, it is also noted that the responses to these developments are very diverse. Those who view the family as the key instrument of social control and traditional socialization become anxious at the thought of any change; they worry that the family may lose its core functions. People representing this position in the U.S. and Europe view family policy as a means of supporting the status quo and, in fact, reversing whatever change has begun.

In contrast, those who actively want change, who favor greater equality for women, and/or greater flexibility in life styles for families and individuals—and those who note that decisions as to living arrangements or labor force participation are of enormous significance in determining family economic well-being—support family policy for its potential in achieving their own goals. Thus, the growth of the feminist movement in the U.S. and Europe during the 1960s and 1970s has clearly contributed to an expanded interest in family policy. Recognizing the complexity of the task of women who would cope with the dual roles of mother and paid worker, feminists have pressured for policies and laws assuring sexual equality, maternity benefits, child care, and various other measures—measures which are usually viewed as at the center of family policy.

The content of family policy envisaged by these disparate groups may be totally different, but the interest in the utility of family policy as concept or organizing rubric, as each defines it, is plainly influenced by the same developments.

Despite the obvious presence of interest (in some places) in increasing the numbers of children born, or the concern with the consequences for children of changes in the family (almost everywhere), interest in helping children per se appears to be of less importance in generating family policy exploration. Child welfare and child development of course remain important and popular fields. And child development professionals in several countries have become more interested in public policy, especially family policy, of late. Moreover, certain research findings and policy stances of scholars are often employed to support policy positions which appear to be taken for other reasons. Several countries illustrate the convergence of child development, population, and labor market policies in supporting broad-based family policies regarding the care of very young children. However, it would require intensive study to sort out fully the significance of each motive.

The conference discussion that followed Liljeström's provocative question confirmed the significance of all these forces. Using another approach, one American participant, reflecting the intense concern on the part of many with the fact that some of the interest in family policy seemed to be coming from very divergent groups, with diametrically opposed values and ideologies, suggested that three different groups could be identified in the U.S. as supporting attention to family policy at present:

1. There are those who view what is occurring as the disintegration of the family. They fear the breakdown in traditional family patterns and ways and see the current developments as a continuation of the turmoil generated first by blacks and youth in the 1960s, followed by other minorities and women in the 1970s. Change in the family, the most important social control institution in the society, is seen as threatening the whole social fiber. For these people, family policy is viewed as a potential strategy for returning to the previous status quo.

2. There are those who would agree that the family is changing but who would vehemently deny that the family is dying. Their position could be described in the terms used by the author of a recent book about the American family in the twentieth century: the family is "here to stay."[15] The position supported by this group is that there is need for extensive reexamination of existing policies which affect the family in order to make these policies more responsive to the needs of different and changing families. These groups see family policy as a useful framework for policy analysis.

3. There are those who have continued to be concerned about problems of inequality and recognize that inequality has a "family component." Certainly, the family is one of the most important institutions for the transmittal of values and of status from generation to generation. Where inequities exist, not only may these, too, be transmitted, but there is no way to eliminate them without in some way affecting the family situation. Furthermore, in some sense, an effort to protect the traditional family is a counterforce to the equality movement, since no one has found a way to minimize the handicap of disadvantaged family status for children if they remain closely tied to the family hearth, or, at least, do not escape from family handicaps. Growing recognition of all of this has led to examination of family policy as a criterion for evaluating public policies in all domains.

Several additional factors were suggested by participants as stimulating interest in family policy:

1. Social policy has emerged as an accepted policy domain in some of

[15] Mary Jo Bane, *Here To Stay* (New York: Basic Books, Inc., 1976).

the socialist countries in the 1970s, as part of the growing recognition that economic change alone would not and could not eliminate social problems. There is need for specific social policy. Family policy began to be explored subsequently in the context of social policy as one approach to achieving a series of societal objectives even though these goals are not necessarily consistent across country lines.

2. There is a growing need for social care services—concrete helping services for the aged and the handicapped—and for recognition that the family is a far less expensive social service provider than public or voluntary agencies, and maybe even a more humane one. Family policy is supported here as providing a strategy for supporting the family in this basic caring role.

Finally, one last factor was suggested as contributing to this international surge of interest by what our Hungarian colleague, Zsuza Ferge, described as an "international contagion of ideas." (This has been described elsewhere by a U.S. political scientist as the process of "societal learning."[16]) It took fifty years for Bismarck's idea about social security to reach the U.S. from Germany. Over half a century later, mass media, jet planes, and international conferences facilitate cross-national discussions and observation. It took a little more than a decade for service programs for the aged in the U.S. to include at least one example of every program that the more advanced European countries had for the aged. In much less than a decade articles on abused children published in different countries all cited the same sources in bibliographies.[17]

Obviously, there is occurring in all our countries an international transmission of social policies, and North America will no longer be left out of the international social policy debate. Central to this debate at present is the question of family policy.

We would conclude our discussion by stating that although certain factors appear to be more or less influential in different countries, no single factor emerges as controlling or determining in any. Policy-making is a complex process. Disparate interest groups and constituencies may support the same policy for different reasons. Policies are adopted to achieve multiple objectives. In identifying factors which seem to have contributed to the up-

[16] Hugh Heclo, *Modern Social Politics in Britain and Sweden* (New Haven, Conn.: Yale University Press, 1974).

[17] For some discussion of these cross-national trends see Alfred J. Kahn and Sheila B. Kamerman, *Social Services in International Perspective* (Washington, D.C.: Government Printing Office, 1977).

surge of interest in family policy we leave to the reader any conclusions as to which may be more significant in any given country. It seems clear to us from interviews, informal discussions, observation, and reading that the development is multidetermined and no single-factor analysis is satisfactory anywhere.

Certain themes are pervasive, however: concern with the effect of changes in family roles and structures; interest in achieving greater equality between men and women as well as between groups; anxiety about demographic shifts; the implication of economic changes for society; and the consequences of out-of-home employment for more and more women. We would posit that it is the interplay among several factors, at the very least, which has led to the convergence on family policy as a possible framework for responding to multiple concerns or a solution for a variety of problems.

Clearly, family policy is in the middle of many societal contradictions. Yet it should be obvious that if the family is a central institution in all of our societies it will be viewed as a critical agent both for those who seek change and those who strive to avoid it.

Part I

EXPLICIT AND COMPREHENSIVE FAMILY POLICY

SWEDEN
Rita Liljeström

THE THREAT OF a dwindling population serves Swedish family policy as its official godmother. It is customary to refer to the 1930s as the decade when this policy was introduced to even out the income differentials between families with none, a few., and many children so as to promote a higher birth rate. The primary solicitude of family policy was for the families with children. Although the child actually was the focus of family policy, it could not be avoided that the desirability of children and concern for their welfare also benefited the parents. After all, the task was one of persuading the adults to want to have children.

Strictly speaking, Swedish family policy has older traditions. Thus the effects of tax policy on families with children were discussed as far back as the 1910s. But if the child is seen as a political object, society's earliest measures related to children who were unprotected by any family, to illegitimate children not acknowledged by society, and to the underage labor of the early industrial period.

It seems fruitful to analyze three themes in the evolution of Swedish family policy:

1. Measures on behalf of the unprotected: child labor, children born out of wedlock, and unmarried mothers
2. Family policy as an instrument for population policy and income equalization
3. Support for equality between women and men: transition from the

DR. RITA LILJESTRÖM is Professor of Sociology, Göteborg University, Göteborg, Sweden.

mother-and-one provider family to families with parents and two providers on an equal footing.

By concentrating on these themes I shall draw the strategic lines rather than paint a full picture of the domain of family policy. For the most part I shall pass by the gradual build-up of reforms having to do with housing amenities and financial aid to students, as well as a discussion of social policy. All these areas have relevance for family policy, although here they form a discreet background.

The societal measures on behalf of the family are taken in the following sequence:

1. Some kind of social malaise becomes politically defined as a societal problem.

2. The government appoints an inquiring body, known as a commission or committee, and issues terms of reference setting forth the aims of work. The commission is manned by parliamentary representatives and experts on the problem area in question. These persons may farm out research contracts, with the resulting studies published as appendices to the commission's report or serving it as a body of underlying evidence.

3. The commission presents its reports with proposed measures in the form of recommendations. The report then starts out on its "submission round," in which a number of institutions, government agencies, and interest organizations offer their opinions and make comments. These submission bodies are either enjoined to answer or are told they have the right to express themselves on the matter.

4. After the submission period expires the matter is ready for treatment in Parliament. By then there will have been time for a substantial amount of debate and opinion molding.

The greater part of research into, and knowledge of, family development in Sweden derives from State-sponsored investigations of family policy (with that term interpreted in a broad sense). My analysis proceeds from this type of material. It is material that has its limitations in that it enters into political argumentation. This is especially evident in goal descriptions, which readily tend to confuse things as they are with how they should be, as well as in a certain ritualization of the knowledge that is produced and carried along from one official investigation to the next.

I here define the family as a household which assumes responsibility for the custody of minors. Definitions of the family, if they occur at all, are adapted to the problems as formulated by the commissions of inquiry. There are families with two parents, families with one adult parent, and families with foster parents. A family may also consist of a married couple, brothers and sisters living together, an adult child living with an elderly mother, and so forth. But children are the real core of family policy. The parents' conditions are largely determined by how their reproductive and productive functions are integrated in society, in its social and moral order. This integration may be harmonious or charged with conflict. When the conditions are such that the presence of children causes conflicts for their parents, a situation will ensue that gives the society cause to intervene. In this sense family policy may be construed as an attempt to resolve conflict, to offer mediating services, so as to bring the interests of parents and children into line with society's interests.

My first theme is chiefly about parents and children who have come in conflict with the society's norms for reproduction, i.e., the demands for conjugal legitimacy.

The second theme has to do with the conflict between, on the one hand, having children and therefore a lower standard of living and a more constrained life style and, on the other hand, no children, or fewer children, and more money and freedom.

In the third theme the conflict is about the difficulties of combining responsibility as parents with participation in production. It should be noted that it is primarily the woman who has had to bear the conflict between parenthood and reproduction as well as between parenthood and production.

These are the conflicts on which the label "woman's question" has been pinned, simply because the conflicts have been settled in favor of the men—at the expense of the women.

Theme 1: Family Policy as Measures for the Unprotected

In the eighteenth-century Swedish agrarian society, child bearing—and hence women, too—was under control. The social control was expressed in three conditions:

1. The birth of a child was to be legitimated through marriage. Children born out of wedlock were "unauthorized" and were to be treated accordingly. Among other things, they lacked the right to inherit from their parents.

2. The young women's chastity was watched. The established church imposed punitive marks of shame and fines. The social sanctions for breaches of sexual morality were harsh and severe.

3. Once pregnant, a woman was duty bound to give birth—under threat of capital punishment for abortion and infanticide.

These implacable rules were effective: only 2.5 percent of the births were illegitimate. Wastage so small could easily be sacrificed on the altar of morality. Even so, infanticide occurred on such a scale that the king found it advisable in 1778 to enact an emergency law on "unknown mothers." The law's aim was to prevent infanticide by guaranteeing an unmarried woman the right to hide and deny her motherhood in order to "give birth to the foetus at an unknown place . . . without anyone's prosecution or inquiry about her person." If the woman so wished her name was not entered in the parish registers, but the child was recorded as having been born of an unknown mother.[1] The mother left with the child a sum of money known as a "foster-home hire" for its upbringing.

This law has been called a class-discriminating statute: after all, a person had to have some money to take advantage of the possibilities that the law offered. It was in force right up to 1915.

As the nineteenth century unfolded with its population pressures, surplus of women, and upcoming industrialization, the old legitimacy order began to dissolve. Each new decade witnessed a rising proportion of illegitimate children. By the turn of the century the authorities perceived the situation to be so alarming that a commission of inquiry was appointed in 1910. Two statistical reports document a survey of the situation for illegitimate children.[2] Perhaps this ranks with the most dramatic and theoretically the most illuminating material that has ever been written about mothers and children. It is not illuminating in the sense that contemporary statisticians can draw conclusions à la the 1970s (besides, the survey is surprisingly unknown today), but in the sense that it lays bare a social rank order of mothers: mothers who have conceived their children in wedlock at the top; premarital conceptions in second place; followed by subgroups of unmarried mothers; and the unknown mothers bringing up the rear. The rank order can be quantified by means of the children's mortality statistics.

The survey embraced all children who had been born out of wedlock in 1889 and followed them up to the age of twenty-one. It exposed the unpro-

[1] Gerald Hafström, *Den svenska familjeratten historia* (Lund: Studentlitteratur, 1965).

[2] "Children Born Out of Wedlock," Statistical Reports, Series A, Vol. I, No. 4 (1914); Vol. II, No. 4 (1916).

tected status of children and mothers, and formed the basis for a family policy through which society begins to replace the father. As a first step, provision was made in 1917 for the interests of every illegitimate child to be looked after by a child welfare officer—by tracing the whereabouts of the father, for instance, and making him liable to pay maintenance. In 1905 illegitimate children were given the right to inherit from their mothers and from their next of kin on the mother's side. It was not until the 1970s that the inheritance right was extended to the father. During the population crisis of the 1930s, when Swedish family policy was officially born, the financial situation of unmarried mothers was improved and there was a campaign to end public discrimination against them. Despite the step-by-step improvement of an income-maintenance system (family allowances, rent allowances, maintenance allowances) to assist one-parent families and the priority given to their children in the society's child care facilities, the standard of living for a family with one parent is still lower than for a family with two spouses.

One of the principles governing the assistance of one-parent families is that such support is intended "to replace the loss of the one parent's breadwinning effort for the child, not to 'pension' the child's custodian throughout the child's growing-up period."[3]

Rates of labor force participation by single mothers with children are extremely high. Although single parents no longer bear the brunt of any social discrimination, the conflicts that two spouses have between their tasks as parents and their tasks in the job world weigh even more heavily on the single parents precisely because the forms of social intercourse are structured in pairs: as a result, the "unattached" mothers are chronically short of time, tied down more to their children, and inevitably more isolated.

As I see it, sexual-policy development theoretically belongs to the domain of family policy. Beginning with official population studies in the 1930s and up to and including sexual-policy solutions to controversial problems in the 1970s, every decade has been strewn with investigations into sexual policy: sexual enlightenment, contraception, and the abortion issue. It has taken a whole generation of political reappraisals to abolish the two outmoded principles for the social control of childbearing:

1. The importance of conjugal legitimacy has declined. Since 1966 the marriage rate has been dropping. At the same time, more couples are cohabiting without having a wedding ceremony. The increase in illegitimate children is exceptional. In 1973 the figure rose to 28 percent of the births.

[3] The Family Policy Committee, "Familjestöd," Swedish Government Official Reports (hereafter referred to as SOU), 1972, No. 34.

2. A survey done in 1971 found that nearly two thirds of the mothers with illegitimate children cohabited with the child's father. In an educated society the inheritance interests and births have been disconnected from family formation and childbearing.

3. Sexuality among young is accepted in the contraceptive society. Sexual enlightenment for children and good contraceptive counseling for teen-agers are well on the way to being put into practice.

4. In 1975 women were acknowledged the right to abortion during the first twelve weeks of pregnancy. Even during the second half of the 1960s the then operative Abortion Act was liberally applied. Forced marriages were abolished for teen-age girls. The principle that every baby should be made to feel welcome was recognized in full.

With all this the conflict between reproduction and parenthood has taken on a new guise. After the social control of fertility was superseded by control with technical aids, the discussion of norms for cohabitation was vitalized even though a great deal still remains unsaid.

Now that measures of family policy have improved women's economic and social status, women are better situated to have children without marrying the father. Society's assistance helps to strengthen the status of the unmarried mother.

On the other hand, the thrust of society's family policy is to put the parents on an equal footing. That in its turn has increased the expectations of a shared parental responsibility and the man's sharing the care of his offspring. Two contradictory tendencies are discernible here. On the one hand, there is the risk that like the unmarried mothers of 1900, the unwed fathers of the year 2000 will be rejected. On the other hand, the debate on the man's emancipation is essentially about his relationship to children.

It is still too early to say anything definite about the consequences for children that flow from weakening conjugal legitimacy. Once regarded as a societal concern, marriage is now construed to be a private affair. That which interests society is the parent-child relationship, not the nexus of woman and man. The types of assistance that both social policy and family policy provide[4] take a neutral stand toward whatever forms people choose for living together. By contrast, the family experts on the Family and Marriage Commission[5] want to safeguard marriage as a legal institution. While admitting that this neutrality might refer to "coexistence on the personal plane," the experts argue that the legislation ought to spell out economic rules which explicitly hold for marriage and which arise out of "the woman's and man's coexistence with family functions."

[4] Ibid.   [5] Family Experts, "Familj och äktenskap," SOU 1972, No. 41.

Cohabitation and legal marriage are controversial issues. To illustrate with the program for family policy formulated by the Swedish Confederation of Trade Unions (LO), cohabitation and marriage are to be equated in all respects. From January, 1977, divorced couples and unmarried parents, whether living together or apart, will be able to share the custody of their children. The parents must be agreed on this in order for joint custody to be possible. No maintenance allowance is payable when divorced or unmarried parents share the custody of their children.[6]

Another area where society had to intervene early to protect minors was the employment of child labor from the nineteenth century to the first decades of the twentieth century. During the nineteenth century the proletariat's children were exploited in mines, sawmills, textile factories and other sweatshops. Not only were they paid miserably low wages but some of them had to support their parents on that pittance. Protective laws were enacted which shortened the workdays for minors, cut down on the night work, and guaranteed a minimum of schooling. The rules and regulations were hard to enforce, and the legal fight stretched out over the decades right down to the 1920s.

If family policy is interpreted to mean measures taken on behalf of children, then Swedish family policy has its roots in keeping watch over the interests of illegitimate children as well as in the protective laws for children whose parents could not offer their progeny a fair measure of security.

Theme 2: Family Policy as an Instrument for Population Policy and Income Equalization

At first the emphasis in child support was put on higher-income brackets, this because the tax deductions favored those who earned higher incomes. With the introduction of a general family allowance in 1948, equal amounts of support were paid for all children. With the addition of a rent allowance, beginning in 1968, family policy shifted its emphasis toward paying higher amounts of support to those in the lower-income brackets.

What arguments of principle have underlaid these shifts of emphasis in Swedish family policy?

A consciously intended family policy in the modern sense started to take shape in the mid-1930s. The world depression and unemployment during the years 1930–34 hit hard at families with children. Some widely

[6] Birgitta Wittorp, "Joint Custody of the Children of Divorced and Unmarried Parents," *Current Sweden*, February, 1977.

publicized studies called attention to poverty and the substandard housing of broad social groups. In 1934 the Myrdals' book *Crisis in the Population Question* heightened the public awareness that something was seriously wrong. All political parties built population planks into their platforms and demanded sweeping measures to deal with this issue.

In 1933 the government appointed the Housing Amenities Commission, followed by the Population Commission in 1935. The task was to promote increased and earlier marriages and a higher birth rate. These goals could be achieved by "reducing the expenses which families incur to raise, nurture and care for children."

The Population Commission saw as the most important cause of the declining birth rate the lower living standard of families with children *relative* to that of the childless at corresponding income levels. On the *quantitative* side, the expenses of families with children would have to be reduced; on the *qualitative* side, the Commission wanted to stress hereditary hygienic and environmental influences, the better to preserve the demographic traits.

The principal result of the Commission's work was to recommend reforms for new mothers. For them and their babies maternity aftercare and child-health centers were established. No charge was to be made for obstetrical services. The Parliament also adopted a proposal for house furnishing loans to newly married couples (1937).

In the 1940s the war and rising food prices were considered to justify doing more on behalf of families with children. A new Population Commission was appointed in 1941 to follow the family reforms enacted in the 1930s. This body worked up to 1947 and submitted a great many reports and reform proposals. But once again the most important reform was undoubtedly the decision to pay national family allowances for all children up to the age of sixteen.

The national family allowances were justified on three grounds:

1. *Population policy*. The allowances would help to counteract the declining birth rate. At the same time, the Commission took a basic stand by saying that quantitative goals in terms of births per year not only were unreasonable but also conflicted with Swedish traditions.

2. *Fairness*. The allowances would further the quest to even out the costs of children so that childless families and families with children could live at the same standard. However, the Commission identified two difficulties: (*a*) there were no unambiguous yardsticks to measure the standard of living; (*b*) evening out the costs of children was hindered by other income disparities in the society.

3. *Social policy*. All citizens would be guaranteed a minimum standard of living. Social policy would protect children from hardship and guarantee economically satisfactory nurturing patterns.

The Commission summarized its rationale in these words: "The cardinal aim is to remove those obstacles of a material nature which now deter far too many families from obtaining the desirable number of children."

Additional protection was extended to families with children with the expansion of social insurance schemes: the 1946 decision on national basic pensions and the legislation on national health insurance in the 1950s.

The Families Commission appointed in 1954 was mandated to enlarge financial support of children to compensate for inflation, and in so doing counteract a relative lowering of standards for families with children.

Public debate on family policy was revitalized during the 1960s. It was dominated by issues of fairness and freedom of choice. The Family Policy Committee appointed in 1965 was mandated to reappraise the balance between different political measures to allow for the financial strength of dissimilar family types. The aim now was to deploy support where and when the needs were greatest. As will have emerged from the foregoing, the earlier discussion had kept two aspects apart: on the one hand, fairness motives as an equalization between childed and childless families; on the other hand, social policy motives as support for low-income groups.

In a report published in 1972 the Family Policy Committee observed that the definition of fairness rests on political value judgments. The notion of fairness can be interpreted to mean a horizontal transfer payment between families with children and childless families earning the same income—regardless of how high it is. But fairness can also be interpreted to mean a vertical transfer payment whereby families with lower incomes receive more support than families with higher incomes.

At this point family policy took a major position on principle. The financial support given to single parents with children and to large families would be strengthened, while it would be slightly reduced for higher-income earners with few children. For this purpose a scheme of paying rent allowances to families with children was devised. The amount of the allowance is determined with reference to income, housing cost, and number of children.

The transition to a more vertically equalized fairness reflects the lost illusions during the second half of the 1960s. In 1965 the government had appointed the Low Incomes Commission to map out the geographic and occupational distribution of low-income groups "with special emphasis on the deviations downward from the average." The Commission (actually a one-

man committee) published a series of reports from 1970 to 1973 which un-
masked the whole picture of how resources were allocated in the Swedish
society. Low incomes and underemployment were both widely diffused, and
it was also clear that the redistribution of incomes under social policy was a
system with no more than negligible redistributive effects.[7]

Ever greater doubt came to be cast on the conventional wisdom which
accepted poverty as a "residual problem" in the Welfare State. The ongoing
debate labeled social policy as the capitalistic system's "charwoman," who
sweeps aside or looks after the human waste that the economic system itself
is constantly generating. In so doing, the critics charged, social policy
helped to reinforce the economic system and to work against the radical
transformation of society.

Instead of regarding poverty as a residue that was on its way out, people spoke more and more of the "new poverty." Some research was
directed to analyzing which factors create poverty and needs for assistance.
The researchers spoke of a relative poverty, which seems to be bound up
with the usage of resources by different groups, with problems on the outlay
side that were particularly caused by ever higher housing costs. The most
adversely affected group consisted of households with only one adult plus a
child, as well as larger households with more children. This new poverty
was to be found in families that did *not* suffer from unemployment or from
alcoholism or other aberrations. Nor were they immigrants; these were families with full-time employed breadwinners who could not make both ends
meet.

The second topic in the family debate had to do with freedom of
choice, defined as "freedom to bring children into the world and woman's
freedom of choice between gainful employment and homemaking." To
quote the opinion of the 1962 Family Welfare Committee:

> To make freedom of choice complete meant giving the families financial secu-
> rity for the number of children they choose even if that works out larger than the
> "normal family's." By the same token, spare the woman from having to choose
> between children and occupation but make it possible for her to have both so
> that she can satisfy herself both as woman and as individual.

In 1964 the Family Welfare Committee arrived at the question of introducing a special care allowance to help cover the costs of minding chil-

[7] Karin Tengvald, "Samhallets krav och de fattigas resurser," Department of Sociology, Upp-
sala University, Sweden, 1976.

dren. This contribution was considered justified on two grounds: first, it would enable mothers to stay at home since it would be best for the children if the mother herself ministered to them during their infancy; and second, it would leave the mother free to choose between homemaking and gainful employment. As envisioned by the Committee, payment of the allowance would be limited to the first three years of a child's life.

Theme 3: Family Policy and Sex Equality

Ideas Behind Transformation of Family Patterns

Today, family policy is actively transforming the family pattern from a unit consisting of a mother and one breadwinner into a two-income unit. Or, to put it differently, it is altering the pattern from a family with specialized roles for the woman and the man to a family with shared roles.

Work in the agrarian society was divided by sex. As more and more of the tasks performed by the self-contained household were taken over by factories, schools, old-age homes, social insurance offices, and so on, the division of labor between spouses also changed in character. Now the households no longer needed the large numbers of adult women, unmarried relatives, and servants who had earlier contributed to the household production. The unmarried women had to go out on the labor market, while the married woman's place was in the home. According to the new industrial ideology, the man's duty was to provide for the whole family.

The ideal picture of the single-income family was nourished by the bourgeois ethos of the nineteenth century. Married women from the working class were very much compelled to work outside the home, but gradually they came to identify their wishes to a great extent with the ideology of the "transitional family."[8] Given the industrial exploitation of women and children in the labor force, the thrust of that day's reform movements was to reconquer "the good home" and "blissful childhood" for the working class in line with the model portrayed by the upper social strata.

As matters turned out, the working class, whose women were forced by economic necessity to work outside the home, did in fact very much identify their wishes with the transitional family ideology. They used a substantial

[8] Alva Myrdal, *Folk och familj* (People and family) (Stockholm: Kooperative förbundets bokfölag, 1944); republished in the U.S. as *Nation and Family* (rev. ed.; Cambridge, Mass.: M.I.T. Press, 1968).

part of their improved living standard for liberating their women from the need to work for others.[9]

Seen from the perspective of social history, what actually happened to the self-contained households?

1. The coordinated work processes were separated into "domestic work" and paid employment outside the home.

2. Since the care and upbringing of children could be combined with the domestic work, children came to be regarded more and more as the exclusive concern of their mothers. The fathers assumed a smaller share of the nurturing function.

3. Adult members of the self-contained households entered into a common social world, where other persons helped the parents mind and train the children for specific tasks. With the division of the work this common base was split up and dissolved. A private life took shape around the domestic chores, whereas organizations and collectives were formed around the job world: work teams, professional groups, trade unions, business firms, and so forth.

Habermas describes the widening spread between private and public in these words:

> To the same extent that the vocational sphere is making itself independent, the family sphere is pushing itself back: it is not so much the loss of producing in favor of consuming functions that characterizes the family's structural change, but rather that it has steadily divorced itself more and more from the functional context of societal work for the most part.[10]

But if the scope of the family's tasks diminished, one aspect was reinforced: the family came to stand for the emotional satisfaction of its members. By and by emotions became the very foundation of the marriage tie.

In the specialized society different subareas began to develop their own ground rules and role relations, all according to the purpose served by their activities. Moreover, the differentiation of activities acted to segment the personality. A modern man has to divide up his personality whenever he goes from one place, group, or activity to another. His different egos need not be interrelated. The labor market assumes that he is able to shift easily between his two roles of jobholder and private person. Profitability and efficiency are the labor market's guiding principles. The growing bureaucratic system requires impersonality and emotional control, obedience to rules and contract clauses, competition for posts and positions, equal treatment of

[9] *Ibid.*   [10] Jürgen Habermas, *Borgerlig offentlighet* (Oslo, 1944).

members in given categories, testimonials by performance, and financial rewards by competence.

The man was the first to become a "modern human being," which gave him a head start. His activities were put into separate, unrelated compartments. With the individuation he was drawn into new social units all by himself. The married woman became bearer of the emotional responsibility, of the family's growing intimacy. All the wife's functions came to concentrate on the family. The roles of wife, mother, and homemaker were interwoven. In this sense she still lived in a traditional world. It now became her role to make good the loss of security in everyday life and in dehumanization of the job world. She stood for love and tenderness in an anonymous world.

This specialization of roles between women and men may be illustrated as follows:

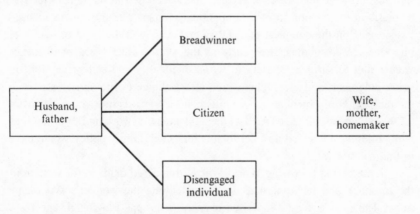

Fig. 1 Role Division: Modern Man and Traditional Woman

The division of roles within the family between a modern man and a traditional woman must be understood in light of the demographic situation prevailing in Sweden for decades as the industrial society evolved (1870–1930). Given a low marriage rate and a late marrying age, the birth rate was bound to be low. The labor market could count on an abundant supply of unmarried women. It follows that the classification by marital status formed the basis for putting women into the respective categories of domestic work and paid employment.

When Sweden was hit by depression and unemployment in the 1930s, a number of resolutions were moved in Parliament to demand curtailing the married woman's right to work. At that time only 10 percent of the married women were gainfully employed. As the population crisis mounted, the situation became even more loaded with dynamite. According to Swedish custom ("don't legislate before you investigate"), the government appointed commissions of inquiry. Alva Myrdal portrays a turning point in the debate:

> At this juncture anything could have happened. The remarkable thing is that, at the crucial moment, the nativity argument was wrested from the hands of the antifeminists and turned instead into a new and effective weapon harnessed to the woman's aspirations. The earlier debate on *the married woman's right to work transformed into a fight for the employed woman's right to marry and have children.*[11]

So rather than curtail the participation of women in the labor force, Parliament in 1937 enacted a law prohibiting the dismissal of any woman who became engaged, married, or pregnant. And that was as far as the women's movement, according to Alva Myrdal, had succeeded in its fight to recover or preserve its position in old occupational sectors. The movement focused its energies on the conquest of legal rights. Although the legal obstacles of importance were abolished as early as the 1920s, other types of obstacles were going to surface: barriers in terms of identity and self-perception, in value judgments and ideologies which affect choice of life style; barriers to the realization of practical opportunities and as regards how different societal sectors are coordinated, such as the adjustment of working life to families with children. All added up to problems for which family policy would have to find solutions.

In the period following World War II, increased demand for women in the marriage and labor markets led to redefining the woman's and man's roles. The marriage rate had risen sharply in groups ranging in age from twenty to thirty-nine years. The population pyramid has changed. Today, the big group consists of women over forty years of age.

The postwar situation has created a boom on the Swedish labor market. Womanpower requirements can no longer be met by unmarried women. The division of labor between the sexes must now be redefined. In the first phase there is a great deal of talk about "woman's two roles." The merits of this dichotomy were challenged by the well-known Swedish writer Eva Moberg:

> Actually there is no biological relation whatever between the functions of giving birth to and nursing children and the functions of washing their clothes, cooking their food and trying to raise them as good and harmonious people. Not to mention the functions of scrubbing floors, washing windows, sewing, shop-

[11] Myrdal, *People and Family*, p. 456.

ping and polishing furniture. The care and rearing of a child is a purely human endeavor and in no way inherent in women's functions as a creature of a particular sex. . . . I believe the concept of "double roles" in the long run may have an unfortunate effect. It preserves the concept that woman has an inherent *main function* by which is meant child care and rearing, creating the home and keeping it together. . . . We ought to stop harping on the concept of "women's two roles." Both men and women have *one* principal role, that of being people. The human role includes as a necessary and moral duty, but also as a rich asset, a glorious experience and much else, the challenge of taking good care of one's progeny.

If you don't admit this, then you ought to realize that you're helping to see to it that woman's liberation will never be more than what it is now: a conditional liberation. Woman has been set free only on the silent assumption that she will proceed with her main purpose, which is to care for and rear children and create their childhood environment. If only she realizes that this is her natural duty, somehow built into her nature as a sexual being, then certainly society acknowledges her as a completely free individual.[12]

The article heralded an intensive debate on sex roles. Shortly thereafter there appeared the Swedish-Norwegian anthology *Kvinnors liv och arbete*,[13] in which Swedish and Norwegian sociologists analyzed sex roles. The term "sex roles" was new to the public debate. It was as though this very designation opened many people's eyes to the fact that what used to be captioned the "woman's question" was actually about a social problem that impacted on men and women with the same force. A fierce debate on sex roles was waged throughout the 1960s.

By the end of the 1960s a radical reappraisal had penetrated Swedish family policy, educational policy, and labor market policy. When in 1968 the Swedish Government presented a report to the United Nations Economic and Social Council on the status of women the following principles for a long-term program were enunciated:

The goal for a long-range program of "women's rights" must be that every individual, regardless of sex, shall have the same opportunities not only for education and employment but also fundamentally the same responsibility for child upbringing and housework. If complete equality is ever to be reached in respect to these rights and responsibilities, there must be a radical change in deeply rooted traditions and attitudes, as much among women as among men, and active measures must be taken by society which will stimulate a change in the

[12] Eva Moberg, "Women's Conditional Liberation," in *Women and People* (Stockholm: Bonniers, 1962), pp. 107–8.

[13] Edmund Dahlström, ed., *Kvinnors liv och arbete* (Stockholm: Studieförbundet näringsliv och samhälle, 1962); published in summary version as *The Changing Roles of Men and Women* (London: Duckworth & Co., Ltd., 1967).

roles of both men and women. The idea that women must be financially supported by marriage must effectively be opposed—even in law, as it is a direct obstacle to woman's economic independence and her chances to compete on equal footing with men in the labor market. By the same token, the traditional duty of the man to support his wife must be supplanted by responsibility, shared with her, for the support of the children. This support of the children should also find expression, from the man's side, in a greater share in the care and upbringing of the children.[14]

To promote the trend toward equality, the government constituted in 1962 the Advisory Council to the Prime Minister on Equality between Men and Women. As the name implies, the Council enjoyed an inside track leading to the inner sanctum, which made it well-placed to watch over the work being done to achieve sexual equality and to submit comments on intended reform, draft laws, and other proposals emanating from the ministries.

The Advisory Council endeavored from the outset to strengthen woman's status on the labor market. In a couple of reports published under contract to the Council, the following view of the goal for equality policy was formulated.[15]

The sex roles have been upheld in that women and men have specialized in different tasks. They have complemented one another. But seldom has attention been paid to the destructive feature of this complementarity. The women stood for everything that bureaucracy and technocracy ignored. They bore a dehumanized society aloft by symbolizing its compensatory and therapeutic core family. The man could perform his traditionally monolithic male role, thanks to a complementary woman's role which answered for all that the male role denies, and vice versa.

If equality is to be realized, women and men must have access to the same life areas (see fig. 2).

But does this not mean that women will also be mentally divided into partitioned roles with very little interconnection, that they will be bureaucratized and performance-oriented, efficient and emotionally impoverished? No, this need not be so, provided it becomes feasible for women and men to combine responsibility for children with participation in working life. The

---

[14] "The Status of Women in Sweden," Swedish Government's Report to the United Nations Economic and Social Council (Swedish Institute, 1968), p. 5.

[15] Rita Liljeström, Gillan Liljeström Svensson, and Gunilla Fürst Mellström, "Roles in Transition," a report to the Advisory Council to the Prime Minister on Equality between Men and Women, SOU 1976, No. 71.

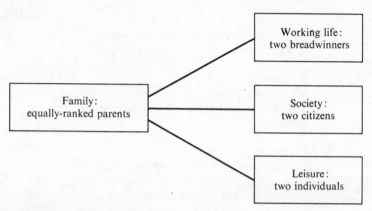

Fig. 2 Shared Societal Roles

full combination also implies that women take part in and leave their imprint on the work of policy-making and culture-creating institutions, and that both men and women are given sufficient time to spend as they see fit: time to establish rapport with themselves; time for personal relations, recreation, and interests. We are forced to reflect on how these partitioned areas relate to one another in our time budget, in traveling distances and community planning, in role expectations and values, and on how obstacles in the form of ownership patterns and power are constituted. Real equality between the sexes must lead to sweeping social changes.

Man possesses development potentials that cover a broad repertoire of personal and societal capacity. This repertoire has been divided into two specialized halves which have restricted one another's human development. The goal for equality is a "whole and indivisible human being," a person whose personality unfolds out of the dialectic between sensibility and objectivity, strength and weakness, rules and exceptions; out of the ability to feel intimacy and command overview, a sense of distance to routine and renewal rather than to reserve a pole for each sex.

Thus defined, the change of roles involves the man every bit as much as the woman. It all boils down to people's capacity to integrate private and public roles, roles in reproduction with roles in production.

Illustrated below is a "repertoire of personal and societal capacity." Every level indicates which abilities, ranging from the most personal to the most general relations, will have to be developed. The researchers declare the following philosophy:

Female specialization
{
Individual
To cultivate emotions and experiences; to look for inner meanings, self-insight

Primary group
To develop enduring personal relations, intimacy, sense of "we" and solicitude for others
}

Male specialization
{
Labor collective
To develop knowledge, methods, and problem solutions; to produce for subsistence and answer for attentions and services

Society
To become aware of larger entities, of conflicts between groups' interests and needs
}

The multifaceted and whole human being's repertoire

We endorse a philosophy that "man's emancipation" is essentially about overcoming the barriers to developing that versatility which lies in a normal repertoire of possibilities. We interpret "the whole human being" to mean the ability to integrate different types of experiences.

We see prime movers of mental growth in the trade-off or balance between contradictions and tensions between different areas or levels. Moreover, we imagine that society will benefit when experiences from different groups and life areas are brought to bear more strongly on the course of events.

If that is the ideology behind the transformation of family patterns, what about the political measures that back up equality between women and men? What do these acts of policy-making look like? Let us begin by looking at the labor market.

Since the mid-1960s we have detected an increasing demand for women in occupations that used to recruit men exclusively. An important cause of this development is the shortage of male labor, a shortage that is expected to become even more pronounced as the 1970s draw to a close. According to labor force surveys the percentage of gainfully employed women has increased as follows:

Changes in Percentages of Women Gainfully Employed: 1965–74

	1965	*1970*	*1974*
All women aged 16–74	48.7	52.9	57.1
Women with children under 7	36.8	49.7	56.7

In the period 1965–74 the number of employed women went up by 300,000, while the number of employed men fell off by 30,000. The two-tier labor market began to stand out as less and less rational.

The Swedish labor market is characterized by a division along sex lines. Slightly more than 70 percent of the women work in about twenty-five different occupations. Men account for a low proportion of employees in these trades. Their job spectrum is a richly differentiated one numbering upward of 300 occupations. Even though the recent developments may have shifted the pivotal weight of these statistics, there are still ample grounds for speaking of two segregated labor markets, one reserved for men and a smaller one for women. While this may not be true in theory, it no doubt holds in practice.

Sweden acceded to the ILO Convention on Equal Pay for Equal Work in 1962. Even though the principle of equal pay for equal work became fully implemented, no more than a slight part of the connection between pay and sex can be eliminated as long as the labor market remains two-tiered. Decisive importance must attach instead to experimenting with counteracting the female-male job split, and to expanding the labor market for both women and men. If traditionally female occupations are going to exert any fascination for men, however, the wages will have to be raised.[16]

Among workers in manufacturing the women earned 79 percent of the men's wages in 1969 as against 70 percent ten years earlier. By 1973 the pay level for women had risen to 85 percent of the men's wages. The Low Incomes Commission found that 67 percent of the extremely low-paid were women. In the group older than twenty-five no less than 80 percent were women. One in every four female wage earners belonged to the low-income bracket, while one of every twelve men could be assigned to this category.[17]

Society and the Parents

"Work for Everyone" is the title of the report published by the 1975 Employment Commission. The government's terms of reference for this investigating body start off with these words:

> Work and its conditions form an essential part of human life. Work is a means of creating a good material livelihood. But work also has an intrinsic value as a

[16] Annika Baude and Per Holmberg, "The Positions of Men and Women in the Labor Market," in Dahlström, *The Changing Roles of Men and Women*, p. 122.

[17] Swedish Labor Market Board, *Women and the Labour Market* (Lund: the Board, 1974).

way toward social fellowship. Work meets one of the fundamental human needs, which is to develop and enrich life.[18]

Where employment policy used to combat joblessness, it now also seeks to get at hidden unemployment by catering to groups who have not actively sought work in the past.

An expansion of facilities to care for the chronically ill, the aged, and children requires heavy increments of staff. Other public services are also looking for personnel. It should be noted that the increase in employment is almost entirely a question of increasing the number of *women* in the labor market.

The combination of Swedish labor market policy with family policy to support the drive for equality between women and men rests on forecasts of full employment in a long-term perspective. Some means of implementing general labor market policy may be briefly mentioned: the system of public employment exchanges; the payment of moving allowances to persons/families who cannot get work in their home town; the provision of free manpower training with subsistence grants payable during the training period; and relief work and sheltered employment for displaced labor or the "functionally" unemployed.

In its 1972 report the Family Policy Committee[19] observed that the increased participation of married women in the labor force was especially striking for the younger married mothers with children of preschool age. At the end of 1971 the ranks of gainfully employed included 47 percent of the mothers with the youngest child under three years of age, 59 percent of the mothers with the youngest child between three and six, 69 percent of the mothers with the youngest child between eleven and sixteen. According to the labor force survey, nearly 55 percent of these women usually work part time.

Even when working full time, moreover, women are paid less on the average than men. A family study indicates that in families where both parents are gainfully employed full time the year round, the husband earns on average nearly twice the income of his wife. It is well-known that the women compensate for their wages by working twice as much in the home!

Thus the Family Policy Committee found that "the most common family pattern nowadays is not a married man with a stay-at-home wife, but a family where both spouses normally work for gain and where the mother in-

[18] Employment Commission, "Work for Everyone," Summary, SOU 1975, No. 90, p. 4.

[19] Family Policy Committee, SOU 1972, No. 34.

terrupts her career once or more often, for shorter or longer periods, as soon as the children come.''

After prolonged debate the decision was made in 1970 to change over to individual taxation. The tax system now postulates that every adult, irrespective of sex, is self-supporting, whereas the earlier tax system assumed that a married man supports his wife. This reform reduced the tax bite for spouses who both earn income compared with families where only one is an earner. Although the reform makes it easier for more married women to enter the labor market, it includes special rules for the benefit of families with one income earner, this is to soften the impact of changing from a single-income family (mother and one breadwinner) to a two-income family.

Another effect of the tax reform was to reduce the bite in lower-income levels while increasing it in the higher brackets—an effect that squares well with the fundamental reorientation of family support toward greater vertical equalization among families with children. The following example clearly illustrates this leveling effect which the tax and allowance system entails for families in different income brackets.

Thanks to the financial assistance program the incomes of families with children earning less than 20,000 kronor a year are increased by about one third after their tax has been subtracted. [As of April 1, 1977, the exchange rate was: 1 krona = $0.24. Eds.] By comparison, those families with incomes over 60,000 kronor per year receive a net reduction of nearly half after taxes and allowances. The original income differentials between families with incomes under 20,000 kronor per year and over 60,000 kronor per year narrow from 1:8 to 1:3 once taxes have been subtracted and allowances added.[20]

Roughly speaking, families with children incur three types of costs: income loss, supervision costs, and consumption costs. Income loss arises when the mother interrupts her gainful employment to look after the children. The thrust of family policy in the 1970s is to lighten the work burden of the two-income family to enable both parents to continue with their gainful employment while their children are growing up. Central government and local authorities are concentrating their efforts on the provision of more day care facilities and other services for the families.

A family survey carried out by the Swedish Central Bureau of Statistics (SCB) estimated the average margin for consumption per child after a stated minimum standard for the parents had been subtracted from the income. SCB then examined which families could afford to support children who in-

[20] Ibid.

volve costs of 200 kronor per month. Among the single-income families as defined above, 28 percent lacked the stated minimum standard. In cases where the one spouse worked part time, the proportion below the minimum standard for children fell to about 10 percent; when both parents worked full time, the proportion below the minimum standard had fallen below 5 percent.

Unless society provides more day care facilities, one of the parents will have to abstain from paid employment so as to look after the children. It is also obvious that changing to the two-income pattern signifies a much greater financial increment than can reasonably come from allowances. Hence the Family Policy Committee assumes that financial assistance within the policy framework should chiefly aim at providing for the children and not at providing for a stay-at-home parent. The special assistance rendered to one-parent families should aim at replacing or supplementing the other parent's breadwinning effort for the child.

With that the Family Policy Committee has taken sides against paying care allowances to parents of small children. The care allowance drew a clear-cut line of political cleavage between the socialist and nonsocialist blocs in the 1976 parliamentary election. All three nonsocialist parties (Center, Liberal, Conservative) campaigned with separate proposals for the design of this subsidy. For their part the socialistic parties (Social Democrat and Communist) saw a risk that the care allowance might preserve the single-income, mother-and-breadwinner family and retard the expansion of day nurseries.

But in January, 1977, when the victorious nonsocialist bloc presented its budget, the care allowance had been excised for reasons of economy. Even so, there are situations where parents need opportunities to stay at home with their children, as when a child is born and during the period immediately following, or when a child falls ill.

As long as the husband was the sole or main breadwinner and it was unusual for married women to work outside the home, the question of income loss in connection with childbirth was a marginal problem. The maternity benefits scheme introduced in 1937 and in force until 1955 contained virtually no protection against income loss. To remedy this deficiency the Family Policy Committee wanted to convert the cash benefits payable under maternity insurance into a parenthood insurance scheme. The parents themselves should decide which one will stay at home to look after the child. Further, the Committee proposed granting parents qualified eligibility for the collection of sickness benefits as though they themselves were sick, in case either of them has to be absent from work so as to minister to a sick child under the age of ten.

The law on parenthood insurance came into force in 1974. Gainfully employed parents are entitled to apportion mutually seven months of "child leave" as they see fit. During this period they receive a daily benefit equal to 90 percent of their regular income. The fathers also share the right to ten days a year when they can stay at home with sick children. The law makes it easier to uphold the equal parental responsibility on the labor market. [By the time this book went to press, the parent insurance had been extended to nine months; part of this can be used to permit part-time work for a prorated period of time. The leave to care for ill children had been extended to fifteen days. *Eds.*]

If both parents work for gain the costs of supervising children will be paid as long as the children are small. But these costs tend to decline as the children grow up, while the consumption costs increase. If these two outlays are weighed together, there is no reason to differentiate the cash assistance payable for children by age.

But under the guiding principles for family policy, it will be up to labor market policy to afford employment to both parents, and an expansion of day nurseries is supposed to meet the need for child care facilities while the parents are gainfully employed. In this way the principles governing labor market policy, tax policy, financial assistance to families, and social insurances have become adapted to a family with two breadwinners and to parents on an equal footing. Proposals to pay care allowances to homemaking mothers have been rejected in the same spirit. Swedish family policy actively contributes toward transformation of the transitional family's sex-specialized division of labor into a new type of family with divided roles. The changing conceptions of parental roles bring children into the center of family-policy debate in Sweden of the 1970s.

Society and the Children

Several official investigations shed light on the child's situation in society. The first task assigned to the Child Center Commission appointed in 1968 was to define goals for the programs in kindergartens and day nurseries, mainly in respect of children aged five and six.

In its first report, "The Preschool," [21] the Commission put forward a

[21] The Child Center Commission, "The Preschool," SOU 1972, No. 26.

pedagogic program and set out the development theories on which the program builds. As part of its overarching goal to give "every child the right to good development potentials," the Commission identified the following pedagogical or educational goals:

1. *Ego perception*. Together with the parents the preschool shall provide capabilities for the child to develop and stabilize a perception of self as an individual.

2. *Communication*. The preschool shall provide capabilities for the child to develop gradually its ability to communicate with the environment.

3. *Concept formation*. The preschool shall provide capabilities for the child to develop a favorable formation of concepts.

Further, the Commission proposed forms of work and a model for interaction between children, parents, and personnel. With the advent of this ambitious program the child center is no longer a parking place for the children while the parents are working, but a development-stimulating milieu whose design wholly proceeds from the children's development needs. The child center is described as a pedagogical adjunct to the family, not as a substitute for the parents.

The second part of the report[22] takes up the organizational aspects and maps out those children with "special needs": children afflicted with handicaps, immigrant children, and children living in back-country areas.

A law on preschooling became operative in 1975. It obligates the local authorities (municipalities) to allot preschool places to all six-year-olds.[23] The municipalities are also required to provide places before the age of six to those children who for physical, mental, social, linguistic, or other reasons are in special need of stimulus and support for their development.

However, children of preschool age are not the only ones who need looking after when their parents are not with them. In 1974 the Child Center Commission presented a program called Children's Spare Time, relating to institutional arrangements for seven- to twelve-year-olds between the time they leave school and the time they return home. The institutions set up for this purpose are called "after-school centers." In addition to recommending the necessary activities and the provision of physical facilities, the Commission outlined a program for training spare-time teachers to be known as "recreational pedagogues."[24]

---

[22] The Child Center Commission, "The Preschool," SOU 1972, No. 27.

[23] Elementary school in Sweden begins at age seven. *Eds.*

[24] The Child Center Commission, "Children's Free Time," SOU 1974, No. 42.

Lastly, in its fourth report, "Education for Interplay,"[25] the Commission outlined a personnel-training program. The key term is "dialogue pedagogics." Words like "reciprocity," "problem orientation," "creativity," "awareness of values," and "dialectics" hint at the spirit of emancipated pedagogics which is here introduced. Although moving quietly, the preschool's pedagogical program for personnel training points to a stinging showdown with features of the Swedish educational system for older children, a cultural revolution that has the toddlers as its stalking-horses!

A report taking upward of 2,000 pages makes one proposal to solve the problems of caring for the children of gainfully employed parents! But how do the solutions square with the reality?

As of 1974, 14 percent of all the Swedish children of preschool age were enrolled in day nurseries and municipally run child-minding homes. In that same year, according to the labor force surveys, there were 417,300 children under seven with mothers in gainful employment. Only 26 percent of the children with working mothers have access to a day nursery or child-minding home. The provision of additional places in day care centers of all kinds has been unable to keep pace with the ever-growing number of mothers in the job world. Even so, the expansion of facilities from the mid-1960s to the 1970s has nearly tripled the number of places in day nurseries.

The government is pushing for a vigorous expansion of day care facilities. About 100,000 more places in day nurseries are expected during the years 1976–80. According to estimates made locally in each municipality, emphasis will be put on the expansion of child-minding homes under family auspices.

Although children in the age range from six months to three years comprise 38 percent of all the preschoolers, only one fourth of the total new increment of places in day nurseries has inured to children under three. At the same time, the rate of growth of labor force participation for mothers with children under three has been outstripping that for other mothers of preschool children since 1970. Nursemaids, relatives, and neighbors have had to step in to care for the smallest children.[26] It is even now apparent that the plans to build more day nurseries will not satisfy the need for places. This should cause no surprise, for the addition of each new place in a day nursery speedily lengthens the queues of children waiting to gain admission.

The shortage of places makes it necessary to assign priorities to admis-

[25] The Child Center Commission, "Education for Interplay," SOU 1975, No. 67.

[26] The Family Assistance Commission, "Förkortad arbetstid for smäbarnsföräldrar, SOU 1975, No. 62.

sions. First preference is usually granted to the children of single parents and to children whose parents are socially disadvantaged, as by nervous complaints, alcoholism, and overcrowding. This procedure is liable to lead to a high incidence of disturbed children in day nurseries.

Before decision was taken to build more day nurseries on a large scale, the public debate was chiefly concerned with the quantity of day nursery places, but once the expansion plans were officially adopted the focus of concern shifted to qualitative aspects. After all, there was no point in discussing the quality of something that scarcely existed! And critical viewpoints were used earlier as arguments against the expansion of day nurseries.

The Family Assistance Committee[27] drew attention to the long hours that many children spend in day nurseries. This investigating body had done a study of stay-in times based on a representative sample of children. The results divulged that slightly more than half of all children spend at least nine hours per day in the day nursery and one-fifth spend at least ten hours. And the younger the children, the longer the stay-in time. Over 60 percent of the children of solo parents spend at least nine hours in a day nursery compared with 45 percent of the children who have both parents. Stay-in times amounting to ten hours or more are most common for children of working-class mothers (27 percent of the mothers).

In recent years demands have been raised in Sweden to shorten hours of work across the board. Most of the talk has been about a six-hour workday for all wage earners. Those who favor shorter working hours have invoked the following arguments:

1. There would be more contacts between children and parents.

2. The sexes could share the housework more equally. Instead of women working part-time and men full-time, everyone would have a six-hour workday.

3. Democracy would be vitalized in popular movements, trade unions, and neighborhood communities.

On the other hand, male voices have been raised on behalf of a four-day week with longer, unbroken weekends.

The Family Assistance Committee did not think it advisable to anticipate a future cut in working hours for everyone, but proposed shortening the hours for parents with children under three. In its deliberations the Committee said that:

> The favorable effect of a good day nursery milieu can be lost if the stay-in time is too long. Be a social and pedagogical program ever so well-thought-out, it will have no efficacy if the children are too tired to assimilate the content.

[27] Ibid.

The long hours that parents put into working and traveling give rise to various problems. . . . the time that parents and children can spend together becomes too short. . . . children and parents are too tired. . . . the day nursery is intended to be an adjunct to the parental home and not to replace it.

The Committee proposed extending the childbirth coverage of parenthood insurance from seven to eight months, adding that one and the same parent may not use more than seven months at the most. This means that the father must use some of the time if the family is going to take full advantage of its benefits. The Committee also proposed a technical solution to enable parents of children under three to reduce their time on the job to six hours per day. The compensation period would apportion 300 days to each parent. Solo parents would of course be entitled to take full advantage of 600 days for themselves.

This proposal stirred up a controversy. The Swedish Confederation of Trade Unions (LO) rejected it, arguing that the reform would not be feasible for their member groups but would lead instead to discriminating against parents of small children in the job world. That would not solve the problem for the worst-off groups.

In the 1976 election campaign the then-governing Social Democratic party went out to the voters with a new scheme devised to make the proposal more useful because of its inherent flexibility. The coverage of parenthood insurance would be lengthened to twelve months—and the parents could decide for themselves how to use the leave before their child reached the age of eight: as unbroken time at the beginning; as a six-hour workday during the child's first three years of life; as a prolonged vacation period (or some other variant) spent with the children. However, two and a half months were reserved for the father and could not be taken by a married mother. Among other things, this provision would make it easier for men to claim child leave.

The time problems still remain for parents of small children. The debate has taken on a more acerbic tone with the LO's demand to keep day nurseries open at night for the children of night shift workers and for that mounting proportion of wage earners whose working hours are scheduled outside ordinary daytime hours. The Social Democratic party itself is split on the question of opening day nurseries at night.

On the one hand, it is argued that demands for efficient job performance should not be allowed to infringe on the rights of children to be in the safe custody of their parents at night; on the other hand, the LO contends that the actual state of affairs is such that parents of small children are overrepresented among night shift workers—some children will inevitably be left alone in the dwelling overnight or will have to sleep in a car parked at the factory. Where does the public interest come in when there is a conflict of interests between parents and the capitalistic economy? Family policy is brushing more and more against the very structure of the job world.

The big wage-earner organizations, the LO and the Swedish Central Organization of Salaried Employees, are important pressure groups in family policy as well. They have devised programs for family policy just as thoroughly as the political parties have done. On issues such as equality between the sexes, the expansion of day nurseries, and a leveling-out of incomes among families with children the socialistic parties see eye to eye with two of the three opposing parties, Center and Liberal. The lines of cleavage are to be found in such things as the attitude toward payment of care allowances to homemaking mothers and opinions on the construction of the reforms. On the level of principles the debate has been about:

1. *Voluntary versus compulsory aspects.* Shall, say, one part of the parental time off be reserved for fathers, or shall fathers themselves decide whether they are interested?

2. *General versus selective measures.* For example, should there be a cut in working hours across the board, or shorter working hours for parents of small children?

3. *How things should be versus what they actually are.* For example, should the nurseries open at night?

There is no doubt but that the scope of the debate on family policy has escalated to a broad public debate during the 1970s.

Measures that have been proposed for children have brought new questions in their train. The quest to integrate "children with special needs" in child-center programs, together with ordering priorities for their placement in preschools, brings to the fore the special activities to uncover the hidden demands on the municipalities. The society's increased interest in public scrutiny raises problems of secrecy and family privacy. Higher standards of educating and training child care personnel, plus the lively debate being waged on the upbringing of children, have made it clear that the parents must be included as insightful partners. This explains the background of the viewpoints put forward by the Working Party for Society's Child Care Facilities[28] on various matters, among them privacy, integrity, activities to uncover the latent demands, and training people for parenthood.

In connection with the 1968 Child Center Commission, a sociological

[28] The Working Party for Society's Child Care Facilities, "Samhällets barnomsorg," SOU 1975, No. 87.

analysis[29] of children's nurturing conditions came out, examining the sociopsychological situation of children and adults in the light of geographic mobility, ideals of social mobility, and the society's functional differentiation. Considering that child psychology has largely moved in a social vacuum, the sociological analysis put the interaction between children and adults in a societal frame of experiences, interests, and dissensions. The Child Environment Commission was appointed in 1973. Its investigative data were called upon

> to illuminate the children's total life situation today, how it has evolved and how it can be made to underpin the ordering of priorities between different political efforts, both within the family-policy reform work and the reform work within other societal sectors. Among other things, the Commission will illuminate which repercussions different alternatives to family-policy measures may have on sectors which lie outside the sphere of family policy proper. For changes in the family-policy area it is also essential to be able to judge how changes in other societal sectors may be expected to affect the children's living conditions.[30]

In 1975 the Commission's first report, "The Children's Life Environment,"[31] was published along with seven reports submitted by independent experts on various topics, notably the physical environment, the working conditions of parents, and child culture. Two of these reports, the one a sociological critique[32] and the other pedagogical,[33] point out the absence of substantive content in the dialogues, communications, and ego perception of the pedagogical programs. The question of value content in upbringing is pointed up by the day nurseries' growing role and by the subject matter of the planned parenthood training courses. Many years ago spokesmen for the Swedish labor movement and the established church had entered into some sort of compact, a "historical compromise," as it were, whose gist was, "If you don't say anything to your children, I won't say anything to mine either." This "agreement" is now called into question.

Public debate on family policy in the 1970s puts stress on holism, qualitative aspects, and ideological values in a way that differs from that in the 1950s and 1960s. When it comes to evaluations of the family policy pursued, one can in a sense regard the recurring official investigations as a follow-up of what has happened in the meantime. As such, a great deal of

[29] Rita Liljeström, "Samhället och barns utveckling," SOU 1975, No. 31.

[30] The Child Environment Commission, "The Children's Life Environment," SOU 1975, No. 30.

[31] *Ibid.*   [32] Liljeström, "Samhället och barns utveckling," SOU 1975. No. 31.

[33] Eva-Mari Köhler, "Barns uppfostran och utveckling," SOU 1975, No. 33.

the subject matter has revolved around measures in the economic and housing amenities area as well as knowledge of demographic conditions and changes on the labor market.

A Glance at the Future

The 1970s in Sweden have on the one hand witnessed the undertaking of vigorous political initiatives to democratize the job world. New laws have been enacted which confer greater influence on the employees but presuppose widespread mobilization of the employees if the legal letter is to be filled with real substance.

On the other hand, several tendencies point away from the job world. To illustrate, there are the proposals to cut working hours across the board; heavy municipal and commercial investments in leisure; men's increased responsibility in the home and as fathers; the public sector's investment in parenthood training; activation of parental collaboration with day nurseries, schools, and leisure activities transcending age limits; and endeavors to expand the social networks around families with children toward integrated neighborhood communities with revitalized participatory democracy.

The participation of parents in the job world and in the development of more open life styles and social networks around the family raise urgent coordination problems—failing this, how are they supposed to perform adequately when the time frame is already squeezed as it is?—and will require vigilance to insure that the quality criteria are met. On the other hand, reforms in the job world and a more open family with several adults who answer for the children are other determinants.

In a future perspective family policy faces some heavy going. Broadly interpreted, family policy has to coordinate its efforts with those of labor market policy—likewise broadly interpreted—in order to solve the composite problems and meet the demands imposed by reorganizing a sexspecialized society into a better integrated and more egalitarian society. Apart from the women, this is also a matter of reintegrating the children in a closer reciprocal action with the adult world, and also of abolishing the injustices that the vertical differentiation of the children's parents now brings in its train.

So much for this vision of family policy. It should not be permitted to hide the fact that there is still a yawning gap both deep and wide between the arguments and political goals of the official investigations and the surrounding everyday reality.

≈2

NORWAY

Hildur Ve Henriksen
and Harriet Holter

IN NORWAY, AS in other Scandinavian countries, the distinction between family policy and other types of social and economic policy is not entirely clear. Measures labeled "family policy" have frequently been introduced to cope with other problems than the family per se; on the other hand, a number of state interventions in economic and social affairs may have had far-reaching effects on family life and the development of the family institution. Norway has developed an extensive system of public social security and health services of which only a minor part is explicitly termed family policy. In the following, we discuss government measures that are officially labeled family policy plus some parts of the social policy system that according to common sense should also be classified as affecting the family institution or certain categories defined by their "membership" in a family (mothers for example).

In any case, government intervention in family affairs is seen by the present authors as lagging behind the changes in family life itself. The considerable shifts in the patterns of marriage and family that have characterized Norwegian society since the beginning of industrialization are mainly results of changes in the production system. It may be true that the family is a strong institution as far as its very existence is concerned—few societies if

DR. HILDUR VE HENRIKSEN is Magister of Sociology, Institute for Social Research, Oslo, Norway.
DR. HARRIET HOLTER is Professor of Social Psychology, University of Oslo, Norway.

any are without some kind of officially recognized family institution—on the other hand, this institution is highly vulnerable to changes initiated in other spheres of society. The strict institutional division between the sphere of production on the one hand and the sphere of reproduction on the other hand that is found in Western capitalist societies is in one sense only apparent.[1] The production system—work life, technology, economic development, the market—more or less determines the patterns of the personal or private sphere. The division between them serves several functions, one of which is to leave the owners and decision-makers in production free to pursue their goals without too much regard for the conditions of reproduction.

Compared to the changes in the concentration of industry, the request for mobility of the labor force, urbanization, and the pursuit of new markets to keep up profit—trends which deeply affect family life—government family policy is of lesser consequence. This policy may, however, enlarge or diminish the effects on the family of developments in the sphere of production. As will be briefly discussed later, this should be the main frame of reference for evaluation of a family policy. The difficulties of evaluations, however, are obvious since the changes in family life are difficult to assess in a precise way, and also because these changes are the result of so many and often invisible circumstances in the economy and technology of a society.

Adding to these difficulties in discussing family policy as a clearly defined topic is the fairly understandable fact that government intervention itself is not guided by any too clear conception of the family or the forces governing the family. Nor are policy-makers too interested or willing to formulate goals or ideas as to what kind of family institution they want to support, *and* why. Norwegian family policy is, then, above all, characterized by a pragmatism that sometimes is reflected in conflicting measures and diffuse ideas about the family.

---

[1] The term "sphere of production" is here used to connote those activities or institutions that function to produce and market goods and services. The sphere of production is characterized by the necessity of producing for profit and by a property system which implies a contradiction between labor and capital. The sphere of reproduction comprises the activities and institutions, the purpose of which is to reproduce labor: the family, the educational system, the health services, the social policy agencies, and social policy apparatus, for example. This sphere is characterized especially by caretaking and socialization.

Historical Antecedents of Norwegian
Family Policy

In Scandinavia the concept of family policy was seriously introduced for the first time at the beginning of the 1930s. A debate on the family institution had for a long time been confined to small circles and was characterized by an ambiguity typical of the culture in the Nordic countries as regards marriage and family life.

This tendency to ambiguity originated in the period of early industrialization—for Norway, the latter part of the nineteenth century. On the one hand, the religious and "folkways" traditions of agricultural society were carried on and supported by—and also in themselves supporting—a patriarchal family pattern. On the other hand, a protest against the norms of the patriarchal family was gaining ground toward the end of the century. This protest was founded in the principles of liberal bourgeois culture. Authors as different as Henrik Ibsen and August Strindberg—among others—were literary exponents of a critical view of the family. Both the adherents and the opponents of the family were looking at this institution from a *moral* perspective. In conservative and religious circles the family was and still is considered of great moral consequence in itself, and also as the basic institution, the institution per se, on which society builds its norms and values. For the liberal protesters against this view, the main point was that the relationships within marriage and the family were based on force and suppression and were thus basically inhuman and immoral. On this score, liberals were joined by left-wing socialists who analyzed the family in the tradition of Marx and Engels.

The family itself, however, remained fairly stable as an institution through the latter part of the previous and the beginning of this century. When it became obvious that the use of child labor threatened to decrease the value of labor considerably, Norway, like other industrialized countries, abolished the use of children in production and, in the same vein, introduced some protective measures for working women.

The first clear sign, perhaps, of the formation of a more "modern"— that is, small, intimate, private nuclear family—in Norway came in the middle of the nineteenth century when single women of the bourgeois were given opportunities to go out into a working life so as not to burden their families economically.

These changes are all part of international trends common to Western industrialized countries in the previous century. Norway was, however, making a unique concession to liberal ideas on the individual and his rights when a law on illegitimate children in 1915 gave these children equal rights with children born within wedlock to the name and inheritance from the father. The status of unmarried mothers was somewhat improved, and at the same time married mothers were given a more secure position. However, these legislative measures were not aimed at the family institution as such, but rather at categories of disadvantaged persons.

Another set of ideas which originated in the liberal bourgeois tradition, but which were more obviously family policy-oriented, appeared in Norway in the 1930s. The chief representative of this view, Margarete Bonnevie, analyzed the situation of women and explained their suppression as founded in the family institution. Consequently, she proposed a number of family policy reforms aimed at facilitating the married woman's entry into the labor force and at the same time increasing the husband's responsibility for the care of home and children. Bonnevie's view did not make much impact at the time, but as will become apparent, similar ways of thinking are being more widely accepted in the 1970s.

During the 1920s and 1930s, however, the growth and increasing strength of the labor movement dominated the Norwegian political scene. The ideas on economic growth and social welfare which developed within Scandinavian social democracy were for several generations to have priority over more specific consideration of the family.

In contrast to the Swedish social democracy, its Norwegian counterpart did not take any special interest in the family in the late 1930s. The birth rates that were one source of increasing concern in Sweden in the 1930s did not apply to the same extent in Norway. Nevertheless, the Swedish ideas and discussions originating in the writings of Alva and Gunnar Myrdal in the 1930s had an effect in Norway as well, but mainly in the period after World War II.

Norwegian Family Policy

The beginning of the postwar period was characterized in Norway by fairly stable family relations, compared to other Scandinavian countries. Being somewhat behind with respect to industrialization and urbanization, and with traditionally strong elements of Low Church cultural influence, the divorce rates, the incidence of illegal abortions, and the number of children born out of wedlock, for example, were relatively low. The number of married women in the labor force was remarkably small. During the 1960s, however, there was accelerated development toward considerable change in these patterns. But the results of these later trends show up in terms of family policy mainly after 1970.

Nevertheless, Norwegian family policy in the period from 1945 to 1970 was characterized by a growing tendency to look at the family and its problems as a public concern. To a certain extent the political character of the family institution became recognized, or at least, the possibility of influencing the situation of the family by means of tax policy, children's allowance, housing policy, divorce and abortion legislation became a matter of serious consideration. It is true that the radical left wing of the Norwegian Labor Party has a tradition of distrusting the family institution as such, and in the 1920s and 1930s the suppression of women and children within the family was viewed by left-wing circles as a result mainly of the capitalist ownership of the means of production. Socialism was regarded as the only way by which the family might be changed into an institution with freedom for all its members. However, the moderate section of the Labor Party, which has been and is the core of the party, never considered the family institution to be a problem of this order and character. On the other hand, neither did the social democracy look upon the family as an important vehicle by which those societal changes should be brought about that were the explicit goals of postwar social democratic labor: a general rise in the gross national product, full employment, redistribution of income between high and low earners, and a certain development of public control over the capitalist economy. A development toward these goals implied to the social democracy that it should improve its policies and secure a decent standard of living for everybody, regardless of the individual's family relationships.

However, since so many of the manifest political goals were centered on the security and well-being of the workers, a policy for those who were either too young or too old or in other ways unable to work had to be developed. In some of these matters, the Norwegian Labor Party was influenced by the ideas originating in Sweden. The Swedish economists Alva and Gunnar Myrdal were among the first in the world to present a systematic analysis of the social and political implications of the population problem, and to suggest practical solutions. Up to this point, the population policy in most European countries had been chiefly of a conservative nature and very often developed within a military and imperialistic frame of reference. The Myrdal paradigm introduced a new way of thinking in that it combined the goal of keeping the birth rate at a fair level with such radical measures as birth control and active support of the family. In 1940 Alva Myrdal presented a family policy program for Sweden which comprised a wide spectrum of measures. The main tenets were: parents should be encouraged to give birth to a reasonably large number of children; free choice of the number of children should be made possible by free access to contraceptives; unwanted pregnancies should be prevented; and a number of educational measures for the family should be introduced in order to give popular information on marriage, birth control, child care, and housing. Support in the form of cash grants to the families according to number of children, as well as measures in the form of in-kind benefits (free school meals, clothing, and so on) was discussed.

In Norway the discussion on the Myrdal ideas was interrupted by World War II. It continued, however, in certain circles, and in the course of the war years a feeling developed in many quarters that the debate on family policy should be kept within a *social-political* frame of reference and not a moral one.

As a Policy for Children
Since equality in standard of living was one of the main goals of Norwegian postwar social policy, the question of redistribution between those with and without children had arisen by 1945. The problem of cash grants versus in-kind benefits (subsidizing housing, school meals, children's clothing, and so on) was given some attention. Those who preferred cash grants were of the opinion that giving support in the form of in-kind benefits was equivalent to taking away the parents' responsibility for the care of their children, maintaining that parents know best what their children need. Those who wanted in-kind benefits stated that such support benefited the children; furthermore, by making use of this measure, the government would be better able to integrate family policy with the general economic and social planning.

In 1946 a law on children's allowances was introduced in Norway as part of the first political program after the war. This program was the result of joint efforts of politicians from all parties, a fact which shows that ideas on the welfare of children were easily introduced in our country.

In the years after 1946 other measures were added to the system of children's allowance, such as social insurance for family supporters, advancing the father's child-rearing payment in cases when the parents have not married, housing subsidies, and health centers for mothers and children. The policies of taxation and of housing were developing a kind of "family-centeredness'' in the 1950s to such a degree that large groups of unmarried persons, both male and female, felt that they were given too small a share of the public benefits and consequently formed an organization to serve as a pressure group to influence the authorities. In general, the type of family policy that appeared in Norway toward the end of the 1940s and in the 1950s had as its main goal the strengthening of the *economic* situation of the family with special regard to the children.

As family policy thus became, basically, a policy for the redistribution of income, the authorities contributed to a definition of family problems as problems of consumption. The debate was partly about the children's standard of living, partly about leveling income differences between families with children and other types of households. The question of how the family as an institution ought to function was only peripherally a matter of discussion in the years immediately following World War II. In family policy, as in other parts of the policy of the Norwegian Labor Party, scant attention was given to the views and principles of the party's left wing.

It is symptomatic that although Norway had excellent experts on sex education as early as the 1930s, the politics of birth control and advice on the use of contraceptives was very slow to develop in our country, compared to elsewhere in Scandinavia. The practical political measures that were introduced supported the traditional view that the family institution should be conserved, and the question of contraceptive methods was considered to belong to the private sphere. In one respect, however, the official family policy constituted a radical break with earlier views and policy, and this was the wide acceptance of a certain public responsibility for the economic welfare of children. One might say that the children were viewed as separate from the family, in the sense that economic child care became part of the public sphere while other elements of the family, such as the marriage relationship and the relationship between parents and children, still belonged to the private sphere.

As a Policy Concerning Old Age and Illness

As mentioned, the manifest political goals of Norwegian social democracy were mainly centered in the life situation of industrial workers, small farmers, and fishermen. During the 1960s the Labor Party introduced, not without considerable political fight, a social insurance system through which all persons above the age of sixty-seven, whether or not they have been employed, receive a pension. Into this system has also been merged other types of social security measures for different groups: unmarried mothers, handicapped and disabled of many types, widows and orphans. Consequently, in the beginning of the 1970s a clause in the family legislation mandating children's responsibility for the care of their old or ill parents was abolished. Along with the pension system certain types of public aid to the old and the disabled have been introduced. Welfare centers, subsidized train and bus fares, old age homes and institutions, support for improvement of housing conditions of old people, and special services in the homes of old people are among these. The attempt to shift the responsibility for the old and the ill from the family to the public sphere is perhaps the most complete and radical political measure toward a "functional drainage" of the family in our time.

As a Policy for Women
Only to a limited extent could Norwegian family policy from 1945 to 1970 be said to address the position of women specifically. The main legal protections of women in marriage were established in the 1920s. Some improvements in the situation of unmarried mothers were made in the postwar period. Furthermore, the public health insurance system which covers the whole population was reformed in 1956 with respect to delivery services, cash contributions to the mother, and free care in hospitals. It should also be mentioned that the child allowances are paid to the mothers.

During the postwar period the number of married women in the work force, especially mothers with small children, was much lower in Norway than in other industrialized countries. Only toward the end of the 1960s did this situation change, and the proportion of married women in the labor force increased from 11 percent to 23 percent during the decade. It is the contention of the present authors that there is a close connection between this increase in married women's employment and the decrease in that part of the male jobholders' salaries which is the "family support" amount. In the 1950s and 1960s a tight labor market and recession tendencies in the economy in general called for a greater part of the female population to enter the work force. Consequently, the "family support" part of the men's wages was reduced (or rather did not increase as much as the cost of living), and families with children could not manage economically unless the mother went out to work. The explanation that has been most widely accepted for the difficult economic situation of families with children is inflation. Inflation, however, can be seen as functional for bringing a maximum of labor supply. Other explanations of the increase in women's employment have been social-psychological, taking into account women's isolated situation and their need to use their abilities. We do not contest these views but we think that they mainly explain the situation of middle-class women. The fact is that the tendency for a large number of mothers with small children to enter the work force was not apparent in our country until the middle of the 1960s, and the problems of working mothers were not an important issue in the official debate on the family before this time. The view that children need their mothers at home was strongly advocated in most political parties, also within the Labor Party.

However, to the extent that it is possible to say that family policy in Norway was influenced by the ideology and theoretical discussion on the position of women, it was characterized by contradictions. On the one hand were attempts to strengthen the mother-child relationship, for instance in establishing health centers for mothers and children. On the other hand, the official authorities expressed faintly positive views on the participation of married women in the labor force. The conflicting attitudes were reflected in the rather weak interest in the building of, and the very slow increase in the number of, day care institutions for children before the 1970s. Until recently, the interest of the official authorities in a systematic analysis of the family institution as such was limited in our country. From the middle of the 1950s the ideas of the sociologist Erik Grönseth on the relationship between the father's provider role, the authoritarian structure of the family, and the suppression of women represented theoretical and at the same time practical suggestions for family reforms: equality between the sexes as regards the responsibility for work both inside and outside the family combined with a child care salary to be paid to that parent who chooses to take care of the child. Grönseth's suggestions presuppose considerable changes in the production system, which in the eyes of politicians and administrators as well as of the representatives of private enterprise was incompatible with a rational and effective use of the labor force. Grönseth's ideas are, however, taken more seriously at present.[2]

The question of a child care salary, or, as it has also been called, a mother's wage, has been discussed off and on during most of the postwar period. But the cost of introducing a child care salary seems almost prohibi-

[2] Erik Grönseth, "Economic Family Policy and Its Guiding Images in Norway," in P. de Bie and C. Presvelou, eds., *National Family: Guiding Images and Policies* (Louvain, Belgium; International Scientific Commission on the Family, 1967); Hildur Ve Henriksen and Harriet Holter, "The Familial Institution—Alienated Labor-producing Appendage to Market Society," in Larry T. Reynolds and James M. Henslin, eds., *American Society: a Critical Analysis* (New York: previously published by David McKay Co., Inc., 1973; copyright, Longman, Inc., 1973), pp. 248–93.

tive. There were and are doubts about the possibilities of financing such a salary, and about the way the financing should be organized: from the general tax budget? Or from the profits of private enterprise? Furthermore, negative views have also been presented. A child care salary may tie married women even more strongly to the home in that it may never be high enough to represent a free choice to most fathers. At the same time, a child care salary may hinder married women from seeking employment outside the home.

The private sphere of Norwegian society has not been influenced by a liberal-bourgeois tradition of sexuality to the same extent as neighboring countries. The changes that took place in marriage legislation in Norway in the 1940s and 1950s must be viewed more as an expression of a desire to strengthen the position of the wife within the family and not as an attempt to liberalize the divorce rules in themselves. Today, there is a certain reluctance in Norway to follow the same course as Denmark and Sweden in the liberalization of marriage and divorce legislation. Furthermore, this fact does not seem to create any serious protests in our country.

In one important respect, the position of the mother was strengthened during the years under discussion. In more than 90 percent of divorce cases the mother is granted the right to keep the children. Also, on behalf of the children's welfare, she will get the family home. It may be a matter for discussion, however, whether strengthening women's position *as mothers* in the long run strengthens their position *as women*. A policy that stimulates fathers to take care of their children may over time be more liberating to women.

Summing up, one might say that the welfare of the children became the focus of family policy from 1945 to 1970. The public authorities took over part of the economic responsibility and the health of children, but did not in other ways interfere in the relationship between parents and children.

Norwegian Family Policy in the 1970s

Since the middle of the 1960s there has been a rapid change in Norwegian family life and an increase in problems, posing questions about the traditional family's possibilities for survival. Family size is diminishing, the birth rate has been declining over the last ten years, the number of divorces has about doubled over a decade, and the number of children born out of wedlock is increasing. The age of marriage is lower than ever before, however; and the relative number of marriages is larger than ever. At the same time, couples are cohabitating more frequently without having confirmed their marriage legally ("uncertified marriages"). The number of spouses in need of guidance and treatment seems to increase, so does the part of the population that seeks psychiatric help—facts which may be attributed to conditions in work life as well as to family and kinship relationships. It may be a matter for discussion and choice of words whether the family as an institution is tending toward dissolution or toward fundamental changes. The present authors have described the development elsewhere as a change toward an individuated, intimate, privatized family type.[3] Of equal importance is the apparent tendency to dissolution of the traditional, stable social networks that have been informal supports of the old family type. The development seems to be part of a possibly transitory breakdown of the more traditional structure of the reproductive sphere. There is no doubt about the tendencies for public agencies and government administration to accept more responsibility for the childbearing and rearing functions in general.

The event originating in the production sphere that has had the greatest effect on the family institution in Norway in later years is probably the change from one-earner to two-earner families. This seems to have influenced most strongly the Labor Party's attitude in bringing family policy into focus. Other trends in this sphere have also been of consequence for the family institution and family policy. One of these is the strong tendency to concentration of production which has resulted in many types of problems: the difficult situation for families who have to move to high-pressure areas and, correspondingly, the problems of families who stay in a local area that loses many of its vital functions, such as schools, places of work, health services, and so forth. It has become apparent that the lack of possibilities for family members to share their daily life has not been defined as a public issue and has not been granted status as an important problem in the same way as the economic problems of the family. The change within the economy in the 1960s and the beginning of the 1970s had as its consequence a severe crisis in family relationships both qualitatively and quantitatively. This crisis seems to have resulted in a change in the nature of psychological and social family problems. Institutions that render psychiatric service to the

---

[3] "Individuation" of the family connotes the process whereby the individual family member to an increasing degree is integrated into other institutions than the family. "Intimization" of the family points to a development of the family institution to become more of a setting for close, intimate personal relations, whereas "privatization" is a (quasi) movement toward a type of social closure of the family which makes public insight into a family out of place. The present authors have developed these concepts in *Familien i klassesamfunnet* (The family in class society) (Oslo: Pax, 1975).

families are growing in number, and the established institutions are more and more trying to help and treat whole families instead of individual family members. This development is characterized by two trends: firstly, new institutions are created, such as family counseling centers; and secondly, the already existing institutions are changing their types of service from giving mostly individual and medical care to treating whole families. The changes in the health centers for mothers and children are an example of the latter trend.

In the beginning of the 1970s this situation gave a new impetus to the principal debate in which politicians also take part, on the family as a social institution. This debate is influenced from three different quarters: in psychiatric-psychological circles the phenomenon of psychic health is viewed in relation to the interaction patterns of family members; in the various groups that are influenced by Marxist ideas the focus is on the relations between family and society; in the feminist movements the interest is in women's position in the family and how this position influences their total life situation.

The State and the Family with Children

In 1974 the Ministry of Consumer and Administration Affairs presented a paper (hereafter referred to as the P.P.) to the Parliament in which the Ministry had carried out an analysis of the situation of families with children.[4] It is of importance to note the reasons that were given by the Ministry for presenting this P.P. In the introduction the Ministry states that the question may be posed whether a clear definition of the official goals of family policy is to be found anywhere in Norway today. The Ministry goes on to say that the resolution agreed upon by the Council of Europe may serve as a basis for the Ministry's own definition of such goals. In this resolution the European Council states that

> the goal of the unity of the member nations in the Common Market is to facilitate the social development of the different members. Such a "social development" is dependent on conducting an adequate family policy which meets the needs of the family both through economic and financial measures that may compensate for the burdens placed on the family; and through an adequate organizing of other services in order that the family as a unit, and its individual members, may have an opportunity to develop fully their capacities within society.

With this goal for family policy the Ministry attempts to shape a new way of thinking about the relationship between the family and the state: the

4 "Barnefamilienes levekar," *Stortingsmelding*, No. 51, 1973–74.

principle that measures for strengthening families with children ought to take the form of cash payments and subsidies is left out, and is replaced by the idea that an increase in the employment of married women in the labor force will be far more effective as a means of strengthening the economy of these families than an increase in the children's allowance. In this connection the Ministry presents its view on the desirability of increasing the opportunity for each individual family member to make a free choice of occupation. It also stresses the importance of making each individual member able to realize his or her abilities and interests, and states that this will strengthen the family institution.

Furthermore, the P.P. states that in order to enable a larger number of married women to enter the labor force, society has to build more child care institutions of different types: day care institutions, leisure-time institutions, playgrounds, youth centers. According to the Ministry, this may also serve the needs of children because the general economic development has led to impoverishment of the types of milieu in which children may play and have fun together. Also, the homes are no longer able to meet the needs of children and teen-agers for social contact and creative play.

With regard to previous principles in family policy, the P.P. proposes certain changes in the definition of what are *public* and what are *private* functions in the care and socialization of children. The state should assume much more responsibility for the social welfare of the younger generations. On the other hand, the economic situation of the family is to a greater extent defined as a private responsibility of parents.

As to the role which the family institution plays in society, the Ministry in parts of the P.P. attributes very important functions to the family: the family is presented as the institution which shall "fulfill the family member's basic need for love, emotional health, and material care and security." The Ministry goes on to state that the family "is the institution that is chiefly responsible for the child's development into a member of society." On the other hand, according to the P.P., families meet with considerable difficulty in fulfilling their functions. In this connection trends like urbanization and industrialization are mentioned as reasons for the change in the ability of homes to create good relations between children and adults or to socialize the children for adult roles. The possibilities of shaping the milieu for the children in order that meaningful activity and social experience are facilitated are also often lacking.

In many ways the P.P. represents a notable advance compared to ways in which previous governments have treated family policy. By presenting this paper the government for the first time made itself available as partner in a discussion on the functions of the family institution and the goals of family policy. Furthermore, some of the problems which the modern family has to cope with are very clearly described in the P.P. One may agree or disagree with the evaluations and conclusions that are drawn by the Ministry, but it may be appreciated that the government presents its views on such a controversial subject.

Relationship between Spouses

One of the most important political initiatives of the Norwegian labor government in the 1970s has been a proposal before Parliament to establish free abortion, and furthermore to present a law about equality of men and women. Both proposals fell through in Parliament, but only by a narrow margin, and the present Social Democratic cabinet seems determined to renew these proposals if labor is still in power after the coming election.

The government got more support when introducing a new law on work environment this year (1977), according to which the rights of women during pregnancy and the postparturition period are extended in important ways. The law also introduces new ways of thinking about the father's role. All employed women get a right to an eighteen-weeks maternity leave. If the woman is married, the couple may decide to divide some of these weeks between them. This is a completely new feature in Norwegian legal rules on maternity leave. However, the law states that the mother is to stay at home for the first six weeks after childbirth, so that the choice between husband and wife is for the remaining twelve weeks. Also, the mother may decide to use part of the maternity leave before delivery, whereas the father is granted no such liberty. During the eighteen weeks of maternity leave the one who stays at home is granted 90 percent of his/her wage. (At the moment, the payment is calculated somewhat differently, but it is expected that the rule of 90 percent of the wage will be introduced in the near future.) In addition to the right to the paid maternity leave, the mother *or* father has a right to take further maternity leave up to one year (eighteen weeks plus thirty-four weeks) without pay but with full job protection. If the wife is not employed, the husband has no right to any maternity leave. But all husbands, whether the wife is employed or not, may take two weeks off without pay, but with job protection. This leave is called "welfare" or "care" leave. In families where the mother is working, the father has a right to this "care" leave in addition to the right to share some of the eighteen weeks with the mother.

The main point in the argument on fathers' rights to "maternity" leave has been that for the sake of the welfare of the baby, fathers must be enabled to establish close contact with their newborn child. But the furthering of equality between the sexes has also been given much weight.

Another law has also been enacted this year, entitling working mothers and fathers to ten days leave a year each for taking care of ill children under the age of ten years.

The current debate in government circles and within the political parties and the labor unions concerns whether to give priority *either* to a further increase in the weeks of maternity leave with pay, *or* to a general reduction in work hours (the six-hour day) for parents with small children. It seems rather unlikely, if the latter alternative is chosen, that the reduction in payment which automatically follows a reduction in work hours can be compensated for. The discussion, however, focuses on the possibility of granting some kind of compensation to low-wage earners. (Special attention is given to groups of women whose work situation is difficult as regards maternity leave: farmers' wives, women working on ships, and so on). It should be noted that the new laws on maternity leave and other facilities for parents cover couples who are not legally married as well as married couples.

The State and Socialization of Children
As mentioned, the public coverage of day care institutions in Norway has until recently been rather incomplete. In 1975, however, the government put into effect a new law on day care institutions in which it is explicitly stated that the municipalities are responsible for securing children a good life situation by constructing and operating day care institutions or by financially supporting the maintenance and operation of such facilities. All municipalities were asked to develop programs for building child care institutions according to research on the need for them. The state will subsidize operating costs and the municipalities may get low-cost loans for the buildings through a state bank.

The government plans to increase the number of places in day care institutions from about 40,000 as of 1975 to 50,000 by the end of 1977—coverage of 11 percent. By the end of 1981 the number of places is intended to be 100,000—coverage of 25 percent. The municipalities are to decide the rate of payment in the public day care institutions according to the economic ability of the parents. The cost of family day care is paid partly by the parents, partly by the municipalities. Through budget procedures the government also subsidizes the municipalities' expenditures for family day care.

Furthermore, the government has recently introduced a new law on health clinics for mothers and children which should increase considerably the number of such clinics. Here all services to pregnant women, mothers and their newborn children, and to children up to school age are free. Free dental care for children in school (to eighteen years) has been in effect for some time. The present trend in the health service is toward paying greater attention to the child's emotional development and the family situation of the child although the control of the child's physical development is still very important. The father is also invited to attend the clinics to a greater extent than before.

The most recent development in policy on children appears in a "Paper on the Situation of Children" presented to Parliament by the Ministry of Administration and Consumer Affairs in 1977. The chief message of this paper is that children as a group must not be isolated from the world of adults. This has two practical implications: The physical planning authorities must take children's needs into account to a much greater extent than before. Children must have sheltered playgrounds, and all building or living quarters must be planned so that there can be a good "neighborhood milieu," especially as regards the needs of children. Furthermore, the parents must be integrated in the milieu of the day care institutions, and also in the different leisure-time activities arranged by the authorities. The municipalities will receive larger grants in order to develop a better local milieu for children. New jobs will be created in the milieu-creating field with special responsibility for the life of young children up to the age of twelve years. The paper explicitly states that the parents must be integrated in these activities. It is obvious that the government has become aware of the growing trend in our society to segregate children and adults and parents and children and that they do not want this trend to go too far. To a certain extent the paper also takes into account the further need for reduced working hours for parents with small children.

Among the issues in the current debate on the situation of children is the possibility of instituting a "parent's certificate" and a "children's ombudsman" in order to secure the rights of children more effectively.

Concluding Remarks

In Norway the 1970s have seen more activity in the field of family policy than any earlier period.

Assessing the effects of family policy on the family institution requires at a minimum the following conditions: (1) a definite goal on the part of policy-makers with respect to what kind of family one is aiming for; (2) some idea or theory about the forces or circumstances that influence family life; (3) some data on, or analysis of, the movements of these forces and of the development of family life itself. None of these requirements is fulfilled in Norway today, and the following constitute only a fragmentary approach to the questions that may be raised.

It seems feasible to discuss the effects of family policy in terms of its influence on: (1) size, recruitment, and legal requirements of family formation; (2) functional drainage and functional renewal of the family institution; and (3) tendencies to individuation and privatization of the family. These elements are overlapping, but no attempt is made here to analyze the relationships and contradictions involved.

It is probably outside the possible range of government policy in a capitalist society to initiate such changes in family patterns as are subsumed above. For example, only when circumstances other than public policy weaken the family's ability to solve the problems of the old or the incapacitated is government intervention established. It seems, however, feasible that government measures may counteract or stimulate somewhat the trends that are already present. It may, for instance, be maintained that Norwegian postwar family policy has contributed to the current change in the image of what a family is.

Since public services and allowances cover unwed mothers and cohabitating couples as well as ordinary families, this may have expanded the concept of "a family" and legitimized otherwise deviant ways of establishing families. A tendency toward a pluralistic marriage and family culture is further stimulated by the official policy. Furthermore, the government initiatives and support of information about the use of contraceptives, and its recent activities in favor of women's unqualified right to abortion, are also contributions to the establishment of a new marriage-and-family culture. Without going too far into this theme, it seems reasonable to suggest that these elements of family policy support women's independence as partners, wives, and mothers, and that the image of marriage as an intimate and mainly emotional bond is underlined.

Family policy measures may, however, be categorized into measures of *substitution* (substituting new ways for old ways of problem-solving), measures of *support,* and measures of *direct maintenance* of families.

A policy of substitution consists of establishing public services that substitute experts, public agencies, courses, and public organized care units for traditional family solutions to given problems. Day care institutions and schools relieve families of part of their socializing functions and belong to a substitution policy which usually supports the tendency to functional drainage of the family. In evaluating this policy, it should be borne in mind that: (1) the development that makes day care institutions a reasonable solution to socialization problems does not originate in government policy; (2) elements of a more collective socializing of children may be highly preferable to a totally privatized socialization in today's families; and (3) the independence of women may be increased by the present Norwegian child care policy.

The supportive parts of Norwegian family policy consist mainly of financial aids, like child allowances and housing subsidies. Such measures may or may not maintain a family institution in the long run; they are certain to make life easier for many families at the moment. Financial support of the type favored by the Norwegian government may be seen as a transfer of means to families so that they are able to fulfill certain functions. In the long run, however, this may not stimulate the family as an institution. On the other hand, money allowances and supportive services also tend to give families new tasks as families, namely, to act as integrating units for the reception of aids and services to the individual and the family as such.

As may be evident from this discussion of Norwegian family policy in the 1970s, direct maintenance measures are more and more the focus of government interventions. The establishment of public family guidance and therapy agencies, the attempt to involve the father in child care by granting leave from work in connection with a new-born child or a child's illness; the attempts—so far mostly on paper—to integrate parents in the public activities and care of children should be seen as a policy aimed directly at maintaining families as social units. This shift toward direct maintenance reflects the severity of the pressures and problems which during the last decade have hit the whole sphere of reproduction and caretaking.

Nevertheless, a maintenance policy is to some degree a contradiction of other features of government intervention in the reproductive sphere. The general social policy has since the 1930s aimed at support and aid to the *individual*, thereby—perhaps an unintended consequence—making the individual less dependent on family and kin and more dependent on public agencies and government bureaucracy. The implication is probably a weakening of the family institution, at least over time. The extensive social insurance system and health services are giving considerable support to the individual with no conditions of family status attached; proportionally few services are rendered to the family as such. In the long run this may be an important contribution of government policy to the changes of the family institution: to stimulate and go along with the tendency toward individuation of the family.

These and other contradictions in government policy that affect family life show some of the difficulties inherent in a Social Democratic administration of a capitalist society. The government cannot prevent the family from changing into that form of social unit which best serves the production system of private enterprise, as long as this system is kept under only minimal public control. It seems possible, however, to put a brake on some of the more destructive tendencies toward isolation of mothers, barriers between children and adults, and keeping women in a dependent and subordinated position in the family and in relation to men in general.

HUNGARY

Zsuzsa Ferge

FAMILY AS A concern for central policy-making was recognized at a rather early stage of development of the Hungarian social system, the People's Democracy, established after World War II. The first Family Act was passed in 1952. Its aim, as stated in paragraph 1 of the law, was "to regulate and to protect the institutions of family and marriage, to assure—in marriage and in family life alike—the equal rights of women, the protection of the children's interests, and to promote the development and education of young people"—all this in accordance with the constitution and the basic tenets of society.

This act was revised and somewhat modified in 1974, but its essential features remained unchanged. To give some idea of the contents of the old and the new act, let me point out the most important changes. The first act abolished all the bureaucratic obstacles to marriage and simplified the formalities. The new version introduced one condition, a thirty-day waiting period before the actual marriage, because the extremely high divorce rate, and especially the high incidence of short-lived marriages, suggested that some marriages were made on a rather sudden impulse.

The new act also regulates in a more flexible way the choice of name of the wife, which is a special Hungarian problem: before the war, the married woman lost her own name entirely, and took over, with a suffix for "Mrs." the *full* (family and first) name of the husband. The 1952 act gave the wife a choice between following this custom and keeping her full maiden name.

DR. ZSUZSA FERGE is Section Chief and Senior Researcher, Institute of Sociology, Hungarian Academy of Sciences, Budapest, Hungary.

The new version retains these alternatives, and offers some new ones, such as a combination of the husband's family name and the wife's first name, and so on. The issue seems to be trifling, but in reality it has many social implications. The suffix for "Mrs."—together with the husband's full name—is the only way to express the married status. Thus renouncing it renders ambiguous the marital status of women, which hitherto has been obvious. This step presupposes, then, a decrease in the public importance of the married status for women.

Divorce was regulated in a rather flexible way by the first act, but divorce by common consent was somewhat difficult to obtain then and became easier in 1974. At the same time, the new act pays more attention to the fate of the children of divorced parents and regulates their placement in a less mechanical way. According to the 1952 act, the boys were usually assigned to the father, the girls to the mother. The new act intends to place the children with the parent who seemingly will provide better care, education, and so forth, and tries to prevent, as far as possible, the separation of siblings.

In addition to these two acts, several measures, such as a general system of family allowances gradually built up since 1945 and a network of child care institutions to alleviate the burden of working parents, are aimed at helping to solve various family problems. Nevertheless, *family policy* as such was nonexistent until the 1970s. This lack is interconnected with the evolution of *social policy* in general. In order to understand the fate of family policy, one must first understand something about social policy in general.

Right after 1945 there was a short period when social policy was extremely active. Besides coping with the immediate and often very great problems caused by the war, it radically transformed the whole prewar system of social policy. This prewar system corresponded to a rather early stage of capitalist development; that is, it had more in common with the laissez-faire period than with the later, more interventionist stages. This means that social insurance was accepted only slowly and reluctantly (especially by employers), so that around 1940 it covered less than one fourth of the population in most fields, and had rather low standards. The main task of social policy was considered to be the alleviation of poverty by means of strictly means-tested selective measures and organized charity. (When a system of outdoor poor relief in kind for the aged was worked out in the 1930s, it was exalted as an extraordinary social achievement and an absolute proof of progress—but nobody inquired among officials about the reasons for massive poverty.) Besides state-organized "charity" and the slowly progressing social security provisions, a great number of voluntary associations dealt with various social problems. Thus, there has existed since 1905 a voluntary Association for Family Protection. However, in the whole period between the two world wars it was first and foremost concerned with the maintenance of the international "power position of the Hungarian race." It set as its main task the reversal of the decline in the natality rate, which was seen as due to immorality and greed (all connected with the spread of employment and the emancipatory movement of women, of course). And the birth rate decline had to be stopped because it threatened, in the long run, "the existence of the race."[1]

The constrained postwar conditions did not allow the creation of a large-scale and generous system of social benefits. But at least the main prewar principles of charity, selectivity, and discrimination that favored white-collar employees against manual workers were eliminated and replaced by an entirely different outlook. Social policy became a public concern, social security principles were accepted and implemented on a large scale, and universal, or at least nonselective, solutions gained ground. Thus, the former antidemocratic, discriminatory aspects were almost automatically eliminated.

All this progress occurred spontaneously, so to say, in the course of the revolutionary upswing that characterized these years. This also means that the theoretical basis, the principles underlying the actions, was usually not spelled out explicitly; that priorities were defined rather heuristically. Nonetheless, the outcome corresponded—almost inevitably—to democratic and egalitarian ideals because of the historical conditions.

The gains made in the three or four years after 1945 proved to be durable. But from the end of the 1940s progress in this field was considerably slowed down. This was due not only to the scarcity of resources created by forced accumulation and accelerated industrialization (although this partly artificial scarcity was at the root of the other problems). There was also the officially held belief that socialist development rendered unnecessary an autonomous social and societal policy. Under these conditions each policy measure—whether economic or noneconomic—was directly motivated by social concerns and therefore could not but forward general social aims. It was also maintained that all social problems, from poverty to alcoholism to delinquency, will automatically disappear with progress, so that there is no

---

[1] *Family Protection: a Struggle against the Decrease of the Birth Rate* (Budapest: Association for Family Protection, 1938), Preface by the Minister of the Interior.

need to pay special attention to them for the short time they will continue to exist. (A naïve, mechanistic materialism and political voluntarism formed the background of these beliefs, but it is not our concern here to elucidate their respective roles.)

These political errors did not mean that socialist social values were entirely lost from sight. Thus the 1952 Family Act stressed rather strongly the equality of women, assured their equal rights within marriage, and had a number of provisions to abolish legal and social discrimination against illegitimate children. Also, several institutions belonging to the realm of social policy continued to mark progress—even if at a slowed-down rate.

However, no attempt was made to take into account in a systematic way the social problems and their interrelations, or the various consequences—intended and unintended—of the different policy decisions. It remained, therefore, a hidden problem for a very long time that value clashes could occur, that the promotion of one ideal may have harmful effects on others. Full employment, for example, an important value in itself, could unfavorably affect family life if coupled with a high rate of commuters. All these elements contributed to the "suppression" of family policy: it could not become explicit while social policy was not, and its complex and synthetic outlook could not be accepted while a more fragmentary approach characterized policy-making in general.

Besides these general problems of social policy there were some additional reasons, connected more specifically with the institution of the family itself, which hindered the appearance of family policy. These reasons were never spelled out either, and official documents never referred to them. In my opinion, however, there *were* reservations, and it is hard to deny that they had some foundation. They were composed of the following main elements:

1. The institution of the family was "oversaturated" in Hungary with religious content. No doubt, its laicization was assured by law after 1945, but it was easy to see that the traditional religious aspect would not instantly disappear; on the contrary, the institution of the family will contribute to its maintenance.

2. The traditional model of the "bourgeois" family had an openly retrograde character, at least in its Hungarian form. It was governed by firmly held authoritarian principles legitimizing the domination of the husband, which permeated the husband-wife relation as well as relations between the generations.

3. In the first years after the Liberation, a highly positive value was at-

tached to the activities taking place in the public sphere, in politics, in the reconstruction of the country, or simply in productive work. The family could not be viewed in those years otherwise than as the stronghold of private life and individualism, diverting attention and energy from public concerns and weakening the collective values.

4. Besides—or behind—these negatively evaluated, but more or less transitory, features of the family was a more fundamental cause for reservations. It has been known for very long—let us say since Plato—that the family is the most important mediator of social positions, of privileged and disprivileged situations, and thereby of the conservation of social inequalities. That is why the communal education of children became, quite early in history, part and parcel of all kinds of radical, even if utopian, ideologies. In the Hungary of the 1940s and 1950s it was obvious that the creation of a system of high-standard communal education was no immediate possibility, and that the institution of the family had to be safeguarded. But still, it could not be accepted with enthusiasm, and was inevitably considered as a necessity to be endured rather than a value to be strengthened for its own sake. This was all the more true because at that time it was entirely unclear what would remain of the family once its productive function was rendered superfluous by industrialization, household chores institutionalized in the interest of women's emancipation, and the education of children transformed into communal education in order to eliminate the conservative role of the family.

To sum up, then, in the decade from the end of the 1940s to the end of the 1950s two main factors barred the way to family policy: the absence of an autonomous social policy on the one hand and the historical problems connected with the class-character of the family on the other. However, both obstacles were slowly overcome.

From the end of the 1950s it was gradually becoming manifest that the previous assumptions about the necessary coincidence of economic and social progress, the spontaneous disappearance of social problems, and so on, were ill-founded, and led in many spheres, contrary to expectations, to an aggravation of social difficulties. Also, the retrograde features of the family, though they did not disappear, began to fade away under the new social and economic conditions. (To give just one example: with the spread of employment and better training of women, and thus their increased economic independence, the former pattern of domination by the husband simply *had* to weaken, and even to disappear in a growing number of families.)

Finally, several new developments began to prove that the family could not be viewed as a necessary evil but as a social institution having a number of important functions, and irreplaceable for a long time. These functions were partly "objective" and partly "psychosocial." The first point may be illustrated by infant care: it turned out that nurseries, at least with their actual organization and pedagogic system, besides being extremely expensive could hardly equal the quality of home care offered in the majority of families. The second point became evident when it could be seen that the private and the public sphere were not necessarily antithetic but could complement each other: the various types of interpersonal relations answer to different social and psychologic needs, and their coexistence is not only possible, but even desirable. Actually, it seems to be a psychological truism that the closer and even the more exclusive the child's early contact with his nearest relatives, the stronger will be his/her affective security, and thus his/her ability to form good human contacts later on will be increased. This may not be an eternal "law," but it seems to hold in any case under present conditions.

The revival of the legitimacy of social policy was followed by a thorough analysis of social reality. This led, in turn, to the recognition that social policy measures may have side effects not necessarily in accordance with the original intentions, and that the various values motivating the decisions may also be contradictory, at least in the short run. It was realized, too, that a number of grave social problems were related to each other, and either their common root was to be found in, or led to, the malfunctioning of the family.

All these events led to the conclusion (among others, of course) that the family, its stability, its well-being, and the prevention of its malfunctioning or disruption were extremely important for the individuals as well as for society as a whole. Therefore, social policy could not ignore this field but had to include it explicitly among its targets.

It was at this point that family policy emerged and became one of the concerns of central policy-making. It is since then, from about 1972 or 1973, that the concept of family policy itself has been *explicitly* used.

Measures Affecting the Family prior to an Explicit Family Policy

The absence of family policy did not mean neglect of the various needs of families, especially since population policy was almost constantly in the limelight, and the majority of measures favoring an increased birth rate benefited the family, too. But the scope of the needs the coverage of which was recognized as a social obligation was, originally, rather narrow. Thus practically from the very beginning of the existence of the actual system it was accepted that, in addition to earnings from work (the main principle of distribution), central redistribution had to cover the basic needs of those who were unable to work because they were too young, too old, or ill. Children undoubtedly belonged in this category, and therefore the family allowance was introduced as a flat-rate, universal benefit for manual workers and white-collar employees in 1946. First because of a general scarcity of funds, and later on because of the political problems already referred to, the amount remained so low up to the end of the 1950s as to make it more a symbol of the commitment of the state than a real help to families. From the end of the 1950s, it was raised several times, reaching an acceptable level in the middle 1960s. However, it is not considered satisfactory yet, and is planned to be substantially raised in the coming years. The successive increases of the family allowance had two priorities: more than average rates of increase were applied to families with more than two children and to families of members of cooperatives, who had a disadvantageous position in the allocation of social benefits until the mid-1960s. They acquired entirely equal treatment in 1975.

Another early sign of the recognition of basic needs was manifest in the price system. Some goods—milk, baby food, children's clothing, and even toys and children's furniture—were and are still rather heavily subsidized.

Child care institutions, from nurseries through kindergartens up to day care centers for after-school hours, are well-known elements of the social policy of socialist countries. I do not deal with them here in detail, partly because their evolution is rather well-known,[2] and partly because their main aim was not so much to help the family as a whole as to forward the cause of women's emancipation and the collectivist education of children. It may be added, however, in order to give an idea of their importance, that 11 percent of infants under three years of age are placed in nurseries, around 70 percent of the cohort from three to six are in kindergartens, and 25 percent of the children in primary schools (aged six to fourteen) benefit from the school day care centers.

The majority of the benefits connected with motherhood—which are actually rather significant—are not directly connected with the family as such.

[2] See Susan Ferge, ''The Development of the Protection of Mothers and Children in Hungary after 1945,'' in Pamela Roby, ed., *Child Care—Who Cares?* (New York: Basic Books, Inc., 1973), pp. 341–96.

The most important of these are: a substantial maternity benefit granted as a citizen's right (although contingent on prenatal medical care); a maternity leave for employed women of twenty to twenty-five weeks with full salary; reduced working hours during the breast-feeding period; an increase in the normal period of paid leave, the number of additional days depending on the age and number of children in the family; up to sixty days per year of leave paid at the rate of illness benefits to allow parents to care for ill children under age three (up to thirty days in case of children aged three to six),[3] and, finally, the child care grant. This latter measure is, however, one of the significant exceptions in so far as family policy is concerned.

The child care grant, introduced in 1967, offers mothers who were gainfully occupied for about a year prior to the child's birth (or were students) the choice of staying home after expiration of the fully paid maternity leave or returning to work. If they stay home, they receive a monthly grant until the child is three years old. The amount of the grant was originally 600 forints and is now 960 forints (almost half of the average salary of this cohort). [As of April 1, 1977, the exchange rate was approximately: 1 forint = $0.05. *Eds.*] Since 1975 this grant has been related to the number of children. Its sum is increased by 100 forints after the second child, and by 200 forints in case of three or more children. If there are more children *under* three, the sum is multiplied accordingly. The grant does not interrupt the employment: whenever the mother wants to work again, the employer is bound to assure her a job similar to her former one. Since early 1976 the mother has had the right to interrupt the grant several times, but only once a year. Also, the years spent on grant count among the pensionable years.

The child care grant is a multipurpose measure, remedying the shortage of nurseries, promoting natality, alleviating the financial hardship of the family that may occur if the mother ceases to be gainfully occupied. In addition, it promotes the home care of small children, thus serving a specific family function.

Despite its positive aspects and its widespread popularity (about 70 percent of young mothers avail themselves of this opportunity), the measure has some retrograde, negative social side effects, frequently analyzed and criticized.[4] Actually, some modifications are projected; one of them is to transform the grant from a maternal to a parental right. This means, it is hoped,

---

[3] The two latter leaves can be used by fathers only under certain conditions, and their transformation into parental rights is currently under discussion.

[4] See Zsuzsa Ferge, "Women's Work, Paid and Unpaid," *Labour and Society* (Geneva), April, 1976, pp. 37–52.

that the main retrograde aspects of the grant—its reinforcement of the old stereotypes about the female role and duties, for example, will be in large part eliminated. Another change envisaged would lower the age limit of children accepted by kindergartens. Thus far, this limit has been set at three years, and younger children go to day nurseries. If the mother wants to return to work after two years, say, this means a rapid change of institutions for the baby—admittedly a severe shock to the infant. Now, therefore, a more flexible arrangement is advocated, whereby younger children can also be accepted by the kindergartens.

Although not strictly to the point, some comments must be added about the child care grant because its Hungarian variant is very often severely criticized by Western protagonists of women's emancipation. These criticisms emphasize the problems already referred to, and lead to the advocacy and eventually the adoption of a much shorter period of leave (one year at most). We read in a recent paper by a prominent Austrian trade unionist:

> In some quarters efforts are being made to get maternity leave extended to three years, but this suggestion is being vigorously opposed by most trade unionists, particularly by women, on the grounds that such a measure would, in all probability, mean the end of suitable employment for skilled or highly qualified women.[5]

This, and many similar arguments, seems to forget that in the majority of industrialized countries the institutional child care programs cover much less than 10 percent of children under three.[6] (In Austria, 2 percent of children aged one to three are covered.) If, then, the maternity leave with work protection ends after one year, the real alternatives are the following: The mother stays at home, without any income, and is forced to give up her employment rights. This is by far the most frequent solution. Another possibility, if the joint income of the spouses is high enough, is to employ a paid "child-minder," usually a woman. This means, therefore, only a switch in the person of the child-minder, without changing the traditional arrangement of women caring for babies, and is contingent on a more or less privileged position. The remaining solution—grandmothers or relatives act as childminders; or, at worst, *ad hoc* solutions—either have even more drawbacks than the former ones or are available only for a small minority.

[5] Edith Krebs, "Women Workers and the Trade Unions in Austria: an Interim Report," in *Women Workers and Society* (Geneva: International Labour Office, 1976), pp. 185–98.

[6] See Sheila B. Kamerman and Alfred J. Kahn, "European Family Policy Currents: the Question of Families with Very Young Children" (unpublished paper, Cross-National Studies, Columbia University School of Social Work, 1976).

I am therefore convinced that until a society is able and willing to create high-quality out-of-home care arrangements for practically all the children of the age cohort, the child care grant, offered as a parental right, with full work protection and so forth, is a better compromise between conflicting aims than the other alternatives actually offered to women.

The measures discussed up to now—with the exception of the child care grant—either were connected with elementary needs or emphasized only one or two targets. In recent years the scope of needs recognized as legitimate objects of redistribution widened, and the central decisions became more complex, trying to reconcile various and sometimes contradictory aims.

The most important new element of recognized need is housing. It is not yet acknowledged as a basic need which has to be covered out of central funds for everybody, but at least the priority of large families and newly founded families is now strongly emphasized, and some financial help is assured to families that enjoy priority. Thus Parliament passed the Youth Act in 1971. The act is concerned with the special rights and opportunities of young people, but there is a clause stipulating that the "State promotes the creation of the necessary conditions of founding a family in case of young people and assures them preferences in the satisfaction of their claim for a dwelling." This act was shortly followed by a government decree elaborating the details of the preferential treatment of large or young families (a reduced lease in case of flat rentals; an increased loan in case of new construction).

Among the newly acknowledged needs subsidized holidays are also worth mentioning. Since the end of the 1940s the trade unions and enterprises have maintained holiday homes. For a long time most of the places were reserved for adults (single or married), and only a few families could enjoy a holiday together with their children. Since the first years of the 1970s there has been a marked tendency to change the pattern and to reserve more places for complete families, with priority for those with several children. (Some enterprises also introduced free holidays or reduced tariffs for large families.)

Probably the best example of the more complex treatment of social problems is the decision of the Council of Ministers about population policy tasks, issued in 1973.

As already mentioned, the evolution of the population was an important preoccupation of the government. Nevertheless, the direct regulation of birth control was viewed in a rather simplistic way. When a slow decrease of the natality rate, combined with the atmosphere of the cold war, incited the government to encourage an increase in the birth rate in 1952, the single measure which was adopted was the abolition of free abortion, without any additional provisions. When this measure was, in turn, dropped at the beginning of 1956 because of the economic and political tensions it caused, birth control was entirely liberalized. This step again stood alone, and was completed neither by institutional marriage and family counseling, nor by the propagation of modern methods of family planning and birth control, nor again by direct and indirect measures favoring families with children. As a consequence of the former rigid administrative intervention and the lack of complementary provisions, abortion became almost the only, and certainly the most important, means of regulating the number of children. In a population of 10 million, the number of abortions approached a yearly 200,000, outnumbering births, and the birth rate dropped to 12.9 per 1,000 in 1962, slowly rising to 14–15 per 1,000 toward the end of the 1960s. But this rate was still too low to insure even the simple reproduction of the population.

Because of the deleterious effects of the high number of abortions and the unfavorable consequences of a decreasing and aging population, the practice of birth control was again modified in 1973. This time, however, the former one-sidedness was avoided and a more complex approach was adopted. The only restriction concerned the entirely free abortion, although the conditions were much less severe than in 1952. (Abortions are permitted unconditionally for women over age thirty-five, or, under this age limit, for those who already have two or three children, if there are health reasons, if the woman is unwed, if dwelling conditions are inadequate, and so on.) At the same time, a number of benefits (family allowances, the child care grant, the maternity benefit, the allowances connected with the illness of the children, the number of paid free days for mothers) were increased, sometimes significantly. Also, the priorities given to families with several children were reemphasized (child care institutions, holiday homes), and a whole packet of decisions dealt with family-planning problems. In this connection the counseling service for the protection of women, established in 1971, was reorganized as a network for "the protection of the family and women," with the explicit task of spreading modern methods of family planning. The purchase of contraceptives was rendered easier and less expensive. It was also decided that the various aspects of family planning and family life—from biological and hygienic to moral and psychological—had to be incorporated in educational knowledge at all levels, in normal and extramural courses alike.

This last decision about population policy is, then, far from being simply natality-oriented. Besides this aim, it has elements which belong to policy in regard to women, to income-maintenance policy, and to family and child welfare. Even employment considerations may be detected in it in case of the child care grant, or educational policy considerations as well, in connection with the new subjects to be introduced in schools.

This complexity suggests that at the beginning of the 1970s natality considerations were already permeated by, and coordinated with, more general family interests, which means that the idea of family policy was already widespread.

The First Governmental Framework for Family Policy

In the course of the previously described evolution the concept of social policy was introduced with increasing frequency. Autonomous sections or departments of social policy were created in the various research institutes and political or administrative bodies from trade unions to various ministries (particularly in the ministries of labor, finance, and health). Among them, the Ministry of Labor was designated as the most important state agency of social policy. Its department of social policy is currently charged with working out the main outlines, the principles, and the short-, medium-, and long-term tasks of social policy.

Obviously, the Ministry of Labor is not the sole responsible organ of social policy, even less is it charged with the execution or control of all the measures belonging to this sphere. But it is assigned a leading role in the conceptualization, planning, and coordination of actions and measures falling within the field of social policy.

As this new department worked out the methods and guidelines for its own functioning, it recognized that family policy could be a very useful umbrella concept for its work. This seemed to be logical on the following grounds:

1. The different government and nongovernmental bodies remain in charge of various subsystems of social policy. Social insurance, for instance, belongs to the trade unions; the health service, together with nurseries and some home services, to the Ministry of Health; other child care institutions to the Ministry of Education, and so on. However, the orientation and the outcome of all these partial policies have to be assessed by the

Ministry of Labor. This can be done in a consistent and unified way if the well-being of the family is taken as a yardstick, if the analysis determines how the different measures affect not only individuals, but families as well.

2. With the unavoidable fragmentation of social policy, some complex issues were lost from sight: the professionally oriented services (health, education) and the specialized, single-purpose benefits (child-related allowances, pensions) did not solve the more complex problems. The most important fields thus left over were the functioning of the family in general—how the conditions of normal existence were assured—and, connected to that, the prevention of malfunctioning if possible, and many-sided, well-coordinated social help once a situation becomes grave.

Both elements proved the legitimacy of a family policy approach, and this was in fact adopted. However, its concepts, its tools, and its methods had to be worked out. In order to accomplish this task in the most efficient way, it seemed rational to make use of the available intellectual resources. That is why the Ministry of Labor decided in 1973 to set up a Forum for Family Policy. The group, formed in 1974, is composed of experts working in government bodies (from the Planning Board to the ministries and councils), in political bodies (the Central Committee of the Hungarian Socialist Workers Party, the trade unions, the National Council of Women), in some of the biggest enterprises, and in research (mainly in some research institutes of the Hungarian Academy of Sciences). The Forum functions alternatively as a study group, a discussion group, or a working party, or its members are asked by the ministry to prepare auxiliary materials.

The department of social policy of the Ministry of Labor became, then, the central government agency of family policy. By setting up the Forum, it triggered interest in this field and catalyzed the theoretical work connected with this issue. It was in this connection that several studies have been or are currently being prepared at the request of the ministry about the desirable aims, the content, and the orientation of family policy. These studies will serve ultimately as raw material for the elaboration of the government program of family policy now under way. They may also be of some interest for their own sake inasmuch as they show the orientation of research and the various approaches used thus far in Hungary.

Nongovernmental Views and Research on Family Policy[7]

One of the studies prepared at the request of the Ministry of Labor was the work of a team composed of L. Cseh-Szombathy (Institute of Sociology), B. Buda (psychiatrist-psychologist), and A. Hajnal (Economic Research Institute of the Planning Board). This study formulates a general family policy model based on a systems analysis approach. The first part analyzes, on the basis of statistical data, the demographic, social, and economic conditions and possibilities of the family. The second part outlines the systems analysis approach, and the third part consists of propositions for further research. (In the near future a secondary analysis of statistical data on the social heterogeneity or homogeneity of Hungarian families will be carried out.) This study has eminently a theoretical relevance, but for the time being its most interesting part, the application of systems analysis to the family, is still in an initial stage.

The study by K. Kulcsár (director of the Institute of Sociology)—after a brief overview of the impact on the family of the changing economic and social conditions—discusses family policy in its relation to social policy. He interprets this relation on two levels. The more general term, "societal policy," defines the system of social goals and affects family policy inasmuch as it stresses the central role of family and deals also with the general situation of the young and the old, of men and women, and of various strata. This approach implies a long view, but very little is known about the evolution of the family in the long run. Therefore, family policy related to long-term social policy cannot do much more than create adequate material, legal, and other conditions in the interest of the *stability* of the family. (The study draws attention to the limitations of direct, legal intervention in family affairs even if it serves stability.)

The second, more restricted view establishes a connection between family policy and social policy, defined as having the task to eliminate, or at least to lessen, income and other differences which arise *independently* of the work done (because of demographic reasons, for instance). The family

[7] In Hungary practically all research is financed by the state budget, although the funds are not allocated directly to the researcher but to institutes of research. Thus in an extended sense all research is "governmental." However, the work done in research institutes is oriented toward new findings which, obviously, do not necessarily correspond to the solutions already endorsed officially.

policy derived from this concept has a "corrective" function to bridge the
gap between groups by means of various benefits in cash and in kind. This
whole task has to be seen in a medium time span, while a longer perspective
was advocated in the first case. Theoretically, dysfunctional families must
be handled by the second type of family policy, too, but before working out
the remedies more should be known about the causes of their inadequate
functioning. At the end, the study stresses the importance of a unified, coherent conception and organization of social policy.

According to a third approach (mine, to be precise), family policy is
part not only of social policy (handling essentially central redistribution), but
also of societal policy in a broader sense (aiming deliberately at the transformation of structural social relations in accordance with socialist aims).
Therefore its main tasks include:

1. The creation of material and cultural conditions which will contribute
   to modification of the former mechanisms that transmit social inequalities from one generation to the next,
2. The creation of legal, cultural, and material conditions which will help
   to render intrafamily relations more democratic.

This seems important, partly from an all-societal viewpoint, because
the character of private interpersonal relations cannot be at variance with the
social relations in the public sphere (or, taking it from the opposite angle,
the public sphere cannot be really democratic if interpersonal relations remain traditional and asymmetrical within the family), and partly because of
the interests of all the members of the family. Nondemocratic family relations create unequal chances for the development of the various family
members;

3. The creation of material and legal conditions as well as public institutions to take over some of the family functions, which will permit the
   family to operate adequately and to assume its actual functions properly.

However, these frames ought not to be too rigid, because further
changes are probable in the functions of the family as well as in the relation
between the private and the public sphere.

All these tasks are extremely complex and require the purposeful utilization of the instruments of practically all the specialized social policy services and branches, not to mention those of some other policy fields, from
regional planning to educational and employment policy. This means that
family policy cannot have a separate, autonomous organization. But the
above considerations have to be reckoned with whenever policy decisions

are made which directly or indirectly may affect the family. It is not realistic to assume, however, that family interests will be asserted spontaneously, all the less so because the implications for the family of a decision in a seemingly remote sphere may not be clearly visible. Therefore a kind of "agency" is needed which would analyze and amend the different decisions if necessary.[8]

One of the studies in this series, which has probably the highest practical relevance, was prepared by Mrs. Anna Gayer, of the Ministry of Labor. According to her, there are two main family groups which may be distinguished, even if only rather crudely. The first and by far the larger group is composed of "normal" families. They may have better or worse conditions, but they are essentially intact, can fulfill their functions, and can cope with their tasks and obligations. The second group is composed of families that are handicapped in some way. This handicap may be due to "social" reasons, such as low job qualifications and low income, or any kind of personal (not directly social) reasons, such as the lack of a parent, illness, or deviances. More often than not families fall into the second group by a cumulation of several handicaps. This second group is characterized by rather bad living conditions and therefore by perpetuation of the "vicious circle," the transmission of disadvantages to the next generation.

As far as deliberate family policy is concerned, it has to concentrate its resources on the second group in the coming years. As long as there is no substantial improvement in their conditions, it seems extremely difficult, and not really timely, to aim at raising the general standards of the first group. The measures to be used in this task are rather varied, ranging from the improvement of working conditions and the vocational training of the young members of the families to redistributive measures and a network of social workers. This network must be composed of specialists as well as generalists, and must make use of various financial and other means in order to give personalized help. An initial step in setting up this network would be to provide adequate training of the would-be social workers.

Let me add that there is an important trend in Western social thinking and sociology dealing with social work. It points out the role of the social services in reinforcing the domination of the ruling class, inasmuch as they extend the control of the dominant group to all areas of life of the dominated groups, and they undermine the self-evaluation and self-respect of the work-

---

[8] The National Council of Women, an elected body representing all the women, is fulfilling this role in the case of gender-related issues. A similar solution would be conceivable for family affairs.

ing class (or the target groups in general) by questioning their specific values and attitudes.

The grass-roots movements in the United States, a number of initiatives of social service people in the U.K., French social workers belonging to the CGT.[9] are reacting against this "trap" in various ways.[10] They usually stress the social determinants of personal problems; they show the manipulative functions of the approach which concentrates merely on the psychological adjustment of the client; they aim at developing the potentialities for self-help, especially by making better known the rights of people and the ways and means of asserting these rights. It is a widely shared opinion in Hungary that if personal social services are to be developed, they will have to adopt this latter approach.

Mrs. Gayer holds that the priority assured to the second, more deprived group of families must not imply neglect of the first one. The study in question emphasizes mainly two issues which require more attention and adequate preparation. One is the occurrence of emergencies, of critical situations, in the life of families that have been functioning adequately. In order to cope with these situations, either specific help may be necessary (as with the first group), or counseling agencies may be very useful. (The actual network for the protection of families and women does not offer practical or psychological counseling in crisis situations.)

The second task for family policy is to work out the ways and means by which family burdens can be alleviated. The assumption underlying this recommendation is that the family cannot be overburdened, that society cannot shift the responsibility for everybody to the active generations. This means that all kinds of services have to be implemented which can effectively and efficiently help the functioning of the families, especially in the care of children and of the aged. Services in this context do not signify institutions (such as separate homes for the elderly), but all types of home labor-saving devices.

In addition to the studies prepared for the Ministry of Labor, other research projects are important even if their explicit aim is not connected with family policy in its strict sense.

---

[9] Radical trade union. *Eds.*

[10] See Peter Townsend, "The Future of Social Services," in *Sociology and Social Policy* (London: Allen Lane, 1975), pp. 27–28; Jeanine Verdes-Leroux, "Pouvoir et assistance: cinquante ans de service social," in *Actes de la recherche en sciences sociales*, June, 1976, pp. 152–72; Richard Cloward and Frances Fox Piven, "The Public Bureaucracies and the Control of the Poor," in *The Politics of Turmoil* (New York: Pantheon Books, 1945), pp. 9–26 and *passim*.

There is an important research project at the Institute of Sociology, consisting of a thorough analysis of ways of life and their transformation. This study deals with, among other things, the evolution of family relations and the changing patterns of family life. The study is headed by L. Cseh-Szombathy, while the family issue is mainly handled by Mrs. Judit Sas, who has done some important pioneering work in the field.[11]

There are also various studies and researches which are indirectly connected with family life and, ultimately with family policy. The connections are visible in the research concerning aging and care for the aged (Cseh-Szombathy), and deviant behavior (R. Andorka, Central Statistical Office). One of the latest works, on children under state care, made a deliberate attempt to bring out the connection between family problems and the necessity of resorting to foster care.[12] The book shows that a vicious circle still exists, leading from the disrupted family life of the parents, especially the state care of one of them, to the same situations in the life of their children. One of the findings here, which is most relevant for family policy, concerns one-parent families. The author shows that with two-parent families foster care of children occurs only if there is an extraordinary accumulation of bad objective conditions plus some deviance (primarily alcoholism). One-parent families, however, especially those in which the father is alone, can hardly avoid resorting to state care of the child because there are no specialized social services to help solve the emerging problems. The systems of wages, of work organization, of institutionalized services, and so on, are all conceived with the "normal," two-parent, and mainly two-earner family model in the background. Therefore the absence of one parent leads not only to financial hardships, which are already partly, and may be more fully, overcome by social benefits in cash. The main difficulty is the absence of one partner in coping with various household chores, even if the partner represents only a passive "presence." (In the normal family, the night shift of one parent, shopping, going about one's affairs, does not mean that the child has to be left alone, but a parent alone has no other alternative for the time being.)

Another huge study program is covering the problem of educational handicaps and ways and means of overcoming them. These researches are

[11] Judit H. Sas, *Életmod és esalád. Az emberi viszonyok alakulása a esaládban* (Way of life and family; the evolution of interpersonal relations within the family) (Budapest: Akademiai Kiado, 1976).

[12] The study was sponsored and the research report prepared by the Institute of Pedagogy of Budapest and headed by György Várhegyi and Katalin Hanák. A book by Katalin Hanák based on these results, and focusing on the family, is in press.

financed by the Ministry of Education and the Academy of Sciences. They are preparatory studies serving to elaborate the coming reform of the educational system. Some elements deal with family conditions and their special impact on school handicaps. (The institutes interested in this aspect—the Institute of Social Sciences of the Central Committee of the Party, the National Institute of Pedagogy, the Institute of Pedagogy of Budapest, the Pedagogical Research Group, and the Institute of Sociology of the Academy—are working in cooperation.) The scope of this research covers the impact of objective life conditions, of various subcultural factors (including the specific situation of Gypsy families), of regional inequalities, and so forth. It is easy to see that they will also yield results directly relevant to family policy.

It is clear from the foregoing description that family policy is understood in various ways, on different levels of social practice, with contents which vary according to the approach selected. However, it is hard to consider these different standpoints as "conflicting definitions," nor are they in collision with each other. They all start from the assumption that *the family*, its normal functioning, the well-being of the family as a whole and of its individual members, has to be made a relevant concern in social and societal policy-making. If there were any real debate going on, it would take place among those who maintain that it is not necessary to coordinate the various decisions with a view of the family because there cannot be any conflicting aims, and therefore no unintended consequences which would be adverse to the family. But this debate does not take place. Even if the second opinion is present in a latent way in many discussions, it cannot be well-supported in the face of former experiences.

Organization and Content of State
Family Policy

The main results and conclusions of the researches and writing are systematically pooled and screened by the Ministry of Labor. They are ultimately used to lay the foundations of government family policy. As mentioned, the Ministry is currently engaged in elaborating the conceptual and organizational frames of this policy, and already it has had an impact on actual policy-making.

Since 1974 the Ministry of Labor has had to submit regularly a report to the Council of Ministers on the actual state of family policy, the main problems to be solved, and the proposed solutions. Since 1975 the Council of Ministers has officially charged the Ministry of Labor with the coordination of family policy issues that arise in the activity of any planning or administrative body with a national scope of authority. It is also assigned advisory functions in these matters.

An important decision of the Council of Ministers instructs all the parties participating in the elaboration of the five-year and long-term plans to prepare a special chapter in each special plan which will summarize all the decisions having implications for family policy. The same decision charged the Ministry of Labor to work out—in cooperation with all the interested government bodies and voluntary (political) organs—the guidelines for family policy to be implemented by employers on the one hand and local councils on the other. From these documents it is possible to infer what definitions are currently used in official family policy, and how it is understood in general. In fact, for the time being, and until the government program is worked out and endorsed, these are the most "official" documents on the matter.

The Directives for Family Policy Work—prepared for economic organizations (enterprises, cooperatives) and issued by the Ministry of Labor in November, 1975—start with a definition of family policy:

> By family policy we understand all the planned, intended effects which aim in a complex way at influencing the life conditions and attitudes of families, in order to assure that the functioning of the family will be in harmony with the requirements of socialist development. Family policy expresses, then, a system of interests relating the socialist state and its institutions to the functioning of the family.

Family policy, therefore, is an element of state or enterprises' social policy.

The first point discussed by the directives deals with the necessity of assuming family policy tasks at the enterprise. This duty stems from the fact that adequate or inadequate family conditions affect very closely the work of the individual so that even the "economic" interest of the enterprise militates for incorporating family policy in the operation of the enterprise. Moreover, under socialist conditions, the enterprise is not only an economic unit concerned only with so-called economic interests, but has to take into account more far-reaching social interests and the immediate or long-term interests of the workers. It also has to become a socialist collective, necessarily interested in the well-being of its members.

True, because of these considerations, the enterprises have carried out important social political functions in the last three decades. The introduction of the family policy perspective means only, as on the national level, that the tasks performed hitherto may be better coordinated, the priorities may be more effectively set, and the resources may be used in a more concentrated way. In this sense the family is looked upon as the *organizing principle* of the most varied social policy actions and measures.

The scope of family policy, according to the "directives," covers prevention in the interest of all the families and complex intervention in case of acute problems. In order to assure adequate operation of this policy, strong stress is laid on participation of employees in providing information about the needs, claims, and desires of the collective; and about special problem cases which may be best known by the closest collaborators. Their participation is also stressed in decisions about the priorities to be adopted, and in carrying out the decisions. If there are families that require constant social help or care, the enterprise may hire social workers for that purpose, or (more frequently) will cooperate with the local council and/or other responsible bodies.

The Directives for the Family Policy of Local Councils—also issued by the Ministry of Labor in November, 1975—are based on the same assumptions and definitions, but elaborate in more detail the importance of coordinated action. This is the core problem in the case of the councils, which for a long time have run a large number of specialized services, the majority of which work directly with the families—without having to deal with the whole family. These special services include: health and education; protection of mothers and children; home care of invalids, the aged, and those on probation; foster care of children; allocation of housing, and so on. These services—visiting nurses, social workers, probation officers—all work practically independently, and if there are institutions like day centers (clubs) for the aged, canteens for children, and so on, they also operate separately. It would be therefore advantageous to organize an exchange of information among those services as well as some coordination of their work. This could help to avoid overlaps as well as flaws, and thereby render the whole system more effective.

These documents suggest that the Ministry of Labor, and government in general, interprets family policy on at least three different levels, or in three different contexts:

1. On the most general level, the family is seen as a basic social institution whose smooth and undisturbed functioning is important not only for the private well-being of its members, but also for society in general. In-

deed, the links between the family and society are extremely strong as shown by the education of children and the production of manpower—functions which are still carried out in a large measure by the family. Therefore smooth functioning has to be assured. The means which may be implemented for this purpose are manifold. They include the utilization of social policy resources as well as the adequate formulation of legal documents (the transformation of maternal rights into parental ones, for example), not to speak of the various possibilities of acting upon the consciousness of people, or the services which may alleviate the tasks of families. The long-term objectives of societal policy which are connected with the family also belong to, this interpretation. However, this aspect, which is rather strongly emphasized by sociologists, is less predominant in actual government programs: the perspective is too remote to be formulated in terms of specific action. But long-term social planning obviously includes the main conditions and requirements of this evolution.

2. The second, more practical interpretation of family policy follows from the first. It refers to the family as the "organizing principle" or the "frame of reference" of all kinds of social policy activities. It explicitly requires that each social policy decision or measure be analyzed from the family angle and its manifest and latent consequences assessed from the viewpoint of family interests.

3. There is a third, more restricted meaning imputed to family policy, corresponding by and large to the traditional concept of family protection, at least on the face of it. The tasks stemming therefrom are connected with the existence of problem families which need—for a short or long period—many-sided social help. If there is a difference in the interpretation of this task as compared to traditional family protection, this is due to the general outlook of social policy under socialist conditions: this policy cannot stop at symptomatic treatment, cannot neglect the causes of maladjustment, and cannot rely solely upon redistribution (and even less on psychological treatment) in coping with social problems. It has to inquire into the causes of the difficulties, and has to envisage the elimination of these causes even if they imply not only the alteration of distribution, but also that of basic social relations.

Family protection is a special concern because actually there is no network of social workers with a comprehensive, general training, and because—as already pointed out—the various specialized social services work more or less in isolation from each other. Whether a separate "fifth" service will be needed[13] to overcome this problem, or whether some other solution will have to be found, is still an open question. It may be added that this third interpretation of family policy is also related to the two previous ones inasmuch as it designates the high-priority areas in the whole sphere of family policy.

As with the various theoretical approaches, so in this case of the practical application of the concept of family policy: these three interpretations are in no way opposed to each other. Rather, they are complementary approaches to a single objective. No doubt it may be somewhat confusing that the same concept is used with several different meanings. The confusion is, incidentally, somewhat increased if we take into consideration that there are a number of other policies—social policy, income policy, standard of living policy—whose content overlaps family policy (and each other). In some cases, attempts are made to define one or another of these policies in an unambiguous way. However, there are no really heated quarrels on these points.

The reason seems to be that while theoretical clarity is of utmost importance in cases of high-level abstractions, and this holds for the definition of the content and aims of the two generic categories of social and societal policy as well, the case is different when we are dealing with the subspheres of either of the broad categories.

The protagonists of all these subspheres prefer action and progress with a theoretically somewhat blurred background to clear concepts without action. The same holds true for all those who advocate one or another interpretation of family policy: they agree on one point, namely, that for the time being the first goal is to have the family policy approach accepted and applied in as many spheres as possible—and strict definitions may come later. The conceptual and factual progress of the last few years seems to prove the soundness of the option. It should be added, however, that the main dangers inherent in conceptual cloudiness can be avoided because the basic social goals (which are better clarified) orient the actions in the various subspheres, family policy among them, and give them a certain coherence.

---

[13] The reference is to an identifiable personal social service system separate from income transfers, health, education, housing. *Eds.*

CZECHOSLOVAKIA

Walter Vergeiner

SOCIAL POLICY, as much or as little as any other instrument for regulating societal processes, is internationalized in the sense that its established elements are held in common with those of other countries. In view of this, social policy is sensitive to changes and trends taking place elsewhere, and postwar development in this respect is a good example of how social policies mutually influence one another.

Joint use of social policy instruments, however, does not imply that they are everywhere handled in the same way or have equal effects as to the social levels they produce. Despite their international similarities, social policies have distinct national differences, due to the ideologies behind them and the targets they have before them. While both these motivations are closely connected, the latter nevertheless depend to a decisive extent on national, economic, social, demographic, and other factors responsible for shaping the patterns of social situations. In consequence, social policy, including the family policy of a country, cannot be viewed under ideological auspices alone, but can be fully understood only against the background of intricately interwoven determinants that act not merely in space but also in the sequence of time.

DR. WALTER VERGEINER is at the Research Institute for Labor and Social Affairs, Prague, Czechoslovakia. The paper expresses his personal views and does not represent an official position.

Historical and General Background

Up to 1918, the territory of Czechoslovakia was part of the Austrian Empire. This involved, apart from the political and national suppression of the Czech and Slovak people, economic disproportions in the structure of the regions inhabited by them. While the western part showed a high degree of industrialization during the nineteenth century, the adjoining sections of the country were predominantly rural areas with various levels of agricultural production. This resulted in differentiated demographic patterns and attributes, some of which had repercussions that are felt to this day.

The past century experienced above all a gradual decline of the birth rate from 43 to 35 per 1,000 and a parallel drop of the death rate from 33 to 24 per 1,000. The result was a fairly constant growth of population at the rate of 10 per 1,000.

Industrialization of the western parts led to labor and population concentration in larger cities which set the pace for the demographic revolution typical of the current century. However, distance from the governing center and other factors were responsible for containing the growth of the cities and checked their expansion to oversized metropolises. This too has affected history, for it has made it possible to avoid the extreme social contrasts and problems connected with intensive urbanization. Ties with agriculture were not severed rapidly, however, and in some aspects were never completely broken, which necessitated a good deal of travel between rural and urban areas. This raised specific problems later on, with the upsurge of female employment in industry, trade, and services prevailing mainly in towns.

Another element pertaining to later development was mass emigration from underdeveloped regions or even from industrial centers following economic setbacks. The depression of the 1930s added to spiritual and political as well as physical emigration, throwing the majority of the German population of the prewar republic into the arms of fascism, making them incapable of living jointly with the Czechs and Slovaks after 1945. Migrations, wars throughout the world, and depressions caused lasting imbalances in the age structure of the population and cast their disturbing shadows for decades to come.

The first independent Czechoslovak republic was established in October, 1918. At that time, the death rate nearly doubled while natality rates averaged 12.6 per 1,000, additional factors that interfered with demographic balances for more than two generations. The creation of the new State gave national freedom to the Czechs but continued to subject the Slovaks to the economic interests of their western neighbors who were opposed to their industrial progress. The years after 1919 temporarily restored the prewar birth rate, which was curtailed again during the 1930s. After the more or less random influences of World War I, the failing economy and political conditions produced the first conscious impulse toward family planning and set the stage for values that were inherent in the period following the country's demographic transformation.

As yet, however, the new demographic trend was still limited to the urban population, whose birth rate (about 14 per 1,000) reached but one-half that of the equally large rural population. The geographical expressions of this were seen in marked differences moving from west to east and correlating with various degrees of economic progress: Bohemia's birth rate averaged 19.4 per 1,000; Moravia's and Silesia's, 22 per 1,000; with Slovakia leading with its anachronical 31 per 1,000.

Structural Changes after 1945

The end of World War II invoked a number of basic structural changes in the political, economic, and social sphere which together and in their interaction had substantial repercussions on family life.

In the political field, the country chose development according to socialist principles which implied the nationalization of industry, finance, and commerce. The economic targets were set on expanding industrial production and on transforming predominantly small-scale agricultural production into large-scale agriculture based on state farms and cooperatives. Achievement of both objectives required priorities in heavy industry, investments in power supply, raw material procurement, and extension and modernization of the infrastructure.

As a result of corresponding plans and their implementation, national income increased nearly five times, industrial output more than nine times, construction tenfold, and agricultural production doubled. In this process, investments were located in such a way as to assimilate the economic levels of the Czech and Slovak parts of the country. All this, together with changes in the ownership of productive wealth, was geared to a general social regrouping. Another aspect of the process was substantial migration from rural

to urban areas, and the social outcome of the economic movement was also
determined by differentiated productivity growth in the various spheres and
industries, as shown in table 1.

Table 1 Social Structure of the Czechoslovak Socialist Republic, 1930–75

	(*Percent of Total Population*)	
Social Group	*1930*	*1975*
Manual workers	57.3	60.5
Other employed persons	6.8	27.8
Cooperative farmers	—	8.9
Other cooperative producers	—	1.7
Small farmers	22.2	1.0
Shopkeepers and artisans	8.2	0.1
Capitalists	5.5	0.0

Today's social structure of the active population consists almost entirely of three groups: blue-collar workers, white-collar workers, and cooperative farmers. [The term "active population" as used throughout this volume refers to the labor force generally and includes the employed, the
self-employed, and the unemployed who are looking for work. *Eds.*] The
working and living conditions of these three groups are equalized to a very
high degree, which is evident from the annual per capita net income in their
respective households (see table 2).

Table 2 Average Income According to Social Group

Social Group	*Annual per Capita Net Income in Czechoslovak Crowns* [a]	*Index 1973 (1960 = 100)*
Blue-collar workers	13,588	166
White-collar workers	16,130	166
Cooperative farmers	16,559	216

[a] As of April 1, 1977, the exchange rate was approximately: 1 crown = $0.18. *Eds.*

The differences prevailing in income are not so much the result of differentiated earnings as of the size and composition of the household, in particular the number of minor children. The first conclusion to be drawn from
this is that any policy of equalizing the living standards of various social
groups must not only avoid differences in earned income but in addition
must operate with positive measures of family policy.

The joint feature of the living and working conditions of the three
salient social groups is the complete separation of work from residence,
which has its particular significance for women, faced with the task of in-

tegrating working and family duties. The scope of this problem is evident from the fact that growing economic potentials led fairly soon not only to full employment but also to almost equal employment rates of men and women, as shown in table 3.

Table 3 Economic Activity According to Percent of Men Aged 15–59 and Women Aged 15–54

	1950	1975
Men	96.4	96.8
Women	54.1	86.5
Total	75.6	91.8

The continuing differences in the employment rate of men and women are mainly due to women who are absent on maternity leave and are, from the point of view of the individual families, of a temporary character only. Typical for Czechoslovakia, therefore, are families with two breadwinners working on an equal footing and receiving equal pay for equal work. Owing to a rational, and partly also to a traditional, division of labor, women are mostly engaged in less strenuous and less skilled work outside industry. This involves lower pay, so that a woman's actual contribution to the family budget amounts to about two-thirds that of the man. In view of this, the temporary loss of a woman's income due to family contingencies, if balanced by social benefits, can be compensated adequately only if the benefits are, if possible, not related to the woman's income. In this instance, unselective social policy has indeed selective functions since it replaces a higher percentage of lower than of higher earnings.

The equal participation of both sexes in economic and social life requires, among other things, assistance in providing for the children while both parents are at work. Assistance is also needed to reduce and simplify household chores, still shared by women to a larger extent than by men. The scope of the problem can be judged from the fact that time spent by women on household duties equals almost half of the labor input in industry and therefore takes a substantial slice of the leisure time of women—and partly, also, that of men. On the other hand, the equal positions of both sexes in other respects, and additional factors that prevail in all highly industrialized countries, lead to democratization of the family and its functions, including family planning. This is further supported by the educational leveling of both sexes, in some cases even the educational superiority of women, which signals possible future problems in finding suitable marriage partners. Girls make up 63 percent of the students in grammar schools; in other medium-grade schools, 55 percent; and in the universities and colleges, 40 percent.

Structure of Population and Family

The shaping of the demographic structure of the population and of its microunits proceeded against this general background and in conjunction with it, but the structure is also the outcome of interaction with inherent demographic factors. The sum total of all this gives rise—sometimes gradually, sometimes more rapidly—to the establishment of replacement patterns which persist under the given conditions and are known by the term "population climate." Changes in this climate are apparent from their effects, which have been observed since 1945 in most industrialized countries, though there are marked differences in the periods when they set in and in their intensity. If these changes produce undesirable repercussions and problems in the general societal setup, governments may resort to action that will probably reverse the process. This is the most general and basic function of family policy, even if not the only or ever present one, and historically speaking it indeed came into being for this and no other purpose.

On the whole, we can observe four stages or patterns of the population climate as they are manifested in varied trends of the birth rate. The *first stage*, commencing in 1945 and extending to the middle of the 1950s, was characterized by rates of more than 20 per 1,000 inhabitants, due to large cohorts of women in the fertile age, to marriages and births delayed by the war. This development was also supported by lowering the marriageable age to eighteen years for both sexes.

The *second stage*, representing a transition to more modern but still acceptable trends, was fairly short and came to an end by 1960. It reduced the birth rate to an annual average of 18.5 per 1,000 and was clearly influenced by the introduction of abortions, practically free of charge and made readily available. However, abortions should not be viewed as the ultimate cause of falling birth rates but only as a ready instrument for regulating family size according to concepts emerging out of more general motives.

Though no one has attempted to make a close analysis of these motives, they may be understood as products of a period of accelerating employment rates of women regardless of age and of equalizing their position in the family with that of men. At the same time, this increased the demands of the nuclear family for separate housing, construction of which had to compete with economic investments and was therefore initially restricted to areas interested in attracting new labor.

This may raise the question as to the nature of the link between the size of the family and the employment rate of women. There is no doubt that the two are related, especially in the initial stages of equalization of the sexes when measures to loosen the connection between women's labor force participation and family size are necessarily incomplete and lagging behind. On the other hand, it must be noted that the correlation between female employment and children is far more complex than it appears at first. It has been proved that what matters is not the lack of time or interest in children but hesitation to allow the high standard of living achieved by two incomes to be affected by the arrival of new family members, increasing expenditures and depriving the family, at least temporarily, of the mother's contribution. Time was necessary to minimize the negative side effects of general female labor and of rising educational standards for family life, and to make the positive implications of equality manifest to everyone.

The *third period* further reduced the birth rate to a critical low (14.9 per 1,000 in 1968) and lasted up to 1970. It has to be projected against the background of intricate economic and political problems connected with slackened economic growth, making the dependency of living standards on family size extremely sensitive. This was particularly true for the young family with partners up to thirty years of age, who reacted promptly to a situation from which they drew only the simplest conclusion.

The *fourth* and so far final *period* started in 1971 and renewed remarkable upward trends (a birth rate approaching 20 per 1,000) of which more will be said when analyzing its salient forces. This is justified by the fact that for the first time demographic processes were regulated quite consciously and comprehensively, thus providing good material for studying the efficiency potential of planned family policy.

The entire period after 1945 had, of course, other significant factors and agents that upset or supported the pattern of the birth rate. After a sharp decrease, the death rate stabilized around 10–11 per 1,000 and was later on influenced by the aging of the population. In conjunction, natality and mortality resulted in natural increases of the population, gradually ranging from 8.8 per 1,000 in the 1950s to 4.2 per 1,000 in 1968 and up again to 8.0 per 1,000 in 1975. Irrespective of these indicators there was a steady increase in the number of marriages per 1,000 inhabitants from 6.8 to 9.5, but at the same time the divorce rate rose from about 14.0 to 21.6 per 100 marriages.

As a result, Czechoslovakia has today close to 15 million inhabitants, with slightly more women—51.3 percent—than men. Children up to fourteen years of age make up 23.3 percent of the population; the senior age groups (men aged sixty plus, women fifty-five plus), 19.4 percent; and the remaining productive cohorts, 57.4 percent. Women prevail most markedly in the senior cohorts with 62 percent, as compared with 48.7 percent in the productive age groups. The average life expectancy of men has risen to 66.9 years and of women, to 73.7 years. Owing to increasing rates of training and education beyond the age of fifteen, and to a growth in the incidence of disability, the actual labor force is about one million (or nearly 12 percent) lower than the number of persons in the productive ages, so that the proportion of working to dependent population equals 1:1.

To complete the picture, it is appropriate to indicate how these general trends are reflected in the family today. According to 1970 census figures, there are about 4.3 million flats, of which 3.7 million are occupied by one family only. Eighty-six percent of all flats therefore house only one family, which stresses the advanced degree of breakup of multiple family households, with all the advantages and disadvantages involved.

According to family allowance statistics, nearly 42 percent of all families with minor children have one child, nearly 43 percent have two children, over 11 percent have three, and the rest have four or more children. According to social groups, the birth rate is highest in the smallest group, that of the cooperative farmers, with 2.57 children, while that of the blue-collar workers, representing the largest group, ranks second with 2.09 children. The white-collar workers have the smallest families, with an average of 1.76 children. One aspect of these differentiated rates is the persisting higher birth rate of people who live in smaller communities—an average of 2.14 children in communities with up to 2,000 inhabitants contrasted with 1.77 in cities with populations over 10,000.

To sum up, Czechoslovakia is a country where families are marked by two jobs and two earned incomes, with an average of slightly more than two children. This is the basis from which family policy has to proceed and with which it has to reckon should it aim at changing the given situation.

Family Policy Development and Present Concept

Family policy is not a monopoly of the twentieth century. What is new in policies concerned with the family today is the range of aspects they cover and the approach to its needs. As any other legislation that forms part of general policy, it not only has its main function but pursues at the same time the interests of the community or of its domineering sections in a wider range. It therefore attempts to influence and regulate the family's behavior according to explicitly stated or silently presumed patterns, and in this respect the concept of family policy not only varies from one social system to the other, but is in harmony with changing needs and also with different stages of the same system.

The oldest measures of family policy defined the family's rights and duties in the social context, regulated the transfer of its property in case of death, and outlined the position of the partners vis-à-vis one another, as well as in confrontation with the outside world. Within this framework, the life of the family remained self-contained, and as a rule law interfered only in cases of neglect or impeded care of the children. This corresponded with conditions under which families were independent economic units but had to become obsolete and insufficient when industrialization involving new modes of work and life put provision and consumption of necessities on a broader, social basis.

We find that in Czechoslovakia, family policy up to 1945 was restricted to regulation of family relations, to modification of labor legislation for women and minors, to legal protection of children who were not properly attended to, and finally, to a few social insurance benefits pertaining to death of the breadwinner and to confinement of employed women. The term "family policy" was completely unknown since everyone was supposed to be his own master and the separate measures molding family situations were not directed toward the family as a unit.

Even after 1945, such a conceptual image was not forthcoming immediately. Fairly soon there was a clear shift from the mere legal definitions of family rights and duties to direct aid in certain contingencies, which primarily centered on the implementation of sexual equality, mainly in the economic sphere. Nevertheless, one of the first measures to be introduced, in the form of family allowances for all employed persons, had a distinctly social motivation in wanting to lessen per capita income differences caused by diverse numbers of children. Further steps improved traditional social security benefits (paid maternity leave, birth grants, and so forth), and at the same time plans were made for the rapid increase of nursery and nursery school capacities. In addition, the gradual process of extending free medical care to all citizens brought even in its initial stages substantial improvements of maternal and child care and related facilities. The range of measures to aid and protect families was rounded out by the Family Code (1963), bringing equal rights and duties to both partners in regard to property, education of children, mutual support, and divorce. The expansion of privileges for women and youth in labor legislation culminated in the Labor Code (1965), and the entire period up to 1970 was further marked by *ad hoc* amelioration of benefits and services relevant to family needs.

It was at this point that the concept of family policy was taking its final shape, subjecting all its aspects and instruments to unified guidance and giving priority to family situations and requirements crucial to citizens and to society as a whole.

This needs further explanation. Reviewing the development of sociopolitical measures in aid of families with children, one cannot help noting a certain coincidence in the sequence and choice of various provisions adhering to traditional instruments from the arsenal of sickness insurance and pension schemes. As a result, family contingencies were seen in terms of various separate groups of families, instead of as stages in the individual family cycle. Thus attention was not always focused on decisive needs but was diverted in too many directions. This hampered the clear determination of priorities and led to dissipating available resources instead of concentrating them with the greatest possible efficaciousness.

As shown by the level of demographic indicators, results were indeed required more than ever. With the birth rate below the limit of plain replacement, inducements were needed in the form of aid capable of contributing to a rapid change in the population climate. This pointed unmistakably to the weak point of family policy, to its more or less equivocal treatment of strongly differing phases of family life. In particular, there was no special concern for the young family which, though meeting the brunt of establishing and equipping a household and raising children, had to do so with one income reduced or temporarily suspended and received, on the whole, no more than families in the advanced and less demanding phases.

The significance of the young family is evident from the fact that married couples with both partners under thirty-five years of age amounted to 900,000 in 1970 and constituted more than one fifth of all households. Families with women in that age span give birth to more than 95 percent of all children. The age of 35 practically terminates fertility, and in consequence, all population inducements must be situated in the preceding period of family life to be effective and also socially justified.

This was the pivot around which the present concept of family policy began to be formulated in 1971. As can be seen, societal interests imprinted upon it the seal of population policy, but further information will prove that it is decidedly more than that.

Elements for the improvement and extension of family provisions were elaborated during the second half of the 1960s, on the basis of a comprehensive analysis of the demographic situation and perspective and of conditions of families with children. Conclusions demanded greater complexity in meeting family needs and stressed, above all, the lesson drawn from past experience: new measures and improvements have in terms of population results only temporary effects and must be renewed regularly and with a view to changes within the family and the society it composes. This is true of positive family policy but may as well apply equally to measures seeking curtailment.

It is for this reason that the new concept came forward not only with new instruments but also with improvement of some of the existing ones. The demand for comprehensiveness was respected by including, among others, measures influencing the population climate not only directly by material aid but also indirectly, by means of public education. In doing so, family policy was specified according to the particular situation prevailing at the end of the past decade and by decisive and relatively effective factors capable of changing it soon. The concept thus arrived at was the basis of a working paper for the Fourteenth Congress of the Communist Party of Czechoslovakia which lent its authority to the solution of the problem and to the measures subsequently enacted.

The concept, as suggested, has definite pronatal aspects and therefore is family and population policy in one. The goal pursued by it does not envisage permanent population growth but seeks to overcome the danger of a threatened deficit by achieving an average birth rate of about 2.5 children per family. This in the end should stabilize the population and safeguard an age structure, thus avoiding future oscillations. It is known that increases followed by rapid decline are apt to upset the economic rhythm, not only in terms of discrepancies between labor demand and supply, but also of volume and structure of consumption. Last but not least, the number of children in the family affects the psychological and moral aspects of family life.

It must be understood that the means chosen for achieving the goal do not rely on coercion. They are inspired by the fact that any family policy, positive or negative—or even the absence of one—is by implication a population policy, tacitly accepting, supporting, or countering population trends. All that is necessary to turn a set of conditions and measures relating to families into family or population policy is to raise them to the level of conscious regulation, and to adjust the instruments with their inducive or preventive elements to what is required. In this respect, family policy is nothing else but macrosocial family planning, and it is indeed obvious that individual family planning cannot be effective without the consent, support, and cooperation of society, of its scientific, medical, legal, economic, and educational bodies. In so far as determining the number of children it wants is one of the basic rights of the family, this right—as any other one—will remain an empty declaration without the assistance of society as a whole.

The second feature of Czechoslovakia's family policy concept is its comprehensiveness, not in the sense of theoretical completeness but in the sense of meeting or influencing all factors and situations that seemed pertinent at the time of its drafting. As pointed out, the *key situation* for decisive demographic behavior is that of the young family with its conflicts between needs and resources. If these conflicts between expectation and reality are allowed to persist, the family is forced to revise its plans by choosing the most convenient solution to restrict its size.

There was of course an awareness of this, but obviously not enough. In spite of the wide range of medical and social aid offered to families with children, there still remained problems in the family. Above all, mothers of newly born children were interested in returning to work as soon as possible after maternity leave, to renew their full contribution to the young household. This was not really helpful to any of the parties concerned, and further measures were therefore required to change the pattern substantially. The measures subsequently adopted were: introduction of low-interest loans for young couples, with repayment reduced on the birth of children; maternity allowances for women giving birth to at least the second child, paid in lump sums up to the second year of the baby. As a rule, the benefit was a follow-up of paid maternity leave and thus substantially extended it. In addition, the birth grant was doubled to 2,000 crowns per child, and family allowances were raised for the second to the fourth child.

The effects of these interventions were indeed encouraging. Suddenly the young family was less pressed for income and time, and the rhythm of the first family cycle became smoother, permitting adjustment. More than 90 percent of women eligible for prolonged maternity leave make use of it by drawing the new allowances,[1] and the first two children are spaced to facilitate steady personal care by the mother during the children's earliest and most sensitive periods of life. Thus admission to preschool establishments is postponed to a later stage, making it possible to transfer the care of children from mere nursing to education. This is in the interest of mother and child and also of society, relatively released from the pressure to build new capacities.

[1] Use of prolonged maternity leave is somewhat lower on the part of professional women.

The lessening pressure to provide preschool facilities is relative since they have not yet reached optimal potentials. Nurseries can provide for over 13 percent of the children between six months and two years of age, but kindergartens are already caring for more than 67 percent of the corresponding age bracket (three to five years). The kindergartens have so far been of a predominantly educational character, and there are plans to make their program for five-year-olds available to all children prior to compulsory education. Because of increased interest on the part of professional families and the fact that preschool establishments are required only temporarily (they become redundant after the ebbing of births in the district or housing center), construction of nurseries and kindergartens is being accelerated with the aid of factories and cooperatives and by mobilizing other than standard forms (micronurseries). The shifting need for places according to the age of the children is mitigated by the preference for combining nursery school and nursery, which enables transformation of one type into the other by means of internal adjustments.

These conflicts and the solutions offered must not be seen as instruments for poverty relief. They are to be understood as levelers of problems, differences, and possibilities that face families with children as distinct from childless families. It is for this reason that benefits and other aids are, as a rule, mandatory rights independent of income. This is true also of assistance to other than young families.

Apart from family allowances, the most important *permanent interventions* are income tax relief and price subsidies for children's clothing. While the former is of course related to income and the sum thereby obtained is larger the bigger the wage, family allowances are unified and their rate depends solely on the number of children. The allowances rise rapidly— from 90 crowns per month for one child to 880 crowns for three children— and thus represent an antidote to income-graded tax relief for which the number of children is irrelevant. While this system is on the whole satisfactory and has recently found acceptance in other countries, there is a strong feeling that the family allowance should reflect the child's age, which more than anything else is a clear indicator of its needs.

A further pillar of the family policy concept is the *housing program,* based on the recognition that lack of housing is not conducive to higher birth rates. This situation that kept down birth rates during the 1960s matured for several reasons: prewar low-quality housing deteriorated during the war and after it, when priority had to be given to restoring and expanding economic potentials. In addition, demands for separate housing for young families became universal, and the process of breaking up the former three-generation family was supported by migration to new industrial centers. Since then, the situation has improved considerably, and it is now possible to assign new housing to young families within short periods—except in the two capitals, Prague and Bratislava.

The social and thereby also the family-political character of the housing problem is apparent from the fact that rents rebated according to the number of children are far below maintenance costs and that only one fourth of all houses are being built by individuals, the majority being put up by local authorities, economic establishments, and housing cooperatives.

Another specific factor responsible for low natality figures was the institution of *abortions* offered practically free of charge and on very liberal grounds. The act adopted in 1957 corresponded with the demand of women for their exclusive right to have wanted children only. It also pursued the aim of abolishing undercover abortions detrimental to the health and even the life of the pregnant woman. In this the act proved so successful that by the end of the 1960s more than one third of all pregnancies were terminated by abortions, making them contraception ex post facto and more convenient than other birth control practices.

It was for this reason that implementing provisions amended in recent years maintained abortions on medical grounds without restriction but somewhat narrowed down other contingencies in which they are permitted by special committees set up in all districts. As a result, abortions dropped by about one fifth and today terminate less than one fourth of all pregnancies.

The next component of the present family policy concept refers to the complex problem of *leisure time* for the parents, particularly the mother. Its complexity is difficult to grasp, and there are no handy measures to tackle the problem. It has been mentioned how the time factor was handled in the case of young families, but other aspects of the problem remain to be treated.

Some of them are of a general nature and found in most countries, while others have their roots in economies with high employment rates of both sexes. This involves, among others, shopping problems. Daily shopping tends to concentrate in two afternoon peaks, marking the end of the workday for factory and nonfactory workers. Women push their purchases of commodities and services into two short periods. Coping with these demands requires a well-planned and capacious network of supermarkets and service facilities that can respond without delay. Time is needed, not only to establish these facilities but also to develop new approaches to delivering consumer services at or near the work place. This, too, may lead to complications, because it increases demands for female labor which can be made available only by transfers from elsewhere. In search of prompt and at least partial solutions, shopping hours were adjusted to meet the situation, but this, too, has its limits under conditions where all facilities are serviced by a staff working a forty-two-hour week, spread over five days. In addition, shopping hours cannot be strained or rearranged indefinitely without impeding the interests and needs of shopworkers who are required in their own families.

Czechoslovak eating habits, relying on elaborate self-cooked meals, call for supplies of semiprocessed goods to save time in preparing the meal. Again, much has been done in this respect in recent years, and here too it is difficult to achieve more because of a lack of labor. Cheap factory and school meals contribute indispensably but are not yet the final answer. Theoretically, modern household appliances have a high time-saving capacity, but though commonly available and used, their practical effects must not be overestimated.

In general, it may be said that so far, leisure time is worth further attention in order to provide more room for self-realization and contacts with children.

The family is not only a unit cooperating in basic essentials but also a structure promulgating *spiritual and emotional values*. As regards the latter, the family has undoubtedly a unique position in laying and integrating foundations, while communication of knowledge becomes more and more the monopoly of the school. Close interaction is therefore required from both if their functions are to succeed, and efforts are made to foster the necessary links (parents' committees and meetings; lectures advising parents on educational problems). It is not without interest to note that the determining factor in forming the child is no longer the educational level of the father but ever more that of the mother as well.

From the very beginning, spouses should be equipped for their role as parents and organizers of a family household. Research proves that this is not always the case. Figures on divorce rates, generally high (2.18 per 1,000 inhabitants), show that in Prague, for instance, 42 percent of all marriage breakdowns occur within the first five years.[2] This indicates that young couples are not always prepared for family functioning, and their physical maturity at an early age does not match their maturity to socialize in the family unit. Analyses of divorce cases indicate that men are not yet up to the

[2] Another alarming feature is that three-fourths of all divorces involve children.

expectation of the now better educated women who feel the contrast between their role as worker and the attention paid to them at their place of employment, and the husband's lack of cooperation and understanding at home. Unfortunately, breaking up the marriage does not solve the problem as a rule, since remarriage proves difficult and if accomplished often ends in another divorce (the proportion of second and further divorces increased on the part of women from 13.1 to nearly 18.0 percent of the total since 1967).

In view of this it has been decided to give more space to these questions (including sex education) in the curricula of all types of schools and to make the family also the subject of general education by art and the mass media. Voluntary organizations (trade unions, youth and women's leagues) are recruited to cooperate and by their special means to stress the value of the family for personal happiness and welfare. All this creates a positive attitude of society toward the family and its needs and contributes to changes in the population climate.[3]

Doctors take their share in biological instruction and in offering contraceptive advice, and for the prevention and treatment of critical situations, marriage counseling centers are being set up in all districts. Both these services have their problems. Medical contraceptive advice has been found to be influenced by the doctor's personal attitude and psychological patterns, a fact which is not apt to evoke confidence on the part of the client. Counseling centers, on the other hand, have not yet become institutions commonly used, which may be due to their isolation, both local and functional, from institutions normally frequented by citizens.

Finally, the Czechoslovak concept of population or family policy has received its organizational basis in the Government Population Commission to coordinate its elements and supervise implementation of measures adopted in diverse competences.

To summarize the concept described, we may discern still another feature characterizing its transformation. While initial stages in the approach to the family, for a comparatively long period, hesitated to employ instruments reacting to crucial family situations immediately, there was greater generosity in appreciating them ex post facto and indirectly. To give one example, it may suffice to compare the relatively short maternity leave, prevailing for more than seventy years, with the far more liberal retirement relief for women that was adopted before, but mainly after, 1945. This is true of most

---

[3] An interesting parallel can be observed between the low natality figures of the 1960s and the overwhelmingly negative treatment of the family in mass media articles and entertainment, in contrast to the situation prevailing in the first half of the 1970s.

countries and may be understood as the result of family policy, having its earliest roots in social insurance with its particularistic approach, incapable of comprehensive treatment of social situations and aiming at compensation of loss instead of forestalling it. New impulses were needed to reverse this conservative image, and the Czechoslovak family policy concept may be considered one of the levers in this direction.

The New Family Pattern

After five years of intensive family and population policy it is now possible to evaluate results and draw conclusions as to its efficiency. Before doing so it seems appropriate to examine whether new and old policy were applied to the same sample, which would make the attribution of credit very simple. Policy concepts and policy-making often overlook that this is hardly ever the case. Social innovations and step-by-step improvements and developments relate, as a rule, to different cohorts, since the ones whose behavior provoked the revision have in the meantime changed, at least in age. In consequence, the new measure now applies to people of whom we know very little, and in times of rapid social development this may lead to serious misconceptions.

To be more specific: the generation of parents whose demographic behavior motivated the new family policy concept was that born before World War II. Everything this generation wanted to have and achieve had to be wrought out of devastation and by mobilizing all available resources for building the prerequisites to gradual future improvements. This was true for the country as a whole and for individual families in particular, and in the latter it evoked in the end self-contained egotism and determination to strive for everything that could be had and that others had. Gradually, there did not seem to be much room for children, and after the acquisitive goals had been achieved it was too late to change one's utilitarian horizon.

However, with the end of the 1960s this generation was being replaced by their children, who are no longer in the same position as their parents were because, among other reasons, they share their property and have their assistance in establishing themselves. In short, they have inherited the wealth acquired by their parents, and for this they did not have to inherit their attitudes. In addition, nominal wages, being two-thirds higher in 1970 than in 1955 (real wages are higher by nearly 60 percent), have since then increased by a further 16 percent on the average. As a result, the average per capita income in 1973 was 86 percent above that of 1960. Thus the base to which the new family policy concept was applied was substantially different from that at the time it was conceived. Though this was not apparent then, the new concept was no longer necessary to bring about changes in the birth rate all by itself, but was in fact meant to preserve the transformed basis. This does not mean that development would have proceeded without it, in particular since it also comprised other than material measures and since it also attacked problems that were not automatically receding in the course of improving income.

The lesson to be drawn from this comparison of two generations is that the questions inquiring into parental motivations cannot be posed abstractly but only in the context of actual conditions, properly analyzed and interpreted. Failing this, policies may be misguided and may disregard factors susceptible to different handling.

The outcome of five years of new family policy is indeed rewarding. The following indicators for the period of 1971–75 are proof of this: the birth rate increased from 16.5 to 19.5 per 1,000, averaging 18.3 per 1,000 for the five-year span compared with 15.5 per 1,000 in the preceding five years. More than 1.34 million children were born, bringing about under stabilized mortality conditions a population increase of half a million people. This represented in 1975 a relative gain of 8.0 per 1,000, compared with 4.3 in 1970. A split-up of figures according to the Czech and Slovak republics shows a rapid closing of the fertility gap between them: the Czech birth rate rose from 15.7 to 19.1 per 1,000 and the Slovak from 18.2 to 20.6 per 1,000. Analysis makes it clear that about one fourth of the higher birth rate is due to larger numbers of women in the fertile age, so that all the remaining share must be attributed to other factors—including new family policy measures.

The only shadow in the otherwise bright development is a rapid increase in the divorce rate: while it averaged 5.9 percent of all marriages that took place in 1965–69, it rose more than threefold, to 22.8 percent, in 1975.

General Observations

The definition of family policy given above is generally accepted, and the only differences that arise refer to the lack of clear distinctions between family and population policy and to the degree by which it stresses its role in implementing demographic targets. This may be understood in view of the situation five years ago, but is open to reappraisal when indicators cease to be the main concern.

In view of the diversity of measures employed by family policy, it cannot be subordinated to other earmarked policies, such as social income, redistribution policy, and so on, but must stand on its own. It is in substance the coordination of pertinent policies that affect family life and interests, either generally or in specific circumstances, and their specific deployment in support of social and individual needs. In view of this, social or income-maintenance policy, family planning, housing, medical care, market provisions, and so forth are part of family policy not automatically, but only in respect to their adjustment to family needs in historic circumstances.

It is for this reason that family policy is not covered by specific legislation and institutions. The adequacy of this arrangement is determined also by the fact that the function of various measures and spheres in relation to the family is not the only one they pursue but merely one of several. The family context of this or that public responsibility may even become negligible or obsolete if the set of conditions that establishes the link begins to reshape. Unification of family measures can best be achieved by suitable organizational procedure, exacting more than advisory competence and requiring permanent and steadily renewed interest of the authorities involved.

Similarly, family policy is multilateral also as regards its scope. It appeals either to the family as a whole or to its individual members, or may even refer to persons outside the family. Formally or legally, family measures and rights usually adhere to one of the parents, while other, less direct connections may be effected by way of specifying social groups (women regardless of their family status) or none at all (action in regard to shopping facilities, housing, and so on). In addressing family members the choice is still very often made under traditional auspices rather than being governed by desirable family roles.

Initially, family policy attempts to mitigate conflicts of interest between family members, and together with universal employment it is indeed the key to abolishing the conflict of unequal sexes. Nevertheless, impacts of the policy vary according to family patterns, as indicated by rising divorce rates. They can be interpreted also as the outcome of sociopolitical measures strengthening independence in case of family failures, even if caused by irresponsibilities. Innovations in family structures, as indeed in all others, remove shortcomings of one type, to create new ones, previously unknown. Still, the latter can be no excuse for tolerating the former but must merely be the impulse for trying to tackle them as well. While traditional conflicts have no secrets as to their substance and origin, new ones very often have, and it takes time to handle them adequately.

New conflicts of interest in the family seem to arise out of the loss of man's monopoly of higher education and of the status involved, and are particularly acute in families in which both partners have higher professional education. In them, persisting patterns and family requirements create difficulties in sharper outline. They may be found in stress for the wife at her place of employment if she lacks support at home—which may also apply to the man—while household chores, however divided, will impinge upon her professional interests. All this will permeate the relationship of the partners, and to find solutions requires qualities and provisions that are not always available.[4] Apart from this, husbands with long professional training create family problems from the very beginning: in comparison with other families, they have to postpone marriage and childbearing, and their total income, though eventually higher, is initially lower than that in other families.

Experience has led to the recognition that families deserve public concern irrespective of their demographic contribution. While the initial interest is indeed the birth rate, with both its extremes, rectifying these causes other problems which, if unattended, can reverse the demographic process. Higher birth rates call, for instance, for immediate and future market provisions, for more preschool and educational establishments, for more jobs, and influence the social welfare expenditure. In order to meet these immediate and future needs and to prevent relapses, the Government Population Commission (GPC) was appointed in 1971 and given an authority which similar bodies had not previously enjoyed. Its function is to inform the government of demographic developments and to advise it on population policy and measures. In addition, it supervises implementation of the measures adopted in this respect and calls on the ministries concerned to attend to problems that do not require intervention of the supreme executive.

The function and work of the GPC is based on a decision of the Central Committee of the Communist Party of Czechoslovakia and the federal government, which also approved its statute to regulate its activities. The GPC is chaired by a deputy prime minister. Vice-chairman and secretary are the Minister and Deputy Minister of Labor and Social Affairs, respectively. This department dealing with labor, wages, and social policy, apart from

---

[4] This dilemma is due to the fact that economic equality of women leads not only to their higher employment rates but also to their shift from employment as domestic servants to other work. After the war, domestic servants were replaced by the grandmothers, who are substantially "rejuvenated" since then and are no longer ready to function in this capacity.

sections concerned with family questions, also maintains the secretariat of the GPC.

Nongovernmental cooperation is most comprehensive on the part of the trade unions charged with administration of sickness insurance for employed persons, which is financed out of the state budget and incorporates some of the essential family benefits. Together with other voluntary organizations (youth, women's league) they participate, in addition, in influencing public opinion and attitudes toward family and parenthood.

At present, there is no conspicuous discussion which would suggest disagreement with the family policy outlined before. Debates center mostly on questions and methods of implementation. This refers, for instance, to expansion of the capacity of preschool establishments, which is now the prime concern of the GPC. The problem has its roots in construction and staff shortages necessitating the introduction of simpler forms of day care facilities and the cooperation of industrial and agricultural organizations. Capacities are particularly lacking in areas of new housing schemes, occupied mainly by young families.

Debate also focuses on the possibilities of evaluating the efficiency of family policies in terms of fertility gains. Recent results would prove them futile. On the other hand, it appears an oversimplification to give all the credit to improved socioeconomic provisions and to exclude from their range merely the influence exacted by higher numbers of parents. If this were the case, it would indeed be possible to predict family policy results, which is hardly feasible, and no attempts have been made to ascertain trends in detail. The connection between policy in favor of families and their reactions to it is tacitly assumed, and this is and will have to be sufficient grounds for making and improving provisions.

On the other hand, experience shows that investigations into the population climate (the readiness of families to have a certain number of children) are apt to uncover the background of their attitudes. If this background unfolds a series of specific salient problems it may well be presumed that their perseverance will preserve the given climate in the future. In this sense, prediction is possible and indeed shows its value.

This can be illustrated by linking up with the next question, that of research. For a long time, opinion polls on the population climate were considered the only pertinent form of population research. Ever since 1956, various samples have been investigated as to the correlations between the planned and ideal number of children and the factors which supported or limited these expectations. Up to 1959, the results of these investigations gave the clear picture of a modern family with more than two children. Since then, numbers have dropped systematically and reached an average of 1.8 children in 1968 in towns, only slightly higher for the rural areas (2.03). The figures on wanted children strongly correlated with the birth rate in this period, which fell from nearly 19 per 1,000 in 1956 to a low of 15 in 1968. According to the respondents, the lower birth rate was motivated by waiting periods for separate housing in the first place. These waiting periods have been contracting rapidly since 1970, and in consequence, planned children again began to surpass the limit of two, forecasting the birth rates that prevail at present.

Gradually, the comprehensive approach to family policy led to more comprehensive research into family problems and to attempts at synthesizing its results. For this purpose, the GPC established a permanent subcommittee on population research—other subcommittees deal with other specific questions—with the aim of coordinating the specialized research projects and of helping to disseminate their findings and conclusions. The wide scope of present research may be gathered from the following classifications of the relevant projects: problems of demographic development; attitude to parenthood and factors influencing it; social situation of families with children; living and working conditions of employed women; population aspects of housing; family education; population aspects of medical care; distribution of population and environment, and so on.

The chief sponsors of these projects are the Research Institutes of Labor and Social Affairs and of the Standard of Living, the Federal Office of Statistics, various institutes of the ministries of education and health, the Ecological Research Institute, the Academy of Science.

Postscript: General and Special Provisions of Direct and Indirect Family Aid

1. The general situation of the family is given by the Family Code in defining its rights and duties, particularly in relation to its members. It states, among other things, what are the equal rights and duties for husband and wife as regards supporting one another and as regards the education of children. Property and income acquired during marriage by either partner is the joint and indivisible property of both of them, and as such it is equally divided on divorce and with respect to the interests of the children.

2. Equality of the sexes is reflected also in men's and women's right to

work and to equal remuneration for work performed. At the same time, the Labor Code takes into consideration the specific working capacity of women and juveniles and contains a number of regulations to protect their health and working contract. Among others, there are provisions that assure privileges to women caring for children as regards their working regime and possibilities of suspending the contract on the part of the employer.

3. The basic right of every citizen to health is implemented by free medical care offered to every citizen regardless of age or work performed. This includes free examinations and treatment, medicine and aids, hospitalization, including operations—all irrespective of duration and cost involved. In case of mother and child, special services assure prenatal and postnatal care, confinement with medical assistance on delivery, and school medical services that specialize in countering possible harmful physical and mental development during school attendance.

There is also a wide range of special provisions in aid of families, taking the form of direct or indirect financial aid and/or services rendered. Instead of using these criteria for classifying them it may be more appropriate to subdivide them according to the period of family life for which they are most typical. If conditions of eligibility are fulfilled, they are of course awarded also to other families.

Provisions for Young Families

1. *Loans to newly married couples.* These are usually applied for on marriage, and eligibility is extended to spouses up to the age of thirty. They are given for building and furnishing houses, and accordingly the low interest varies from one to 2.5 percent. The amount claimed may reach 30,000 crowns. On the birth of a child, 2,000 crowns are written off for the first child and 4,000 crowns for each subsequent child. The arrival of children also postpones installment payments and the maturity of the loan.

In addition, there are loans at 2.7 percent interest to finance building family houses or cooperative flats.

2. *Compensation for reduced earnings.* A sickness insurance benefit is given to pregnant women or to working women up to nine months after delivery if for medical or other reasons they have to transfer to other work with lower income.

3. *Birth grants.* At rate of 2,000 crowns for every child, grants are given at childbirth to every economically active woman and to the wife of every active man.

4. *Paid maternity leave.* Working women who give birth to children

are entitled to maternity leave for a period of twenty-six weeks (single mothers and in case of multiple birth, thirty-five weeks). Four weeks of this leave are to be taken before the expected confinement. During this leave women are paid maternity benefits at the rate of 90 percent of their previous net income.

5. *Maternity allowance.* At the expiration of the maternity leave, employed women may apply for a maternity allowance at the rate of 500 crowns a month, if they deliver a second child or further children. Unemployed women may apply from the day of the child's birth. The allowance is paid up to the second year of age of the youngest child.

6. *Nursing allowance.* Women or men who are required to be absent from work because of nursing a sick child or caring for another sick family member are eligible for a nursing allowance at the rate of the sickness benefit for a mandatory period of three days and three optional days. Single mothers may have the allowance extended to a total of twelve days.

7. *Preschool facilities.* Nurseries and kindergartens have priorities for children when both their parents are employed or when only one parent is looking after them. Care provided in these institutions is free of charge, and small contributions requested toward meals are graded according to per capita income.

8. *Special services.* In the form of institutional care, infants' homes, children's homes, and homes for defective children are available as a rule for one-parent families or inadequate families, or for handicapped children.

Provisions for All Families with Children

1. *Family allowances.* This direct aid in cash is given on behalf of all children up to the age of sixteen or twenty-six, for further vocational training. The allowance amounts to 90 crowns per month for one child, 430 crowns for two children, 880 crowns for three, and 1,280 for four (240 crowns for each additional child). For disabled children, the allowance is increased by 300 crowns. Semiorphaned or fully orphaned children are entitled to orphans' pensions, and a means-tested children's allowance is usually awarded to single parents who do not receive child support from the other partner.

2. *Income tax relief.* Family allowances are supplemented by income tax relief awarded usually to the parent with the higher income. This rebate is not graded according to the number of children but increases in case of disability or the support of other adult family members.

3. *Rent rebates*. Uniform rates are fixed for all flats. They differ only according to the standard of the flat as defined by four categories. If the proportionate space per occupant exceeds that prescribed, this is taken into consideration as well. From the rate thus ascertained, rebates are given on behalf of children, ranging from 5 percent to 50 percent according to their number.

4. *Fare rebates*. Public transportation offers free or half fares to children up to ten years of age and rebates at the rate of 15 percent to 25 percent to all pupils and students. There are similar rebates for persons who need to travel to and from work.

5. *Subsidized commodities*. Comparatively low and stable prices for essentials are paired with price subsidies of children's clothes and footwear.

6. *Purchases by installments*. Purchases of commodities, such as household equipment, textiles, television and radio sets, and so forth, can be made by installment payments in the form of low-interest loans granted by the savings bank.

7. *Free education*. Compulsory and higher education of all types is free of charge. During the former, textbooks and utensils are provided free of charge and during the latter, stipends are available and offered either by the state (social stipends, scholarships for prescribed marks) or by prospective employers.

8. *School meals*. Meals are provided by every type of school and served at prices that cover 60 percent of the cost. About half of all pupils and students make use of this scheme.

9. *Factory luncheons*. Most places of employment provide meals at low prices for their workers and staff. Together with school meals they reduce cooking considerably in households and are an essential condition for maintaining high female employment rates.

Provisions for Old Families

Income maintenance during old age or other long-term contingencies is safeguarded by the pension scheme that covers all economically active persons. A uniform scheme is in force for all employed persons and members of cooperatives. Its main features are low retirement ages (fifty-five and fifty-eight for miners and other strenuous occupations, sixty for other men, and fifty-three to fifty-seven for women, according to the number of children raised). The rate of the pension depends on gross income and the period of work or other credited activities achieved. For instance, three years are credited to women who interrupt work because of child care. In relation to net income,[5] the pension amounts to the following percentages (see table 4) after thirty-five years of employment or credited periods:

Table 4 Income and Pension

Gross Income in Crowns	Pension as Percent of Net Income
1,000	70
2,000	72
3,000	59
4,000	52
5,000	47

In addition, social assistance administered by the local authorities provides supplementary aid in cases of need and especially social services that deal mainly with the requirements of the chronically ill or lonely pensioners. Local committees also organize recreational and cultural services in the form of pensioners' clubs and provide free or cheap vouchers for these services in normal establishments. Apart from this, there is a home-helpers scheme, and pensioners are of course included in free medical service.

[5] After deduction of income tax only; there are no contributions on behalf of social security.

FRANCE

Nicole Questiaux and Jacques Fournier

A POLICY IN favor of the family emerged in France during the first half of the twentieth century, more precisely in the years 1938–46.

Up to 1914 there was nothing of consequence to be noted, although in 1902 and 1912 official commissions endeavored unsuccessfully to survey the depopulation problem. A few isolated measures were taken in an endeavor to answer the specific needs of the poorer families, who became entitled, in 1913, to draw assistance benefits when they had more than four children. Civil servants [1] also were gradually allowed to claim a supplementary allowance to cover the cost of bringing up a family.

During the years 1919–24, the mood changed. Some help had been provided during World War I for the families of servicemen; the loss of lives had been severe, and a change in the political majority had brought into the first government of those *bloc national* Ministers known as *familiaux* because of their commitment to this sector of the electorate. The Superior Council for Natality had been set up and invited to review the over-all aspects of the problem.

But realizations remained fragmentary, even symbolic: here a family medal, there a national Mother's Day. More practical were the reduced railway fares for large families and exemption from conscription for some of

NICOLE QUESTIAUX and JACQUES FOURNIER are Maîtres des Requêtes au Conseil d'Etat, Paris.

[1] Teachers, railway workers, and servicemen were the first to benefit from advantages which were extended to all civil servants in 1917.

their children. As a moral boost for the family, abortion and even contraception propaganda were severely repressed (Law of July 31, 1920). However, materially speaking, the sole effect of the national law for encouragement to large families was to establish a minimal allocation (90FF per year, enough to buy 75 kilograms of bread) for families of four children and over, when their income was below taxable level.

This was also the time when a system of family benefits for wage earners in industry and commerce was instituted. However, this was done privately. Some employers came to accept the idea that wages could be related to family expenses, whether for ethical or practical reasons. They joined forces in compensation funds, first established in 1918 in Grenoble, Lorient, and Roubaix Tourcoing. Through such funds, contributions were levied on wages and redistributed in the form of family benefits. In this way employers were not penalized because of differences in the number of children of their personnel, as might have been the case if they had set up separately a supplementary wage scheme.

But the new scheme itself was not compulsory, and differences continued to affect competition between affiliated and nonaffiliated firms. After some measure of development, the system could not meet its own obligations. As usual, the smaller or medium-sized concerns refrained from joining, and toward the end of the 1920s a mere 30 percent of the wage-earning force benefited from the system. The amount of the individual allowance remained low, since only 2.7 percent of the corresponding wages went to the contributions.

However, this private initiative did give rise to the first important public intervention in the field. Affiliation was made compulsory when, by the Law of March 11, 1932, and to consolidate an agreement reached in 1929 between the Funds (*caisses*) and the administration, all employers were required to contribute. This law is contemporary with legislation concerning national insurance, dating from 1928. The difficult working conditions related to the economic crisis had given good grounds for intervention from the state.

From now on, all wage earners, whether employed in industry, commerce, or even agriculture (under special provisions), were entitled to family allowances. But the implementation of the law was slow and encountered great hostility in some occupations.[2] The Funds remained under the sole supervision of the employers and were free to determine the level of protec-

---

[2] Obstruction from garage owners was remarkable. Through various legal devices, its members succeeded in evading their legal obligations until the immediate prewar period.

tion. The legislature was content to set minimum standards in conformity with existing practices. The total number of beneficiaries thus increased from 1,800,000 in 1932 to 5,400,000 in 1938, at which time total contributions amounted to 3 percent or 3.5 percent of the wages.

Families were not to have first-rank priority among the beneficiaries of the new social policy introduced in 1936 as a result of the political victory of the Popular Front. Significantly, the substantial increase in wages then decided upon did not concern family allowances. This oversight was repaired here and there through arbitration, the new procedure established to rule industrial relations. But 1938 witnessed capital developments concerning the place of the family in official policies. Changes occurred in two phases.

First, the allowances system was notably improved through the decree (*decrets lois*) of 1938. Minimum rates were made uniform at departmental level and substantially increased. Added benefits, related to the presence of the mother in the home, were made general. All in all, from the beginning of 1937 until the end of 1938, allowances rose by 142 percent, which was two or three times the increase during the previous twenty years. For the first time benefits were extended to independent workers; farmers and rural craftsmen were, however, subjected to a means test.

The decree of 1938 was concerned exclusively with the allowances scheme. But the following year a comprehensive family policy was defined in terms of a code for the family by the decree of July 29, 1939. Prepared by a small group of members of Parliament and public officials meeting in a High Committee on Population, this enactment drew its inspiration from concern about the birth rate. It did, however, deal with different aspects of family problems. Materially, family allowances were extended to the entire active population. The allowance for the first child, however, gave way to a very substantial "premium for the first birth," admittedly meant to encourage young couples to bear children sooner. There was an increase in rates for families with more than three children, and tax remittances were provided for. But the legislature was also concerned with moral support to the family through several measures concerning abortion, contraception, alcoholism, and immorality. The law went so far as to encourage peasant families to attain or maintain their traditional way of life. The law concerning adoption was improved upon. A whole new field relating to child welfare was explored. Support was provided for families in difficult circumstances, and alternate means were considered when the family failed to meet its responsibilities.

One could now speak in France of a proper family policy. For the first time, on June 5, 1940, a minister for family problems figured in the last government of the Third Republic. The Vichy regime, with its revealing motto, "Work, Family, Country," was, of course, ready to take on this heritage while giving it its own direction. The family was now the pillar of the social organization. Family associations were compulsorily federated and given official status. Fathers of large families were given representation in numerous organs, including town councils, and received credits toward promotion in the civil service. What was encouraged was one particular type of family in reaction to any contemporary signs of change. Divorce was strictly prohibited during the first three years of marriage, women were strongly encouraged to remain in the home. This accompanied a persevering income policy for the family, advantages were maintained and even increased, and the civil servants received in 1942 a family income supplement which was added to the family allowances.

The family policy could have been discredited because of its relationship with a government marked by extreme conservatism and its collaboration with the occupying power. This was not the case. Of course, some of the more reactionary aspects did not survive, but what had been attained was kept and even reinforced. One of the questions underlying this discussion is whether there still is a policy supported by a political commitment. There was undoubtedly such a commitment in 1945 and 1946, and action in favor of the family was one of the main components of the over-all social security system then installed in France.

As one can see, policy for the family emerged over a relatively brief period, and this was the doing of governments of very different political orientations: the radical center at the end of the Third Republic, the conservative right wing during the Vichy regime, the leftist Socialists at the beginning of the Fourth Republic. From the start, family policy was designed in a more structured manner and carried more content than in neighboring countries. There are reasons for this.

The Need for Social Protection

Family policy can be described as one of the means through which the community may intervene in the field of social protection, and social protection did in fact develop as a form of public intervention in France, as in other countries, during the first half of the twentieth century.

We have given an explanation for this elsewhere and shall briefly summarize it here.[3] What are now described as social questions, social problems, and social policies gradually appeared in the middle of the nineteenth century in parallel with the development of industrial capitalism. Intervention in the social field was the necessary answer to the change in social structures and way of living brought about by the development of this new economic organization. Such intervention was made necessary whenever Adam Smith's "invisible hand" appeared unable to smooth the consequences of change. In other words, the law of the market, concentration in private enterprise, and forced changes in employment conditions, had been of such consequence that reaction on the part of the public was inevitable; this in turn had forced an answer for the community, an organized answer in the shape of a social policy.

Historically, the first step was taken when the social field encompassed the problems of labor as related to industrialization, the concentration of the working force in big towns and its exploitation. The family as such was not considered to be directly involved. Of course, measures were taken to control working conditions for women and children, and this was not without implications for the family. But labor legislation was concerned with the worker as an individual, or workers organized in their unions, not with their families.

Family problems were more directly dealt with at a later stage when the field of social policies extended to a new domain, that of social protection. Before then, some measure of security had been insured privately through the mechanisms of inheritance, saving, and hard work, or through family and local solidarities. The new mode of production made all these inefficient. When the population gathered in large cities, neighborhood links were severed, and it became more difficult to survive in the face of difficulties. Wage earners, now the growing majority of the working population, were strictly dependent on their salaries, and, finally, the monetary disorders which appeared after World War I destroyed individual savings. In France, the point of no return was reached in 1900–30, when industrial income became more important than income from agriculture. Urban population exceeded rural population toward 1930, and the number of wage earners in industry and commerce was 7,600,000 in 1901, 10,500,000 in 1931.

It is no surprise that in the same period there had to be some measures to protect individuals—and first of all, wage earners—from many risks. These dealt first with industrial injuries, as early as 1898, then with pensions in 1910. Ill-health was covered in 1928. Family expenses were addressed, as

[3] Nicole Questiaux and Jacques Fournier, *Traité du social* (Paris: Dalloz, 1976).

we have noted, on a compulsory basis in 1932. Coincidence is not an explanation, and things could have been very different. Whereas during the nineteenth century, labor legislation applied solely to individuals, leaving it to them whether to maintain a family with their wages or by means of the substitute income provided by the community, this was not now the case, and the idea of compensation for family expenses asserted itself despite the warnings of liberal economists. Leroy-Beaulieu, for instance, wrote in 1896:

> This theory of a family wage is nothing less than the socialist theory of wages related to requirements. It leads straight to collectivism, because it cannot be applied by private persons and can only be put into place by the State, distributing all the work and all the wages.[4]

Social protection tended to make use of the family for reasons related to change in the family itself, particularly to the attention that was now being focused on the child.

The Change in the Family

For an entire school of thought, represented first by de Bonald, then by Le Play, who greatly influenced the French family movement up to and even after the Vichy regime, the nineteenth century had witnessed the decline of the family. The blame was laid on the Civil Code decreed by Napoleon; although it had not adopted some of the extravagant ideas of the Revolution, it imposed equal division of property among the children, and this was deemed fatal to paternal authority and to continuity in heritage.

Divorce, widely authorized under the Revolution, more restricted but permitted under the Civil Code, suppressed by the Restoration in 1816, reinstated by the Third Republic in 1884, was considered another cause of instability. The fall in the birth rate was considered to be a consequence of loose living and individual selfishness. The goal of any family policy could only be to protect the family from those threats and to go back to a traditional model, that described by Le Play as the patriarchal family, a family founded on paternal authority, indissoluble wedlock, unrestrained childbirth, and intangible inheritance.

Contemporary historical studies, such as the works of Philippe Ariès,[5] do not leave much of this theory standing. Of course, the family changed

---

[4] Paul Leroy-Beaulieu, *Traité théoretique et pratique d'économie politique* (Paris: 1896).

[5] Philippe Ariès, *Histoire des populations français* (Paris: Éditions de Seuil, 1971).

greatly in France during the nineteenth century, but change did not necessarily mean weakening family ties. Ariès compares the old-fashioned family to what he calls the contemporary family. The first knew nothing about contraception and grew according to biological laws. But it was not in any particular way a home, a refuge for its numerous children. Most of them left it early, and family ties were spaced out. One or two heirs remained to take charge of the inheritance. The family was not preoccupied with education, and children were brought up as their environment led them to be, or were placed in another family.

A new type of family appeared in the eighteenth-century bourgeoisie. It developed during the nineteenth century and spread widely to the working classes who, by the end of the century, were just emerging from poverty. This family was interested in the child, its future, its education. The ties within the family were now essentially sentimental. It had become a center of social relations and a refuge from the outside world. The role of the mother as mistress of the house and educator was magnified, and if she bore fewer children, it was so that they might be better cared for.

In such a context, the economic function was losing its importance. Anyway, there were fewer family firms because of the expanded wage-earning force. More and more often, the father worked outside. But the family developed its recreative role and also, although this is sometimes denied, its function in education. The family came to cope with new duties related to the presence of children at school, and the longer these duties lasted the longer parents and children lived together.

This family was prepared to take up a function of protection. This need did not concern old people so much as previously; thus they often were separated from their children and were now entitled through the pension scheme to a more autonomous existence. But it did apply very directly to the children, for whom the family felt responsible and for whom it provided a more economical and efficient arrangement for social protection. Nothing much had come out of the farfetched educational theories that had been the fashion with some of the educational communities in the eighteenth century. On the contrary, progress in social science had stressed the importance of familiar surroundings and of the parental image in the shaping of young personalities.

The individual and the community had agreed to implement the protection of childhood and youth through the family. This is why a "family" component appears in the social security systems. But why has that component developed further in France than in other countries? Why does France have a more structured policy in this field? Undoubtedly, this is due to demographic preoccupations.

Preoccupying Demography

Demography has made considerable progress, and we now have the necessary instruments to describe and understand past movements of population. A recent report of the National Institute of Demographic Studies (INED)[6] presents two different indices—a short-term index, called the sum of reduced births; and a long-term index, the total number of descendants of a generation—and both indices shed new light on what has really happened to procreation habits during the last century.

But contemporaries had their own view of things, and to understand what this has meant for family policy one must look at things through their eyes. Until recently, the only indicator referred to was the gross birth rate, and perception was greatly influenced by events of national history. Franco-German antagonism weighed heavily on contemporary judgment.

It was in the second half of the nineteenth century, and particularly after the defeat in 1870, that the first voices were raised to denounce the risks of "depopulation" that can be seen in the data assembled in table 1.

Table 1 Demographic Evaluation in France During the Nineteenth Century

	1866	1881	1900	1911
Number of births	1,006,000	937,000	827,000	603,000
	1856–67	1871–80	1891–1900	1901–8
Gross birth rate in percent	26.7	26.5	22.1	20.9
	1806–11	1841–50	1881–90	1891–1900
Annual population growth in percent	50.0	41.0	17.0	7.0

Pr. Richet, in the *Revue des deux mondes* in 1882, and books such as Rossignol's *A Country of Bachelors and Only Sons* in 1896 followed this perspective. Nationalism had its say in the matter. If France intended to reconquer Alsace and Lorraine, she needed more children. The first pressure group in favor of families was the National Alliance for the Increase in the French Population created in 1896 by Alphonse Bertillon, and in the 1900s

[6] Institut National d'Études Démographiques, *Natalité et politique démographique* (Paris: Presses Universitaires de France, 1976).

official commissions were given the task of studying the problem. But these initiatives did not create a real change in public opinion. Things were to change much later.

We now know that the fertility rate was already recovering with the generations born in 1896 who had reached the childbearing age when World War I came to an end. But this reversal of the trend was not visible in the statistics between World War I and World War II because they naturally enough reflected the trend from past generations. On the contrary, the birth rate had continued to decline in a way which appeared to be more and more worrying, even catastrophic—it was no higher than 14.6 percent, one of the lowest in the world, on the eve of World War II—and for a few years the number of deaths even exceeded the number of births. France seemed to be losing substance at the time when, as a country of low density compared to its neighbors, it felt the menace of the doctrine of "living space" which Hitler's Germany was developing in accordance with its territorial ambitions.

The alarm was raised. This was undoubtedly the reason for the new policy adopted in 1938. But the new line might not have been so well received if it had not been in accordance with the change in attitude toward natality which was now characteristic of the new generations. In other words, family policy and its demographic content were not set up to counteract an evolution but, on the contrary, in a more and more favorable context. This climate persisted in the years that followed. Signs of a higher birth rate, interrupted by mobilization, reappeared after 1952. This explains why the direction remained the same after the war, although the political majority was not so much committed to the family. But at the time, there was need for reconstruction, and the big social reforms appeared to insure both employment and security for the new generations.

The Family Movement

The background described so far tends to leave a relatively minor role to the family movement in shaping family policy. But it makes it possible to understand the evolution of this movement and to explain why some of its favorite themes were taken up by schools of thought which might otherwise have been inattentive or even hostile.

In the nineteenth century, as we have noted, the family was more or less a right-wing cause. Family was associated with monarchy, religion, property. Revolution was a form of parricide. There seemed to be a relationship between the execution of Louis XVI and the revolutionary law authorizing divorce by mutual consent and denying the authority of the head of the family. Those who struggled for family rights, not only the ultras of the Restoration but also Le Play and his sociological school, and even Albert de Mun, or de La Tour du Pin and the first Social Catholics, decided to return to the reforms of the Revolution. They did not accept the republican policies on marriage, divorce, or the suppression of the privileges of the first-born. Yet this stress on the family theme is not incompatible, at least to begin with, with noble indifference to the real problems of family life. In his study, which favors the family movement, Robert Talmy notes about the monarchy of July,

> the strange contradiction of a regime which elevates the family to the rank of an institution and yet leaves the working class families to face the most severe material difficulties while an exaggerated attachment to their savings draws the leading classes to a neo-Malthusianism.[7]

When a proper family movement did take shape around 1900, when a certain number of pressure groups set promotion of the family and defense of its interests as their field for action, they had to cope with this heritage. Undoubtedly, the natalists of Bertillon's National Alliance and the family spokesmen of the first militant associations of large families were now ready to act within the laws of the republic and to insist on material claims. The Alliance campaigned for tax reform. Captain Maire, spokesman for one of the more active associations, favored the slogan, "Large families are creditors of the nation." But the family as an institution was still in the foreground. Catholics, who were at the time in close touch with the right-wing movements, were predominant in the associations. In Parliament, although some left-wing members did join the group for the defense of the family in 1919, nationalists were more often than not the spokesmen for the family movement. An important congress on the family was held in Lille in 1920 under the chairmanship of General de Castelnau. It proclaimed, in a solemn declaration, the rights of the family, "founded on marriage, bound by hierarchy under the paternal authority." Among the rights claimed, with tax reform, was the family wage; one can also note mention of free transmission of the family heritage and the institution of a family vote, a system which would have given the father the right to vote in strength proportionate to the number of his children.

[7] Robert Talmy, *Histoire du mouvement familial de France* (Paris: UNCAF, 1963).

At the beginning of the 1920s, the family movement remained in close relationship with the more conservative forces. But this was the time when things were beginning to change slowly due to several influences:

1. It appeared that Parliament was not ready to move toward institutional reform. Proposals in favor of the family vote met with no success.

2. The growth of the movement had tended to displace its gravity center. After 1920, new family associations were created, and they were not, as before, limited to large families. All families were now invited to join. These new associations made up the General Confederation of Families under the guidance of Abbé Viollet, and they now took their place beside the National Federation of Associations for Large Families. These new associations were more interested in the social aspects of the family problem. And things went the same way when, in the 1930s, workers' family associations of a more popular nature, such as the Workers' Christian League, joined the movement.

3. The trade unions' attitude also tended to change. With one exception, the less important French Confederation of Christian Workers (CFTC), they had so far been hostile to family benefits. They saw them as a way to deter the workers' movement from action and to maintain low salaries. But hostility was to give way to action in favor of a change; in 1923, the General Confederation of Labor (CGT) made family benefits part of its program on condition that they were to be distributed on a national basis and no longer through a system in the hands of the employers.

As the family policy was turning in the prewar years to questions of income and standard of living, and gradually was giving up the idea of an ideal model for the family (benefits were now to go to children born out of wedlock), public support grew accordingly.

The Vichy regime could have handled things in a way which might have compromised the whole family policy. But the reasons for such a policy were still there. And it happened, politically speaking, that one of the three most important political parties born of the Resistance movement, the Popular Republican Movement (MRP), had taken up the family theme as its own. It was influential in the transition to the present system.

THE PRESENT SYSTEM OF PUBLIC INTERVENTION
IN THE FAMILY FIELD

As we have stressed, French family policy was shaped as a system of public intervention at the end of World War II. This system has remained in operation in its essentials, which does not mean that it has not shown some form of evolution.

Principles and Framework
of Public Intervention

Four main points should be made here:
1. France openly favors a family policy.
2. This policy is directed not to a single aim but to several aims.
3. It involves specific institutions.
4. It is the result of converging and also contradictory pressure from the political and social forces in French society.

Family Policy Favored
A policy for the family is generally recognized as one of the country's social and economic needs, both officially and by a consensus of opinion.

The preamble of the French Constitution of October 27, 1946, which also figured in the 1958 Constitution, advocates among the principles which are particularly to be stressed at the present time the idea that "the Nation insures proper conditions for the well-being of the individual and the family." Such a policy is defined and implemented at governmental level. One can refer to the decree of December 24, 1945, which defined the mission of the Minister of Health who was then responsible for family problems. It was up to him to "study, with all ministers concerned, and to coordinate principles and implementation of a policy to protect the family, encourage the birth rate and insure that families are given the necessary means to bring up their children." The terms of reference of the authorities concerned, whoever they may have been under different governments, have never really changed. In June, 1976, again, the President of the Republic, speaking at the thirtieth anniversary of the Family Associations' Union, declared:

> The family is one of the basic institutions for the development of the human being and for the stability of society. This is why I am committed to strengthening the institution, by way of the global policy for the family duly discussed with the family associations.

Official statements of such a nature do, without doubt, have some effect on reality. An important proportion of the nation's resources is spent on these actions. There may be some discussion on the content of the policy, not on the need for a policy. This is true of the opposition as well as of the governing majority. The current Common Action Program of the left-wing parties deals on one of its first pages with family benefits and later, in a brief chapter, with other measures covering family needs.

The picture, however favorable, does have some drawbacks. First of all, family policy is not entirely coherent. It pursues several aims at the same time: social and demographic action *for* the family but also *on* the family. Its efficiency varies according to the different sectors of intervention; among all the actions which are of consequence for the family, a nucleus is definitely inspired by family policy (family benefits, tax rebates, and services for the family). But in fields such as education, health, and housing other considerations may compete successfully with the aims of the family policy. The great variety of agents implicated in the policy do not necessarily tend to act in coordinated fashion.

We also have to face the question whether family policy still has the same force that it had thirty years ago. All in all, family policy has declined among the priorities of social reform. Is this acceptable? Should a new priority be formulated for the family? This is one of the themes actually under discussion.

Aims

The aims of the family policy are not easy to describe, because they are not always explicitly formulated. Public intervention certainly intends to act in favor of the family. It is less easy to say whether an action *on* the family is also intended, with the view to encouraging a definite type of family.

The family is officially supported because, as is often said in speeches, it is the basic cell of society. Individuals find in the family the most commonly recognized shelter, and a frame for their activities. The family insures the upkeep and upbringing of the children. It is a center for sentimental relations, sociability, and solidarity. For these reasons it deserves support from the community.

Material support is provided through family benefits and services for the family. The aim is either to relate family income to the number of children, or to provide services that are not available on the market, or that are inadequately provided (home help, day care, education).

But the support to the family is also of a moral nature. It aims at giving the family the capacity and discipline to face its mission in society. The state tends to act then, as often in France, as guardian. Marriage counseling services are not very much developed, but there is a national network of social services, medical consultations, and more and more psychological and educational services; all these are directed to the health, well-being, and education of the child. And because in a way the family is, whether one likes it or not, associated with morality, different forms of "action against immorality" are usually placed under the banner of family policy (such as the censorship of films or of publications directed to young readers).

This is where policy infringes on intervention in the family. The state moves out of its neutral attitude and reacts to the type of family that modern society seems to shape. But it is not able to put much pressure on the family. Intervention is accepted as long as it concerns the family's attitudes to children. Parents must care for their children, and the legislator intervenes restrictively (to stop mistreatment of children), or positively (to insure compulsory education). The community may substitute itself for the family, when the latter is not up to its task, by instituting some form of guardianship for family allowances or by placing the child in another home.

The duty of solidarity is spelled out by law as the *obligation alimentaire,* which means the obligation to provide for the worker and members of the family. It covers not only minor children but all members of the family. But legislation has tended to demand less from the family by way of help due to adults; if a means test is necessary, the law tends increasingly not to include the resources of the family. The family is more free than it was to choose whether it should help its own members.

Family policy is also not indifferent to the size of the family. This was to be expected when one of the reasons for intervention was the decline in the birth rate. Today the state still tries to encourage families to have a given number of children. How many? Perspective changes. It used to be more than three children. Now the public authorities are focused on the second or third child. The family is encouraged to bear those children and bring them up. But which family? Should it be only the legitimate family? Should it be the couple living together? Or the unmarried mother? What relationship should be expected between parents? What is the proper balance between family life and professional activity? Here family policy has given up trying to refer to a model and has to adapt to different family structures.

This has long been the case for the natural family, which has been entitled for many years to the same help as the legitimate family. However, natural parents did have to wait until 1975 to be officially represented in the family associations.

Things have moved more slowly, and the role of the woman still remains under discussion. Family policy used to be inclined toward the model of the housewife held to her household tasks and the upbringing of her children. This is why, even in 1945, legislation favored a special education for young girls, and why some family benefits were limited to the nonworking mother. But things have now moved far enough to encourage authorities to adopt a more neutral attitude.

Institutions

Family policy may also be characterized by its institutions. These can be described at three levels: the public agencies responsible for formulating and implementing governmental decisions; the Funds forming the social security system; and probably the most original aspect of the French organization, the family associations which have been invested with an official role of representation.

1. No single agency is entitled to deal alone with the family. Family problems are covered by several ministerial departments in separate administrations. [Although the precise French term is *Direction,* we have used "administration" throughout. *Eds.*]

a) The Social Welfare Administration, usually part of the Ministry of Health, is sometimes given, as at present, quasi-ministerial status in the shape of a Secretary of State. Here we find the Sub-Administration of Family and Childhood. This governmental agency has first-rank responsibility in drafting family policy. But it has no jurisdiction over family benefits.

b) Family benefits are covered by the Administration of Social Security, which is sometimes under the Minister of Health; at other times, and for the moment, under the Minister of Labor. It includes a Sub-Administration for Pensions and Family Benefits.

c) The Administration of Population and Migration is usually under the Minister of Labor. It takes responsibility for population problems and supervises the INED and the secretariat of the High Committee on Population.

Other ministries are involved with family problems, in particular the Ministry of Education, which is very important in France, where the education system is centralized. The Ministry of Finance and the Department of Social Affairs have a role in coordination; the first, in controlling short-term economic effects of social policies and the second, in preparing long-term plans.

This brief description may give an impression of confusion. As a reaction to this, and to satisfy the family organizations, a Consultative Committee for the Family was created in 1971. Its members are experts, interested civil servants, and representatives of the associations. This institution seemed, for some time after it was created, to be somewhat neglected, but the government has now made up its mind to refer to it most questions of importance.

Locally, questions relating to family policy are dealt with in the *départemente* ("county") Administrations of Health and Social Welfare. [Although not fully satisfactory, this is our phrasing for *Direction sanitaire et action sociale. Eds.*] These bodies are the local representatives of state agencies involved in social affairs, and on the other side the Regional Administrations of Social Security supervise the family allowance funds, as they do all social security bodies.

Finally, there is scope for intervention by the local government councils. The *départements* contribute to the state's action in the social field. The town councils have more autonomy and can choose a large variety of actions related to education or to family services.

2. Family benefits are administered not by public agencies but by the family allowance Funds, which are theoretically governed by representatives of the interested parties (employers, wage earners, family associations). They are organized on a local and national basis.

This is not an organizational form unique to family allowances. It is also employed for the other branches of the social security system. The family branch was, like the others, reorganized in 1967. Each branch was then made more autonomous financially, and employer representation was reinforced. Employers were a minority in the immediate postwar years, but they now hold half the seats on the boards and are able to form a majority with the more moderate trade unions.[8]

It is important to remind the reader that the autonomy of the family branch inside the social security system was one of the issues under discussion in the postwar years. The trade unions and left-wing parties favored single funds covering all forms of risk. But the family associations and the MRP party intervened to maintain a separate organization, first as a temporary measure (Law of August 22, 1946), then definitely (Law of February 21, 1949).

As are all social security bodies, the family allowance Funds are strictly supervised. The administration lays down all the rules under which benefits are awarded. But the Funds do enjoy some autonomy in their social welfare

---

[8] The boards of the family allowance Funds include twenty members: nine from various groups of employers and self-employed, nine from the unions, and two from family associations. The system of designation by the organizations has replaced direct election, and the number of seats attributed to each organization is determined by the government.

and health activity, where they are free to spend a small percentage of the contributions according to their own decisions. They can then allocate supplementary benefits or finance grants and loans for equipment and services. The National Family Allowance Fund, whose role is to coordinate the local Funds, and which has some resources at its disposal, can thus have some say in family policy. The administration cannot entirely ignore what happens in this separate field of action.

3. We have so far covered organizations which do not deal exclusively with family problems. This is not the case with the official representation of families organized through the *départemental* unions and the National Union of Family Associations (UNAF).

French law often gives a privileged position to the so-called "representative" organizations. But usually—and always in the field of labor problems—the normal rule is pluralism.

In the field of family policy, on the contrary, the *départemental* unions and UNAF enjoy a real privilege. Family associations are entitled to make representations to public authorities only if they are affiliated with these unions. They are represented in due proportion to their membership; the members themselves, through the mechanism of the family vote, are entitled to a number of votes related to the number of their children.

UNAF and UDAF (the *départemental* unions of family associations), as specified in Article 3 of the Family Code, act in a consultative status on all questions involving family policy. They are the official representatives of families and send delegations to all interested bodies, commissions, and councils. There are about a hundred of those at national level. They have the legal right to represent family interests before all courts. They also administer their own establishments at the request of the public authorities.

The institution does savor of the corporatism which, under the Vichy regime, was dominant in the origins of the family movement. But it also respects pluralism. The family unions have not entirely superseded the family movements. The influence of the movements has been recognized on a recent occasion; the board of UNAF is now constituted partly by persons elected in the *départemental* unions, partly by persons designated by national movements.

At the same time, by virtue of this same Law of July 11, 1975, associations have opened their doors to married couples without children and to all persons with the legal responsibility for children, even, with some restrictions, to foreign families. The right to vote has been given to each parent and not only, as before, to the head of the family.

The unions can count on financial stability not only through the contributions of their members, but through a share (3 percent) of the family
benefits. They run some risk of sclerosis through their privileged status, and
also because they have to express a moderate view which may be common
to all the families represented. Moreover, their militant membership is narrow: only 400,000 families belong to the associations. There are five times
more in parents' associations related to the school system, and consumer or
environment protection associations compete with the family associations, as
do the trade unions.

In spite of this, the institution shows vitality. Together with their representative role, the family unions have created useful services: information
services for the family, cultural activities in some cities or suburban areas,
protection of family benefits, and so on. UNAF takes positions which have
to be taken into account by the government and the political forces. It initiated its own internal reforms in 1975, which shows it was not entirely out
of touch with change in the movements it seeks to represent.

Family Movement a Unity?

All this could give the strong impression that the family movement is a
unity. This is only partly true, for instance, when it is necessary to claim a
larger financial stake in favor of families. But there are also differences
which reflect contradictory social and economic influences. The family can
be an important issue in their confrontation.

Differences are apparent inside the movement itself. One can distinguish a large center which is content with the form of representation, but not
insensitive to change (Federation of French Families, National Confederation of Rural Families, and several smaller associations). A conservative
wing consists of the National Confederation of Associations of Catholic
Families, whose real aim is to promote the values of marriage and of a
stable, united family focused on childbearing. The more working class
oriented and syndicalist federations constitute a progressive wing, more interested in concrete action in connection with the trade unions and left-wing
parties.

In the small world of the family movement, one does not find a reflection of the sharp national differences between right- and left-wing political
forces, with employers on the one side and most of the trade unions on the
other side. The contradictions which in France are characteristic of the
workers' situation do not reappear here. Tension is, in a way, underplayed,

because of a common reference to the same values and to specific institutions. They are not absent, however, in the controversies underlying family policy.

For the moment, two points can be stated. First, the family problem does not have first-rank priority for the large professional organizations or unions. This is true for the employers' movement. Employers still prefer to increase direct wages rather than to see the same effort go through a national redistribution mechanism. But it is also true for the workers' unions. For them also attention should first be paid to direct wages; even in the field of social security demands affecting pensions and the health service are often considered more important than those which concern family benefits.

On the other hand, if one were to characterize the attitude of the political parties toward the family, one could say that today none of them is committed, as the MRP was in 1945, to be the privileged representative of the family ideal. The left, as the right, speaks of the family, but not in the same way. The right will still be inclined to insist on the institution of the family which must be respected and preserved. The left will stress the necessity to create better material conditions for the family. The word itself has more echo, as public opinion surveys show, on the right than on the left. But the real problems involved are a concern for both the left and the right, each camp carefully trying to express the consequences of its more fundamental choices.

The Different Sectors of Intervention

Family policy covers a number of goals which are the explicit objectives for programs and policies deliberately designed to achieve them. The more important of these are: income maintenance; the family's way of living; social action directed toward the family; family and housing policy; and family and the education system.

Income Maintenance

Family policy in France is essentially an income-maintenance policy. The support of the child is a heavy burden on the family budget, and this is sufficient grounds for social transfers in favor of the family.

There is no consensus of opinion on the cost of a child. The INED has suggested the following scale. Theoretically, if a couple spends 100FF, a family's expenses rise to: 127FF for one child; 154FF for two children; 181FF for three children; and 208FF for four children. [As of April 1, 1977, the exchange rate was: 1 French franc = $0.20.]

Paul Paillat, author of these studies, notes that they do not give a proper picture of the needs of the older child. According to UNAF, in 1975, the cost of the child was very much related to its age, amounting monthly to: 320FF under six years of age; 530FF under ten years of age; 740FF under fourteen years of age; and 980FF under eighteen years of age. The social indicators related to the Seventh National Plan (1976) refer to the following consumers' scale:

One adult	1.0
Another adult	+0.7
Child aged 10 to 15	+0.5
Child aged 2 to 9	+0.4
Child under 2	+0.2

Controversy is never very far in this type of analysis. Forms of consumption are definitely different in the different social groups, and their expectancies concerning the needs of their children vary even more. Scientifically, one can admit this, but it is more difficult to publicize the results of such studies. The public might very well conclude that all children do not have the same value for the commentator.

On the other hand, all studies on family income must be put in the perspective of the family cycle. Families are not really interested in comparing their situation at a definite moment with that of all other families: for them, the upbringing of children is a long-term task involving restraint and planning for sixteen to twenty years. What is also important is the direct family income during this same period. Promotion, work opportunities for women, length of the educational obligations, all have influence on the capacity of the family to face its obligations.

The cost of a child is also a controversial issue among organizations. Family associations and trade unions base their campaigns concerning the cost of living index, wages, or family allowances on different evaluations. UNAF evaluated the monthly budget of a family with two children, in July, 1976, at 3,335FF (or 3,900FF if the children were teen-agers); the same figure became 5,000FF for the National Confederation of Popular Family Associations. At that time, the official cost of living index was 167 (on the basis of 1970 prices); it varied from 176 to 198 if one referred to cost of living increases calculated by UNAF or by the trade unions on their particular family budgets.

Everyday experience does not always confirm the views of statisticians. This is why family policy has given up any official evaluation of the cost of a child. These uncertainties, however, do not deter it from trying to compensate for that cost. This is done in two ways. Family allowances are allocated by the social security system, and a tax remittance system adjusts the general income tax in favor of the family.

Family allowances. Under the generic term "family allowances," and through the social security system, families benefit from a variety of allowances. The two most important ones[9] are the family allowance properly speaking, plus single-wage-earner's allowance. The latter recently (1977) became a complementary family allowance payable whether there is a single wage in the family or both parents are wage earners. Families receive, in this way, a supplementary income which they are free to spend as they please.

Several principles are involved, and their interpretation has changed with time. The aid is related solely to the presence of a child; all children are termed equal. The allowance is granted to all children concerned, on a uniform basis. It does not take into account differences in the income of parents or in their social status.

But, and this comes from its history, the aid is also part of a supplementary wage scheme. It is financed through the social security system; funds come from contributions and are in that way related to the income of active workers. That is why the beneficiaries expect a relation between the aid and their real wages.

The system is, then, a compromise, and has not overcome all its contradictions. It has also been corrected over the years for demographic reasons or, more simply, through lack of funds.

Family allowances are granted to the children of a parent who is employed or is unable to work; who lives in France with the children and has at least two children in charge. As one can see, this is a very comprehensive rule. Children considered as being in charge include: children up to the age of sixteen and a half; up to eighteen if they are in apprenticeship; or up to twenty for the child pursuing his studies or incapable of working.

In spite of the work basis of the French system, the right to family allowances has always tended to extend as far as possible. The definition of work as a condition was stretched far enough to cover all marginal situa-

[9] They do not include an exceptional allowance granted to all families drawing allowances, in September, 1975. This premium of 250FF aimed to encourage spending in the face of the economic crisis. It has not been renewed.

tions; and from January 1, 1978, all children will be entitled to the benefit irrespective of the employment status of their parents.

In this way we have arrived at a situation where about 13 million children draw allowances. These do not include the first child.[10] This is the first sign of an intention to favor large families, or at least families with several children. This appears also in the way the allowance is calculated. The allowance is a fixed percentage of a basic monthly salary, the base being determined by government decision. The percentage amounts to 22 percent for two children, 59 percent for three, 96 percent for four, and 33 percent for each extra child. As one can see, the intervention is focused on the third child, and differences related to the place in the family of the child are higher than they were originally. Children over ten and over fifteen draw a supplementary 9 percent and 16 percent respectively.

Equality comes to the foreground again, however, when one considers the basic salary. There is only one basic salary scale for all families. Differences related to geographic situations have been progressively eliminated. The base is fixed annually. It is not legally related to real wages and it is decided by the government, whereas free discussion is the rule concerning wages. But, of course, beneficiaries cannot remain indifferent to the relation between the allowances and real wages. The monthly basic salary is at present 768FF, less than half of the minimum legal wage and roughly a quarter of the mean wage.

The rule of equality, which one could have considered to be characteristic of the French system, has now been somewhat modified. This is visible when one comes to the single-wage-earner allowance. This allowance has been thus far added to the family allowance when the family has only one source of work income and has at least one child. For the single child, however, the benefit is limited to the child of a single parent, to the handicapped child, or to the last child still in care of a family that has reared several children. As before, the allowance is also a percentage of a basic figure determined by government decision: 50 percent when there is a child under two years of age; when there is no child under two, 20 percent for one child, 40 percent for two children, and 50 percent thereafter.

This allowance has had a difficult history. Originally, it openly favored a definite way of life for the family, with the mother remaining in the home. But although it was widely granted to families where the mother had no

[10] This is why, according to 1970 European Economic Community figures, the percentage of children drawing allowances in the 0–19 age group in France is 85 percent, below rates in Denmark and the Netherlands.

need to work, the amount was progressively reduced. The Law of January 3, 1972, introduced a complication by creating a means test for this allowance. To insure proper selection of beneficiaries, the allowance was reduced for families whose income was above a certain level,[11] related also to the number of children at home, while it was increased for the poorer families, those below the taxation level.

The single-wage-earner allowance and the supplementary allowance are calculated on a different basis and are much lower than that of the family allowance itself. The supplement amounts to 50 percent of the base and is due when there is at least one child under three years of age or four or more children. About 2,500,000 families actually benefit from the single-wage-earner allowance itself and 900,000 from the supplement.

It is possible to know approximately the mean amount which actually went to each family in 1970 and the number of families in each category (see tables 2 and 3). The mean annual wage was then around 16,000FF.

Table 2 Mean Amount of Allowance According to the Size of the Family, 1970 (*in FF*)

Number of Children	Family Allowance	Single Wage Earner	Total
One	—	573	573
Two	1,161	819	1,762
Three	3,497	1,060	4,353
Four	5,560	1,071	6,511
Five +	8,760	1,118	9,741
All families	3,009	881	3,257

SOURCE: National Institute of Statistical and Economic Studies (hereafter referred to as INSEE), *Données statistiques sur les familes*, 1970.

Table 3 Number of Families Benefiting from the Allowances

Number of Children	Family Allowance	Single Wage Earner	Total	Percent
One	—	756,000	756,000	15.4
Two	2,166,000	1,538,000	2,166,000	44.1
Three	1,126,000	909,000	1,126,000	23.0
Four	461,000	401,000	461,000	9.5
Five +	396,000	348,000	396,000	8.1
Total	4,149,000	3,952,000	4,905,000	100.0

SOURCE: INSEE, *Données statistiques sur les familles*, 1970.

[11] 34,560FF annual income for a family with two children, and so on.

A rough comparison allows us to say that in 1976 a family of two children with the single-wage-earner's allowance was entitled to about 8 percent of the mean wage, 16 percent with the supplementary single-wage-earner's allowance. In 1970, the same family drew about 10 percent of the mean wage.

Important changes have now been introduced by law to be implemented in 1978. The single-wage-allowance disappears, as does the children's allowance, to be replaced by a new allowance. This *complément familial* (complementary family allowance) will amount to 340FF on January 1, 1978. It will follow the increases in the basic salary for the family allowances and will be paid, whether the mother works outside the home or not, to families with a child under three or with at least three children. The means test is preserved, and the income ceiling will be the same as that now in effect for the single-wage allowance; the ceiling will be raised by 15 percent when there are two wage earners in the family; and the ceiling will follow the increase in real wages. Single-parent families will be entitled to a supplement of 50 percent of the allowance.

For the moment, two statements seem to be essential: (1) The aid is not negligible, especially for the lower income groups. (2) The population supports this form of social transfers.

But aid to the family has not paralleled increases in real income, and particularly the rise in wages. This is indubitable even if there is some con-

Table 4 Family Allowances, Wages, and Retail Prices (*Base 100 in 1946*)

Years	Family Allowances		Hourly Wage	Prices
	Two Children [a]	Five Children [b]		
1946	100.0	100.0	100.0	100.0
1950	235.4	257.7	277.5	294.4
1955	347.9	434.2	489.2	382.0
1960	380.4	496.9	731.3	519.1
1965	448.6	719.0	1,062.2	624.7
1970	508.0	920.3	1,614.6	728.0
1973	564.4	1,102.0	2,268.5	941.0
(1975) [c]	638.8	1,376.6 [d]	3,169.3	1,190.8

SOURCE: Jean Jacques Dupeyroux, *Droit de le sécurité sociale* (6th ed.; Paris: Dallez, 1975).

[a] Family allowances plus single-wage-earners' allowance plus compensatory benefit for the handicapped.

[b] The same plus two supplements for children over 10 and children over 15.

[c] This table has not been continued officially since 1973 because of the variety of new allowances which do not follow the same rate of increase.

[d] Including the increased single-wage-earner's allowance.

troversy between the government on one side, the family movement and the opposition on the other, as to the importance of the lag behind wages. Indeed, the figures in table 4 are clear.

The conclusion is the same if one relates family benefits to all social benefits, or to direct income (see table 5).

Table 5 Purchasing Power of Direct Income, Social Benefits, and Family Benefits (*Base 100 in 1962*)

	1962	1963	1968	1969	1970	1973
Direct incomes	100	105.9	136.3	143.6	153.8	175.9
Social benefits	100	112.6	164.9	177.9	189.5	232.3
Family benefits	100	108.8	128.2	131.9	130.5	141.9

Reference years have been chosen according to the trend noted for family benefits: the index rose in 1963, remained stable until 1968, rose again in 1969, and then lagged again until 1972.

In nominal value, the mass of family benefits has had an annual 10 percent rate of increase since 1970, while the corresponding rate for wages is 14.6 percent. This is easy enough to understand. There is no fixed link between family benefits and real wages, or even between them and the ceiling wage, which is the limit for pensions, and other social security benefits. The government, in its successive decisions, has tended to follow the rise in prices rather than the rise in real wages. This has been somewhat corrected lately as regards the particular evolution of the increased single-wage allowance, which seems to have moved up more rapidly than prices.[12] But this is not really visible in the mass of the transfers, and it is not possible to predict the impact of the new ceiling-based child care allowance.

The quotient familial (*family tax benefit or deduction*). Income maintenance is also insured through the fiscal system, and income tax rebates constitute an essential feature of aid to the family. This is so because of their impact on the material situation of families and also because of their political importance in the French context.

The mechanism is simple. Taxable income is divided into shares; each parent has one share, each child half a share. The progressive income tax is then calculated according to the more favorable rates in effect for a lower income level. For instance, in 1976 a married taxpayer with two children was expected to pay the amount of income tax indicated in table 6.

The significance of these measures is seen in information from the 1970 income surveys shown in table 7.

[12] Following the rate of increase of the minimum wage.

Table 6 Income Tax (*in FF*)

Income	One Share	Three Shares
20,000	2,568	118
50,000	13,783	5,143
100,000	38,075	21,351

Table 7 Income Tax in Percentage of Income, According to Income Level and Number of Children

Annual Income (*in FF*)	Number of Children						
	0	*1*	*2*	*3*	*4*	*5+*	*Mean*
Less than 3,000	—	—	—	—	—	—	—
3,000–6,499	—	—	—	—	—	—	—
6,500–9,999	0.8	0.2	0.1	—	—	—	0.6
10,000–14,999	3.3	0.8	0.4	0.2	0.1	—	2.2
15,000–19,999	5.5	2.3	1.1	0.7	0.3	0.2	3.3
20,000–29,999	7.8	4.7	3.5	2.2	1.2	0.5	5.3
30,000–59,999	12.4	8.7	7.5	6.6	6.0	3.8	9.5
60,000–99,999	20.1	16.4	14.3	12.8	11.4	9.5	16.2
100,000 or more	31.6	28.7	25.7	25.1	23.6	20.8	27.9
Mean	8.6	8.2	7.6	6.9	6.5	4.2	8.0

SOURCE: INSEE, *Enquête sur les revenus de 1970.*

The state thus implements a very important policy in favor of the family through the *quotient familial*. It was estimated in 1966[13] that if these measures had not been taken, the number of poverty families with four children would have doubled. The burden on the budget grew from 3.4 billion francs in 1968 to 6.5 billion francs in 1973, which is practically +90 percent at a time when the gross amount of taxable resources had increased by only 17 percent and the number of dependent children had not changed. Seven and one-half million families are actually affected. Particularly since family allowances are not included in taxable income, the fiscal system is a very important instrument of family policy. The relative significance of the different forms of intervention has changed since 1945. Originally, the equally distributed family allowances were by far the bulk of the nation's effort. At the present time they represent about 20 billion francs, while the means-tested allowances amount to 12 billion francs and the tax rebates to 9 billion francs.

Opinion is on the whole favorable to the *quotient familial*. The approach is not, however, above criticism. It does not consider the cost of the

---

[13] There is no more recent information.

child and its place in the family; and it is certainly an advantage for the higher income groups. This effect goes even farther than it appears initially. Families who are way under taxable level are in no way in a better situation than the taxpayers without children in the same income group. Also, for fiscal reasons, the student who pursues his studies is regarded as dependent, and more often than not he belongs to the higher social group. This is why this "multiplying quotient" is sometimes severely criticized. An expert report on taxation in 1974 even came to the conclusion that advantages given in this way to the higher-income families were the most favorable in a group of countries including Europe and the U.S. To attenuate these effects, some reforms have been attempted, but they meet with strong opposition from the higher wage earners. The latter, noting that their wages are reported by their employers, so that they are responsible for payments for taxes and contributions to social security, want to preserve the status quo.

An adjustment is, however, necessary. The *quotient familial* deals only with income tax. But the French tax system leans heavily on the sales tax, and families are large consumers. According to the only published study (1967), the mean amount of sales tax paid by families does not vary much according to the number of children. It even seems to diminish with the size of the family because of the place taken by food in the family budget; food products are relatively lightly taxed in the French system.

According to INSEE (*Enquête sur les revenus de 1970*), as soon as the family has more than three children, the balance between family allowances and taxes becomes favorable, except for the higher-income classes.[14]

The studies carried out in 1976 on social and economic indicators connected with the Seventh National Plan suggest another analysis. Table 8 gives in nominal value the amount of family benefits paid to fourteen typical families; in each family situation, benefits are compared according to the social and employment status of the head of the family. Four categories are listed: higher executive, lower executive, clerical worker, and blue-collar worker.

Families in the medium-wage group, from the lower executive class, are losers. Higher-income groups and workers benefit from the system more or less equally if the family is large (three or four children). The aid does seem to have some corrective effect on the hierarchy of real incomes when the family has one or two children. And these effects have definitely been accentuated in recent years; this reflects both the impact of the *quotient*

[14] Above 60,000FF annual income.

Table 8 Family Benefits[a] for Fourteen Typical Families, 1976 (in FF)

Number of Children	Social Group	1970	1971	1972	1973	1974	1975
One child under 2	Higher executive	2,382	2,635	2,372	2,452	2,634	3,018
	Lower executive	2,133	1,922	1,792	1,824	1,999	1,548
	Clerical worker	2,366	2,462	2,529	2,723	2,993	3,161
	Blue-collar worker	2,066	2,122	2,253	2,341	2,647	3,956
First child under 2; second between 2 and 5	Higher executive	4,630	4,996	4,863	5,217	5,954	6,858
	Lower executive	3,992	3,816	3,777	3,882	4,152	4,617
	Clerical worker	4,250	4,477	4,597	4,873	6,386	8,064
	Blue-collar worker	3,836	4,058	5,031	5,920	6,841	7,887
First child under 2; second between 2 and 5; third between 6 and 9	Higher executive	7,430	8,001	8,184	8,803	9,810	11,338
	Lower executive	6,897	6,834	6,906	7,216	7,694	8,374
	Clerical worker	6,487	6,926	7,881	8,945	10,525	12,145
	Blue-collar worker	6,030	6,355	7,482	8,561	9,994	11,539
First child under 2; second between 2 and 5; third and fourth between 6 and 9	Higher executive	9,793	10,585	11,408	12,464	13,397	15,404
	Blue-collar worker	8,301	8,795	10,079	11,294	13,286	15,399

[a]Family allowance, single-wage-earner allowance, and increased allowance, housing allowance, quotient familial.

familial and of the means-tested allowances, which leave out middle-income families regardless of the number of children.

Families' Way of Life

What has been said so far about income maintenance, although it is the nucleus of family policy, does not exhaust the field of intervention. Family policy covers a series of actions directed toward facilitating daily living for the family or even suggesting a pattern. Goals here go beyond financial aid, and the substance may be an issue for controversy, since questions are raised about the natalist content of the policy or the expected role of the mother. The French policy encourages childbearing and values the role of the woman in the home. But policy is also influenced by changing attitudes; this explains some form of hesitation and even contradiction when demography has to cloak itself with discretion and when the state is expected to be neutral in the face of the changing status of women. The aid tends to become more diversified. Instead of coming up against too controversial issues, it prefers to explore in a practical manner a series of specific needs for the family. Instead of pressing a solution, it offers a variety of services among which, one hopes, each family will be more or less able to choose.

Family policy does bear the mark of the demographic preoccupation. Several of its aspects imply a definite encouragement to childbearing. Allowances are granted before birth to encourage the pregnant mother to submit herself to medical supervision. A postnatal allowance has taken the place of the old maternity allowance, which used to be related—rather too insistently—to a short gap between successive births. Today, this premium is paid on all births. All this is not so important as the principles which exclude the first child from allowances or relate the rate of allowance to the place of the child in the family. And now young men who are fathers before the age of twenty-two may dispense with military service.

The same concern appears each time family policy deals with the maternal function. The single-wage allowance was originally a grant to the housewife. We have seen how it was subsequently made available to all mothers regardless of their income and also how, in an increasingly unfavorable context, the authorities allowed this form of aid to dwindle and subjected it to a means test. But the level of the allowance continued to reflect a refusal to choose. Even when it was increased for the lower-income group, and grew slightly more rapidly than the other allowances, it was never meant to be a substitute for a second source of income. We are far from having a maternal wage which, according to certain sectors of opinion, could be a proper payment for work by the woman in her home. The mother of a family who has brought up several children does benefit in the pension system from two extra years of insurance per child. This does not go so far as to consider all the years spent bringing up the children as equivalent to years of work. However, the at-home mother has long received more consideration from family legislation than does the mother who works outside; the latter had to wait until 1972 to receive an allowance for child care. This, too, was subject to a means test. Ceilings were first extremely low, and if one considers that this allowance goes to families who have, in general, two sources of income, selection seems to be more severe when the mother works outside than when she stays at home. As a result the number of beneficiaries remained small until recently—about 33,000. In 1976 the allowance amounted to about 300FF per month; income ceilings (when the family has two sources of income went from 40,000FF yearly income for the first child to 90,000FF when there are five, and so on. The recent substitution of the *complément familial* for both the single-wage and the child care allowance results in a more simplified form of benefit; in addition, it permits the government to maintain a far more neutral stance toward child care. Two objectives are achieved. Help goes where it is needed most: to families with very young children and large families. Second, although the ceiling rates are expected to be more favorable to single-wage-earner families, both one- and two-earner families are eligible, and the objective is to provide support for low-income working mothers also.

In addition to this particular family allowance, some measures have been taken to reconcile maternal tasks with working conditions. They concern labor law and have been recently brought up to date. First, a woman who gives birth is eligible for a maternity leave, six weeks before the birth of a child and eight weeks after the birth, and during this leave the working woman is entitled to a social security benefit equivalent to half her wage, within the limit of the social security ceiling wage. Some women contend that it would be preferable to have a longer period after the birth, and many people agree that this leave should be considerably extended. Among all the measures which might show a new interest in the family, this certainly would be one of the most popular. A recent court decision concerning the auxiliary public employees is a sign of this interest. The law had omitted to provide this form of protection for them, and the Council of State, which is the higher administrative court, decided that the right to maternity leave was a general principle of law, applicable even without specification.

But the most frequent cause of stress for the working mother comes when she is back at work and needs to get leave for her child care duties. Several collective agreements permit her to take unpaid leave without running the risk of breach of contract. This was first made possible in the civil service: leave can be extended for two years and the right to promotion was partly maintained. But an important move was made in 1977 when a parent's leave within the limit of two years was made possible both for mother and father in all salaried positions. So far the scope of the new system will cover, however, only firms employing more than two hundred.

To go further, and allow some form of payment during extended child care leave, as has been done in a very few industrial sectors, would require public action through the social security system. Proposals have been made by the Minister of Health and the Secretary of State on the Status of Women and also by the Opposition (there is a proposal from the Socialist Party). Both parents would, under these proposals, be entitled to the benefit, and the idea seems to be popular with many families.

Traditionally, a pregnant woman benefits from special protection at work. She may not be employed during her maternity leave; nor is she permitted to do specific types of work, such as carrying heavy weights. These laws were rounded out in 1975 by an important rule concerning recruitment. A woman is not obliged to declare her pregnancy to her employer, and she is entitled to come back to the same job at the end of her maternity leave. This is, of course, aimed at facing some of the realities of discrimination. However, even the most concerned defenders of the working mother do not wish to go too far toward special protection, in case they deter employers from recruiting women in general. The trade unions and the feminist movements are cautious in the face of any form of discrimination at work, even that in favor of women. This explains why part-time labor seems to be generally favored by public opinion. However, it has not yet spread much. Employers find it difficult to organize, even when the employer is the Minister of Health responsible for family policy, who did try to set a good example in the civil service. Workers' unions fear that part-time labor may compete successfully with their collective interests, the same work being produced, in fact, for half the salary. In this debate, the mother's family difficulties are not the focus of discussion. However, it is probably because of the pressure of family responsibilities that a large number of workers are interested in flexitime arrangements now in place in some large firms.

The conclusion is that the population issue tends not to disappear but to become more subtle. Public opinion expects authorities to be neutral and to respect each family's outlook regarding its plans for childbearing and the mother's activity.

In regard to this, no fact has more significance in the French context than the recent abortion reform. The Law of January 17, 1975, put an end to restrictive measures which went as far back as the 1920s. This did not come about without qualms concerning the birth rate, and the new legislation will be reviewed after a trial period of five years. The number of abortions was thought at the time to be about one third of the births, and many thought that in the French context, particularly because of the Catholic church's negative attitude to contraception, abortion was in fact used in a clandestine manner as one of the most important instruments of family planning. In spite of this, the restrictive legislation fell apart in the face of medical progress which had facilitated abortion and under the pressure of a large sector of feminine opinion, going far beyond the influence of feminist movements.

After much agitation, the law finally passed by Parliament is being implemented with caution. Abortion can be performed only in hospitals or in supervised establishments—and part of the medical staff does not hide its opposition. Another law (December 4, 1974) has encouraged the creation of family planning centers, and contraception is now reimbursed under the health service.

If all these measures had worked out in accord with the authorities' expectations, abortion should have been kept to a minimum rate. However, in the last two years not enough has been done in the field of family planning counseling. The delay seems to have affected the number of abortions, which amounts officially to about 45,000 in a year. This is a source of concern to the natalists.

The question has, for the moment, lost its dramatic implications. But this recent experience illustrates some of the hesitations that underlie family policy. At the moment nobody is really convinced that purely natalist measures are of any use, but nobody dares to touch them in case this disrupts family attitudes.

The authorities are more sure of themselves in a rather practical and modest type of action. Instead of trying to influence the family, they take it as it is and endeavor to meet some of its everyday needs. In this field of action, one finds a whole variety of interventions either related to an event in family life or put to some special use. They take the form of money benefits, or free access to services, or services accessible through some form of contribution. In this last instance, contributions are often calculated on the basis of the *quotient familial* method.

The same variety characterizes activities of authorities in charge of income support programs. There can be benefits due by law under certain conditions or granted according to the discretion of the responsible body, which may be the social security organization or the local decentralized councils. In this way, family allowances financed through the social security system also include some specialized allowances. We have said that the allowance itself is raised in the case of the older child. When his parents' income is under a fixed ceiling, he also benefits annually from an allowance covering the cost of schoolbooks, and so forth. A special education allowance is provided for the orphan and handicapped child.

We have stressed the role played by the social security funds in the fields of health and social welfare (*action sanitaire et sociale*). They may award extra benefits in special cases and make grants for equipment and services which might be useful to the family. They actually dispose of funds which permit quite a wide scope of intervention: 4.72 percent of contributions levied on wages plus 1.8 percent of the personal contributions of employers and independent workers. A complementary 0.4 percent of the first type of contribution and 0.2 percent of the other go to support an original form of action, the "service benefit." This aims at taking responsibility (within a ceiling of 30 percent, of the cost for the family) for certain social services, such as home help and child care, social centers, special housing services for young workers. The funds are also allowed to pay into this benefit whatever they may save on administration and the interest on loans. All this amounted, in 1974, to about 2 billion francs roughly divided into three unequal shares: 40 percent went to building; a slightly smaller share, to the functioning of the establishments and services; the rest, to the supplementary benefits.

This twofold intervention of individual aid and community services also characterizes the intervention of the local authorities. In France, these were very much involved in the social assistance system, which has maintained its traditional role in spite of the development of social security. This allows some families without resources to claim aid from the community. Aid is granted after an individual screening at the local level, but funds come from the three budgetary sources: the commune, the *département,* and the state. This national assistance covers 650,000 children—3.9 percent of the population under twenty.

Through its local bureau of social aid, the commune also has quite considerable possibilities of granting several different forms of aid and of organizing services for the local population. Crèches and social services, sometimes organized through a social center, are the most frequent forms of intervention at this level.

While it is difficult to cite all the types of intervention, two classifications may be of interest. First there is, at all levels, some debate as to whether it is more useful for the family to draw supplementary money allowances, which leave it free to spend the sum as it wishes, or whether funds are better employed in organizing services open to all families. Concerning the first type of action, many plead that the family is the best judge of its own needs. To draw a supplementary allowance, however, families have to submit to close examination of their income and personal situation. Aid in the form of service benefits from experience and encourages families to use the most satisfactory ways of dealing with their problems. But it is often considered costly, especially as personnel expenses tend to draw heavily on the budget of the Funds or the local authorities. Also, it seems that the more affluent or educated families tend to know how to use these services much better than those who ought to have first priority.

Secondly, these interventions have two different goals. Some of the services answer some of the very common, everyday needs of the family: housework, child care, vacation. Others are more ambitious because they aim at helping with exceptional hazards facing the family. The family then becomes the object of a special social policy.

The commonest forms of intervention are: home help, crèches, vacations, and social service. Home help services have developed because of the difficulties of urban life. It has grown more and more difficult for the family to count on its wider circle of relations or on neighborhood help in case of emergency. This form of aid means that the mother may be replaced at home for a limited period of time after she has given birth to a child, is sick, overcome by exceptional difficulties, or has to pursue vocational training. It is a more ambitious form of aid than the simple housework aid given to the aged. The family home help has been trained for the purpose over an eight-month period and has an official certificate of competence. In 1975, 6,000 or 7,000 persons worked in this field.

This intervention aims at dealing with crises in the family. But the family also requires everyday help to look after young children. In France, families use a very large variety of solutions. According to a study published in the consumers' monthly *Que Choisir?* 85 percent find their own solutions:

they have someone at home or place the child with a private person. The situation of children under three cared for outside their homes may be described as follows: 40,000 are in *crèches collectives* (center care); 18,000 are in *crèches familials* (supervised family day care); 100,000 are with their grandparents; 200,000 are in the *écoles maternelles* (public nursery school); 500,000 to 600,000 are in licensed and unlicensed family day care, some of which has recently been given a form of status and recognition.

The center care functions under very precise rules. It has to have a trained director and a given percentage of personnel in relation to children served; the number of children is limited to forty; the hours are strict, and so is medical supervision. It eliminates children who might be slightly sick. There is some controversy about the crèches which is not without social and political undercurrents.

Everybody agrees that there are not enough places. Requirements evaluated as far back as 1970 showed the need for some 150,000 places. On January 1, 1975, 873 crèches were functioning and had places for 40,888 children. This means one place for every sixty children under the age of three. This situation has led to setting up crèches in private homes. There are 17,373 of these. A group of supervised persons functions in this way in their own homes. Also, the nursery schools have been instructed to open their doors more widely to children between the ages of two and three. A teacher assisted by one untrained helper may be responsible for forty children in these facilities.

Why are there so few crèches? This service is considered costly, particularly because it is not possible to ask the family to pay for it in proportion to its real cost. The fee depends on family income and is on a progressive scale. In 1975, it ranged from 3 to 32FF per day. Several studies have proved that costs per day and per child are generally high and vary, regardless of the quality of the service, in a way that is sometimes difficult to understand. Table 9 cites costs for 1970.

From there on, many rush to the conclusion that it is much more economical for the mother to stay at home. That is why the development of this

Table 9 Cost of Child Care per Day and per Child (*in FF*)

	Public Crèches	Private Crèches	Supervised Family Day Care
Cost	30.15	22.51	21.97
Grant from the responsible body	19.44	6.97	9.22
Family participates	8.76	16.31	11.13

form of service has only recently been given priority rank, under pressure from the growing active female population. Twice, in 1971 and 1974, a credit of 100 million francs was allocated from social security funds to boost public aid.

Vacations, as Kahn and Kamerman have already noted,[15] are an original element of the French service picture. This form of service is so popular that a rule had to be set requesting the Funds not to spend more than 30 percent of their social and health funds on allowances enabling families and children to go on vacations.

A new form of service has recently come into favor: the social center. It meets new expectations from the population, which is more and more ready to take some forms of social service into its own hands. A social center is a service open to all residents of an area, urban or rural. In general, families are the most frequent users. The center covers a geographical sector and employs qualified social service personnel, but it also involves users in its activities. The users do not have any preconceived idea of their requirements, but they find the entire variety of local services assembled in these centers: home help, pedagogical advice, family planning, medical supervision, and so forth. There are 528 such centers, 162 of which are directly organized by the Funds. The financing is only partly covered by the 10 million francs of service benefits allocated by the Funds, and the centers remain very dependent on grants from the local councils and also on contributions from the users. In 1976, the Minister of Health allocated special, limited, funds to add to the service benefits. One third of the centers will probably receive this encouragement.

The sum of actions and services directed to the family is the concern of one of the priority programs of the Seventh Plan. The French planning system does not, in general, imply an obligation to relate public expenditure to the priorities laid out for the five years covered by the plan. But such exceptional obligation is assigned for a limited number of priority programs, among which the family program is included. In the next five years, 1,005 million francs will be spent by the national budget on the family (this means 5,000 new places in crèches each year, for example).

Social Action Directed Toward the Family
The family per se is also a target of broader social welfare policy. In France, where a junior Minister is in charge of this department, this means action

15 Alfred J. Kahn and Sheila B. Kamerman, *Not for the Poor Alone* (Philadelphia: Temple University Press, 1975).

directed to individuals or groups with a view to preserving their capacity to adapt to life in society. The Minister himself prefers to describe his task as the prevention of risks and handicaps which might, if they were not faced, put the community in a difficult situation.

In this way, the family is the instrument through which the community tries to cope with some of these problems. For instance, it still has an overwhelming responsibility in caring for a handicapped young person or adult. If the family is no longer able to take charge of its old people, new responsibilities are created for the country, and if the family is incapable of performing any of its tasks, children are taken in hand by the community. Some families are vulnerable and cannot attain stability without outside support.

Recently, these different problems have come to the foreground, but this does not mean that a solution has been found for all of them. One realizes their seriousness when one notes the increase in the number of children who have to be placed outside their families: 130,000 are in institutions and 200,000 in foster homes. French law also allows for measures of guardianship of family benefits when authorities have reason to fear they will not be spent in the interest of the child.

Fears concerning juvenile delinquency are periodically expressed, and one does not need to agree about causes in order to recommend preventive action. France has traditionally developed social services. *Assistantes* and *assistants sociaux* (social workers) form a real profession numbering 20,000. Their casework, directed to individual situations, or their community action, directed to groups, is very often related to family problems. This is, in particular, the case when these social services are organized by the family Fund or by the local Council. Another interesting example can be given with regard to a special field: action concerning migrant workers. After much hesitation, instructions were given in 1967 to encourage family immigration: any migrant who is working regularly, has been in the country for a year, and has proper lodgings and a stable income is entitled to bring his family into the country. He then receives a premium benefit of about 1,000 FF, the family is allowed a maximum of sixty hours of free family help plus some training in the French language and in health education. Migrants can call upon a specialized social service. Clearly, the family appears to have some merit in the eyes of the French community as an intermediary in helping to avoid problems created by the presence in the country of a large group of migrant workers.

It appears, however, that some families are expected to carry out very difficult tasks. Aid to the family is certainly not sufficient when a handicapped child has to be dealt with, or supported even after he has grown up. In spite of recent reforms, which will increase social expenditure in this field by nearly 2 billion francs, the burden still weighs heavily on individual families.

The new Law of June 13, 1975, will be entirely implemented in 1977. The family allowance system will then take on the financing and administration of a new scheme for the handicapped. For handicapped children a specialized education allowance will now be granted, regardless of the parents' means, and will replace all the different forms of aid now in force. This aid [16] does not in any way cover the exceptional expenses related to the care of handicapped children. It is meant to continue, when the children become adults, in the form of a minimum guaranteed wage related to the official minimum wage. For the moment, it has only been possible to allow for the handicapped adult half of the minimum worker's wage. This is due if the handicapped person is unable to work or at least unable to make a living from his work, and if his personal income is below a fixed ceiling. The French population includes about 2 million handicapped people under retirement age, and of course the family will still bear a large share of their upkeep.

The mother of the handicapped child does, however, have all the years spent in bringing up the child taken into account in relation to her pension. Since 1970 treatment in specialized homes has been taken over by the health service and is entirely free. The problem, however, is that of finding a place for a severely handicapped patient. Existing resources are deemed to cover only one third of the need. Here there still seems to be a wide scope for further development of family policy. Public policy has, on the other hand, given up encouraging the family to cope with older people. Today a very small number of people over sixty-five live with their children, and isolation of the elderly is a growing social problem. Nothing of consequence has been done to help families who might be prepared to deal with this problem. In particular, there are no special housing facilities for families wishing to keep an older parent, or for providing temporary relief during vacation time for families who care for handicapped elderly people. A new allowance has, however, come into force for the single parent with children; it insures a minimum guaranteed income if resources are insufficient. [17]

[16] Thirty-two percent, 56 percent, or 80 percent of the basic salary for family allowances, according to the child's handicap; this means from 222FF to 555FF per month.

[17] One hundred and thirty percent of the monthly basic salary for family allowances for the parent (902.85FF) plus 44 percent for each child (305.58FF).

The Family and Housing Policy

Support of the family is definitely one of the aims of housing policy. Until now one of the family benefits based on the same source of financing, that is, the family allowance system, has constituted the most original instrument of public intervention in this field.

Housing needs are met in France through the private market, but the community intervenes in two ways. First, there is a public housing scheme financed from budgetary funds or by inexpensive loans; the number of children is one of the priority conditions which gives access to this less expensive sector.

On the other hand, the housing allowance is a money benefit which adds to the other family allowances. But it must be spent on housing, and was in fact created in 1948, when there was a general rise in rents. This is a rather sophisticated allowance as it tries to combine several criteria: size of the family, income, and the share of this income that the family is ready to spend on the type of housing which is appropriate to its needs.

The aim is to compensate for the family's housing expenses. But for many years the benefit went only to families who could already draw upon the other family allowances. They were also expected to pay rent or to acquire property, and to be ready to spend on this a given percentage of their income—a percentage which varied according to the size of the family. The lodging must conform to definite health and tenancy standards. The allowance amounts to a fraction of the difference between the rent actually paid and this minimum theoretical rent, and this fraction is itself related to the number of children. Since its initiation, this allowance has been constantly reexamined with a view to relating it better to income and rent levels.[18] But a real change has been on the way since 1972. Since then, the allowance has been granted not only to families but also to the aged or the handicapped, to young workers, and to young couples married for less than five years or couples or single persons who may have a child, a parent, or a handicapped person in their charge. These new categories compete with the larger families for the same financial resources, and things may go even further with a proposed reform of housing policy. It has now been suggested that a grant, subject to a means test, should become the essential instrument of all housing policy. It would still be managed by the Funds, but it would be financed both by the social security contributions and, in some way, by the budget.

Nothing can be said yet about these perspectives, which might curtail

---

[18] Example: A family with three children pays 700FF monthly rent and has an annual income of 28,400FF. Allowance amounts here to 170FF per month.

all direct intervention by public authorities. The funds distributed through the new allowance would be employed by beneficiaries in the normal housing market.

The present-day experience has closely related both family and housing policies and, if it is coming to an end, the reasons probably do not really involve family policy. This form of intervention has been quite costly; the funds going to the housing allowance amount to nearly 12.3 percent of the total of family allowances. But this increase in costs has been due more to the rise in rents than to the number of beneficiaries. The allowance was given, in 1973, to 1,780,000 families, which amounts to about 11 percent of the beneficiaries of the family allowance system.

Three points must be made here. The technique is ingenious, because it encourages the family to spend in such a way as to have proper housing conditions. But this is paid for by complex rules of distribution which tend to limit the efficiency of the aid. The amount of the allowance is also probably not high enough, for one can note that the percentage of the family budget spent on housing does not really increase with the number of children. This percentage was about 17 percent of the budget for a family with two children in 1972 and did not seem to increase much with the size of the family.

Public intervention in the field of housing policy has been somewhat criticized recently by official reports which underlined the fact that the poorer families were not the first to benefit from the aid, and that the effort expected from them seemed to diminish when income increased. The housing allowance did not counterbalance the cost of housing in improved areas or in new buildings. It seemed to drop as soon as the family tried a somewhat better solution than that of finding housing accommodations in the most subsidized area. Allocation rules tended to exclude the old, small, and uncomfortable lodgings which were used by the poorer families, and on the contrary the higher-income families living in new constructions had benefited from this help more than the others.

This criticism is in the background of current reforms. They may not, however, be inspired chiefly by family needs. As for families, they remain very much aware of everything that might be done to give them access to proper lodgings; questions of priority rules, the quality of the subsidized housing, and accommodations are very often raised by family association spokesmen. In spite of the links formed over the past twenty-five years between housing and family policies, the family still seems to have claims that have gone unnoticed.

Family and Education

The extensive system of free education in France does, of course, help greatly in the upbringing of children. This is true, not only in the case of compulsory education, but also in kindergartens and universities. Even private schools, whether religious or not, may make an agreement with the state which then gives them a grant to cover costs. This gives the family a very wide range of choice.

It is not feasible here to deal with all the problems in the education system which might well be of interest to the family. Three points seem to have a special importance:

1. The impact of the community's expenses in the field of education is in some way related to social status. The family always has to bear the cost of the upkeep of the child, and after the age of sixteen the child benefits from free education only if the family can go on keeping him or can do without an extra source of income.

A relatively modest system of grants does help the family in its efforts concerning education. Grants are given to children at school, and to young people in universities or training colleges, when the family's means are inadequate. The amount varies according to the size of the family. In 1972–73 the amount was about 527FF in secondary schools and 3,477FF at higher-education levels. In 1974–75, the scale applicable to university students went from 2,160FF to 5,508FF. Forty percent of children in secondary schools and 15 percent of university students draw grants. This over-all percentage has not notably increased in recent years: it has in secondary schools, but seems to be decreasing at higher education levels. These measures, along with the help given to cover transportation costs and the upkeep of children away from home, amount to about 6 percent of the budget of the Minister of Education.

The grant system is being discussed at the university level. Should it not become a system of study allowances, also subject to a means test? In this way a student, who now has full legal rights at the age of eighteen, would have his situation considered independently from that of his family. For the moment, however, a high proportion of students comes from families in the higher income groups, and it is deemed somewhat artificial to judge their situation independently when it is thanks to family support that they are able to continue their studies.

Grants, and help to children pursuing studies, do no more than attenuate social differences. Families remain unequal within the education system, if one considers the number of children and the social status of the family head. This can be seen when one applies two criteria to the situation: length of studies and cost to the community of the education of a given child. The percentage of young people between the ages of sixteen and eighteen pursuing studies varies considerably according to the father's profession, as does also the type of diploma obtained. A recent inquiry at the national level on attainments of school-age children and another carried out by the Ministry of Education on a group of children followed throughout their studies both come to the following conclusion: "Whatever the social origin of the family may be, children's success in school studies, in primary schools at least, is primarily related to the fact that they come from small families. This is even more noticeable in the poorer class living in urban areas."[19]

This situation can be described in financial terms. A higher proportion of public funds go to children in the higher social groups because, for them, the period of studies is generally longer. However, the hierarchy is not as widely open as the income scale itself, and at the compulsory education level, public intervention tends to correct differences without suppressing them.

2. Despite the importance of education for the family, family policy is not really planned in relation to the educational system, nor is this system organized in relation to family needs. This is true of the programs and also of the institutions. The first question, which concerns pedagogic research, cannot be gone into here, but it is astonishing that two policies can develop in such closely related fields without organized contact. The only bridge goes through the parents' associations, which flourish in educational establishments. Since 1968 their elected representatives have had a seat on the different boards of the education system, and are officially consulted.

3. France is rightly proud of its kindergarten education system. The *écoles maternelles* are open to two and one-half million children between the ages of two and five. Their methods are original and intended to suit each child's personality. More and more people are convinced that this form of education intervenes at a sufficiently early stage to affect some of the causes of discrimination or inequality in society. The families themselves certainly attach the utmost importance to this service.

This form of education, which is not compulsory, tends to cover the entire population in spite of difficulties in rural areas. In 1973–74, 74.4 percent of the children were at school at the age of three; 94.4 percent at the age of four; and 100 percent at the age of five. These schools also provide a

19 From an internal government document.

most useful service by caring for children under school age, and their efficiency regarding educational aims has now been proved. A higher proportion of children who have gone through the *maternelle* have a normal course of study later than those who have not made use of it.

The family tends to hand over its pedagogical responsibilities to the school system earlier and earlier. This "socialization" of children is considered to be an asset to them, and here again, the more affluent or more educated families are the first to understand this and thus to make use of existing services. This appears in statistics: in 1972–73, a large proportion of agricultural families and a notable proportion of the working class had not yet made use of the *maternelles*. As has already been said, the situation is now improved.

The child who learns in its own family how to make contact with the world outside will make better use of the preschool system. He finds within his family that essential form of support which gives him access to the educational system whenever and wherever necessary. It is certainly at this stage, when family and education overlap, that opportunities for each child are definitively decided.

A Comprehensive Approach to Family Policy

One way of getting an over-all view of family policy is to look at the financial picture. This will enable us to point out the place of family policy in social expenditure, its evolution, the peculiarities of its financing.

As we have said, the most important source of financing is social security contributions: 9 percent of wages, with a ceiling of 38,000FF per year, go to the family allowance system; contributions levied on employers and independent workers vary according to their income.

Table 10 recapitulates the different allowances as forming part of the family allowance system; it concerns the general organization of social security, covering all salaried workers in industry and commerce.

A more comprehensive overview is provided by table 11, which is derived from the national social accounts report.

The national budget's contribution to family policy goes first to subsidies for the special system of family allowances relating to those in agriculture, and then to some of the other special organizations. It also covers costs of assistance benefits, school grants and, as we have said, tax rebates under the *quotient familial*.

Table 10 National Family Allowance Fund (Caisse Nationale D'Allocations Familials) 1974 Expenses (*in 1,000FF*)

Administration		1,452.99
Social welfare and health [a]		1,471.76
Family benefits		
Family allowance	15,065	
Single-wage-earner allowance	3,563	
Indemnite compensatrice	942	
Prenatal and maternity allowance	1,432	
Maternity leave	166	
Special allowance for handicapped	20	
Extra benefits	54	
New allowances		
Supplementary single-wage		
allowance	1,958	
Orphan allowance	417	
Handicapped children	38	
Handicapped adults	110	
School expenses allowance	464	
Child care	79	24,000.00
Miscellaneous		1,292.00
Housing allowance		4,491.00
Total		32,707.75

[a] "Social welfare and health" designates the form of intervention carried out by the Funds at their *own* initiative, as described above.

Table 11 Transfers to the Family, 1974 (*in 1,000FF*)

Health fund and maternity benefits	3,168.62
National family allowance fund	25,124.00 [a]
Agricultural (salaries)	1,211.59
Agricultural (growers)	2,171.78
Military fund	28.15
Civil servants	1,404.21
Utilities	169.70
	9.18
SNCF (rail)	242.91
RATP (Parisian local transport)	29.28
Local councils	6.30
Medical proprietary	12.68
State	12,861.34
Local councils	691.92
Total (correcting for duplication)	45,870.76

Source: Ministry of Finance, Paris.
[a] Not including administration and housing.

Table 12 Family Benefits as Percent of National Income (1972)

France	4.1
Germany	2.2
Italy	2.3
U.K.	1.7
Netherlands	3.1

SOURCE: Common Market Social Survey, 1975.

Table 13 Expenses Related to Family Policy in the "Social" Budget of the Nation

	Percent of Total "Social" Expenditure	Percent of Gross National Income
1968	21.47	4.58
1969	19.48	4.03
1970	18.70	3.88
1971	19.66	4.21
1972	17.93	3.94
1973	17.96	4.04
1974	16.96	3.95
1975[a]	15.35	4.12

SOURCE: Ministry of Finance, periodic statements on the social budget or the social accounts.
[a] This year shows a fall in production, which is why the percentage of social expenditures in the gross national income rose from 23.28 percent in 1974 to 26.82 percent in 1975.

Expenses related to family policy amount to 15.36 percent of social expenditure,[20] and if the French situation is compared to neighboring Common Market countries, it still remains true that special emphasis is apparent for family policy in this country. (See tables 12 and 13.)

But the family's share in social intervention seems to be shrinking. Table 13 gives the expenses related to all family benefits and to tax rebates.

The decrease of the family policy share in percentage of total social expenditure is remarkable and regular. The same regularity is not so apparent in the second column. The gross national income does itself vary, and such other "social expenses" as health and pensions have increased more rapidly than has the gross national income. The percentage going to the family may appear stable, or may be slowly decreasing, while family policy's share in the nation's social effort has become much less important.

If the comparison is limited to allowances per se in industry and commerce (and excluding the *quotient familial*), the share of the family over a longer period has been practically cut down by half. (See table 14.)

[20] French "social" expenses in 1975 comprised more than 26 percent of the gross national income, more than the national (state) budget.

Table 14 Social Expenses Related to Family, Health, and Pensions as a Percent of Total Social Expenses

	1960	1970	1975
Family	35.3	24.3	18.8
Health	31.6	35.2	63.2
Pensions	17.4	19.8	23.0

SOURCE: Ministry of Finance.

There are several explanations for this change in relative situations. One is the effort made for the family in neighboring countries. Aid to the family has increased notably in Germany, Belgium, and the Netherlands. In France, on the contrary, it has encountered competition from other forms of social action (social policy. *Eds.*) in a context where the government does not accept more extensive commitments in the social field. During the same period, France was the country in which public expenditures did not increase. Pressure toward economy had to find outlets somewhere, and family policy was subject to some cutbacks. Proof of this appears with the fall in the percentage of contributions going to family allowances; initially fixed at 12 percent, they reached a maximum of 16.75 percent in 1958, then gradually fell to 14.25 percent in 1959, 13.50 percent in 1962, 11.50 percent in 1967, 10.50 percent in 1970, and 9 percent in 1974. This was done to allow a transfer of contributions to the other branches of social security.

The financial picture is relatively clear. It is more difficult to unravel governmental and administrative responsibility for the decisions taken.

Family policy is definitely a form of *public* intervention. The private sector, and particularly the interested associations, seek only to bring pressure to bear on decisions taken at governmental level; or they are responsible for the administration of facilities and services which are, essentially, financed by grants from the public sector.

There of course are public authorities who assume direct administration of establishments or services. Town councils, Funds, the administration of aid to children organized in the "assistance" systems of the department, the schools and the education administration create and administer such establishments and services. Their actions develop within the limits of the budgetary authorizations.

All this is really secondary compared to the mass of money directly transferred to the family. The most important decision concerning the family is that which fixes the percentage of contribution from wages (and the wage ceiling) which feeds those transfers. This is part of social security policy and also of fiscal policy, and always involves considerations that go far beyond family issues. The *quotient familial*, for instance, is one of the Finance Minister's responsibilities. It raises important political questions because it concerns taxation of the higher-income groups among salary earners. The percentage of contributions and the level of social security benefits are decided by the government as a whole. This decision is initiated by the Minister of Labor, who supervises social security. It is very much influenced by what economists consider to be industry's capacity to pay, and by the financial pressure inside the social security system, where the health and pensions branches are constantly in need of funds. And here again, reactions from the more affluent salary earners, who do not like to see the ceiling wage move in accordance with the rise in salaries, are extremely important.

Family policy also tries to encompass decisions of the Minister of Housing or of Education. In the absence of official coordinating structures this task is accomplished by defining common aims for some of these actions at the governmental level. This is where the Minister of Health, who is officially responsible for family problems, operates. His capacity for direct action, however, is very limited; in fact, he has direct responsibility for only the unit concerned with service to children. Thus his authority depends very much on his being on good terms with the other ministers. His relations with the Minister of Labor may be very close, and the latter may accept from his colleague a large measure of initiative in the instructions given to the social security system. Relations with the Minister of Housing are usually not so well-established, and the Minister of Health also has to take other governmental opinions into account. The Secretary of State on the Status of Women (when there was such a ministerial post) had some say in these matters. But in all cases, one Minister simply has to be convinced—the all-important Finance Minister. This explains why critical policy decisions always are taken by the government as a whole. It cannot be otherwise.

Decisions are often "prepared," technically, at the level of the Planning Commission. This organization set up special commissions to think out long-term problems relating to family policy before enactment of the Sixth and Seventh Plans.

Preparatory work for the plan makes it possible to take a global approach to family problems and to relate them to other long-term tasks. The Commissariat is not the only place where this is possible, however. INED, in its research and in its advisory capacity to the government, does not limit its scope to a strict interpretation of demographic problems. The National Institute of Statistical and Economic Studies (INSEE) is also increasing its statistical output in the social field by publishing selected statistical information which is commented on in *Données sociales, 1973–74,* or in *Documents statistiques sur les familles.*

The National Family Allowance Fund and the UNAF also have their own research services. Their boards take a stand on family problems in the name of families.

Planning, in the French sense, provides opportunity for consultation with these different organizations and for putting all this information together. This is the material the government uses to set down the aims of family policy, aims which in turn appear in governmental declarations often made at the highest level.

For example, on December 5, 1970, when speaking at the twenty-fifth anniversary of UNAF, the President of the Republic, Georges Pompidou, stated:

> The State is under obligation to create material and moral conditions favorable to the family way of life. This not only means social justice, but also measures to oppose the break-up of the family. This means, in my mind, that the family has to be recognized not only as a social reality but also as an institution with which the State has to deal through adequate means of representation. Family interests, thus duly recognized, must be met by an active policy involving family allowances, housing facilities, child care, education, training for the handicapped, employment for young people. The time has come to imagine, in the field of family policy, techniques which elsewhere have been called "progress contracts," the aim being to insure that family allowances are stable in real value and grow more quickly for the underprivileged.

In June, 1976, his successor also spoke of a global family policy and four definite objectives for governmental action:

1. To replace all means-tested allowances by a single allowance to be given to all families with incomes under a relatively high level, so that two thirds of the families would be included
2. To define a social status for the mother of the family
3. To help both parents to reconcile their vocational and family activities more successfully
4. To adapt housing policy to family needs.

He concluded by saying that the government has deliberately chosen a global policy, hoping to "trigger off a really favorable reaction among all responsible bodies and the citizens themselves." This speech came after a debate in Parliament where the government had been criticized for not giving the family enough place in the plan and had to present a corrective statement to the nation's representatives:

The Plan should include a new family policy, and this must be the first amongst significant actions which will, in the 1980s, give economic growth a new direction. This is also necessary because of another serious cause for worry: the birth rate has been falling in France for several years.

This led the Minister of Health to offer the Parliament these proposals, giving two directions to family policy. The first consisted of accepting "a more open family structure, which is what the French people want":

We do not want to limit the liberty of women to choose a vocational activity, the autonomy of young people, or to impose upon the French natalist obligations which they do not understand. The Government has chosen to adopt a new legal frame for the family institution.

The second thrust would "support a balanced family policy rather than to concentrate all the efforts on money benefits, especially on family allowances." This balanced policy is developed in the priority program for the Seventh Plan.

These citations are characteristic of the way the policy has recently been formulated. Civil servants, when they come to express themselves publicly, are sometimes more skeptical. Jean Michel Belorgey writes:

Reflection on family policy, which is over and over again taken up and never comes to a conclusion, would make people think of a cemetery of good intentions. Everyone can recognize his own pet project, the brazenly natalist program for prenatal medical supervision or vaccination against German measles, the old-fashioned program for maternity centers, the civic program concerning the rights of mothers to increased pensions, etc.[21]

Whatever one may think of the distance between formulation and action, the aims of family policy have remained those that history brought to the foreground: demography, social justice, social stability. It is with regard to these aims that we must try to sum up the results.

RESULTS AND PERSPECTIVES

A Balance Sheet

Family policy clearly has achieved some success with regard to some of its different aims from its origins until 1976. The record does not, however, appear to be entirely convincing.

[21] Jean Michel Belorgey, "La Politique sociale" (Paris: Seghers, 1976).

The Demographic Objective

The decline of the birth rate has not been successfully counteracted. INED (1976)[22] sums up the situation in the following terms:

> In all developed countries, fecundity has declined in a marked and continuous manner since modern times. This trend in Europe lasted until the generation of women born at the beginning of the century. It was then reversed and an ascending phase covered a period of thirty years. It then gave way to a new trend of recession which it seems was only at its first stage. In some countries this recession has brought fecundity to a level lower than any observed so far, lower than what is required to renew generations. In other countries such as France, where the upward trend had gone higher, fecundity has not yet fallen below the danger line, but the decrease is very definite and it may well be that the evolution will finally be the same, with some delay. In other words, the total family reared by successive generations of women goes from 3.3 children for the generation of 1850, to 2.0 for generations of 1895–96. Then this number increases, over thirty years, to achieve the maximum of 2.64 children (generation of 1928–30). The trend reverses again, the women born in 1943 have had 2.35 children.

The report concludes that long-term changes show a great regularity, but this does not exclude very noticeable oscillations of the short-term index, which reversed very suddenly in 1964. This is why the report, very cautiously, does not deny any effectiveness of family policy. Its authors believe that the rise in fecundity between the years before and after World War II may not be due to the family policy, for the same phenomenon was apparent in other countries. But the highest level achieved, 2.6 children per family, was higher than in comparable countries. Also, the increase was more noticeable for salary earners in the private sector than in the public sector, and this could be related to the fact that the family allowances system, which had originally benefited civil servants, was extended to salary earners in private industry during the period under consideration.

Family policy appears to be simultaneously the reflection of a favorable climate and perhaps an agent of change. It may have helped to encourage a trend. It did not, however, succeed in opposing the reversal apparent since 1964 and an evolution which experts deem to be both permanent and of concern. The same experts are at a loss, however, to understand why the birth rate suddenly rose in 1976, and caution is the only admissible attitude at this stage.

[22] *Natalité et politique démographique.*

Social Justice

Aid to the family is redistributed from couples or single persons without children to those who have to bear expenses related to family. One does not expect this operation to benefit the higher-income groups and to be detrimental to the less affluent families.

Income statistics are not very satisfactory; available data do not always permit distinctions related to the size of the family. We have noted that the impact of income maintenance is apparent. But it does not entirely compensate for costs. If one analyzes the family's spending capacity, expenses per person tend to diminish with the size of the family. (See table 15.)

Large families have to economize on housing, and a notable proportion of them still lives in crowded conditions. When there are more than three children, families do not have as many automobiles as families with fewer children. Even health expenditures seem to diminish, although one does not know whether the family has to practice economy or does not have the same attitude toward ill-health.

INED published figures in *Population*, June, 1971, which showed a relative decrease in family income over a certain period of time. In 1950, an

Table 15 Annual Consumption by Consumer Unit[a] According to Size of Family

(Head of household less than 35 years old)

	Average Household	No Children	One Child	Two Children	Three + Children
All expenses	15,251	16,822	12,934	11,606	9,195
Housing[b]	2,592	4,183	2,282	1,913	1,491
Food	5,541	4,690	4,346	4,023	3,591
Clothing	1,475	1,771	1,262	1,173	968
Transportation and telephone[c]	2,011	3,000	2,036	1,781	1,096
Entertainment[d]	915	985	802	750	590
Health and personal care	1,293	896	905	902	696
Miscellaneous[e]	1,425	1,295	1,300	1,064	762

SOURCE: P. Longone, *Population et Société*, INED.

[a] A Consumer Unit equals 1 for a single adult, to 0.7 for persons more than 14 years of age living in the household, to 0.5 for children less than 14.

[b] Including household equipment, rent or mortgage costs, outside maintenance about 30 percent.

[c] Especially automobile, both purchase and maintenance.

[d] Including television, movies, hobbies, tobacco, etc.

[e] Vacations and household help, for example.

unskilled worker with four children, whose wife did not work, had an income level which represented 53 percent of that of a corresponding couple without children. This percentage fell to 39 percent in 1970. For the more qualified worker, the corresponding indexes were 52 percent in 1950 and 40 percent in 1970.

INED has also tried to compare typical situations over the period 1950–61. A group of specialized workers is considered to have had the same promotion experiences at work. The wives are assumed to be unskilled workers employed full-time as long as there are no children, part-time after the arrival of the first child, and then assumed to refrain from any outside work after the arrival of a second child. The study assumes that one of these families has no children over the period; its income level increases by 80 percent. In another family, a single child is born in 1951; its income level increased by 10 percent. In the third family, two children are born in 1950 and 1955; the income level falls by 4 percent.

The financial assistance given does not seem to compensate for inequality between families. We can refer here to the social indicators research carried out in connection with formulation of the Seventh Plan. It was noted that the intermediate income groups did not seem to benefit from the system and that correction of inequalities seemed to benefit families with one or two children mostly.

From the same source, we can give an indication of disparities in income per person before and after the transfers. The reference is to the family of the untrained worker whose wife stays at home and who has two children. (See table 16.)

Here, transfers do seem to narrow the gap between families without children and those with children, and this is more noticeable in the case of the lower-income group, because the family benefits constitute a relatively large share of their income. Differences between families of the same size whose head may be, in one case, a worker, in another a higher-salary earner, also appear to be slightly attenuated. The study also reveals how slight the redistributive impact of family policy has been. In 1970 the income ratio between higher executives and workers was 4:1. Family policy brought it down to between 3:4 and 2:9, depending on family structure. The same figures for 1975 are 3:8 before transfers and 2:9–2:6 after family policy transfers. The impact of family policy on the wage ratio has remained very much the same despite all the reforms carried out during that period to introduce a more selective policy and therefore a greater redistributive effect. These tables do not take into account freely dispensed services such as

Table 16 Index of Income by Consumer Unit According to the Type of Family
Before (1) and After (2) Transfers

(Index 100 = situation of a family with 2 children,
head of family a worker, wife with no professional activity) [a]

Type of Family	1970	1975
Higher executive, wife active,	(1) 785	(1) 732
no children	(2) 612	(2) 462
Higher executive, wife active,	(1) 667	(1) 622
one child	(2) 450	(2) 404
Higher executive, wife inactive,	(1) 576	(1) 538
no children	(2) 396	(2) 354
Higher executive, wife inactive,	(1) 688	(1) 657
one child	(2) 351	(2) 312
Higher executive, wife inactive,	(1) 607	(1) 381
two children	(2) 305	(2) 271
Higher executive, wife inactive,	(1) 369	(1) 327
three children	(2) 275	(2) 266
Higher executive, wife inactive,	(1) 305	(1) 286
four children	(2) 251	(2) 223
Worker, wife active,	(1) 236	(1) 239
no children	(2) 178	(2) 176
Worker, wife active,	(1) 201	(1) 203
one child	(2) 153	(2) 162
Worker, wife inactive,	(1) 161	(1) 161
no children	(2) 110	(2) 109
Worker, wife inactive,	(1) 120	(1) 120
one child	(2) 108	(2) 106
Worker, wife inactive,	(1) 86	(1) 86
three children	(2) 96	(2) 95
Worker, wife inactive,	(1) 75	(1) 75
four children	(2) 96	(2) 92

SOURCE: INSEE, Commissariat au Plan.
   [a] Annual income of the family chosen as reference was in 1970: 5,869 FF before transfers;
7,362 FF after transfers. In 1975: 10,795 FF before transfers; 13,763 FF after transfers.

education, which may benefit the higher-income groups where children take
up longer studies.

All the problems of method are far from being solved in implementing
policy. It would appear that the redistribution aspect is somewhat disap-
pointing. It is generally recognized that the antiredistributive aspect of the

fiscal policy more than counterbalances the selectivity introduced at the other end. This leads a certain number of specialists to conclude that too much emphasis should not be laid on redistribution: our family policy is there to answer family needs, and if one wants to redistribute, one should use the fiscal system separately.

It is certain in any case that families not only react to the sums redistributed through transfers; they are as much influenced by the level of direct incomes. Decisions concerning promotion, access to a second source of income, comparison between the situation of couples with or without children at the same income level, are every bit as important as the level of transfers. And there is one important consideration in the background: the family is very much concerned with its accumulated capital and its capacity to transfer it through inheritance. Family capital may be one of the real causes of social rigidity in France. Very little is known about its importance and its distribution among families.

In such an uncertain scene, it is not surprising that family policy can become, more often than not, a source of confrontation between different social groups. Policy may favor one or the other, according to the weight they carry politically.

Social Stability
In spite of the general belief that French society is undergoing rapid change, the family as an institution appears to be remarkably stable. Neither marriage nor family is rejected, and the family is not really denied its role in individual security and well-being. The marriage rate has remained remarkably stable,[23] and recent trends, which might show a slight decrease in this rate, are not sufficiently confirmed to allow comment. Divorce remained at the stable level of 10 percent of marriages from 1950 until 1965, and only recently has it increased to about 13 percent—a low rate if compared to that in the U.S., the U.S.S.R., and Scandinavian countries.

Philippe Ariès thinks that the family was responsible for many forms of progress during the nineteenth and twentieth centuries: less crime, less alcoholism, increased education. These signs still seem to persist, even if sociologists point to causes for worry. It is a fact that education has progressed, even at preschool age, with the full support of the family. Of course France is not exempt from some of the well-known consequences of urban life. The Minister responsible for social welfare wrote in 1974 that the

[23] Between 8 percent and 9 percent of the men and 7 percent and 8 percent of the women are unmarried at age fifty.

number of children who had to be taken in care by social services, who ran away from home, or who had shown signs of delinquency had more than doubled in the previous ten years. Even so, absolute figures remain rather low: 300,000 children were abandoned or removed from their families in 1972; 160,000 were considered to be in moral danger or delinquent; 70,000 were runaways. Blame has not been laid on the family but on industrialization and urban life. In the collective study *La Famille*, this is described in striking terms:

> The family does not survive too well in large, urban concentrations of population, overcrowding is visible and to live in a crowd does, in fact, create isolation. It seems impossible to avoid the breaking up of relations with the elderly, who are left to themselves, while many young people miss the relationship with their grandparents.[24]

This judgment does not imply a criticism of family policy. Such policy seems to accompany the underlying changes in society rather than to shape them. We find it difficult fully to unravel what is cause and what is consequence in the French experience; this is one of the interesting subjects for comparative study.

Trends of Change

Evidence of change nonetheless creates uncertainty. Women are participating in the labor force much more than previously, the biological function of the family is changing, parental roles are not immutable. All this is the cause of some tension which cannot but reflect on family policy.

Feminine Activity

What is important is not only that 44 percent of women ages fifteen to sixty-four are now employed. In France, the movement seems irreversible because it affects all social groups, and particularly those which seem to act as initiators of new social trends. The new trend is very noticeable in the younger age group, particularly those between twenty and twenty-nine. It involves married women more and more often, irrespective of the fact that they have children. The classical image, which had women working until their marriage, stopping then, and coming back into the labor force after having brought up their children, is becoming obsolete. In age groups 25–29 and 30–34, labor force activity rose between 1968 and 1974 from 52.2 percent

[24] "Famille et Espace Social," *La Famille* (Paris: Hachette, 1975), pp. 261–94.

to 61.4 percent and from 44.6 percent to 55.8 percent. Fewer and fewer women look upon their contribution to the family budget as incidental. This is particularly true of the more educated woman and is also related to the occupation of the husband. Labor force participation rates rise in proportion to the husband's income, reach a maximum at the intermediate level, and then decrease.

All this tends to show that whether it may be for material reasons or through women's desires to make the best of the education they have received, a fundamental change has occurred in the French woman's attitude to work. This is reflected in opinion surveys, and is shown in the INED study of May/June, 1975. The public is 64 percent favorable to the employment of married women, and the percentage of favorable answers rises to 78 percent with young people and to almost 70 percent in the more educated or higher-income groups. At the same time, however, 82 percent feel that it is preferable for the mother to devote herself entirely to her child until it reaches the age of two or three.

Family policy has to take the time budget of the working mother into account. Everything tends to show that in French society, reconciliation of the two roles is not an easy task. In her work, the woman is handicapped by child rearing, and she appears to work less than the men and to be absent more often. It is true that there is a relation between this and the age or number of children. However, the handicap diminishes when the woman is better qualified. Any type of interruption of activity (part-time work, return to work at the age of thirty-five) is followed by direct or implicit discrimination.

Family life itself also has to adapt. The time devoted to housework is greatly reduced. This is particularly true of younger women who, between the ages of twenty-one and twenty-four, spend five hours a week at these tasks, while older women spend eight hours a week doing the same work. Women at home and women who work outside tend to use the same household equipment, but women at home more often also have domestic help. This, of course, is related to their husbands' incomes.

Insecurity, discrimination, and other difficulties met in the labor market necessarily affect women's private life. This is why what is done to facilitate the working mother's task may become very important for the future of family policy.

The Planned Family
Couples marry younger; the average age of marriage for first marriages fell between 1960 and 1970 from 26.1 to 24.4 for men, 23.5 to 22.4 for women.

This trend tends to become more uniform: it affects all social groups and appears in the different regions of France. Couples also live longer and may expect a significant period of life together after the years devoted to bringing up the children.

At the same time, in France as elsewhere, attitudes toward sex are changing. More children are conceived before marriage. However, there is no spectacular increase in illegitimate births. There is no way of knowing exactly how many irregular unions are, in fact, stable or whether communes represent more than an exceptional solution fashionable in some circles. But since 1970 all the younger couples are systematically more favorable, or declare that they are more favorable, toward sexual freedom for the woman and to living together before marriage. Sexual life begins earlier. It has its place outside wedlock. What was hidden is now openly recognized. But at the same time, the married couple is valued, not only because of the parental role, but as one of the forms of individual fulfillment.

Public opinion respects the family and would like to reconcile, in its image, sex and security. Tensions would not be of much consequence if the family had not radically changed its attitude to childbearing. In France, it is a great change that family planning should have become at the same time both easy and open. Not only is contraception practiced as it has always been, but each couple openly claims the right to decide on the size of its family. Policies must take this into consideration, and this means uncertainty, because just as there may be a model consumer's attitude, there appears to be a model family attitude. Perhaps this is why the family with two children born at relatively close intervals is now in such favor.

The abortion pattern is difficult to interpret: at present there are 45,000 legal abortions a year since the new law was passed. Does this mean that abortion is becoming a normal family practice? Will it increase when the law is properly applied all over the country? Will it attain its aim, which is to be an answer to distressing circumstances, whereas normally, properly informed couples will use other contraceptive methods? Is this the beginning of a rise in the number of abortions, which might constitute a dangerous evolution and precipitate reaction? The experts do not have the answer to these questions.

Roles within the Family

A very cautious evolution of the legal status of the family certainly reflects change in roles. Legislation which had deemed divorce to be based on the faults of the interested parties did not survive. In fact, before any changes were made in the law, the courts had come to allow divorce in 95 percent of the cases, which was a way of tolerating divorce by mutual consent. This has been the rule since 1975, under the form of divorce by joint action or declaration.

Since 1965, reform of the marriage law allows the wife to administer her own property, particularly the funds coming from her occupational activity. Since 1970, she shares her husband's responsibility as head of the family. Things may be moving even more rapidly as far as attitudes are concerned. Not all women are sympathetic to the themes developed by the Movement for the Liberation of Women or by groups like the League for the Rights of Women. But these themes are making headway. Young people are being brought up in coeducational schools. It is no longer generally accepted that decisions concerning the wife's work, the family budget, or even the husband's employment are made by the husband alone.

Reform has not yet succeeded in eliminating disparaging pictures of feminine roles from schoolbooks, but this is attempted more and more frequently. There is also reform relative to the child's status. In 1970 it was ruled that parental authority is exercised in the child's interest. Discrimination due to conditions of birth has almost disappeared in the case of natural or adopted children.

But reform concerning the age of majority appears to be even more radical. This was reduced to eighteen years by the Law of July 5, 1975, affecting 2,400,000 young people. It brought with it not only the right to vote, but also many possibilities which had not even been envisioned: the right to leave the home, to get married, to open a bank account, to be liable, to make a contract.

Political expression, in fact, had been ahead of the law. Both the young and the very young had expressed political views about conscription and other matters and had recourse to action even in the *lycées*. There is a form of criticism of the family in all this: young people seem to reject their parents' right to decide on all of their interests. The new law is, in this sense, a form of clarification.

The young adult tries to affirm his identity between the family and the educational system. Problems concerning young people as a group may set a limit to family policy. All this is not without ambiguity. For young people in France, "protests" are still a social reality. They often come from the students, and if their everyday needs are met by the family, it is easier to find time for protesting. Many young people move without transition from the family circle to the labor force. Their family has done what it could in a sometimes difficult environment, and the young do not tend to hold it responsible for their difficulties. They prefer to blame the political or economic system in which they have to live.

Generations overlap but do not live together. Only 8 percent of households choose this way of living, and it seems that smaller families are not able to cope with responsibilities for older people. In any case, French society now has to take the problem of isolated persons into consideration. The family as a resource is not a solution for all elements in the population. Surveys concerning retired persons tend to show that isolation is a great cause of poverty. In Paris and in the other cities the lonely widow more than any other category is condemned to reduced circumstances and pushed into a marginal situation.

The future is not clearly outlined. For some, the family is an outmoded hierarchy; for others, it is the last refuge for privacy. There are as many prophets of the disappearance of the family, in a society where each one will seek his own way to happiness, as there are experts ready to predict the reinforcement of the family as a healthy reaction to present-day working and living conditions. Anyone involved in family policy must live with this uncertainty.

Controversies

Experience has shown the apparent capacity of family policy to weather social and political changes. In spite of this, three areas of controversy are apparent at the present time among all those interested in family problems, whether they are pressure groups, political parties, technicians, or government officials. These differences concern the importance to be given to demography, attitudes toward feminine employment, the distribution of public aid between social groups. The lines of cleavage do not necessarily coincide. People may find themselves in one group concerning one of these problems and in opposing groups in relation to another. And on each subject, a similar objective can carry opposing technical implications. Controversy among specialists adds itself to political controversy. And above all, more general questions are now open: Need family policy be reaffirmed in 1978? Does it require a new boost? A formal political commitment?

A New Start for Family Policy?
The fall of the birth rate and the decreasing share of family allowances in family income have led some political speakers, whether in the Government

or the Opposition, to claim that a new commitment to the family is now necessary. This would certainly mean a substantial increase in the share of the nation's resources devoted to family policy; there can be no miracle, no result, without paying the cost in terms of contributions drawn from the economy.

In the actual governing majority, M. Michel Debré is the apostle of this cause. For him, who after World War II spoke of a France with a hundred million inhabitants, demographic preoccupations are essential. His analyses often show concern about the family as an institution.

In the Opposition, the commitment to family is based rather on a preoccupation with social justice. Proposals are made to counteract the deterioration of the family's spending capacity; and a marked increase in family allowances is then suggested relating such allowances to wages.

All of these hopes have little chance of becoming realities. Factors which still tend to weigh the other way remain very important. The French government has, for several years, shown a determination to restrain the increase in public spending for social policies. In other words, it is not ready to increase the tax burden, which is now about 40 percent of gross national income.

Public expenditure goes to public services and to social transfers. The first group of expenditures is relatively low in France compared with neighboring European countries, and cannot suffer further reduction. The second group can hardly be increased very much and, within the sums going to transfers, the family competes with the health service and pensions. In these two fields there is considerable financial pressure because of increasing costs of medical services, the lowered retirement age, and the increased pensions. The wages going to the family have few chances of increasing and may even again be restricted. In this case, the Government has no scope for substantial increase of the total going to the family and it can only try to make better use of it by assigning it differently.

The consequences of this situation are admitted by the political authorities. They note that social expenditure in France tends to conform more and more to the same pattern as in neighboring countries, and they believe that the increase in direct wages (well above the poverty level—which is not, however, defined) has made action in favor of the family less necessary.

Could a change in the government majority mean a change in orientation? It is difficult to answer this. It could be that a left-wing government would not feel committed to such a rigorous view of the over-all tax burden. It could, then, accept an increase in public expenditure, and this might make more room for family policy. But it would also have to respond to other claims in social fields. All this would add up, and decisions would then be very much influenced by the workers' unions which appear, at least for the time being, to give some priority to health and the retirement age. Even if, through a change in the majority, the country were committed to spend more on its social policies, the priorities might not be fundamentally different from what they are today.

Birth Rate Policy or Family Policy?
Some of those who have recently expressed their anxiety concerning the fall in the birth rate would like to see family policy take a definite natalist turn.

This would mean concentrating the effort on encouraging a second and a third birth. Most couples do have one child. At the other end of the scale, very large families of four, five, and six children do not constitute a realistic model in present-day France. Encouragement would probably prove inefficient. A family of two or three children may be an acceptable model; and the aim might be to get to the stage where every couple would have two children—better still, three. This would imply concentrating income-maintenance aid on these families. One would also need to understand why couples do not rear families of this size. The study of the INED shows that it is the difficulty in reconciling maternity with work outside that deters many women from having more children, rather than problems related to housing or education. It is possible to carry on both activities as long as there is only one child. It becomes more difficult to do so with the arrival of the second, and practically impossible with the third. This is where intervention would be needed, either to discourage the mother from working or to provide the necessary facilities so that she could carry on both activities.

Two main objections arise in this context. First, technically speaking, we are not really able to understand the relation between family policy and attitudes to childbearing. In 1976 the birth rate suddenly appeared to rise again in a way which specialists are quite incapable of explaining. Can one really believe that measures concerned with the percentage of the benefit going to each child actually do influence attitudes? It might be easier to understand the impact of measures concerning the woman at work. Policies applied in Czechoslovakia and Hungary, where a woman can temporarily leave work after having a child without losing her salary, are believed, in France anyhow, to have a direct effect on natality.

Politically speaking, however, the public is not ready to accept measures too indiscreetly directed toward encouraging childbearing. INED's

1975 survey shows that 50 percent of the persons who are ready to express an opinion on this point think that the state should not intervene in order to stop the decline in the birth rate. Nothing could be more revealing than the position taken by the family movement itself. It used to be unashamedly natalist; now it offers a family policy (which it favors) as opposed to a natalist policy (which it excludes). And the President of the Republic, speaking to UNAF in 1976, was careful to make the same distinction, because his listeners expected it. The inspiration behind the lower *complément familial* is similarly revealing.

This does not mean that preoccupation with the demographic situation has disappeared. But this preoccupation needs to be supported by other arguments. It will color the nation's attitude to the labor force activity of women, but it will not lead to financial enticements. Even the difference made between children, with no benefit for the first child and more for the third, is disliked by the public. This is one of the reasons UNAF states that the problem is to encourage the first child and that if the first child is easily managed by his parents, they have more reason to have a second and a third. The Opposition party has also tabled a reform extending the allowance to the first child. This is a response to the view that the community should not try to influence the attitudes of the couple but only help them in proportion to the responsibilities they have decided to assume.

Labor Force Participation for Women and the Maternal Function
The authors believe that labor force participation by women is a long-term trend of French society and that it would be vain to try to go against it. Policy must therefore take it in its stride.

This view is not unanimously shared. The maternity wage proposal reflects the intention to encourage the more traditional family model where the mother remains at home to bring up her children. Here again these views have little chance of becoming law because the idea prevails that policy must be neutral as regards mother's work outside the home. One may, however, have different interpretations of neutrality.

The idea of a maternity wage, which was put forward by UNAF, was adopted in 1973 by the Consultative Committee on the Family and followed by a legislative proposal signed by 112 members of the Government majority. At first view, this would appear to be nothing more than an evolution out of the single-wage-earner's allowance, granted to the parent who does not have employment, or who has a job which is insignificant. But it is a fundamental change if the maternity wage is granted to the large majority of families and on the express condition that the mother remain at home. This is the case where this proposal is concerned. It has been suggested that the wage be fixed at a high enough level to compensate for the income the mother would give up. Some suggest half the minimum wage, the Consultative Committee proposes three quarters, and the proposal itself suggests that a salary amounting to the minimum wage should be granted without any time limit after the birth of the third child.

Whatever the amount and duration of such aid may be, it would mean a very big share of the family policy budget (25 billion FF if the allowance amounted to half the minimum wage). The authors of the proposal suggest that it is consistent with a movement in opinion which would recognize domestic work at its proper value, and they hope to find support in the feminine electorate. They also are responsive to the view expressed in opinion surveys which, while accepting outside work for women, prefers to see her free to devote herself entirely to her very young children.

This of course means moving away from the neutral attitude which inspires family policy at present. This was the cause of the slow reduction of the single-wage-earner's allowance, and such a reduction was made possible only because it did not meet serious public opposition. Today, a reversal of this trend is opposed by the two largest trade unions and a large section of feminist opinion. They denounce any approach which they believe will lead the beneficiaries to a mistaken view of their interests. They say that the maternity wage is not really a proper salary since the amount does not compensate for the loss of a second source of income and is financed through the social security system, not directly through the economy. Young women who might have the opportunity and the desire to have outside employment could be encouraged to leave it in a way which would prevent them from ever taking it up again. It would appear that this proposal is just a means of solving an employment crisis while compromising all the woman's chances of going back to work or of obtaining experience and promotions. And what is actually known about the new attitudes of women does lend force to these arguments.

At any rate, the Government has not taken up this proposal. Another measure has been developed: the complementary family allowance which is now to take the place of the single-wage-earner allowance and the several allowances related to the care of children. If a couple has a young child,[25] or three or more children of any age, the community allows parents to choose

---

[25] Under three, the age after which most children can attend the free public nursery school, *école maternelle*.

between two solutions, both of which imply obligations: either to care for the child(ren) themselves by giving up a source of outside income, or to work outside and pay for the child care. Of course, the assumption is that the more spent here, the more the rearing of children will be encouraged; in short the demographic preoccupation reappears, but no one pattern is encouraged. The help is expected to cover the cost of an activity deemed useful by the community: the care and education of the young child in his family. The proposed allowance amounts to half the minimum wage, with an income ceiling allowing about two thirds of covered families to benefit.[26]

The Opposition did not oppose this proposal. Indeed, a proposal coming from members of the Socialist Party had suggested that, up to the age of three, a "supplementary care allowance" should be added to the family allowance whether the mother works or not. The difference might come from the fact that for the Government, the new allowance would be the backbone of any new effort in favor of the family, while for the Socialist Party the family allowance itself, which in its view should be granted to *all* children, remains central.

The left-wing parties have overcome their reluctance to interfere with working conditions for women, and more and more often their proposals imply new obligations for employers. For instance, they include among their proposals a longer maternity leave and also the right to a child care leave (which has recently become law). It is interesting to note that the favorable vote was related to the extension to both parents of rights initially provided only for the mother.

Family Policy and Income Redistribution
There are three ways of relating the amount of the aid to the family to the income of beneficiaries. They are all simultaneously referred to in the present policy.

First solution. Aid is equal for all children and does not vary according to income. The idea is that the community should cover the cost of the child and that this cost should be evaluated objectively on the basis of identical needs. We have seen that this has been the case for the family allowance, properly speaking, sometimes for the single-wage-earner allowance, and, theoretically, for universal, free services such as education.

Second solution. Aid increases with income. This is not meant to be a paradox. This solution is not without justification for those who note that

---

[26] A sensitive point is the relative level of income ceiling applied to families with a single or two sources of income; actual figures tend to favor families where the mother is at home.

more is spent on the child when the income is higher. If one wants to relate the level of income of the family to the income of persons without family obligations in all social classes, more must be given to those who earn more. This is the principle behind the *quotient familial*, the family tax deduction.

Third solution. Aid increases when income is lower. Family policy is then employed as a form of redistribution of income, and expenditure is concentrated on the lower-income groups, the others being expected to support their families through their direct wages. This is the significance of the means-tested allowances or of the fees demanded for some family services.

The relative importance of the three techniques has changed over the years in a way which can be described schematically as follows: In 1945–46, solution number one prevailed, because the family allowances were the core of the policy. Progressively, with the development of direct income and the lag of the family allowances behind wages, solution number two became more important, and now, through the recent reform, the third solution has led to a more rapid development of the means-tested allowances. This is why we have come to the present situation where the intermediate income groups seem to be losers.

What might a proper direction be today? Positions are not clearly defined. Each solution has its supporters, and there does not seem to be an agreement to give up any of them. The problem is, then, the relative place of each in any future evolution. This uncertainty is reflected in opinion surveys. Only 16 percent of the answers favor equal allowances for all, but only 18 percent favor allowances concentrated on the lower-income group. Actually, 64 percent favor the status quo. And if questions concerning the tax system had been raised, the responses might also have approved the system now in operation.

So far, the public authorities seem to be oriented toward increasing the part played by solution number three. The reasons are financial, for they do not envisage an increase in over-all expenditure. If the same amount is to be spent more efficiently, one can only think in terms of selectivity (means-testing). Ideologically, this attitude is not in contradiction with liberal economic theory which believes that family needs can be satisfied in an increasing number of situations by direct income.

However, there are two limits to such an orientation. First, since the middle-class groups have not benefited lately, they will probably not be excluded from any new measures such as the complementary allowance. Also, there will be controversy about the antiredistributive effects of the present tax deductions. It seems that many would accept a tax reduction related uniformly to the costs of a child. But the higher salary earners constitute a pressure group which vigorously opposes any change here.

In the Opposition, positions are not always clearly defined. Preferences still seem to favor the first solution. This means, of course, granting benefits even to the richer families. But this could be alleviated by action on direct income and by including the benefits in taxable income. This would permit the state to recover some of the benefits granted to the higher-income groups. And from that side comes the proposal that the present *quotient familial* should give way to a fixed tax reduction related to the number of children.

The principles involved are different here. Means-tested allowances are looked upon as an old-fashioned, bureaucratic form of assistance and, because families are continually obliged to justify their resources, are considered incompatible with dignity. If selectivity is necessary, it is thought that this should come preferably through the tax system, which takes an over-all view of each family's situation. It is also clear, although this is not always specifically stated, that the left wing favors a relative increase of indirect income through collective redistribution instead of counting only on the direct income provided by returns from labor or capital.

Part II

FAMILY POLICY AS A FIELD

6

AUSTRIA

Edith Krebs and
Margarete Schwarz

THE CONCEPT OF family policy is relatively new in Austria. Although formulated in the years after World War II, it was not mentioned in the federal constitution. However, certain family policy measures such as cash assistance and tax reductions had been introduced earlier. In general, family policy is widely understood by all political parties to encompass all steps taken deliberately by the state and society to protect the interests of families and to enhance their condition. There is not, however, an official definition of family policy in Austria.

Family policy benefits are generally limited to the two-generation family, the basic family unit. More and more of these benefits are extended to the single-parent family of one parent and offspring. Recently, serious consideration has been given to the proposition that the family is a unit throughout its life cycle. This interpretation is a significant departure from the idea of the family as young married couples with infants or couples with growing children.

Some fundamental legal and social changes are under way which will have profound effects in the areas of social, health, tax, and housing policies and specifically in the area of family law. The revisions have been initiated despite the fact that the Austrian federal constitution of 1920 does not men-

DR. EDITH KREBS is Director, Women's Section, Chamber of Labor, Vienna, Austria. DR. MARGARETE SCHWARZ is Representative of the Women's Section, Chamber of Labor, Vienna.

tion family policy. Hence it does not assign the responsibility for family policy either to the federal government or to the provinces.

In fact, the judicial process has rested the responsibility for family law with the federal authority. Moreover, the federal authority is responsible for safeguarding the family, whether by granting assistance, providing payments or tax relief for persons caring for children, or by measures designed to protect the working mother. These include regulations concerning prenatal care and maternity leave benefits provided by social security. They also provide for the mother's release from work in order to care for a sick family member and for payments to women employees after childbirth. The provinces are mainly responsible for infant welfare, kindergartens, and the establishment of student shelters and similar facilities. In addition, family planning and counseling services, although financed by the federal government, can be administered by the provinces, local communities, and even by legally constituted organizations. However, there are fundamental differences in the scope and goals of family policy as seen by conservative and Catholic groups on the one hand and by the federal government on the other. Basically, these contradictory attitudes reflect the inherently different conceptions held by the conservatives and the socialists of the society as a whole. The socialists, despite their firm allegiance to the Austrian state, continue to regard the social order as capitalistic and as having class differences. On the other hand, to the conservative politicians the main distinction, at least theoretically, is between families and nonfamilies. Hence, the conceptions of family organization diverge widely, ultimately leading to the question: what is a family?

The family associations (conservative) regard all social measures as utilitarian and are concerned solely with the effects of such measures on the family. The socialist faction supports only a limited number of narrowly defined family policy measures, while all other political activities are focused on the entire Austrian population or on particularly disadvantaged groups, which by no means comprise only families. The federal government regards the problems of the family as a part of the general problems of society, since the well-being of the family is inseparable from the material welfare of the entire Austrian population. Recognizing the necessity of numerous measures directed toward the family, it very clearly supports the view that the best form of assistance to the family is provided by extending the welfare state.

In this perspective, the government has a social commitment to create the necessary conditions for future generations to grow up "healthy" in the sense of the definition of the World Health Organization. Appropriate steps should be taken to ensure the necessary knowledge, training, and skills, especially through benefits of educational measures, to enable them to shape their lives and to make the greatest possible contribution to the enhancement of the economic and cultural development of Austria. This helps to explain that, in contrast to the conservative politicians and family organizations, the government views family policy efforts from the perspective of the child and not of the whole family. Thus on the occasion of a family policy conference held in 1967, Dr. Gerhard Weissenberg, then Minister for Social Affairs, explained:

> Our concern is aimed primarily toward the standard of living of the child; the concern of the family organizations is aimed primarily toward the standard of living of the guardian. While in our view the necessary Equalization of Burdens on Families Act is an expression of solidarity in behalf of the child, others are more concerned with the equalization of burdens on persons having many children versus those having no children, which results in children being provided at best indirectly with assistance. Often the assistance does not reach the children at all. . . . If our main concern is directed toward the child, then the next logical recognition is that we must provide for each child the same initial opportunities that affect his subsequent development. But in order to create these conditions, the first goal of our family policy must be to produce equally accessible social benefits. . . . The great social function of our family policy consists in the extension of social benefits.

While at the beginning of the 1950s the newly emerging term "family policy" was mainly understood to mean granting assistance and tax relief to the family provider, a new direction for family policy was delineated in the statements by Dr. Weissenberg.

Austria's Assistance Program

In order to make an appropriate evaluation of Austria's assistance program, which is serving an increasing number of children, a brief review of its development is in order.

The challenge was to resolve the conflict stemming from the development of an efficiency-directed policy while remaining committed to the principle of the survival of the family. A family wage plan that would make larger payments to the family provider than to the single person could not be conceived. Nor could incentive pay alone solve the problem of the family provider's greater burden. Nor could it impede the material decline of the family with children in comparison with the needs of single persons or childless married couples. Both the United Nations Declaration on Human Rights and the European Social Charter state that the wages of an employee must be high enough to assure the existence of the family.

In a market-oriented economy, therefore, other appropriate measures must be instituted to supplement incentive, either through direct financial contributions or by payments in kind in order to assure the welfare of the family and of the child in particular. Efforts were made after World War I to assist the more burdened family by means of a child allowance. In 1948 legislation was passed to provide assistance through the Food Assistance Law. This provision, originally created solely for families of employees and further developed in subsequent years, was followed by the Child Assistance Law. Both laws were finally supplemented in 1954 through the Equalization of Burdens on Families Act in order that other segments of the population might enjoy some form of assistance, although in lesser amounts at that time. The two forms of assistance were merged over the years, and finally funds were allocated for financing assistance. A unified Assistance Law has been in effect since 1967 for all levels of the Austrian population. The Equalization of Burdens on Families Act continues to be financed largely from an employer contribution (based on an employee salary waiver incorporated in the wage and price agreements) with a supplement from income taxes. There are also small contributions from farmers and from the provincial government. (See table 1.)

The 1975 analysis of income and expenditures by the Fund for the Equalization of Burdens on Families gives an overview of changes in family policy in Austria since 1970, that is, since the change in political makeup of the government in favor of the Socialist Party. Cash payments have been increased and, as mentioned by Dr. Weissenberg, are directed more toward the child. Assistance payments progressivity has been decreased wherever possible [in favor of equal support for each child. Eds.], while expenditures for benefits in kind, to help children directly, have been increased.

Hence during this period, maternity assistance was increased from 1,700 to 2,000 schillings in 1970 to 4,000 schillings in 1973, and finally in 1974 to two payments of 8,000 schillings each. The Mother-Child Pass, which was introduced in 1973, is integrally related to the over-all health policy. This relationship was specified by Dr. Ingrid Leodolter, Minister for Health and Environmental Protection:

The infant mortality rate at the time I assumed the duties of Minister [1971] was 26.1. It was reduced to 20.5 in 1975 and to 18.3 in 1976. Altogether it was possible to reduce infant mortality by about 30 percent. Similarly gratifying is the evidence that since the introduction of the Mother-Child Pass and other supporting measures, injuries resulting from treatment and permanent injuries have been eliminated to the same extent.

Table 1 Equalization of Burdens on Families Act Revenue and Expenditures (in billions of schillings)[a]

	1970	1975
Revenue		
Employer contribution[b]	7,103.9	14,382.3
Contributions from payroll and income taxes, from investment returns, and from corporate income	620.0	1,175.2
From agricultural and forestry enterprises	67.6	65.9
From the provinces	124.8	127.7
Total	7,916.3	15,751.2
Expenditures		
Family assistance	6,931.3	10,813.2
Maternity assistance	186.4	1,270.8
School transportation assistance	—	119.5
Free transportation for pupils	—	1,337.4
Schoolbooks	—	901.2
Mother-child pass	—	350.0
Total	7,117.7	14,861.3[c]

[a] As of April 1, 1977, the exchange rate was: 1 schilling = $0.06. *Eds.*
[b] Employer contribution is the employees' salary waiver resulting from wage and price agreement.
[c] Slight discrepancy in totals in original. *Eds.*

Measures introduced in 1972 to provide school transportation assistance, travel passes, and free schoolbooks to students at all levels reflected an additional concern of the federal government to create equal opportunities and possibilities for children from different social strata. Rural youth, severely disadvantaged prior to 1972, benefited noticeably from the availability of free transportation and books. These measures were of especial benefit to girls, who comprised the other disadvantaged group in terms of educational opportunities, and provided effective support to an emerging need to meet their educational needs. Females make up more than half of the students in Austrian secondary schools that offer general education as well as more than 40 percent of the students enrolled in advanced technical institutes and academies. The almost simultaneous creation of school assistance, home assistance, and study assistance was another outstanding factor in the increased numbers of students from rural areas and in the numbers of female students.

This development and the new trends to be discussed are partly expressed in the government statement of November, 1975:

> . . . The main emphasis in family policy during the past legislative period was on the improvement in provisions for the pregnant woman and newborn child as well as on measures designed to secure greater equality of opportunity in the education of children.
>
> In accordance with the principle of equality of opportunity, allowances are made for children both in the area of financial support for the family and in the income tax law, using a proportionate tax consideration that is to a large extent independent of the parents' income. This principle of providing equal support to each child to the greatest extent possible will be amended in the future by further improvements in the Equalization of Burdens on Families Act. Assistance already introduced for families having special problems—such as families with handicapped children and one-parent families—is to be maintained and extended.
>
> The planned advance of outright maintenance for children will provide the one-parent family with the security of knowing that the maintenance is dependably and regularly available.
>
> The family counseling centers now in operation have proved to be of genuine value to the population. Hence the further extension of these facilities is to be accorded special attention. Information about family planning is similarly to be extended.

Family Counseling Centers

The government's emphasis on its growing ability to help and counsel the socially disadvantaged is also evident in the structure and extension of Family Counseling Centers in Austria. In 1974 a federal law authorized the establishment of federally financed Family Counseling Assistance Centers. There are now 120 such centers in Austria. Provinces, local organizations, and hospitals as well as private organizations and church groups serve persons in need, with complete anonymity, advise and counsel on varied questions concerning partner relationships, family planning, family matters, problems of single mothers, and so on. The state supports only those family counseling centers and nonprofit organizations that meet certain minimum standards in facilities and personnel.

New Regulation for Termination of Pregnancy

The extension of these facilities in Austria is one of the supporting measures of the new regulation for termination of pregnancy made in accordance with the major reform of criminal law in 1974. The new legislation decriminalizes the termination of pregnancy. It permits a pregnancy to be terminated during the first three months: (1) to avoid serious danger to life or severe harm to the physical and mental health of the woman; (2) if there is serious danger that the child would be severely harmed mentally or physically; (3) if the prospective mother is a minor. In all these cases, termination of pregnancy must be performed by a doctor.

Maternity Leave and Emergency Assistance

The emphasis on assisting the socially disadvantaged is also clearly expressed in the regulation of maternity leave benefits and emergency assistance for single mothers. Maternity leave benefits are available, upon compliance with certain conditions, to any mother who is employed. This assistance is so designed that any woman whose husband provides materially for her and the child receives a smaller amount than a woman who is alone or whose husband is either unable or unwilling to provide child support. The single mother is entitled to receive emergency assistance from unemployment insurance up to the child's fourth birthday. In order to qualify, however, the mother has to prove her inability to secure proper care for the child, hence the impossibility of her accepting employment.

Advance on Maintenance Payments

In November, 1976, a measure was passed to make aid more effective in family emergency situations. An innovation in Austrian law, it permits the granting of an advance on maintenance payments to children whose fathers renege on their responsibility for their support. The law's premise is that minors have a claim against the state for advance payments under certain conditions. The amount is limited, and the disbursement of funds is handled by the court that has jurisdiction. It is already evident that this measure is valuable, an ideal approach in providing effective financial assistance to single mothers and their children. The advance payments are drawn from a fund set up for the Equalization of Burdens on Families Act. The same fund also provides for family assistance, maternity benefits, schoolbooks, school transportation, and (in part) maternity leave benefits.

Apart from these and other measures for the socially disadvantaged, a strong political consensus about the family is undeniable and is expressed in sociopolitical and tax measures as well as in legal precepts and decisions concerning the family. An important sociopolitical consideration is the constantly increasing need for protection of the working mother, which is supplemented by resolutions governing maternity leave benefits by means of an extended system of assistance and payments in kind as well as by appropriate tax measures. All such family policy measures—apart from school, home, and study assistance—are granted to each child upon compliance with certain conditions, regardless of the amount of income or maintenance obligations. Hence the measures are independent of income.

Social Welfare Measures

Social welfare measures for the family in the various provinces, however, are for the most part income tested and mainly affect the socially disadvantaged. But in Vienna and a number of other cities a health service is available to all mothers. Every pregnant woman who submits to certain examinations receives a packet of baby clothing of considerable value. Pregnancy counseling centers, schools for expectant parents, and prenatal counseling centers ensure health care for pregnant women and infants as well as training young parents in all aspects of hygiene, nutrition, and psychology essential for the child's well-being. The facilities of the youth agencies are primarily intended for those children and youth who either have no family or whose family is not in a position to provide care and training. These measures and/or their implementation are regulated by the social assistance laws of the individual province.

Kindergartens and Day Nurseries

Kindergartens are still considered among the social welfare measures for children. In the view of politicians and of qualified professionals in the field, however, kindergartens more properly belong in the field of education. Kindergartens are now thought to have less of a caretaking than a training and educational function, especially in providing preschool training for children from socially disadvantaged groups.

In 1973 there were 153 day nurseries, mostly public, in Austria. However, the demand far exceeds the facilities. At present a nursery's service is limited to the children of working parents and single mothers. In contrast to kindergartens, these are not regarded as a supplement to family training or as preparation for school but, despite their predominant excellence, merely as a substitute for home care where there is none.

In 1973 there were 2,236 kindergartens in Austria. Some provinces have an ample number of spaces, but in others there is still an inadequate number. In the fall of 1977, Vienna had a kindergarten place available for every five- and six-year-old child.

Goals of Family Policy

The goals of Austrian family policy require additional comment.

The right to marriage and family is not mentioned in the federal constitution, hence neither marriage nor the family has special constitutional guarantees. Nevertheless, all political factions in Austria support a policy of protection and promotion of the family. The party in power regards it as a fundamental goal of family policy to facilitate the establishment of a family by anyone who wishes to do so, and to assist such persons toward a position that will permit them to raise the number of children they desire in social conditions that accord with their preferred standard of living.

Austria applies the concept of family policy in a restricted manner and considers all assistance to be guided by its present sociopolitical goals. Additionally, Austrian law has always attempted to the greatest extent possible to enact consistent federal regulations for all branches of law. This is in conformity with the Austrian federal constitution; thus the basic legal regulations are the same for all Austrian citizens. The special regulations made specifically for mother and child constitute exceptions to this principle and are explained in greater detail in the Summary of Family Policy Measures.

Taxes
Only in matters of tax law and housing is no consideration given to the single parent and child. On essential matters the whole family is taken into consideration, and appropriate relief is available. The primary concern is with deductions for children entitled to support and with unemployed wives. At issue also are tax measures for promoting home construction, particularly for providing extremely low-interest loans and graduated rent assistance based on income and number of children.

Traditional Role Concepts
Another essential point concerns possible differences in interest and interest conflicts between marital partners and between parents and children. Dif-

ferences of interest and interest conflicts occur mainly in regard to the position and responsibility of the woman in the family. In Austria, traditional role concepts, according to which the man must earn and the woman must care for the household and the children, are still strongly entrenched despite the fact that the percentage of working women is just as high as in the past. About 53 percent of women aged fifteen to sixty work. The number of working wives varies between 40 percent and 50 percent according to age. In 1976, 39 percent of the labor force were women. As a result, in many instances the woman must assume all housekeeping and child-training responsibilities even if she is employed. This usually leads to constant overexertion and results in a relatively high incidence of disability. Public opinion, in principle, concedes a woman's right to work but in effect constrains all but the single woman in the exercise of this right. Gainful employment is acceptable for the married woman but is almost entirely rejected for the mother. These traditional role concepts are still maintained in many families, with the result that the majority of boys as well as the majority of girls continue to be strongly inculcated with bourgeois, cliché role concepts. Despite the constantly increasing demand in Austria for education of women, girls frequently pursue only a short course of study or seek less qualified occupational training than boys do. The continued practice of providing one-sided training for girls at all levels leads to further entrenchment of an outmoded role concept rather than to a new definition of the woman's role. Almost 90 percent of all female apprentices continue to be trained in typical "female" occupations such as sales work, dressmaking, beauty parlor employment, and so on. Women comprise the majority of students in the general training classes in secondary schools but continue to be a smaller and smaller minority in mathematics classes, in advanced technical training institutes, and in technical and pure scientific fields at the university. Yet, constant improvement in their education contributes to a change of consciousness.

Of special importance to the change in the woman's image is the surprising increase in the number of female academicians, which doubled from 1951 to 1971 while the number of male academicians during this period increased by only 17 percent. Changes being made in the portrayal of women in schoolbooks will surely lead to a more reality-oriented idea of the effect of women on society.

Family Law
Family law often exhibits quite significant differences in regard to the sexes. At present, the Parliament is completing reform of family law. The first

large section, the regulation of the legal relation of marital partners to one another, was completed in 1975. This was preceded by a reform of the statutes pertaining to illegitimate children in which, however, there was no fundamental alteration of the basic assignment of male and female roles. The reason is that in the very nature of this legality no essentially divergent opinions could emerge.

The reform of the legal system governing relations between husbands and wives has created far greater problems. To date, the man's role has been to head the family and, in principle, to support the family. Correspondingly, the wife had to assume the husband's surname, follow him to his place of residence, obey his orders, and keep house.

By contrast, the new law views marriage as a partnership with shared duties and obligations. The spouses choose freely the extent of each one's participation in the support of the family as well as in other tasks. The legal reforms were extended to allow the engaged couple to declare their intention to retain the woman's maiden name as the family name after marriage if they wish to do so. Similarly, the woman's obligation to obedience was eliminated. The husband's right to independent ownership of the common marital dwelling to the disadvantage of the wife was eliminated. It is easy to understand that those who perceive the social order as inherently patriarchal would hardly accept these reforms. In particular, they have most vigorously opposed and even ridiculed the change in the right to choose the family name. As they see it, frequent use of this right would lead to the end of the "ideology of the son and heir." All sides uniformly agreed only that maintaining the household and rearing children are completely valid contributions toward support of the family. Current revisions in the legal status of the legitimate child lead still further to the view of marriage as a partnership. Today the father retains and exercises full "paternal authority". In the future, both partners will have the same parental rights and duties, and the child, from a certain age on, will also have specified rights.

The first part of the reforms of family law should necessarily be viewed from the perspective of the long-term effects, and thus their potential influence on the institution of marriage cannot be predicted. But the second part is of immediate importance, especially for the mother. Previously, unlimited parental authority obtained in all those instances in which the marital partners no longer had a good relationship with one another. This usually had a disastrous effect on mother and child in dissolved marriages. In the future, in the event of divorce, full parental rights and duties will be held by the parent who is responsible for the care and training of the child. As a rule, therefore, the position of the divorced wife and mother will undergo considerable improvement. This is also of special importance in terms of family policy, for to a large extent it is precisely the children of divorced parents who require special consideration by society.

While these changes in family law are or will be fundamental changes in the areas of role allocation and prestige, the main issue in the last section of the reformed family law concerns very specific matters, essentially material questions. The law that has governed inheritance up to the present does not provide for a statutory claim by the surviving member of the marriage. In extreme instances this can lead to a situation in which a wife of many years, upon the death of her husband, can lose to another woman the entire inheritance to which she was without a doubt morally entitled. In the future this possibility should be eliminated through a statutory claim of half of the amount to be distributed. In the event of the dissolution of the marriage, there should be a claim on property acquired in the marriage. In other words, the wealth acquired in marriage should be divided equally, or at least according to a prescribed formula. This would put the wife in an incomparably better situation. At the same time, this regulation would signify the end of the last great bastion of male dominance in the family. These regulations will therefore undoubtedly require still more time for negotiations in order to make them acceptable to those who, either because of financial interests or their adherence to an outmoded social tenet, cannot or do not wish to accept this new principle.

Allowances have already been made for the principle of marriage conceived as a partnership in income tax law and in family assistance law that provides an elective claim on family-related payments by the husband or the wife. However, another wide legislative area of the social insurance law remains totally oriented toward the husband's responsibility to support the family. Consequently, attempts are being made to reconcile the new family law and this area of law. The transition to a partnership arrangement in health insurance law—assuring the right of the husband to be insured by the working wife—can be realized without too many difficulties. This is not the case, however, with the pension insurance law, which de facto recognizes widows but not widowers. An equalization of the right of the widower with the right of the widow in reference to a pension is hardly in the realm of possibility, considering the present financial state of pension insurance. The elimination of the widow's pension is inconceivable both for reasons of principle and because even employed women are poorer insurance risks as a result of housekeeping and child-rearing duties incumbent upon them until now and, too, as a result of the biological fact of motherhood. In addition, because women are mostly disadvantaged in terms of salaries, they attain much lower bases of valuation for pension incomes. A commission under the chairmanship of the Minister for Social Administration is at present examining possible solutions to this difficult problem of adapting social insurance to the new principles of family law.

Another noteworthy measure was enacted into law in January, 1977, which could either ferment or resolve conflicts within the family. It provides for a maximum of one paid week of nursing leave to each employee, regardless of sex, in the event that a live-in dependent requires care. An investigation by the Chamber of Workers and Employees for Vienna in 1954 showed that 54.9 percent of the mothers but only 3.4 percent of the fathers assumed the actual care of ill children of kindergarten age. It further learned that most of the fathers who actually assumed the nursing tasks belonged to the better-educated classes. Another study reached the same conclusion that it is the father with a high school or university education who is most willing to share in the care and training of children. To be sure, there is frequent conflict between employed parents over the issue of who is to care for a sick child. To date, the working wife almost always assumed this duty, even with the certain knowledge that her chances for job promotion might suffer. The legislation now offers a possibility for both parents to respond to such emergencies, which will probably mean that in view of all the disadvantages to their work lives, many women will no longer be willing to assume the care of a sick family member. Developments are awaited.

Family Policy and the Government

Family policy is regarded as a responsibility of the government both by the current administration and by the more powerful political factions within the country. As mentioned earlier, neither the federal constitution nor the basic law of the state mentions the concept of the family. However, since Austria ratified both the United Nations Charter and the European Social Charter, it guarantees Austrian citizens the rights and basic freedoms spelled out in both documents. Assistance to the family is therefore regarded as the responsibility of the public sector: the federal government, the provinces, and the communities. The most essential family policy measures are explained in further detail in the Summary of Family Policy Measures.

Both the government statement and the platforms of the three large parties of Austria express a clear commitment to assisting the family. Hence the

Socialist Party included in its 1958 Vienna platform the following statement
in the chapter entitled "Questions Concerning Women":

> The Socialist Party of Austria recognizes the economic and social necessity of
> the employment of women. It demands the social recognition of housework, it
> values motherhood as a social achievement. . . . Mothers of small children
> should not be compelled for financial reasons to seek employment. Security
> within the family is a basic condition for the harmonious development of chil-
> dren. . . . Strengthening of the family is primarily a moral and social issue for
> the entire population. The establishment of families should be supported. The
> community should assume the support of a person deprived of family and
> thereby obviate problems of social adjustment and loneliness. . . . Mother and
> child should be given special social protection. The Socialist Party of Austria
> considers it a duty of society to create both in the city and in the country facili-
> ties of sufficient scope to meet the standards of modern medicine and welfare
> for the purpose of providing counseling services and care for pregnant women
> and mothers, for providing pediatricians and dry nurses in every Austrian dis-
> trict, for constructing specialized children's hospitals in large cities, establishing
> special departments for children in hospitals serving smaller areas.

The Austrian People's Party similarly affirmed its support for assistance
to the woman and the family in its 1972 Salzburg platform, which includes
the following statement:

> The Austrian People's Party supports a partnership type of relationship between
> the sexes. This requires a new conception of the roles of husband and wife in
> the family and in the areas of culture, education, the economy, and public life.
> Social services must be designed in such a manner that the woman having fam-
> ily responsibilities has the possibility of deciding freely whether or not she
> wishes to be employed. The willingness of the mother to dedicate herself for
> years to the mental, spiritual, and physical well-being of her children must be
> valued and supported as a social achievement of benefit to the entire population.
> The family must also in the future fulfill vital responsibilities. It should continue
> to be the first and decisive training center for the child. The family should offer
> growing children security and recognition, transmit an orientation toward ethical
> values and community relatedness, and provide training for democratic respon-
> sibility. One-parent families have a special claim to protection and assistance.

The Freedom Party of Austria supported the following position in response to these questions in its discussion proposal for a Manifesto of Freedom in 1972:

> We support equal rights for men and women. Mainly the woman, as the mother,
> needs society's protection. . . . The mother or the person who, in the absence
> of the mother, takes the mother's place is of fateful significance for the sub-
> sequent development of the child. The main goal of family policy must be to
> strengthen the family in such a manner that it can fulfill its social functions. The

establishment of a family requires more than mere financial assistance from the state. . . . We affirm a natural attitude toward sex life and conscious parenthood. . . . Based on the predominant contemporary practice of women working outside the home, girls and young women as well as young men must be trained in accordance with their talents for optimal employment. Girls entering the labor force should also be trained in knowledge and skills that will enable them to cope with family responsibilities.

The Family Advisory Council

The Family Policy Advisory Council was established in 1967 in the Office of the Federal Chancellor, reflecting the support of all important political factions of Austria. This occurred primarily in the absence of a unified agency responsible for family policy. The following ministries are involved actively in questions of family policy: the federal ministries for finance, education and art, social administration, health and environmental protection, justice, construction and technique, as well as the Office of the Federal Chancellor. This Advisory Council has the task, upon request of the Office of the Federal Chancellor, of providing expertise on economic, social, legal, and cultural matters affecting the family. It can, however, also initiate proposals and applications to the Office of the Federal Chancellor. It is also responsible for the examination and evaluation of suggestions and demands made by family organizations. Usually, ten representatives of the family organizations belong to the Advisory Council. In accordance with their statutes, they work on behalf of economic, social, legal, and cultural matters of the family and comprise a broad representation of interests in the family. The Advisory Council also includes one representative from employer organizations and one from worker organizations. The Advisory Council consists of a maximum of fifteen members and is headed by the Federal Chancellor or a representative appointed by him.

In addition to the Advisory Council, three large family organizations are concerned with questions of family policy: the Austrian Friends of Children, the Catholic Family Organization of Austria, and the Austrian Family Alliance. The largest organization is the Austrian Friends of Children, which is close to the Socialist Party of Austria. The Catholic Family Organization has a particularly close relation to the Catholic church, while the Austrian Family Alliance attempts to maintain an attitude of neutrality and to be nonpartisan. The activities of these organizations are mainly financed by member contributions, donations, and public subsidies. To be sure, the political parties are also concerned with problems of families and women (as shown by their platforms), as are various interest groups, especially those representing workers (particularly the women's and sociopolitical departments). Political parties and other interest groups are active in presenting requests and proposals to the federal ministries responsible for problems of families and of women, in submitting evidence, in providing counsel and training, as well as in publicity work.

The concerns of the various parties and organizations in regard to family policy do not differ greatly, as evidenced in their respective platforms. However, in the conduct of daily politics they express extraordinarily different ideas of possible solutions to single issues. The Austrian Family Alliance, the Catholic Family Organization, the Austrian People's Party, and the Freedom Party share the same position concerning payments by the Fund for the Equalization of Burdens on Families Act. All these organizations regard the sole purpose of the fund to be that of making cash payments to the family. The Austrian Friends of Children as well as the Austrian Workers' Board and the Austrian Union Alliance, as the most important representatives of worker interests, and the Socialist Party, as the ruling party, support the position of the former social minister, Dr. Weissenberg, placing primary emphasis upon payments in kind rather than upon cash payments as a means of granting all children the same benefits and allowances. Sharp contrasts emerge in political discussions of these two points of view. The former position demands higher cash payments, including payment of training assistance to mothers who have given up jobs for the sake of the children, and the payment of maternity leave benefits to women farmworkers. The workers and the governing party are more in favor of pressing for the extension of payments in kind. At present they are attempting to replace tax relief for the family with a larger amount of assistance for each child in order to provide adequate material support if possible to those children whose parents do not earn enough to be entitled to a tax deduction for a child. Further details include the position of the more conservative family organizations, which favor cash payments to cover at least 50 percent of the child's expenses and a progressive scale according to the number of children. The ruling party and the Austrian Friends of Children favor equally high assistance for each child and maintain that the 50 percent coverage has already been partially exceeded through benefits in kind and by various other family benefits. These groups also reject the idea of granting maternity leave benefits to women farmworkers. They maintain that the purpose of these benefits—to make possible close contact between mother and child among women who work at some distance from home and who are subject to direct supervision—are not applicable to women farmworkers.

If family policy is understood in the larger context of a family-related social policy, a whole complex of problems with particular relevance to the family provokes heated discussion. This is the case at present in Austria, where questions concerning school, job security, women, family law, pension financing, and taxes are among the most important issues.

Education

The importance to the family of the school and the range of its program is evident. If both parents are employed, there is a need for different kinds of schools than now exist in the larger part of Austria. Despite the fact that four out of ten women are employed, with the exception of a few schools, mostly denominational, there are *de facto* only the schools that are in session for a half day only. As a result, an adult, usually the mother, is required to be home in the afternoons and to assist with school homework. As an alternative to the half-day school, an attempt is being made to introduce a kind of school that is in session for the whole day.

The opinions of both major political parties as to whether schools should be in session for a whole day or a half day diverge. The care of pupils for a whole day is also regarded from the standpoint of the greatly increased demands on students.

The problem of providing children with sufficient kindergarten and preschool facilities in Austria has not been solved, apart from the example of Vienna previously mentioned. Several provinces have a far from adequate number of day care centers; in the majority of instances, they have only half-day kindergartens. As a result, it is extremely difficult to employ women in these areas.

The necessary revision of teaching materials to deal with the roles of the man and woman and the conception of the working world as it is taught in school are the main problem discussed at length both within and outside the family, and particularly by persons in the field of education.

Employment

Another matter of fundamental importance to the welfare of the family is the guarantee of a high level of employment. Thus far, Austria has successfully maintained close to full employment, although there are areas in which for structural reasons difficulties emerge in obtaining appropriate jobs for women and youth. Through the introduction of state measures for improving the job market, it has been possible to a large degree to make jobs secure and, through occupational training, retraining, after-school training programs, and other new programs, to equip workers with skills to make them employable.

Independence of Women

In all discussions about the family, considerable weight is accorded the question of the increasing independence of the woman in Austria. Although the percent of male and female workers in Austria has remained almost unchanged since 1910, the employment of women, especially married women and/or mothers, was hitherto regarded as a passing evil to be eliminated as soon as possible. This attitude has changed, however, in the last decade. The employment of women is now not only taken for granted but is officially regarded as one of the main reasons for Austria's high living standard and is supported by the state, especially in the field of education and in job market policy.

A change in consciousness among most company managements and in the skilled trades has not yet occurred, however, as is evident in the greatly diminished earning and career opportunities of the Austrian woman discussed in the 1975 Report on Women by the Federal Government. Certainly the attitude of a large number of women toward employment has changed. An inquiry conducted in 1974 by the Institute for Empirical Social Research revealed that 41 percent of the employed women polled gave as one of their reasons for working "the pleasure and joy of working." Concern about their old age likewise is a weighty factor in the considerations of many of the somewhat older women, as shown by the fact that 29 percent mentioned providing for their old age as one of their reasons for working. Other reasons not related to the family, such as pleasure from coming into contact with other people, greater independence, and so on, were noted. As many as 21 percent cited greater independence as one of their main reasons for working. A hardly perceptible change of great significance can be concluded from the poll, indicating that a growing number of women accept their own employment for personal reasons rather than as a supplement to the man's income.

The consciousness among males, on the other hand, which similar investigations has revealed, has by no means changed as much as that among women. Although hardly detectable in public, to the attentive observer this is shown in the very evident dispute in many groups, especially wealthy, male-dominated groups, that oppose a greater equalization of rights of the woman in the marriage and particularly oppose the prospects of greater material demands by the woman in the event of divorce.

This tenaciously conducted battle for a real improvement in the position of women also includes much attention to the struggle to broaden the range of occupations open to them. Recognizing that the traditional restrictions in the employment of women constitute one of the reasons for their weak financial position, worker organizations, especially their women's departments, along with the Ministry for Social Administration to which the Job Market Administration belongs, are attempting to open up occupations that until now remained, if not *de jure, de facto* closed to women. The first successes are beginning to take place in the metal trades. Similarly, the reduced bans against women working which went into effect recently can be regarded as suitable instruments for opening up previously legally closed occupations.

In addition to implementing the equivalent training of girls and boys and striving for more and better job opportunities for girls, the problem of the mother who has many children must be solved in the future. The state and communities are already assisting these persons in every conceivable manner. Still, this problem shows clearly that its origin is in the changed status of marriage from an institution which supported the woman to a partnership in which both sexes share tasks. Although it is possible that both parents in small and medium-sized families may be gainfully employed during relatively short working hours, the practice is hardly conceivable for large families. Support for these persons, who are not very numerous in Austria, will certainly be the topic of extensive deliberation in coming years.

Consequences of Family Policy

The consequences of family policy measures on the family are not only constantly discussed in the mass media but above all are the subject of numerous debates in the Family Policy Advisory Council, in Parliament, and of course in family and women's organizations. The first Report on the Situation of the Family in Austria appeared in 1969, and the publication of a second Report on the Family is planned by the federal government for 1979. Along with the 1975 Report on Women, it will undoubtedly contain important statements about the extent of change that has taken place in the situation of the family and, in particular, of the child in the last decade.

In addition, both research conducted at universities and empirical social research are strongly preoccupied with questions concerning families. The work of the Central Office of Austrian Statistics is of special importance in providing accurate family-related data. A governmental office responsible to the Office of the Federal Chancellor, it conducts censuses, gathers statistics on marriage, divorce, births, consumer research, and carries out micro-census research about certain topics (the workload of employed women, social contacts of families, and so on). Research on statements concerning the consequences of family policy measures and/or possible evaluations of future measures are similarly conducted by these agencies. In addition, the Institute for Higher Studies, the Boltzmann Institute, the Academy of Sciences, the Austrian Institute for Health, the Economic Research Institute, and numerous other institutes and advisory councils are extensively concerned with a multitude of questions within this complex. The results of this research are usually published in professional journals and given wide coverage in the mass media, resulting in the strong popularization of these questions.

The distribution of responsibilities between the federation and the provinces, which is confusing for the non-Austrian, frequently results in a certain fragmentation of measures relevant to family policy. Questions of responsibility were therefore only briefly touched upon here wherever it seemed necessary for the sake of clarity. Despite similarities in policy statements issued by the large parties, family organizations, and worker organizations, there are sharp differences among these groups concerning the role of the man and that of the woman within the family and in economic life. Once again it should be mentioned that the process of self-discovery of the woman in Austria, especially among the younger generation, has made considerable progress in the last ten years. On the other hand, it cannot be denied that the traditional idea of the woman's role held by the man is still predominant. Although many women demand a change in the image of the man's role, these demands are hardly given serious consideration by men. But as long as there is merely an attempt to change the role of the woman in marriage, family, and in the entire economic life without pressing for abandonment of the fixed role assigned to the man, a genuine change in the position of the woman and in the interrelationships of all family members cannot occur. The process of bringing about a change of consciousness, reflecting an understanding of democratic cooperation in the family, professions, and society, will not be successful unless a change can also be effected in the consciousness and patterns of thinking among men in possession of power concerning their function and role.

This great task, although primarily directed toward mothers, presupposes appropriate preparation in the family and in school. While this can hardly be accomplished in most families because of the traditional role concepts, a broad, unexploited field is opened up for the school. A family policy conceived as part of a comprehensive social policy must therefore give first priority to this task of the school, since without it all efforts concerning the welfare of children and parents would essentially be restricted to the material realm.

SUMMARY OF FAMILY POLICY MEASURES

Special Family Services[1]

Marriage Assistance
On the occasion of a first marriage, a husband and wife who are residents of Austria have a right to marriage assistance of 7,500 schillings per person, or a total of 15,000 schillings. Request for payment is filed at the Office of Residency.

Family Counseling Centers
Family Counseling Centers were established to provide better information about birth control, supply those who desire children with the necessary information, provide information about family problems and all rights associated with motherhood. By 1977 there were 120 Family Counseling Centers in Austria. The Federation merely provides support for this program, since in accordance with the Austrian constitution the Board of Health is administered by the provinces. Only nonprofit Family Counseling Centers that meet certain minimum standards of personnel are supported. The Counseling Centers are run by the provinces, communities, hospitals, churches, and private organizations.

Protection of Mothers
Austrian regulations concerning protection of pregnant women and mothers within certain periods of time after delivery of the child apply to all gainfully employed women.

For the entire duration of pregnancy and up to four months after delivery (in the event of maternity leave, up to four weeks after its conclusion) there is almost complete protection against termination of employment and

[1] These family services were created after World War II and are specifically designated as such. The over-all summary is as of March 31, 1977.

dismissal. The employer must be advised of the pregnancy or delivery or be notified of the employee's condition within five working days after she files for the benefit. Bans against, or restrictions on, work apply to pregnant women and to mothers up to twelve weeks after delivery. Heavy physical work, especially carrying heavy loads, constant standing, working with radiation, working in dust, heat, and dampness, and working overtime, at night, and on Sundays and holidays (with limitations, however) are forbidden. In general, any work that could jeopardize the health of the mother or of the child is prohibited.

The prescribed term during which work is banned or restricted begins eight weeks before delivery and ends in cases of normal birth eight weeks after delivery. In cases of premature birth or multiple births (and in the future probably also in cases of Caesarian section), the term during which work is banned or restricted is extended to twelve weeks. In those cases in which danger to the life or health of mother or child is confirmed by medical specialists, an absolute ban on work is in effect from the day such evidence is submitted. During the period of an absolute ban on work, the average payment for the last thirteen weeks or, as the case may be, three months before the start of the ban on work, continues to be paid by health insurance.

Any mother who resumes work at the end of the term during which work is banned or restricted is entitled to time for breast feeding. During a work period of up to four hours daily, this amounts to forty-five minutes; during eight hours or longer, two forty-five minute periods, or one and a half hours daily. This time is paid in full.

Maternity Leave
In addition to the time after delivery during which work is banned or restricted, the mother has a right to maternity leave that may at the most last to the end of the child's first year. She is protected against dismissal during this period, and financial support is provided by unemployment insurance. Mothers under the age of twenty-one must have been employed for twenty weeks in work covered by unemployment insurance; all other mothers must have been employed for fifty-two weeks in the previous two years in work covered by unemployment insurance. Special regulations apply to apprentices and to certain groups of female students preparing for social professions. Maternity benefits for single mothers and for women whose husbands have a limited income and/or do not provide for the child at present amount to 3,974 schillings; for all other mothers the amount is 2,659 schillings. The

maternity benefits are pegged annually according to a certain formula. Payment is dependent upon proof that the child lives in the household of the mother and is cared for most of the time by the mother herself. Adoptive mothers are also entitled to maternity benefits.

Emergency Assistance
Emergency assistance from unemployment insurance is provided at a maximum to the end of the child's third year when it can be proved that a single mother whose maternity benefits have run out cannot make arrangements for the child's care, hence cannot be referred by the Employment Office. The amount of assistance is based on the mother's estimated income. At the most, the entire amount of the unemployment benefits is paid out.

Delivery Assistance
This assistance is granted to Austrian citizens and to foreigners who, it is assumed, will remain in Austria permanently. Adoptive mothers as well as natural mothers are entitled to the benefit. Delivery assistance amounts to 16,000 schillings and is paid in two installments of 8,000 schillings each. The first installment is due after the birth of the child, the second upon completion of the child's first year. The condition for granting the first installment is the completion of four medical examinations of the mother during pregnancy and an examination of the infant in the first week after birth. The second installment is due after a Mother-Child Pass has been submitted in proof that the required examinations of the infant were completed during its first year.

Family Allowance

As a contribution toward the expenses of child rearing, a family allowance is usually paid until the child reaches nineteen. All employed persons, including self-employed persons and farmers, can apply for this benefit if the child lives in their household, is either under age or is receiving vocational training, or, because of a handicap, is incapable of earning. Included are the parents' own children, grandchildren, stepchildren, adopted children, and foster children. The recipients of social insurance payments (especially women on pensions) can also claim this assistance. The monthly installments, actually paid fourteen times annually, are as follows:

Table 2 Family Allowance Installments

	Schillings
For one child	450
For two children	940
For three children	1,530
For four children	2,040
For each additional child	540
For each severely handicapped child	900

Payments of assistance are made on the basis of the Assistance Card, usually obtained from the local office responsible for such matters and in other instances, from the tax office. Monthly payments are made to dependent employed persons and recipients of pensions and welfare and other social benefits by their payroll departments. The companies making these payments are reimbursed by the respective official financial agency. Self-employed persons receive quarterly payments from the revenue office.

The Fund for Equalization of Burdens on the Family was created for the purpose of financing family assistance, maternity assistance, a small amount of maternity leave payments, free school transportation, and schoolbooks. The Fund receives allocations from the following sources: from the employee's salary waiver amounting to 6 percent, which is in the form of the Employer's Contribution made to the Finance Ministry; from a 3 percent income tax; from a contribution from agriculture; and from a small amount, which has remained the same for years, paid by the provinces on the basis of population.

Student Transportation Passes and School Travel Assistance

Students up to age twenty-eight are entitled to the School Transportation Pass. If it is not possible for them to use public transportation, various organizations (communities, community organizations, school sponsors, parents' organizations) can rent a vehicle to provide transportation. The Ministry of Finance will pay a certain amount toward such rental. School transportation assistance can be claimed if the distance to school is at least three kilometers and there is no public transportation available, if no vehicle is provided by an organization, or if the pupil lives in an institution or boarding school. The amount of support is determined by the distance between school and place of residence.

Free Schoolbooks

Books required for school use are provided free of charge to students in compulsory intermediate and secondary schools. The school issues book coupons that can be used at bookstores. The practice of providing free schoolbooks facilitates social equalization among children from low-income and high-income families. Outmoded schoolbooks are gradually being replaced with realistic, relevant texts that are better suited to contemporary society. Special importance is placed upon such topics as the modern idea of marriage, family, and the woman's role in society.

School Assistance

School assistance can be claimed for students at or beyond the tenth-grade level if they are socially disadvantaged Austrian citizens, have a good school record, and attend compulsory intermediate or secondary schools. The amount of assistance is based on the parents' income and the number of dependent persons living in the same household.

Housing Allowance for Students

Housing allowances can be granted to students at or beyond the tenth-grade level if they are Austrian citizens, have a good school record, and attend compulsory intermediate or secondary schools. The condition for receiving housing assistance is that the student live away from home because the school is too far away to permit daily commuting.

The amount of the housing allowance is based on the parents' income and the number of dependent persons living in the same household.

Study Assistance

This assistance is granted to Austrians studying at scientific institutes, art academies, teacher training schools, institutes for advanced social professions, theological seminaries, vocational training schools in agriculture and forestry. The condition for claiming the assistance is financial need and a good school record. The amount is based on the parents' or the spouse's income.

Travel Reductions on Austrian Railroads

Families with at least two children for whom a family allowance is received can obtain, upon showing the Family Card, a 50 percent reduction on the price of tickets on the Austrian Federal Railway and on privately owned railroads as well as on all domestic bus lines of the Austrian Federal Railways and Mail. The Family Card may be obtained at the railroad station. To qualify, the recipient must be a parent taking a trip with at least three eligible family members.

Other Social Policy Measures

Vacation and Special Paid Leave
A minimum of four weeks' paid vacation is granted. A fully paid leave of one work week per work year is provided for the purpose of caring for ill family members living in the household.

Severance Pay upon Birth of a Child
Women who have been employed by the same employer for a minimum of five years can claim, after the birth of a child, half the severance pay that would be due in the event of their dismissal by the employer. To qualify, the woman must resign during the period after delivery when work is banned or restricted or, in the event of having claimed maternity leave, she must resign within six months after delivery of the child. (More favorable regulations are offered by collective contracts, service organizations, and shop agreements.)

Tax Concessions[2]
A tax deduction is allowed for each child as well as for the unemployed mother. The tax deduction now in effect for each child who is eligible for a family allowance amounts to 4,000 schillings annually. Each parent can claim half of the special deduction. The unmarried mother is granted the full amount of the child deduction. The married mother who does not work is granted a tax deduction of 2,200 schillings annually. Maternity benefits are not counted as income.

The Social Security System

The Austrian social security system includes four fundamental components: health insurance, accident insurance, pension insurance, and unemployment

[2] A change in the wage and income tax system that anticipates a transition from tax allowances granted to cover expenses of children in favor of a corresponding increase in assistance has been worked out by the Ministry of the Treasury and is under discussion.

insurance. Public service employees are not covered by unemployment insurance, for they cannot be dismissed from their jobs. Unemployment insurance benefits relevant to the family—specifically maternity benefits and emergency assistance for single mothers—have been mentioned. Public service employees receive assistance comparable to maternity benefits paid by unemployment insurance in the form of checks issued by their payroll office. There is no regulation, however, covering female public service employees comparable to that providing emergency assistance to single mothers. And since public service employees cannot be dismissed, none is necessary.

The Austrian social security system is a compulsory insurance system supplemented by voluntary health and pension insurance as well as through the inclusion, at no extra cost to the family, of the insured man in the majority of payments made by the separate branches of insurance. Payments applicable to the family made by the separate branches of insurance are as follows:

1. Health Insurance

Payments are made in the following cases:

a) Illness: medical care, medication, and therapeutic aids

b) Work disability as a result of illness: sickness payments, family support, day-to-day money, hospital care in some instances

c) Pregnancy: medical or midwife assistance, medication and therapeutic aids; hospital care (including maternity hospitals); maternity benefits (not for dependents or the self-insured); delivery grants

d) Death: funeral allowance.

Illness. The right to claim insurance payments is in effect from the first day of being insured. Claims for health insurance payments can be made on behalf of a dependent family member (fulfilling household responsibilities) in instances of illness, pregnancy, and death. These payments are granted without special contribution toward insurance of a family member; that is, without an increase in insurance rates. The following are considered family members: the wife, children, and grandchildren; the mother, daughter, or sister of the insured person, provided any one of these keeps house for the insured without remuneration. Children and grandchildren are considered eligible family members up to the end of their nineteenth year. Maternity benefits, with the exception of maternity benefit payments, are also available to dependent family members. (For the amount and length of time maternity benefit payments are made, see the details concerning prenatal care.)

One form of payment specially designed to meet the needs of the family is family money. Sickness payments, which are a partial substitute for absent earnings, are on principle suspended during the hospital stay of an insured person. If the insured person is responsible for family members, family money, which is one third of the so-called "basis of evaluation," replaces sickness payments. Supplements to family money are paid according to the number of family members.

Pregnancy. The insurance covering pregnancy becomes effective at the beginning of the eighth week prior to the expected date of delivery. If the insured woman or the insured man whose wife is pregnant has terminated the insurance earlier, but the insurance contract has been in effect for at least six weeks, or in the previous year for twenty-six weeks, maternity benefits are still due. This holds even if the insured person becomes jobless immediately after termination of the insurance and if the birth occurs within six weeks after termination of insurance. Benefits may be claimed for a ten-day stay in a hospital or maternity hospital. A single payment of at least 1,000 and no more than 2,000 schillings, depending upon the special conditions of the individual policy, is made upon delivery.

Death. A payment to cover burial expenses is made upon the death of the insured person or of a close relative. This amounts to twenty-five times the basis of evaluation (higher payments can be established by the individual health insurance policies). In the case of a woman on a pension, the payment is simply equal to the monthly pension.

2. Accident Insurance

All categories of accident insurance benefits are provided: family money and day-to-day money as well as special support, supplementary grants for child support, assistance to widows, burial expense payments, survivors' pensions, and pupil accident insurance.

The regulation here concerning family money and day-to-day money is different from the regulation concerning medical insurance but serves the same purpose. The insured person or his immediate family can additionally be granted special support related to the severity of an injury or as a result of lengthy treatment.

Disability pension. An additional provision of accident insurance is a disability pension, payable to a person injured in an accident or suffering from work-related injury or illness. If the person is severely injured, an additional pension is paid as well as a supplementary payment for child support amounting to 10 percent of the pension up to the end of the child's eighteenth year. For vocational training or in situations of inability to earn, this child support can be extended beyond the child's eighteenth year.

Burial expenses. Payment from accident insurance for burial expenses can be appropriately increased by taking into consideration the financial position of the surviving family. This payment includes an allowance for transporting the corpse.

Widow's assistance. Widow's assistance is paid when the widow of a severely injured man is ineligible for a widow's pension because the death of the husband was not the result of an accident at work or a job-related illness. In such cases, the amount granted is 40 percent of the basis of evaluation.

Widow's pension. The widow's pension is payable throughout her life. It amounts annually to 20 percent of the basis of evaluation. If the widow loses one half of her salary, or reaches the age of sixty, the pension is increased to 40 percent of the basis of evaluation. Although the pension is terminated upon remarriage, under certain circumstances it can be reinstated in the event of the death of the new husband or divorce from him.

Orphan's pension. An orphan's pension is paid to children of the deceased in the amount of 20 percent of the basis of evaluation (if both parents are deceased, the amount is 30 percent). As a rule, the child receives the orphan's pension until he is nineteen. Under certain circumstances there is the further possibility of drawing a parent's or a sibling's pension.

Students. Finally, since 1977 coverage of students is included in accident insurance. They receive medical treatment; in the event of complete destitution they receive a guardian allowance. Austrian citizenship is not a condition for receiving accident insurance benefits by pupils attending compulsory schools, secondary schools, and teacher training schools, but it is a prerequisite for university-level students.

3. Pension Insurance

Pension insurance provides the following: retirement pension; early retirement pension in the event of unemployment; or, if the condition has been in effect for a long period of time, disability or occupational disability pension; survivor's pension; and the handling of widows' pensions.

Retirement pension. This is payable to men upon reaching sixty-five and to women upon reaching sixty. If unemployed, men can claim the early retirement pension upon reaching sixty; women have the right to claim the early retirement pension at age fifty-five if they have been collecting unemployment payments for at least fifty-two weeks within the previous fifteen months. Financial benefits are paid for equivalent periods of time.

If the insurance policy has been in effect for a long period of time, the early retirement pension can also be claimed by men at age sixty and by women at age fifty-five if they can prove 420 months of insurance coverage and if 24 monthly compulsory insurance payments within the previous 36 calendar months can be documented.

Disability pension. This pension is paid not only in the event of lasting or temporary disability but also upon the death of the husband to the surviving wife over age fifty-five if she has given birth to at least four living children. If a disability pension, an occupational disability pension, or a retirement pension is granted, child support supplements are granted in specific situations in the amount of 5 percent of the basis of evaluation for each child who has not reached the eighteenth birthday (more if the child is going to school or is unable to work).

Widow's pension. This pension amounts to 60 percent of the retirement pension, the disability pension, or the occupational disability pension to which the insured had a claim or would have had a claim at the time of his death. If a widow remarries, the pension is reduced to 70 percent of the initial sum. If the new marriage is dissolved by death or divorce, the claim to the widow's pension left by the first husband can be reinstated under certain conditions.

Orphan's pension. This is paid to a child who has lost one parent. The amount is 40 percent of the pension due the deceased parent or which would have been due him. If the child has lost both parents, the amount of the orphan's pension is computed at 60 percent.

4. Unemployment Insurance

Unemployment benefits are paid to unemployed persons who are willing and able to work and have been covered by unemployment insurance for a certain period of time. Eligibility is based on the length of time the person was insured. Supplements are provided for family members.

Emergency assistance. This assistance is granted after termination of the claim on unemployment insurance and amounts to at least 75 percent of the unemployment compensation. It similarly provides family supplements.

Women who are receiving emergency assistance are at a disadvantage in comparison with men. This inequity is an exception within Austrian social insurance law.

Family Law

The essential features of Austrian family law have been in effect for more than 150 years and are therefore to a large extent not in accord with contemporary reality. Since 1925 Social Democratic women of Austria have attempted to bring about fundamental reform of this field of law. These efforts were interrupted by National Socialism and the war. A renewed attempt was begun in the 1950s, but so far only two important fields of law have been regulated—illegitimacy and the legal position of marital partners in relation to one another. In addition, a federal law covering the granting of maintenance support was passed. Maintenance support assures support to children whose fathers do not provide for them. These children, who must either be Austrian citizens or stateless, have a claim on the Federation to an advance of the maintenance legally due them. No claim on a maintenance advance exists, however, if the child lives in the same household with the defaulting supporter or if the child is placed in a shelter or with foster parents. Such advances may not exceed 1,897 schillings per month; payments are adjusted annually. The Youth Office having jurisdiction over such matters must collect from persons obligated to provide support the amounts already paid out and reimburse the Fund for the Equalization of Burdens on Families, which supplies the maintenance advance.

Legal Position of the Illegitimate Child
In 1970 the legal status of the illegitimate child and of the child's mother was greatly improved. The most important precepts of the new law are briefly as follows: The child continues to take the maiden name of the mother. In terms of support and care, the illegitimate child is placed in an equitable position in comparison with the legitimate child, using as criteria the life situation of the father, the mother, and the needs of the child. The mother continues to be primarily responsible for the care and training of the child. The father has the right to participate to a limited extent in the training of the child. Full parental rights are still denied the mother, and for this reason official, legal guardianship is in effect upon the birth of an illegitimate child. However, the mother has a legal claim to be appointed guardian of the child if she is considered fit and if she can meet the standards for the care and training of the child. In such an instance, the Youth Office can be appointed special counsel with the main responsibility to determine paternity and to implement the child's claims to support. The right of an illegitimate

child to inherit continues to be limited. Only in the event that the father leaves a widow but no children entitled to the estate does the illegitimate child receive that part of the estate which otherwise, if the widow is alive, would fall to his descendants or to lateral relations of the deceased.

Legal Position of Marital Partners
in Relation to One Another

In 1975 the Parliament passed a law concerning the new legal status of marital partners in relation to one another. The legislation changed the definition of marriage conceived along patriarchal lines to marriage conceived as a partnership. Its most important features are:

The personal rights and duties of marital partners are basically the same. This principle provides the basis for each partner's right to gainful employment and for mutual responsibility in providing support. In pursuit of their mutual interests, the partners must take each other and the well-being of the child into consideration. The wife no longer must unconditionally follow the husband to the place of residence chosen by him. The principle of the shared family name was retained though the engaged couple has the option of deciding to use the woman's maiden name as the family name. Both parties must contribute to their support according to their abilities. Housework and the care and training of children are considered a contribution toward support. If a husband is unable to contribute toward living expenses because of some severe ailment, for example, he has a claim to support by the wife. In conformity with the idea of a partnership, if both husband and wife are employed, both must share in the housework. If only one of the partners is employed, the other must keep house. Finally, the legislation provides for protection against one-sided disposition of the married couple's residence.

Two additional legal areas are now under consideration by Parliament. The government's bill concerning the legal status of the legitimate child is soon to be enacted. The other government-sponsored bill deals with the effects of marriage on financial arrangements and with questions of inheritance and will probably require longer deliberations.

7

THE FEDERAL REPUBLIC OF GERMANY
Friedhelm Neidhardt

FAMILY POLICY IN the Federal Republic of Germany (F.R.G.) appears as an admixture of postwar decisions and current attempts to solve new problems. It is difficult to identify its contours, and it is impossible to understand its tendencies and contradictions, without referring to the historical context.

Postwar Sources of West German Family Policy

Historical Background

Private and public relationships of the family seem to have been determined for many years by the family experiences of people during World War II and in the postwar years. Family sociologists [1] convincingly stressed the fact that in the totalitarian atmosphere of public life in Nazi Germany and the largely anomic state of the economic and administrative structures in the 1940s, the institution of the family and the larger kinship group proved to be the only intact social system for overcoming the ideological pressures and the material problems of daily life. Society regressed to the primitive mechanisms of survival and to the "primordial" basis of its structures, upgrading the family as the most elementary unit.

It seems plausible that these experiences reestablished a traditional kind

DR. FRIEDHELM NEIDHARDT is Director and Professor of Sociology, Sociological Research Institute, University of Cologne, Cologne, Federal Republic of Germany.

[1] Helmut Schelsky, *Wanglungen der deutschen Familie in der Gegenwart* (Dortmund: Ardey, 1953); Gerhard Wurzbacher, *Leitbilder gegenwärtigen deutschen Familienlebens* (Dortmund: Ardey, 1954).

of *Familiensinn* (family consciousness) within the public and that the public too supported some sort of family bias within the newly developing politics of the West German Federal Government after 1949. There was a consensus of all major parties that the Constitution of the F.R.G. should include the explicit norm: "Marriage and family are under the particular protection of the state order."[2] And very soon, in 1953–54, came the institutionalization of a specialized family ministry of the federal government with the formal "task to cooperate in administrative and legislative matters with the competent departments in order to assure the observance of the particular family interests."[3]

Ideological Factors
Within this institutional frame was another factor that decisively influenced the interpretation of the constitutional norm and the implementation of family policy. For the first two decades, the West Germans were governed by Christian Democrats, and up to 1969 the Secretary of the Family of the federal government was selected by this party. Thus, there evolved a rather cohesive ideological background for the practice of family policy, and this background has been determined by the moral philosophy of the Christian churches—both Protestant and, even more, Catholic.

The effects of this circumstance can be summarized thus:[4]

1. The family was viewed as a "natural order,"[5] as a "donation of God"[6]—as a collectivity that in its "essence" is to be absolutely respected and unreservedly stabilized. A relatively restrictive "marriage and family law that protected the continuance and cohesion of the family"[7] was one of the consequences of this paradigm.

2. Because of the "natural" character of the family the state had to avoid direct intervention in the free play of family life processes. Family policy was mainly seen as the attempt to countervail and correct those societal influences that tend to destroy the traditional structures of the family. It

---

[2] Art. 6/I Grundgesetz of the F.R.G.

[3] Jutta Akrami-Göhren, "Die Familienpolitik im Rahmen der Sozialpolitik mit besonderer Berücksichtigung der Vorstellungen und der praktischen Tätigkeit der CDU" (dissertation, University of Bonn, 1974), p. 261.

[4] For a polemical analysis of the Christian Democrats' family policy see Dietrich Haensch, *Repressive Familienpolitik* (Reinbek: Rowohlt, 1969).

[5] See Franz-Josef Wuermeling, *Familie—Gabe und Aufgabe* (Cologne: Luthe, 1963), p. 107. Wuermeling, a Christian Democrat, was the first and long-time Secretary of the Family.

[6] Helmuth Begemann, *Strukturwandel der Familie* (Hamburg: Furche, 1960), chaps. 4, 5, 12.

[7] Wuermeling, *Familie—Gabe und Aufgabe*, p. 167.

was logical, then, that governmental activities, besides affirming the family as a central element of the state order, concentrated on providing direct cash benefits: on the one hand, payments thought to compensate for some of the family costs of child rearing (child allowances), and on the other hand, subventions for building, buying, or renting houses or apartments.

3. Together with the programmatic reduction of governmental intervention in families, private welfare organizations, especially religious ones, were financed and otherwise supported to do social work for families and to provide counseling, socializing, and leisure-time services and facilities. That the government did not aim to control these intermediary "free forces" corresponded to the officially acclaimed "subsidiarity principle" which affirms the primacy of the voluntary (originally religious) agencies over the public.[8]

In sum, in the postwar period of the F.R.G. there developed an explicit family policy that was both highly institutionalized and decentralized and, therefore, rather obscure. For ideological reasons, and supported by recent historical experiences, this family policy explicitly approved of the family in its traditional structures. It restricted itself to activities that were absolutely supportive of these structures.

A family policy of this kind scarcely would have survived until the end of the 1960s if the situation of the family had not appeared to be mainly unproblematic. Marriage rates were extremely high; divorce rates became very low; the birth rate stabilized on a medium level; and the number of illegitimate births dropped constantly until 1966 (see tables 1–3). The indicators of family well-being did not signal disturbances that could stimulate mobilization of a government policy to intervene in the traditional structures of the family system.

The situation changed in the mid-1960s. The reconstruction period of West German society which led to the normalization of public and private life was running out. Problems which remained latent as long as there were objective grounds for the subjective feeling of progress in many aspects of life now became manifest. Obviously, some of these problems concerned the institution of the family, and they stimulated new tendencies in family policy.

Context for Family Policy

Family Indicators
Several new developments can be observed in many fields of West German society since the second half of the 1960s. Illegitimate births as well as

[8] *Ibid.*, p. 103.

Table 1 Divorce Rate, 1950–75

(per 1,000 inhabitants)	
Year	Rate
1950	1.69
1955	0.92
1960	0.88
1965	1.00
1970	1.26
1973	1.46
1974	1.59
1975	1.73

SOURCE: *Wirtschaft und Statistik* (Bonn: Statistisches Bundesant, 1977), No. 2, p. 85.

Table 2 Birth rate, 1950–75

(per 1,000 inhabitants)	
Year	Rate
1950	16.2
1955	15.7
1960	17.4
1965	17.7
1970	13.4
1975	9.7

SOURCE: *Statistisches Jahrbuch 1976 für die Bundesrepublik Deutschland* (Bonn: Statistisches Bundesant, 1976), p. 67.

Table 3 Illegitimate Birth Rate, 1950–75

(per 100 births)	
Year	Rate
1950	9.73
1955	7.86
1960	6.33
1966	4.69
1970	5.46
1975	6.12

SOURCE: *Statistisches Jahrbuch 1976*, p. 67.

divorce rates rose (see tables 1 and 3). At the same time, there emerged, especially among subcultures of students and intellectuals, a commune movement that experimented with a type of private life understood to be an alternative to the conventional forms of family life. Although this movement remained in the minority, it succeeded in catalyzing criticism of the family and upgrading it to a public issue. Finally, the birth rate dropped constantly, and it is now below the so-called "demographic replacement" level (see table 2).

In accordance with social science theories[9] these occurrences were generally interpreted as indicators of family problems centering on the roles of children and wives. In many more or less scientific reports, and in numerous mass media accounts, psychic disturbances, school difficulties, and a wide range of social problems of children were explained as being caused, among other reasons, by psychological elements in family life, especially in the lower classes. On the other hand, the rising movement for emancipation of women publicized the female dilemma as between household and work and added considerably to the denunciation of conventional "repressive" family structures.

Of course, all this cannot be considered to have been enough to wrest governmental politics from their bureaucratic controls. There is, certainly, no automatic relationship between the existence of social problems and political efforts at problem-solving. Especially in those cases where there is an ideological basis for policies, the governmental apparatus does not prove to be very sensitive to outside stimuli. In spite of this, West German family policy has somehow changed since 1969 in the direction of new kinds of problem-solving, at least in its explicit goals. This cannot be explained without considering further factors.

First, there is evidence that family-dependent problems of children and wives have been perceived as affecting some of the hard-core interests of the social system and its political powers, and therefore they were defined as matters of public concern. Most influential seems to have been the fact that the public perceived some connection between socialization problems of the family—above all the chronic undersocialization of lower-class children—and the functioning of the economic system. With alarming concepts like *Bildungskatastrophe* (educational catastrophe), it was stated that the West German system of higher education was greatly underdeveloped in comparison with that of the U.S. and Soviet Russia; that a far too small percentage of the younger generation completed secondary and university education;

---

[9] For the diffusion of scientific results in the field of family affairs the two family reports of the federal government, both prepared, and the latter written, by social scientists and other experts seem to have been rather influential. See *Erster Familienbericht: Bericht über die Lage der Familien in der Bundesrepublik Deutschland* (Bonn: Bundesminister für Jugend, Familie und Gesundheit, 1963); *Zweiter Familienbericht: Familie und Sozialisation—Leistungen und Leistungsgrenzen der Familie hinsichtlich des Erziehungs- und Bildungsprozesses der jungen Generation* (Bonn-Bad Godesberg: Bundesminister für Jugend, Familie und Gesundheit, 1975).

that, therefore, there was large loss of potential talent; and that this must be very disadvantageous for a country which, in a rapidly developing world economy, is dependent on compensating for its lack of natural resources by the production and exportation of know-how.

During recent years, furthermore, for the first time in the postwar history of the F.R.G., there has developed a lively debate about population problems, centering on the effects of a very low birth rate on economic and general welfare. Finally, it can be assumed that there is a growing recognition that the constraints imposed by household and family responsibilities on professionally educated wives and mothers have public costs in addition to private ones. If, for example, only one third of all female physicians actually work in their profession—and this is the case in the F.R.G.—then it is impossible not to think of the wasted investments of time and money that the other two thirds represent. Thus, there are certain politically significant links between familial problems and societal interests. Undoubtedly this relationship stimulated and catalyzed some of the initiatives that mobilized West German family policy in the last few years.

New Programmatic Elements

A second stimulus came from the fact that since 1969 Social Democrats (in coalition with their junior partner, the Free Democrats) have taken over the federal government and its family department. This change of the ruling party permitted and promoted new accents in family policy.

1. Although the Social Democrats accept the constitutional guarantee of special state protection of the family institution,[10] they tend to prefer a more liberal definition of family groups and a less ontological and more functional view of the family's relevance[11] than do the Christian Democrats.

2. In accordance with their equality formula, Social Democrats stress the individual rights of the traditionally subordinate family members, namely, children and wives, and are highly sensitive to family problems caused by the class structure of West German society.

In order to arrive at their political goals, Social Democrats are more inclined to build up public institutions outside the family for the sake of individual family members' interests—even if this should cause a certain loss of traditional family rights and tasks.

[10] In their Godesberg Program of 1959 the Social Democrats postulated: "State and society have to protect, further and strengthen the family."

[11] For details see the party document "Familienpolitik der Sozialdemokratischen Partei Deutschlands" (Bonn-Bad Godesberg, 1972).

Of course, as soon as Social Democrats took over governmental power, such preferences led to some changes from the postwar style of family policy. Even the Christian Democrats, stimulated by the accumulation of the somewhat new family problems referred to above, had previously begun to modify their policy, too. In fact, the earliest and perhaps most interesting document of a new "rational family policy" stems from Mrs. Aenne Brauksiepe, the last Christian Democratic Union (CDU) Secretary of the Family, and was published in 1969, some months before her retirement. Here Mrs. Brauksiepe, warning against an overestimation of the collectivity aspect of the familial institution,[12] urged "the protection of children against the misuse of parental power,"[13] stressed "the important role of preschool education outside the family,"[14] and advocated policy activities in favor of a greater equality of life chances for children. Meanwhile, official party statements of the Christian Democrats acclaimed—with some ambiguities—these principal positions.[15]

Controversies

On the surface, then, there seem to be "astonishing convergences" between the family programs of the main parties.[16] This is especially true when the comparison is made on the basis of abstract party declamations. But recent controversies show that programmatic divergences are still alive when specific governmental decisions need to be taken. So, the 1976 election campaign included bitter polemics on topics in the wider field of family affairs, namely, the new divorce law and new legislation on abortion. It is probably the rather conservative influence of the Catholic church that hinders the Christian Democrats from being as adaptive and flexible as more pragmatically oriented politicians would like the party to be.

In so far as the Catholic church is able to control some parts of the electorate, its influence also affects the Social-Democratic Party (SPD) to some degree. This might be one reason for some differences between the party

---

12 "The family will meet its present requirements only if it enables its members, the wife and children as well as the husband, to develop their individual personalities." Aenne Brauksiepe, "Grundsatzfragen künftiger Familienpolitik," Sonderdruck aus dem Bulletin des Presse- und Informationsamtes der Bundesregierung, No. 41 (1959), p. 13.

13 Ibid., p. 12.   14 Ibid. p. 9.

15 Compare, for example, the Christian Democratic Union, Leitsätze der Familienpolitik (Bonn, 1976).

16 Klaus Wahl, "Familienpolitik in der Bundesrepublik Deutschland," in H. Braun and U. Leitner, eds., Problem Familie—Familienprobleme (Frankfurt and New York: Campus, 1976), p. 183.

line and the government's actual strategy. Obviously, in the eyes of the party dogmatics the SPD ministry moves too cautiously and not "progressively" enough.[17] In fact, it can be argued that the programmatic concepts of the SPD have been translated into family policy measures only to a slight degree. The corrections since 1969 do possess some consistency, but they did not change the *status quo ante* in a fundamental way. The structure of postwar family policy is still dominant.

This is by no means surprising. Aside from the fact that policy-making within a settled system always is—and perhaps should be—some kind of "piecemeal" procedure,[18] the family policy structure of the F.R.G. possesses a particularly high degree of inertia because of immobilities that are built into its institutional arrangements and do not allow great leaps for any of its beneficiaries.

Institutional Bases and Organizational Problems of Family Policy

Government Mechanisms

Without any doubt, there is an explicit family policy in the F.R.G. Since the family is explicitly legitimized by the constitution, it is not happenstance that the government includes a specialized family ministry (unified with a department for youth and, for some years, with a department for health). There are specific party programs for family policy; a 1965 decision of the Bundestag requires the federal government to submit a report on the situation of the family by an expert commission every four years, supplemented by a governmental statement on the problems that the report highlights.

The functioning of family policy is, however, structurally impaired by organizational dilemmas, the most fundamental of which probably is based in the field of family policy itself, namely, the diffuse nature of family affairs. The family as a small living unit is a place where the private consequences of practically the total output of societal institutions and processes are somewhat manifested and must be integrated with some kind of individual life style. Other policy fields refer to specialized institutions and to spe-

---

[17] See for evidence Katharina Focke and Dieter Greese, "Diskussion 'Familienpolitik,'" *Die Neue Gesellschaft*, XXIII (1976), 92–102. Informative in this respect is also a comparison between the party document (SPD, "Familienpolitik der Sozialdemokratischen Partei Deutschlands," Entwurf der Partei-Kommission für Familienpolitik, 1972) and the government's declaration on family policy in *Zweiter Familienbericht*, Part I.

[18] Karl R. Popper, *Das Elend des Historizismus* (Tübingen: Mohr Siebeck, 1965), pp. 47–57.

cific functional processes: defense, economy, agriculture, justice, housing, labor, and so on. They are differentiated according to special functions that constitute their genuine core problems.

Difficulties in Defining Family Policy

Within a government's department structure it is rather easy to define the identity of the organizational units that are related to them. This is not the case with family and family policy. Family policy tends to be as diffuse as its object, the family. In other words, because the family constitutes itself as the private integration of the almost total range of public influences, virtually all family policy problems are genuine problems of other branches of policy.[19] A family ministry, then, can be considered a governmental department for everything—or nothing.

In the F.R.G. the formal responsibility of the family department always came close to the latter pole. The 1975 family report states: "The responsibility for practically all legislative initiatives that are relevant for family policy is outside the family department"—with only one exception, namely, the authority for child allowances.[20]

Certainly, the principle that all relevant policy matters are decided within the cabinet by majority vote insures that the Minister of Family Affairs and his apparatus exert some influence. But it is evident that the family ministry, lacking the prerogative to prepare and propose such decisions in almost any substantial field, is very weak within the give-and-take processes of competing departments. Family policy interests, therefore, do not seem to be very well represented—if they are not precisely parallel with the interests of other fields of policy.

The consequence is that family policy is highly structured by the exigencies of other departments. Schubnell and Borries proved this in their 1973 analysis of governmental family aids. They showed that the bulk of those activities the federal government itself labeled "family policy" was actually motivated and qualified by employment aspects, economic interests, social policy intentions, and other criteria.[21] It is plausible, then, to hypoth-

---

[19] The Secretary of Family, Katharina Focke, touched on this phenomenon with the concept of family policy as a "cross-section task."

[20] *Zweiter Familienbericht.*

[21] Hermann Schubnell and Hans-Joachim Borries, "Hilfen für die Familie. Systematisch-statistische Zusammenstellung" (unpublished paper, Wiesbaden, 1973); Hermann Schubnell and Hans-Joachim Borries, *Materialien zum Zweiten Familienbericht der Bundesregierung* (Munich: Deutsches Jugendinstitut, 1976), p. 12.

esize—as the Family Report Commission did—that the internal consistency of family policy measures must be rather low.[22]

Interest Group Power

I do not think that the structural weakness of family policy manifested in this way is due to the programmatic neglect of family policy affairs by the government and the political parties; the strong family bias, especially of the Christian Democrats, would be a counterargument to this sort of explanation. More convincing seems to be the attempt to correlate the phenomenon with fundamental features of the political mechanism. In parliamentary systems like that of the F.R.G., the output of the political system is certainly heavily influenced by the capability of interests to organize themselves and to generate power by their command over sanctions. In this respect, the structural base for family policy is not very powerful. Of course, there are the churches, but their family interests are limited and, mainly, conservatively defensive, so that they behave like veto groups with the result that they are more apt to immobilize than to activate a "rational family policy." On the other hand, there are family organizations, mainly religious ones, but their membership is very small. Unlike the unions and the numerous economic lobby groups, they scarcely possess the resources to influence the government by threats. Therefore, whenever family policy is confronted with a considerable demand for problem-solving, normally it is dependent on mobilizing or finding similar interests in other departments and then adapting its own interests to the evolving course. This may be called the hitchhiking fate of family policy.

Decentralization of the Family Policy Structure

In West Germany the family policy system is extremely decentralized. On the one hand, due to the constitutional principle of federalism, there is an intricate division of labor among the federal government, the eleven state governments, and the immense numbers of communes. In some branches of housing policy, in practically all fields of education policy (including kindergarten), and in many areas of family-relevant social policies, the federal government is not authoritatively responsible, but—to the degree of its own financial involvement—may make claim only to cooperation and participation. Considering that many if not most state and commune governments are under the control of a competing party, it is clear that the achievement of

---

[22]*Zweiter Familienbericht*, p. 77.

country-wide consensus and coordination is a real problem—ending all too often in keeping things as they are.

Nongovernmental Units of Family Policy

The voluntary welfare agencies constitute a further element within the family policy system, and not a slight one. In some fields, such as preschool education, counseling, parents' education, and family vacation services, these welfare organizations, and especially the church-affiliated ones, are actually dominant. Recently, research ascertained[23] that in the F.R.G. voluntary agencies administer almost 31,000 institutions for children, youth, and families with more than 1.6 million places. They employ more than 200,000 people specialized in these activities.

Of course, there are important functional reasons for delegating the carrying out of social work, with its necessarily personalized service tasks, to intermediary "free forces" of society. They have the advantage of being able to balance bureaucratization and spontaneity much more than do administrative units of the state. Furthermore, they do have the extremely valuable potential to recruit and activate volunteers more easily, thereby bridging the gap between anonymous secondary institutions and informal primary group involvements.[24] On the other hand, it can be dangerous, if the autonomy claim of these organizations hinders cooperation and even clarity. It seems to me that the present situation displays some examples of this. The cost of the current degree of decentralization is obvious in terms of the consistency, mobility, and control of the family policy system.

Central Issues and Main Activities

Definitions of Family Policy

Structural problems of the family policy organizations, of course, do influence the content of family policy. This can be seen on the most fundamental level, namely, the working definition of family policy.

There are, on the theoretical level, some concepts that describe family

---

[23] Frantz-U. Willeke, "Die kollektiven Leistungen der Wohlfahrtsverbände für Kinder, Jugendliche und Familien" (paper for the Wissenschaftliche Beirat of the Family Ministry, Heidelberg, 1976).

[24] Willeke found "that in the 'open social work and health service' of the German Red Cross no less than 75 percent of the 2.3 million hours of employment in 1972 were performed by people on an honorary base." *Ibid.*, p. 13.

policy as a qualified kind of "intervention in the structure and functions of family."[25] Within the actual praxis of policy, there appear, however, implicit versions of a concept that seem to be very loose and imprecise. In their content analysis of governmental documents on "family aids" Schubnell and Borries found that there is no "uniform definition of 'family' and 'family service.' "[26] The government, for example, declares certain general occupational training programs, health services, pension payments, housing aids, and so forth, as elements of its family policy, although the individual claim on it is not bound to the family status of the entitled persons or is only peripherally so bound. Obviously, the fact that these and many other governmental activities for the most part favor persons who are family members is taken as a sufficient criterion for defining such activities as part of a family policy. When about 85 percent of all people in the F.R.G. actually play family roles, this definitional procedure, to be sure, produces an activity profile of West German family policy that looks very impressive and that serves the public relations interests of the government very well. But it does not indicate that the working definition of family policy is sufficiently clear-cut.

Contrary to this procedure and for the sake of the following analysis, it seems necessary to confine family policy to those activities that are determined by specific family criteria. Family policy, as a field of activity, then, could be defined as the totality of all measures which—in an objectively discernible way—refer to the family as a family and to family members as family members. This, however, is not enough to construct a conceptual scheme that produces systematic family policy analysis.

Activity Dimensions of Family Policy

The existence of family policy itself is dependent on some goal assumptions, explicit or not. It rests on the supposition that it is desirable to structure the private zones of individual lives into family units which, therefore, have to be supported. Accordingly, family policy is bound to make decisions on three activity levels, at least: (1) Family policy must define its specific goal unit, called family. (2) Family policy must deliver services for the family

[25] In several publications Wingen developed the most comprehensive attempts to define family policy and its possible instruments. See Max Wingen, *Familienpolitik. Ziele, Wege, Wirkungen* (Paderborn: Bonifacius, 1965); Max Wingen, *Familienpolitik—Konzession oder Konzeption?* (Cologne: Bachem, 1966); Max Wingen, "Familienpolitik," in Siegfried Keil, ed., *Familien- und Lebensberatung—ein Handbuch* (Berlin: Kreutz, 1975), p. 352.

[26] Schubnell and Borries, *Materialien zum Zweiten Familienbericht der Bundesregierung*, p. 8.

system (family system policy). (3) Family policy must make sure that family systems really prove functional for the private lives of their members; and eventually it has to support those members who are in danger of being repressed by the internal dynamics of family life (family members policy). Along such lines our analysis identifies, describes, and comments on the most important topics and activities in West German family policy.[27]

Working Definitions of the Family

First, there is a dilemma linked with any kind of family policy: the more family policy actually supports the family, the more it will discriminate against private groupings which are similar to families in their recruitment and their problems but which are not labeled as families. Traditionally, children who do not live with their own legally married parents have been the primary victims of rigidly narrowed family concepts. In two respects, the West German government has continued to widen its working definition of the family unit to the point where formal discrimination has ceased to exist. On the one hand, in 1976, the Parliament passed a law removing the few remaining reservations which distinguished adopted children and their families from "normal" ones. On the other hand, by legislation passed in 1969, the family status of single parents and their children—in 1975, 7.2 percent of all family groups—was formally upgraded so that they have exactly the same claims on governmental support as others.

In this way, the government broadened its object definition further. Some limitations, however, still remained. For example, while a single mother and her child are perceived as being a family, a man who lives with them without being husband and father in the legal sense is not acknowledged as being a family member—with the consequence that privileges resulting from legalization by marriage are not granted: for example, certain tax reductions and all allowances, which vary with the number of family members. In this respect, the SPD secretaries deviate from SPD party pref-

---

[27] The most complete recent governmental description of the official family policy can be found in Bundesministerium für Jugend, Familie und Gesundheit, "Stellungnahme der Bundesregierung zum Bericht der Sachverständigenkommission," in *Zweiter Familienbericht*, pp. v-xxvii. Whether the governmental statement of 1975 can be judged as an adequate response to the family report of the experts' commission (*Zweiter Familienbericht*) is instructively analyzed in Franz Xaver Kaufmann, "Zum Verhältnis von Soziologie und Politik—Das Beispiel Zweiter Familienbericht," in *Zeitschrift für Soziologie*, V (1976), 301–6.

erences.[28] In the party paper on family politics it is proposed that families be defined in the widest sense as "living units of one or more adults with children which are expected to last."[29]

It seems to me that ideological reservations aside, administrative reasons provide the main arguments against such a proposal. The point is that the exigencies of all large-scale bureaucracies demand that they work with formally defined entities. A grouping whose fundamental relationships, those between men and women and adults and children, are not somehow legalized, and thereby stably defined, is hardly manageable within formalized administrative procedures.

Family-System Policy

By widening the definition it became possible to support the family unit with fewer discriminatory effects. The new government, however, did not support the family without further corrections, stressing some new aspects and, more implicitly and only very slightly, neglecting some old ones. Concerning those activities directed to the family unit as a uniform collectivity, the new government was not impressive in extending its family policy activities or expanding relevant public expenditures. It was, however, very careful not to frustrate vested interests. On the one hand, the "classical" instruments of West German family policy were not given up: family allowances, financial assistance for housing, supports for institutions that counsel and educate parents or offer family vacations. In fact, such activities still absorb an overwhelming portion of all the money the government spends within the field of family policy. On the other hand, it would seem that the government somewhat reduces the relative share of those expenses, compared with the output in other branches of governmental activities.[30]

Obviously, the government concentrated on expanding the total extent less than it did on redefining the quality of its family system service. In this qualitative respect, a certain trend is observable. There are indications of governmental attempts to reduce some of the middle- and upper-class bias of

[28] Focke and Greese, "Diskussion Familienpolitik," p. 92.

[29] SPD, "Familienpolitik der Sozialdemokratischen Partei Deutschlands," p. 7.

[30] The effects of this can be seen in the fact that, for example, the 1975 rise of the *Kindergeld* within the system of *Familienlastenausgleich* was, by far, not enough to compensate for the increase in costs that the families were experiencing. The present rates are, then, not at all above the average when compared internationally. For the first child the family receives DM 50; for the second, DM 70; for the third and each further one, DM 120. [As of April 1, 1977, the exchange rate was: DM 1 = $0.42.]

the former family policy system. This is most definitely the case with respect to the regulation of those payments intended to compensate for some of the family costs of child rearing (child allowances). The former system partly worked with relative reductions of taxes. With the progressive tax-rate system, the poorest families did not gain anything, because they did not pay taxes, but the rich gained a great deal. This anomaly was completely abolished by instituting payments of equal amounts. Another example indicating a similar tendency, but with fewer effects, can be discovered in governmental housing policy. Here, the early Christian Democratic strategy favored families in the social strata that expected to acquire their own homes.[31] Meanwhile, starting around 1969,[32] the governmental orientation shifted somewhat to the solution of housing problems of the poorer classes. New efforts that favor certain categories of "problem families" (foreign workers and other marginal groups) point in the same direction without being significantly effective thus far.

"Family Members" Policy

The main line of substantially new strategies of problem-solving, however, was developed in regard to "family members" policy, understood as the totality of actions geared to family members in order to balance their individual rights and duties. The government repeatedly pointed out that the Constitution of the F.R.G. not only guaranteed the specific protection of the family but also created individual rights,[33] and that therefore the government is obliged to balance the one against the other.

This task, evidently, is not an easy one because there is no one-to-one correlation between the family's and the family members' well-being. Social science research has pointed out the possibility that under certain conditions the equilibrium of the collective family system can be reached only by severely repressing one or more of its individual members.[34] This, it seems,

---

[31] Wuermeling, *Familie—Gabe und Aufgabe*, pp. 150, 156.

[32] Brauksiepe, *Grundsatzfragen künftiger Familienpolitik*, p. 21.

[33] Bundesministerium für Jugend, Familie und Gesundheit, "Stellungnahme der Bundesregierung zum Bericht der Sachverständigenkommission," p. vi.

[34] For example, see several articles in Gregory Bateson *et al.*, *Schizophrenie und Familie* (Frankfurt: Suhrkamp, 1969); Horst Eberhard Richter, *Patient Familie. Entstehung, Struktur und Therapie von Konflikten in Ehe und Familie* (Reinbek: Rowohlt, 1970). A sociological interpretation is given by Friedhelm Neidhardt, *Die Familie in Deutschland. Gesellschaftliche Stellung, Struktur und Funktion* (4th ed.; Opladen: Leske, 1975).

is a forceful argument for supplementing a system perspective by a member perspective within family policy.

The government worked on family membership problems in two ways. On the one hand, two legislative acts redefined and regularized the possibilities of dissolving a family unit whose personal difficulties have reached a point where the conflicts between its members have destroyed the probability of normalizing family life. First, new divorce regulations somewhat liberalized the right of husbands and wives to leave a family they themselves define as definitely broken. Second, the government passed a law intended to improve the protection of children; one of the consequences was that guardianship courts got more power to take children out of a family if their well-being was in danger because of the family situation.

Family Policy Goals
The latter activities can only be measures of ultimate intervention. More important must be the efforts to preserve families by strengthening their capacities to balance the various members' interests and wants by themselves. In order to obtain such goal, the government, on the other hand, did something to overcome the traditionally patriarchal order of family life by redefining the normative and actual roles, especially of wives and children.[35] All parties explicitly consent to a principally egalitarian concept of family life,[36] and they, too, unanimously agree to the rule that "the well-being of the child is the primary goal of family policy."[37] This basic consensus, of course, does not exclude bitter polemics between the parties whenever the consequences of violating these principles must be faced.

On the normative side of the problem the government worked with legislative initiatives that completed the legal emancipation of wives[38] and that are intended to upgrade the formal family status of children. However, only one phase of actual situations can be influenced by modifying legal conditions. A more difficult task is to arrange socioeconomic factors so that they really support the normatively prescribed ones. Here, the problems

---

[35] Husbands whose roles are necessarily involved are rarely mentioned. They form a residual category within present West German family policy.

[36] CDU, *Leitsätze der Familienpolitik,* p. 6; SPD, "Familienpolitik der Sozialdemokratischen Partei Deutschlands," p. 10.

[37] CDU, *Leitsätze der Familienpolitik,* p. 8.

[38] "Erstes Gesetz zur Reform des Ehe- und Familienrechts," effective from April 8, 1976.

largely remain unresolved. They are manifesting themselves mainly in the mother-child relationship.

The present problems of the mother-child relationship seem to be determined by the facts: (1) the child is considered to be heavily dependent on diffuse relationships, mainly with the mother; (2) a significant and perhaps rising percentage of mothers obviously perceive the maternal role as not sufficiently serving their own identity demands; (3) the compatibility of the mother role and the out-of-house activity roles is poor. On all these levels policy interventions, theoretically, can take place. What is done in the F.R.G.?

On one level, it can be thought that the mother could be relieved of her primary responsibilities to her children by transferring them, for example, to the father or to institutions outside the family. In the F.R.G., however, the father is not seriously expected to take the mother role, nor is any outside institution. Even in cases where institutional support is granted the mother is still considered the central reference person for her child.

On a second level, a strategy for upgrading the mother role might be a reasonable approach to solving the problem. But the possibilities are structurally limited. An actual loss of relevance of the mother role resulted from central features of a universal modernization process and was determined by the development of social differentiations that transferred a number of family functions to outside institutions. This process cannot be significantly reversed. Yet, it seems to be relevant to differentiate the resulting mother-role problem in relation to a specific time period. In the first years of a baby's life the mother probably is meaningfully employed as mother. The problems arise when the child inevitably is integrated into the social life outside the household and less and less frequently asks for its mother.[39] The mother-role problem, then, usually turns out to be a career problem. This role is one of the very few in our society whose fate is determined by some kind of negative seniority principle, namely, by a progressive loss of status and functions. Considering this time criterion, it might be necessary to differentiate concepts of problem-solving according to certain phases. This, in fact, is a procedure acknowledged and practiced by West German family policy. All parties agree that mothers with children under the age of three should be handled differently from mothers with children above this age. All

---

[39] Research done by the Family Report Commission proved a very high correlation between dissatisfaction of unemployed mothers and the age of their children: the older the children, the less satisfied are mothers with their family role. (*Zweiter Familienbericht,* p. 116).

parties, moreover, propose to upgrade the mother role in the first phase by giving the mother an income for concentrating on, and "working" with, her child.[40] The government, however, has responded vaguely and has not announced any future initiatives—in part because of the magnitude of the financial consequences.[41]

There is a third level of intervention: efforts to enlarge the compatibility of inside and outside family roles by some integrating measures. This is discussed mainly with reference to the relationship of mother roles and out-of-family working roles of women. Concerning the conditions of work, the government evolved a position in favor of an expanding supply of part-time jobs—without being able to do very much to realize its objective. The government also points to the existence of the fourteen weeks of paid maternity leave and the further five days of paid leave in case of a child's illness; but it does not plan to expand those periods, which do not seem impressive when compared with international standards.[42]

Public efforts in support of the family obligations of employed women must also be differentiated according to the time criterion. Opportunities for institutional care for children above the age of three have been significantly enlarged within recent years. In 1970 only one third of all children aged three to five found places in kindergartens; in 1976, the number was almost 70 percent, and further growth is planned.[43] On the other hand, the facilities for mothers with children under the age of three are few. In 1972 there were no more than 600 day care centers, with about 19,000 places.[44] Less than one percent of all children in the lowest age group could have formal daytime care outside their own family.

Of course, the federal government is not responsible for these conditions, because day care centers are the responsibility of the states and the

[40] CDU, *Leitsätze der Familienpolitik,* p. 8; SPD, "Familienpolitik der Sozialdemokratischen Partei Deutschlands," p. 4.

[41] Bundesministerium für Jugend, Familie und Gesundheit, "Stellungsnahme der Bundesregierung zum Bericht der Sachverständigenkommission," pp. x, xvii.

[42] Sheila B. Kamerman and Alfred J. Kahn, "European Family Policy Currents: the Question of Families with Very Young Children" (working paper, Columbia University School of Social Work, New York, 1976), p. 17.

[43] The rising percentage of children going into the kindergarten is, however, not a valid indicator of public efforts. The percentage rise is, to be sure, in large measure due to the fact that, dependent on the falling birth rates, the absolute number of children between three and six in 1976 was significantly lower than in 1970. *Bundesregierung,* p. xix.

[44] *Zweiter Familienbericht,* p. 123.

communes. The central government is able only to initiate demonstration projects, programs to be tested because of their innovative quality. On the basis of this formal prerogative, the central government initiated the family day care mothers experiment (*Tagesmütter*) for some children of working mothers.[45] Although this project includes fewer than 200 children, the public has been so critical that it appears to be highly improbable that a formal family day care program ever will become institutionalized on a broader scale in the F.R.G.

Table 4 Daytime Care for Children under the Age of Three of Working Mothers, 1975

Source of Care	Percent of Children
Mother	17.6
Grandparents	45.6
Other relatives	6.6
Older sisters or brothers	2.5
Friends, neighbors	4.4
Specialized persons	7.2
Other families	6.1
Various institutional arrangements	12.6

SOURCE: R. Pettinger, "Erwerbstätigkeit von Müttern mit Kindern in den ersten Lebensjahren," p. 6.

It is clear that mother-and-child problems largely remain unresolved, especially for families with children under the age of three. For these age groups the state heavily relies on the primarily private arrangements made by the family. Such arrangements have been made by more than 30 percent of mothers with children under the age of three who work outside their own households (see table 4).[46]

In this respect, grandparents play a rather active role in the F.R.G., obviously much more so than in other countries.[47] In almost half of all cases of working mothers with children under the age of three, grandparents are giving daytime care. Nevertheless, it is not known, and scarcely can be controlled, to what extent private arrangements really function when they do

[45] Deutsches Jugendinstitut, "Zwischenbericht über die wissenschaftliche Begleitung des Modellprojekts 'Tagesmütter' " (paper, Munich: DJI, 1976).

[46] Rudolph Pettinger, "Erwerbstätigkeit von Müttern mit Kindern in den ersten Lebensjahren" (paper prepared for the Wissenschaftliche Beirat of the Bundesministerium für Jugend, Familie und Gesundheit, Munich, 1976).

[47] Compare Canadian data in Andrew Armitage, "Canada," in this volume.

exist. In addition, there remain all those instances where private arrangements cannot be made.[48]

Evaluations, Instruments, and Research

Evaluations

It is difficult to estimate the precise effects of certain circumstances on the whole range of family life.[49] In part, the difficulties of evaluating family-relevant topics are due to the particular attributes of the object itself. The family appears to be a diffuse object with broad and varied dimensions and somewhat cross-cutting lines of individual interests. This means that any factor exerts a plurality of effects with possibly divergent loads and with rather complex feedback processes. Therefore, family policy interventions in family life are difficult to assess.

Additional problems, however, arise from the fact that in the F.R.G. the family policy system appears to be relatively obscure, so that it is even difficult to identify the exact nature of policy-induced factors which operate on the microsocial level. Because of the high degree of decentralization and the rather low degree of coordination, as we have seen, there are many possibilities that programs will conflict and that there will be divergent interpretations of any one program in the policy system. For example, the Family Report Commission pointed out that on certain levels of income distribution the accumulation of uncoordinated financial aids can lead—in extreme cases—to a situation where recipient families ultimately possess more income than do higher-earning families of otherwise equal status,[50] an outcome certainly not intended by the government. There also are examples in the fields of family counseling and parents' education: the almost anomic market transmits more or less contradictory concepts of proper family life and family role behavior, with the probable effect that families subject to these stimuli become highly uncertain about what to do.

Instruments

During recent years the government itself stimulated and often financed evaluation studies concerned with this problem area. These studies, how-

---

[48] The Family Report Commission empirically proved that about 20 percent of the mothers who do not work outside their household wish to do so. (*Zweiter Familienbericht*, p. 124).

[49] Perhaps this is the main reason for the relatively high degree of ideologization within the field of family policy.

[50] *Zweiter Familienbericht*, p. 77.

ever, concentrated less on system effects of family policy than on the effects of single instruments. Here some first results can be reported.

Within a certain range of family problems, any government has the alternatives of working on problem-solving either by offering universal public services and facilities or by giving direct cash benefits ·to families with problems. The latter approach has the advantage of a relatively high probability of reaching those categories of families that should be supported. The difficulty is that the actual use of the money provided these families hardly can be controlled, and therefore it is uncertain whether problem solutions really are attained. It is, for example, questionable whether families use housing assistance for housing or child allowances for children. Current research by F. Kaufman et al. probably will clarify these matters.[51]

Research

On the other hand, the dilemma of a universal service strategy seems to be that, in part, it may serve a selected clientele. As research demonstrates,[52] child care, preschool, counseling, and related services and similar facilities barely reach even those families that the programs intend to reach because of the severity of their manifest problems. The government, therefore, is supporting some experiments which attempt to test new and better forms of delivering public services in this field.

Another question concerns the quality of efforts that these institutions exert when they are used. In this respect, the government is supporting research by Kurt Lüscher[53] that intends to assess the so-called "Parents' Letters," a special kind of newsletter distributed periodically to all parents during the early years of parenthood.

In general, there is a growing awareness that a family policy declared to be "rational" must incorporate scientific evaluation research.[54] The federal government, therefore, has financed a special research institution, the Deutsches Jugendinstitut in Munich. It places and supports an increasing

[51] Alois Herlt, Franz Xaver Kaufmann, and Klaus-Peter Strohmeier, "Öffentliche Sozialleistungen und familiale Sozialisation. Zur Analyse der Wirkungen familienpolitischer Massnahmen," in Klaus Hurrelmann, ed., *Sozialisation und Lebenslauf* (Reinbek: Rowohlt, 1976), pp. 243–59.

[52] Franz Pöggeler, ed., *Wirklichkeit und Wirksamkeit der Elternbildung* (Munich: Deutsches Jugendinstitut, 1976), Klaus Wahl, *Familienbildung und -beratung in der Bundesrepublik Deutschland* (Stuttgart: Kohlhammer, 1973).

[53] Kurt Lüscher, "Das Sozialisationswissen junger Eltern" (unpublished paper, Constance, 1976).

[54] Hans Ulrich Derlien, *Die Erfolgskontrolle staatlicher Planung* (Baden-Baden: Nomas, 1976).

number of projects in other institutes; it has activated a scientific advisory board of some twenty experts that tries to give some advice on family policy matters; and it constantly communicates with the expert commission which—every four years—submits a family report to the federal government and to Parliament.

Of course, it is an unsettled question as to which policy functions science actually can exercise. The specific rationality of science, naturally, is not identical with the specific rationality of the policy subsystem, and communication between the two is full of sheer "noise."[55] It is possible, however, that the external pressures on both sides will stimulate communication and improve it. This is somewhat under way currently in the Federal Republic of Germany.

[55] Hannes Friedrich, *Staatliche Verwaltung und Wissenschaft* (Frankfurt: Europäische Verlagsanstalt, 1970); Friedhelm Neidhardt, "Sozialisationsforschung und Politikberatung," in Friedhelm Neidhardt, ed., *Frühkindliche Sozialisation* (Stuttgart: Enke, 1975), pp. 1–6; Friedhelm Neidhardt, "Systemtheoretische Analysen zur Sozialisationsfähigkeit der Familie," in Friedhelm Neidhardt, ed., *Frühkindliche Sozialisation*, pp. 162–87; Max Wingen, "Bedingungen und Probleme sozialwissenschaftlicher Familienpolitikberatung," in Christian v. Ferber and Franz Xaver Kaufmann, eds., *Soziologie und Sozialpolitik, Sonderheft 19 der Kölner Zeitschrift für Soziologie und Sozialpsychologie* (Opladen: Westdeutscher Verlag, 1977), pp. 629–49.

POLAND

Magdalena Sokołowska

THE FAMILY IS broadly defined in Poland today. The term is applied to one-parent families, including those with children out of wedlock, and also to childless couples. Family allowances are paid for all adopted children and for foster children as well. The term "household" is usually used for statistical and social-political purposes. The terms "household" and "family" are often used interchangeably. In 1976 one-person households amounted to 16.0 percent of all households, while families constituted 98.4 percent of households composed of more than one person.[1]

Perspectives on the family are to be found in the important legal provisions. In the constitution of 1952, Article 67 reads: "1. Marriage and family are under the care and protection of the Polish Peoples Republic. Special state care is supplied to large families. 2. Birth outside wedlock does not limit the rights of the child."

In the new constitution (1976) Article 67 is considerably extended. The following sentences were added:

> 3. It is the parental responsibility to rear children to be righteous and aware of their obligations as citizens of the Polish Peoples Republic. 4. The Polish Peoples Republic assures realization of support rights and obligations. 5. With concern for family well-being, the Polish Peoples Republic with the participation of the citizens supports construction of different forms of flats, especially cooperatives, and establishes rational distribution according to existing resources.

DR. MAGDALENA SOKOŁOWSKA is Professor, Institute of Sociology and Philosophy, Polish Academy of Sciences, Warsaw, Poland. The author is indebted to Dr. Irena Reszke for her collaboration.

[1] Census, 1970.

In 1976 the Parliament approved expansion of the family and child care code. This was the fourth revision of the basic principles of family law in the Polish Peoples Republic. The main points of the third enactment adopted in 1965 were: (1) liberation of family relations from the domination of irrelevant property rights; (2) equal rights of marital partners and all children; (3) the child's welfare as the decisive premise for most solutions of family conflicts.

The amendment was proposed, as one of the deputies stated, "for the sake of the family and its stability, for children who need increased care, for more efficient solutions of the care, support, property, and housing issues." He referred to the social policy of the Polish United Workers Party, which stresses the role of the family and the social position of the woman as mother, and he observed profound interrelations between the form of the family and its functioning on the one hand, and the social life of our country and personal feelings of individual happiness on the other.

General principles of the previous family code have been retained, but some topics are further elaborated and/or expanded, such as foster care (the foster family), so-called "full adoption," sharing a flat during the divorce trial and afterward; and a particularly careful analysis was made of any divorce when children were involved. The postulate of equal rights and responsibilities of marital partners is fully respected in the family code. In Poland equality of the sexes in family law has already been achieved.[2]

The child's well-being and its correct socialization are among the most important objectives and standards in developing family policy. The child's well-being is generally identified with that of the mother. Possible differences of interests or conflict of interests between mother and child are not taken into consideration. On the other hand, a possible conflict of interests between marital partners is recognized. Both of them are obliged to care for the children and to participate in household chores. This responsibility applies, at least theoretically, to husbands and wives equally, especially if both are breadwinners. Avoidance of this obligation might be considered by a court to be a reason for divorce with a statement indicating the liability of the negligent party.

In the case of conflict of interest between mother and child on the one hand and father on the other it is mother and child who are taken care of by the legal regulations. This is reflected in the support law. Also in the crimi-

[2] Equal rights of women are also respected and implemented in citizens' rights, in civil rights, and in the law that regulates inheritance.

nal law sanctions of imprisonment and custody are provided for those who persistently decline to pay support—men more often than women.

The concepts of family policy also can be found in the speeches of the political leaders. Excerpts from two speeches by the First Secretary of the Polish United Workers Party are quoted:

> In our whole social policy we pay great attention to strengthening family ties, to improvement of mother and child care, to creation of the best possible conditions for personal development of children and youth. This corresponds with the social needs, with the development of our nation, with the general expectations in our country.[3]

> Family fulfills and will fulfill the irreplaceable function in the formation of the character of man. There is no socialist society without a stable, strong and spiritually healthy family. We disregard theories of the alleged inevitable crisis of family ties flourishing on the capitalist ground. The people's state—we ascertain it explicitly—will strengthen, support and care for the Polish family. It is because such policy satisfies the most vital interests of our nation.[4]

Emergence of the Concepts of Social Policy and Family Policy

The concepts of social policy and social planning entered the official vocabulary in Poland after December, 1970. Previously, "policy" was almost synonymous with economic policy and "planning" with economic planning. Social problems were believed to be negative consequences of the capitalist system in Poland until World War II and of the war itself. It was assumed that they would gradually disappear, somehow automatically, under the new system.

A fundamental turning point came in 1971. It was described by a well-known Polish sociologist:

> The events of the end of 1970, the cause of which was attributed by the party to improper economic and social policy, effected an essential change in this sphere. The plenary session of the Polish United Workers Party Central Committee at the end of December 1970 and beginning of January 1971 advanced the postulate of changing that policy and basing it on rational foundations.[5]

[3] At the seventh convention of the Polish United Workers Party.

[4] To the Polish women, March, 1975.

[5] Jan Szczepański, "The Political Test of Social Sciences," in A. Podgórecki, ed., *Utilization of the Social Sciences* (Wrocław: Ossolineum, 1973), pp. 19–28.

These "rational foundations" had to correspond with the current situation. In 1945, Poland changed its political, economic, and social order and within three decades has been transformed into a modern, industrial state. The old philosophy aimed at helping "the poor" was practically useless; but this kind of social intervention had long traditions in prewar Poland. Moreover, there was an orientation directed toward remedy of the acute problems and breakdowns of particular people. Obviously, such things are not limited to "the poor." However, they involve a specific group of people who need help for special reasons and under special circumstances. The nature of such problems changed over time, and it is still changing, but the idea remains that social policy means action to provide help for individuals (and, more recently, also families) in trouble. Countless programs were (and are) at work in this area, and are still expanding.

However, this type of social intervention had also some negative consequences for the society generally. For instance, industry used to include working mothers in a specific group of people in trouble (and troublesome). Maternity and child rearing were assumed to be the purely individual problems of female employees and a burden for industry. The phrase "troublesome worker" has appeared in relation to working women.

It was a fundamental change in this approach which characterized the huge program created in the early 1970s and gradually implemented step by step. The emerging concept of social policy has been directed to the whole society, to average people under ordinary circumstances. In the official declarations social policy is called "the instrument for realizing principles of social justice and equalizing chances and opportunities." It encompasses, among others, social security, employment policy, health policy, housing policy, and so forth.

The concept of family policy emerged simultaneously. The family was the logical alternative to the previous individualistic approach. Therefore, the social policy became "saturated" with family content. There is no clearcut, unequivocal definition of family policy, and it can hardly be delineated from all the policies mentioned above as well as from several others. Frequently the concept of social policy is used interchangeably with the concept of family policy.

There are two idioms often used in the popular formulations: "to strengthen the family" and "help to the family." Thus the trade unions pointed in their platform of December, 1976, to actions which are directed toward strengthening the family, creating ever better living and child rearing conditions. The participation of trade unions in the development and implementation of the social program of strengthening the family and in the comprehensive services for it is an everyday responsibility for us. One should spread the idealistic-moral principles which promote the integration of family life, raise the feeling of responsibility of family members for its unity and the life success of all its members.

Consequently, the following goals are specified: concern for the young mother and her child rearing, effective help to young families (especially in the area of housing); development of housing projects; development and activation of the social-educational life in the housing estates; improvement of the cultural, educational, and health institutions as well as of trade, services, and transportation.

The concept of "help to the family" was accentuated in the speech of the head of the League of Women at the session devoted to "the definition of the League of Women's obligations related to strengthening the family's educational function" in November, 1976. The following dimensions of activities were specified:

1. The preferred economic dimension: social achievements of the working people including a wide scope of benefits for the woman-mother, the development of care and educational institutions, that of housing, supply,[6] and services.[7] This kind of help to the family, its rising standards, making the household chores easier, the chance to take personal care of the child while the continuity of employment is preserved, more time for leisure and culture —contributes to the higher level of family functioning, directs its orientation toward the nonmaterial sphere of life and enriches its interests.

2. The second dimension of help to family strengthening, of the activities aimed at its stability and correct functioning, is the improvement of law, of its coordination with family life, development of counseling, and diffusion of the society's legal culture.

3. The third dimension consists of the broad action of the social institutions, that of the educational authorities and mass media related to broadening parental pedagogic knowledge.

4. The next sphere of activities on behalf of family strengthening, including its educational function, is . . . the rise of demand for the correct attitude in the family unit and responsibility for rearing children—that of a party member, a worker, an activist.

5. And finally is the dimension of action which prevents the impact of a demoralized family by means of pulling out the child and undertaking to develop substitute forms of rearing.

[6] Of stores in material goods, food, etc.

[7] Laundries, for instance.

It seems to me that in Poland the family content in social policy occupies relatively more space than in several other countries. The Polish historical experience must be at least partly responsible for this phenomenon,
which may facilitate understanding of the present Polish situation.

For more than 120 years, from the end of the eighteenth century until
1918, Poland did not exist on the map of Europe, and what had once been
Poland fell under three different political and economic systems: Russia,
Austria, and Prussia.[8] For many years there were no independent political
institutions or Polish schools, and the Polish language was banned for some
time, even from the church. During this period the family remained the main
national institution and the "fortress" of the national spirit. The cultural
heritage, preserved in families, maintained the unity of the divided nation in
the absence of schools and cultural institutions. Oppression and hostility
toward the oppressors made for a strong family bond. A family protected its
members against the outer world and assumed some of the functions that in
the free countries were performed by other institutions. Educating youth in
their native language, history, and literature was felt to be a responsibility of
the household, not only among the nobility, but among the working class
and the peasants as well.

Such an overgrowth of the family functions was caused by the peculiar
political condition of the country. By the twentieth century it had become an
anachronism, incompatible with the trend of evolution in other European
countries. It came to an end after World War I, when Poland again became
independent.

During the Nazi occupation in 1939–45 the family household again
started to fulfill multiple functions, and the family was again the most important national institution. Centers of political and military underground organizations were located in private homes. Cultural life and the widespread
unofficial educational system, including high schools, were continued in
private homes as well.

After 1945, especially during the early 1950s, during the rapid industrialization of the country, the notion of family was suppressed. Mass media
propagated the model of a citizen—a member of the collective working
team. It was industry, the working place, which deserved public attention.
The family context of human life emerged in mass media only in the 1960s,
and it has occupied ever more space since then. Nowadays it is the family

---

[8] The following historical overview is taken from Magdalena Sokołowska, "Poland: Women's
Experience under Socialism," in Janet Zollinger Giele and Audrey Chapman Smock, eds.,
Women—Roles and Status in Eight Countries (New York: John Wiley, 1977), pp. 349–50.

("the panacea for everything," as some sociologists used to call it) which has replaced the working team of the 1950s. This attitude seems to express a comprehensible, perhaps temporary, societal reaction to the previous years. Programs directed to the family meet a warm response from the population. It is the family and its needs which became the pivotal point for social planning and important economic decisions.

Family Policy as Women's Policy

Two family members are clearly preferred by family policy: the woman and the child. Each of them is differently addressed: whereas the child is approached *through* the mother, as explicitly or implicitly dependent on her, the woman is an independent, manifest object of the government's policy on behalf of the family unit. Family policy in Poland is inseparable from women policy. The full and widely used definition of family policy is "women and family policy." It is true that women policy is also one of the crucial components of family policy in several other countries. However, some national peculiarities are responsible for this special Polish emphasis. It is the historical and cultural heritage which undoubtedly is one of the most important factors.[9]

The Historical and Cultural Heritage
Women's high position in the family is one of the characteristic features of the Polish national culture. However, the family and the informal social circles were in the past the only areas of women's activity. Conditions of life under the partition of Poland (1795–1918) militated against development of an inner-family democracy. Owing to the preponderance of the agricultural population, the patriarchal family was the dominant form of family life. The members of the worker's family enjoyed more individual rights, but here too reigned a strict differentiation of family roles based on sex. The wife-mother occupied a high position in the household, to such an extent that there was frequent reference to a "matriarchy," and during periods of unemployment she became the only breadwinner. But the matriarchy was limited to home, divorced from contact with the world, which was totally the domain of the male. Women were relatively most emancipated in families of the intelligentsia where changes in the pattern of life were visible.

[9] Magdalena Sokołowska, "The Woman Image in the Awareness of Contemporary Polish Society," *Polish Sociological Bulletin*, XXXV, No. 3 (1976), 41–50.

Between the two world wars about 6 percent of the population belonged to the intelligentsia. The most numerous class was the peasantry. There was never an organized feminist movement in Poland.

The Polish population is more than 90 percent Roman Catholic. The powerful Roman Catholic church had a very strong impact on the nation's life through 1,000 years of Poland's history. The Roman Catholic church is the irreconcilable advocate of social life based on the strict separation of the sexes, with the woman's role severely limited to the family and home, and the man assigned to the occupational and political spheres of the wider world. While all religions share this attitude toward women, the Roman Catholic church seems to be the most conservative in this respect.

In Poland, "sexist" attitudes are an ingredient of the cultural tradition and heritage. Gallantry, "cavalier" manners and behavior, and romantic chivalry are almost basic features of the traditional Polish male personality. Until World War II this was characteristic behavior only in the upper classes. After the war it became a widespread pattern in all classes and strata. The ideal woman in Poland has characteristics which traditionally prevailed in the peasantry and the working class. Polish men in leading positions still admire the image of a wise woman ("female wisdom"): brave, hard-working, economical, self-denying, and devoted; guardian angel of children, the aged, and the sick in the family; ruler of pots, pans, and washtub; confidante of man's troubles, his life companion. It is certainly difficult for them to accept a different image: not so much that a woman should have education and a washing machine instead of a washtub, but that she be a partner in family, professional, social, and political life instead of a "life companion."

There are now, in all social strata, some generally accepted norms regulating male-female relations and behavior which are based on these deeply rooted traditions. The male plays the role of a "cavalier." For instance, he kisses the woman's hand at home, at the workplace, at the professional meeting, as an expression of welcome, farewell, sorrow, gratitude, and so on. The political leaders also observe this custom. In addition, a man is expected to bring flowers on any number of occasions. Perhaps this is the reason for the nationwide warm acceptance of International Woman's Day on March 8. It became a "flower day," swamped with flowers given by men to "their" women: wives, sisters, friends, supervisors, subordinates, and so on. Women respond to this chivalry by dressing, making up, and behaving in a "feminine" way.

It may be clearly seen how difficult it was to impose the Marxist doc-

Proportion of Women Graduates at the Third Level by Field of Study, 1970

Field of Study	Percent
Medical sciences	82.4
Education	78.3
Humanities	67.4
Social sciences	62.8
Natural sciences	60.4
Fine arts	48.5
Law	43.8
Agriculture	40.8
Engineering	24.7
Total graduates	57.0

trine regarding the position of women and family under socialism on the Polish historical and cultural heritage. In the early 1950s, this doctrine was rigidly applied. However, in the late 1950s the traditional context started to play a more important role. Contemporary Poland is characterized by innumerable and often contradictory processes occurring simultaneously, which reflect both the continuity of tradition and the rapid social and cultural change.

The Present Educational and Occupational Position of Women
Women's position today reflects the social change. In 1974 women constituted 42.1 percent of the economically active population. Their economic activity lasts throughout their life without any break during the childbearing years.

There are relatively few differences in the level of general education of men and women in Poland, especially in younger age categories. The high proportion of women among students graduating from Polish educational institutions at the third level is striking (see the table). This high rate is unusual, compared to that in other countries, especially if the field of study is considered.

Even in comparison with countries like Finland,[10] which is internationally high in such fields as law, natural and medical sciences, and engineering, the Polish proportions are much higher. In the natural and social sciences there is a female majority of graduates, in addition to the tradi-

[10] Elina Haavio-Mannila, Magdalena Sokołowska, "Social Position of Women in Finland and Poland: Changes and Trends" (paper presented at the Finnish-Polish seminar on Social Structure and Social Changes, Vouranta, Finland, 1976).

tionally feminine fields of the humanities and education, which are female-dominated in Poland as in many other countries.

The education of women is one of the great attainments in policy of the socialist state: (1) It equalized the educational level of the two sexes. (2) There are fewer elements of discrimination against women in the educational system than in several developed countries. (3) As is known, education is a driving force of change in the attitudes and behavior of individuals and groups: it creates possibilities of choice, shapes the way of life. It is to the credit of socialism that Polish women for the first time in history share en masse this priceless good.

On the contrary, the domestic and family sphere reflects continuity of the old tradition.

Fluctuation of Women Policy

As is known, constitutions contain fundamental legal norms based on given ideology. In the socialist countries equal rights for women is one of the main values raised to the dignity of law. Precise guarantees of the postulate of equal rights and determination of the conditions for implementation of this statutory principle are characteristic of the constitutions of socialist countries. The paragraph on equal rights was elaborated in the new Polish constitution (1976), and it reads: "Citizens of the Polish Peoples Republic have equal rights regardless of their sex, birth, education, occupation, nationality, race, religion and social background and situation." Paragraph 66, dealing specifically with women, remained unchanged (1952):

> 1. Women in the Polish Peoples Republic enjoy the same rights as men in all spheres of life: state, political, economic and cultural. 2. Equal rights for women are guaranteed by: (*a*) equality with men in the right to work and remuneration according to the principle "equal pay for equal work," in the right to rest and recreation, social security, education, to distinctions and awards, to public office; (*b*) mother and child care, protection of pregnant women, paid maternity leave before and after childbirth, expansion of the network of maternity services, nurseries and kindergartens, development of the service and catering establishments.

However, a new statement has been added in 1976: "The Polish Peoples Republic strengthens the position of women in society, especially that of mothers and working women."

Changes in the constitution over time reflect transitions in the state's ideology and the social policy originating from it. Thus, the guarantees of women's equal rights in the constitution of 1952 stressed the domain of work and were intended to make employment accessible to women, whereas the word "mothers" has been used in the constitution of 1976 and is mentioned on an equal basis with "working women."

The last thirty years brought a polar change in the declared models of women's position in the society, as expressed in the press and other publications.[11] Four main viewpoints have emerged:

1. The years 1947–54 were characterized by the desire to achieve the maximum activation of women, in which connection the role of women as members of the socialist society was strongly emphasized.

2. In the next few years a new model was projected, stressing the woman's family role, thus automatically lowering her vocational-professional role.

3. Roughly from 1958 to the end of the 1960s there was a tendency to harmonize both viewpoints without favoring either one.

4. At the beginning of the 1970s a new approach was applied, focusing on an active pronatalist population policy. It seems that recently a still new trend is developing and that it is marked by the growing availability of individual options.

From each viewpoint flow different principles of social policy. In the first period the need was strongly stressed for building nurseries, kindergartens, and other facilities that would liberate women from "household slavery." In the second period resources were limited for those facilities and directed rather to increasing wages and family allowances. In the third period the approach was somewhat undecided, but the expansion of nurseries and other helping institutions was still held down.

In the fourth period there was a trend to limit the employment of certain groups of women, this time for demographic reasons. The press devoted ever more space to the problems of the family, which was treated as woman's domain; it was stressed that women had the right to choose either gainful occupations or household work exclusively, the prestige of which has clearly risen; the biographies of mothers with many children were published; the molding of opinion on the upbringing of the young generation left no doubt that it is regarded as the responsibility of the mother; the designation "family head" in relation to a male—husband/father—appeared in the press again after many years of absence. However, in the last year or so, there is again a different trend. On the one hand, there are several new regulations that make it easier for mothers to stop working periodically, and on

[11] Jerzy Piotrowski, *Women's Gainful Employment and the Family* (Warsaw: Książka i Wiedza, 1963).

the other hand, the helping institutions are increasing in number. Moreover, the pronatalist propaganda in its former form is slowing down.

Population Policy

The Polish demographic situation looks rather good. The rate of population increase for the last few years was 0.9 (1.02 in 1975). The age structure places Poles among the "youngest" societies in Europe. The rate of reproduction amounts to 1.05, and the demographers expect this situation to last for at least the next fifty years.

Both rates reflect the fact that the Polish Peoples Republic today belongs to the developed countries. In 1955 the rate of population growth was almost 2.0, and rapid decrease since then has made some people worry about the nation's future. In the last few years, there was a stormy debate in the press and in numerous agencies, centered on the problem of securing the desired number of children in the Polish family and on devising a pronatalist policy that would be effective in the near and the more remote future. While almost all disputants favored such a program, they differed considerably both in their assessment of the Polish demographic situation and in their predictions up to the end of this century as well as in the nature of their proposed pronatalist policies and the means which should be provided. It is interesting to note that not a single woman participated in these deliberations in the press. The disputants were demographers, statisticians, planners, journalists, and the undefined people involved in the issue on patriotic grounds. For two or three years the debate was dominated by the last group, which succeeded in creating a highly emotional atmosphere. The increase of the population was assumed to be an issue of the highest national importance and priority, and as is usual in such cases, it was women's rights other than child bearing and rearing which were questioned. The ideas presented varied from the extreme of opposing generally gainful employment of women in certain age groups to the moderate viewpoints seeking solution in part-time jobs, which still are unpopular in Poland.

This kind of debate is no longer taking place. Now numerous articles written by professionals, mostly demographers, are published in the press. They hold the opinion that there is no reason to worry about the Polish procreational situation. However, at the same time, they specify conditions which should be provided for the family, especially for the young family. For instance, one demographer believes that the opportunity resides in comprehensive economic transformations, a radical improvement in the living standards which would make for even fuller satisfaction of non-essential wants, in the development of the network of services, and in better housing. It is only then that the effectiveness of various incentives can be increased, it is only in such conditions that one can launch an active pronatalist policy, and it is only then that it will not prove fatal to the welfare of women![12]

This approach is congruent with the comprehensive social and family policy launched in 1971.

One particular issue deserves special attention, namely, the fact that relatively fewer children are borne by women with higher education. This seems to be a particular source of trouble for several people. One demographer writes as follows:

The question of the genetic quality of the nation is a very difficult one. Should it be evaluated through the prism of the social, class-strata structure? Partially yes. This is the field where doubts and problem-seeking are justified. For instance, why among 239,000 women with higher education employed in the national economy almost 100,000 have no children whereas a half of them are under 30 years of age and one third are in the 30–44 age group. This already is a big social problem![13]

The all-Polish representative study revealed that women aged twenty-one to forty-seven who used to continue their careers had on an average one child less (1.98) in comparison with those who used to work for a short period of time or not work at all (2.98).[14] The author is of the opinion, which is generally shared by sociologists, that women who continue to work, usually the relatively higher educated, represent the growing group of the population that is realizing a modern style of life; the small number of children in the family belongs to this pattern. A comprehensive family policy may perhaps change this pattern in the long run. It is worthwhile to note that the Governmental Population Commission in Poland, appointed in 1975, three months before the Population Congress held in Bucharest, is acting as the advisory body to the president of the Cabinet Council. It is aimed at promoting and coordinating the comprehensive population policy in the country.

Family planning in Poland is at the early stage of its development. Only

[12] Stefan Klonowicz, "The Infants Weekly," *Polityka*, Vol. XLVIII (1971).

[13] Franciszek Stokowski, "Can the State Impel Child Bearing?" *Magazyn Rodzinny*, No. 3 (1976).

[14] Adam Kurzynowski, "Genesis and Perspectives of the Gainful Employment of Married Women in Poland" (dissertation, High School of Statistics and Planning, Warsaw, 1977).

about one half of the married couples use any contraceptive or any means of contraception. The pill is used by about one percent of women in the age group of fifteen to nineteen.[15] In this situation, it is the termination of pregnancy which remains the most popular means of birth control. The law that legalized abortion was enacted in 1956 and almost immediately became a subject of constant debate and of periodic waves of open criticism. The critics seem not to observe that the legalization of abortion affected neither the birth rate nor the health of the female population. It caused a significant decrease in illegal abortions, which resulted, among other things, in fewer deaths due to abortion. It is the powerful Roman Catholic church which violently attacks the abortion law, by numerous methods, as well as individual opponents who do it in a more obscure way. In 1973 the Parliament examined "the socioeconomic and health effects of the implementation of the 1956 law" and decided against amending it. However, it urged the necessity of developing a comprehensive population and family policy and recognized that fundamental to such a policy was the implementation of a wide social program to improve protection of women and children and the living conditions of families.[16] In 1976, the Secretary of Health and Social Welfare took the floor in the debate in the press. He pointed to a slow but continuous rise, since 1970, of both birth and population increase rates due to: (1) the increase of the relative number of women in the childbearing age, and fertility rates; (2) the effective social policy since 1971 which contributed to higher standards of living; and (3) improved mother and child health protection.[17] However, it seems that this was not the final voice in the debate, and it will be continued further. The firm attitude of the state authorities concerning this issue should be stressed.

Child Care and Child Rearing

There is an extensive volume by Adam Kurzynowski, who for several years has engaged in a pioneering type of study in the Polish Peoples Republic.[18] Almost all data presented in the following section are taken from it.

---

[15] Magdalena Sokołowska and Barbara Lobodzińska, "Contraceptives and Termination of Pregnancy," *Problemy Rodziny*, LVII, No. 1 (1971), 50–55.

[16] Jan Rosner, *Polish Reports*, in Alfred J. Kahn and Sheila B. Kamerman, eds., *Cross-National Studies of Social Service Systems* (New York: Cross-National Studies, Columbia University School of Social Work, 1976).

[17] Marian Śliwiński, "The Demographic Future of the Nation," *Trybuna Ludu*, November 9, 1976.

[18] Kurzynowski, "Genesis and Perspectives of the Gainful Employment of Married Women."

In 1970 employed married women constituted 68 percent of all married women in the productive age and 25 percent of the total labor force as compared with 4 percent in 1950. This rise involved all age groups. In 1970 childless women constituted 26 percent of the employed married women (29 percent in 1960); mothers of one child, 35 percent versus 32 percent; of two children, 28 percent versus 25 percent; of three children, 8 percent versus 10 percent; and of four children and more, 3 percent versus 4 percent.

There are two main reasons for married women to seek jobs: demand for their work by industry and economic pressures on their families. In the last thirty years several ups and downs related to the demand have occurred due to the various fluctuations in the national economy. However, the years 1971–75 were characterized by a rapid development of the economy accompanied by a rapid rise in the demand for women's labor. In comparison with 1970, the percentage of working women in 1971–75 increased by 27 percent, and in 1975, for the first time in several years, there were many more jobs available for women than there were women seeking employment. It is predicted that by the year 2000, employed married women will amount to about 80 percent to 90 percent of all married women in the productive age. It is exactly the present proportion of employed married women with third-level education: in 1970 there were 89 percent of such women at work.

The last five years were marked by a fundamental change of the state's approach to women's work: since 1971 the family, including children, housing, household, and so on, is considered as a unit.

Maternity and Maternity Leave
The prestige of motherhood has been dramatically elevated in the years 1971–75. A completely new tone has been established in the official declarations and has started to ring out in the mass media. The public was not accustomed to it for many years. However, I believe that the majority of the people like it. Mother's Day has become a celebrated holiday. Two quotations illustrate the atmosphere related to it. The first is a fragment from a daily newspaper column commenting on the Mother's Day celebrations on May 27, 1976. The second is an excerpt from the Trade Union Declaration accepted by the Congress in 1976.

> "Gratitude, respect and wishes to the mothers on their day." The whole society, all generations have expressed their greatest gratitude and respect, their very best wishes to mothers on their Day. The children have expressed their deep feelings by offering flowers and gifts; the adults, in ceremonial meetings and occasional musical performances, as well as in the intimacy of home.
>
> Mother's Day celebrations have given the occasion to think over how to

make it easier for a woman to combine the respectful duties of motherhood with the difficulties of carrying on her vocational activities.

Woman-mother plays an essential role in establishing the family and its rearing functions. Trade unions will continue the efforts to improve life and work conditions of working women, to establish their vocational and social position, to give special support to women who are the only breadwinners for the family and their children.

Trade unions' initiatives will tend to facilitate the household management carried on by women. This should be the objective of the development of services and supply of devices facilitating household work as well as the supply of consumption goods.

Together with the administration trade unions will act on behalf of the children-rearing women who are gainfully employed. Trade unions together with the executives and local authorities will actively support the development of nurseries and kindergartens, especially in the new housing estates.

Effective help to mothers rearing children up to two years of age demands improvement of the system of family allowances and other financial help which makes it possible to withdraw from employment for a certain time span and to obtain part-time jobs.

Cooperating with the Socialist Youth Federation and especially the Pathfinders' Organization and Association of Children's Friends as well as housing cooperatives the trade unions will contribute to the development and improvement of the various forms of children's and youth's vacations and leisure, to the full utilization of the educational potential of those forms and to proper medical care during the holiday.

The text of the Trade Union Declaration is rather unconventional. It is written from the standpoint of family policy and therefore approaches more broadly the traditional area of trade union activities. Also it mirrors the present attitude in the field of family policy which is directed almost exclusively to women.

Maternity leave and maternity allowance. The up-to-date legislation related to maternity and child care has been comprehensively described elsewhere.[19] In the years 1971–75 it was significantly expanded. At present, women on maternity leave in the course of one year constitute about 7 percent of all female employees—about 350,000.

Unpaid child care leave. This leave is granted to all mothers who wish it. First established in 1968 for one year and extended in 1972 to three years, it enables a woman to utilize it in the course of her child's first four years. It entitles her to all rights and benefits due to the working population. It is expected that a partial remuneration for at least one year will be an-

---

[19] See Rosner, *Polish Reports.*

nounced soon. A child care leave is now utilized by about 30 percent to 35 percent of working mothers, who take it directly after their maternity leaves.

Nurseries
The number of nurseries and places increased substantially from 1947 to 1975. Coverage is now approximately 8 percent for the children under three. About 20 percent of the working mothers with children of this age were served. However, the dynamics of this increase differed in four main periods: (1) the years 1945–49 were characterized by a rapid increase; (2) 1950–55 showed the most rapid expansion; (3) 1956–70 had a slow growth; (4) 1971–75 again had a much more rapid increase, three times that in 1965–70; also the rate of increase in 1971–75 was the highest since 1955.[20]

Kindergartens
Kindergartens serving children over the age of three are very numerous in Poland, chiefly in urban areas. In 1975 two thirds of the children between the ages of three and seven attended kindergarten. However, here too the rate of increase in kindergartens and kindergarten places varied over time, accelerating sharply between 1970 and 1975.

Demand for Nurseries and Kindergartens
It is assumed that in the coming years from 35 percent to 40 percent of women will utilize a child care leave. In the 1960s about 30 percent used to stop working for a certain period of time after their maternity leave. Women whose husbands had a relatively higher income utilized this leave more frequently. Therefore, it seems that at least one year of a child care leave (which now amounts to three years) should be covered by an allowance possibly equal to the woman's earnings. The demand for nurseries will depend partly on the solution of this issue.

Further, it is assumed that about 30 percent of families outside agriculture with a wife-mother in employment will solve their child care problem with the help of their parents and/or of other people, mostly relatives. Three-generation families constitute about 18 percent of the urban families in Poland. In addition, there are at least 8 percent of two-generation families (so designated because the oldest generation lives separately) where the grandparents also take care of a baby or a small child. The remaining 4 percent are made up of families living in the rural communities (but employed

[20] There were 1,246 nurseries at the beginning of 1977 with 86,000 places.

outside agriculture) where three-generation families are much more frequent.[21]

Therefore, there are approximately 35 percent of families with mothers utilizing a child care leave and 30 percent solving the problem by their own means—a total of 65 percent of families with children under age three. What about the remaining 35 percent, or 362,000 families? One hundred and nine thousand send their children to day nurseries; it is not known how the remaining 253,000 care for their children.[22] Assuming that all of them would like to have their children in nurseries, the estimated number of places needed would be 253,000 or about 280,000 if the present overcrowding were liquidated. It is hardly possible to answer this question at the present time, for at least two factors unknown at the moment certainly will play a definite role: on the one hand, a paid child care leave which might diminish demand, and on the other hand, a better quality of nurseries, with elimination of their current inadequacies, might increase the popularity of this institution. Anyway, there should be about three times more places in nurseries than there are currently.

The demand for kindergartens can be estimated more easily. First, the assumption can be made that all families with children of preschool age wish to have their children in kindergarten, which has become a widely accepted institution. In 1975 there were 1,226,000 children of employed mothers in kindergarten; there will be 1,353,000 in 1978. In 1975 there were 669,000 children of preschool age. Therefore, the number of available places should be doubled. Only children of working mothers are considered in this estimation. However, according to the far-reaching plan of the state the institution of kindergartens is going to be an integral part of the national educational system. Plans have already been made for a general kindergarten education for children aged six, a year before entering school. Consequently, younger children also will be included in the preschool education program. Obviously, a much larger supply of kindergartens will be required.

Family Allowances

Child Allowance
In 1971 the basic reform was initiated with the objective of decreasing economic differences between families earning the least, and having many

---

[21] Nowadays, the contribution of domestic servants plays an insignificant role. There are only 44,548 such persons in the country; almost 20 percent of them are in Warsaw.

[22] A study aimed at answering this question is now being carried out by Adam Kurzynowski.

children, and all other families. The first stage of this reform consisted of increasing allowances for children in families earning the least and having three or more children. In the second stage, in 1975, all families earning the least, regardless of the number of children, obtained an increased allowance. This new allowance is paid to families where the monthly income for one person does not exceed 1,400 zloty. [As of April, 1977, the tourist exchange rate was: 1 zloty = $0.03. *Eds.*] Such families are entitled to a monthly allowance which amounts to 160 zloty for one child, 410 zloty for two children, 750 zloty for three, and 360 zloty for each additional child.

The Support Fund
Since 1975 a special law has been in force "aimed at increasing care of children and of other persons in a difficult financial situation due to inability of enforcing support payments and at raising the responsibility of persons obligated to pay support." This law is directed to women mainly, to the single family, and to breadwinners who are abandoned or divorced and bringing up children, and those who are caring for children out of wedlock. It also concerns support payments due to the husband from his wife or to parents from their children. It is the state which provides payments for those who earn less than 1,400 zloty monthly and are unable to collect support.

The Support Fund is a complete novelty in the Polish legislation and it has been in force for only two years. However, its popularity is rising. Whereas in 1975 there were 50,000 persons benefiting from it, in May, 1977, this number amounted to 76,000. Some new instructions added at the beginning of 1977 extended the number of people entitled to benefits from the fund: the child allowance, which is paid to families where the monthly income for one person does not exceed 1,400 zloty, is not at present included in the upper limit of 1,400 zloty. The state as an obligee is able to enforce support much more efficiently than the particular individuals. In 1975 the sum enforced amounted to 26.5 percent of payments, and in 1976 it exceeded 40 percent.

Child Care Leave
All working mothers with children up to age seven are entitled to two days yearly of the fully paid leave.

Sick Child Care Leave
All working mothers are entitled to a fully paid (equal to the sum earned monthly) sick child care leave up to sixty days yearly. Previously, it was only thirty days, and blue-collar working mothers were entitled to a benefit amounting to 70 percent of their wages.

It is interesting to note that a sick child care leave originally was provided for a parent taking care of a sick child. The decision as to whether the mother or the father would care for the child was left to the parents. However, in 1973, the Ministry of Health and Social Welfare distributed a circular to all its units ordering them to grant the leave and the consequent benefit to mothers, and to fathers only exceptionally: when a father proves that the mother is sick herself or absent, and that nobody else is available to care for the child. One reads in the circular: "It is indisputable that the mother has special predispositions to take personal care of the child. For the child's sake, the leave from work related to care of a sick child should be granted foremost to mothers . . ." The press still reports on the various ups and downs of particular fathers whose right to take care of their sick child has been denied.

Benefit for a Handicapped Child

This benefit has been provided since 1975 for such a child up to the age of sixteen, regardless of the family income. It amounts to 500 zloty monthly.

The maternal and child health care system in Poland has been described elsewhere.[23]

Housing

It is only in the last five years that the issue of housing has been identified by the state authorities as a matter of top priority. For the first time a centrally planned housing policy has been established in Poland. It is closely related to family policy and constitutes one of the pillars of the social policy initiated in 1971. Huge housing programs have been launched all over the country, and they are realized systematically. Over 80 percent of the urban population now live in independent flats. The demand still exceeds supply and it has been estimated that not until around 1990 will the basic housing needs of the population be met.

Housing for young married couples as well as for families with many children deserves special attention from the state because it is still a serious problem. A couple childless after two years of marriage has to pay a special tax, but some couples have had to postpone having a child because of their bad housing conditions. Eighteen percent of the newlywed couples possess

---

[23] Rosner, *Polish Reports.*

an independent flat, 57 percent live in a separate room in a nonindependent flat, 18 percent share their room with other people, and 7 percent still live separately while waiting for their flat.[24] The waiting time takes several years. However, numerous programs and actions both at the national and local levels are operating to provide flats for young couples. They are put at the top of the waiting lists and get priority in purchasing furniture. The supply of furniture still is too limited, mostly due to a dramatic rise in the number of families that have received new flats since 1971.

Household

According to the 1964 Family Code, a housewife is an equal marital partner, and a woman's exclusive devotion to the family role is considered a "fulfill-ment of the citizen's obligation to work."

Housing conditions are still difficult although they improved significantly during the last five years. Approximately two thirds of the urban flats are composed of two or three rooms and are inhabited by three or four persons. All flats in towns have electricity; approximately 75 percent have running water; 50 percent have a bathroom and toilet; 36 percent have central heating; and 40 percent have a gas cooker.[25]

Household living is a field where change occurs rather slowly and where family policy has been the least effective so far. Home tasks demand much time and energy because there are few household devices, limited canned food supplies, and the daily shopping takes much time and effort. Dinner, the main meal, is cooked daily by 90 percent of the urban families; laundry is done at home by approximately 80 percent (more than 90 percent of the urban families possess electric washing machines, but only a few are fully automatic). Clothes, especially for children, may be made at home. Approximately one third of the families cultivate a garden plot, owned or rented.[26]

Over 70 percent of wives-mothers in these families are gainfully em-

[24] Zbigniew Smoliński, "With What Do the Newlyweds Start?" *Trybuna Ludu*, July 30 and 31, 1977, pp. 30–31.

[25] Adam Andrzejewski, "Social Aspects of Housing Policy," in A. Rajkiewicz, ed., *Social Policy* (Warsaw: Państwowe Wydawnictwo Ekonomiczna, 1976), p. 259.

[26] Danuta Markowska, "The Contemporary Family in the Light of the Social Science Findings" (paper presented at the conference on Summary of the Scientific Findings on Women, Maternity and Family, Polish Academy of Sciences, Warsaw, 1976).

ployed. However, the burden of housework generally is borne by the house-wife, whether she is employed or not—70 percent to 90 percent of these chores are performed by her. Participation of household members is only subsidiary.[27] The fact that the employment of an exemplary mother does not harm the family is particularly stressed in the mass media. Especially men-tioned are the good cooking and special dishes enjoyed by the family.

The care of the old and the sick also belongs to women. About 55 per-cent of the people over sixty-five in towns live with their children. If care is necessary, it is assumed, in this order, by wives, daughters, and daughters-in-law.[28]

The burden of Polish women is recognized and highly regarded. They are distinctly mentioned, praised, and thanked for their merits and contribu-tions in the official speeches and swamped with flowers on International Woman's Day and on Mother's Day.

The term "woman's question" still is frequently used. "Woman's question" in the Polish Peoples Republic today involves questions of nur-series, kindergartens, the social services, food and meal services, consumer services, the production of household equipment, and the like. It has be-come commonplace that these are specifically for women, provided by soci-ety in order to lighten women's heavy burden.[29] The mass media often use the slogan, "Let us help the working woman." For example, the Warsaw daily paper reports that the car enterprise won the contest organized by trade unions under the title "Let us make the life of working women easier" because "it took care of leisure for children and families and . . . provided a store and kiosks within the factory." The same newspaper brings a mes-sage concerning an exhibition which was organized under the same slogan and consisted of facilities "serving women's work in the household." An-other daily reports that the trade union units in enterprises initiated new forms of leisure for women—for instance, holidays for mothers where they can take children with them—and that special sanatorium treatments for mothers are provided which enable them to have their children accompany them to the health resort.

However, as has been pointed out, contemporary Poland is character-

[27] Jerzy Piotrowski, *Family Needs Resulting from an Increased Employment of Married Women: Adequacy of Existing Resources to Meet These Needs: Report of Research* (Warsaw, 1969).

[28] Jerzy Piotrowski, *Old People in Family and Society* (Warsaw: Państwowe Wydawnictwo Naukowe, 1973), pp. 185–86, 201.

[29] Sokołowska, "The Woman Image. . . ."

ized by innumerable processes, often contradictory, occurring simultaneously, which reflect both the continuity of tradition and the rapid social change. In March, 1976, shortly before International Woman's Day, a statement by Halina Skibniewska, vice-president of the Parliament and a professor of architecture, was published in all the newspapers:

> There is no woman's question in Poland, but there are questions of maternity, of the help for family, questions of the marital partnership where the responsibilities are divided between husband and wife. There is the question of a faster moving away from the patriarchal family ideal where all contributed to the success of the male. There is also the question of help for a single mother and a single father.[30]

Employment

Legislation

Whereas the family law applies in Poland to both partners equally (although implicitly mostly women are concerned), regulations related to employment are addressed explicitly to women. As in the other developed countries numerous regulations are provided to protect maternity. And as everywhere it is extremely difficult to tell which ones really protect woman's biological system and which are factors of subtle discrimination. They are hardly consistent. For instance, since the early 1950s women have had work on night shifts, yet the long list of occupations prohibited to women has not been revised for twenty years despite the modernization of technology. While emphasizing the need for special treatment of pregnant and nursing women, the regulations are extended to all categories of women, which limits their opportunities in employment.

Part-Time Jobs

These proved to be rather ineffective, marking a difference between Poland and many other countries. In 1971 a special resolution in this area was undertaken by the Council of Ministers, but the situation remained unchanged: at present only approximately 6 percent of all gainfully employed women work on a part-time basis. In addition, more than 50 percent of them are in the older age brackets, with the most numerous group aged sixty to sixty-four. The part-time jobs are mainly intended for the young wife/mother.

[30] Halina Skibniewska, "Family and the Role of Women in Poland," *Zycie Warszawy*, March 3, 1976.

However, they are rejected by young women for several reasons, career orientation being one of them. In other words, a part-time job keeps one's vocational position low, constitutes a definite barrier to advancement, and so on. Moreover, the functioning of the household is affected by the part-time job of a wife/mother to almost the same extent as by a full-time job whereas the economic rewards are much smaller.

An attempt to develop crafts work at home does not show any significant rising trend. This kind of work was mainly intended for young mothers who stay at home for one to three years because of the unpaid maternity leave. However, it is mostly the older women, especially pensioners, who are interested in this activity.

The Social Fund

In 1973 a so-called "social fund" was established in all enterprises as a means of satisfying social needs of employees and their families. The enterprise utilizes its social fund under supervision of the local (within the enterprise) trade union organization. The fund may be used for building or buying lodgings for the employees, for building and operating nurseries and/or kindergartens, canteens and/or buffets, holiday and recreation centers, and so forth.

Mother as the Sole Earner

Among all Polish families, approximately 13 percent constitute one-parent families, mostly headed by women. In 1960–70 such families increased by 40 percent. They are overrepresented in the low-income families bracket.

The "solitary mothers," as they are called in Poland, were under special social care and assistance both in employment and outside it prior to the emergence of family policy. For instance, the law prohibits firing a solitary mother. She has priority in utilizing the social fund, in receiving lodgings, unpaid vacations, placing her children in nurseries and kindergartens, and so on.

Government Mechanisms and Processes

The formal organization of the social services in Poland has been described elsewhere.[31] It is the Ministry of Labor, Wages, and Social Affairs which is the chief promoting and coordinating body of the country's social policy.

[31] Rosner, *Polish Reports.*

The Support Fund[32] illustrates how a social benefit gets established. The Support Fund suits this purpose because it is a new institution, not loaded with historical ballast.

In 1971–72, the trade unions, social welfare agencies, and women's organizations started to report on the difficult situation of women-mothers in one-parent families. These reports were based on observation of the life conditions of such women. They looked for help ever more frequently. Although support from the financially stronger marital partner (usually the man) is authorized by family law, many deserted families were unable to receive it. Reports and resolutions concerning this issue were directed by the state authorities to the "team for the program of help to families with many children and other low-income families living in difficult conditions." Such a team was created in 1972 at the Ministry of Labor, Wages, and Social Affairs. The material received by the team was approved and further elaborated, and the first version of the proposed new program was then discussed with the Ministry of Social Justice and the Social Security Agency as well as with trade unions, women's and welfare organizations. Subsequently, the proposal was presented to the Council of Ministers, and then, in the framework of a whole package of the urgent social issues, it became the subject of a debate at the Twelfth Plenary Session of the Central Committee of the Polish United Workers Party which approved its basic principles. Afterward, the preliminary versions of the legal act as well as of the executive regulations were formulated, and opinions of all ministries, the local authorities, the trade unions, and the social scientists were collected and analyzed. The corrected text was returned for final approval to the Council of Ministers, which next directed it to the Parliament, where it was revised by several commissions. Finally, the text was passed by the plenary session of the Parliament. The very last phase involved publication of the executive rules and training of a group of the Social Security Agency's employees. And the Support Fund started to operate.

After two years of observation some regulations were modified in the sense that more families became eligible for the fund. This was performed by a "team for coordination of accomplishment of the social policy toward woman and family in the period of the Women's Decade 1976–85." Appointed by the Prime Minister, the team began to function in the second half of 1976. It is thought to be a long-term activity aimed at realizing the ideas of the United Nations General Assembly. As is known, it recommended that the member countries establish governmental bodies to initiate and coordi-

[32] Based on Henryk Białczyński, "The Security of Existence," *Magazyn Rodzinny*, July, 1977.

nate activities toward the family. This proclamation came together with the fast developing activity in the field of family policy in Poland.

Views of Social Scientists and Research
on Family and Family Policy Issues

Social Scientists

Social scientists, in common with over 90 percent of the working urban population, are the state's employees. Research institutions, publishing houses, and the mass media are all state-funded. Nevertheless, the published views of the social scientists and the findings of their research often differ considerably from the official declarations, resolutions, statements, and so forth in the field of family policy.

The social scientists in the Polish Peoples Republic are characterized by their particular pragmatism, which consists of their concentration on the development of society as a whole and their involvement in current social problems. Also, they are constantly preoccupied with the question of practical application of their activity, which mainly means not only the direct implementation of their research findings, but first of all the impact on public opinion and consciousness. This is precisely the area which makes the position of the social scientists in Poland quite different from that in the Western countries. The researcher ("the scientific worker," as he/she is called in the Polish Peoples Republic) enjoys very high prestige. The university professor ranks unchangeably at the top in the numerous studies of public opinion on occupational prestige, and it is the very fact of being a professor that counts, no matter whether natural or social sciences are involved.

Since about 1971 the social scientists have more frequently taken over the floor on the issues of family and family policy. Their views can be detected in various debates going on in the mass media, in the reports or replies to several inquiries made to them by the government, parliamentary, or party bodies, and so on. The opinions of Jan Szczepański, a well-known sociologist, written on behalf of one of the government agencies, are presented below. Szczepański assumes that the principles of family policy should be based on a family model liberated from the feudal-traditional relicts; that is, family policy based on the principles of partnership of man and woman in a family, with equal rights and responsibilities. He then delineates the following domains of family policy.

1. *Education*. It is necessary to introduce well-prepared programs on family life into the school. These programs should stress home economics and teach rational consumption patterns aiming at educating consumers (there are 10,000,000 housekeepers in Poland, men and women) who should know how to make rational decisions related to consumption and to be able to create the necessary base harmonizing the economic policy in the microscale with that in macro.

2. *Housing*. Both construction and furniture industries should provide lodgings corresponding with the social function of the family. The social cost of ill-adjusted housing is much higher than the expense related to building functional flats.

3. *Health.* Health care is covered in the family policy of our government. Numerous legal acts provide a broad scope of services for women-mothers and children. However, insufficient means often prevent these postulates from being fully implemented. Especially a long-term program to combat alcoholism should be immediately put into operation under auspices of health services and the Ministry of Labor, Wages, and Social Affairs.

4. Also, there are plenty of legal regulations related to working women, and this issue is under the constant attention of trade unions. It is the homemaker who is ignored. However, numerous studies indicate that this is just the person who deserves attention from the legal viewpoint.

5. An attempt should be undertaken to estimate the social loss caused by the educational ignorance of parents. If only intuitively, this is a serious factor contributing to the process of leading youth astray and to juvenile delinquency. Actions related to the development of nurseries, kindergartens or any other form of child and youth care cannot be fully effective unless parents are prepared for educational collaboration with these institutions.

6. Care for the "disabled" families (chronically ill, mentally and physically handicapped, etc.) also presents an important set of problems.[33]

In 1975, the leading official daily, *Trybuna Ludu,* invited a large group of people to answer the question of what a socialist family means to them. No rules and preconditions had been set up, everyone wrote whatever pleased him or her. The responses were published in the daily and later edited and published in a book.[34] The authors of fifty short papers represent a diverse body of academics and practitioners, sociologists, psychologists, economists, educators, demographers, physicians, government officials, activists, journalists, parents.

All social scientists contributing to the work expressed their view that public discussion on the contemporary Polish family is useful because it may

---

[33] Jan Szczepański, "On the Question of Women and Family Policy."

[34] Bolesław Kosterkiewicz, ed., *Socialist Family—What Should It Be?* (Warsaw: Książka i Wiedza, 1976).

help the development of the family model in actual social, economic, and cultural conditions. In one particular paper[35] the author states that there is a tremendous need for such a model because of basic changes which occurred in the life of each family due to changes in the macrosystem of Poland. However, there are no adequate proposals for dealing with the marital-family living of the postwar generation. Sociological research indicates that the examples of the parental families are obsolete to a great extent. Something new must be created since even a "good" family home only rarely is sufficient to offer patterns useful for the future life of our youth. Public opinion gives little inspiration to this question. As is known, the family has emerged relatively recently in the mass media. Moreover, its emergence is not tantamount to systematic knowledge of interfamily relations and of the function of a citizen in his/her family group. Such knowledge still remains incomplete.

The author of another paper[36] points to the negative consequences resulting from the image of the traditional family which still persists in the social consciousness. In spite of the constantly growing number of working wives-mothers who have a definite education and occupation, the majority of publications devote too much space to the "negative consequences of women's work" which result, apparently, in the lack of time for raising children. Basic social values of mothers' work are underestimated, namely, those brought home by active participants in the broader life. This is precisely what largely enriches the upbringing processes. In addition, mothers' work creates conditions for the mutual understanding of all family members who increasingly are involved in life outside the home.

As is seen, social scientists devote much attention to the traditional prejudices and stereotypes which still prevail. One of the sociologists[37] points to two matters deserving attention: that ability and knowledge of a modern family life are neither inborn nor inherited, and that the social equality of men and women has not yet been achieved, especially in the family. It is exactly at the new stage of development of the socialist family where the process of the social liberation of women should take place.

An interesting approach to the family is offered by a sociologist[38] who observes that the family is usually considered to be "a dependent variable,"

[35] Magdalena Sokołowska, "Where is the Father?" pp. 99–102.

[36] Danuta Graniewska, "Work and Family," pp. 207–10.

[37] Jan Malanowski, "Self-conscious Cooperation," pp. 178–81.

[38] Jan Szczepański, "To Start from Home," pp. 31–66.

an effect of the various societal activities. However, family itself is a powerful "independent variable," and it could be, if rationally used, a factor in speeding up the societal transformations.

Research

Numerous studies carried out in Poland contain "family" in their titles. The family is investigated by several disciplines, such as sociology, economics, psychology, law, pedagogics, medicine, and others. In addition, there are various subdisciplines, for instance in medicine, which also center on the family: psychiatry, epidemiology, pediatrics, obstetrics and gynecology. Needless to say, the family is understood and conceptualized differently in the particular disciplines, subdisciplines, and by individual researchers. The studies vary from the highly specialized ones which are published in the professional journals to the problem-oriented, practical works. They are often published in the popular scientific monthlies, in the widely read weeklies, in the daily press, and they are presented on the radio and television when the particular studies are quoted or their authors are interviewed. Such studies have a definite impact on the social consciousness and indirectly influence social and family policy. The trouble is that in Poland, as elsewhere, knowledge of the family is inconsistent, fragmented, and often contradictory. For instance, in previous years there were numerous studies carried out on the effects of mother's work on the well-being of her children. Such studies frequently come to opposite conclusions. The psychologists and obstetricians are inclined to suggest that mother's work by definition is harmful for the children, whereas the sociologists and epidemiologists are less pessimistic. One can but wonder what premises should be adopted by family policy if it would tend to rely on research.

Several studies give alleged support to the simplistic opinions, quickly spread and likely to be quoted, about the negative consequences of a lack of motherly care. For instance, some psychologists express quite peculiar ideas resembling those that contributed to creation of the feeling of guilt which plagues thousands of mothers in the U.S. who seek career opportunities. On the contrary, an observation based on an all-Polish study that for approximately 30 percent of the children, rearing conditions in nurseries are better than at home passed almost unnoticed.[39] Also little attention is paid to the fact that it is the household and not child care and rearing that occupies a major part of the mother's time at home. Such a conclusion derives from

[39] Jerzy Piotrowski, *Family Needs.*

numerous studies that examine the time budget of several groups of women.

The sociologists, economists, and demographers have collected an impressive body of knowledge about Polish families. The bulk of it, especially that in the sociological studies, has a "basic" character. They aim to increase the knowledge of society and are not directly applicable to any policy. But numerous studies are practically oriented and can be used in family policy. For instance, the social scientists have investigated the effects of married women's work on various aspects of their family life; the time budget of gainfully employed marital couples; the social situation of single mothers—the only earners. Also relevant for family policy is research on the normative models functioning in the consciousness of the defined social groups confronted with their real patterns of family life, and with the official normative models reflected in family law, and models propagated by mass media.

In the sociological studies the family is approached as the object of various state-societal efforts; the consequences of such operations on different aspects of family functioning are investigated. So far, in only one project has an opposite direction of the conceptualization been applied: in a nationwide study devoted to changes occurring in the consumption patterns of the over-all society under the impact of the household.[40]

The sociology of the family has developed apart from research on the broadly conceived social, occupational, economic, and cultural structure. Such studies constitute the mainstream of the sociological investigations in the Polish Peoples Republic. Also, research on women is isolated from the core of the general preoccupation of the social scientists. Those works are labeled "women's studies" and, as in other countires, are written mainly by women about women for women. In 1976 this situation began to change: in at least two all-Polish studies on migration and social mobility sex started to be differentiated and analyzed along with such typical variables as education or occupation. Also, for the first time, two papers, one dealing with the societal position of women and another devoted to the family, were included in the program of the macrosociological seminar on the social structure and social change in Finland and the Polish Peoples Republic.[41]

[40] Jan Szczepański, "Expected Changes in Consumption Patterns, Cultural Needs, and the System of Values in Polish Society" (unpublished report, Institute of Philosophy and Sociology, Polish Academy of Sciences, Warsaw, 1977).

[41] For a paper on the social position of women see Sheila B. Kamerman, "Public Policy and the Family," in Jane Roberts Chapman and Margaret Gates, eds., *Women into Wives* (Beverly Hills, Calif.: Sage Publications, 1977), pp. 195–214. See also Rita Jallinoja, Jerzy Piotrowski, and Veronica Stolte-Heiskanen, "Marriage and Family" (unpublished paper, 1976).

The Center for Research on the Contemporary Family attached to the Association of Family Planning is the only center in Poland devoted to the systematic study of the family. This active group assembled various specialists, theoretically, empirically, and practically minded, and transformed family into an interdisciplinary study area crossing the institutional boundaries. The Center is simultaneously engaged in rigorous research and acts as a platform for frequent meetings and vigorous discussions. The leadership of the local branches of the Association for Family Planning plays an important role in the dissemination of information.[42]

In addition, there is another group of people deriving from the orientation of "social policy" which has a long tradition in Poland. In its present form it embraces representatives of several disciplines and practical areas, such as law, economics, city planning, administration, finance, sociology, psychology, pedagogics. Its scope and orientation are rapidly changing into an interdisciplinary complex which includes both diagnostic and prognostic dimensions, with the aim of coordinating the total social policy at the macro-community and micro-level. It is the committee—Poland 2000—appointed by the Polish Academy of Sciences. The research and writing of this group are of particular importance since they include people who occupy posts in the problem-oriented research institutes subordinated to the particular ministries, and positions in the Party, in the administrative agencies, and in the social associations. Thus, they themselves are promoters of social and family policy.

[42] In this connection the role of the women's press should be mentioned. It is one of the crucial channels for dissemination of knowledge and shaping of public opinion in both a progressive and a well-balanced way. Particularly, two women's weeklies, *Przyjaciółka* (Friend [a female]) and *Kobieta i Życie* (Woman and life) play a significant role. The first is designed mainly for the rural areas, for relatively less educated readers. Its circulation of 1,300,000 copies is the largest of all weeklies in Poland. The second is intended for a more sophisticated public. Its circulation amounts to 650,000 copies, which are sold immediately. The survey carried out by its editorial board revealed that each copy is read by approximately ten people and that men constitute about 40 percent of the readers.

FINLAND
Jarl Lindgren

AS IN MANY other countries, concern about the population growth acted as godfather to Finnish family policy. During the 1920s the decreasing birth rate was regarded as an alarming phenomenon, reasons for which and consequences of which were debated both among medical researchers and economists. Attention was also given to the prerequisites for practical population policy and the measures it calls for. In this respect, special mention should be made of a broad program proposed by Arvo Ylppö, professor in pediatrics at the central hospital of the University of Helsinki, and intended to further child care. Since, according to him, one could not increase the birth rate, all attention should be focused on decreasing the death rate, especially the child mortality rate. This program, which was to be realized during the following decades, was in a way the origin of maternal and child care in Finland.

The actual family policy awakening, however, took place in 1934 when the chief actuary of the Central Statistical Office of Finland, Gunnar Modeen, gave a speech on the future population development of Finland and the economic consequences. This speech, which aroused a great deal of attention, was based on a population prognosis covering the entire country and revealed that our population would decrease in the near future and would never reach the four million mark. Modeen emphasized that an increase in population strongly affects economic progress. If our population growth should slow down, this would have a harmful effect on the economic development

DR. JARL LINDGREN is Director of Research, Population Research Institute, Helsinki, Finland.

of our country. Many researchers and representatives of public life hurried to give their opinions on this matter. The importance of the population question and the necessity of population policy measures were generally recognized in the debate in the newspapers in 1934–35. According to Lento,[1] the fact that our population would never reach the four million mark was the most important reason that the speech aroused so much attention among the public. The general public had, of course, heard rumors of a decrease in the birth rate, but the matter had not been presented in such an alarming light before.

This interest was fostered by corresponding developments in our neighbor to the west, Sweden. Only a month after Modeen's speech Alva and Gunnar Myrdal's book *Kris i befolkningsfrågan* (Crisis in the population question) appeared in Sweden. The lively debate in the Swedish press caused by the book, the numerous bills in the Swedish Parliament, and the resultant measures no doubt affected the formation of opinion in Finland also.

Modeen's speech is generally held to be the signal for the beginning of family policy in Finland.[2] One did not have to wait long for practical measures. In 1935, the Finnish Parliament requested the government to give attention to population questions, to sponsor studies to determine the proportion of families with many children among the lower-income groups in Finland, what kind of circumstances they lived in, and what measures should be undertaken for their support. In line with the example given by Sweden the government established in 1937 a special committee to study population questions.

In 1935 and during the following years many family policy bills were presented to Parliament. From the point of view of families with children, the most important results were the raising of income tax deductions for children. Another important reform was, however, the levying of an additional tax, the "bachelor's tax," on those who did not have a family or responsibility for looking after close relatives. In 1937 a law was passed on maternity benefits, according to which support could be given to mothers in poor circumstances. Mothers with little or no means were also guaranteed a cost-free childbirth.

It is obvious that the family policy in Finland during the 1930s closely followed the development in Sweden where several measures especially con-

---

[1] Reino Lento, "Väestöpoliittisen ajatustavan synty ja tähänastinen kehitys Suomessa," in *Väestöliiton vuosikirja I.* (Helsinki: 1946).

[2] See Pekka Kuusi, *Social Policy for the Sixties: A Plan for Finland* (Helsinki: 1964), p. 176.

cerned with maternity and child care and tax reforms were enacted. The emphasis was laid on reforms aimed at improving the living standard of families with low income. However, the measures carried out were rather modest and could be described as more formal than actually effective with regard to their fundamental aim, to promote a higher birth rate. This prudence as to family policy expenditures was at least partly due to the recession in the mid-1930s and the worsening international situation in the latter part of the 1930s which necessitated increased defense expenditure.

Equalization of Family Burdens

World War II, which began in the fall of 1939, was a hard blow to the nation, and the debate on population questions was intensified in the pages of newspapers and magazines as well as over the radio and in private circles. In February of 1941 several civic organizations established Väestöliitto—the Population and Family Welfare Federation. This independent organization with its semiofficial standing has since then played a significant role in the development of Finnish family and population policy. According to the rules of the Federation, its task is to "spread information on the significance of the size and quality of the population for the existence of the nation as well as for its material and emotional development."

Among the first tasks of the Federation was to deal with the problem of the equalization of family burdens. Immediately after it was founded, the Federation began to disseminate systematic propaganda in favor of equalization. The first results were reached in 1943, during the war, when the Law on Family Subsidies was passed. The purpose of the family subsidy system was to help low-income families with at least five children. Thus, Finland in a sense was the first Scandinavian country to adopt an actual process of equalizing the financial burdens of families.

In 1947, the idea of "family wages" was launched by Finnish employers' organizations, obviously influenced by the Swedish family allowance system introduced the same year; that is, children's allowances were suggested as an alternative to general wage increases. The objective was to avoid a new inflationary wage-price spiral. Despite their adherence to the principle of equal pay, the labor organizations were definitely interested in such a remarkable social benefit. The government hastened to take advantage of this situation, decreeing in September, 1947, that a system of "family wages" to employees with families would be adopted in the whole country. The system was shortly replaced by a general scheme of children's allowances covering the whole population and all children.

At the same time that the equalization of family costs gradually found acceptance, maternal and child care were improved. A law providing communal maternal and child care centers enacted in 1944 decreed that the centers were mandatory in every community.

Thus the general system of equalization of family costs which came in force in 1948 was fundamentally based on neither family policy nor social policy. The nature of the reform was almost solely connected with wage and economic policy. Even if the impetus to the child allowances system was of a wage policy nature, the arguments for it were basically demographic. However, more and more often social policy motives were brought up. The cost of children should be evened out so that families with children could live on the same standard as childless families.

Structural Change in Social Development

Since the 1950s social development has been characterized by a noticeable change in structure. The determining feature has been a decrease in the population in sparsely populated areas, and a growth in population centers of different sizes. The proportion of the population engaged in agriculture has diminished rapidly, while that in industry and the service trades has increased. During the mid-1960s even the state undertook measures to get agricultural production to correspond to domestic consumption. These included, among others, measures to decrease the size of cultivated areas. While 46 percent of the economically active population were working in the agricultural sector in 1950, the corresponding figure in 1975 was only 16 percent.

Even if the movement of labor to rapidly growing industries characterized by high productivity has been an important factor in the increase of well-being, the rapid structural change raised several difficult problems. In sparsely settled Finland giving up agriculture almost always entails a change in residence. As a result, internal as well as external migration became more and more lively. Those in the most sparsely settled east and north of Finland moved to the already noticeably urbanized and industrialized southern part of the country, or, to a great extent, to Sweden.

It has been necessary to build new service facilities, dwellings, and roads in the urban centers. The newcomers have had difficulties in adjusting themselves, and there has been a shortage of housing. The drawbacks of migration were especially evident in the abandoned areas.

The reconstruction after the war did not allow for improving social policy. However, in the 1960s when the economic growth in Finland had reached a relatively high level the pressure for increasing income transfers to nonactive population groups became greater and greater. Clearly, employment and labor force policy had to be intensively developed during this time of structural change. The health care which, compared with the other Scandinavian countries, had been modest and imperfect became now a rapidly expanding part of our national economy. In 1964 the general law on health insurance came into force. In 1972 a new national health law was enacted according to which the municipality must take charge of the health care of the inhabitants, transportation of the ill, school health care, and dental hygiene in its area.

In the field of policy that affects retired people, the benefits granted by national retirement pensions which had been very unsatisfactory were improved continuously. In 1960 a general employment pension came into force, and in time this was enlarged to include more and more sectors of society.

While in 1960 slightly more than 9 percent of the gross national product (GNP) was used for income-transfer programs, the corresponding portion in 1974 was a bit more than 16 percent (see table 1).

Table 1 Percent of GNP Expended for Family Policy and for Social Policy

	Social Policy	Family Policy
1950	8.3	3.7
1955	8.8	3.3
1960	9.4	2.4
1965	11.0	2.5
1970	14.2	2.0
1974	16.4	1.6

Income redistribution mainly directed to the retired, the work disabled, the ill, and families of widows resulted in a regression in the field of family policy proper during the 1960s. From 1950 to 1970 family policy expenditures declined from 3.7 percent to 1.6 percent of GNP. The real value of child allowance decreased, and only minor reforms were enacted. Thus in 1961 a special child allowances law came into force, the purpose of which was to give support in connection with care and raising of a child by families in difficult straits. At the beginning of 1962 a law on housing subsidy to families with children was enacted according to which a housing subsidy can be given to those who live in rented housing.

The increasing emigration at the end of the 1960s and the continuously decreasing birth rate forcibly drew attention to population questions, and in the 1970s a possible rearrangement of family policy became a frequent topic of discussion. One evident result of this was the day care law which came into force in 1973, the purpose of which was to make day care programs a general social service system. In 1973 also the Parliament accepted a government proposal according to which an increased child allowance would be paid for children under three years of age. Further, equalization of family financial burdens has been extended to some degree under the present law.

In political circles opinion has become more favorable toward family and population policy. Many political parties have adopted a population and family policy program, and many members of the current Parliament have, when interviewed, emphasized their desire to improve family policy. The motives have more often been a fear of a labor force shortage and the threat of a decrease in population than the idea of fairness; that is, society should reimburse more of the expenses accrued by families with children than it now does.

Content of the Finnish Family Policy

Family Policy Concept

"Social policy" is the term for the manifold work carried out by the Finnish society through which society tries to improve the conditions of those in difficulties or in need and of those who live in inadequate social conditions. More and more, when a certain minimum standard of living is gradually insured, the realization of economic and social equality has risen to the fore.

According to the Finnish system, social policy can be divided into the following sections:

1. Social security policy, which is the main part of social policy

    a) Social insurance: insurance against unemployment and illness; old-age security in which the insured himself, his employer, and in some cases also the state share the financing

    b) Social assistance which is financed by general taxation: maternity benefits, child allowance, student grants, and invalid benefits

c) Social service: maternity and child clinics, home help service, and child care programs

d) Social welfare: child, youth, or vagrant welfare

2. Labor policy: protection of workers, working agreements and labor force policy

3. Health welfare

4. Housing policy.

Parts of the following can also be included in social policy:

5. Education policy

6. Regional planning, the problems of which are perhaps mainly dealt with in cultural and economic policy.

In Finland, family policy is not a separate sector of social policy nor does it seem to belong to any other sector of societal policy. An official definition of family policy is also lacking. Family policy is mainly an operational aspect which can be added to different measures taken by the authorities regardless of what area of societal policy these measures come under. The main family policy measures are included in the social policy sections.

Armas Nieminen,[3] who was the first in Finland to make a more thorough examination of family policy, felt that it was a part of population policy but at the same time also a part of social policy. According to Nieminen, population policy, which means affecting the development of quantitative relations within the population, can be considered an independent branch of societal policy. And again, family policy, the support of families, is to be considered one of the means used in population policy. Family policy, however, is also social policy, because it includes the application of a social aspect to the section of society formed by families and aims at insuring them a reasonable standard of living, security in a social sense, and happiness. As a part of social policy, family policy aims in this way at achieving fairness for families, and as a part of population policy, it aims at keeping the birth rate sufficiently high and the size of families large enough. Family policy can thus be treated as an independent sphere in the social policy system; but, equally as well, separate, in connection with different sections of social policy. Nowadays, family policy measures are generally considered as income maintenance or social service.

As to the content of family policy, Riitta Auvinen,[4] without taking a

[3] Armas Nieminen, *Mitä on sosiaalipolitiikka* (Helsinki: 1955).

[4] Riitta Auvinen, *Tämän päivän sosiaalipolitiikka* (Helsinki: 1971).

stand on how it fits into social development policy, notes that family policy includes all the aims and measures whose purpose is to aid and support the formation of a family, its preservation, and its development economically, spiritually, and as a healthy body.

The Family Council—an organization founded in 1973 by the Finnish Population and Family Federation and the Finnish Cultural Foundation and dissolved in 1976 after having fulfilled its task to obtain information in the whole field of family policy and to initiate proposals in this sphere—defined family policy as "the whole formed by all actions taken to create the prerequisites for the realization of favorable family life enriching human relations and offering favorable ground for growth" and aimed at "the realization of the potential of family life and helping out those who are most in need.[5]

Hence family policy contains both direct and indirect measures. The sphere of the indirect family policy measures is very difficult to limit. However, it can be seen to include all supportive action taken by society meant for all citizens regardless of whether they have a family or not, but which at the same time improves the position of families. On the one hand, one point of departure for family policy is the examination of society's expectations regarding the family. Here family policy is to be understood as government action aimed at affecting the family. On the other hand, another point of departure could be what the family expects and hopes for from society, thus in a way rising to the society level from the inside. Here the examination starts by looking at the consequences or the demands from the family level on all of societal policy. In practice, the objectives of family policy must be defined as lying between these two extreme alternatives.

Even if the Family Council was inclined to see family policy as including all measures aimed at affecting the family both directly and indirectly, and even if it currently seems to be the tendency among theorists to see family policy in its broadest sense, most of the measures which indirectly affect the life of families are not in general, at least among social administrators, considered as family policy. Hence family policy—meaning only measures that affect families with children—excludes most indirect measures such as educational policy, housing policy, old-age security, and labor policy which, however, undoubtedly contribute to the welfare of families. The disbursements noted in the social expenditure statistics under the heading

[5] Perheneuvosto, "Perhepolitiikan tavoiteohjelma" (unpublished, Helsinki: 1976), p. 6.

"Children and Families" may give a picture of the prevailing concept of what the Finnish view could consider as family policy:

Maternity allowances and benefits
Day care centers for children
Family day care
Child allowances
Child care allowances
Prepayments of child support
Child welfare
Child guidance clinics
Children's homes
Training schools
School meals
Home-help services
Vacations for housewives and children.

Family guidance can also be added to this list. For the time being it is practiced mainly by private organizations and municipalities.

Family Policy Motives
In Finland, population policy aspects have always been strongly emphasized when outlining family policy reforms. That was also the case in the report of the Committee on the Equalization of Family Burdens published in 1966,[6] the first and only committee report to date which has attempted to draw up a total plan for Finnish family policy. This report stated that the most important basic motives of family policy are the safeguarding of a basic standard of living for children, equal opportunities for development for all citizens, and protection of the growth of both the population and the labor force. One concrete objective of family policy presented in the report was the insuring of an annual population growth of at least over one-half percent. This could, according to the committee, take place primarily by making more effective equalization of financial burdens in families with a large number of children.

Population policy aspects are also evident in the report of the Child Day Care Committee,[7] where it was noted that child day care services are one form of family policy support, through which society is trying to help families with children. A well-cared-for family—a goal of family policy—af-

[6]*Komiteanmietintö* 1966:A7, *Perhekustannusten tasaus komiteanmietintö, 1971* (Helsinki, 1966).

[7]*Komiteanmietintö* 1971:A20, *Lasten päivä haitokomiteanmietintö* (Helsinki, 1971).

fects, in turn, the structure of the population and the labor force, guaranteeing steady population development and the opportunity to practice a balanced and predictable labor policy, which in turn has a positive effect on all phenomena in the cultural and economic life of the country.

Close connections between family policy and economic policy can also be seen. This connection has been brought up especially by Pekka Kuusi, who outlined the general trends of the Finnish social policy in the 1960s and whose influence on the development of Finnish social policy has been striking. He especially emphasized that income equalization serves to support economic growth by mobilizing human resources and stabilizing consumer demand.[8] Kuusi saw social policy as a means to increase the economic growth and to heighten the standard of living of the population.

Even if population policy motives and economic aspects have appeared to be of great importance in the debate concerning improvement of family policy, the social policy aspects, and partly also health policy aspects, have more or less directly motivated the family policy measures.

In Finland, where the individual-centered conception of society is prevalent,[9] meaning that society is obliged to support the welfare and comfort of its citizens, the individual's right to freedom of choice is often emphasized and used in the debate on family policy reform. In a pluralistic country such as Finland where social reforms could be described as compromises between the political parties and the interest groups, such as labor organizations, a reform is forced to be more or less neutral.

This neutrality has been discernible in the current debate concerning support to parents with small children.[10] This benefit gives parents better opportunities to choose the kind of care they want for their children. The principle of neutrality is also visible in the maternity benefit, which from its beginning in 1937 has been paid either in the form of a maternity pack containing clothes and items necessary for the care of the baby or in cash.

Clearly, measures intended to level out expenses incurred by having children are neutral when paid in cash and not in kind, and when one disregards the possible implicit population or economic policy idea. These measures have also generally been regarded only as a way to increase the consumption capacity of families with children. Nor has it been considered

[8] Kuusi, *Social Policy for the Sixties*, p. 94.

[9] *Komiteanmietintö* 1971:A25, *Sosiaalihuollon periaate. Komiteanmietintö I. Yleiset periaatteet* (Helsinki: 1971), p. 8.

[10] *Komiteanmietintö* 1971:A20 and *Komiteanmietintö* 1976:42, *Perhekasvatustoimikunnan mietintö.*

meaningful to link them to income and thus make them a general income-transfer measure.[11]

Even if the decision-makers' fundamental motives in proposing a family policy reform may have been of a demographic or economic nature, the explicit arguments formulated nowadays in committee reports and official proposals and documents are those of fairness, democracy, freedom of choice, and so on; in other words, motives that belong to the field of social policy.

Also, in the proposals made by members of Parliament family policy motives have been mostly formulated as social policy.[12] Earlier, reference was often made to the necessity of a vertical equalization of differences in the standard of living. This motive played a very important role, especially during the first years of Finnish family policy, when about two thirds of all family policy proposals emphasized the necessity of supporting poor families. The horizontal equalization motive has been brought up both during the postwar years and during the past few years. Recently, interest has been directed toward young families. Emphasis has been given to the fact that the position of young families with children is difficult in the society, as their income is low but their expenses high.

Sometimes even if the effects are not the opposite of what the official motives had hoped for, they are nevertheless often more numerous than expected. Day care illustrates this. In the government's proposal to Parliament children's day care was motivated from a family point of view, by the fact that an increasing number of mothers of preschool age children are employed and the daily care and education of their children must be left to someone else. Thus the day care system could be considered an attempt to further the current trend in development and to adjust families to it. But with this reform, society also tried to take into account at the same time not only demands by families but also demands made by the economic development. Explicitly, the motives were improvement of the standard of living of families, primarily through the parents' own work. There are, however, strong economic motives in the background, such as that of insuring society a sufficient supply of labor.

Measures on behalf of one-parent families and families with a disabled child which usually are considered as family policy measures could, however, be classified as social policy proper since they are intended to relieve

[11]*Komiteanmietintö* 1971:A25, p. 25.

[12]Leena Suominen, "Family Policy Motives behind Proposals in the Finnish Parliament," in *Yearbook of Population Research in Finland* (1975–76) (Helsinki, 1976), XIV, 30–41.

families in special difficulties. Benefits related to maternity have apparently been based to a great extent on public health motives.

The debate preceding a family reform often shows that the measures intended to support families with children are for the most part multipurposed, accentuating different motives from time to time. However, they are perhaps usually the result of international influence. The reforms, even if in a more modest form, have usually been directly borrowed from Sweden, which in Finland is considered the model of the welfare state. Hence a new reform and clearly also the motivation behind it could be considered as the result of the cooperation between the Nordic countries. But the development in other countries also has an impact on Finnish society, where influences from the outside world quickly make themselves felt. Especially in the last years Finnish society has proved to be very open-minded toward international influences while searching for aims, objectives, and means.

Family Policy in Action

The Mechanism of Policy-making

According to the Constitution of Finland, the Parliament in session represents the people to whom the power of the state essentially belong. The Parliament has been regarded as the most important political institution of Finland. Before a new social measure can be applied, therefore, it must be presented to Parliament and receive its approval.

Often the government or a ministry appoints a committee to study a current issue. The committee discusses the issue and submits its report to the sponsor which appointed the committee. After the report has completed a round of authorities and offices for judgment and statements of opinion, the government can make a proposal to Parliament for the enactment of a new law. A member or group of members of Parliament can also make a proposal to Parliament. Hence, matters can be initiated in Parliament through two channels, as a government proposal or as a proposal initiated by members of Parliament. Generally, a number of members sponsor a proposal. The number of proposals made by a Parliamentary faction or group of factions is rather small, and so most of the proposals are so-called "private" proposals.

In addition to the public authorities and the political parties the labor organizations are active in social welfare and often take the initiative in important social welfare reforms. The inspiration and initiative given by private bodies have also been very important. Through their initiative social welfare programs are often adopted by the authorities.

The Administration
The national authority for administration of social policy affairs is the Ministry of Social Affairs and Health. The National Board of Social Welfare handles the direct supervision and promotion of social security, which includes the measures considered as family policy proper, excluding maternity and child clinics which belong within the sphere of the National Board of Health. The boards are subordinated to the Ministry of Social Affairs and Health, which handles legislation on social security, budgeting, and major appointments. Hence there is no organization on the national level which takes care of, and specializes solely in, family policy questions. However, to a great extent the promotion of family policy is dealt with by the Finnish Population and Family Federation, whose research institute specializes in family and population policy and demography.

Social security comes under local municipal self-administration. Originally parishes of the Lutheran Church, the municipalities are the basic units of local government. The communities enjoy a high degree of self-administration. The policy-making body of a municipality is its council, elected by direct popular vote. Executive powers are entrusted to the municipal board and various specialized boards. The council appoints these boards for four years at a time, approves the annual budget, and levies a local income tax on the inhabitants, this being quite separate from state taxation. The members of the council and of the boards represent local political groups.

For the local administration of social welfare, assistance, and services every municipality is obliged to appoint a social welfare board and a board of health. Detailed instructions on the local administration of social work must be laid down in the bylaws of the municipality. Appeals against decisions of the social welfare board can usually be made to the provincial administration and appeals against decisions of the National Board of Social Welfare to the Supreme Administrative Court.

Family Policy Measures
Finnish social policy has been built up gradually as economic resources and political conditions have allowed. Policies of support for the family could be divided into: (1) measures aimed at equalizing the costs to families of rearing children, (2) social and economic benefits related to maternity; (3) special allowances to meet special problem situations; (4) measures which indi-

Table 2 Family Policy Expenditures in 1975

	Million Marks [a]	Percent
Payments aimed at equalizing family financial burdens	1,120	48.7
Child allowances	706	30.7
Housing subsidies for families with children	107	4.6
State tax rebates for children	307	13.4
Maternal and child programs	516	22.4
Maternity allowances and benefits	258	11.2
Children's day care	285	11.2
Other family policy expenditures	510	22.2
Child care allowances and child's supplement to family pensions	79	3.4
Prepayment of child support	35	1.5
Communal home helpers	108	4.7
Vacations for housewives and children	14	0.7
School meals	274	11.9
Child welfare	154	6.7
Total	2,300	100.0

SOURCE: Ellala and Kotiranta, pp. 57–58.

[a] As of April 1, 1977, the exchange rate was: 1 Finnish mark = $0.26. *Eds.*

rectly ameliorate the situation of particular families although aimed at other objectives.

As table 2 indicates, the measures aimed at equalizing family expenses incurred by having children—chiefly child allowances—form the main part of family policy expenditures. Consequently, Finnish family policy could probably be described as being above all a policy designed to equalize the burdens of families with children.

The responsibility for financing family policy measures resides primarily with the employers. In 1975 their contribution was 44 percent of the total expenditures. The proportion paid by the state and the municipalities was about the same size, or 25 percent, while the employees contributed only 6 percent. Most of the measures are financed by the state and the municipalities together. Hence the cost is paid equally by the state and the municipalities together whereas the municipalities are mainly responsible for the financing of children's welfare and school meals and the state is entirely responsible for housing subsidies. However, child allowances, which are the largest item, are paid for in total by the employers.[13]

[13] Esa Ellala and Maija-Liisa Kotiranta, *Social Expenditure in 1974 and Preliminary Data for 1975.*

Even if these measures constitute the greatest part of family policy expenditures they are relatively modest income transfers from the family point of view. They are not big enough to remove the obstacles of an economic nature which prevent families from having the desirable number of children, which was the original aim.

Benefits related to maternity and child care and child upbringing are of a more intervening and influential nature. Maternity benefits as well as maternity and child clinics could be regarded more as public health policy than family policy. Their impact on child and maternal mortality has also been significant, and thus they have been worthwhile population policy measures.

It should be mentioned that a family policy payment is nearly always paid to one member of the family and not to the family as a whole. Child allowances, for example, are paid for the support and upbringing of the child, maternity benefits are paid to each expectant mother, and so on. The only support paid formally to the family is housing subsidies. Here, a "family" means people living together in or out of wedlock in a common household, including at least one child in the care of the head of the household or of someone living with the head of the household on a nontemporary basis.

Measures aimed at equalizing family maintenance costs. The most significant measures for equalizing family maintenance costs are child allowances, which are paid by the state to the mother for the support and upbringing of children under sixteen years of age. Every child living in Finland is entitled to this allowance. The general rule is that the child allowance is paid to the mother or some other adult who is providing for the child. At first, the child allowance consisted of an equal payment for each child of the family, but since 1962 it has been graded according to the number of children. Since 1973 an increased child allowance has been paid for children under three years of age.

When child allowances were introduced in 1947 in Finland the object was to avoid a new inflationary wage-price spiral. Thus this reform which has been so far the greatest in the family policy field in Finland was carried out without paying attention to the fundamental problem of family policy: equalization of family expenses incurred by having children. Even if later its equalizing aim was emphasized there has never been any real attempt to decide how high a standard of consumption should be insured to families with different numbers of children. As the child allowance has never been connected to any index the result has been a large fluctuation in its real value depending on the economic situation and political compromises. Today the value of the child allowance is about 10 percent of the average maintenance cost of a child.

Since the size of the child allowance depends solely on the number of children, its relative value is less the higher the income of the family. Its redistribution effect is on the horizontal level, for the means used to cover the cost of child allowances are included in the social security contribution charged to employers, and the social security contribution affects the wage standard of employees with children and those without to the same extent.

Earlier, the value of the child allowances was followed more intensively than nowadays, indicating that child allowances have been more or less accepted as additional income in general, given with no specific aim to families with children. It is likely that in most cases child allowances are used as additional income to cover expenditures of the whole family.

Housing subsidies represent quite a different category of family policy measures paid for a special purpose, the subsidization of housing costs of low-income families. A family with at least one child under sixteen, with a yearly income or property not exceeding a limit defined in the regulations, is entitled to a housing subsidy from state funds. The term "child" can also include a dependent person under twenty who is continuing full-time study or training, or who is incapacitated. Housing subsidies can also be paid to a family with children whether they live in rented housing or in their own home.

Housing in Finland is quite expensive by general European standards because of various factors, including severe climatic conditions. Dwellings are often too expensive for the proper housing of large families, especially in urban areas, and quite a large number of families have to live in houses or flats that are too small so that they can meet other urgent living expenses. Owing to the very rapid structural change caused by intensive migration, there has been a housing shortage in cities and towns which may have created dissatisfaction and contributed to a lessened willingness to establish families and to a desire to postpone having children; society has not been able to adjust itself to the rapid structural change in the housing policy sector. Certainly, the housing subsidy could be considered an important measure which is nevertheless inadequate since it cannot remove the housing shortage which has made the housing problem, especially of young people, difficult to solve.

In 1976 a new tax system came into being, that of separate taxation. There was an increase in the size of deductions for children. In addition to child deductions, a family with children has the right to deduct from their taxable income in their state and municipal tax returns a so-called "special work income deduction," if both spouses are employed.

Tax deduction for children has been the subject of criticism because families with small incomes could not get full benefit of it. As a child allowance, the amount could be considered mainly a horizontal income tranfer from families without children to families with children or from families with few children to those with many children. However, the tax deduction is quite small and constitutes only about one tenth of the average maintenance cost of a child.

Social and economic benefits related to maternity. The family policy introduced in the 1930s was mainly a motherhood policy and the maternity benefit inaugurated in 1937 was the first major family policy reform. Today all mothers qualify regardless of economic position. The only formal requirements are that pregnancy has lasted at least 180 days, and that the woman before the end of the fourth month of pregnancy is medically examined at a maternity clinic where assistance and guidance on health care are given during her pregnancy and for the first two weeks after confinement.

Maternity benefits are paid either in cash or in the form of a maternity pack. The pack, which contains clothes and other items for the child and is valued at about twice the cash payment, is intended to give guidance to the mother in the care of the baby. The cash payment equals about three days' average industrial pay.

In the child clinics each child is examined by a doctor at least three times during the first year, and at least once a year afterward. There are also supplementary checkups by the clinic nurse at frequent intervals. All services given by the maternity and child welfare clinics are completely free of charge.

M ·rnity and child clinics have contributed to a high level of guidance and support for the general health of mothers and children by reducing infant mortality in Finland during the last decades to one of the lowest in the world. The maternity benefit, whose cash value is rather low, has been more important as a public health measure than as a measure of equalizing family expenditures, for the examination of the expectant mother is a precondition for the collection of the be ·fit. The high level of maternal and child welfare has also been considered one of the essential preconditions for the economic growth in Finland.[14] However, it appears that the child clinics are not adequately prepared to deal with issues concerning the psychological development of the small child, and problems of this kind are becoming more apparent as the basic physical problems are taken care of. It is likely that more attention will be paid to psychological problems and their treatment in the

[14] Kuusi, *Social Policy for the Sixties*, p. 226.

future. Maternity and child clinics will be able to offer specialist and consultant services in psychology as well as in physiotherapy, dentistry, and pediatrics.

More and more improvements have been made in maternal and child welfare. Maternity leave has been lengthened to 174 days. During this period every woman is entitled to a maternity allowance of about 30 percent to 50 percent of an employed woman's average daily pay. If the mother is the principal or sole family earner she is also entitled to a "provider's allowance." This maternity allowance is paid to all women who give birth to a child. Those who are not economically active are given the minimum maternity allowance, which is about one fourth of the minimum wage.

In 1973 new legislation was brought into effect to make up the deficiencies in children's day care provision. The intention was to make such provision a public social service available to anyone in need of it. Every municipality is now liable by law for the provision of sufficient day care centers or family day care to meet the municipality's needs. Under the new law day care has to be arranged primarily for children who need it from the social and educational viewpoint. Day care service fees are rather inexpensive and are graduated according to the financial situation of the parent or guardian; in some cases the service may be free of charge.

All children under seven are eligible for day care centers, and they must be grouped according to age in each nursery. The law also regulates family day care: the maximum number of children in such a group is four, including any children of the person in charge. Day care in families can be guided or supervised. Guided family day care is run by the municipality, so that the fee is the same as that in a day care center. Supervised day care is run by private individuals, and the fee is determined by supply and demand. This makes it noticeably more expensive than family day care or day care centers. There are also clauses that control the activities of small play groups and the level of supervision.

Although the Children's Day Care Act was passed in 1973 and the number of day care centers has steadily increased, the need for day care is substantial. It is estimated that only one half of the need is satisfied by this institution regulated by the law. The scarcity of public day care implies that day care service is given mainly to children from one-parent families, low-income families, or families in special difficulties. To a very great extent middle- and high-income families are forced to use day care run by private individuals (table 3) where the fee may equal the taxed minimum wages of a married woman.

Table 3 Forms of Day Care and Their Estimated Use

	Children	Percent
Day Care		
All-day groups	34,500	15
Half-day groups	27,000	11
Guided family day care	20,000	9
Supervised day care	40–60,000	21
Domestic employees	30–40,000	15
Parent, relatives, etc.	52–83,000	29
		100

SOURCE: Iiris Niemi and Leena Suominen, *Suomalainen lapsiperlu* (Helsinki: Perheneuvosto, 1976), p. 40.

Different child care alternatives, especially for small children, have been debated for a long time. A comparison between the future need and supply of the day care services in Finland also shows that it might be difficult to limit the development to the projections made by the Board of Social Welfare.[15] If future demand for labor surpasses the supply, the demand for day care places will be much greater than now anticipated. However, the current recession may have changed the situation.

Among the alternatives to day care institutions particular mention has been made of a special care allowance to parents with small children. It has been suggested that it be realized in the following way: maternity leave—or parental leave—will be lengthened to one year, and after this the opportunity to take child care leave without pay and without losing one's job will be offered to either parent until the child is three years old. Another alternative for parents of small children is part-time work, and more flexible working schedules.

Special allowances and services. In certain difficult family situations the public authorities will give support in the form of home help. The law provides that a municipal home help can take over the regular duties of a housewife, especially in large families, if the mother is ill, pregnant, suffering from stress, needs a holiday, or is incapable of carrying out her ordinary duties for other reasons. Home help is normally given for two weeks only in any one family. It is a free service for persons of limited means, but generally the municipal council will charge a moderate fee fixed by the Board of Social Welfare.

A bill now under preparation is likely to extend home-help services to

[15]*Työvoimaministeriö, Työvoimatarpeet ja työmarkkinoiden tasapainottomuudet,* V. 1975– 1980; *Työvoimaministeriö, Monistettuja tutkimuksia,* No. 16 (Helsinki: 1975).

anyone who occasionally needs help in the home and is unlikely to cope with personal or family problems without some support.

Especially in big cities the scarcity of home-help service has been severe because of the increasing labor participation of women with children; the noticeable immigration of young families to cities, which leaves grandparents and relatives who might have assisted in case of illness far away in another part of the country; the necessity to use home helps for the growing number of elderly people, and so forth. As in all fields of social service there seems to be a multiplying need also for home helps which it has not been able to satisfy partly because of the scarcity of human resources but partly also because of the legislation which obliges the municipality to employ only a minimum number of home helps.

Among allowances intended to support families in special difficulties special mention should be made of the "care allowance" and prepayment of child support. Since 1970 a care allowance has been paid for the support of severely handicapped children living at home. The purpose is to help meet the inevitable extra expense arising from special care and treatment, including physical therapy.

Because collecting maintenance payments from the person decreed responsible for child support (divorced fathers and fathers of illegitimate children) may be an arduous and time-consuming task, the social officials can make a prepayment of child support to the mother of the child. The same official then collects that sum from the person who is responsible for maintenance. The purpose of the prepayments is to insure that payments are made for children whose parents or guardians are alive, but whose payments have been unsatisfactorily arranged. Prepayments of child support are paid out of municipal funds each month for a child under eighteen years of age born in or out of wedlock. If the child for some reason is not entitled to prepayments of maintenance, child support is paid out of public funds with certain restrictions.

Indirect economic support of the family. Several general welfare policy measures, particularly in the field of public health and education, such as scholarships, school meals, free health services for children, and so forth, also contribute to the economic support of the family. Since they are generally considered to belong to other sections than family policy they are not discussed here.

However, comparable with the measures directly aimed at equalizing family burdens is the school reform that has gradually been introduced in the country. This reform combines the four-year primary school and the five-year junior secondary school into a free, compulsory, comprehensive school. It means not only equalizing opportunities for obtaining the basic knowledge required in society but also better health care for children and the possibility for every child to receive a free school meal.

Current Debate on Family Policy

During the past few years the most important family policy reform under discussion has been the expansion of child care alternatives by supporting the care of children at home. Other important questions have been the improvement of family guidance and the realization of education in family and human relations, not only in basic and vocational schools but also in adult education. This training in family and human relations, which in principle is included in the basic school curriculum, is still in the planning and experimental stage. Among other questions under discussion and consideration is the development of social security for housewives.

Child Care Support for Small Children

Child care support for small children, termed "mother's wage," has been under discussion in Finland ever since the 1950s. Originally it meant a social allowance or an increased child allowance given to mothers of small children, and at that time it was assumed that the mother would stay home to take care of her children. Later on, the term came to include support intended for all mothers caring for small children, even for mothers who hold jobs outside the home.

The support for small children has mainly been justified by child care and educational and economic views. It has been considered desirable that as long as the child is small he should be cared for by his own mother. Thus the mother or, as has been emphasized during the past few years, either parent must be given the opportunity to care for his/her own child by giving a big enough allowance so that the parents do not feel that they have to work while the child is small.

The support has also been considered as compensation for the work which the mother does at home for the benefit of her child. It has still been deemed justified that families who care for their children at home should also benefit from support given by society, not only those families whose children attend day care centers maintained by society. Since day care maintained by public funds is expensive, it has further been deemed economically more profitable to care for children at home than to keep them in day care centers.

In its report the Committee for the Equalization of Family Burdens [16] called for the implementation of the mother's wage. This wage would be payable to not gainfully employed mothers with small children. The motive behind the committee's recommendation was that every mother should have the opportunity to take care of her child at least during the child's first three years of life. The Committee on Children's Day Care [17] also proposed a care allowance to be paid for all children under the compulsory school age. This allowance was seen as justified because of the occurrence of childbearing and the need for child care at the very time that parents' incomes are lowest and they are establishing a family and buying a home. However, the Children's Day Care Act was passed by the Parliament, but the bill on care allowance was not.

In 1974 the Ministry for Health and Social Affairs appointed a committee, [18] one of whose tasks was to search for a mother's wage system that would grant mothers better opportunities to stay at home and take care of their own children. According to the committee, child care support should be primarily given for all children under three years of age. Thus conditions would be created for parents to take care of their children at home, at an age when their home environment generally is their most natural growth environment. Care support should be equal to the smallest maternity allowance (360 mk/month in August, 1976.). Care support should also be paid for children between the ages of three and six who because of illness risk or abnormality would be best cared for at home. To qualify for care support for a first-born, the parents, or at least the mother, should participate in the child's care in an acceptable manner and should take part in a child care course.

The care support would be paid only to families whose child is not attending an all-day care center supported by society. Those who do take advantage of such all-day care would not have the right to receive care support; instead, the support would be paid directly to the entity responsible for the day care. The years that the parent stays at home and receives child care support should be taken into account as years entitling the parent to a pension.

During the past year the question of care support has been making the rounds for judgments of opinion, and in the fall of 1976 the Ministry for

[16] *Komiteanmietintö* 1966:A7.   [17] *Komiteanmietintö* 1971:A20.

[18] *Komiteanmietintö* 1976:42.

Health and Social Affairs decided to set up a three-year experiment in some municipalities to get an idea of the social and economic effects of the care support. The suggested practice of paying wages to mothers has also received a good deal of criticism. This criticism has come primarily from those who strive for equality between the sexes, but to a certain extent also from labor organizations and leftist parties. Doubts have mainly centered on whether the mother's wage would benefit those families most in need of this kind of support and whether it would improve the status of women.

The Committee on the Position of Women in the Finnish Society[19] took a negative stand on the mother's wage issue in the form suggested by the Committee on the Equalization of Family Burdens. It was felt that a mother's wage paid by society would be fairly small in any case, compared to the wages of employed women, and there was doubt whether it would increase the choices available to women, particularly to those who absolutely need the income from their jobs. The same kind of criticism has also been made of the suggested care support.

To support the care of children under school age at home in families of small means and with several children, however, about ten rural communes and two cities pay a kind of communal mother's wage or home-care support. The idea of paying such a support is mainly of an economic nature: it is cheaper for the community to pay the support to the mother than to arrange day care for her children when she is working outside the home, especially if the mother lacks professional training. The granting of this support is based on the principle of individual care and depends on need as rated according to statistics provided by the Social Welfare Board.

Family Guidance

In its report the Committee on Family Education[20] suggested ways to improve and expand the system of family guidance. The committee maintains as its main principle that a diversified society should be able to offer different types of family guidance services, and these services should be supported by society.

By family guidance the committee refers to the kind of activity which by means of advice, suggestions, and discussions strives to improve the relations between family members. Thus family guidance also consists of information concerning personal relations as in legal and social aid matters, but it does not consist of economic aid.

[19] *Komiteanmietintö* 1970:A8, *Naisten asemas tutkivan komiteanmietintö* (Helsinki, 1970).

[20] *Komiteanmietintö* 1976:42.

The committee also examined different alternatives in improving the organization of family guidance on the part of the social welfare boards, health boards, and child guidance clinics. The basis for the alternatives was that family guidance is not restricted to family guidance centers; all the occupational groups that come in contact with people, as, for instance, social workers, health care workers, parish workers, lawyers, and teachers, have to work out family problems. For this reason the committee felt that family guidance and its study belong to everyone whose work is helping people, and therefore no collective body can practice family guidance as its exclusive right. The municipality must, to the best of its ability, arrange matters so that family guidance is available to its residents to the degree and in the forms of activity necessitated by the needs of the people.

Consequences and Implications of Family Policy

The effect of certain family policy measures is nearly impossible to ascertain exactly for there is always a legion of other circumstances and factors working at the same time in the same or the opposite direction. One can only try to imagine what direction the effects of the measure will take.

The fact that family policy in Finland has been built up gradually as allowed by economic resources and prevailing political conditions also contributes to making family policy measures an overlapping and incomplete system difficult to interpret. An exhaustive and thorough analysis of the Finnish family policy and its effects is also lacking. Before a new measure is applied, however, a committee is ordinarily formed to draw up a plan for the measure. The committee, whose members usually represent both expert authorities and different political parties, make studies to clarify the measure, interview experts, and so on. They also may order a survey to estimate its probable effects.

Attempts have further been made to clarify how different measures have affected different population groups, different-sized families, and so on. The main interest has been in seeing how various subsidies have increased the family income. It has of course not been possible to clarify to what degree a single measure has brought about the demographic or economic effect which was the motive for the application of a reform. It has only been possible to acknowledge that a measure has contributed to the development.

Most of the research on family policy has been done at the research department of the Ministry of Social Affairs and Health and at the Population Research Institute of the Finnish Population and Family Federation.

Finnish family policy has mainly been considered a part of social policy, and its measures as well as its motives have been typical of those of social policy in the Nordic countries. In other words, it has contributed to the goal of social policy, "to increase equality by improving the standard of living of its citizens."

Generally, family policy measures, and income transfers in particular, could be considered relatively small and insufficient so that the psychological significance of these income transfers probably has often been larger than their economic significance. However, the general rise in the standard of living and the rapid improvement in other social policy fields have compensated to a great extent for the slow development of family policy income transfers and in some cases made it less necessary to improve family policy payments. Thus, enacting a public health insurance system almost always means more money for the care and upbringing of children.

Increasingly, with the rising standard of living the quality of life has come within the sphere of family policy. One significant question is how men and women can have equal opportunities to participate in work and social life on the one hand and family life on the other.

Family policy could be said to have contributed actively to leveling out differences between the sexes. This holds true especially with regard to children's day care, tax reform, and also to the increasingly more effective birth control with access to effective contraceptives and practically free abortion. The participation of married women in the labor force has been especially facilitated. The participation rate of all women aged fifteen to seventy-five capable of working is 71 percent (or 58 percent of the whole female population). Women, however, do not participate in social life to the same extent as men. In families where both parents are gainfully employed the wife usually does more work at home than the husband. Wives still live in a traditional world.

Gradually the debate has focused more and more on questions of how the care and upbringing of children and their socialization can be organized in the best possible way. During the 1970s the Finnish society has been apt to enact far-reaching social policy reforms whose realization, however, must be postponed into the future because they compete for society's scarce resources. This implies that the Parliament is forced to abstain from enacting new laws on social reforms.

❧10

DENMARK

Jacob Vedel-Petersen

DANISH USAGE HAS no official definition of the term "family policy" nor has the concept any generally accepted meaning. Nevertheless, the expression occurs repeatedly in political discussions and is commonly used in the Danish language. No attempt will be made here to define the concept, but family policy will be described, based on the accepted use of the term.

In Denmark, family policy concerns measures in support of families with children, and the objective is to lend support to parents in their function as parents. Family policy refers to a series of measures designed to support the family and also covers statutory provisions regulating relations between individual members of the family.

A "family" in the political sense in Denmark is typically a two-generation unit, parents and children. Measures in support of families that assume responsibility for care of their older members would scarcely come under the heading of family policy. They are more a phase in care of the elderly, since their aim is not to support the primary family but to utilize its resources to overcome the isolation in which the elderly find themselves in Denmark. In this manner the elderly are provided with a less expensive and more humane form of care than they could otherwise have in a nursing home or housing built specially for the old.

The emphasis in Danish family policy has been placed on families with young children and children of school age. The age range for children in a family-policy context extends from conception to fifteen to eighteen years. Aid for older juveniles will frequently come under the heading of support for

JACOB VEDEL-PETERSEN is a Program Director, Danish National Institute of Social Research, Copenhagen, Denmark.

young adults, and many of the benefits and allowances are linked to their education, thus considered more as an aspect of education policy than family policy. Admittedly, the purpose of the latter category of allowances is analogous to that of the benefits available under family policy, but they are granted to the young people themselves. Moreover, it is not a condition of eligibility that recipients live within the primary family. However, the distinction is not hard and fast.

Thus we find that a family in the context of Danish family policy has two generations: father, mother, and children (or expected child); unmarried mothers or fathers with children (including unmarried expectant mothers without children); foster families; and adoptive families. Some problems of classification occur with common-law marriages (unmarried people living together and having children). In certain cases, such as in an evaluation of emergency needs, they are regarded as formally married, while in others the mother is considered in the category of unmarried mother with children. At various times in recent history certain groups—families with an unmarried head of household, including young unmarried mothers; families with many children; and economically poor families—have been the subject of special social welfare measures.

Family policy measures may be directed toward the family as a group or toward individuals within the family; a family-oriented measure is one that aims at supporting parents in exercising functions allotted to them within the context of parental authority.

Statutory Provisions Relating to Marriage

It is a statutory requirement under Danish law that both parties should be at least eighteen years old at marriage. However, exemption from this rule is frequently given, mostly on account of the woman's pregnancy. Exemption is granted after a study of each case and an assessment of the parties' maturity and their ability to maintain themselves, including the question of housing. Parental consent will be taken into account but is not necessary for exemption to be granted.

In Denmark a minor does not automatically come of age at marriage. The basic principle of equality of the spouses (equal rights of individual persons) is expressed in the legislation concerned with matrimony: the man and the woman owe each other mutual support and are jointly responsible for the welfare of the family.

Husband and wife are both under obligation to the best of their respective abilities to contribute toward upkeep of the family, including the children. It is the duty of every man and woman, so far as the state is concerned, to support his/her spouse and children under the age of eighteen. This support may take the form of cash or work within the home.

Parental authority over children born to the marriage is shared jointly by the parents. Parental authority over children born out of wedlock is the exclusive right of the mother.

The duty as parent includes an obligation to look after the child and a right to decide its personal affairs.

The duty of supporting the child rests upon both parents—including the unmarried father. But in his case the support will be converted to a fixed payment of maintenance.

If the parents fail in their duties toward the child, the authorities are invested with the power to assume care of the child and, if necessary, have the child removed from the home.

Children are under no financial obligation to their parents. In effect, they must fend for themselves from the age of eighteen, since the parental duty of maintenance is deemed to cease at that point. In addition, under the parental authority, parents can decide that their children will not stay in school longer than the statutory period of nine years. This would compel the child to be self-supporting from the age of sixteen, if he wished to continue his education beyond that age.

Danish law has no provisions requiring children to support their parents in old age. This obligation lies entirely with the state.

Marriage can be permanently dissolved by annulment or divorce and provisionally suspended by judicial separation.[1]

Judicial separation can be obtained when both parties are agreed in their desire for separation or when one party demands a separation, and the marital relationship has broken down irrevocably.

The law provides the following grounds for divorce:

1. After separation of one year, either party can apply.

2. When there is adultery by one of the parties, the other party can apply.

3. When the parties have been living apart for three years on account of incompatibility, either can apply.

4. When one party deserts the home for a period of two years, the other can apply.

[1] Statute No. 256, June 4, 1969.

5. When one party is declared insane or given a prison sentence of a certain severity, the other can apply.

6. When there is cruelty on the part of one party toward the other or toward the children, the other can apply.

7. When one party is declared missing, the other can apply.

It will be observed that the present legislation does not permit divorce without a prior period of separation unless one of the above-mentioned circumstances is present even when the couple agree in their desire for a divorce; but it is a point worthy of discussion whether the new Matrimonial Act should not, in fact, permit divorce with immediate effect.

It is a special feature of Danish law that divorce and judicial separation can be obtained by license without the formality of passing through the courts. Actually, the great majority of divorces and separations are by administrative license.

Of the above grounds for divorce, only the first (59 percent in 1970) and the second (37 percent in 1970) are of any practical significance. Few divorces are granted on other grounds.

When a couple obtain a judicial separation and divorce, the following points have to be decided:

1. How property is to be divided between them
2. Who is to have custody of the children, if applicable
3. Whether one party should pay maintenance to the other.

Under Danish law there is community of property: everything owned by the husband and wife on their marriage or acquired later becomes their joint property.

While the marriage is still in effect, however, each party may freely use and dispose of that part of their joint property that he/she owns, in other words, whatever he/she brought into the marriage or acquired during it. He/she can sell or use it, and his/her creditors can base their claims on it. To safeguard the interests of the other party, right of disposal is subject to certain restrictions. For example, one party cannot without the other's consent sell a house which serves as the family dwelling.

If the marriage is dissolved by separation, divorce, or death, the jointly owned property is divided into two equal portions irrespective of which one of the parties earned most during the marriage. Under this arrangement the wife is assured one half of the joint property even though she has had no form of gainful employment during the marriage. Division of the estate is usually conducted privately. Only about a thousand estates in divorce are administered by the courts.

If desired, husband or wife (or both) can draw up a marriage settlement in respect of their property or part of it, stipulating that the property is the sole and indivisible property of whoever makes the settlement (the same arrangement can be made by means of a bequest or by a gift to one of the parties). The significance of separate property in law is that such property is not subject to sharing when the estate is broken up. The separate property is withdrawn in advance by its owner.

Marriage settlements that establish separate property are a rare occurrence, found in less than 10 percent of all marriages.

The family dwelling will usually go to whichever party is granted custody of the children—or to the party to whose business enterprise the dwelling is attached. In the absence both of children and a business establishment, it will be allotted to the party whose name is stated in the title deed or lease. If it is a house belonging to one of the parties and included in the joint property, the other party must naturally be granted financial compensation, usually in the form of a mortgage deed.

The principle in law with regard to custody of the children is based on what is best for their welfare. Any "blame" on either party for collapse of the marriage is left out of the question. Generally speaking, young children up to two years of age are awarded to the mother.

Although in principle the law makes no distinction between the parents, in practice, custody of the children is most frequently awarded to the mother, who is still considered the parent most capable of bringing up the children. If the husband and wife disagree on custody of the children, divorce cannot be obtained by administrative license but must go before the courts. The parent who is not granted custody is usually awarded right of access to the child. He/she must also pay maintenance for the child.

Since April 1, 1976, the standard rate of maintenance which a husband must pay for each child in the custody of his wife has been D.kr. 3,636 per annum while the corresponding rate payable by a wife for each child in the custody of the husband is D.kr. 2,412 per annum. [As of April 1, 1977, the exchange rate was: 1 D.kr. = $0.17. *Eds.*] If children's maintenance is not paid by the set date, the local authority can advance the money on behalf of the child and then recover the outstanding payment(s) from the defaulting parent. If parents have incomes above what the law considers modest, the standard rate of maintenance is increased by a certain percentage. The higher rate is fixed according to the payer's income irrespective of whether the payer is the father or the mother. Maintenance payments are deductible from the payer's taxable income.

Husband and wife are free to agree whether one should pay maintenance to the other and, if so, how much and for how long. In the event that they make no arrangement about maintenance, the court will decide whether either should pay to the other and, if so, for how long. The amount is fixed by an administrative authority.

In deciding whether either party should pay maintenance to the other, the court—as stipulated by law—will consider the duration of the marriage and the individual's means of providing for himself/herself at a level not too far below the standard during marriage. Often the amount of maintenance is fixed for a specific period of years to help the recipient through a course of training or education or until he/she has found suitable employment. Although the law is neutral in its wording, using the term "spouse," it is almost invariably the wife who receives maintenance benefits. The amount is fixed after a detailed assessment of the personal and financial circumstances of husband and wife respectively. In practice, the main criterion will be their respective incomes (or potential income, if employment capability is utilized). The level of expenses, on the other hand, plays a less important role, except for the duty of maintenance toward children of the marriage. In the case of incomes in the medium range, the amount of maintenance will probably be in the region of one fourth of the differential between the incomes of the payer and the payee. But the total maintenance commitments of the payer to children and/or spouse will seldom exceed one third of his/her income. This sum can also be deducted from the payer's taxable income, and maintenance is registered and taxed as ordinary income for the recipient.

A commission report in 1974 on the status of women in Danish society found it appropriate in principle that maintenance contributions should be abolished completely. However, the Commission on Family Affairs recommended that the rule should be retained for the time being until the family and social pattern had been sufficiently amended to insure that marriage did not to any serious extent restrict women's earning capacity more than men's. On the other hand, another commission appointed by the government recommended retention of the maintenance system, largely on the same grounds, but with a time limit on the maintenance period.

Family Facts and Figures

The population of Denmark was 3.8 million in 1940 and rose steadily to 5.0 million in 1975. However, the number of marriages did not increase correspondingly. It was 35,000 in 1940 and 31,000 in 1975, and there has been a marked drop in the past few years. On the other hand, there has been an increase in the number of common-law marriages. The average age of women at the time of marriage has remained virtually unchanged.

The number of divorces has risen quite steeply: from 3,500 in 1940 to 13,000 in 1975, with a sharp upward swing in recent years. Over the thirty-five-year period divorced women have displayed a rapidly declining tendency to remarry; they elect rather to enter into common-law marriages.

The number of births was 70,000 in 1940 and 72,000 in 1975. The figure for 1976 will be substantially lower than for 1975. Birth control has become much more widespread since 1940 (including use of the pill, which was generally released in 1966), and Denmark legislated abortion on demand in 1973 (25,000 abortions were performed the following year). The relative drop in the birth rate is substantial, and in recent years it is women in the very young and the thirty-five to forty-five age groups who have been giving birth to fewer babies. If the present birth rate continues unaltered, the population level will peak in the 1990s and then begin to decline.

In Denmark in 1975 there were 506,000 children up to six years of age; 565,000 aged seven to thirteen, and 445,000 aged fourteen to nineteen. In the same year 43 percent of the children lived in one-child families, 37 percent in families with two children, 14 percent in families with three children, and 6 percent in families with four or more children. The majority of young Danish women wish for and expect to have two or three children. There are children in only half the households in Denmark. This proportion will probably drop in future as families are reduced to two and three children and because births are concentrated among women in the twenty to twenty-nine age group.

The *first child* is usually born very early in the marriage: more than two thirds of all married couples have their first baby within two years of marrying; 40 percent expect the baby at the time of marriage. Rather less than 20 percent have their *second child* within eighteen months of the first; 40 percent wait from eighteen months to three years. The interval between second and *third child* varies considerably, with the average interval greater than between the first and the second child.

The general pattern of birth timing in the family's life shows that a youthful age at the time of marriage is very often associated with premarital pregnancy, short intervals between births, and more than the average number of children. Thus women who marry in their teens in particular have to cope with a heavier burden of dependence at an early age.

In 1940 8 percent of all births were illegitimate; this figure increased to 11 percent in 1970 and 22 percent in 1975. As many as 90 percent of all unmarried mothers live in a common-law marriage. Many of them enter into a formal marriage later—either with the father of the first child or, quite often, with another man.

The Aim of a Family Policy

Family policy in Denmark for many years has *not* been designed to secure a specific, high level of births. With an adequate domestic population growth and a positive population explosion elsewhere in the world, the question simply has not applied. However, the problem of a declining population may well develop again in view of the drastic fall in the Danish birth rate. A debate is already under way, although in a form different from that of the 1930s. Some people see the declining birth rate as the result of the insipid family policy pursued by government, especially cuts in investment in day care institutions. What causes anxiety is not so much a steadily dwindling population as the policy of public belt tightening which impairs the conditions under which the present generation of children will mature and is moreover seen by women's liberation supporters as a blow to equality for women.

Eugenic considerations, although to the fore a generation ago, have played no part in recent Danish family policy.

Family policy over the past few decades has been founded on a variety of basic standpoints on which it was possible in principle to obtain fairly broad agreement. They are to some degree overlapping, but each has its own special value:

1. *The general view that burdens should be shared.* Having children represents an economic load that weighs heavily upon most families, particularly the young family which is in the process of establishing its roots and has relatively low earnings. It is reasonable to spread the load, with childless couples and single persons contributing to those with children, and families with children having recipient status as long as they have dependents—and becoming contributors once the burden of child-raising has lifted.

2. *The narrower view of preventing risk.* Support should be given to society's weaker families—those with very low incomes, those with more than the average number of children—and the unmarried mother or father. The standard of living in such families can be so low as to present a hazard

to the healthy development of the children. It is a well-known fact that illness and socially negative deviations occur especially frequently among children of such families. It is vital that help should be given at an early stage, while the children are still children, so as to remove the risk that poverty will extend its influence into the next generation.

3. *The idea that all children should have the same opportunities in life, regardless of their origin.* This is a broader social view aimed at securing for the children of less affluent families access to such facilities as health services and schooling of a standard equal to that enjoyed by the children of more affluent homes, or to raise the housing standard of the less well-off above the level they themselves could pay without some kind of support.

4. *The view that parents should be safeguarded against discrimination on account of their children.* At work and in matters of housing, the expectant mother or mother of small children must be protected from losing her job because of pregnancy or child care, and it must be insured that families with children are able to rent decent homes.

5. *The view that children are our future.* This is a powerful factor in a country whose sole natural raw material is its human resources. Important phases in the development of these resources occur in childhood and are to a large extent dependent on a happy life, the standard of living, stimulation, and socialization within families. Measures that help families solve the problems presented by a modern society will thus be important to tomorrow's society. This view motivates measures which are not directly granted to the family; for example, kindergartens may be seen as a direct contribution to the child. Holders of this viewpoint see payments and other contributions made directly to the family as going to the family not as the end, but as the instrument of redistribution of wealth between adult and child generations. Kindergarten and similar facilities are a means of passing the cultural heritage from one generation to the next—possibly in a better manner than the family home can achieve.

These views do not per se give rise to any great disagreement, but in the process of transforming them to practical politics, ideological and economic conflicts can emerge.

Danish family policy is rooted primarily in the general theory of the need for social and health measures: protection of the weak, prevention of faults in development, and the equalization of income differentials. And in recent years there has been the question of influence by the traditional education policy in Denmark. As poverty-oriented problems have gradually been overcome, the spotlight has turned more and more upon the child's mental development and education. While measures to eliminate social imbalance in the higher levels of the schooling system are—as already indicated—considered part of the country's educational policy, the provision of kindergartens and other day care institutions for children under the obligatory school age and in the early school years still comes within the framework of family policy. Powerful forces have demanded that educational day care institutions should be available to *all* preschool children on the grounds that the educational programs offered by these institutions are an asset to the child's development.

Basic elements in Danish family policy can thus be traced back to aspects of social, health, and educational policies. On the other hand, it is less easy to pinpoint political intentions designed quite specifically to further the interests of the family as a middle-class institution with special ethical values.

It is true that statutory regulations relating to family matters have been drawn up with the traditional family in mind and that new family-type units, such as the common-law marriage with children, find themselves at odds with those rules. On the other hand, as the number of common-law marriages is on the increase, it is likely that an attempt will be made to solve their legal problems in as neutral a manner as possible, without discriminating against the new forms in favor of the traditional. The resistance of religious interests in this debate is unlikely to be of any great significance.

It is also correct that a rising divorce rate and a rise in the number of children necessarily removed from their homes and placed in institutions will be seen as signs of difficulties facing the family and symptoms of an abortive family policy. But this is due more to unease at the social, economic, and psychological consequences of divorce and our knowledge that it is difficult to establish an adequate adolescent environment for children outside the family than to any worries on behalf of the traditional family as cultural torchbearer and sacred institution.

It could also be stressed that our relatively well-developed policy of day care facilities favors those families who have their young children cared for a few hours daily or for the whole day outside the home, and also those families in which the mother takes a job outside the home. The public subsidy paid to these institutions is, of course, financed partly by those families in which the mother stays home and looks after the children. But this fact does not justify a conclusion that it is the stated aim of Denmark's family policy to have children brought up in public institutions and mothers employed outside the home. What has happened is that the day care institutions originally set up as necessary social measures for looking after the children of lower-class working wives during the day have come to embrace the educational philosophy of Montessori, Froebel, and others, and emerged as day care centers as we know them today. These are now of such quality that even a large proportion of those families that believe a mother's place is in the home and that the upbringing of children is primarily the duty of the family nevertheless feel that their preschool children benefit from the facilities of a kindergarten, at least for a few hours a day.

Moreover, it may be observed that numerous schemes over the years have extended and still extend assistance to the unmarried or otherwise single mother. However, it would be wrong to imagine here any intention of fostering breakdown of the traditional family-unit pattern; the desire has merely been to aid particularly deprived groups. The fact that it gave rise to no special political upheaval is perhaps due to the Danes' relaxed attitude toward religion, sex, and the family institutions; on the other hand, it should not be seen as a deliberate attempt to dissolve the family.

However, it is irrefutable that measures in support of the single mother, such as higher rates of the child allowance, rent subsidies, free or partly free day care services, and perhaps assistance toward her own education or training, may have encouraged many young people to delay marriage for some years. But this was not the design of such measures, and receipt of benefits and allowances of this type by unmarried partners living permanently together has been viewed in some quarters as contrary to the aims of those measures. In a social sense, therefore, common-law marriages have come to be regarded on the same footing as traditional marriages. This has given rise to vigorous protest since it means that the social authorities can decide whether a woman is living permanently with a man and sharing his household (this is the distinction between genuinely single persons and unmarried persons living in a common-law marriage). The decision has been attacked by the popular press as "bedroom snooping" and considered an unwarranted invasion of a woman's privacy.

The important point, however, is that the resentment that arose toward common-law couples was due not to the fact that they were living together without the formality of a marriage certificate but that some of them were presumed to be abusing certain social schemes aimed at helping other and definitely needy groups. There was a feeling of injustice that the woman who was unmarried but living permanently with a partner should not only be better off financially than her married sister but enjoy just as favorable social and economic conditions. Admittedly, in the eyes of some Danes the married mother is perhaps a little "nicer" than the unmarried mother living "in sin," but this fact has no great political significance; the principle of justice, on the other hand, carries a good deal of weight.

The formally married, middle-class family as an institution and its preservation or otherwise have not constituted the central theme in the debate on Danish family policy. Clearly, there has been debate, and there have been extreme views of every shade, but it has not been an element of any importance in family policy. The family is more an instrument and means than the end itself so far as family policy is concerned, in recognition of the importance of the family to the child, and the family's suitability as a basis for achievement of the main adult-life objectives.

Principal Elements of Danish Family Policy

Let us examine some of the chief elements of Denmark's present family policy. It will be noted that the majority of them are financed from national taxation.

Family Allowance
The basic family allowance is paid in respect of all children whose father and/or mother are married or living in a situation comparable with marriage. The allowance is approximately D.kr. 1,650 per child per annum.

A supplementary family allowance is paid instead of the basic allowance for children whose parents both receive a retirement or disability pension and for children of single mothers and fathers who do not live in a situation comparable with marriage. The supplementary allowance is D.kr. 2,475 per child per annum.

A special family allowance *in addition to* the basic or supplementary allowance is paid for the children of widows and widowers, children of invalid or pensioner parents (D.kr. 1,820, or half that amount if only one parent receives a pension), to illegitimate children for whom no one is found to be liable (D.kr. 3,630 per child per annum), and to orphans (D.kr. 6,000 per child per annum).

Moreover, an extra allowance is paid to all single mothers or fathers who are already receiving the supplementary allowance; only one such extra allowance is paid per household, regardless of the number of children. This was introduced to compensate for certain income tax increases for this group which were the unintended consequence of a government tax reform.

The allowances are paid until the child reaches the age of sixteen (the special family allowance, however, is paid up to the age of seventeen years).

Children in the sixteen to seventeen age group used to receive all forms of allowance, but they were denied the basic and supplementary allowance in the latest round of government economies, and instead the government introduced a youth allowance with a maximum of D.kr. 7,000 per annum per youth. This is graduated according to the family's income: it is phased out completely if the household income exceeds D.kr. 70,000 or if the young person earns more than D.kr. 15,000 per annum.

All family allowances are adjusted by 50 percent of the index of retail prices, and they are not included in the family's taxable income. The basic family allowance is not a large amount (a skilled worker in Denmark in 1976 earned an annual salary of approximately D.kr. 80,000), but it is free of tax, and for households with lower-middle incomes it is not entirely insignificant.

It will be noted that until April 1, 1977, the family allowance scheme made a payment to all families and a supplementary payment to certain groups presumed to be especially deprived.

It has been questioned whether it is reasonable that families with high incomes should also receive the basic allowance, and whether it would not be more reasonable to graduate the amount according to income and raise the amount paid to the less affluent families. Actually, a decision has been made as part of the current government cutbacks that effective April 1, 1977, the basic allowance will be reduced for incomes above D.kr. 110,000 per annum; that is, taxable income, which is substantially lower than gross income. This is a break with the tendency for social allowances and benefits to be paid universally, as is the case with the retirement pension. It is claimed that it is easier to administer when the allowance is paid to all; that eliminating those with high incomes does not save a great deal of money; that an allowance made to all is a right whereas an allowance only to the less affluent becomes a form of public assistance; and finally, that it is politically easier to introduce an allowance to all rather than only to a part of the population. The compromise between these two views expressed in the incomes graduation after April 1, 1977, is, however, relatively insignificant since few families have a taxable income above D.kr. 110,000. The result is, therefore, that the idea of leveling out the social imbalance, at least as far as the basic allowance is concerned, has been lost, and it has simply become a general aid toward coping with the expenses of virtually all families with children.

The supplementary and special allowances are in most cases paid to families with rather modest incomes and are therefore an important factor in the economy of these families.

Family allowances have been reduced and adjusted on a number of occasions in recent years as part of the general economies of changing governments. As a consequence, allowances of a family policy nature are in practice subject to a good deal of political maneuvering.

Housing Policy

Laws and regulations that favor the housing conditions of families with children relate in Denmark only to rental dwellings; families who wish to own their own homes have no better standing in the market for owner-occupied homes than people without children. Rental dwellings are situated chiefly in towns and suburbs and account for about half of all homes in Denmark.

A very large proportion of rental dwellings has been built by nonprofit housing associations. The share has fluctuated at various times, but at present it represents the majority of all rental dwellings. Nonprofit housing associations enjoy certain privileges; they are tax exempt and can obtain concessionary borrowing terms. On the other hand, they must undertake to build homes suitable for low-income families, and in their renting policy they must pay special attention to the needs of families with children, unmarried mothers, pensioners, and others with low incomes.

The system of nonprofit housing has existed for many years and currently extends to half of all rental housing in Denmark. It has helped bring about more reasonable conditions and more sanitary housing, and has been a valuable asset in securing good housing for the weaker families, especially those with children. However, the problem today is that even nonprofit housing associations are unable to build homes at prices the low-income family can afford.

In addition to nonprofit housing, there are statutory provisions for rent subsidies for families with low incomes and children: subsidies are available in respect of either private or nonprofit housing. Rent subsidies require that the dwelling be of a certain minimum size in relation to the size of the household and meet a certain standard; these requirements are designed to help families with children obtain decent housing. The amount of the rent subsidies depends on the total family income, the amount of the rent, and the number of children receiving child allowances. The subsidy amounts to a maximum of 15 percent of the rent plus a further 15 percent for each child.

All things considered, Denmark has a relatively high standard of housing. The housing shortage following World War I has gone completely, many of the oldest and most dilapidated dwellings have been demolished or rebuilt, and many of the poorest quality housing areas have been renewed. Very few families with children remain in substandard dwellings, such as overcrowded homes with more than two persons per room, basement apartments, vacation cottages, homes without sanitation.

On the other hand, it must be recognized that home construction plays such a vital role as regards both employment and the national economy that housing is a field in which powerful political muscle is flexed, with only lip service paid to the interests of family policy. The extent to which these interests should be accommodated is therefore a constantly recurring issue in Danish politics. The situation alters from year to year. For example, in the most recent round of political negotiations on housing (eleven political parties are represented in the Danish Parliament and compromise is therefore essential), it was agreed that a large number of dwellings in private rental properties could be put up for sale as condominiums, thus changing status from rented to owner-occupied homes. Prices are very high, and many families cannot afford to own their own homes. Conceivably, this decision may in the long run mean that many of the rental homes will vanish from the pool of rental accommodations available to young families. Young families with children will thus be prevented from occupying many of the higher quality homes.

Day Care Institutions

Day care facilities are available in the following forms:

1. *Day nurseries (crèches).* These facilities are for children from birth up to the age of two or two and a half years. Most are open eight to ten hours daily. Approximately 8 percent of all children in this age group attend day nurseries.

2. *Subsidized family day care.* Authorized and supervised family day care is mostly for children under the age of three years. Approximately 8 percent of all children under three are in local-authority approved family day care.

3. *Kindergartens.* These institutions, open for the most part from 7:00 A.M. to 5:00 P.M., and some for a half day only, are for children aged two to two and a half until they start school at about seven years of age. Some 30 percent of all children between the ages of three and seven attend kindergarten.

4. *Youth centers.* These day care institutions are for school children

aged seven to fourteen years before and after school hours. They are open all day, but attendance is highest in the afternoon, from the time the children are finished in school until parents come home from work. About 6 percent of children in the seven to ten age group attend youth centers.

5. *Age-integrated institutions*. This form of day care institution for children up to fourteen years of age is open all day. It is regarded as having much greater educational value than those that are divided up according to ages. The intention is for future institutions to be age-integrated if at all possible. So far, only 4 percent or 5 percent of all children in day care attend such institutions.

All these institutional forms of day care are open to children of all families, but children of single heads of households are given first priority, followed by the children of working mothers. Regardless, a large number of the children are from homes where the mother is home all day.

Central and local government defrays 80 percent of the cost, the remainder being paid by the parents. The parents' share, however, is still quite high, and—depending on a means test—the authorities may pay 90 percent or 100 percent. About 11 percent of parents enjoy these facilities free of charge, and 14 percent pay a reduced rate.

The rather high parental share of payment does, however, have an unfortunate result. The parents who send their children to day care institutions are either in the low-income bracket and get a substantial or complete rebate, or they are in the high-income bracket and can afford to make full payment. Middle-income families, on the other hand, find themselves between two stools: they get no reduction and they find the cost steep. In many cases they have no alternative but to rely on less qualified day care arrangements or let their children look after themselves while the parents are at work.

Day care institutions are found primarily in urban and suburban areas, but there can be widely varying facilities available, depending largely on the prevailing attitude of local authorities. With the changing structure of employment in rural areas the need is rising there for similar facilities. Parents in rural surroundings are coming more and more to acknowledge that their children can benefit from the stimulation they receive at a kindergarten, youth center, and so on. However, it will be some years before this need is fully accommodated.

Denmark's day care institutions originated as social facilities for the children of the working classes and working mothers, but also as half-day kindergartens, first and foremost with an educational objective. In some countries these two forms have survived as separate types of institutions, but in Denmark they have gradually become one as middle-class wives entered the labor market and demanded high-quality day care facilities. Half-day kindergartens do still exist, depending on local requirements, but in principle institutions are identical as regards technical facilities, staff, educational objectives, and so forth. The families who use the institutions differ, of course, according to the residential area concerned, but generally speaking it has been possible to avoid having institutions that care for low-status children and another set of institutions for middle- and high-status children.

The number of day care institutions has increased rapidly over the past decade as more and more women have gone out to work. The proportion of working women in the twenty to twenty-nine age group is 70 percent. Many take jobs for compelling economic reasons, others to satisfy a rising level of consumption, and still others out of fear of losing touch.

The policy will still be to open more day care centers in the years ahead, but the rate of increase has slackened markedly in response to the sluggish state of the economy in recent years. In general, political willingness to open new day care institutions has been closely geared to industry's need for female labor.

In the 1960s and 1970s the demand for places in day care institutions considerably outstripped the supply, partly because of the rising number of working mothers, partly because mothers who remained at home wanted their children to enjoy the benefit of educational stimulation in day care institutions. There still is a widespread belief in the beneficial effect of day care facilities, especially the kindergarten.

Denmark has trained a large number of day care teachers in a three-year course. These teachers have become organized into a militant professsional body, and many are outspokenly left wing. Previously, the most common source of disagreement between the parent's ideas of upbringing and those of the day care teacher was that the latter was more permissive and liberal with regard to activities, courtesy, social relationships, and emotional reaction. This phase appears to have passed. On the other hand, many young teachers are critical of society and adopt a socialist attitude toward their work with children. This fact has undoubtedly been one reason that certain local authorities have hesitated to set up day care centers, preferring instead to organize day care facilities in private homes, with family day care mothers. However, there have rarely if ever been disputes of any kind between parents and day care institution personnel that have developed into out-of-hand situations. Largely speaking, relations between the institutions and the parents are good, and the latter have secured statutory representation on the governing committees of their respective institutions. Parents in almost all social groups have come to appreciate the significance of education for the young child. Usually parents also want preschool children to learn something and undergo preparation for school.

Some institutions are owned by Christian organizations, others by Social Democratic bodies or various private interests. Many are owned and run by local authorities. Social Democratic facilities were set up as an alternative to the Christian institutions; however, there has never been any great ideological conflict between them, and there are few significant differences in everyday management.

Day care by private families has always been strictly a private arrangement between a working mother and, for example, a neighbor. In response to the drastic shortage of day care facilities in the 1960s, this form of day care was introduced as an emergency measure under local-authority control. Family day care mothers were appointed by the local authority, homes were inspected and evaluated, and they became subject to supervision and inspection by the local social authorities. Parents paid the same amount they would have paid to a regular day care institution, the local authority meeting the balance. As indicated, it was an emergency arrangement, designed chiefly for children up to the age of three. However, it does not seem probable that this form of day care will give way to regular institutions in the foreseeable future. It is a cheaper arrangement for the authorities and is flexible enough to cope with a fluctuating demand. Parents were initially rather skeptical of the family day care system, but attitudes have changed; for one thing, it is easier to make individual arrangements regarding delivery and pick-up times with a family day care mother than with an institution. And some children do get on better in smaller groups.

Youth centers look after school-age children outside school hours. They are frequently located in the most densely populated areas of town. In many cases they receive children whose social adjustment and development are threatened; many of the children have been ordered by the social authorities to join youth centers because they show signs of asocial tendencies or because their parents have demonstrated a lack of ability to take proper care of them. In many instances, such an order is issued as an alternative to removing the child from the parental home. The youth center is considered to have had considerable prophylactic importance. Unfortunately, however, it is an institution that seems to have difficulty in attracting and holding children in the eleven to fourteen age group.

Apart from these institutions, a number of schools maintain recreational facilities for children after school hours. There are also many clubs for school children. These institutions vary considerably in quality. Children are under no obligation to attend, as is often the case with youth centers. This aspect is attractive to the child but worries the parents who spend all day at work: there is no one to keep an eye on the child's activities in the afternoon. Here, the parents' desire for safety conflicts with the child's need for liberty. The low attendance of children above the age of eleven at the compulsory youth center would seem to indicate that the children have won.

Health Centers

The expectant mother is entitled to three medical examinations free of charge during pregnancy and two after the birth. She is also entitled to free examinations by her midwife during pregnancy.

Ninety-four percent of all births take place at institutions, clinics, or hospitals at no cost to the mother. Midwifery services in the event of home birth are free of charge.

The maternity leave in connection with the confinement and the size of the economic support to be granted depends partly on the woman's connection with the labor market and partly on the size of her income. If she is a wage earner and employee she will in certain cases receive fourteen weeks maternity leave with full pay; in other cases she can get five months leave and be paid half of her usual salary. If she is a factory worker she can get fourteen weeks maternity leave without salary but with a daily allowance, generally 90 percent of her usual income. If the woman is self-employed or employed in family business or trade she has the right to get economic support for four weeks after the confinement.

The child is entitled to free medical examinations at the age of five weeks, five months, ten months, fifteen months, and twenty-four months. It then has an annual checkup until school age. The family gets all the usual vaccinations (diphtheria, tetanus, polio, whooping cough, and smallpox) free of charge.

Whether the family wishes to make use of these medical services is a matter for it to decide. They are most widely used during the child's first year of life (up to 75 percent of all infants, dropping to about 50 percent by the child's sixth year). There is some indication that the most socially deprived families tend to make relatively less use of the system than the more affluent. This fact has occasioned some consternation concerning child health in families with substandard living conditions, especially in rural areas.

It should be observed that while preventive medical examinations of young children were undoubtedly of vital importance in earlier times, it is seldom nowadays that they reveal a morbid condition not already ascertained by some other means. There have been proposals that the purpose of these examinations should be redirected: instead of being exclusively concerned with the physical health of children, they should place more emphasis on the child's mental development and the family's social situation.

Virtually all local authorities have a system of health visitors who make regular calls at homes where there are newborn babies, checking their health and advising the mother. The health visitor scheme was introduced in 1937 to reduce what was then a relatively high rate of infant mortality.

Whether the family wishes to receive a health visitor is a voluntary matter, but the system is free of charge and popular, and 98 percent of families in local-government areas which have these visitors do take advantage of the arrangement. Formerly, the visitor made many calls, most frequently at the start and then at longer intervals. The frequency of visits was then the same for every family. Frequency is now more flexibly matched to the needs of the individual family, and if a need is registered, visits can be continued beyond the child's first year up to school age, when examinations are taken over by the school doctor and school nurse.

For many years stress was laid on promoting the infant's physical health, but there is a growing effort to direct the health visitor's interest to the child's mental development, the emotional relations of mother and child, social conditions generally, and the importance of environmental factors for the well-being and development of the young child.

The annual school medical checkup can have the child referred to his own doctor or to any one of a number of institutions for handicapped children. Free dental care is also being introduced at most schools throughout the country.

Since 1973 abortion has been available on demand for any woman during the first twelve weeks of her pregnancy. After twelve weeks abortion is granted subject to special authorization and an assessment of the general condition. The operation must be conducted at a public hospital and is free of charge.

There has been some resistance to abortion legislation by religious and medical circles. Its passage and implementation, however, reflect the consistent advance of the preceding decade toward more liberal abortion laws, the desire to stamp out illegal abortion, the strongly voiced views of the women's liberation movement, the fact that easier access to birth control methods in low-income families was a sound means of maintaining a better standard of living for children already born, the wish to avoid social misery in low-income, large families, and finally, it was a reflection of the fact that for many years population stagnation was not seen as a problem.

It is believed that abortion on demand has eliminated the back-street abortion and reduced the number of spontaneous abortions. In 1975 there were 27,884 legal abortions in Denmark.[2] It has been judged that this figure was somewhat higher than the sum of formerly illegal, legal, and spontaneous abortions, but it is impossible to say precisely how much higher.

Single Heads of Family
In principle, families with unmarried or otherwise single heads are treated on an equal footing with other families. In various respects, however, they have enjoyed special forms of assistance. As already noted, they receive higher rates of family allowance, they have priority in allocation of day nursery and kindergarten places, and housing legislation makes extra allowance for single-status heads of family (provided these are genuinely single and not living permanently with or sharing a household with a partner).

Children born out of wedlock enjoy the same legal rights as legitimate children. They succeed to the property of their mother and father. Paternity is considered established if the putative father acknowledges liability. Paternity can also be established by the courts. In both cases the child enjoys the same legal status.

Until recently Denmark had a special institution known as Maternal Aid, which had centers throughout the country to assist the unmarried mother with establishing paternity, finding living accommodations, buying equipment and other supplies for the expected baby, and—especially in the case of the very young unmarried mother—planning an education or job training. Low-income married couples could also apply to Maternal Aid for assistance.

The organization has now been disbanded and its duties delegated to the social welfare section of each local authority. This has also increased the range of assistance available to the individual client.

The situation of the unmarried mother over the past few decades has

---

[2] "Statistiske efterretninger 1976," No. 75.

improved vastly, the stigma of former times having been largely removed. She enjoys better social conditions and is integrated much more readily into society on an equal footing with its other members.

Child Welfare

Whether child welfare comes under the heading of family policy is debatable. However, certain aspects of it serve to illustrate the Danish view of the relationship between family and state or local authorities.

Child welfare is based on a complex of legislation, regulations, and institutions aimed at helping children and parents who are unable to look after their children or give them decent conditions and a good upbringing. This form of welfare is administered by social committees in the municipalities.

Typical cases for consideration by the committee are, for example, parents who on account of illness, lack of housing and so forth, are unable to look after their children; or children whose antisocial behavior demonstrates that their parents have lost control of them; or families in such deep social distress, perhaps on account of alcoholism, criminal behavior, or prostitution, that their children's development is threatened; or cases in which a child has been neglected or physically or mentally mistreated to the extent that its well-being is in jeopardy.

In such circumstances a number of courses of action are open. For example, a caseworker may be delegated to the family and establish regular contact; use may be made of advisory clinics, temporary or more prolonged placement of the child in an institution or foster home; or financial assistance may be given to the family if in this way removal of the child can be avoided.

The character and effect of these facilities have been more or less unchanged for many years, although there have been improvements and an expansion in the system. The significant change, however, is in the balance of power between authorities and the family.

Three principles have become more and more firmly established through statutory amendments over the past thirty or forty years. This is true especially of removal of the child from the home, which is the measure that interferes most with the integrity of the family and has the widest ranging consequences for parents and child. Removal from the home because the parents are temporarily unable to care for their children (on account of the parents' illness, for instance) presents no problem; the difficulty arises when the home is subject to long-lasting social or psychological defects.

1. The first principle concerns collaboration with the parents. For-

merly, parents who neglected their duty toward a child were considered morally inferior persons, and every step was taken to save the child from their harmful influence by placing the child at a great geographical distance and for a long period. Gradually, however, it was realized that it is difficult to reestablish and treat children whose development is in jeopardy if the parental relationship is not positive. Cooperation with the parents has thus become a major factor in such cases, both prior to placement, if applicable, and during the period the child is away from the family. The parents are encouraged to maintain contact with the child, and every effort is made, except in extreme psychopathological cases, to foster the family's sense of togetherness and unity.

2. The second principle is that of replacing compulsion wherever possible with voluntary collaboration. The regulations provide that a child can be placed outside the family with or without the consent of the parents. Previously, it was official policy primarily to remove children from difficult families without parental consent. This practice created an uneasy, hostile attitude among the public toward the child welfare authorities. It was as if the authorities removed children from their parents and never returned them. The regulations, however, and the practice have been changed; it is now practice to avoid compulsory measures if possible and to encourage parental cooperation. It is still possible to remove a child from home without parental consent, but the number of compulsory removals has been sharply reduced. This has enhanced the standing of the child welfare authorities in the eyes of the public.

3. The third principle is based on consideration of the family as a cohesive unit. This idea is evident throughout the latest batch of social legislation. It assumes that problems and social deviations in a family may be traced to one or more members of the family although the cause of such problems may actually rest in the behavior and affairs of other members of the family unit. Perhaps it is not the brooding schoolboy who needs treatment but his alcoholic father. The latest statutory measures on the social front offer a wide choice of remedial courses after a dynamic examination tends to show where the fault lies, irrespective of how the problem first came to light or who showed the symptoms. Under this principle the family is no longer regarded as a collection of individuals comprising father, mother, and a few dependent children but as an organic unity in which—for better or worse—the individual members influence and are affected by one another.

In a family policy context the idea may not be revolutionary, but the philosophy has not been practiced previously in Denmark as a basis for the country's social legislation. In a sense, the public and social authorities intrude more deeply than before into the private domain of the family, but it is hoped in this way to replace the treatment of symptoms with the treatment of causes.

Many years are likely to pass, however, before the social administrations are fully capable of building up the practice envisaged by the law.

Controversy

The preceding account of Danish family policy may possibly have left the impression that the subject is without controversy. This is conceivably true in the sense that family policy in Denmark is based on theories and philosophies of social, health, and educational policies broadly supported over the past forty years. It is also correct that the mainstream of debate in Denmark has not been colored by the emotional, ethical, and religious issues and attitudes toward the family as an institution that we know from other countries. This does not mean, however, that divergent views on these issues and attitudes do not exist in Denmark, but they have been voiced on the sidelines only.

However, the subject has its tense moments. Some of the problems that produce friction, both at a political level and internally within the families, are:

1. What should be the aim of a family policy?

   a) Should it support the traditional family with a working father and a mother who stays home and looks after the children?

   b) Or should it help the family to liberate both parents and let them both get out to work, by looking after and educating the children during the day?

   c) Or should family policy aim at dissolution of the traditional family?

   d) Or should family policy remain neutral toward such issues?

The first view (*a*) is held by relatively few and strongly conservative circles.

The second (*b*) is supported by the broad center of the Danish political spectrum, including the ruling Social Democrats, partly on pragmatic grounds: the family must be helped to make its way in a modern society.

The third (c) is at present held only by women's liberation extremists and far left wing interests.

The fourth view (d) is supported by broad, moderately conservative circles. This has found expression especially in the debate on day care institutions. By way of generous public subsidies to these institutions, support is given to families with two working parents—to which families with a home-bound mother must contribute. This is considered unjust, and advocates of this view suggest instead that the family allowance should be increased substantially and that those parents who wish to have their children in a day care institution should then pay the total cost of running the institution. In this way, it is claimed, family policy would take a neutral stance in relation to families' various wishes as to whether only one or both parents should have jobs outside the home. As a matter of fact, this proposal favors the traditional form of family with the mother working at home. Wives who work outside the home would get even less remuneration from their employment. It is bad enough that they are not permitted to deduct from their taxable income the cost of using a day care institution.

Another proposal for solving the same problem is for all families to be allocated three hours daily free of charge in a day care center for each child in its relevant age group. If the family wanted to use the institution longer than the three hours daily, it would have to pay a considerably higher fee than at present. Even if 10 percent of all day care places were earmarked for free allocation on an all-day basis to families with very low incomes or families whose children are judged to benefit from a full-day service (children of mentally afflicted parents, for instance), the system could be implemented for about the same budget as today's day care facilities. The system would afford all children the benefit of subsidized day care facilities.

This proposal is criticized for favoring highly qualified women whose earnings are high enough to permit them to pay for children in day care institutions beyond the free hours while penalizing women on a modest hourly wage, either by forcing them partly or completely out of their jobs or by obliging them to let their children roam the streets during the time after the free hours.

Whether a Social Democratic or conservative view of day care institution policy should prevail is important only as long as there is a shortage of facilities. The day Denmark has an adequate supply of low-cost facilities to meet its needs there will be no conflict in principle; the two groups agree that all children benefit from a few hours a day in a kindergarten and that parents should preferably be free to choose whether both or only one goes out to work. While the shortage of day care institutions persists, however (and this is likely to be the case for many years), the proposals aimed at neutrality on the question of parents working outside the home will be conservative because they allocate a larger share of public funds to the more affluent, and it will probably also serve as an obstacle to permitting women to free themselves from the kitchen sink.

2. The parents' relationship to the labor market is also fraught with conflict, particularly while the children are still young.

Employers wish to have a stable labor force for eight hours per working day. While the children are small, it is difficult to cope with housework, family life, and bringing up children satisfactorily when both parents are at work all day. Many families would like an arrangement whereby the husband works full time while the wife has a part-time job—but it may not be easy to find part-time work. Trade unions have displayed no special interest in the part-time employee. For one thing, they have regarded the part-time worker as a possible source of wage depression; moreover, it is difficult to organize part-time workers into trade unions; and finally, there is the traditional attitude that if women want equality with men, they must work on the same terms as men. This latter view is taken particularly by women's industrial organizations, and in this they are supported by the contemporary women's liberation movement, whose advocates reject the theory that women should be happy with marginal, part-time employment. But these fronts are gradually gathering momentum. There is not the same willingness to give way to the requirements of the labor market; and there is an increasing desire to demolish the rigid framework surrounding the male domain. In practice, 50 percent of the women are employed in the service industries, hospital training, the social sector, and so forth.

The conflict inherent in the various factors—the requirements of industry; the needs of the family and care of the children; a woman's right to work and pursue a career on the same footing as men; and a man's right to family life on an equal footing with women—is one of long standing, but its arguments have been growing in volume and there would still not appear to be any satisfactory solution in sight. Housework and care of children within the home have not hitherto been reckoned in cash terms, but when mothers take their place in industry, the cost of this work must be met in some way. Central and local authorities cover some of the cost by subsidizing day care institutions, but in the present situation the outstanding balance is paid for by women's overtime hours in the home and the very long hours spent every day by children in day care centers. In many families these economic burdens are considerable and questionable, and there is a need to allocate them more uniformly either by transferring part of the load to the authorities or by inducing the employer to take his share.

3. Individuals and families without children have interests that differ quite considerably from those of families with children. This applies generally to the investment of public funds, and it applies locally in the allocation of housing, use of recreational space, construction of safe routes (to and from school) for children, and so forth.

It is only in the past few decades that parents have been able to carry a bit of weight as a mutual-interest group cutting across party lines. Elected parents have joined the executive and management committees of schools, day care institutions, children's homes, and have also had an opportunity of gaining direct influence in local tenants' associations.

Parent associations have also appeared to represent parents with children in day care institutions and parents with handicapped children. Some of the latter have had particularly effective influence.

It should also be mentioned that the heavy demand for day care institutions—especially during periods of labor shortage—has generated broad political agreement in the Parliament on legislation which stimulates construction and expansion of these facilities. On the other hand, once passed through the Parliament, such legislation is then administered by local authorities—and there are big differences in attitudes toward day care institutions. As a result, the number of day care places per capita fluctuates immensely from one local government area to the next. Until recently there were even local authorities who suggested that their single-status heads of family could place their children in foster homes and similar institutions in order to allow the parent to go out to work. This, of course, would have saved the authorities the expense of setting up day care facilities for these children. However, it should now be impossible for any similar situation to arise.

Whether the mutual interests of families with children can hold their own against people who do not have children will no doubt be revealed in the decisions of the next decade with regard to how families with small children are to be assisted and how the relationship of parents of these children to the labor market is to be adjusted and safeguarded.

4. How deeply into the family should society penetrate with its assistance, supervision, and so forth?

Some people believe that society is under obligation to extend wide-ranging assistance to the family, especially in respect to the children, who are the weak and dependent parties. In order to be able to exercise this support and take corrective action to help families before they slip too far into a dangerous situation, society has to obtain the right of supervision and receive information from many quarters. And help should be brought to the family in the form of visits, family advisory services, private teaching facilities in the home, accompanied if necessary by an order to parents with regard to the upbringing of their children and admission to a day care institution or treatment by a consultant clinic.

Other people believe that society should interfere as little as possible with family life; assistance should be minimal and in the form of general measures. It is an aspect of the family's privacy, and outside action, advisory services, treatment, and so on, do more harm than good. In some of these circles, psychiatrists, psychologists, teachers, social experts, and social workers are viewed with the utmost skepticism. Personal responsibility for one's own life and for the lives of one's family, they feel, must not be undermined.

The first of these standpoints may be placed, largely speaking, in the center and left of the political spectrum; the second is to be found on the right. However, the extreme left wingers share conservative skepticism toward "psychotechnocrats," although their motivation may not be the same.

The latest round of social legislation is based principally on the first of these opinions, but as the law is administered by the local authorities, practice will in many cases tend to become more conservative.

The chief problem is not one of choosing between compulsion and free will, for the principle of voluntary action is firmly established in Danish society. The dispute rests in the fact that the first group views the family as a dynamic unit which largely determines the fate of its individual members, and there is therefore a need to protect and aid the weak. The predominant view in the second group is that officialdom should not interfere with the integrity of the family, which should be left to act on its own resources. The problem as the first group sees it is how to make contact with families that lack resources as well as the knowledge and courage to seek assistance; the main problem for the second group is to avoid lifting responsibility from people and offending those who could have managed independently.

To whom do the children belong? Society or the parents?

5. Certain conflicts also exist between parents, on the one hand, and children and young people, on the other hand. Many parents are heavily committed at work to earnings, consumption, and furtherance of their careers, and have difficulty finding time to look after their children and take

part in their upbringing. The children, for their part, need to spend a lot of time with relaxed, balanced parents. This conflict can be settled by economic measures only when lack of parental contact with the child is due purely to the fact that the parents are forced for economic reasons to work a good deal outside the home. In cases where neglect is due to a deeply felt need on the part of the parents to take part in business and industry, it is highly unlikely that an order for one of the parents to stay at home will produce a beneficial result for the children. An attempt must instead be made to compensate the children for this lack by providing them with facilities that take the place of the missing parental functions.

In the relationship between parents and young persons in the family a conflict may arise as to who is to use the funds paid to the family for upkeep of the young. Until a few years ago a family allowance was also paid in respect of children aged sixteen to seventeen. It was contended that many young people received the allowance directly from their parents and spent the money on luxuries for themselves. The money therefore did not form part of the family budget or help ease the breadwinner's burden. When it became necessary to trim government spending a few years ago, it seemed only right that a majority of the Parliament should vote for abolition of the family allowance for these older children on the grounds that it was merely luxury pocket money. Its place was taken by a youth allowance, paid after a means test to families that need it; those families that could afford to let their children spend the family allowance no longer received an allowance, while young people in low-income families or young people living independently could continue to get help.

6. Just as the question arises of how far society should interfere in the family's affairs, it is justifiable to ask how far and with what purpose society should step into the child's life. Should society aim primarily at allowing the child to become a healthy, adjusted, and productive citizen, or should it insure a happy childhood straightaway? Is childhood principally a preparatory stage for adulthood, or is it an independent phase of life with its own values and needs? Strictly speaking, the problem is a variation of the adult-child conflict mentioned earlier. The children are the adults' future breadwinners.

The peculiar factor in the problem is that while at the family level the child carries a certain "political" weight and influence, at the societal level the child is powerless, a virtually nonexistent political force.

There is no doubt that proposals for measures for the benefit of children are much more likely to gain support when the motivation is that children thus develop faster, become better adjusted, learn more, and are better prepared for school and work than if the proposals are motivated merely to help children become happier and more content and aimed at improving existential values. Obviously, society's educational institutions must strike a balance between these two standpoints. But there are powerful backers—parents, teachers, the labor market—for the first viewpoint, and there is a risk that the early childhood years will become subject to the same principles as those in the adult world concerning efficiency and competition. The unexploited resources for learning and preparation in early childhood will be drawn into the race for production, and it is perhaps futile nostalgia to fight for preservation of the world and special values of childhood.

New Trends

Each of the latest trends in the field of family policy raises new problems or accentuates old ones:

1. The birth rate is declining. There are fewer conceptions and many abortions, and family wishes with regard to the number of children are modest.

The reason for this state of affairs is not immediately clear. It can, however, reach the point where it becomes a problem, and in that case it will probably result in improved assistance for families with children.

2. Divorce is on the increase, marriage on the decrease, more illegitimate children are being born, more couples are choosing to live permanently together without the formality of a marriage certificate. All of this indicates a breakup in the traditional, tightly knit family.

These factors vary in character. In some cases they may be the reasonable consequence of general development; in others, the result of imbalance and unreasonable living conditions. In any event, they necessitate reflections on the causes and on any necessary countermeasures—and thought should also be given to the possible effects upon the children's development.

The rising number of broken and irregular family formations accentuates such issues as changes in the concept of ''breadwinner,'' alterations in the father's legal status in respect to the child he may have outside his marriage, and possibly new methods of securing the children's right to contact with the father who is not a member of the household.

3. Dilution of family life, the dwindling number of useful joint family functions, the many families with just one or two children, women's entry into the labor market—all these factors have served to undermine the family

as a basis for the social lives of young and older children. This brings up the question of whether the family can be given better conditions for an enriched life together or whether society should aim at day care institutions which take over the individual's social life in an environment with close and stable emotional ties and with functions and responsibility extending deeply into the traditional areas of parental function and responsibility.

4. Poverty in the traditional sense, if not overcome, is at any rate on the decline in families with children. The chief problems are no longer poor nutrition, unsanitary homes, and disease but nerve-straining working conditions and impoverished conditions for psychological and social development. There are very few poorly clad, poorly fed children in schools and day care institutions. On the other hand, many children come from stress-ridden, understimulating homes, devoid of contact. The consequences for the child's development are considered to be no less serious than the effects of pecuniary poverty in earlier times. However, the combination of poverty and psychological/emotional neglect is the worst.

This fact has led people to wonder whether prophylactic medical examinations, health visitors, and school doctors should not turn their attention more to the emotional circumstances of the family and be retrained to help cope with this type of shortcoming.

Additional light is also brought to bear on the question of which educational programs the day care institutions should rely on in order best to assure the child's cognitive, emotional, and social development. It has long been recognized that children from stress-filled, poorly functioning homes are the minimum achievers in school and frequently drop out before completing their course. It was thought that this could be counteracted in day care institutions for preschool children by preparing them for school, especially through cognitive development programs. There is doubt, however, as to whether such programs provide adequate help for children who are starved for contact, and whether they would not be better served by programs designed to satisfy their need for contact and to straighten out and develop their emotional and social personality functions.

Family Groups in Real Jeopardy Today

Finally, let us look at some family groups that may be presumed to live under especially exhausting conditions or otherwise present special hazards for the future of their members, particularly the children.

1. *Families with heavy work burdens in conjunction with stress and distressed family life*. In this situation the parents are reduced to mere money earners, and there is a risk that contact with both young and older children will be neglected and that there will be general discontent on the part of the parents.

2. *Poor families, including the newly poor*. The burden of economic support falls especially heavily on these families, and there is a risk that their standard of living will drop dangerously low.

3. *Families hit by unemployment*. Unemployment of either the mother, father, or both parents has negative consequences as regards the individual's feeling of adequacy, the family's economy, and the whole family life generally.

4. *Families which are culturally and/or geographically isolated*. Even in cases where family life is balanced and harmonious, the situation can be restrictive and a threat to development of the children.

5. *Families which do not have the time, capacity, or urge to look after their children*. This type of family is found at every level of society, and the situation can affect both young and older children.

6. *Unmarried/single heads of family*. Their problems are more or less covered by the above points.

7. *Families in critical situations*. These are families suffering from death, divorce, imprisonment, and so forth.

8. *Families with alcoholism problems, mental affliction, children with handicaps*. These families are found throughout society.

9. *Emotionally unstable families*. This type of family, with friction and conflict between the parents and possibly with the children, is found at all levels of society.

General Future Objectives

The list of endangered families or hazardous situations leads naturally to a list of specific objectives for future family policy. The following are the author's own ideas in general—with apologies for their utopian nature:

1. To give all parents the opportunity to have at least one of them spend at least half of every day with their children under the age of two years, without economic loss and without losing status at work.

2. To insure that men and women have equal opportunity to have contact with their children and participate in a satisfying family life.

3. To give all children over the age of two years the opportunity of spending three or four hours daily in an educationally stimulating day care institution at no cost to the parents.

4. To insure that children whose parents both work full time outside the home are allocated day care facilities which are capable of assuming some of the traditional parental functions and helping to develop the child's over-all personality, including basic social and emotional development and intellectual stimulation.

5. To insure that older school children and young people, once they grow up and leave the family, do not end in a vacuum but can associate with environments that permit further social development, functional meaningfulness, and identification/integration with the adult world.

6. To try to influence family formation by attempting:

   a) To discourage very young women from having children until they have defined their identity as adults and until they have a permanent relationship to vocational training or a job

   b) To reduce the number of marriages likely to fail

   c) To reduce the number of unnecessary divorces, that is, those where the husband and wife have nothing to gain by divorce

   d) To limit the harmful effects of necessary and unavoidable divorces

   e) To facilitate necessary and healthy divorces, those through which the parties improve or salvage their lives.

7. To insure that children of common-law marriages and other new forms of living are not worse off than other children as regards legislation and social measures.

8. To insure flexibility of social support measures which permit families to arrange their lives according to their personal resources and attitudes, differing from family to family and from one period to another; and with regard to the needs of the children, which differ from child to child and from time to time.

9. To safeguard childhood's own intrinsic values, its pace, its richness of imagination, its creativity, its curiosity, and its humor; in other words, to enable the child to stimulate its parents toward being good parents.

Part III

IMPLICIT AND RELUCTANT FAMILY POLICY

UNITED KINGDOM
Hilary Land
and Roy Parker

BRITAIN HAS NEVER had an integrated set of social policies explicitly termed *"family* policies." Unlike many other European countries, Britain has never had a government minister whose title included the word "family," or even "population." Forty years ago when, as now, there was growing concern about declining birth rates in many European countries, the British government, unlike the governments of Sweden, France, Belgium, Italy, and Germany, did little to design directly pronatalist policies. Alva Myrdal in her study of family policies in a number of countries at that time, concludes:

> England never came as near as even Weimar Germany to visualising an integrated family reform policy. The strong impact of individualism in English social philosophy may have been to some extent responsible, as family values have never been stressed in English public life.[1]

However, although it may be true that family values have never been *stressed* in our social legislation, it would be quite wrong to conclude that British social policies have not been based on certain assumptions about both the pattern of responsibilities and dependencies within marriage and the

HILARY LAND is Lecturer, Department of Social Administration and Social Work, University of Bristol, Bristol, England.

DR. ROY PARKER is Professor, Department of Social Administration and Social Work, University of Bristol, Bristol, England.

[1] Alva Myrdal, *Nation and Family* (London: Kegan Paul, Trench, Trubner, 1945), p. 9.

duties of parents for their children or vice versa. These assumptions usually remain implicit in the legislation and are rarely articulated by those responsible for their administration. There are at least three reasons for this.

1. There is a widely held view that family life is, and should be, a private matter. An eminent political scientist recently wrote: "Can anyone dispute the fact that much if not most, private action and personal relationships are outside State control?"[2] The family is regarded as a vital, intimate sanctuary from the harsh economic world, and therefore the state should not intervene. Every piece of legislation believed to affect the relationship between parents and children or between husbands and wives, ranging from the introduction of state-financed old age pensions and school meals at the turn of the century to the more recent divorce and abortion law reforms, has had to overcome considerable opposition in order to establish the legitimacy of such intervention.

2. The family is perceived to be a fragile institution which must be protected. Therefore, social policies which can be presented as a means of counteracting the allegedly destructive effects of economic change on the family are more likely to be considered legitimate and therefore to win support from those who determine policy changes. As Richard Titmuss wrote:

> The rapidity of change in highly industrialised societies during the last one hundred years has put the family on the defensive—it is in this context that we need to see the social services in a variety of stabilising, preventive and protective roles.[3]

On examination, what is being protected are particular patterns of responsibilities and dependencies within the family and a long-established division of labor between the sexes and between generations. By presenting these as "natural" or "normal" the state can support and sustain them without appearing intrusive, thus preserving the illusion that the family is a private domain. At the same time, such strategies deny that there is an ideological dimension either to family life or to the policies themselves. Great care is taken in the delivery of services and benefits to the family not to upset the pattern of power and dependency within it. The debate in Britain in 1976 about the introduction of the child benefit scheme provides an excellent example.

3. A range of social services has been developed for adults and chil-

---

[2] William Robson, *Welfare State and Welfare Society* (London: Allen and Unwin, 1976), p. 15.

[3] Richard M. Titmuss, *Essays on the Welfare State* (2d ed.; London: Allen and Unwin, 1963), p. 117.

dren who are defined as being "without a family" or without a "normal" family: they are presented as facilities for *individuals,* and often abnormal or deviant individuals at that. The problem of establishing the legitimacy of state intervention is, thereby, considerably reduced. Of course, everyone has a family at the point of birth, and very few lose all their relatives while still in infancy, but by steadily narrowing the definition of family (or at least the "normal family") it has been possible for the state to provide a wide range of benefits in cash and kind without appearing to impose or undermine family values. At the same time, the boundaries of those family obligations which are thought to be important have been emphasized and sustained.

The full extent and nature of family policies in Britain may become apparent once the camouflage is removed. This can be done, but only by the close examination of a variety of policies, many of which do not appear directly relevant to family issues. Attention to the detail reveals the embedded assumptions. That is the approach we have adopted here. As a result, it has not been possible to look at more than three main groups of policies, those concerned with (1) social security and taxation (income maintenance); (2) housing; and (3) the provision of supplementary or alternative care. We are conscious of all that is omitted: family law; the impact of health care policies on families; employment policies; education.

Income Maintenance and Marriage

Family policies are often discussed in the context of demographic objectives, and therefore the term "family" is defined as parents and dependent children; that is, the nuclear family. As a result, the policies so identified are those which either concern the responsibilities and costs of parenthood or affect the relationship between parents and their children. This is a narrow view of the family, for it overlooks other stages in the family cycle which are not only important but, for most people, may also last longer than the stages during which young children are present. Childbearing and child rearing are being compressed into a shorter period: fertility within marriage starts later than it did and it ends earlier. A recent study of demographic trends concluded that "it looks as if fertility is virtually completed by the time the woman is aged 29 and the marriage has lasted ten years."[4] At that

4 David Eversley, "Demographic Change and the Demand for Housing," in Martin Buxton and Edward Craven, *The Uncertain Future* (London: Centre for Studies in Social Policy, 1976), p. 32.

age a woman can expect to live another forty-five years. The average age of fathers at the birth of *all* children in 1973 was 29, and at that age men have a life expectancy of more than forty-years. One- and two-person households have increased in number (see table 1), and those comprising parents and children have declined.

Table 1 Household Composition (Great Britain)

Households	1961	1971
No family (single or unrelated adults residing together)	16.8	22.2
Married couple, no children	25.6	26.7
Married couple with children	48.1	43.0
Lone parent with children	6.7	6.7
Two or more family house-holds	2.7	1.4
Total	100 = 16.2 million	100 = 18.3 million

SOURCE: Office of Population, Censuses and Surveys, *Social Trends,* No. 7 (London: Her Majesty's Stationery Office, 1976), p. 73.

The 1971 census showed that of the 18.3 million households in Britain only 50 percent consisted of parents and children; 27 percent contained a married couple only; and 22 percent were either one-person households or unrelated adults living together. In 1961, when there was a total of 16.2 million households, the figures were 55 percent, 26 percent, and 17 percent respectively. These figures mean that active parenthood does not last all or even most of a man or woman's married lifetime. It is therefore important to examine and understand the needs and obligations that are presumed to arise from marriage quite separately from those that are presumed to arise from parenthood. If we fail to observe this distinction marriage will too often be equated with parenthood. Moreover, examining the family only at the child-bearing stage of the life cycle not only obscures the distinction between marriage and parenthood but also results in overlooking the obligations and relationships between adult children and their middle-aged or elderly parents. Here we attempt to disentangle the needs and duties assumed to be associated with marriage from those associated with parenthood with reference to social security and fiscal policies.

The British system of social security, including both contributory social insurance and means-tested benefits, has been based on certain assumptions about the family. Since 1601 our public assistance legislation has defined those family relationships that carry with them both rights and obligations to financial maintenance. The law specified the relatives from whom the authorities that granted assistance to a poor person could seek reimbursement. Over the years the extent of such liability has been reduced. Since 1948 only the obligations which spouses have to maintain each other and which parents have for their dependent children remain. Other assumptions about relationships within families have been less explicit but no less a fundamental feature of social security policy. For example, the Victorian system of relief for the poor (the Poor Law), which took the form of institutional care in the local workhouse (indoor relief) or the payment of cash grants (outdoor relief), assumed the universality of the two-parent family: a family which was both stable and largely dependent upon the father's earnings. The major problem of poverty was therefore believed to be that of the able-bodied but unemployed male; it was he who had to be assisted, but without undermining his incentive to work. As a result, the needs of women and children without husbands and fathers who were capable or willing to support them were regarded as exceptional or peripheral.[5]

The reality was very different. Men's wages were often low and irregular, and the probability of sickness or death much higher than today. The Board of Guardians that had to administer a system of relief to the poor in each parish (the smallest administrative unit in Britain) had to deal with substantial numbers of women and children who were not or could not be dependent upon men. This posed very real problems because it was feared that if the separated wife or even a widow were given financial help this would undermine the obligation that men had to work in order to support their families. Widows were sometimes refused benefit for six months after the death of their husband, and separated wives had to prove that the separation had occurred at least two years previously. Unmarried mothers caused even greater dilemmas. They were precluded from claiming maintenance, either directly or through the Boards of Guardians, from a man who was the father of their child but to whom they were not married, because to have allowed them to do so would have been an "infringement of the exclusive privileges of the married state" and therefore "a direct attack on that insti-

---

[5] As Beatrice and Sidney Webb commented in their extensive review of Poor Law policy:

> "With regard to the treatment of women, it cannot be said that the Report [on the Poor Laws] of 1834 afforded much guidance to the central authority. . . . In this Report, the single independent woman is nowhere mentioned. The wife is throughout treated exactly as the child; it is assumed that she follows her husband. . . . With regard to the really baffling problems presented by the widow, the deserted wife, the wife of the absentee soldier or sailor, the wife of a husband resident in another parish or another country—with or without children—the Report is silent." Beatrice and Sidney Webb, *English Poor Law Policy* (London: Longmans, 1910), p. 36.

tution.'' [6] The difficulties posed by lone mothers are extensively documented in the Poor Law records, and the resulting policies varied from one part of the country to another; but nearly all treated the unmarried mother harshly and only offered her the workhouse.

In time the needs of some categories of women were met quite outside the means-tested benefit system. Widows, for example, were eventually acknowledged as needing *and* deserving assistance. In 1925 the national insurance scheme introduced widows' pensions for widows whose husbands had made the necessary contributions. Beveridge, who in 1942 wrote the report on social security which formed the basis of most of the postwar social security legislation in Britain, recommended that similar help be accorded to women whose marriages ended in divorce or separation. However, his proposal for a separation benefit failed to win sufficient support, not least because ''if separation benefit was made too readily available in cases of separation or desertion it might have the antisocial effect of encouraging the breakup of marriage.'' [7]

Today our social security policies are nationally, not locally, determined; but one-parent families still present difficulties for our social security system. The number of them dependent on the means-tested supplementary benefits scheme (the successor to the Poor Law) has doubled in the last ten years; [8] the number of divorces has doubled since 1971, and although many men and women remarry (in 1974, 28 percent of all marriages in England and Wales were remarriages), for short periods between marriages they may need financial help from the state. At any time about half of all one-parent families are dependent on supplementary benefits. In 1973 the Finer Committee on One-Parent Families proposed a special guaranteed maintenance allowance for all one-parent families, including unmarried mothers, but this has yet to be implemented. Interestingly, in Britain the solution to the problem of lone mothers is perceived more in terms of how best to remove barriers to their remarriage rather than to overcome obstacles to their increased participation in the labor market.

---

[6] An extract from the Poor Law Commissioners Annual Report, 1840, quoted by Morris Finer and Oliver McGregor, ''The History of the Obligation to Maintain,'' in *Report of the Committee on One-Parent Families*, II, Cmnd. 5629 (London: Her Majesty's Stationery Office, 1974), p. 118.

[7] *Ibid.*, p. 146.

[8] In 1965, 110,000 one-parent families (5.3 percent of all claimants) received national assistance (now called supplementary benefits). In 1975, 281,000 one-parent families, or 9.7 percent of all claimants, received supplementary benefits.

However, the group of women which was and has remained largely invisible in our social security system is the great majority, namely, those who are married and living with their husbands. Social security policies assume that they are dependent on their husbands and that if they have paid employment their earnings are not a vital part of the family income. Consequently, unemployment and sickness among married women have not been defined as problems which warrant income support. Maintaining the family income has been interpreted first and foremost to mean maintaining the *husband's* income and earning capacity. Thus when the actuarial advisers to Lloyd George's government were devising the first national unemployment and health insurance scheme in Britain in 1911 they wrote:

> Married women living with their husbands need not be included [in the insurance scheme] since where the unit is the family it is the husband's and not the wife's health which it is important to insure. As long as the husband is in good health and able to work, adequate provision will be made for the needs of the family, irrespective of the wife's health, whereas when the husband's health fails there is no one to earn wages.[9]

As a result of such convictions, arrangements to include casual workers in the unemployment benefit scheme specifically excluded married women; in any case, upon marriage all working women lost the right to benefits based upon the contributions they had made before marriage. The insured (that is, working men and women who paid contributions) had the right to free medical treatment, but the so-called *family* doctor did not provide his services free to the nonworking wives and children of his male patients until after World War II when the National Health Service became available to all.

Yet, contrary to the assumptions which these examples reveal, many families were not dependent solely on the man's earnings. For instance, an analysis of the returns of the 1911 census showed that on average the husband's or father's earnings accounted for 70 percent of a working class family's income and that only 41 percent of families were dependent solely on the earnings of one man.[10]

Participation by wives in the labor force continues to grow (see table 2).

---

[9] Quoted in Bentley B. Gilbert, *The Evolution of National Insurance in Great Britain* (London: Michael Joseph, 1966), p. 315.

[10] Arthur Bowley, "Earners and Dependants in English Towns in 1911," *Economica*, May, 1921, p. 101.

Table 2 Wives'[a] Economic Activity Rate by Age: 1961 and 1971 (England and Wales)

	Percent Economically Active	
Age	1961	1971
Under 20	42.7	41.4
20–29	34.9	40.2
30–39	32.4	45.8
40–49	37.7	57.6
50–59	29.4	49.5
60+	6.9	13.7
All ages	29.4	41.8
With dependent children	25.2	38.6
With no dependent children	33.6	44.8

SOURCES: *1961 Census,* "Household Composition Tables, 10% Sample," Table 44; *1971 Census,* "Household Composition Tables, 10% Sample," Table 50.
[a] Married but separated women excluded.

Today in Britain many more married women have paid employment outside the home than in the 1920s and 1930s. The 1971 census showed that over half of all married women under sixty (the retirement age for women) were economically active. In 1974, the seven million working wives contributed on average 25 percent of the family income, and half a million of them were the sole or primary earner.[11] In many families the wife's contribution, although smaller than her husband's, may be vital to keeping them out of poverty. The Department of Health and Social Security (DHSS) showed that in 1971 the number of poor two-parent families with fathers in full-time employment would have nearly *trebled* if the father's earnings had not been supplemented by the mother's.[12] Nevertheless, recently a Minister of State to the DHSS wrote in justification of not paying to the unemployed or sick married woman additional allowances for her children, which automatically added to the *father's* unemployment or sickness benefit: "It is normal for a married woman in this country to be primarily supported by her husband, and she looks to him for support when not actually working rather than to a social security benefit."[13]

Thus, assumptions about the nature of the marriage relationship have

[11] Lynn Hamill, "Wives as Sole and Joint Breadwinners" (unpublished paper, Social Science Research Council, Social Security Workshop, 1977).

[12] Department of Health and Social Security (DHSS), *Two Parent Families and Their Needs* (London: Her Majesty's Stationery Office, 1971), p. 14.

[13] Brian O'Malley, a Minister of State to the DHSS, in letter to Women's Liberation Campaign for Legal and Financial Independence, May 14, 1975.

changed very little, and the dependency of married women is still regarded as a central feature in social security policies, in spite of the fact that 1975, the International Women's Year, saw major changes in income-maintenance legislation and passage of the Sex Discrimination Act

We have now entirely abandoned the principle of flat-rate benefits in return for flat-rate contributions in our social insurance scheme. Instead, all contributions are earnings-related (5.75 percent of earnings up to a ceiling of approximately one and a half times average male industrial earnings). This means that men and women with the same earnings pay the same contribution. However, until April, 1975, when the scheme became fully earnings-related, men had always paid a higher contribution than women, not on the grounds that on average their earnings were double those of a woman's but because, as Beveridge explained in 1942, unlike women, "men are contributing for themselves and their wives as for a team."[14] This meant that when a man became sick or unemployed he claimed benefits for himself plus additional dependency allowances for each child, and for his wife if she was not in paid employment. Similarly, when he retired he drew a pension for himself plus an allowance for his wife (which was equal to about 60 percent of the single person's pension).

All married women could choose not to pay full contributions to the national insurance scheme (this was known as "the married woman's option") and to rely instead on their husband's contribution record for a pension as his dependent and thereby forego entirely any sickness, maternity, or unemployment benefit in their own right. Three quarters of married women chose to opt out of the national insurance scheme, and there was much to encourage them to do so. They received a lower rate of sickness and unemployment benefit than their single sisters and had to satisfy much tougher conditions in order to qualify for a pension in their own right. In the light of this, the flat-rate contribution seemed to be a disproportionately high proportion of their earnings.

This choice is to be withdrawn, starting in May, 1977, but only slowly. Any married woman or widow already exercising her choice to opt out will be able to continue to do so provided that she does not leave the labor market for more than two years. However, on examination, although any newly married woman will contribute on exactly the same basis as her husband, she will not receive the same benefit. The level of benefit she attracts for herself will be the same as that of a man or a single woman, but, unlike

[14] William Beveridge, *Social Insurance and Allied Services* (the Beveridge Report), Cmnd. 6404 (London: His Majesty's Stationery Office, 1942), p. 50.

her husband, she will not automatically receive additional dependency benefits for any of her children. Neither will she be able to claim a dependency
benefit for her husband unless he is incapable of paid employment, whereas
he only has to show that his wife is not working, not that she cannot do so.
In time, as more and more married women collect insurance benefits in their
own right when unemployed or sick, the need for dependency benefits for
spouses will be reduced. Meanwhile, there are clear inequities arising from
the assumption that a wife's earnings are only supplementary. Similarly, the
need for additional dependency benefits for children will disappear when—
and if—the new cash allowances for children called "child benefits" take
the place of family allowances and become large enough to replace the extra
benefits currently paid for children in the national insurance and supplementary benefit schemes. The principle of paying a cash allowance for children
which is high enough to meet the subsistence cost of a child irrespective of
the marital or employment status of the parents is one of Beveridge's underlying principles which has yet to be implemented. However, until that
happens it will be necessary to supplement child benefits. To do so only during a period when the *father* is sick or unemployed underlines the view that
men support families whereas women take paid work only to support themselves unless they have a chronically sick or disabled husband who is incapable of paid employment.

Other changes were introduced in the social security legislation passed
in 1975, and they too were based on certain assumptions about the responsibilities and duties arising from marriage. For example, there is now a non-
contributory invalid care allowance which is paid to those who have to give
up paid employment in order to care for a sick or elderly relative (cousins
are excluded, but stepbrothers, half brothers and sisters, and in-laws are included). This will help single men and women whose contribution toward
the care of their chronically sick and disabled kin has hitherto received no financial acknowledgement. However, they will have to give up paid employment (defined as earning more than £9 a week) in order to qualify for the allowance of £10.50 [As of April 1, 1977, the exchange rate was: 1£ = $1.72.
Eds.]; but this new allowance will not benefit the one in ten women in paid
employment who also has the care of an elderly or infirm relative, one in
seven of whom are so severely handicapped that they require all duties to be
performed for them. Married women are excluded from this provision altogether. In a recent test case a national insurance commissioner reversed a
decision to pay an invalid care allowance to a young married woman who
looked after, but neither lived with, nor was maintained by, her severely

disabled husband. In doing so he explained that married women had been specifically excluded from this benefit on the assumption "that a married woman would not usually work and therefore would not lose wages or rights to national insurance benefit."[15] The DHSS seems to ignore the fact that economic activity rates for childless married women under forty years of age are nearly the same as those for single women and that increasing numbers of women are combining paid employment with motherhood so that by the time their children are of secondary school age over half the mothers are back in the labor market. In other words, the majority of married women now have paid employment for most of their married lives. If a private organization attempted to discriminate against women on the grounds of their marital status in this way they could be prosecuted under the Sex Discrimination Act. However, the social security system is specifically excluded from the requirements of that act.

The unpaid work of married women caring for sick and elderly relatives continues to be taken for granted except in one small way. Under the 1975 Social Security Pensions Act women who stay at home in order to care for children (up to the age of sixteen) or sick or elderly relatives will be credited with national insurance contributions so that their rights to a retirement pension will be maintained. The regulations covering this new measure have yet to be published, but although it is clear that single men will also be credited with contributions when home responsibilities keep them from paid employment, it is by no means certain that the provision will include the married man who chooses to stay at home to look after children while his wife takes paid work.

Another recent change recognizes, for the first time, that a man may be economically dependent on his wife. Widowers' pensions have been introduced into the social security system, but only for those men who are already retired[16] or who are permanently sick or disabled. Only the husband who cannot be expected to take paid employment himself is acknowledged to be dependent upon his wife. This, of course, in no way undermines "the widespread view that a husband who is capable of work has a duty to society as well as to his wife, to provide the primary support for his family."[17]

The British social security system does not recognize that most married

[15] London *Times*, January 8, 1977.

[16] A man who is the survivor of a pensioner couple will have a dual entitlement to the earnings-related additional pension which they have both earned, subject to the maximum amount which any one person can draw.

[17] O'Malley, letter to Women's Liberation Campaign for Legal and Financial Independence.

couples share the economic support of their families and that some may wish to share responsibilities for domestic work: breadwinners are male. Only women care for children, the sick, and the old, and if they have paid employment this must take second place to their domestic duties. In reading the social security legislation it would be hard to deduce that the "typical" family consisting of a man in full-time employment, the woman as a full-time housewife, and two dependent children has been, at any point, a minority of families (10 percent in 1971). Neither would it be apparent from the way the legislation is framed that in 1971 one in six households (excluding pensioner households) relied almost entirely upon a woman's income for support and that the majority of these households contained dependents.[18]

A study of British fiscal policies, which allow the taxpayer to offset against his (or, less often, her) taxable income allowances in recognition of certain specified family responsibilities, reveals similar underlying assumptions about the nature of the relationships between men and women in the family. Married women's paid employment is accorded greater recognition than in the social security system because, as a government discussion paper states, "the needs of the economy require the continued employment of large numbers of married women and the system must be such that they feel it is worth their while going to work."[19] Nevertheless, the marriage relationship is assumed to be one in which the husband is the primary breadwinner and his wife, irrespective of whether she has earnings or an income of her own, is his dependent. *All* married men can, therefore, offset a larger allowance (£1,085 in 1977 compared with £735 for a single person) against their taxable income than single men because it is assumed that "a man with a wife to support has clearly a lower capacity to pay tax than a single man."[20] In 1974 the cost in foregone revenue of the married man's tax allowance was £1,100 million. With the latest increases announced in the 1976 budget it must cost something in the order of £1,400 million. In other words, the tax subsidy to marriage is almost as great as the tax subsidy to parenthood (that is, the cost of foregone revenue represented by child tax allowances).

The British tax system aggregates the income of husband and wife and

[18] See Hilary Land, "Women: Supporters or Supported?" in Diana Barker and Sheila Allen, eds., *Sexual Divisions in Society* (London: Tavistock, 1976).

[19] Green Paper on *Proposals for a Tax-credit System* (London: Her Majesty's Stationery Office, 1972), p. 18.

[20] "Select Committee on Tax-Credit," *Evidence* (London: Her Majesty's Stationery Office, 1973), II, 360.

considers that it belongs to the husband, who is therefore liable to paying the tax on it because, it is argued, the family constitutes a single spending unit. Yet "family" is very narrowly defined to mean only husband and wife; children's income has not consistently been aggregated with that of their parents. With graduated rates of tax this would mean that a married couple would be worse off than two single people living together. However, ever since 1942, "as a concession to stimulate the movement of married women into employment,"[21] the tax relief offset against a married woman's earnings has been equivalent to a single person's allowance. In other words, a married couple pay less tax than two single people. But it is the tax position of the husband, not the wife, which improves upon marriage. Since 1972 married couples have been allowed to opt for separate taxation, but only on the wife's earned income. However, because the husband loses the married man's allowance, unless both are paying high rates of tax it is better not to choose to be taxed separately.[22]

The assumption that the husband is the head of the family is underlined in a number of other ways. Only the husband can sign their joint income tax return unless the wife has opted for separate taxation and/or separate assessment. Should too much tax be deducted from a woman's pay, the rebate may be sent to her husband because, legally, it belongs to him. Even if the marital home is jointly owned it is assumed that he will claim the tax relief on the interest element of the mortgage payments.

The way in which dependent relatives allowances operate provides further evidence that it is the marriage relationship which makes a woman a dependent so far as the Board of Inland Revenue is concerned. Under the present system a taxpayer who is supporting a dependent relative (widely defined to include cousins and other extended kin) may claim tax relief up to £100 a year. Normally, a dependent relative must be incapacitated either by old age or infirmity, have an income equivalent to the National Insurance basic pension, *and* be in receipt of some income from the taxpayer concerned. However, the taxpayer's mother or mother-in-law, irrespective of her age or state of health, is by definition a dependent relative if she is widowed, divorced, or legally separated. The unmarried mother, however, is

---

[21] Richard Sayers, *Economic Policy 1939–1945* (London: His Majesty's Stationery Office, 1950), p. 113.

[22] In the first year of operation only 17,000 couples elected separate taxation. (Separate *assessment,* which allots a portion of the tax allowances to each spouse in proportion to their respective incomes without altering their total tax bill, has been possible for a long time but very few people know about it.)

not. She will have to prove old age or infirmity, on the grounds that because she has never been dependent on a husband, her son or daughter cannot be regarded as replacing the maintenance provided by a former or deceased husband.

The development of tax relief for the employment of housekeepers also illustrates assumptions about the work that men and women do within the home. This particular concession, which was introduced in 1918, was initially only available to widowers who relied upon housekeepers to care for their children. The housekeeper had to be a female relative resident in the taxpayer's home. She did not have to be remunerated. At the start the allowance was £25, the same as that for a wife. A year later it was extended to childless widowers. In 1920 widows with children were allowed to claim such an allowance as well, and, rather surprisingly, in 1924 childless widows were included. This last measure was regarded later as an anomaly for which it was "difficult to find any rational purpose," as the Inland Revenue Staff Federation told the Royal Commission on Taxation of Incomes and Profits, because "it is not the death of a spouse but the lack of a *wife* who can keep house which may necessitate a housekeeper."[23]

During World War II the tax relief for housekeepers was extended so that it became available to taxpayers with children who employed any resident housekeeper, provided that if the taxpayer was a man his wife was permanently incapacitated or dead—but not separated or divorced. A woman on her own with children could claim the housekeeper's allowance only if she were totally incapacitated or supporting herself by full-time paid employment. (The wife of a permanently disabled man *cannot* claim for a housekeeper even if she is in full-time employment.) The definition of housekeeper was broadened to include nonrelatives, but they had to be female. All these rules are still applied, and in 1973 tax concessions of £100 on behalf of 100,000 housekeepers were claimed. Since 1960 single parents without resident housekeepers can claim an additional tax allowance. This has been increased in recent years so that they now receive, in effect, the same personal tax allowance as a married man.

Our examples serve to indicate the dominant assumptions which are made about the nature of marriages. It is quite clear that both fiscal policies and social security arrangements take for granted that upon marriage a woman becomes dependent upon her husband and also that she does the

[23] "Royal Commission on the Taxation of Incomes and Profits, 1951–55," *Evidence* (London: Her Majesty's Stationery Office, 1953), III, 18; italics added.

housework and cares for the children. If a substitute is needed because she becomes disabled or dies, then only a female housekeeper will do.

Income Maintenance and Parenthood

The most generous form of support to parents is given by means of our income tax system (although, as we discuss below, this is under review). When it comes to recognizing the needs of parenthood, in practice the father's claims to tax relief take precedence over the mother's. He claims the tax allowances in respect of his legitimate children unless he agrees that the mother may do so. The deserted wife may find that her husband continues to claim these allowances even though he is contributing nothing toward the children's maintenance. In such circumstances, although the mother may be allowed to offset these allowances against her earnings, this is at the discretion of the Board of Inland Revenue, which does not, in any case, require evidence that a father is helping to maintain his children. Proof that they are his legitimate children or that he has legal custody is all that is required. Just recently, a study of grants to students in higher education, the level of which is assessed and determined by parental income, showed that seven out of ten students did not get their reduced grants made up to the full amount by their parents despite the fact that all those parents (mainly fathers) would have been benefiting by at least £127 a year (the value to the basic rate tax payer of the tax allowance for children aged sixteen or over and in full-time higher education).[24] This will change when the child benefit scheme is fully implemented, but interestingly there has been little criticism of the tax system which requires so little evidence of maintenance. In contrast, cash benefits for the children of the poor have always been subject to much greater scrutiny.

The next most important benefit for parents is the family allowance, although in Britain family allowances have never been generous. They were introduced in 1945 for a variety of reasons, including the desire to encourage parents to have more children. The wartime coalition government accepted them primarily as a means of combating wage inflation by reducing the need and demand for larger wages for workers with families. At the

---

[24] The child tax allowances for the year ending on April 1, 1977, were £300 for a child under eleven, £335 for a child aged eleven to sixteen, and £365 for a child over sixteen. The basic tax rate which applies to the first £5,000 of taxable income was 35 percent.

same time, they were seen as preserving work incentives for men by recognizing family responsibilities both in and out of work (the unemployment benefit included dependency allowances for a wife and children, with the result that the income of the unemployed low-wage earner with a family could be close to that when he was working). Family allowances were also aimed at reducing poverty among children. Only a minority of the political interests supported them as a means of recognizing and improving the status of the mother as a worthy end in itself. However, those who were concerned to reduce the dependence of women on the father of their children did succeed in getting the allowance paid to the mother.[25]

Family allowances differ from other social security benefits in several important ways. First, they are paid irrespective of the employment and marital status of the child's parents. Second, they are the only allowances paid directly to the mother irrespective of the presence or absence of the father. Third, they have not been subject to the regular annual reviews that all other social security benefits receive and have only been increased five times since their inception in 1945. Finally, unlike other dependency benefits for children, the first child is excluded and the value of the flat-rate allowance (currently £1.50, which is taxable) is nowhere near the subsistence cost of a child (the supplementary benefit system provides tax-free allowances for children ranging from £3.60 to £7.80). Only in 1975, thirty years after their introduction, was legislation passed to extend the allowances (to be called child benefits) to the first child. The debate last year on how and when to implement the Child Benefit Act, 1975, reveals some important assumptions about the family.

The purpose of the Child Benefit Act, said Barbara Castle, Secretary of State to the DHSS who steered the bill through Parliament,

> was to concentrate the help government gives to the family through family allowances and child tax allowances in a single cash benefit for all children in the family payable to the mother and untaxed. Only by the father giving up his tax relief was it possible to finance the mother's need properly. And only in this way was it possible to end the absurd anomaly whereby those who need the most help get the least because they are too poor to pay tax.[26]

This act makes it possible to simplify the complex and often inconsistent methods by which the state adjusts family income to family size—but only if

[25] For a full account of the introduction of family allowances in Britain see Phoebe Hall, Hilary Land, Roy Parker, and Adrian Webb, *Change, Choice and Conflict in Social Policy* (London: Heinemann, 1975).

[26] Barbara Castle, "The Death of Child Benefits," *New Statesman,* June 4, 1976, p. 736.

changes are made in the income tax system at the same time. In this sense it was the same as the Conservative Party's proposal to introduce child tax credits as part of their tax credit scheme (a form of negative income tax). The issue was complicated because tax changes are the prerogative of the Chancellor of the Exchequer, not the Secretary of State to the DHSS or the cabinet. But more important, the reform involved a transfer of income between husband and wife as his net pay was reduced because he paid more tax and she collected larger cash benefits for the children. (Family allowances, and in future child benefits, are paid weekly in cash at post offices.) The opposition which this redistribution of income within the family aroused nearly wrecked the whole scheme.

In the April budget of 1976, the Chancellor of the Exchequer *increased* child tax allowances "as part of the compensation for accepting a low pay limit which," he said, "I am offering the Trades Union Congress."[27] This meant that the impact of withdrawing child tax allowances on men's take-home pay when child benefits were introduced would be increased, and at a time when their real wages were falling. Of course, the *family* income would be increased, and one of the issues was how large the child benefit should be. However, after some underhand dealing with trade union leaders and in the cabinet, it was revealed later[28] that the government decided to drop the scheme because it "would have imposed an excessive strain on the pay policy." The cabinet had come to this decision having been told that,

> on being informed of the reduction in take-home pay, which the child benefits scheme would involve, the Trades Union Congress representative had reacted immediately and violently against its implementation, *irrespective of the level of benefits which would accompany the reduction in take-home pay.*[29]

So it appeared that however much extra cash the mother collected in the form of child benefits so that *total* family income was substantially increased, the male unions would oppose the scheme on the grounds of the transfer from "wallet to purse."

The question of whether to increase the father's take-home pay or the mother's cash allowances is not just one of principle. Pay rises are not nec-

[27] *House of Commons Debates,* April 6, 1976, Vol. 909, Col. 274.

[28] Minutes of the cabinet meetings were leaked and reported in an anonymous article, "Killing a Commitment: the Cabinet v. the Children," *New Society,* June 17, 1976, pp. 630–32. See also "Purse or Wallet? How the Cabinet Did a Switch-Sell," London *Sunday Times,* June 20, 1976.

[29] "Killing a Commitment," *New Society,* June 14, 1976; italics added.

essarily shared within the family. Two large surveys in 1975[30] showed that on average husbands passed on half their pay rises to their wives for the housekeeping. Altogether, one in five mothers had received no increase in housekeeping over the previous twelve months, and for larger families and the low-paid the proportion was nearer a third. Another recent study showed that less than half of wives even knew what their husbands earned.[31] The widely held assumption that financial resources going into the family, irrespective of their source and to whom they are first paid, are very largely pooled and shared among members of the family according to some collective notion of their needs is received wisdom but patently false. But as Galbraith has written, "the household in the established economics is essentially a disguise for the exercise of male authority."[32] Any policy which does not collude with this disguise and, as in the case of child benefits, attempts directly to protect women and children, particularly in poor families, from the impact of inflation, runs into considerable opposition from those powerful groups representing the interests of men. Male wage-bargaining strategies in Britain have been based on the argument that they require wage increases (as well as higher wages than women) because they have families to support. Moreover, many men clearly still wish to retain control over how much money their wives receive.

In the event, the government was persuaded to adopt a modified version of the original child benefit scheme[33] but the necessary tax changes had to await the 1977 budget. Meanwhile, the Chancellor of the Exchequer is expressing much concern with the low tax thresholds, particularly for the family man. The question of redistribution *within* the family is likely to remain an issue in Britain.

In spite of their very different histories the details of both the social security system and the income tax system reveal certain clear and persistent assumptions about the economic relationship between husband and wife and

[30] The National Consumer Council, *For Richer, for Poorer* (London: Her Majesty's Stationery Office, 1975).

[31] Occupational Pensions Board, *Equal Status for Men and Women in Occupational Pension Schemes,* Cmnd. 6599 (London: Her Majesty's Stationery Office, 1976), p. 171.

[32] John Kenneth Galbraith, *Public Policy and Public Purpose* (London: Penguin Books, 1974), p. 52.

[33] For a full account of the child benefit debate in 1976 see Hilary Land, "The Child Benefit Fiasco," in Kathleen Jones, ed., *Yearbook of Social Policy* (London: Routledge and Kegan Paul; 1978). A child benefit of £1 tax free will be put into effect for all first children in April, 1977. Income tax allowances for children are to be reduced by £104 for first children and £130 for all other children.

about the division of unpaid labor in the home. At the same time, an unequal marriage relationship is preserved. Social policies which impinge on the family have not been allowed to interfere with work incentives for men. Indeed, we would argue that by assuming an unequal economic relationship between men and women, the man's *duty* to participate in the labor market is reinforced, and although his wife may take paid employment too, her first duty is to care for her husband, children, and sick or elderly relatives. The view that a woman's wage is merely supplementing a man's or is only for her sole support perpetuates low wages both for women and for those men who are not able to bargain for wages high enough to keep themselves and their families. At the same time, such policies accord with an ideology that sustains men's dominance over women both in the home and in wider society.

Housing Policy and Families

It is not only in the fields of social security and taxation that there are underlying but systematic assumptions about marriage, parenthood, and the family. Upon closer examination, British housing policies too can be seen to be shaped by a pervasive conviction that certain kinds of family should be accorded priority. Take the example of public sector housing, which accounts for about a third of all dwellings. Although in practice "council housing," as it is more often called, is for working-class people,[34] it is also characteristically for nuclear families; that is, married adults with dependent children. This group has been granted precedence in allocation procedures, and the dwellings themselves are mostly of a "normal family size."[35] Both supply and distribution have reflected a widespread belief that public sector housing *ought* to be for nuclear families.

The view that council housing should be reserved for families with children wherever possible has been a recurring theme in both local and central government policies since the 1920s. A key policy statement at the end of World War II, for example, insisted that "the Government's first objec-

[34] Until 1949 council housing was restricted to the "working classes," although the term was never defined. Nowadays there are no restrictions; the only criterion is "housing need," again not specifically interpreted.

[35] Note the considerable criticism of high-rise council flats because they are "unsuitable" for families. See Pearl Jephcott, *Homes in High Flats* (Edinburgh: Oliver and Boyd, 1971).

tive is to afford a separate dwelling for every *family* which desires to have one.''[36] Such a policy may seem entirely reasonable and unremarkable except that, by definition, it excludes other kinds of households: in particular, couples without dependent children as well as single people. ''Most single people,'' said a government handbook of the same period, ''will continue to find their own accommodation as lodgers,'' although adding that some provision might have to be made for single women.[37] Clearly, however, those single people were not expected to become lodgers with families in the public sector. Legislation explicitly prohibited it without the local authorities' permission, and housing managers were advised that ''taking in lodgers and sub-letting was not in the interests of good management.''[38]

In the numerous local systems for organizing waiting lists for public housing and for determining priorities, various ''rules'' evolved. Admission to the general list was often limited to married couples and single parents with children, although in some areas engaged people were allowed into the queue. Actual allocation was, and is, frequently settled by awarding points for different aspects of housing need but with heavy emphasis placed upon overcrowding and children. Although childless couples are not debarred from council housing, they are rarely able to accumulate sufficient points to rise to the top of the waiting list. This is generally regarded as ''fair.'' In this respect it is illuminating to recall the passionate sense of intolerable injustice which arose when, in Northern Ireland, a new council house was allocated to a single Protestant woman in the face of Catholic family needs. Indeed, the report of the committee which was set up to investigate the outbreak of violence in the province suggested that this housing incident was one of the sparks which set ablaze the smoldering bitterness.[39]

Family priority in the allocation of public housing is so familiar and unexceptionable that its size and importance as a policy are liable to be overlooked; but it must be remembered that the other two thirds of the British

[36] Ministry of Reconstruction, *Housing,* Cmnd. 6609 (London: His Majesty's Stationery Office, 1945), p. 2; italics added.

[37] Ministry of Health and Ministry of Works, *Housing Manual* (London: His Majesty's Stationery Office, 1944), p. 230.

[38] Ministry of Health, Second Report of the Housing Management Sub-Committee of the Central Housing Advisory Committee, *Housing Management* (London: His Majesty's Stationery Office, 1945), p. 21.

[39] Government of Northern Ireland, *Report of the Commission into Disturbances in Northern Ireland* (Cameron) Cmnd. 532 (London: Her Majesty's Stationery Office, 1969), chap. 3.

housing market are located in the private sector.[40] Although the owner-occupier market also supplies predominately family-sized housing, no special priority is accorded to families with children. Entitlement is by purchase irrespective of social circumstances. That is not to say that building societies and other mortgage institutions do not take these things into account. Their policies tend to favor younger male adults receiving higher incomes who are married or about to be married. Indeed, the chance of a couple obtaining a mortgage may be enhanced by their *not* having dependent children so that both of them are able to work full time. In the privately rented sector, too, there is evidence that families with children are discriminated against, except at the cheapest and the most expensive ends of the market. Letting by the room is generally the most profitable system, but one which militates against families unless landlords are prepared to flout the legislation against overcrowding.[41]

There are good reasons why nuclear "family priority" should have become a central feature of building and allocation policies in the public housing sector. Three in particular deserve mention.

1. The gap between minimum required housing standards and the ability of lower-income earners to pay for them was especially wide for families with children because income per head was proportionately less than in other kinds of households. The public sector, with the aid of subsidies, enabled that gap to be bridged without lowering standards or raising wage levels. The problem was accentuated in those periods when opportunities for mothers to add to the family income (for example, by employment, home work, or taking in lodgers) declined; when the school leaving age was raised; when the income tax penetrated further down the income scale; and when housing standards were raised (mandatory space heating in all new council dwellings, for example).

---

[40] In fact, the dominance of the private sector is even greater than this fraction suggests because mobility is higher than in the public sector, hence more vacancies are created for reallocation. In the *General Household Survey*, 1973 (London: Office of Population Censuses and Surveys, Her Majesty's Stationery Office, 1976), it is reported that 69 percent of heads of households in the public sector had not moved in the previous five years. For owner-occupiers with outstanding mortgages the proportion was 56 percent and in the privately rented furnished, only 13 percent. The tenants of unfurnished privately rented accommodations and owner-occupiers who owned outright, however, were less mobile than public sector tenants: 75 percent and 85 percent respectively had not moved in the previous five years (table 2.24, p. 49).

[41] See, for example, *Report of the Committee on the Rent Acts* (Francis), Cmnd. 4609 (London: Her Majesty's Stationery Office, 1971).

2. There were, at various times, connections between this "family policy" in public housing and demographic policies. Here, for example, is an extract from a Scottish report in 1950:

> The most important phase of a family's life, from the point of view of the community, is the period during which its children are being born. Under overcrowded and unsatisfactory housing conditions, the family is subjected to two adverse influences. The children are exposed to . . . physical and moral dangers . . . and the parents are discouraged from producing children. The first of these influences has always operated although it is no more tolerable for that reason; but the second, the deliberate limitation of families, is a feature of this century. . . . *all we need to discuss is the way in which a wise allocation of houses can help to rectify this trend.*[42]

3. A third reason for the willingness to give priority to families with children in public housing policy may be found in concern about various social ills. Even the twentieth-century shift of social diagnosis toward the internal operation of the family as a source of these ills did not diminish the importance attached to good accommodations as a foundation for sound family life and the proper upbringing of children. As one of the earliest industrialized nations we have long been influenced in public policy by the problems associated with urban slums; not only those of squalor and disease but of criminality and disorder as well.[43]

Such are some of the historical antecedents that have influenced contemporary public housing policies. So far as allocation goes, these are *still* family-centered, as the most recent report on the matter points out: "Few local authorities provide accommodation for single people . . . they generally concentrate their resources on providing housing *mainly for families* and the elderly."[44] This last observation, however, indicates one of two ways in which the "family monopoly" is being moderated.

Whatever our allocation policies may be today, time poses a problem;

---

[42] Department of Health for Scotland, Scottish Housing Advisory Committee, *Choosing Council Tenants* (London: His Majesty's Stationery Office, 1950), p. 29; italics added.

[43] Our most recent report on the child health services, for example, reasserts the conviction that "space and amenities are necessary for family relationships and well-being" and expresses concern that whereas 6 percent of all households in Great Britain were overcrowded in 1973 the proportion for families with three or more children stood at 23 percent. *Fit for the Future: the Report of the Committee on Child Health Services* (Court), Cmnd. 6684 (London: Her Majesty's Stationery Office, 1976), I, 33.

[44] Ministry of Housing and Local Government, Ninth Report of the Housing Management Sub-Committee of the Central Housing Advisory Committee, *Council Housing, Purposes, Procedures and Priorities* (Cullingworth report) (London: Her Majesty's Stationery Office, 1969), p. 104.

for today's young families become tomorrow's elderly tenants, and eventually single tenants.[45] Our demographic history means that the weight of this problem is being felt now, and for a decade or two it will become heavier. The underoccupation of council housing by old people receives regular public attention[46] although there is, in general, much less underoccupation in this sector than among owner-occupiers. Nevertheless, concern about the "problem" in the public stock of dwellings has been one of the reasons that local authorities have embarked upon supplying smaller and purpose-built dwellings. These enable older tenants to be transferred (if they are willing) from family housing, which can then be reallocated to families with young children. Progress is slow, and we may do well to count the emergent costs of a family-oriented housing program which has bequeathed us this and the related situation of estates (housing developments) which lack a mixture of ages and household types.

The second way in which the family priority policy has been eroded is through more recent programs of replacement. The slum clearance drive of the 1930s mostly rehoused families; indeed, at that time the payment of subsidies to local authorities was restricted to this purpose. Since then, however, local authority responsibilities for rehousing have been more broadly defined, and clearance areas have tended to be more heterogeneous, containing more old people and single-person households as well as groups of students and other young people. In order to get ahead with their clearance activities local authorities have felt obliged to provide smaller units of accommodation and make allocations to households without children, especially to the elderly.

The priority in allocation accorded to families with dependent children has not been extended to rent policies. Rent has only been adjusted to family size in a haphazard and rudimentary fashion, if at all. Until 1972 there was

---

[45] In 1973 (*The General Household Survey*, 1973), 37 percent of the heads of households in the publicly rented sector were sixty years old or more. Fifteen percent of local authority tenants were single old people. See also tables 2-1 and 2-20 for demographic data on the elderly.

[46] See, for example, the Report of the Scottish Housing Advisory Committee, *Allocating Council Houses* (London: Her Majesty's Stationery Office, 1967). It points out that there is a "difficulty created by the fact that the early post-war schemes were designed to cater almost wholly for young and growing families. As the children of these schemes reach maturity and leave home, extensive underoccupation by elderly parents begins to take place . . ." (p. 19)

It is noteworthy that according to bedroom standards for measuring underoccupation, the proportion of households with two or more bedrooms beyond requirements was: 14 percent in the public rented sector; 20 percent among those renting privately unfurnished accommodations; 23 percent among owner-occupiers with an outstanding mortgage; and 39 percent for those who owned outright. (*General Household Survey*, 1973, table 2.9.)

no nationally agreed scheme for determining rent reductions. In some cases tenants *without* children at home have benefited most from rent subsidy because the assessment of ''need'' has not been based upon a calculation of income per head; nor is it now. But the picture is complicated by the definition of income. For example, wives' earnings have been included in assessed income for purposes of fixing rent levels, although in their case the first few pounds are discounted. It could be argued, therefore, that rent policies in the public sector (and since 1972 in the private as well) have discouraged wives from going out to work except to earn very small or very large amounts. The family that was not so discouraged would face rent increases linked to the additional ''family income'' up to the maximum rent and probably lose, or have reduced, other means-tested benefits as well. These are by now familiar features of the ''poverty trap''; that is, the situation in which poorer people find themselves worse off as a result of earning more. This arises partly through the payment of extra income tax[47] and partly through the reduction of means-tested benefits like rent allowances.

In general, then, public housing provision and allocation policies in Britain have favored families with children, and in consequence they have been mildly pronatalist. ''Housing need'' has been interpreted in ways which emphasize marriage, child rearing, and a family size which is neither too small nor too large: standard-sized families for standard-sized houses.[48] Almost no provision has been made for three-generation households. What little larger accommodation has been available has been allocated to large nuclear families, although even here the supply has been inadequate. Hardly 3 percent of local authority dwellings built since the war have had four or more bedrooms.[49] Obtaining a council house depended mainly upon the membership of a conventional nuclear family, preferably intact. Both points schemes for determining priority and local residence qualifications, for example, tell against one-parent families.[50] In our view, a particular *family* policy may be discerned in the public sector of housing. It is rarely acknowledged as such.

Apart from the example of housing, British social policy provides few

[47] See Frank Field, Molly Meacher, and Chris Pond, *To Him Who Hath: a Study of Poverty and Taxation* (London: Penguin Books, 1977).

[48] See Hilary Land, *Large Families in London* (London: Bell, 1969), for a discussion of some of the problems facing large families in gaining access to adequate public houseing.

[49] See Cullingworth report, pp. 92–94.

[50] See DHSS, *Report of the Committee on One-Parent Families* (Finer) Cmnd. 5629 (London: Her Majesty's Stationery Office, 1974), I, 381–85.

instances where eligibility for a social service depends upon recipients actually living in or as a "normal" family. Indeed, there has been a marked reluctance to develop policies which assist families to care for their dependent members.

Care of Dependents

General support services, like public housing, have tended to be restricted by a rather narrow conception of the family. Attention has been concentrated upon families with dependent *children*. Yet there are other extensive family responsibilities, among which the care of specially dependent or handicapped *adults* is profoundly important. On the face of it, this too warrants general support from social policies.

The amount of support and care which the female members of families provide for their old and disabled kin is vast, as study after study has shown.[51] Families are reluctant for the old or severely subnormal to enter residential homes or long-stay hospitals; they give dedicated nursing care to the chronically sick and dying[52] and they are ready to offer help which is needed when the time comes for relatives to be discharged from hospitals or convalescent homes.[53] A high proportion of adults who do stay in hospitals or residential homes for unnecessarily prolonged periods have no spouse or close kin.

A few facts help to illustrate these points more fully.[54] In 1971 about a quarter of all old people in Britain actually lived with their children, or their

[51] See, for example, Enid Mills, *Living with Mental Illness* (London: Routledge and Kegan Paul, 1962): "The single patients were mostly devotedly cared for, even at the expense of other members of the family, *so long as their mothers still lived*" (p. 67; italics added); B. Issacs, "Geriatric Patients: Do Their Relatives Care?" *British Medical Journal*, IV (1971), 282–86: "Neglect of old people by relatives, who were for the most part themselves middle aged or elderly, was rare."

[52] See Ann Cartwright *et al.*, *Life Before Death* (London: Routledge and Kegan Paul, 1973): "The overwhelming impression . . . is of the extent of support provided by relatives, friends and neighbors to people in the last years of their lives." (p. 162).

[53] See Michael Meacher, *Taken for a Ride: Special Residential Homes for Confused Old People* (London: Longmans, 1972): "The willingness of families to accept back an aged member after hospital convalescence, or a reluctance to part with them initially for institutional care, has been repeatedly confirmed by research." (p. 446)

[54] For a good discussion of families and their elderly and mentally handicapped members see Robert M. Moroney, *The Family and the State: Considerations of Social Policy* (London: Longmans, 1976).

children with them.[55] In the case of the handicapped elderly who were not living in institutions, this proportion rose to 36 percent and for the very severely handicapped to 50 percent.[56] Nevertheless, it is plain from the evidence that "elderly people living alone or with their spouses are much more likely to be provided with state help. If the elderly person is living with relatives, especially children . . . [public] service is withheld on the assumption that the family will provide the needed care."[57] Hunt's study of the home help service in 1967 indicated that the most common reason for refusing an application was that there were children, usually daughters, in the house or the local area.[58] In Sunderland, Rees discovered that "if an applicant had a daughter living within the boundaries of the county borough home help was not normally granted."[59] A similar conclusion was drawn in Shanas's study of three countries which pointed out that welfare services for the elderly "tend to reach people who lack a family or whose family resources are slender, or they provide specialised services the family is not equipped or qualified to undertake."[60]

A similar though somewhat less pronounced pattern emerges from studies of the physically and mentally handicapped. We know from Harris's inquiry, for example, that there is a greater likelihood of handicapped people receiving health or welfare service if they live alone than if they live with relatives.[61] Yet, at the same time there is public recognition that "inevitably

[55] Central Statistical Office, *Social Trends,* No. 6 (London: Her Majesty's Stationery Office, 1975), table 2.32, p. 78.

[56] Moroney, *The Family and the State,* p. 44. Adapted from figures in Amelie Harris, *Handicapped and Impaired in Great Britain* (London: Office of Population Censuses and Surveys, Her Majesty's Stationery Office, 1971).

[57] *Ibid.* Moroney points out: "Hunt found that 71 per cent of recipients of the home help service were living alone and only 2.2 per cent were living with their children. Wager found that 72 per cent of home help recipients lived alone and of those . . . who lived with children, none received home help or meals and only 4 per cent were receiving home nursing services." (p. 56)

[58] Audrey Hunt, *The Home Help Service in England and Wales* (London: Office of Population Censuses and Surveys, Her Majesty's Stationery Office, 1970), pp. 338–39.

[59] Anthony M. Rees, *Old People and the Social Services* (Southampton, England: Southampton University, 1976), p. 89.

[60] Ethel Shanas *et al., Old People in Three Industrial Societies* (London, Routledge and Kegan Paul, 1968).

[61] Harris, *Handicapped and Impaired in Great Britain.* See also Moroney, *The Family and the State,* chap. 4, for a discussion with respect to the mentally handicapped child.

the presence of a severely handicapped child or adult causes great strain on the family as a whole."[62]

One of the clearest confirmations of our theme is to be found in the history of services for children deprived of a normal home life. Local authorities have received children into public care either on a voluntary basis or through a court order as a clear *alternative* to parental care. In the case of children committed to care by juvenile courts (either because they were in need of care or protection or because of delinquency), almost all parental rights and duties are transferred along with them; a notable exception being the parents' duty to make a means-tested financial contribution.

Once a child is in long-term care there is little evidence that the social services succeed in retaining contact with the parents or that they involve them in reviews or in planning for the child's future.[63] The encouragement given to a rapid growth of foster care after World War II (from 35 percent in 1949 to a peak of 52 percent in 1963–65) could certainly be regarded as a form of "family policy," but one which highlighted the replacement of the child's own family.[64] The more recent decline in foster care (to 32 percent in 1975) is probably accounted for by changes in the 1969 Children and Young Persons Act which brought many adolescent offenders into the "in care" category and by difficulties in recruiting foster mothers rather than by a marked departure from "replacement" practices. This is not to deny that much emphasis has been placed upon the desirability of reuniting children in care with their own families where and whenever possible.

There is also now much discussion of "shared care" in this and other spheres of social need. Yet, as we have argued, the state (both centrally and

[62] DHSS, *Better Services for the Mentally Handicapped,* Cmnd. 4683 (London: Her Majesty's Stationery Office, 1971), p. 3. Evidence to back this view is now plentiful: for example, Eileen Younghusband *et al., Living with Handicap* (London: National Bureau for Co-operation in Child Care, 1970).

[63] One recent study of foster care, for example, showed that 54 percent of the children never saw a parent and a further 30 percent saw then only infrequently. Martin Shaw, Kathleen Lebens, and Ann Cosh, *Children Between Families* (Leicester: University of Leicester, School of Social Work, 1975), p. 17.

[64] See Roy Parker, *Decision in Child Care* (London: Allen and Unwin, 1966); Jean Packman, *The Child's Generation* (Oxford: Blackwell and Robertson, 1975). Child care statistics for England and Wales are to be found in *Children in Care,* an annual white paper (1976, HC 506). For Scotland they are contained in Social Work Services Group and Scottish Education Department, *Scottish Social Work Statistics.* In 1976 there were 100,000 children in public care in England and Wales (a little over 7 per 1,000 of the age group at risk) and in Scotland in 1974 there were 21,000.

locally) has hitherto tended *either* to assume responsibility for child care or leave the family to cope as best it can until crisis or tragedy occurs. It was not until 1963 that local authorities could actually spend public monies on preventing children from being received into care or appearing before the courts by providing support for their *family*. Of course, prevention is a difficult and elusive concept, but those services which would generally be considered as contributing toward its attainment have been slow to develop, despite the rhetoric of public pronouncements.[65]

Take the example of day care for children under five (the preschool population). In 1974 there were 12,000 "priority" children on waiting lists for local authority day nurseries in England and Wales.[66] The more general picture is equally vivid. In 1945, after wartime expansion, there were 1,300 local authority day nurseries for some 63,000 children; by 1974 those figures had fallen to 500 and 25,000 respectively.[67] In Scotland in 1973 there were only 69 local authority day nurseries, providing 3,350 places, although Glasgow alone has a child population under five of nearly 65,000.[68]

By contrast, the number of nursery *education* places for the age group from two to five in England and Wales has doubled from some 200,000 in 1945 to about 400,000 in 1973. However, the most notable increase has been in the rise of private nurseries and private child minding. In 1949 some 7,000 children under five received day care in private nurseries; in 1974 there were over 360,000. Fewer than 2,000 children were known to be looked after on a daily basis by child minders in 1949; by 1974 the number stood at 87,000, although both figures are undoubtedly a considerable underestimation because of the extent of "illegal" (that is, unregistered) child minding.

In 1974 approximately a third of all children under five in England and Wales were known to be receiving some form of day care outside their families. But use increased sharply with age: only 4 percent of those under one

---

[65] "Where children are concerned the main objective is to help families provide a satisfactory home . . . and enable children to stay with their families except where it is against the child's interest." DHSS, *Priorities for Health and Personal Social Services in England* (London: Her Majesty's Stationery Office, 1976), p. 64.

[66] DHSS and the Department of Education and Science, *Low Cost Provision for the Under Fives* (1976), p. 2.

[67] These and statistics which follow are taken from Jack Tizard *et al., All Our Children: Pre School Services in a Changing Society* (London: Temple-Smith/New Society, 1976), pp. 229–31.

[68] Social Work Services Group and Scottish Education Department, *Scottish Social Work Statistics, 1973* (London: Her Majesty's Stationery Office, 1975), p. 7.

year; 8 percent of the one-year-olds; 19 percent of the two-year-olds; 47 percent of the three-year-olds; and 72 percent of children between four and
five.[69] The over-all proportion of 32 percent also hides another important
fact. Almost half of these children were attending schools run by public education authorities (predominantly the three- and four-year-olds); almost all
the rest used facilities provided by the private or self-help sectors. Only 3
percent were looked after in public day nurseries. The distinctions are important, for they suggest that the state is unwilling to share the *care* of
younger children with parents. That need is met largely by private facilities
or is legitimized by being classed as *education;* an established and accepted
realm of state intervention. A Department of Education and Science (DES)
policy paper recently emphasized the aim to provide universal nursery education (usually part-time) for all children from three to five whose parents
wanted it.[70] Another statement by the DES was at pains to explain that nursery education is regarded as

> clearly distinct from the aims underlying the provision of care facilities . . .
> only a minority of children require full or part-time day care. . . . for all or part
> of the period from birth to five . . . the *care* needs of these children are *dif-*
> *ferent in kind* from both their own and other children's educational needs.[71]

Again, we feel that it is plausible to interpret this pattern of day care
policy in Britain as indicating a reluctance on the part of the state to share
the care of young children with mothers except where it can be regarded as
falling into areas of special or professional competence like education or
medicine. Care and nurture of babies and infants must usually remain the
clear responsibility of the family. Mothers should be encouraged, it would
seem, to stay at home to care for their children during their early years. It is
noteworthy that where *care* services are provided they are charged for on
test of income, whereas services classed as *education* (except at the higher
level) are free.

These examples illustrate the fact that at least in the sphere of social
care the state has been disinclined to offer services unless a family's ability
to care has crumbled or disappeared through death or incapacity. Services
are commonly provided on terms which assume that the "ordinary" family
care system has in some way failed or collapsed. As a result, British social

[69] DHSS, *Low Cost Provision for Under-Fives,* table 1, p. 8.

[70] Department of Education and Science (DES), Circular 2/73. See also DES, *Education: a
Framework for Expansion* (London: Her Majesty's Stationery Office, 1972).

[71] DHSS, *Low Cost Provision for Under-Fives,* p. 25; italics added.

services have tended to develop in such a way that "classes of persons in need and categories of disease were treated; not families."[72]

Our thesis, then, is that the state has, over long periods of time in Britain, been prepared *either* to assume major or complete responsibility for the care of the dependent *or* to leave that responsibility squarely and unambiguously with the family. This should undoubtedly be regarded as a family policy, for it affects both relationships between men and women and between the young and the old in families and rests upon assumptions about how they do or should work. It now behooves us to consider how this position may best be explained.

One approach might be developed from H. G. Wells's observation that many are fearful that in seeking to save the family they should seem to threaten its existence.[73] Alongside the wish to see the capacities of families strengthened by help from public services has gone an apprehension that too much help would erode the sense of family responsibility. The debate about the financial liability of relatives, for example, swung back and forth in the history of our Poor Law, too much enforcement being thought as dangerous as too little.[74]

The sense of family responsibility for kin has been conceived to be in a state of "precarious balance," too much assistance added to either side of the scale being thought likely to precipitate an avalanche of abdication. Should this occur, then the family in its conventional form, and the unequal relationships within it, would be endangered. If one accepts this fear as a political reality, it helps to explain why state help with the personal tasks undertaken by family members, notably women, needs to be defined as exceptional or else disguised as something which is not easily generalizable to a wide spectrum of family roles and tasks: for example, as education, medical treatment, or "community care."[75] It may also explain why no public service in Britain bears a name which suggests the availability of a general family service. Only in the voluntary sector do we have organizations like Family Service Units or the Family Welfare Association. Underlying this set

---

[72] Titmuss, *Essays on the Welfare State*, p. 21

[73] H. G. Wells, *The New Machiavelli* (London: Penguin Books, 1966), p. 306.

[74] See, for example, G. Drage, *The Problems of the Aged Poor* (London: Adam and Charles Black, 1895), pp. 104–14; DHSS, *Report of the Committee on One-Parent Families,* Appendix 5, pp. 85–149.

[75] We would argue, in contrast to Moroney, that the quest for "community care" has depended heavily on family care.

of beliefs, we suspect, is the conception of the family as an essentially fragile institution.

One might also discover an explanation for the state's reluctance to "share care" in the related problems of scarce resources and rationing in nonprice systems.[76] Were families to provide markedly less care, the "welfare state" would be inundated by a tidal wave of extra demands; or so it is assumed. With rising rates of perceived dependency and economic stringency this prospect is even more likely to be viewed as a threat to established (and expected) public services, with all the political upheaval which this would create. We stress "perceived" dependency, however, because the actual number of people in the labor force labeled as "productive workers" represents a social category capable of various redefinitions. Retirement and educational policies, as well as policies concerning married women in the labor market, serve to fix our ideas about the scale and nature of dependency.

Having said that, the fear that there would be an undue escalation in public expenditure and taxation if families do less is a political fact. Yet the conclusion is by no means self-evident. We provide massive subsidies to marriage in its present form; for example, by way of married men's income tax allowances which now cost around £1,400 million a year (almost as much as the child tax allowances). A new balance of family responsibilities or structure could conceivably lead to savings in public spending, especially in tax allowances.

Less speculatively, it is quite clear that our social services have to be rationed in some way or other; priorities have to be fixed.[77] Individual need can conveniently be equated with the absence or incapacity of supporting family members, albeit a range of rather complicated and ambiguous situations thereby has to be defined more simply and crudely classified. As we have suggested earlier, for example, need may be as great where families look after their handicapped relations as when the handicapped person lives alone. To assume that the latter has a greater prima facie need is both convenient and probably in accordance with popular conceptions of justice. It switches attention away from the needs of the family as a whole toward the needs of particular individuals.

[76] See Roy Parker, "Social Administration and Scarcity," in Eric Butterworth and Robert Holman, eds., *Social Welfare in Modern Britain* (London: Fontana, 1975), pp. 204–12.

[77] DHSS, *Priorities for Health and Social Services in England* (London: Her Majesty's Stationery Office, 1976).

A third possible reason for the state's tardiness in sharing care is almost certain to be found in assumptions about the proper generational and sexual divisions of responsibility and hence in the work that men and women are generally expected to do within the family and the labor market. Marriage (and the marriage vows) purports to offer a unique relationship of mutual aid based upon an intricate network of dependencies, especially for the women. It seems to us significant that where the state *has* intervened to offer general support to the family (income maintenance or housing, for instance) the conventional roles thereby buttressed are those of husband and breadwinner. The state less readily shares, let alone takes over, the caring and nurturing work usually ascribed to the dependent wife. Support for the family would seem to be regarded as best achieved via the husband, with least risk to his dominant position. This may be because the subordinate position of women in marriage, and hence in the family, is implicitly seen as an indispensable yet brittle keystone to the maintenance of long-established inequalities within wider social and economic institutions.

Lastly, we might suggest that the existence and power of a professional interest in the supply of care services add a further dimension to possible explanations for the unwillingness of the state to facilitate "shared care." To be a professional is to fulfill an expert role. It does not readily encourage the sharing of responsibility with lay people. Nor are many of our helping professions much accustomed to giving the kind of simple physical aid that is often required. Historically, at least, professional status has seemed to be found *outside* families: in clinics, therapeutic communities, fostering and adoption work, in hospitals and schools. Once outside the immediate family context, it has also been easier to identify and treat an "individual" patient. As well as aiding the rationing process, this has fulfilled purposes for the family which Laing and others have discussed in an illuminating fashion.[78]

The rise of the "caring professions" has also exposed a contradiction in public views about the competence of families, especially the female members. On the one hand, considerable work is expected of the family in looking after specially dependent members. Yet there is a Rubicon which once crossed places skill and competence with the professionals, thereby (however unintended) devaluing the capabilities of ordinary families, especially women. The relationship of the professions and families seems to reflect and reinforce that of the state and families.

The idea of shared care is now a more common and accepted principle of the social policy debate in Britain; but the practice develops slowly,

[78] For example, Ronald D. Laing, in *The Social Situation* (London: Tavistock, 1968).

perhaps for some of the reasons that we have suggested. Many unanswered questions still remain; for instance, about the creation of dependence and about just *how* care is shared and with whom. Do sharing policies serve only to privatize a family's caring capacities, or do they help to generalize them? Hadley and Webb have noted recently in relation to the elderly that "one of the dangers is that where a marriage has been an effective support for people in their youth and middle age, to the exclusion of other strong relationships, it can be a most unsatisfactory basis for approaching old age."[79] In any case *should* we devise policies which rely upon or sustain the present high level of commitment and dedication to the well-being of close kin? What are the costs and long-term implications?

Postscript

We made clear at the beginning that we would deal only with a limited number of social policies affecting the family. It may be useful, however, to indicate briefly some other major issues which warrant the close examination and analysis we were unable to give them.

We have tried to expose some of the underlying assumptions about the nature of relationships between the sexes and the generations within the family and have shown how these have acted as important (but not the only) determinants of the pattern and extent of a variety of social policies. We have done little more than indicate how these may relate to inequalities between men and women and young and old in the wider society in general and in the labor market in particular. If this is to be done, then the illusion that the family is a private domain somehow separate from other aspects of social, political, and economic life must be abandoned, along with the view that family policies are quite distinct from other social and economic policies. Although we have implicitly criticized the obscure nature of the ideological dimensions of a selection of British social policies as they affect the family, we recognize that at least there has been little pretense in Britain that it is possible to separate out "family policy." The interesting question is what purpose and whose purposes are served by ignoring or keeping hidden these ideological dimensions.

In stressing that the family is not an institution somehow apart from the rest of society we are not saying that the relationships and division of labor

[79] Roger Hadley, Adrian Webb, and Christine Farrell, *Across the Generations* (London: Allen and Unwin, 1976), p. 198.

within it are totally determined by the particular economic system of that society. Although we pointed out that in order to establish the legitimacy of
social policies which would affect family responsibilities and relationships,
such policies have been *presented* as a means of counteracting the ill effects
of economic changes, whether or not economic change has had a destructive
effect on the family is an empirical question. It is a question to which insufficient attention has been paid because, in accordance with the view that the
family is fragile and somehow declining in its capacities, especially to care
for kin, the answer is too readily assumed to be in the affirmative. However,
the historical evidence which has been examined calls into question the view
that the support offered by kin declined as families were exposed to the effects of industrialization and urbanization.[80] What is clear is that the nature
of the bargains struck and the exchanges offered between family members
altered as their relationship to the labor market changed. For example, the
paid employment of married women in factories a hundred years ago enabled their families to offer support to elderly kin (especially female kin)
who could make an indirect economic contribution to the household by looking after the children and doing the housework. During periods of recession
when married women were laid off from factories, masters of workhouses
found that they "had had a large increase in the number of older and
widowed women . . . no longer wanted to mind the home and children
while the mother went to the mill."[81] In other words, contrary to conventional wisdom, increased employment of married women outside the home
facilitated rather than hindered mutually supportive relationships between
kin. In Britain the proportion of elderly cared for in institutions is *half* what
it was at the turn of the century, and yet it is widely assumed that many
more old people today are abandoned by their families. What is interesting,
as Richard Titmuss has pointed out, is that the view that family life has so
changed that families accept far less responsibility for aged parents was also
prevalent at the turn of the century.[82]

In addition to issues concerning changes in the participation of the
young, the old, and women in the labor market there are other aspects of
economic change which need to be examined for their differential impact on
family members. The family is often equated with "home," meaning a

[80] See, for example, Michael Anderson, *Family Structure in the Nineteenth Century* (Cambridge: Cambridge University Press, 1974).

[81] *Interdepartmental Committee of Inquiry into Physical Deterioration,* Report, Appendix V,
Cd., 2175 (London: Her Majesty's Stationery Office, 1954), p. 127.

[82] Titmuss, *Essays on the Welfare State,* p. 19.

place which is stable in the geographical sense. It is believed that frequent moves, although good for workers, are bad for families: meaning women, children, and the elderly. Our educational system is based on the implicit assumption that children move infrequently during their childhood. Mobile children, such as those of families in the armed forces, therefore pose very real problems, and for them the stability of boarding school education may be offered. Because of the preoccupation with nuclear families our housing policies have not, in fact, helped the old to stay close to their adult children, and yet the *family* is blamed for failing to care for elderly kin.

We have emphasized the importance of sex and generation as ways of unraveling the relationship between the state, the family, and the economy. In analyzing this relationship we suggest that the family should not always be considered to be the dependent variable. The persistence of fears about the ill effects of economic change on the family points to the need to take account of beliefs about patterns of dependency and the division of labor within the family and the extent to which they may actually modify the process of industrialization and economic development as well as act as important determinants of the development of state social policies. As a recent study of social theory and the family concludes:

> Some of the concern about women and children working in 19th century factories was not just about the hours and working conditions but about the fact that they were there at all and these concerns provided an occasion to dramatise the values of family life and sexual relationships which, it was felt, were being threatened by this particular feature of the factory system.[83]

In order to take the analysis further we need to examine the very statistics which we use. The data we collect are based upon definitions which themselves are liable to hide the very dimensions we wish to expose. For example, this is how the government's General Household Survey defines "the family": "In general families cannot span two generations; that is grandparents and grandchildren cannot belong to the same family."[84] Thus it is not surprising that we have been unable to discover from the official statistics how many elderly people live with their married children or their married children with them. Similarly, the census definition of "chief economic supporter," by giving precedence to full-time over part-time, male over female and older over younger workers, insures that the majority of bread-

---

[83] David Morgan, *Social Theory and the Family* (London: Routledge and Kegan Paul, 1975), p. 212.

[84] Office of Population, Censuses and Surveys, *General Household Survey,* 1973, p. 135.

winners are counted as male. The otherwise valuable Family Expenditure Survey allows us to differentiate the recipients of income but gives no indication of who in the family spends (or saves) it. There are many other examples.

Fifty years ago, Eleanor Rathbone, who championed family allowances in Britain for many years, wrote:

> I doubt whether there is any subject in the world of equal importance that has received so little serious and articulate consideration as the economic status of the family—*of its members in relation to each other and to the other units of which the community is made up*. I say "articulate consideration" because what appears haphazard in our present arrangements for the family is probably the result of more deliberate purposing and choosing than appears on the surface, but it has been a subconscious and therefore inarticulate purpose and choice.[85]

We believe that she might well have made the same comment today. However, the hidden dimensions of the family and family policies are beginning to be exposed, understood, and challenged. A resurgent women's movement has provided much of the impetus for these reexaminations by insisting that the roots of women's subordinate position in society lie in the family.

[85] Eleanor Rathbone, *Family Allowances* (2d ed.; London: Allen and Unwin, 1949), Introduction, p. i; italics added.

～～12

CANADA

Andrew Armitage

THE FAMILY HAS not been a major focus for the development of Canadian social policy. The development of social policy has tended to be problem- or issue-oriented, concerned, for example, with poverty, crime, or illness. At a formal level, the family has been less recognized as a major focus for the development of social policy than have such other demographic groups as the elderly or children. The agencies that have served the family have tended to be residual in their form; for example, child welfare agencies or family service agencies provide services which only come into operation in situations of family problem or family breakdown. A much larger group of services, such as those in the health care, education, income security, and housing fields, recognize the existence of families in the entitlements they provide or the general policy direction they pursue. Yet they appear to have no deliberate policy objectives for the family, since they are concerned primarily with the social or economic issues that define the service in question. Furthermore, there are major areas of social affairs in which a policy that affects the family is established by corporations operating in the market economy. For example, the lending policies of banks and trust companies determine access to mortgages. In turn, these policies affect the access of families to housing. The Canadian government does not formally endorse corporate policy-making; on the other hand, a lack of government intervention is an implicit endorsement. Through such mechanisms, policies that affect the family are established without direct government action—and sometimes without government knowledge.

DR. ANDREW ARMITAGE is Professor, School of Social Welfare, University of Calgary, Calgary, Alberta, Canada.

The search for Canadian family policy is a task that requires examination of a large number of diverse and scattered actions with implications for family functioning rather than explicit objectives for the family as a part of Canadian society. Nevertheless, there are some important exceptions to this general pattern:

1. *The Vanier Institute of the Family.* The Vanier Institute of the Family was founded in 1963, supported by a major grant from the Canadian government. The purposes of the Institute have included research into Canadian families and life styles, the development of educational materials, and the study of Canadian social policy as it affects the family. The Institute has thus provided a positive focus upon the family per se. The intent of this focus has been to insure that the family remains a major focus of Canadian life and social development.

2. *Family policy in Quebec.* The government of the Province of Quebec has had a more concerted and deliberate set of policies bearing upon the welfare of the family than the provincial governments of the English-Canadian provinces. Policy in the areas of family law, income security, education, and the organization of the social services has been influenced by deliberate family-centered objectives. Furthermore, these objectives have principally a national or cultural purpose bearing upon the preservation and development of a distinct French-Canadian society.

3. *The women's movement.* A third major influence upon the development of a more positive family policy has come from the women's movement through such bodies as the Royal Commission on the Status of Women in Canada.[1] The gradual, but continuing, emancipation of women from financial dependency and social subordination to men has demanded that fuller consideration be given to formal social policy for the family. The traditional form of the family is based upon assumptions of the roles of men and women, which women have increasingly challenged. As a consequence, a whole series of social policies in the areas of family law, income security, and social services has come under scrutiny. These policies have often been found wanting from the perspective of women's emancipation, and hence reform and change directed toward a more deliberate and formal family policy have come under consideration.

[1] Royal Commission on the Status of Women in Canada, *Report* (Ottawa: Information Canada, 1970).

The Canadian Family

A sociological study of the family has not been the foundation upon which Canadian social policy affecting the family has been developed. One might argue that ought to be the case for the future, but it has not been the case in the past. However, social policy has been influenced directly and indirectly by assumptions and perceptions concerning the family. The sociological literature is broad and heterogeneous, and we cannot hope to produce here the overview of the literature that is provided by such writers as Elkin[2] or Ishwaran.[3] Instead, three major subjects pertinent to the development of Canadian social policy will be considered.

Definitions and Cycles

There are many perceptions of what constitutes "a family." Narrow definitions, built on legally verifiable relationships, provide only a partial presentation of the idea of "a family." For some, a family can be based on homosexual unions, or communal living arrangements. For many more, a family exists even though there may be no legal marriage between the spouses or legal adoption of dependent children.

According to the census of Canada, "a family consists of a husband and wife, with or without children who have never married regardless of age, or a parent with one or more children never married living in the same dwelling. A family may also consist of a man or woman living with a guardian child or ward under 21 years for whom no pay was received."[4]

Table 1 shows that a great majority of Canadians live in family situations as defined in the census definition. Nevertheless, the percentage of single persons is rising. In addition, of the five million Canadian families at the time of the 1971 census, 9.4 percent were one-parent families.

Approximately 80 percent of one-parent families are headed by the mother. One-parent families are caused (1971) by: death of a spouse (47 percent); divorce (12 percent); separation (34 percent); birth out of wedlock (8 percent).

One in five Canadians is living outside traditional family units, and the proportion of such persons in the Canadian population is increasing. The ori-

[2] F. Elkin, *The Family in Canada,* study commissioned by the Canadian Conference on the Family (Ottawa: Vanier Institute of the Family, 1964).

[3] K. Ishwaran, *The Canadian Family* (Toronto: Holt, Rinehart and Winston of Canada, 1971).

[4] Census of Canada, Definitions, 1971.

Table 1 Families and Single Persons, 1961 and 1971

Year	Total Population	Families	Single	Percent Single
1961	18,238,247	16,095,721	2,142,526	11.7
1971	21,568,315	18,852,110	2,716,205	12.6

SOURCE: Census of Canada: Family Data, 1961, 1971.

gins of this trend are partly demographic, for an increasing proportion of the Canadian population is in the elderly age groups. However, part of the trend is also social and is related to the rising divorce rate, greater participation by women in the labor force, and a trend toward more women raising children on their own.

The marriage rate remains very high in Canada. The age of marriage for women is stable at a median age of 21.2 years (1973). The age of marriage declined during 1921–61 and has remained constant since. However, the number of divorces has risen rapidly. In 1941 there were 112 divorces for every 100,000 married couples. In 1973 there were 650 divorces for every 100,000 married couples, with divorce rates in Alberta, British Columbia, and the Yukon Territory exceeding 1,000 divorces for every 100,000 married couples.[5] Furthermore, growing numbers of divorces involve children: in 1973, 56.6 percent of all divorces, compared to 45 percent in 1969. Social legislation affecting divorce has been changed in Canada, making divorce easier to obtain. However, it seems much more likely that this change has allowed marriage breakdown to be legitimated and recognized rather than having any positive relationship to marriage breakdown per se. Rates of remarriage following divorce are also high, particularly for men.

The size of Canadian families with children has declined from 3.9 persons (1961) to 3.7 persons (1971).[6] Canadian fertility rates are now very much lower than they were during the 1950s for women of all age groups. At one and the same time, the age of a mother at the time of the birth of her first child rose from 22.4 in 1966 to 23.2 in 1973, and there is a particularly sharp decline in the birth rate for women over thirty. Thus, Canadian women are both delaying having children and restricting child bearing to their twenties. The only fertility-related statistic that has increased since the 1950s is the rate of illegitimate births. The number of illegitimate births per 1,000 unmarried women was 12 per 1,000 in 1951, 20 per 1,000 in 1970,

[5] *Perspectives Canada* (Ottawa: Statistics Canada, 1974).

[6] *Ibid.*

and 17 per 1,000[7] in 1972. The increase between 1951 and 1970 may have been influenced by a reduction in family pressure on women to marry in order to legitimize a child. The decrease from 1970 to 1972 is probably a consequence of the more ready availability of abortion.

Putting these trends together, they represent very considerable change in the Canadian family. Living as part of a traditional two-parent nuclear family with children is part of the life experience of far fewer Canadians than was true during the 1950s. Childless families are much more common both in the age group from twenty to twenty-four and in the age group over fifty. Young married couples are delaying having children, having fewer children, and are stopping having them earlier. The family unit is more likely to be broken but then may be joined with greater frequency to a member or members of another family. One-parent families, as opposed to two-parent families are more common as are persons who live in nonfamily situations. Although it is too extreme to say that the traditional family is disappearing as a major social unit of Canadian society, it is also too complacent to say that it is simply adapting to a new set of conditions. Although the family remains the principal unit of interpersonal relationships, the extent of its dominance is declining as more Canadians than formerly live in other than traditional families or singly.

The Labor Market and Urbanization

Between 1951 and 1971 the Canadian population increased from approximately 14 million to more than 21 million persons. Approximately 75 percent of this growth was the result of a natural increase, with the remaining 25 percent due to immigration. However, this population increase has not been evenly distributed throughout Canada: it has been concentrated in Ontario, Alberta, and British Columbia and in urban rather than rural areas. This pattern has been the result of the economic development of the Canadian economy, related to the extraction of natural resources and to a major expansion of the service sector of the economy.

These forces have expressed themselves in relation to the family primarily through opportunities for employment and economic advancement. Some effects on the family include high physical mobility, longer periods of educational dependency, and higher female participation in the labor force.

Study of physical mobility shows that in five-year periods approximately 50 percent of the Canadian population change their place of resi-

[7] Gail Cook, ed., *Opportunity for Choice* (Ottawa: Statistics Canada, 1976).

dence. Of this total, approximately 60 percent move within the same metropolitan area or municipality, approximately 30 percent move within the same province, and 10 percent move between provinces.[8] The extent to which this high mobility is disruptive of community participation and kinship relationships is not clear. It certainly contributes to a society in which building new social relationships, both formal and informal, has to be a continuing occupation.

Postsecondary education of persons between the ages of eighteen and twenty-two also has an influence upon family function. One effect is to delay departure from the family of origin. A second effect is to promote nonfamily living situations, and the third effect is to produce reciprocal dependencies between husband and wife during the first phase of family formation.

Finally, labor force participation of women has risen sharply from around 20 percent in the 1950s to 35 percent in 1973. Labor force participation by women is highest in the areas of greatest economic development. In both Ontario and the far Western provinces, labor force participation by women approximates 40 percent, whereas in other regions of the country it approximates 30 percent.[9] These high rates are only partly income-related; 25 percent of women with husbands in the highest income group are in the labor force. Furthermore, labor force participation affects women in all stages of the family cycle. Despite the absence of well-developed day care facilities, 32.6 percent of women who have children below school age are in the labor force. The labor force participation of increasing numbers of women is a matter of necessity for some; for others, it is a matter of choice and opportunity. Employment is central to having an independent identity in our society. It provides an alternative to the frustrations of the traditional roles of mother and housewife. It provides an escape from the perhaps unfortunate but nevertheless real stigma of being "just a housewife." It also provides the only way whereby many young families can purchase their own homes. The effects of these changes upon family living standards, the demand for such social utilities as day care, and the design of income-security programs are considerable. These changes also affect the policies of commercial corporations: mortgage lending policies are based now on two-income families. Indeed, it is difficult to discern the extent to which such

[8] M. V. George, *Internal Migration in Canada* (Ottawa: Dominion Bureau of Statistics, 1970).

[9] Cook, *Opportunity for Choice.*

changes have responded to social change, as opposed to having consolidated or even produced social change.

Ethnicity and Kinship

Canada is not only an immigrant country but a country that embraced the idea of a multicultural mosaic rather than the idea of a melting pot of different cultures. Until the 1971 census it was not possible to class one's ethnic origin as "Canadian" in the Canadian census, and Canadian sociology has concentrated much of its attention along ethnic lines.

The family is a central institution in the transmission of ethnic identity, cultural heritage, language, and patterns of association. Evidence as to the persistence, or breakdown, of kinship and ethnic patterns is conflicting. On the one side, there is evidence of a marked decline in the number of residential extended families and a corresponding rise in the number of nuclear families and single-person situations. Further, the data on residential mobility suggest that physical association is now harder to achieve. On the other hand, there is considerable sociological evidence of the persistence of modified extended family ties.[10] These are seen in patterns of recreation and vacations. They are also seen in patterns of correspondence and long-distance telephone calls. Furthermore, the higher divorce rate and the increasing occurrences of one-parent families may tend to increase contact with kin. Finally, the decreased bitterness of separation and divorce, and the greater chance of remarriage of divorced persons, results in an expanding category of "extended family person," the ex-wife or husband and the step-father or stepmother.

Most immigrants to Canada adopt English as their working language and are assimilated into the English-Canadian majority. Despite the readiness to accept different cultural patterns, the major trend would appear to be in the direction of gradual assimilation of immigrant minorities. This would also appear to be true for French-language minorities outside the province of Quebec and the immediately adjoining area of New Brunswick.[11]

The French-Canadian Family

The French-Canadian family has held special status in the history of Quebec and in the preservation of a distinct linguistic and cultural heritage in North

[10] S. Parvez Wakil, "Marriage and the Family in Canada," in Ishwaran, ed., *The Canadian Family.*

[11] *Perspectives Canada* (Ottawa, Statistics Canada, 1973), chap. 11.

America. From the conquest of Quebec by England until the quiet revolution of Quebec in the 1960s, the Catholic church had a major influence upon Quebec family patterns. This influence supported rural rather than urban living, extended families, a high birth rate, preservation of French language and culture, and the continuation of Catholicism. Assimilation with the English Canadians was rejected. The political and legal status of women was low. It was not until 1940 that voting rights were granted to women in Quebec, and the legal rights of a married woman with respect to her own property were severely limited. On the other hand, the role played by women in French-Canadian society within the home was highly regarded. In French-Canadian literature, women are shown to have forceful character, initiative, and decisiveness, but they were expected to show these characteristics either at home or in religious orders and not in secular or political society.

Despite this distinct ascription of role to Quebec women, the sociological evidence of their labor force participation is similar to that for Canadian women as a whole. In 1911 the participation rate for Quebec was 16.19 percent when it was 16.18 percent for the whole of Canada. The respective 1961 rates were 27.91 percent and 29.45 percent. More broadly, the French-Canadian sociologist Philippe Garigue concludes that:

> Traditional French-Canadian culture has had traits that allow individual French Canadians to adapt themselves, without too great an effort, to industrial change. French-Canadian culture is a variation of the total North American culture, not something completely different from it. The social forces affecting French-Canadian culture and families are similar to those affecting Canadian families as a whole and the responses of the families to them are also similar.[12]

The birth rate in Quebec has fallen sharply along with the birth rate in Canada as a whole, and the average size of a Quebec family (3.9 persons) approximates that of Canadian families as a whole (3.7 persons). Analysis of difference in family size appears to show more effect from urban-rural difference than from French-English differences.

Nevertheless, at the political level, changes in the French-Canadian family have been more seriously considered than those in English-Canadian families. The reason is that the changes threaten the continued existence of a distinct French language culture and identity patterns. Family mobility threatens the opportunity to raise children in a French-language milieu. The assimilation of most immigrants into the English language culture threatens

[12] Philippe Garigue, "St. Justin: a Case Study in Rural French-Canadian Social Organizations."

the dominance of the French language and culture within the city of Montreal. The declining birth rate combined with the pattern of immigrant assimilation to English-language groups makes it probable that the French language will be spoken by a decreasing percentage of the Canadian population in the future. The emancipation of women from the traditional motherhood roles creates uncertainty as to how a distinct cultural heritage will be transmitted. These factors all affect social policy in Quebec and create a greater consciousness of the need for family policies that provide for continuity in the national and cultural roles that the family has traditionally fulfilled in Quebec society.

The Native Indian Family
The Native Indian and Inuit family has been much less the source of deliberate social policy attention than the French-Canadian family. However, the sociological data indicate basic and continuing differences between the Native population and the majority of Canadians. Particularly important is the much higher birth rate among Indians—more than twice the Canadian average. This birth rate results in a much younger population with 45 percent being under age fifteen compared to less than 30 percent for Canadians as a whole. Native families are much more likely to have rural residence and are disproportionately represented in the far North and in the rural areas of the Western provinces. The Federal Indian Act recognizes special inheritance rights for Native persons, distinction of legal status, and special rights to collective property.

Leaders of the Native people have shown increased militancy and urgency in seeking to preserve and develop their distinct cultural background. In these discussions, primary attention has been paid to tribal patterns and to historical patterns of land use. The Indian and Inuit people are extremely diverse, being drawn from different areas, having different cultures and languages and different contemporary political and cultural objectives. Nevertheless, the continuation of distinct patterns of family life is also part of what the Native peoples seek for themselves. The development of family policy in Canada needs to take account of the particular situation of these people.

Data on the Canadian Family
There are three principal sources of research-based data on the Canadian family. The first of these are the social data published by federal and provincial statistical agencies. Statistics Canada regularly publishes the following reports on Canadian families:

Survey of Consumer Finances
Estimate of Families in Canada
Low-Income Families
Immigrant Families
Expenditure Patterns
Income of Families
Vital Statistics

The Census of Canada, 1961, 1971, and so on, provides additional data on: family composition, mobility, ethnicity, language, income, employment, and housing.

Provincial sources supplement this federal data. The Statistics Canada publication *Perspectives Canada* (1974) provides a compendium of these and other Canadian social statistics. Analysis of these statistics is largely external to the statistical agencies, but there have been some excellent monographs commissioned and published by the agencies concerned.

A second major source of data is the service output data from Canadian social programs. These data are much less uniformly conceptualized, organized, or catalogued than the basic statistical data. With some care, the analyst can begin to assemble data on the operation of Canadian social programs and their impact on the family, but all too often firm conclusions are impossible. Greater attention to consistency in conceptual approaches, definition, and data collection patterns would be of major value in assessing the relationship of programs to family welfare.

The third major data source is the specialized, usually sample-survey-based, studies of professional sociologists. Access to these studies is aided by publications of the Vanier Institute of the Family that provide catalogues of Canadian family studies. Access is also possible to selected studies through such books of readings as Ishwaran's *The Canadian Family*.

There have been a number of projects, most notably by the Economic Council of Canada, Canadian Council on Social Development, and the Social Science Research Council of Canada, that have examined the case for the development of a series of Canadian social indicators. However, no such set of indicators has yet been designed.

Canadian Social Policy and the Family

Canadian social policy has been developed primarily around distinct policy issues, and acts of intervention. British North America has been interpreted as providing primary provincial jurisdiction over social policy. Hence, the early development of Canadian social policy is concerned with voluntary, municipal, and provincial actions. Nevertheless, some social policy fields (e.g., immigration and services to native peoples) are federal responsibilities under the British North America Act. In addition, there has been a continuing process of development of federal policies and programs that either provide support to provincial policies or take over full responsibility for social policy. This latter tendency is particularly marked in those fields of social policy for which the federal power over monetary and fiscal policy is critical, such as income security and housing. It is much less evident in such fields as family law, for which federal resources are less needed.

The analysis of Canadian social policy has been organized in relation to these basic divisions in the development. That is to say, there has been a primary concern with social and economic issues and a secondary concern with how response to these issues is to be divided among different levels of government.

This pattern of development and analysis has tended to divert attention from the collective impact of separate policies upon distinct demographic groups, including the family. Thus, this is an initial attempt to survey social policy and its relationship to the Canadian family and does not have a series of established analyses to draw upon. As a consequence, some of what follows has to be speculative, hedged with such loose phrases as, "it would appear that the intent with respect to the family was" or, "the likely impact upon Canadian families was . . ."

Our basic approach is to examine major social policy fields and indicate whether they contain explicit family policy objectives, assumptions concerning the family, or consequences for the family. The major fields to be examined are: family law; income policies and poverty; and personal social services.

Family Law

"It is in society's interest to maximize the number of stable marriages within the community . . ." [13]

Jurisdiction over family law is generally provincial in Canada. Provincial law governs matrimonial property, the conditions for marriage, adoptions, and child welfare. Federal laws governing divorce, and maintenance after divorce, are interpreted in courts administered by the province, the judges of which are appointed by the federal government.

This primary provincial jurisdiction permits the existence of two sepa-

[13] "Special Joint Committee of the Senate and House of Commons on Divorce: Report," Ottawa, 1967, p. 44.

rate legal systems affecting the family in Canada. In Quebec the basis of the law is the Quebec civil code, promulgated in 1866 and based on the structure of the *Code Napoléon*. In the other provinces, the basis of the law is the English common law.

The complicated jurisdiction over Canadian family law introduces a complexity in the development and administration of the law that is unknown in unitary states. In several provinces, unified family courts are being considered as a desirable way to simplify the administration of the law and to make legal decisions more responsive to the total welfare of the families affected.

Marriage. Provincial law governing the "solemnization" of marriage has been primarily concerned with the conditions of minimum age and parental consent. In the absence of parental consent, the minimum age is twenty-one in seven provinces; eighteen in two provinces; and twenty-one for men, eighteen for women, in Prince Edward Island. With parental consent there is further variation. In five provinces the minimum age is sixteen, in one it is fifteen, and in one it is fourteen. Three provinces have no minimum age, and under the Quebec civil code the minimum age is twelve for women and fourteen for men. There is a variety of statutes governing who may consent, and also giving special recognition to the situation of the pregnant minor.

The Royal Commission on the Status of Women in Canada[14] argued for a single minimum age of eighteen. The commission rejected the arguments for parental consent and/or marriage on the grounds of pregnancy. Instead, the commission argued in favor of a marriage age sufficient to insure a minimum maturity on the part of both partners. The commission saw its recommendation as designed to protect the young girl who is more likely to be pressured by family or circumstances into early marriage.

There has been no action by provincial legislatures on the commission's recommendation.

The situation of the registered Indian woman who marries other than a registered Indian man is unique in that she loses her Indian status. This does not apply to the registered Indian man, for he retains his Indian status. The Royal Commission on the Status of Women recommended that "an Indian woman upon marriage to a non-Indian be allowed to: (*a*) retain her Indian status and (*b*) transmit her Indian status to her children."[15]

---

[14] Royal Commission on the Status of Women in Canada, p. 234.

[15] *Ibid.*, p. 238.

There has been no action on the commission's recommendation.

Matrimonial property. The English common law provinces, following the precedent of English legislation, enacted legislation during the latter part of the eighteenth century that provides for a married woman to have independent property, enter into contracts, and so on. In Quebec it was not until 1964 that an act was passed establishing the full legal capacity of married women.

The establishment of women as legally separate from their husbands provided for their independence with respect to their own property. The situation of common property is more complex. This is due partly to the inevitable confusion of ownership between a married couple, partly due to the fact that their contributions to the family may be different in kind, and partly to the fact that their separate situation only becomes an issue when the marriage is being terminated.

The Quebec civil code has provided for a number of possible ways of treating joint property. Up until 1970 there were basically two marital regimes, one based on separation of property or variation thereof established via a notarial marriage contract, and the other a statutory community of property system established automatically in the absence of a notarial contract. In 1970, a new legal regime, "the partnership of acquests" was brought into force. This regime allows the woman to act as a person legally separate from her husband, and provides for an equal distribution at dissolution of all property that has been acquired during a marriage. However, a couple may enter into a notarial contract to establish some other system of property division.

The English common law provinces have no comparable system for the division of property acquired during a marriage. If the property is jointly held, an equal division is made. However, if the property has been acquired under one spouse's name, then his or her right to the property is primary. In a recent case in Alberta, the wife of a rancher endeavored to obtain an equal share of the ranch's assets on the grounds that she had made an equal contribution to its development and management. This was refused on the grounds that "she had only done what any ranch wife would have done."[16] Rights to property are also affected by such considerations as who left whom, the contribution each partner made to the dissolution of the marriage, and so on.

The Royal Commission on the Status of Women in Canada recom-

[16]*Murdoch and Murdoch,* Alberta Supreme Court, 1975.

mended a system of equal division of accumulated assets [17] as best providing for equal but separate recognition of the spouses. This recommendation has been considered by a number of provincial law commissions. The general trend of the commission reports is to support the Royal Commission's view, subject to a number of special conditions, such as the extent to which it should be applied to present as opposed to future marriages. Legislation to establish a system based on this approach is before the Ontario legislature and is under consideration in a number of other provinces.

Divorce and custody. The Divorce Act (1968) provided broader grounds for divorce in Canada than those previously accepted (adultery, sodomy, bestiality, and rape). In particular, "marriage breakdown" resulting from a series of factors, and evidenced by a three-year separation period, was recognized as ground for divorce. The number of divorces granted annually has risen sharply.

However, the present law still retains the concept of fault and represents a compromise between those who argue for a law based solely on individual contract. Discussion of the divorce law has tended to favor a further liberalization. This could take the form of a reduced period of separation as evidence of breakdown (the Royal Commission on the Status of Women recommended one year [18]), and a no-fault approach to the act of dissolution.

During marriage, both partners enjoy equal guardianship and custody rights to their minor children. At dissolution of a marriage, guardianship and custody rights are most frequently decided by mutual agreement between the spouses. Alternatively, guardianship and custody may be established by court order. In some provinces, special provisions are made to represent the children's interest in such proceedings; in British Columbia the Superintendent of Child Welfare is required to make a report to the court.

Maintenance. The obligation to support one's immediate family is explicit in both federal and provincial legislation. Six Candian provinces have legislation requiring children to support their aged or dependent parents. Such legislation is rarely enforced. In some situations, adult children are the indirect beneficiaries of state provisions for the aged. On the other hand, the maintenance obligation within the nuclear family remains mandatory.

While the nuclear family is together, enforcement of the maintenance obligation is rarely necessary. However, when there is separation or divorce the partners have to decide their continuing financial obligations to each

---

[17] Royal Commission on the Status of Women in Canada, p. 246.

[18] *Ibid.,* p. 258.

other by mutual agreement or, alternatively, have them decided by court order.

The judicial guidelines are that such orders should be "just and reasonable, having regard to all the circumstances of the case such as the conduct of the parties, the age and number of children, the respective financial ability of both spouses or the possibility that the wife works."[19] Orders may be varied as the circumstances of either partner change.

The major problem with such orders is the difficulty of enforcing them over time. The problem of enforcement is partly due to the changing circumstances of the former spouses and the usual waning of the husbands' voluntary compliance. This is compounded by the fact that legislation is provincial. The difficulties of enforcement between provinces constitute an invitation to evasion by those so inclined.

The difficulty of collection is further sharply compounded by the problem of poverty. A man needs a substantial income to keep two households out of poverty. If his former wife has to apply for social assistance, the usual practice is to deduct the value of the private maintenance payments from the assistance grant. This places the former husband in a situation in which his payment merely reduces the province's payment to his former wife. Reciprocally, the former wife gains nothing from the husband's payment. As a consequence, failure to comply voluntarily increases sharply as the wife turns to public agencies for support.

This failure to fulfill maintenance obligations leads to political and public concern for the added burden thereby imposed on the public purse, and to a search for more effective enforcement mechanisms. The Ontario Law Reform Commission[20] advocates a system of payments with the court as an intermediary. The court would initiate action if there was non-compliance.

However, the problems of the private maintenance system at poverty, or near-poverty, income levels are too fundamental to permit remedy simply by a greater emphasis on enforcement actions. It would appear that consideration should be given as to whether the private maintenance system has a role to play at poverty or near-poverty income levels. Such consideration should precede consideration of enforcement actions; actions that are often unproductive, as when the husband moves or is jailed for noncompliance.

Canadian family law evidences a conservative tendency toward the

[19] *Ibid.*, p. 249.

[20] Family Law Project, *Study on Support Obligations,* Part II (Toronto: Government of Ontario, Queen's Printer, 1969), XII, 596–606.

preservation of the traditional family units that constitute a declining proportion of Canadian families. This tendency is seen in the compromise evident in divorce legislation between societal and individual interest; in the slow pace of reform legislation that would give women a more equal position to men in families; and by the emphasis upon enforcement in maintenance obligations.

There is little evidence of positive policy; instead, there is a slow and reluctant yielding to sociological change that always leaves family law a decade or two behind the developing nature of family relationships. Meanwhile, the unintended consequences of laggard legislation include practices of duplicity, legal manipulation, and avoidance.

Although historically the Quebec civil code has been even more conservative than the English common law, this is now no longer the case. Indeed, in some fields (e.g., matrimonial property), the Quebec legislation provides a legal structure more in keeping with the contemporary nature of family relationships than that provided in the other provinces.

Income Policies and Poverty

Canadian social policy dealing with income is basically reactive to the distribution of incomes created by the operation of the market economy. Such market incomes take no account of financial dependency or need. Therefore, such incomes are unrelated to any view of family welfare.

Social policies have been introduced in a number of forms that are designed to modify the distribution of income between individuals and over the individual's working life. Some of these policies have explicit reference to the family; others are based on some assumptions about the family; while others have consequences, sometimes unforeseen for the family. The principal examples of such social policies are: minimum wage policies, tax policies, child allowances, poverty lines, social allowances, pension policies, and unemployment policies.

Minimum wage policy. A minimum wage policy has been developed in Canada chiefly to provide protection for workers against exploitation at very low wage levels. Conversely, opposition to minimum wages has come from employers of low-wage labor and from concern that a high minimum wage level would contribute to unemployment.

Minimum wages are mainly determined by provincial regulations and vary widely. At their highest—$3.50 per hour, in British Columbia—they provide an annual income that is inadequate to meet most estimates of family need. There is little evidence that minimum wages are related to any ideas on family income. Many minimum wage, or near minimum wage, levels are found in the service industries where the labor force is predominantly women. Whereas a proportion of these women are dependent on their wages for a family income, the majority are second wage earners within their family units.

The effects of minimum wages, and changes in the minimum wage level, on family incomes is a subject worthy of closer scrutiny, and more explicit policy.

Tax policies. Canadian tax policy was extensively examined by the Royal Commission on Taxation.[21] The commission proposed that the family be recognized as the basic income and expenditure unit for tax purposes. This led the commission to propose that the income of husband, wife, and minor children should be aggregated for tax purposes and taxed on a single schedule—different from that applicable to individuals. The commission also proposed that all gifts, inheritances, and so on within a nuclear family be tax free.

In introducing legislation, the Canadian government accepted the latter recommendation but rejected the concept of an aggregated family income for tax purposes. As a consequence, family members continue to be taxed as individuals subject to deducations from taxable income for dependents. These deducations are valued at (1976): $2,000 basic personal exemption; $1,830 married examption; $390 for children up to sixteen years of age; $720 for dependent children over sixteen. In addition, certain other family-related expenses, such as child care expenses or payments to elderly or handicapped parents, may be deducted from taxable income—subject to limits on the maximum value of such deductions.

The history of these deductions and their value is obscure. Although the personal exemptions are sometimes referred to as related to the concept of exempting a subsistence level of income from tax ''in principle,'' in practice one cannot find any attempt to relate the levels to any clearly articulated standard. The Canadian Council on Social Development and the National Council of Welfare have both advocated family tax policies that would exempt poor families from taxation through a system of tax credits rather than

[21]*Royal Commission on Taxation* (Ottawa: Government of Canada, Queen's Printer, 1966).

deductions from taxable income.[22] The advantage of a tax credit system is that it would provide a tax exemption for dependents at a single basic value. The present system of exemptions from taxable income provides the greatest value to those with the highest incomes and is thus a regressive part of total tax policies.

However, no action to incorporate these principles into tax policy seems likely in the near future. Tax policy will likely remain poorly related to the family and unrelated to income policies as a whole. Tax policy is always subject to the limitation that it cannot confer positive benefits unless there are special provisions to make unused tax credits refundable to the families or individuals involved.

Although income tax policy is primarily federal, Quebec has retained its own provincial income tax, separately administered and collected. Sales taxes are levied by both federal and provincial governments, and real estate taxes are levied at the municipal level. This complexity of taxing authority impedes the introduction of concerted tax policies of any form.

Child allowances. Family allowances were introduced in Canada in 1945, principally as an economic measure designed to buttress spending levels during the postwar readjustment period for the Canadian economy and not as a deliberate policy to strengthen family life. The value of family allowances has been adjusted on several occasions and in 1976 had an average value of $22.50 per child. Family allowances are paid for all children in the family unit. An average value for family allowances is set through federal government permission to the province of residence to vary the value of individual payments in accord with either the child's age or the position of the child in the family. Most provinces either pay the average value to all children or make only minor modifications. Quebec, however, has a significantly different approach to the distribution of family allowances.

The intent of family allowance policy outside Quebec is not completely clear. Family allowances have never been adequate to cover child care expenses at poverty-line levels. In addition, there is excellent documentation to show that flat-rate family allowances are only weakly redistributive between income classes.[23] In 1971 the federal government proposed to scale family

[22] Canadian Council on Social Development, *The Social Implications of Tax Reform* (Ottawa: the Council, 1970); National Council of Welfare, *The Hidden Welfare System* (Ottawa: the Council, 1976).

[23] Antal Deutsch, *Income Redistribution through Canadian Federal Family Allowances and Old Age Benefits* (Toronto: Canadian Tax Foundation, 1968).

allowances to income in the proposed Family Income Security Plan.[24] Legislation for this purpose was introduced but allowed to die when Parliament was dissolved. Opposition to the scaling of family allowances was based on constitutional grounds, the danger of stigma, and the increase in administration costs. Furthermore, a similar positive effect could be obtained by making family allowances high and subject to taxation. The measure also failed to pass because its effect would have been to strip middle- and upper-income earners of their family allowances. This was not judged to be the most popular move to precede the forthcoming election.

Canadian federal family allowance policy provides an example of a family policy that has become firmly enmeshed in its latent consequences. For example, family allowances are received primarily by mothers, providing them with a source of income and some limited independence from their spouses.

The Royal Commission on the Status of Women argued for a program of federal child-care allowances, payable to the mother, and valued at $500 per child per year. No action has been taken on this proposal.

Quebec family allowance policy has an independent set of objectives. The basis of these objectives is to provide special support to large family units and it is implicitly related to a positive population policy. Quebec scales the federal payments to family size and makes an added contribution to their value from provincial sources (see table 2).

Table 2 Family Allowances in Quebec, 1975–76: Monthly Benefit Rates (*in dollars*)

	Quebec	Canada	Total Value
First child	3.68	13.25	16.93
Second child	4.92	19.87	24.79
Third child	6.14	32.84	38.98
Each subsequent child	7.36	36.16	43.52

SOURCE: Quebec Pension Board, "Annual Report 1975/76; Quebec Family Allowance Plan."

The origin of this positive set of policies may be found in official policy statements of the Quebec government.[25] The value of family allowance payments even in Quebec remains far below the incremental costs associated

[24] Department of National Health and Welfare, *Income Security for Canadians* (Ottawa: Government of Canada, Department of National Health and Welfare, 1971).

[25] *Guidelines for a New Quebec Family Allowance Policy* (Quebec: 1969); Commission of Inquiry on Health and Social Welfare in Quebec, *Report* (Quebec: Government of Canada, 1971).

with maintaining one child at the poverty line. These approximate $1,000 per child per year.

Poverty Lines

The poverty of one in five Canadians has been a major social problem since the 1960s. There have been several different approaches to dealing with the problem, not all of which are directly relevant here. However, several features of poverty have particular relevance for the family.

Poverty lines are based on family needs and expenditure patterns. When these standards are applied to survey data it is found that families with dependent children are somewhat more vulnerable to poverty than other Canadians (one in four is in poverty). This vulnerability increases rapidly as family size increases. In addition, the one-parent family is particularly vulnerable to poverty (one in three is in poverty).[26] The poverty of family units has been considered to be a more serious social problem than the poverty of individuals because of concern that a dysfunctional life style may be developed in such families and transmitted through their children.

In partial response to these views of the impact of poverty upon families, the recommendations of the Senate Committee on Poverty included the development of a negative tax income-support program for all families, but for individuals only over the age of forty.[27]

Despite much discussion of poverty lines, and debate as to how they can be established, the minimum standard of living for Canadians is, in practice, set by provincial social allowance policies. The levels of payment under these policies are substantially lower than the poverty-line family incomes proposed by the Senate Committee on Poverty or the Canadian Council on Social Development.

Social Allowances, Federal Income Support, and Supplementation Proposals

The provincial social allowance programs are cost-shared by the federal government through the Canada Assistance Plan. The basis for eligibility and the value of allowances is the need of applicants. Need is determined by the provincial department to which application is made. This leads to a diversity of definitions of eligibility and of allowance levels in the different provinces. A recurrent problem is that in many provinces the approved levels of assis-

[26] Special Senate Committee on Poverty, 1971.

[27] *Ibid.*, Recommendations.

tance fail to incorporate a reasonable allowance for the costs of shelter. This creates a situation in which recipients live in inadequate housing and are vulnerable to exploitation and discrimination by landlords.

Beginning in 1973, the government of Canada, in cooperation with the provinces, initiated a major review of income-security policy. By early 1976, proposals for a revised system based on a support program for the dependent, and a supplementation program for the marginally employed and full-time working poor, was presented to the public. The supplementation program was proposed for "families with children and singles and couples over 54."[28]

No legislation based on those proposals is in sight.

Pensions. The Canada Pension Plan and the similar Quebec Pension Plan are the major Canadian social insurance programs for old age, survivors, widowhood, disability, and orphan benefits. These plans are based on a traditional view of the family; that is, a breadwinner's pension is to provide for the spouse's needs.

The Royal Commission on the Status of Women drew attention to the fact that this assumption about dependency and the employment-related basis of contributions resulted in housewives having restricted access to the plan. Furthermore, in the event of separation or divorce they lost a pension right designed for their need as well as that of their spouse.

In response to these concerns, amendments to the Canada Pension Plan are now before the Canadian Parliament. These provide for splitting Canada Pension Plan credits on divorce or annulment. Also, a woman who leaves the work force to raise children (under age seven) may drop out those years from her lifetime earning record and thereby protect the value of her pension.

There are other features of the Canada Pension Plan that warrant scrutiny from a family policy perspective. These include the inadequate levels of benefits for widows and orphans. Disability benefits are faced with unique questions of their own, primarily because there are a number of other disability-related programs—the total effect of which is uncoordinated and unplanned.

Unemployment insurance. Unemployment insurance is not basically a family-related program. However, the design of the program does contain some direct family-related provisions, some family-based assumptions, and some latent family consequences.

[28] Communiqué, meeting of federal and provincial Ministers of Welfare, Ottawa, June 1–2, 1976.

Provision within the unemployment insurance plan for maternity benefits is the major example of a direct, family-related provision. Its inclusion in the unemployment insurance scheme is arguable. More attention would probably be given to maternity benefits if they were provided through a separate program. The present provision of benefits up to fifteen weeks was considered inadequate by the Royal Commission on the Status of Women. The Royal Commission argued for eighteen weeks for the extension of coverage to those who stop work temporarily during pregnancy and to those who are already on unemployment benefits at the time of confinement.[29]

The family-based assumptions within the unemployment insurance program primarily relate to benefit levels. The maximum unemployment benefit level in combination with family allowances approximates some estimates of a poverty-line income for a family of four. This approximation may be coincidental, and it is not recognized in any policy statement.

The latent consequences of unemployment insurance for family welfare occur chiefly through the effects of the plan's operation upon two-wage-earner families. In such families, there is often some discretion possible with respect to the second income. This is particularly the case where the loss of the second income can be partly covered by unemployment benefits. As a consequence, there is some unintended use (abuse?) of unemployment insurance during temporary leaves from the work force. The taking of such "leaves" is not permitted, but effective policing and control are impossible when unemployment rates are high.

Income programs and poverty lines contain many assumptions about the needs of families and the levels of support they should provide. These assumptions are not always clearly expressed but can be inferred from the value of benefits and conditions of eligibility.

Within the general framework a number of specific examples of policy can be discerned in which the family is perceived as a major target for intervention. These examples include Quebec's family allowance program, the proposed federal supplement program, and the maternity leave provisions of the Unemployment Insurance Act.

The Canadian women's movement is the major advocate for a number of modifications in the Canadian income-security system that have primary reference to women's situations but many implications for families. These include the proposed child care allowances, division of Canada Pension Plan credits, and proposals for better maternity coverage.

[29]*Ibid.*, p. 85.

Finally, the individual operation of specific programs, and the cumulative effect of the operation of a series of programs, can be seen as having a series of unintended consequences for Canadian families. Issues worth study are the impact of social programs on two-income families, the effect of social programs upon the control of family incomes between the spouses and on role expectations, and the effect on families of abrupt changes in living standards due to unemployment, sickness, disability, and so forth.

Personal Social Services

Personal social services in Canada are scattered among different organizations whose primary mandate is usually related to action on specific social issues. Typical organizations that provide personal social services include provincial social allowance departments, child welfare agencies, mental health agencies, family service agencies, and so on. All these services are organized on a primarily "residual" model, designed to assist after family breakdown rather than to support family life. During the last ten years a growing perception has been that these services share a number of common features and functions. This permits their analysis as a whole, and action has been taken in a number of provinces to promote their administrative consolidation. Responsibility for personal social services is for the most part provincial, with the federal role most often expressed through cost-sharing programs designed to promote some degree of uniformity in service access and standards.

In 1975 the Canadian Council on Social Development completed a major study of the personal social services.[30] Much of the contents of this section is drawn from that study. The personal social services, their purposes, financing, and so on have also been the objects of study through the federal-provincial working paper, and task forces, on social security in Canada. The work of the federal-provincial review is now complete, and a Canadian federal Social Services Act is being prepared for presentation to Parliament.[31]

One might have thought that this intense period of activity concerning the personal social services might have had specific reference to the family

[30] H. Philip Hepworth, *Personal Social Services in Canada* (Ottawa: Canadian Council on Social Development, 1975).

[31] "Working Paper on Social Security in Canada," 1973); Communiqué, meeting of federal and provincial Ministers of Welfare. [This initiative was aborted.]

as representing the major unit of informal association to which these services relate. However, such has not been the case. The relationship of personal social services to the family closely parallels that found in the income-security field. That is to say, policy and programs contain a number of implicit assumptions about the family that occasionally are focused on specific policies. They also contain a number of consequences for families which are most often unplanned and unattended.

Family life education. Concern with family life education is expressed through a loose network of local family life education councils, the principal function of which is to encourage local educational authorities to incorporate some family life material in their curricula. The councils also promote some developmental, small-group activities for married couples; relate to churches, community associations, YWCAs, and so forth; and respond to local issues that affect the family.

At the national level the family life education movement is focused on positive features of family life, and its educational strategy is basically designed to prevent social problems and to assist the adaptation of the family and social institutions to contemporary society. The impact of family life education is difficult to assess. The movement does not have specific goals for family life in Canada other than that it should be "better." However, more than one approach can be conceived, and indeed should be open for discussion, examination, and adoption.

Family planning and abortion. The educational aspects of family planning are a specific type of family life education. However, there is a separate network of local, provincial, and federal family planning associations. These are voluntary agencies, supported in part by government grants.

In addition, there is a series of family planning services organized under public health service auspices, university health departments, major public hospitals. These services supplement the activities of physicians in private practice who provide by far the greater part of family-planning advice and services. The supplementary services are useful because of their better contact with specific population groups—university students, for instance.

Support for these services comes partly from such shared-cost programs as the Canada Assistance Plan, partly from a variety of health auspices, and partly through the direct work of the family planning division of the Department of National Health and Welfare.

Abortion tends to be treated euphemistically in this service network.

The law dealing with abortion in Canada was changed in 1970 so that abortion becomes possible when a panel of physicians attested that the mother's "health" was "endangered" by the pregnancy. The law has led to a variety of practices and wide variations in access and eligibility criteria as different medical committees interpret "health" and "endanger." However, the law has been viewed as too liberal by a number of public groups who oppose abortion outright or in other than extreme circumstances.

The Royal Commission on the Status of Women in Canada recommended a simpler procedure, based on a woman's wishes during the first twelve weeks of a pregnancy. The commission also proposed some changes in the criminal law to clarify the right of persons to seek their own sterilization.[32] A media campaign against the availability of abortion under the present law makes such legislation unlikely at this time.

The impact of improved family planning information and services is clearly associated with the very rapid drop in the Canadian birth rate during the last fifteen years. However, ambivalance continues in the provision of information and services to young women to offset the rising number of illegitimate births.

Day care and homemaker services. These essential social utility services are not well-developed in Canada. Their relationship to family functioning becomes more critical as women's participation in the work force increases, but the need for these services is much broader. Typical important uses of these services include the family where the mother is sick; the family where one or more children are retarded, handicapped, autistic; and the family that is isolated from kinship or community support—all conditions which can cause an unacceptable level of stress for parents. All these situations are magnified when the growing number of one-parent families is considered.

In 1975 an estimated 250,000 children under the age of three had mothers in the labor force. Approximately 4.7 percent of these received day care services. Of some 312,000 children aged three to five of working mothers, a little over 17 percent were in day care programs. Over half of each of these age groups were cared for in their own homes; the major form of out-of-home care for both groups was family day care.[33]

The Royal Commission on the Status of Women in Canada advocated a national day care act and concerted planning to insure that the opportunity to

[32] "Working Paper on Social Security in Canada," pp. 281–86.

[33] *Status of Day Care in Canada, 1975* (Ottawa: Department of National Health and Welfare, 1976).

place children in organized child care arrangements would be available to all Canadian families.[34] Similar recommendations have been made by a series of national and provincial bodies that have studied the availability of day care and homemaker services.

Action to expand the network of day care and homemaker services proceeds slowly. Opposition not only is due to the cost of such services but relates to traditional views that a mother should be at home. The proposed federal personal social services act would provide federal support for day care services. At present, support for such services is limited to poor people. However, initiative in developing services and a portion of the cost of service remain local or provincial responsibilities. The fiscal situation of municipal and some provincial governments insures that the best that can be expected is a continuation of the slow progress toward a more adequate service network.

Family counseling services. Family counseling services are provided under a number of organizational auspices of which the most important are community- and hospital-based mental health programs; provincial and municipal public assistance and child welfare agencies; and the nongovernment family service agencies. These services share a "case" orientation to intervention and service provision. Demand for these services appears to exceed their supply, for waiting lists are common. Services are provided primarily by social workers but also by clinical psychologists and psychiatrists. At a methodological level there is a shared interest, and some competition, between the professions in the field of family therapy.

Although these services are differently organized, and require different skills, in other ways they share many characteristics with the social utility services. One could expect that most families will at some points in their history benefit from professional counseling. This is all the more the case when divorce is common and people face the difficult legal and emotional problems of separation and readjustment.

The funding of these services has been principally "problem"-oriented, with mental health services carrying increasing responsibility. A proposed new federal Social Services Act could provide the broad-based funding mechanisms necessary to the support of a family counseling service as a social utility.

Child welfare services. Child welfare services in Canada have been generally organized in response to the problem of the abused or neglected

[34] Commission on the Status of Women in Canada, p. 271.

child. The service is directly related to family failure. The boundary line between child welfare services and juvenile delinquency services is often difficult to perceive for the older child, and in some jurisdictions these services are closely associated with each other.

Both services are based, too, on statutory powers of intervention and in that way differ from the social utility services. Policy dealing with such services has the protection of the child and/or protection of society as its primary objective. Within both services, stress is placed upon trying to work with the family within which the problem originally occurred. However, for a variety of reasons—urgency of the problem, limited resources to work with a family, expectations incurred by involving authorities—a not unusual course of events is that intervention leads to separation of children from their parents.

One might hope that a better developed set of social utilities, supportive to family functioning, might make it less necessary to take action under statute in the extreme situations to which child welfare authorities have to respond.

The problem of services to the deliberately abused child has received special attention in Canada. Action in this field has taken the form of education of professionals to recognize the abused child and parents, changes in the law to provide reporting of suspected cases to a central registry, and rehabilitative programs. Even in cases of deliberate abuse, there are opportunities to improve family functioning and reduce abuse through the provision of alternative care, homemaker and counseling services.

The provision of adoption services, and services to unmarried mothers under child welfare auspices (the usual pattern), involves a conflict of interest for the service providers. In most situations, the welfare of the child is seen as best provided for through relinquishment and adoption. However justified this view, the consequence is apparent in the neglect of services for the unmarried mother who keeps her child. A rising proportion of unmarried mothers are keeping their children and raising them, at any rate for a period of time, alone. Special supportive services for unmarried mothers (single parents) who follow this course do not exist. Furthermore, the general-purpose social utilities that might fill this gap are not well-developed.

The abused wife. Physical violence within the family is not confined to children. The wife is an equally common victim. Furthermore, some women may be so trapped by their total social situation (no close relations nearby, no money, lack of access to courts or law enforcement agencies) that they are in effect captives.

In partial response to these circumstances, women's groups in a number of Canadian cities have been organizing telephone services for women who may be faced with abuse. In addition, there has been a growth of "transition houses for women," group living homes for women and children who have been forced to flee and have no one to turn to for refuge. Such homes also provide for the destitute woman and child who may have great difficulty finding accommodations outside close kinship or friendship patterns.

These emerging services are examples of a voluntary service development, prompted and organized by the women's movement, but directly related to family welfare.

Institutional services for children. The problems of some children are too severe to be coped with within the family, however well that family functions, and however adequate are the supportive family services. Thus, as a last resort, a series of institutional services for children is essential. There are three main categories of institutional services: services for the physically handicapped—usually special chronic-care hospitals for children; services for the mentally retarded—usually large institutions, although there is increasing emphasis upon smaller institutions, community foster homes, and community supportive services; services for the emotionally disturbed and/or delinquent child—usually with an emphasis on treatment and a secure environment.

Institutional service is viewed as a specialized resource of last resort. There has been increasing emphasis on group homes and on the recruitment of professional foster parents to provide child care services in such homes. In due course, the insight into effective parenting that should follow from this development will need to be made available to all parents through family life education.

The emphasis that has been placed upon taking all possible measures to keep a child in his own home—failing that, to place him in a home where professional parenting will be available—and only as a last resort and in specialized situations to use institutions to care for children, is a reflection of the high value placed on the family.

The multiproblem family. During the 1960s the multiproblem family was the focus of much research. Concern originated with the perception that a rather small group of families had patterns of functioning that seemed to need the perpetual intervention of social agencies. The intervention frequently involved not only numerous and lengthy contacts but also contact with more than one service agency. Furthermore, intergenerational patterns of agency use could be traced.

Initially, the problem of the multiproblem family tended to be defined as a challenge for intensive casework services. The design of experiments was thus preoccupied with the effectiveness of casework services in obtaining measurable improvement in family functioning. The conclusion of such experiments invariably produced only marginal evidence of change in family functioning as a result of casework intervention.[35]

However, a by-product of this research was to increase awareness of the nature of relationships that tend to be built over time between social agencies and their clients. Some features of multiproblem family functioning could be related to the multiproblem focii of agency development and intervention. The unsettling question was asked: could the multiproblem family be the product of a service structure, the latent effect of which was to reinforce pathology rather than promote health?

Thus, concern with the relationship between services and the multiproblem family contributed to the interest in delivery system reorganization of the personal social services.

The personal social services are in an important transitional state from problem-focused services toward social utility services. The pace of change, however, is slow, and the changes are as much the result of administrative advantages, possible fiscal economies, and the assertion of professional hegemony as they are the product of a response to changing family needs. Even in Quebec, where reorganization has been most thorough, and where the family has been the subject of more policy attention than in other regions of Canada, the reorganization of social and health services is not related to a particular set of family policies.

Evidence of the need for a different set of relationships between families and the personal social services is not hard to find, and the Canadian women's movement has been particularly active in bringing major service gaps to public attention. Resources to close the gap still appear to be lacking. The proposed new federal Social Services Act is to be welcomed, for it will provide a more broadly based mechanism for cost sharing in personal social service development. However, effective use of the act will depend upon provincial and local initiative.

Consequences for the family of the poorly developed state of the supportive utility services can be viewed as including an unnecessary level of stress, anxiety, and bitterness. More seriously, it is quite likely that the

[35] United Community Services for Greater Vancouver, Area Development Project, Research Monographs I, II and III (Vancouver: United Community Service, 1968) provide examples of such research.

weakness of the supportive services leads to more than needed use of statutory powers of intervention, and institutional care services for children. The latent consequences of the present organization of the service system may include reinforcing rather than alleviating problems in family functioning.

Housing, Health, and Educational Services

Each of the housing, health, and education fields of social policy could be the subject of the type of examination of social policy, and its effect on the family, that has been discussed here. However, space will permit only brief references to these fields.

Housing. One of the basic guidelines for Canadian housing policy has been that each nuclear family should be able to form an independent household. Thus, census data on doubled families have been regarded as indicators of overcrowding. Target projections for housing unit construction have been based on a formula that incorporates this assumption.

As the cost of housing has risen, there has been a tendency by lenders to revise mortgage policies so that families can qualify on the basis of two incomes rather than one. This has permitted many middle-income families to obtain housing but requires both spouses to remain employed. The shortcomings of Canadian housing policy for families occur primarily for family units whose total income is too low for them to create an effective demand for rental or owned accommodation of reasonable size and quality. Both federal and provincial governments conduct a number of subsidy programs designed to make housing more readily available to families with lower incomes. Some of these programs are specially designated for families with children. However, for families in the lowest two-income quintiles the subsidies are frequently inadequate. The poor are too poor to qualify for assistance! There is some public housing in Canada that provides subsidies sufficiently substantial to reach the poor; however, the number of such units is completely inadequate to house the number of families in need of accommodation.

Data on housing standards, crowding, and so forth during the postwar period have shown a record of improvement. However, such improvement that has occurred coexists with very poor housing for the poorest Canadians, both those who live in major cities and those who live in rural areas.

There has been a rapid increase in nonfamily households in Canada from 13.3 percent in 1961 to 18.3 percent in 1971, according to the Census.

This expansion is another indication of the tendency for many Canadians to live in other than families. The concurrent reduction of multiple family households from 3.7 percent in 1961 to 2.0 percent in 1971 provides further evidence of the decline of residential expanded family living patterns. These changes are not the result of deliberate social policy. Instead, they express the result of market choices made by individuals and families in the context of rising living standards.

Finally, there have been significant changes in the form and location of family housing. These changes have not been the result of any deliberate planning but are the secondary consequences of inattention to the social changes that result from activities in the private sector. Two such changes are: the consequences for families in central city areas that result from high-density, high-rise living; and the consequences for suburban families of increased traveling time and decreased access to community facilities.

Health. Health policy and practice have, especially since the late 1950s, shown a fairly marked trend away from a family orientation. If anything, they are oriented to the individual, and perhaps even more so to the type of care and method of practice that most suit the health professions.

An important factor in this shift, though in the light of experience in other countries certainly not the sole factor, has been the method of funding health care. The Hospital and Diagnostic Services Act, 1958, provided virtually free hospital services through a federal/provincial cost-sharing arrangement. During the ten (and in some provinces, more) years which elapsed between passage of this act and implementaion of the 1966 Medical Services Act which covered medical services, there was a significant shift toward institutional forms of care, particularly in acute-care hospitals but also through the growth of other residential health provisions, such as extended care units and nursing homes.

The coming of Medicare, which provided an alternative free or insured service, had some effect on slowing down this process, but two other factors offset this.

First, the method of delivery of medical services was itself showing a shift away from a home-based family service to a surgery- or clinic-based individual service. At the level of delivery or primary medical care there is no requirement, or even expectation, that all the members of a family will normally be served by the same physician. The postwar trend has been away from the family physician toward specialization in primary medical care, with the patient being left to select his doctor on the best basis he can.

Medical care is not now commonly offered at home. House calls by doctors are at a low level. Ordinary sickness is dealt with in the surgery. Major illness is cared for, and the two main life events—birth and death—take place in, hospitals.

Second, the lack of resource allocation for home care services in the main federal plans seriously retarded parallel development of this type of provision which would have offered an alternative to hospital or other institutional care.

The remnants of the family support system remained with the public health services, with their child health clinics, school health services, and home visiting and care programs which have maintained a strong family orientation. However, public health is the poor relation in the health field; further, it tends to arouse professional opposition when it tries to extend its role.

The late 1960s and the 1970s have shown a fairly significant effort to return to more family-based health care. The impulses at the political level seem to have come from escalating health costs rather than from a conviction on family policy, though the arguments in favor of family health care have been used to "sweeten the pill" for opponents of change:

1. There has been a steady development of home care programs, either through extension of existing programs, or through new provisions. Initially, these were often directed to the acutely ill to prevent the necessity for hospitalization or to enable early discharge from hospital. Gradually they are being extended to assist the chronically ill. However, it cannot yet be said that there is a policy of consistent family support to enable it to deal with illness and continuing stress. The trend toward home care was initially funded outside the federal/provincial cost-shared programs, but new cost-sharing agreements in 1977 will enable allocation of federal resources to this area.

2. The medical profession itself has viewed the trend toward overspecialization with concern, and a number of medical schools have introduced specialization in family practice in their curriculum. Other attempts to upgrade the status of general practice are under way.

3. There has been a serious attempt toward development of community health centers and multiservice centers with a family-oriented approach. Progress here has been slower than was hoped, but the trend can be expected to continue.

4. A new status is being given to public health programs, particularly those geared toward health promotion. A federal government working paper, "A New Perspective on the Health of Canadians," produced in 1975, ac-

tively promotes this approach. While the working paper is in many ways in-dividual- rather than family-oriented, some of the policies emerging can be expected to assist the return toward a more family-based service.

The results of this examination of Canadian social policy support the view that the family is more often the recipient of social policy initiative than the basis for the planning of social policies. In the main, Canadian social policy shows much more evidence of the influence of assumptions about the family, and latent consequences for the family, than deliberate planning for the family. Where there is evidence of deliberate planning for the family it can be traced to nonfamily movements or interests. The two major examples in Canada of such interests are the national policies being pursued in Quebec, and the policies designed to emancipate women. Both these sets of interests have implications for families and lead to proposals and actions that are deliberate.

When the changing sociology of the family is compared to change in social policy assumptions and programs there are evident frictions. Canadian housing policy appears to assume that adequate housing is a right for those families that are based on two average incomes, yet no concerted effort is made to assist with the inevitable child care costs that result. Canadian in-come-security policy appears to be based in part on assumptions about fami-lies, and in part on assumptions about individuals, with little recognition of the confusion in allowance levels that this creates. Canadian family law ap-pears to be oriented to a traditional view of family responsibilities and dependencies despite extensive sociological data on the existence and growth of other types of intrapersonal relationship and practice.

Given the high value that Canadians attach to individual freedom it seems unlikely that a deliberate set of policies designed to strengthen the ''traditional'' family (or any alternative) would receive wide support. How-ever, the case for policies that are more attentive to the situation of Canadian families (including the many variations therein), and more concerted in their total effect, appears to be excellent.

One might have hoped that Canadian social policy, and Canadian pub-lic opinion, would have been affected to some extent by the Vanier Institute of the Family. However, the imprint of the Institute on social policy is hard to discern. Yet the case for a public body that is informed on patterns of family life, monitors government and commercial family policies, and pro-poses alternatives, would seem to be excellent.

~~13

ISRAEL

Marjorie Honig
and Nira Shamai

ISRAEL DOES NOT have an explicit family policy, nor is there a well-defined set of goals regarding the family. Nevertheless, concern for the integrity and well-being of the family enter implicitly in several policy areas, and the importance of the family at the level of personal preference as well as national interest is readily acknowledged. The route by which Israel arrived at this stage will be given considerable attention, in part because economic and social legislation is better understood in the context of the society in which it develops—government policy is, after all, derived from a country's particular history, its goals, and its special set of strengths and weaknesses—and in part because the recent history of Israel offers some interesting developments with respect to the role of the family and, a topic closely related, the role of women in the family and in the larger society.

One of the first questions which arises in relation to government policy toward the family is why the government should foster the family as a social

DR. MARJORIE HONIG is Director, Division of Basic Research, Bureau of Research and Planning, National Insurance Institute, Jerusalem, Israel.
NIRA SHAMAI is Deputy Director General for Research Planning, National Insurance Institute, Jerusalem.

The authors wish to express their appreciation to Naomi Kies of the Bureau of Research and Planning, National Insurance Institute; to Zohar Karti, Director of the Department for the Promotion of Women's Employment, Ministry of Labor; to Lesley Hazleton, Abraham Doron, and Jona M. Rosenfeld of the Hebrew University School of Social Work; and to Ora Ahimeir of the Prime Minister's Commission on the Status of Women.

unit at all. Does the family have any particular advantage over other forms of social organization in instilling cultural and moral values and assuring social cohesion? Are there any viable alternatives capable of carrying out the traditional tasks of the family?

The early years of Israel offer an interesting experiment in one form of alternative, the collective settlement called the kibbutz. The founders of the kibbutzim, socialists from Eastern Europe and Russia, viewed the closely knit, nuclear family as an obstacle to the achievement of the ideal larger community. They consequently removed from the family most of its traditional tasks. Child rearing and education became communal concerns. Most household tasks were assigned to the collective, and all decisions concerning the earning and distribution of income were made on a collective basis. Loyalties to the larger community were fostered, and potentially competitive ties to the nuclear family were discouraged.

The kibbutz population represented a small minority of the early settlers in Palestine, as it today represents a small minority of the Israeli population. The kibbutz, however, represents a still thriving experiment in several issues of interest: alternatives to the nuclear family, attempts at nontraditional division of duties among family members, and the interplay between ideology and practice.

For the majority of the early settlers, the nuclear family held a more important place than that accorded it in many Western societies. Jewish tradition for centuries had emphasized the family as the central unit in the social structure, and most settlers in early Palestine retained these attitudes. Even here, however, the family underwent a reformulation. While Zionist ideology was not concerned with the role of the family per se, Zionist egalitarian ideals had direct implications for the way in which family life was organized. Belief in greater equality between the sexes, economic and political roles for women outside the family, and even the increased independence of children were incorporated into the traditional view of the family. The nuclear family emerged very strong but different.

Thus, in Israel, attitudes toward the family have tended to collect at the extremes, and may provide a unique focus for many of the issues involved in this discussion. In addition, there has been in Israel a rather provocative development concerning another aspect of the family. Undoubtedly, the most important factor leading to changes in the nature of the family in the last half century has been the changing role of women in society, in particular their increased participation in the labor force and the resulting pressures for greater equality in all areas of life. The early kibbutz placed very heavy stress on sexual equality, a natural partner to the reduction in the role of the nuclear family. The division of labor was carried out without regard to sex. The government of the kibbutz was shared among men and women, and women had equal political weight in all decisions. Outside the kibbutz as well, working women's organizations developed early, stressing the role of women in the labor force and opposing all forms of discrimination on the basis of sex. Women participated in the underground defense of the country and after the establishment of the state in 1948 were routinely drafted into the army. Indeed, the image of the girl soldier and of the woman who served as Prime Minister, Minister of Foreign Affairs, and Secretary of the largest political party, Golda Meir, have become clichés of the Israeli woman. Yet today, on many objective grounds, Israeli women do not fare much better than their counterparts in other Western countries.

Some of the arguments which have been advanced for this process of diminishing sexual equality will be discussed, in particular as they relate to underlying changes in the nature of the family over time.

Early Attitudes Toward the Family

No reader will be surprised to learn that the population of Israel is heterogeneous. The early settlers in Palestine at the turn of the century were urban intellectuals from Eastern Europe and Russia interested in creating an egalitarian society and, for some, a collective socialist society. During and following World War II, European Jews from all backgrounds came as refugees to the then British Mandate. The Jewish populations of the Arabic countries in Asia and Africa, uneducated and unfamiliar with modern conditions, were brought to the new country after the founding of the state in 1948. In addition to these Jewish populations there was the Arab population of Israel.

These groups represented the extremes of political ideology and economic and social sophistication. So it is not surprising that attitudes toward something as fundamental as the role of the family should take on extremes as well. For the Jews from Arabic countries and for Israeli Arabs, the family occupied the central role usually accorded it in traditional, less-developed societies. The family, often the extended family, was the focal point of social, economic, and political life. For the Jewish population in particular this importance was heightened by the role played by the family throughout centuries of Jewish religion and custom. And for most Jews from Europe as well, the family held a dominant role, reinforced by experience as a minority group where the family often served as a buffer against the hostile larger society.

For most of the population of Israel the family probably played a more important role than that accorded it in most Western countries. These attitudes toward the importance of the family carried implications for the role of women as well, of course. Within the populations from Asian/African countries, Jews and Arabs alike, and for much of the European Jewish population, the woman's role was contained within the family, with little room for a political or economic role outside the home. The extremes of this attitude can be found in Israel today in Jewish religious orthodoxy, where the woman's role is strictly confined to bearing and raising children and managing the household. Education is separate for boys and girls and the curriculum widely disparate. While the role of the woman within the family is broad in its powers, outside the family it is negligible.

The family was accorded a much different role in the early kibbutzim, collective communities ranging from 100 to 2,000 persons. In these settlements, the closely knit, nuclear family was looked upon as a threat to the development of the larger community.[1] Accordingly, the role of the family was minimized and the traditional tasks of the family were turned over to the community. All property belonged to the community and all needs were provided for by the community. Moreover, the community, through its general assembly, decided on what should be provided. Although each family had its own room or rooms, children from infancy were raised separately in a communal children's house with other children of their own age group. Children visited their parents several hours daily, but were raised as a group by members of the community assigned to the task. The community was run as a single household where meals were prepared and served in communal rooms. Clothing was purchased and laundered by kibbutz members assigned to the task.

Membership regulations of the kibbutz required each able-bodied adult member, regardless of sex, to work a full-time schedule of tasks assigned to him by a central committee responsible for the division of labor in the community. Accordingly, all women were members of the labor force and were expected to participate in the heavy manual work of reclaiming and cultivating the land, construction, and road building. Similarly, men were allocated work in the kitchens and the laundry.

---

[1] Not all kibbutzim subscribed to these views regarding the family. Most notably, those formed by religious groups did not accept them.

Even without the emphasis on sexual equality which accompanied the goal of income equality, it is clear that the communal structure of the kibbutz had far-reaching implications for the role of women. The traditionally female tasks were carried out by the community. More important, the communal production and distribution of income meant that the woman was economically independent of her husband. In addition to having an equalizing effect on the balance of power within the family, this independence had implications for the dissolution of marriages. Widowhood or divorce on the kibbutz did not result in a decline in a woman's standard of living, as in other societies.

The early emphasis on sexual equality was reflected outside the kibbutz as well. The full political rights of women in the pre-state Jewish political framework to vote and to be elected were attained as early as 1920, despite the strong opposition of orthodox religious groups. Women shared fully in the settlement and underground defense of the country before the establishment of the state and were drafted into the army from 1948 on. In 1921 the first conference of working women was held. The Working Women's Council aimed at broadening vocational areas in which women would be accepted and at providing vocational training which would allow women to engage in agriculture and manufacturing. Agricultural training homesteads for women in the 1920s, for example, produced reserves for later cooperative farming settlements. From the start, the Working Women's Council, along with other major women's organizations, established all-day prekindergarten nurseries throughout the country, enabling mothers to enter the labor force.

Thus, there was a strong emphasis on a major role for women outside the family. While the nuclear family retained its importance for the majority of the population—the nonkibbutz population—the emphasis on women in the labor force and in political life clearly had an impact on family life outside the kibbutz as well.

The Process of Nation-building:
Economic and Political Factors

The two opposing attitudes toward the family and the role of women which coexisted in the early years of the country—the centrality of the family, derived from the traditions of the Jews and their experience throughout history as a minority group and, at the opposite extreme, the kibbutz's early suspicion of the family as an obstacle to communal life—were the two ideol-

ogies brought to the country. The very process of building the country, however, brought into play several forces which left a strong mark on both attitudes. The first of these was an economic requirement to increase the level
of output and the standard of living of the population. In the early days this
took the form of increasing agricultural output through irrigation, swamp
drainage, and improved production methods. Later, it followed the usual
patterns of early industrialization. The need to enlarge the economic base of
the country both for security reasons and to absorb large-scale immigration
required a strong ideological emphasis on the value of work. This extended
to women in the labor force as well. Work outside the home acquired high
status, which was implemented by the early emphasis on women's equality.
While the family remained important, the "woman's place is in the home"
ideal never became instilled as the natural order of things. To the contrary,
this attitude was associated with immigrants from Asian and African countries and was considered outmoded. The entry of such immigrant women
into the labor force was regarded as the first sign of successful adaptation to
Israeli society. Only among the extreme orthodox religious groups was it
considered ideal that the woman have no independent role in society. Although she might work outside the home, it was never far outside—a fam-
ily-owned shop, for example—and this never extended to an independent
social or political role.

The second requirement in the new land was to increase the size of the
population. Based on security considerations in the early days, it became a
desire to replace populations lost in World War II Europe. It was a personal
goal, as European Jews sought to rebuild from the remnants of their families; it became a collective goal as well, to rebuild the Jewish people.

For women, the two goals were of course contradictory. Women were
at the same time expected to participate fully in the labor force and to bear
and rear four or five children. The strength of the double-role ideology in
Israel today—woman as worker and also as superperfect housewife—can
undoubtedly be traced back to these early conflicting pressures. Israel is not
alone in this phenomenon, but the intensity of the attitude is unusual for a
country which refrained from idealizing the woman's role in the home.

The third requirement of the new country was the absorption of large
numbers of impoverished immigrants, those from Europe immediately after
World War II and those from Middle Eastern countries following the establishment of the state. Between 1948 and 1955, for example, 400,000 immigrants were brought to Israel from North Africa and the Arab countries of
the Middle East, increasing the population by roughly a third. A large part

of the enormous task of integrating these families, unfamiliar with modern living conditions, into Israeli life fell to the women's organizations. One result of this was a significant shift in the focus of these groups away from women's rights in the labor force to the instruction of immigrant women in modern homemaking.

The last factor influencing the role of the family and of women in the family was the continual state of war and the pervasive influence of the military. Israel has experienced four wars since 1948 and numerous conflicts in the pre-state period. In all of these, casualties were high relative to the size of the country.[2] The population of Israel is 3.5 million compared with a combined total of 50 million in the surrounding Arab nations. Military and security matters therefore continue to be of overriding importance, involving not only large economic costs but, more important, high costs in terms of time and lives.

Such factors cannot fail to have a strong influence on family life. All Israeli males at age eighteen are drafted into the army for three years. All males to age fifty-four are subject to one and a half to two months per year of army reserve duty. This places serious constraints on women to remain in the home. Moreover, the increased probability of loss of husbands and sons leads to an awareness of the importance of the family and, probably, to higher birth rates. Lastly, the importance of the army cannot help but produce a masculinity cult, as well as a heightened awareness of the uneven burdens placed on men and women with respect to the military.

As in any other country, outside influences have shaped the underlying attitudes and ideologies. What makes Israel a special case in this respect, perhaps, is the force of these factors: rapid economic growth, intense pressures on families to bear more children, and harsh security requirements.

Policy and the Family

Israel began with two contradictory attitudes toward the family and two contradictory attitudes toward the role of women in the family and in society. Both extremes were influenced by economic and political forces peculiar to Israel. In addition, these opposing attitudes naturally influenced each other.

---

[2] The casualty rate in the Yom Kippur war (1973), which lasted only seventeen days, was higher than the total number of deaths in Vietnam relative to the U.S. population over the entire course of U.S. involvement in the war.

With respect to the importance of the family, it is clear that the kibbutz-based notion of the inferiority of the nuclear family as the prime social unit has given way to a more traditional attitude toward the family's role. Over time, the kibbutz population has remained constant—roughly 3 percent of the total population. The more radical ideas of the kibbutz, including the attitude toward the family, did not have wide appeal in the rest of the population.[3] Moreover, within the kibbutz itself, the role of the family has expanded. Children's time with parents has increased significantly, and many of the household tasks previously allocated to the community have been returned to the family. Many kibbutz children now sleep in their family's living quarters, for example, and the pattern is spreading rapidly.

The more traditional attitude of the importance of the family has held its own, despite the pressures of the kibbutz and the more recent pressures of industrialization and geographical mobility.[4] It is probably safe to conclude that the role of the family is stronger in Israel than in most Western countries. Close family ties are maintained, and the family is an important center of social life. Israelis tend to marry early, divorce with less frequency than their counterparts in other Western countries,[5] and almost never elect not to have children. Government policy reflects these attitudes, as would be expected. Income maintenance is based on a universal program of family allowances; housing policy is directed almost solely toward families; and policy with respect to working women tends to concentrate on child-oriented measures.

The trend in attitudes toward the role of women is more complex. Both extreme attitudes have moved toward the center. The traditional attitude regarding woman's place in the home has lost ground, and there is an acceptance among the sons and daughters of immigrants from the Arabic countries, if not among the parents, of the appropriateness of woman's employment outside the home. Much of this change in attitude can be attributed to the early emphasis on women's equality and much, undoubtedly, to the pressures of an increasing standard of living. For the lower-income popula-

[3] The influence of the kibbutz with respect to egalitarianism and social morality has been enormous, however. Today, the kibbutz population is roughly 100,000 persons in some 240 settlements.

[4] Admittedly, the adverse influence of mobility is likely to be minor in Israel, a small country with closed borders.

[5] The divorce rate in Israel is 0.9 per 1,000, compared with 2.1 in Great Britain, 3.1 in Sweden, and 4.6 in the U.S. *United Nations Demographic Yearbook*, 1975.

tion in particular many of the products of an advanced economy can be purchased only with the contribution of the wife's earnings. This development is not surprising and is not unique to Israel.

What is more surprising is that there is probably less sexual equality in Israel now than existed fifty years ago. The early emphasis on division of labor without regard to sex, the accepted notion of woman's participation in the governing of the kibbutz, and the early pressures to eliminate sex discrimination in the labor force have all but disappeared.

Yet it is probably fair to say that Israeli women have a stronger subjective feeling of equality than women in most Western countries.[6] They are, for example, drafted into the army at age eighteen for a period of twenty-four months.[7] They are expected to manage the affairs of their families and also work outside the home during the long periods of their husbands' reserve duty. Moreover, the "feminine mystique," glorifying women as full-time homemakers, was never a factor in Israel, nor is the infant advertising industry capable of promoting such sex typing in the near future.

In addition, a "male culture" centered on sports activities and public bars never developed in Israel, so that leisure activities tend to be shared by men and women.[8] These preferences more than likely have their roots in Israeli youth culture, which is decidedly coeducational. Boys and girls participate together in youth organizations and spend their time in joint hiking, cultural, and scouting activities. These activities tend to create an atmosphere of mutual respect not based exclusively on sex appeal and sexuality. Hence the Western woman's plight of being perceived mainly as a sex object does not seem to be true in the case of the typical Israeli woman.

Moreover, socialistic norms of class equality, which find their expression in a relatively small wage differential and minimal status distinction between people of different occupational rank, have a leveling effect on the rank differentials between the sexes as well. The status and income differential between a doctor (usually a man) and his nurse (almost always a woman) in many countries is substantial and has the effect of creating social distance. This is much less true in Israel.

[6] Much of this section and the general discussion concerning the role of women in Israel owes a large debt to an excellent paper by the late Dorit Padan-Eisenstark, professor and head of the Behavioral Sciences Department at the Ben-Gurion University of the Negev at the time of her death. See "The Uneven Pace of Equality," *KIDMA—Israel Journal of Development*, Vol. II, No. 3 (1975).

[7] This was increased from twenty months following the Yom Kippur war when it was decided that women had been underutilized by the army.

[8] This is less true for the population from Asian/African countries.

For these reasons the Israeli woman may consider herself on a more equal footing with men than her counterpart in other Western countries. On other grounds, however, she fares no better than other Western women. With respect to professional attainment, Israeli women hold the same small proportions of various professions. They are only 7 percent of all lawyers; 5 percent of engineers; 7 percent of school principals and supervisors; 31 percent of all physicians (but primarily in local health clinics rather than in hospitals); and 22 percent of university faculty members, but only 2 percent of those with professorial rank.

Furthermore, the double-role ideology, which sees woman's employment as an addition to her central role as housewife and mother, is as prevalent in Israel as elsewhere. Several studies indicate that successful Israeli career women have a larger than average number of children and are intent on keeping a perfect household, as if to prove that their success is not at the expense of their "primary" role.[9] The possibility that homemaking and child rearing could be a joint obligation of the spouses plays no role either in the Israeli family or in government policy.

Even within the kibbutz, the early gains by women have given way dramatically. Women are now concentrated in the child care and service facilities and the men in the agricultural and industrial work. This trend is more surprising, given the persistence of ideological commitments in other areas of kibbutz life.

Israeli women, in other words, are not better off than their counterparts in other Western countries. Neither are they worse off. However, the question arises as to why their relative position is not stronger, given the fact that Israel antedated many other countries in its positive ideology toward sexual equality and its many practical efforts to implement that ideology.

Several explanations have been offered to account for this phenomenon. The diminishing equality between the sexes in Israel is clearly a complex issue and well beyond our scope here. However, the issue itself and the factors involved are clearly pertinent to the basic discussion of the changing role of the family.[10]

[9] For a discussion of career women in Israel see, for example, Dorit Padan-Eisenstark, "Career Women in Israel: Their Birth Order and Their Siblings—Group Sex Composition," *Journal of Marriage and the Family*, XXXIV (1972), 552–56.

[10] The reader is referred to several analyses: Ada Maimon, *Women Build a Land* (New York: Herzl Press, 1962); Lionel Tiger and Joseph Shepher, *Women in the Kibbutz* (New York: Harcourt, Brace, Jovanovich, 1975); Yosef Criden and Saadia Gelb, *The Kibbutz Experience: Dialogue in Kfar Blum* (New York: Herzl Press, 1974); Rivka Bar Yosef and Ilana Einhorn Shelach, "The Position of Women in Israel," in S. N. Eisenstadt, Rivka Bar Yosef, and Chaim

The arguments take essentially three forms. The first emphasizes the fact that full sexual equality was never achieved, nor really intended, in the early kibbutz for several reasons. To begin with, the concept of sex equality in the initial stages of the kibbutzim was "male-biased." The ideology elevated the masculine standard in personality characteristics, aptitudes, and occupational roles to a single and superior norm for both men and women, thus relegating all traditional female attributes and roles to a second-rate status.

> This masculine heroic image was part of the Zionist ideology which tried to set up an ideal image of the "new Jew" as a farmer and armed defender of his country, excelling in physical prowess and combat bravery. This ideal of the "new Jew" was, in fact, a counter-image of the intellectual and physically unassertive Jew of the European ghetto. Moreover, while women were expected to work in "masculine" farming occupations requiring strenuous physical work, men were expected to play no more than an auxiliary role in the communal services, and nobody ever thought that baby and infants' care might also be a man's work. Hence when the children were born and the service sector expanded, it was the women who were expected to carry most of the added burdens. It was at this point that the "exodus" of women from the fields to the kitchen started.[11]

As the major concern of the kibbutz shifted from the harsh physical conditions of the early years—the reclamation of swamps, widespread malarial infection, lack of water, and harassment by hostile neighbors, conditions which required the participation of men and women alike—to the more prosperous years with larger settlements and larger families, the need for housekeeping and child care services grew and women found themselves back in their traditional roles. Soon, services and education became the women's central occupational domain. They had, in effect, exchanged their traditional feminine household duties for collective ones. They began to question whether, in a situation in which household tasks were to be their lot anyway, they would not prefer the traditional private duties to the new collective ones. Thus began the return to the nuclear family. The kibbutz had succeeded in changing the woman's role without at the same time changing that of the man, and consequently never moved very far from a traditional division of labor.

Adler, eds., *Integration and Development in Israel* (Jerusalem: Israel Universities Press, 1970); Judith Krausz, "The Role of Women in Israel's Development," *KIDMA—Israel Journal of Development*, Vol. II, No. 3 (1975).

[11] Padan-Eisenstark, "The Uneven Pace of Equality."

The second line of reasoning tends to emphasize the forces at work in society at large: the distraction of women's organizations from the role of women in the labor force to the introduction of new immigrants to modern homemaking; the centrality of the army, which cultivated a male culture and solidarity and emphasized the unequal military burden of men and women; and, in particular, religious extremism. Besides its discriminating legal aspects, certain Jewish rituals tend to symbolize and perpetuate women's traditional, unequal role. The absence of a special ritual signifying the birth of a daughter, contrasted to the major celebration of the rite of circumcision after the birth of a son, is only one example. In contrast to modern trends among many Jewish communities elsewhere which have started to revise women's place in Jewish rituals, traditional discriminatory practices largely prevail in Israel.

The final line of reasoning suggests that the major innovations in women's life in the kibbutz failed to stimulate new social patterns primarily due to the preferences of the women themselves for the more traditional female work roles. These preferences, the argument goes, are the product of millennia of evolutionary development in which the biological differences between the sexes produced one sex, the female, more inclined and more suited to child rearing and domestic tasks. It was the women themselves, and not the men or society, who turned their backs on the early efforts toward equality.[12]

Whatever the factors, diminution of sexual equality has left its mark on policy toward the family and toward women. In general, policy has reflected the dual status of women by concentrating female employment policies on child-oriented programs, such as subsidized child care and special working provisions for mothers. Little attention has been paid to other areas of employment policy, such as wage or promotion discrimination or the encouragement of joint husband/wife responsibility for child care. The attitude that woman's central role is one of child rearing and household management has prevailed in the population and has been reflected in policy.

Current Policy Questions

In 1975 a high-level commission on the status of women was appointed in conjunction with International Woman's Year. In the absence of an office

---

[12] This argument is developed in Tiger and Shepher, *Women in the Kibbutz*.

concerned with the interests of the family and due to the natural link between the role of women and the family, this commission has been the
source of much of the current discussion concerning the role of the family.

The commission has confronted some of the difficult issues involved in
formulating policies directed toward women in the labor force and women in
the family. What is the proper role of the government in fostering the notion
of joint husband/wife responsibility for child care, for example? Should the
revolution start within the family itself, or is it government's role to encourage changes by offering various economic incentives: work leaves for care
of sick children for men as well as women, leaves for men following the
birth of a child, and so forth?

Policies of this nature emphasize the equality of men and women. An
alternative argument can be made for recognition of the essential differences
between men and women; in other words, a government policy to compensate women for their special role as producers of the nation's children. This
line of reasoning lies behind compulsory maternity leaves, shorter working
hours for women in the period following childbirth, and work leaves for
child sickness.[13] An interesting issue which arises in this context is the
proper agent for compensation. If employers are forced to compensate
women for the special costs they bear as child bearers and child rearers,
there is an incentive for them to discriminate against women in hiring. In
Israel, employers absorb the cost of shorter working hours for women in the
year following childbirth (one hour less per day), and have acknowledged a
reluctance to hire women for this reason. This is particularly striking in a
country where employers lose on average a month and a half per year of
male workers' time due to military reserve duty. However, while employers
bear the cost of decreased efficiency due to interrupted work schedules, the
government rather than the employers bears the direct cost of compensation
to the workers for lost wages.

Another conceptual issue which arises is the proper division between
the family and society with respect to bearing the cost of children. The nation's children are clearly a public good, even in countries without a pronatalist policy. On the other hand, it is not for patriotism alone that families
rear children. The question then arises as to how much of the cost of children should be borne by members of the society who do not derive private
satisfaction from children.

Other issues currently under discussion include the government's role

---

[13] An interesting illustration of this conflict is that the same legislation—prohibition of night
work for women—was treated as positive and protective, and negative and paternalistic, respectively in two consecutive articles by women in a recent journal.

in more explicit recognition of the value of woman's work in the home by social security coverage for housewives; legalized abortion for reasons other than the health of the mother; legal aid in cases concerning sex discrimination; and the desirability of instituting a system of quotas for women in workers' councils and in the lists of political parties.

The Family in Israel

The preceding discussion has attempted to elicit from the experience of Israel some insights into the modern role of the family and the role of women within the family. Israel has witnessed various attempts to move away from traditional concepts regarding both, with varying degrees of success. Obviously, it is difficult and more than likely unwise to generalize on the basis of these experiments. Nevertheless, we offer some concluding remarks concerning the family and the role of women which seem pertinent to the experience of Israel.

First of all, the nuclear family survived a concerted effort to bypass it in favor of a larger social unit. That the ideas of the kibbutz regarding the family did not spread to the rest of Israeli society is not surprising. The kibbutz, after all, was quite revolutionary in all its aspects and, perhaps predictably, of limited appeal. What is more pertinent is that the early attitudes did not survive in the kibbutz itself where conditions were most propitious. It is possible, of course, that these strong preferences for the nuclear family are particular to Israel only. That they exist in Israel is of little doubt, however.

Secondly, and regardless of what other reasons there may be, it appears that the failure to divide the tasks of child care equally between men and women in the early kibbutzim played a major role in the breakdown of sexual equality. In a broader context, as long as women are first and foremost responsible for the rearing of children, they are constrained from full participation in the labor force. They are less likely, for instance, to undertake the initial concentrated investment in education and training required for the modern labor force and thereafter to gain the important early years of work experience which are necessary to capitalize on the initial investment. They are, in addition, less likely to undertake the extra commitments of time and energy required to achieve even limited success. And as long as women do not achieve economic independence through the labor force, they are not likely to achieve full equality. The real requirement, it appears, is not so much a change in the role of women as a change in the role of men.

In addition, it seems that sexual equality is more easily attained in a framework of coeducation and coeducational leisure activities for the young where all aspects of life are shared from an early age. In Israel there are other reasons as well for the absence of a strong male culture, but the methods of organizing the young loom very large.

Nevertheless, the future of the nuclear family in Israel seems fairly secure. The significant changes are more likely to appear in the roles of men and women within the family.

Current Policy with Respect to the Family

The maintenance and promotion of the family per se do not constitute an explicit policy goal in Israel. There is no office guarding the interests of the family, and "family well-being" has never been included in anyone's list of the national goals. However, it is possible to venture, given the place accorded the family in the national mentality (despite the early efforts of the kibbutz movement) that explicit recognition of this type might be redundant. It is quite possible that this is the case in most countries. However, the traditional importance of the family is heightened in Israel by the special role it has played in the history and culture of the Jewish people.

Despite the absence of explicit recognition, it is possible to identify in all areas of social and economic policy a concern for the family. Family allowances form the basis of income-maintenance policy; housing assistance is directed almost solely toward families; and child care facilities are designed not to replace the family but to aid and supplement its traditional role. In many cases it is impossible to separate those policies designed to aid the family per se from those directed to individual members of the family. There are few policies, however, which aid the individual *against* the interests of the family. Social security pensions for working wives, for example, are not related to the amount of the spouse's pension. Public welfare support does not discriminate against families with employable male heads, as in the U.S.[14] Income tax returns are filed separately for husband and wife. In other words, there are few incentives for the dissolution of marriages or the retardation of the formation of new families.

The picture is less clear with respect to the definition of the family, that is, the recognition in matters of policy of changes in the underlying nature of

[14] For an analysis of the effects of such programs on family stability see Marjorie Honig, "AFDC Income, Recipient Rates, and Family Dissolution," *Journal of Human Resources*, IX (1974), 303–22.

the family. For most policy purposes, single-parent families or families with unmarried parents are treated equivalently to the traditional husband/wife family, as in tax and income-maintenance policy. However, since all matters concerning marriage and divorce procedures are relegated to religious courts, Jewish religious law, which poses special constraints on the rights of divorced women and widows, prevails. Divorced women may not marry a member of the priestly class, and widows without sons are required to marry their husband's brother if he is unmarried. While the restrictions in these special cases may be avoided, and without loss of rights in all areas of civil law—by marriage or divorce outside Israel in the first case, for example— the procedures are costly both financially and emotionally. However, efforts to introduce the alternative of civil marriage and divorce for the nonreligious population have consistently been defeated due to the religious political parties' strategic role in forming the governing coalition of minority parties.

There has been, moreover, no attempt to provide special consideration to single-parent families for expenses relating to their particular status, such as additional child care requirements, counseling, and so on, as has been done in several other countries.

Policy toward women, on the other hand, has been more explicit, especially as regards their role in society at large. Voting rights were attained early in the century; special laws regarding working conditions were established soon after; and discrimination on the basis of sex was prohibited after the establishment of the state. In addition, there has been considerable legislation concerning the rights of women within the family, directed largely toward protecting the rights of Arab women and Jewish women immigrants from the Middle Eastern countries: prohibition of polygamy, marriage before age seventeen, and unilateral divorce; and the establishment of free and compulsory education for boys and girls.

Women in the Labor Force

Since the increasing participation of women in the labor force has been one of the major factors leading to changes within the family, and in the role of the family in society, it is perhaps appropriate to start with this area.

Women constitute about one third of the civilian labor force, and about a third of adult women work outside the home.[15] As elsewhere, the partici-

---

[15] In 1974 the labor force participation rate of all women aged fourteen to sixty-four years was 0.34. Among Jewish women, the participation rates for married women in 1975 with one child was 0.46; two children, 0.40; and three and more children, 0.24. The rate for Jewish married women born in Israel was 0.47; born in Asia/Africa, 0.22; and born in Europe/America, 0.34.

pation rates of married women in particular have risen dramatically in the post-World War II period. In 1955, for example, 25 percent of married women in Israel aged fourteen and above were in the labor force, compared to 33 percent at present. Not surprisingly, wide ethnic variations exist. The participation of Jewish women immigrants from Middle Eastern countries is low, and that of Arab women even lower. This stems from the traditional attitudes of these populations concerning woman's "proper place," as well as the more modern constraints of large family size and low educational attainment. What is important to note is that the participation rates for daughters of the Jewish women in this category do not differ from those of the rest of the female population, and well-educated young Arab women are making strong advances in this direction.

Policy in this area has always been to encourage women to enter the labor force and has been concentrated in family-oriented policies, such as the provision of subsidized child care facilities and special working conditions for women with young children. Much less attention has been given to family-neutral policies, such as the assurance of nondiscriminatory wage and promotion policies or the encouragement of professional goals for women in early education. Israel, it is true, is not alone in this approach; nor has it been accidental. The dual goals of female labor force participation and a high birth rate have led to an emphasis on easing the difficulties of labor force entry for women with children. The emphasis in the early years on non-sex-stereotyped occupational division, moreover, does not find its counterpart in current policy.

Israel is well-known for its network of excellent kindergartens and part-time day care centers, both private (but government regulated) and public. The majority of these have been established and operated for several decades by the women's organizations with extensive government support. As of 1973, roughly 80 percent of three-year-olds and 90 percent of four-year-olds attended half-day kindergartens, with efforts being made to reach the remaining children. Private kindergartens are also available for two-year-olds but on a more limited basis.

With respect to all-day child care facilities, it is an explicit policy goal to meet the full demand for such facilities, estimated at roughly 85 percent of all families with young children with working mothers. Less than one half of these places are currently available, serving 25,000 children. This compares with a total of only 6,900 places available in 1970.

What is perhaps more important is that the major constraint on full utilization of day care centers arises from scarce resources rather than reluctance to use such facilities. In contrast to many Western countries in which, until the last decade, attitudes toward institutional care were adverse, a positive attitude toward sending children to outside care has prevailed in Israel from the early years of the country. This stems in large part from the attitudes toward family and communal life held by the early settlers and expressed in the social organization of the kibbutz, and in part from the early intention, maintained to the present, to use the child care facilities for educational as well as caretaker purposes.

There is a strong emphasis on the use of professional personnel in all kindergartens and day centers, and private kindergartens (those outside the framework of the major women's organizations) are government regulated. There has not been to date an analysis of the costs and benefits of providing public child care of such high quality relative to private alternatives, nor has there been an attempt to separate total costs between caretaker costs and those which can be attributed to the educational purposes intended. Construction costs of the facilities are financed primarily by the government, and the government plays a major role in covering operating costs as well. Monthly fees to each family are income-conditioned, dependent on the mother's earnings alone; husband's earnings and other family income are not considered. (This policy, by the way, reinforces the notion already strong in the population that child care costs are to be borne by the mother rather than jointly by husband and wife.)

Resource limitations have resulted in a concentration of full-day child care services in poorer neighborhoods, where there is special emphasis on providing disadvantaged children with compensatory educational and cultural programs. For the most part, middle-income parents must resort to more expensive private arrangements during working hours.

Several additional policies concerning the employment of women have been family- or child-oriented: mandatory three-month maternity leave with nearly full pay; job guarantee for one year following childbirth for women who decide not to return to work immediately; shorter working hours in the year following childbirth; in the civil service, reduced hours for women with at least two children under the age of twelve; and work absence for mothers due to the illness of children.

Policy regarding female labor force participation has been almost solely family-oriented, directed to encourage the employment of women outside the home but not at the expense of a lower birth rate. That the birth rate has fallen considerably despite these policies is not surprising. Several other trends have worked in the opposite direction, including the increased value of women's time due to higher potential wages resulting from higher educational attainment. Nevertheless, it has been the intention of government policy to attempt to offset these influences.

Demographic Policy

Perhaps the most explicit intention of the government to alter incentives with respect to the family has been its demographic policy. In the early years of the state this took the form of a simple pronatalist goal of increasing the number of births. In more recent years, with increased recognition of the links between large family size, low income, and cultural disadvantage, pronatalist goals have been focused on the middle-income, small family, nevertheless recognizing the difficulties of devising effective policies with such a selective goal.

However, even in the earlier period, policy tended to concentrate more on exhortation than on financial incentives regarding children. Relative to several other Western countries the demographic policy in Israel has been muted. Although the income-maintenance system was developed in the late 1950s on the basis of universal child allowances, the value of the allowances remained small. As late as 1969, child allowances for a family of four children amounted to only 8 percent of the average monthly wage in Israel, compared to 37 percent in France, 23 percent in Sweden, and 15 percent in the United Kingdom. Only with the growing awareness of the relationship between family size and poverty, and the efficiency therefore of a program of income transfers based on numbers of children, did the value of the allowances become significant. Child allowances, in other words, became important primarily as an instrument of income-maintenance policy as opposed to demographic policy. In 1975, allowances for a four-child family amounted to 28 percent of the average wage.

Although the relationship between child allowances and the birth rate has not been established empirically,[16] many countries have used this measure expressly as a pronatalist instrument. Israel, in comparison, has made relatively minor use of it.

Furthermore, the absence of government support of family-planning programs stems not from pronatalist opposition in general, but rather from the opposition of religious groups who view family planning as contrary to religious prescripts. The role of religious political parties in the government

---

[16] For an analysis of the relationship between child allowances and the birth rate see Marjorie Honig, "The Effect of Child Allowances on Fertility" (discussion paper, National Insurance Institute, Jerusalem, 1974).

precludes the adoption of widespread birth-control information programs on an official basis despite strong support within the government. Nevertheless, a program of nationwide family planning clinics is being initiated, to be operated by semipublic institutions, and several government agencies are involved in various aspects of family planning on a smaller scale. The use of contraceptive measures is widespread throughout middle- and upper-income groups, and distribution is officially encouraged. The issue of sex education in the schools is under discussion.

There is currently a program of special loans and mortgages for small families who wish to enlarge their present housing or move into larger houses. This policy is designed specifically with a selective pronatalist goal in mind, and research is being conducted to determine the impact on the birth rate of the families participating in this program.

Income Maintenance and Tax Policy

Since 1959 the income-maintenance system in Israel has been based on a program of universal child allowances, with special emphasis on large families. The government's interest in fostering the family is evident not only in the fact that the program is universal rather than income-tested—it is not, in other words, a public welfare program designed only for the low-income population—but also in its emphasis on child allowances rather than alternative forms of income maintenance, such as wage subsidies or public employment programs. In addition to the emphasis it places on the importance of the family, the program proves to be an efficient mechanism for alleviating poverty since a large part of the low-income population in Israel consists of large families.[17] As mentioned above, the value of the allowances has increased considerably over time. The following table indicates the current value of the allowances relative to the average wage for various family sizes.

Child Allowances as a Proportion of the Average Wage, 1976

	Number of Children							
	1	*2*	*3*	*4*	*5*	*6*	*7*	*8*
Percentage	4.4	8.8	7.6	28.0	38.3	49.8	61.2	72.6

A major change was introduced into the income-maintenance system in 1975 with the integration of the income-maintenance and tax systems. One

---

[17] The other major group constituting the poverty population is the aged, who are covered by a universal flat-grant benefit and a supplementary income-tested program.

of the most important effects of this change was to increase effectively the value of child maintenance to low-income families. Prior to the reform, child support had consisted of a mixed system of direct, nontaxable cash grants to large families, taxable grants to families of one and two children, and tax exemptions for children in the income tax system. The system of tax exemptions was particularly regressive since the value of the exemption was positively related to income level. High-income families subject to high marginal tax rates received, in effect, larger reductions in their tax bill than lower-income families. Families below the tax threshold, those who paid no taxes, received no benefit from the exemption.

The 1975 reform converted the mixed system to a unified program of tax credits based on child allowances. Under a tax credit system, as opposed to tax exemptions, benefits based on the number of children in the family are subtracted not from gross income (to obtain the amount of the family's taxable income), but from the family's tax bill. In this way, families of the same size but different income levels receive the same reduction in the amount of the taxes they must pay, that is, the same monetary benefit from the program of child allowances. Families below the tax threshold, whose tax bill is zero, receive a cash payment from the system.[18]

The new system, therefore, is constructed as a universal demogrant based on the number of children. It is clearly a family-oriented program; individuals or childless couples do not receive benefits under this program. (They may, however, be eligible for categorical programs, such as assistance to the aged, survivors, or disabled.) There is, as well, income-tested support available to individuals or families whose combination of earnings plus support from categorical programs is not sufficient for their needs— large families in which the head may be unemployed or whose total earnings are low. This program is available to all families; it does not exclude families with an employable (though not employed) male head, for example.

The system of child allowances/tax credits, the categorical aid programs (aged, disabled, workmen's compensation, unemployment), and a program of maternity allowances are administered by a single government agency, the National Insurance Institute. The maternity program, clearly a family-oriented policy, covers all costs of childbirth in hospitals, gives cash grants to the mother for clothing for the infant, and replaces 75 percent of the woman's wage for the twelve weeks following childbirth.

The program to cover in-hospital childbirth costs was initiated to en-

[18] The administration of the system at present is somewhat different, but the principles follow the discussion above.

courage hospital childbirths and was directed particularly to the Jewish immigrants from Arabic countries and to the Arab population. Nearly all Jewish births now take place in hospitals, and the proportions for the primarily rural Arab population have increased from 4 percent in 1948 to 89 percent in 1973. Infant mortality among the Arab population has been reduced from 60 per 1,000 to 31 per 1,000 in the same period.

The reform of 1975 substantially increased incentives for women to participate in the labor force. Sizable tax deductions for working women were introduced to compensate for the extra costs of housekeeping and child care. In addition to the regular tax credits for each child in the family, a man with a nonworking wife is allocated two personal credits and a credit for his wife. If the wife works, the husband receives two personal credits; the wife herself receives two personal credits plus an additional credit for each two children. Prior to the reform, a system of separate tax filing for husbands and wives was instituted to insure more equitable tax treatment of the wife's increment to family income.

Divorced women, and women of any marital status with a court order for child support, are guaranteed monthly support payments under a program established in 1972 by the National Insurance Institute. Court-determined alimony or child-support payments, or proportions of such depending on the other income sources of the woman, are paid directly by the Institute to the woman in cases where the husband fails to meet his financial obligations. In this way, women are relieved of the costly and lengthy process of suing nonsupporting husbands; such proceedings are initiated directly by the Institute. All divorced women are eligible for the program, regardless of whether their divorce was obtained in the religious courts or in civil courts. In addition, widows are covered under a universal flat-grant program and a supplementary income-tested program under the old-age and survivors program, survivor's benefits under workmen's compensation, or assistance from the Ministry of Defense if the husband was killed in military action.

Housing

Housing policy in Israel is explicitly directed toward families. Single persons are eligible for assistance only in special geographical areas and under limited conditions. On the other hand, single-parent families (widowed, divorced, or unmarried) with children under the age of twenty-one were recently included as eligible under the most extensive program of housing assistance, that directed toward young couples.

In general, housing policy has as its goal the provision of a home for every family, preferably on an ownership basis. The government has consistently pursued a policy of heavy subsidization of owner-occupied housing at the expense of rental housing, partly on ideological grounds of curbing growth of a landlord class and partly to encourage stable neighborhoods. The consequent lack of rental housing has placed a heavy financial burden on low-income families and on young couples in particular, and the government has responded with additional assistance in this area. Assistance has included public construction, public purchase of privately constructed flats, mortgages and loans for purchase and/or home improvement, as well as the provision, in the last resort, of low-rental, long-term lease housing. In principle, any family which does not own its own home or apartment is eligible for some type of assistance. The extent and terms of assistance depend on family size, present living conditions, and family income. It is assumed that parents will assist children in the purchase of homes but understood that the larger the family, the less the expected assistance.

Housing policy is linked to demographic policy to the extent that special attention is paid to the housing needs of large families. However, since large family size is strongly correlated with low income and other characteristics of poverty, it is not clear at which point demographic policy leaves off and income maintenance begins. One program, mentioned above, is specifically pronatalist in purpose. Families with two or three children are given special assistance for enlarging their living quarters or relocating in larger homes, on the assumption that the additional space will encourage one or two additional births. Whether the desired births actually occur is the subject of ongoing research.

Until recently, housing policy was directed toward the Jewish population. Originally, this occurred because of the emphasis on housing the large number of Jewish immigrants, particularly from the poorer Middle Eastern countries; later, because of the emphasis on alleviating urban slum conditions (roughly two thirds of the Arab population live in rural areas). Assistance to the Arab population was confined to a limited loan program to individual home builders and to non-Jews who served in the army. In 1976 eligibility to additional housing assistance programs was extended to the Arab population.

An interesting facet of housing policy has been the encouragement, perhaps unwittingly, of the nuclear family pattern at the expense of the extended family. Standards adopted for public housing in Israel are rooted in Western culture: multifamily dwellings with sufficient living space for each individual; separation of eating, sleeping, and entertaining areas; and individual sanitary facilities. This has involved a major change in the life style of the populations from Asian/African countries accustomed to living in an extended family setting where cooking and sanitary facilities were shared and households included several nuclear families. Among the many factors influencing the tendency toward strengthening the nuclear family and weakening bonds of kinship with members of the extended family, housing policy has undoubtedly played a role.

The Family within the Law

Legal concepts in Israel relating to the family and to women are a unique mixture of religious custom, British law from the period of the Mandate, and some of the most advanced legal practices to be found in Western countries. The latter include blameless divorce by mutual consent, a wide variety of pragmatic grounds in contended divorces, full legal property rights for married women, and equal child-custody rights of parents. The former derives from the absence of civil marriage and divorce for the Jewish population; in other words, the relegation of matters concerning marriage and divorce procedures to religious courts. (For the Arab population, marriage and divorce are dealt with in Arabic courts within the framework of civil law.) In practice, it is possible to avoid the special restrictions due to the reliance on religious custom in the rabbinical courts. Thus, a divorced woman may marry a member of the ''Cohen'' family (the priests in Jewish tradition), or any Israeli may marry any other Israeli without going to the religious courts by marrying in nearby Cyprus, for example, or by means of a marriage contract drawn up by a lawyer. These marriages are legally binding and do not lead to a loss of civil rights for the parties involved. Any issue concerning the marriage with the exception of a subsequent divorce proceeding, may be taken to civil courts. The numbers affected in these special cases are small. The major constraint arising from the absence of civil marriage and divorce is the requirement for nonreligious couples, representing the majority of the Israeli population, to comply with religious procedures.

In other aspects, Israeli law has acted to protect the rights of women within the family. Such legislation was necessary in light of the paternalistic social patterns among Jewish immigrants from Middle Eastern countries and the Israeli Arab population. Soon after the establishment of the state in 1948, the practice of polygamy was prohibited, as was the practice of child marriage. Divorce at the sole discretion of the husband was also banned. The rights of children against abuse by parents were also insured under the law.

The rights of women within the larger society were also guaranteed. Full political rights in the pre-state framework were attained in 1920 and were ratified as a matter of course with the establishment of the state. The Proclamation of Independence states that Israel "will maintain complete social and political equality for all its citizens regardless of religion, race, or sex." These conditions were made legally binding by the Law of the Equality of Women in 1951, which insured that "there will be one law for women and men. Every legal action and every judicial provision which discriminates against a woman, as a woman, is void."

The laws dealing with the rights of women workers contain certain limitations on the employment of women and have been the object of considerable disagreement among women themselves. The issue, as discussed above, concerns the desirability of treating women workers as equal to male workers in all respects, as opposed to the explicit recognition of biological differences and the additional responsibility of women as child bearers.

Education

Second only to the importance of the family, education has played a major role in Jewish tradition. In religious communities in Europe, the division of duties within the family was predicated on the necessity of religious education for the male members of the household. The complete management of the household was allocated to the woman to leave the male free to study religion and philosophy. This practice is still observed among the orthodox religious population today, and education for male children, carried out in separate schools, is far more extensive than that provided for girls.

For the majority of the population, however, the importance of education was reflected in the early adoption in Israel of free and compulsory coeducational schooling through age fourteen. This policy was opposed to the short-term interests of a segment of the population, since child labor was widely practiced.[19] The policy was also designed to promote greater equality between the sexes for those sectors of the population for whom education for girls in elementary schools rose from 15 percent in 1948 to 87 percent in 1973 and now reaches nearly 100 percent in urban areas. In the isolated rural villages the percentage is considerably lower.

There has also been improvement at the level of secondary education although not so marked. In higher education there has been progress as well

---

[19] Prohibition of the employment of children under the age of fourteen and compulsory education for children under the age of fourteen were adopted simultaneously.

but on a limited basis. In 1952 there was a single Arab female student at the Hebrew University in Jerusalem, compared to 200 in 1974.

With respect to the low-income, "culturally-deprived" population in Israel, the educational system has been viewed as an alternative superior to the family for purposes of socialization. Approximately 6 percent of all children under the age of eighteen are in boarding schools, and roughly 80 percent of these are considered deprived according to various criteria.[20] Among thirteen- to seventeen-year-olds, nearly 20 percent are in boarding schools. Both figures are high by international standards. Moreover, the schools are not financed privately as elsewhere but are highly subsidized from general government revenues. The explicit purpose of the schools has been to remove the children from family influences which have been considered adverse, either because of broken homes, excessive burdens on the parents because of family size, or the incapacity of the parents to instill desired moral and social values. Recently the policy toward children under eight years has been reversed, and they have been returned to their families with special compensatory daytime schools provided. In development towns as well, where the population consists mostly of immigrant families from Asian/African countries, criticism has been voiced that the educational system bypasses the family and considers itself the prime mechanism for socialization.

With the exception of the boarding and religious schools, schools in Israel are coeducational and foster an emphasis on joint male-female activities. This is continued in the youth clubs, which play a major role in the life of Israeli teen-agers.

Health

Although Israel does not yet have a comprehensive health insurance system, the network of government subsidized sickness funds covers nearly the entire population and provides full coverage up to and including long-term medical needs.

The health system is general in nature and has no particular policy orientation toward the family. There is in Israel, however, a special and extensive service directed toward the care of women during pregnancy and following childbirth and to the care of small children. The system is financed jointly by the central government, the municipalities, and the nonprofit hos-

---

[20] The remaining 20 percent are children with special needs, such as the deaf, blind, or retarded, or are in special religious or military schools.

pitals and is based on a widespread network of clinics. The clinics are used by all income groups, essentially free of charge, and provide convenient and efficient gynecological care in the pre- and post-childbirth periods for women, and for young children, regular examinations, inoculations, and complete preventive care. The clinics have been particularly effective in the lower-income neighborhoods where they have provided direction in modern health and child care methods, in addition to their principal medical functions.

Other Social Services

The network of social welfare services operating in Israel comprises a large number of formal organizations differing in their fields of activity, their goals, and the manner in which those goals are achieved, and in the population with access to these agencies. The sector includes at one extreme large bureaucracies serving a wide section of the population; at the other extreme are local offices with small operating budgets and staffed by volunteer workers. Accordingly, it is impossible to identify social service "policy" in general, and in particular to discriminate policy directed toward the family as opposed to individuals within the family.

In general, the agencies operating in what might be called the "economic sphere," as opposed to the provision of physical and mental health services or special care for the aged, for example, are concerned with the family as a unit.[21] These agencies range from the Ministry of Social Welfare, which handles the bulk of public welfare support for families not covered, or not covered sufficiently, under the major income-maintenance programs. The services provided by this agency are directed to the family and include monetary allocations and in-kind benefits, as well as family counseling, legal aid, and placement of children in child care facilities and foster homes. The underlying ideology is to assist the family to every extent possible, but to provide alternative care for individual members when the family is unable to fulfill its basic functions.

In contrast, the social service agencies operating in the areas of health and socialization—provision of outpatient and hospital care for physical and mental health problems, child welfare services, programs for retarded children, and so on—are directed, more appropriately, to individual family members.

[21] The terminology and much of this discussion are based on Jona M. Rosenfeld and Lotte Salzberger, *Family Needs and Welfare Provisions* (Jerusalem: Hebrew University School of Social Work, 1973).

The Military
The military has traditionally made an effort to relate to the families of servicemen. Family visits on a regular basis are encouraged, and families are invited to the ceremonies that mark the various stages in basic training or career programs. Families dependent on the financial support of draftees are covered under an income-maintenance program provided by the military, and special programs are available to assist the families in other needs as well. Considerable assistance and attention are given to the family by the military in case of injury or death of military personnel.

The topics covered here constitute the major areas in which the government, explictly or implicitly, has had an impact on the well-being of the family. In the case of Israel, it is probably correct to conclude that the government has not promoted extensively the interests of the family; nor has the family been ignored. Furthermore, the direction which future policy regarding the family will take is not clear at present. As in all countries, this is likely to depend in large part on the evolution of the family itself.

≈14

THE UNITED STATES

THE UNITED STATES does not have an explicit national family policy, and there is apparently no strong constituency currently urging one. However, in recent years some influential voices have proposed or even predicted systematic attention to the family as a primary object of public action.

Thus, one leading child development psychologist called upon a subcommittee of the United States Senate to consider "the construction of a family social policy at the national level." At the same hearings a prominent black scholar, urging "enhancing family life as a major goal of federal policies," suggested "the development of a comprehensive and coordinated family policy."[1] A leading black public official discussed before the National Urban League her concern for the black family, expressing preference for measures to support the family in its child-rearing, educational, and socialization roles as an alternative to governmental programs, while stating that "government policies should have to survive a family impact investigation."[2]

Even earlier, Daniel Patrick Moynihan had written an introduction to a new edition of Alva Myrdal's *Nation and Family* and urged that "the programs of the federal government . . . be designed to have the effect, directly or indirectly, of enhancing the stability and resources of the Negro

[1] Edward Zigler, former director, U.S. Office of Child Development, and Andrew Billingsley, testimony on *American Families: Trends and Pressures,* 1973, Hearings before the Subcommittee on Children and Youth of the Committee on Labor and Public Welfare, U.S. Senate, September 24–26, 1973 (Washington, D.C.: U.S. Government Printing Office, 1974), pp. 81–97, 302–30.

[2] Eleanor Holmes Norton, July 1975, Atlanta (unpublished). Mrs. Norton is now chairman, Equal Employment Opportunity Commission, Washington, D.C.

American family." While fully aware of elements in the ethos and the polity militating against explicit attention to the enhancement of the family, Moynihan expressed hope for "new departures" since "a nation without a conscious family policy leaves to chance and mischance an area of social reality of the utmost importance, which in consequence will be exposed to the untrammeled and frequently thoroughly undesirable impact of policies arising in other areas."[3]

But the question of family policy is not being debated as an issue of blacks or indeed of minority group members or of the poor alone. To the extent that some spokesmen raise the question of family policy they clearly address the situation of all Americans. Both Vice-President Walter Mondale, chairman of the 1973 Senate hearings, and President Jimmy Carter have urged consideration of the impact of government programs and proposed policies on family life. The President has pledged to "chart a pro-family policy."[4]

Hence there is no federal family policy, but the need for such policy is discussed, sometimes urged, and increasingly predicted. Where it is seriously considered, even in a limited and partial sense, as in 1974 and 1975 hearings to evaluate modest social services legislation, the outpouring of strongly felt and often irrational negative responses through the mails and newspaper columns from selected parts of the country suggest that the subject also touches deeply felt strains of the ethos.

Lack of Comprehensive, Explicit Federal Family Policy

The lack of a comprehensive, coherent policy does not signify absence of public dedication in the U.S. to the family as a primary societal unit.

President Lyndon B. Johnson echoed the sentiments of a long line of presidents, senators, congressmen, and Supreme Court justices when he said:

---

[3] Daniel Patrick Moynihan, *The Negro Family: the Case for National Action* (Washington, D.C.: Office of Policy Planning and Research, U.S. Department of Labor, 1965), p. 48. See also Daniel Patrick Moynihan, Foreword to Alva Myrdal, *Nation and Family* (Cambridge, Mass.: M.I.T. Press, 1968), pp. x, xvii.

[4] "Statement by 'Candidate' Jimmy Carter on the American Family," Manchester, N.H., August 3, 1976.

The family is the cornerstone of our society. More than any other force it shapes the attitudes, the hopes, the ambitions, and the values of the child. When the family collapses it is the children that are usually damaged. When it happens on a massive scale the community itself is crippled.

So unless we work to strengthen the family, to create conditions under which most parents will stay together—all the rest, schools and playgrounds, public assistance and private concern, will never be enough to cut completely the circle of despair and deprivation.[5]

Later, affirming a "national commitment to providing all American children an opportunity for a healthful and stimulating development during the first five years of life," President Richard Nixon vetoed proposed implementing legislation as not "true and tested" and in "the absence of a great national debate upon its merit and broad public acceptance of its principles." Among other things, he argued that "for the federal government to plunge headlong financially into supporting child development would commit the vast moral authority of the National Government to the side of communal approaches to child rearing and against the family-centered approach."[6]

The family and concern for its continuity are strong motives in the U.S. The family's functions are understood and valued. The ambivalence and opposition are, rather, to general public intervention, particularly at the federal level, or to particular policies or programs which are defined as potentially of negative impact upon the institution.

In short, the ethos is either negative toward, or, at best, ambivalent about, the notion of comprehensive explicit family policy at the higher levels of government. It is readily mobilized in opposition to new initiatives. On this, there is not only the evidence of the historic record—a family policy has not been proposed or enacted as such—but also the consensus of scholarship.[7] Indeed, all three major strains in the American tradition have contraindicated formal family policy: democracy, individualism, humanitarianism. The individual has been encouraged in this tradition to break away from the constraints of his family past, to make his own destiny in accord

[5] Lyndon B. Johnson, "To Fulfill These Rights," Howard University, June 4, 1965, as reprinted in Lee Rainwater and William L. Yancey, *The Moynihan Report and the Politics of Controversy* (Cambridge, Mass.: M.I.T. Press, 1967), p. 130.

[6] Richard Nixon, veto message, December 9, 1971, as reported in the *Public Papers* for 1972, pp. 1174–87.

[7] For a summary see Nathan E. Cohen and Maurice F. Connery, "Government Policy and the Family," *Journal of Marriage and the Family*, Special Issue: Government Programs and the Family, XXIX (1967), 6–17.

with his personal merit, to participate on his own responsibility, to build his own associations. The economic development of the country, responding to the opportunity offered to exercise individual initiative and talent and premised on individual opportunity and responsibility for one's personal destiny, has been rooted in social, economic, and geographic realities. The ethos has worked. It has been consistent with a religious heritage which also focused on individual merit and salvation.[8] The exceptions and casualties in a milieu featuring individual successes could be ignored in the face of an over-all record. Even charitable and human responses to casualties have tended to take the form of individualistic assessments and aid: one differentiated the "worthy" and the "unworthy."

The traditions are long and deep. Schorr quotes Calhoun, pioneer historian of the American family: ". . . it was the democratic disposition to deal with individuals, not families."[9]

In brief, we agree with Moynihan in the assessment that there is need to distinguish "between a generalized cultural piety about family life and specific social policies directed to family concerns. The two need not be complementary; most often, in American experience, they have been in conflict."[10] Laissez-faire democracy reacted against the family as carrying forward the continuity of the aristocracy and in any case objected to public involvement in private matters of which family life is the prime example. America avoided choosing among a diversity of immigrant traditions by refusing to endorse any particular family pattern. It interpreted European political history and responded to the growth of Catholic political power in the U.S. by associating interest in the family with political conservatism.[11] Because much of the early European family policy was pronatalist, liberals almost uniformly assumed that family policy meant opposition to abortion, divorce, family planning; in their assessment they ignored an equally interesting Catholic tradition which said that "the family was the basic unit of society and that nothing—neither the freedom of enterprise, nor the power of political parties—nothing was so important."[12]

But the absence of coherent, comprehensive, explicit federal family

[8] Cohen and Connery refer to major elements in the tradition. *Ibid.*, pp. 6–10.

[9] Alvin L. Schorr, quoting Arthur W. Calhoun, *A Social History of the American Family* (1917), in "Family Values and Real Life," *Social Casework,* LVII (1976), 397.

[10] Daniel P. Moynihan, *The Politics of a Guaranteed Income* (New York: Random House, 1973), p. 21.

[11] *Ibid.*, pp. 21–23.

[12] Moynihan, Foreword to Myrdal, *Nation and Family,* p xi.

policy does not signify that there is absolutely no family policy in the U.S.
True, there is no comprehensive, over-all national policy. Yet there are
many social policies relating to family concerns and, as we shall note, they
are often recognized and dealt with as such. Particularly since the mid-
1930s, as federal authorities have responded to crises, needs, problems, and
change, there has been increasing acceptance of specific actions as long as
they were not part of any grand design called "comprehensive social planning" or "family policy." Each initiative is or has been fought and debated
on its own terms, in accord with the context of its day; and actions are seldom justified or even conceived as a component of a coherent policy. Opponents sometimes have attacked the totality with characterizing terms ranging
from "welfare state" to "socialism"; but the public at large has recognized
the process as largely pragmatic and remedial, lacking a general design. Indeed, the family-relevant impact of programs might be quite extensive and
yet ignored because not recognized, and if recognized, considered nonetheless secondary. Or, as in the day care veto referred to, programs indeed
might be cited and blown up for political effect if that served a given objective. A reservoir of powerful feeling about such matters is surely present and
can be unleashed.

As noted subsequently, there have been occasional explicit and quite
manifest policies and many implicit family-relevant initiatives in income-
transfer programs, child development legislation, health programs, housing,
and in the general (personal) social service and delinquency programs—to
offer an incomplete list. And there have been "scares" about day care, family planning, abortion, and income maintenance in connection with measures
which have alerted the opponents of family policies in government.

The reality is even more complex. The U.S. is a federal republic. As
Krause notes in his basic text, the Tenth Amendment reserves to the states
most of the powers in the field which have become known as family law.
States, in turn, are also constrained by the due process clause of the Fourteenth Amendment to the United States Constitution.

Consequently, there is a rich tradition of state programs and laws which
may certainly be described as embodying relatively extensive and quite explicit family policy (although not covering the entire domain as generally
defined). As stated in 1971 by Justice Hugo L. Black, once dissenting and
once speaking for the majority:

> . . . It is not by accident that marriage and divorce have always been con-
> sidered to be under state control. The institution of marriage is of peculiar impor-

tance to the people of the States. . . . The States provide for the stability of their social order, for the good morals of all their citizens, and for the needs of children from broken homes. The States, therefore, have particular interests in the kinds of laws regulating their citizens when they enter into, maintain and dissolve marriages. (*Boddie* v. *Connecticut*)

. . . .

. . . the power to make rules to establish, protect, and strengthen family life as well as to regulate the disposition of property left in Louisiana by a man dying there is committed by the Constitution of the United States and the people of Louisiana to the legislature of that State. (*Labine* v. *Vincent*) [13]

For reasons not at all obvious most U.S. writers about family policy have neglected to consider and analyze state laws and provision. Yet brief consideration suggests the significance within family policy of the laws of marriage, divorce, annulment, abortion, parent-child relationships, adoption, foster care, child abuse and neglect, waywardness, and emancipation of minors. As much may be said of laws relating to legitimacy and illegitimacy, child support, artificial insemination, and alimony. To this one may add the role of the state in exercising options and therefore deferring or shaping many of the substantive specifics in federal-state programs in which funds are matched and the range of state choice is significant. Included here, for example, are: supplementation to Supplementary Security Income (SSI) programs for the aged, blind, and disabled; Aid to Families with Dependent Children (AFDC); unemployment insurance; housing; a variety of education programs; a diversity of health programs.

While within a given state there may be a tendency to accent specific themes (the sanctity of marriage and a refusal to permit its easy dissolution, for example, or the assurance of public assistance income at a level which reflects actual family subsistence needs), no state is known to seek over-all policy coherence or harmonization. In general, policies and programs grow by accretion. Yet states and their considerable involvement in family policy should not be ignored in any overview.

Indeed, there is rationale for the primacy of the state in many domains: a diverse society wants pluralistic solutions on subjects of great impact on primary group life and child rearing. The states reflect the range of ethnicity, religion, origins, and demographic characteristics in the U.S. From this perspective it is therefore fortunate that a major part of state business is

---

[13] Both cases quoted, with more complete citations, by Harry D. Krause, *Family Law: Cases and Materials* (St. Paul, Minn.: West Publishing Co., 1976), p. 224.

social welfare,[14] including matters of family policy, and that much policy and most implementation are left to the states.

On further examination, however, the argument has its flaws. States are within themselves hardly homogeneous in population. State policy which is attractive to one subgroup may be anathema to another, and there are citizens who find themselves disadvantaged because of their state of residence. State resources are less adequate than federal for meeting many needs. Considerable geographic mobility, a national system of communication, and mass media create what is in many ways a national community in which family policy on the state level, whether fragmented or relatively more comprehensive, is seen by many citizens as disadvantage rather than boon.

The Fourteenth Amendment and other clauses have inspired individual and class action through the courts to challenge state laws and programs. Consequently, whether on grounds of "equal protection" (which in some cases becomes the banner for territorial justice—an equal status, whatever the state of residence) or other legal grounds, the federal government finds itself as the locus of family policy by Supreme Court decision. A core of family policy had gradually emerged in this new fashion, even if seldom conceptualized as such. Special note is here taken of family planning, abortion, integration of educational facilities and housing—all major and potent domains. The status of women in the social insurance system is also being changed in the courts, perhaps preliminary to legislative overhaul. Individual and group rights, challenging state-level family policies, help shape new components of national family policy; again, not comprehensive, but becoming more so.

At the same time, another process which expands federal involvement proceeds as it has for almost fifty years. Despite constitutional protection of state powers, the Congress has responded to interests that are national in enacting federal legislation and has been upheld therein by the courts: social security, minimum wage, health insurance and assistance (Medicare and Medicaid), safety and environmental legislation, and so forth—in short, policies and programs not specifically addressed to the family but with major impact on family members and on the family as a unit. Despite the ethos, if constrained by it, and certainly not comprehensive or unitary, federal family policy and policies continue to evolve by court decision and by legislative action and provision. Meanwhile, states continue, too, to develop and ad-

---

[14] Two thirds of state and local expenditures in fiscal 1976.

minister policy and programs while the courts affirm and elaborate the rights of children, mothers, and adolescents *as individuals,* through a new series of protections. Certainly, it is a mixed picture, as attention continues to place the family, and the question of government and the family, at stage center.

What Should Be Discussed?

If a country has an explicit and comprehensive family policy, it specifies the domain through which that policy is to be implemented. The scope of a survey is thereby delimited. The U.S. does not have such a national family policy. Those explicit policies which are identifiable are never conceptualized in their totality; state policies exist in several specific fields but are not national, comprehensive, or even mutually consistent since few states think of themselves as having policy in this sense.

All of this poses a question for our overview: what fields are relevant? We have chosen to ask whether explicit or implicit family policy may be found in the "obvious" fields—domains selected in other countries as vehicles for explicit policy, and/or domains hypothesized as of major potential, having direct, visible impact on primary group life, particularly the social services (using the term in its broad, international meaning).

We do discuss taxation, income security, housing, health, education, and personal social services, but do not cover such potentially interesting fields as transportation, agriculture, commerce, environment, and so forth.

Following our survey of what must, then, be defined as the "obvious" and "traditional" sectors, we turn to another way of completing the picture: a brief overview of policies and programs affecting individual family members other than male family heads. The premise is that the way in which these potential target groups are approached may also reveal the presence or absence of a family perspective in program and policy development.

In surveying the several sectors we focus on the extent to which the family is the center of attention in each of the major fields, on the extent to which the family is employed as a vehicle for policy objectives, and on the degree to which family well-being in some sense has become a criterion for social policy.[15]

[15] The present overview is based on available materials and sources: our long-term and detailed independent research assessments of a series of domains from a family policy perspective are continuing.

The Demographic Backdrop[16]

The total population of the U.S. was estimated to be 214.4 million as of January 1, 1976. During 1975 the population grew by four fifths of one percent, which was slightly higher than the growth rate for each of the three previous years but considerably lower than in 1970 (1.09 percent).

Both birth and death rates reached their lowest levels in American history in 1975. The birth rate was 14.8 per 1,000 population, a slight decrease over the previous three years but a considerable loss since 1970 (18.4). The death rate continued to decline, if only slightly, from 9.5 per 1,000 population to 8.9 in 1975. Although there was a slight increase in immigration in 1975 as a result of the influx of Vietnamese refugees, the over-all rate of population increase (births, less deaths, plus immigration per 1,000 population) has declined from 10.9 in 1970 to 8.1 in 1975. The present age structure of the population is such that it will be many years before the U.S. attains "zero population growth," even if the present low birth rate continues. The current total birth rate, continuing the decline of the last decade and a half, is, however, well below the rate of 2.1 which is required for natural replacement.

If one projects family size from the preferences of young wives, the two-child family seems to be the preferred family size of the future. Young women under 30 have had fewer children than their counterparts in 1960 or 1970. Moreover, the preference of young married women under 25 suggests that future birth rates will decline even further, lower even than the rates established by women whose peak years of childbearing occurred during the

[16] This largely descriptive section is designed to provide only a general context for our overview of government and the family in the U.S. Indication of possible future changes, emerging demographic trends, and so forth, are not discussed here. (But we note some signs in 1977—for which final data are not yet available—of possible birth rate increases, slight marriage rises, and a divorce decline.) Such developments, their implications, and related questions have been saved for a subsequent paper which will have, as one of its major foci, demographic trends and developments related to the family and their implications for public policy. See U.S. Bureau of the Census, *Current Population Reports,* Series P-20, No. 292, "Population Profile of the United States: 1975" (Washington, D.C.: U.S. Government Printing Office, 1976); U.S. Bureau of the Census, *Current Population Reports,* Series P-20, No. 291, "Household and Family Characteristics: March 1975" (Washington, D.C.: U.S. Government Printing Office, 1976). We are indebted to the Bureau of Census staff for review of this section and some updating.

To facilitate comparability with other countries covered, we have for the most part reported 1975 data.

depression years of the 1930s. In 1976, the average number of births expected by these young women during their lifetime was 2.1, approximately one less than that of older women who had already borne nearly all the children they expected to have. Neither childlessness nor the single-child family seems to be a growing preference. In contrast, larger families of three or more children will probably be increasingly rare, if these preferences become reality.

Children in the age categories under 18 are all members of declining cohorts (from a total of 69.7 million in 1970 to 65.1 million early in 1976). By contrast, the aged population has increased and is expected to continue to increase. There are now 22.4 million people 65 and older, representing 10.5 percent of the population, an increase of 21 percent between 1960 and 1970, and an increase of over 12 percent since 1970. This growth is partly the result of the decrease in the number of births and partly because of the decline in the mortality rates of the aged since 1970. In the last five years, the median age of the population has risen almost one full year, from 27.9 in 1970 to 28.8 in 1975.

The movement of the large birth cohorts of the 1950s into the productive age groups and the decline in the number of children under 18 has somewhat offset the effect of the growth in the number of aged in the population. As a consequence, the over-all dependency ratio (the total population under 18 and 65 and over per 100 population aged 18–64) has dropped from 78 to 71 between 1970 and 1975. In assessing this, however, it is important to note the composition of this measure. To obtain a more accurate picture one must look at both the child dependency ratio (the population under 18 per 100 aged 18–64) and the aged dependency ratio (the population 65 and over per 100 aged 18–64). Between 1970 and 1975, the child dependency ratio declined sharply from 60.8 to 53.1, while the aged dependency ratio increased slightly from 17.4 to 17.9. Projections for the year 2000 are an over-all dependency ratio of 63.2, composed of a child dependency ratio of 44.2 and an aged dependency ratio of 19.

The characteristics of households and families have been undergoing substantial changes in recent years. The number of divorces exceeded one million in 1975, the highest number ever in U.S. history in a one-year period, while the number of marriages, two million, was the lowest since 1969. Young adults are continuing to increase their tendency to postpone marriage (40 percent of the women aged 20–24 and 60 percent of the men of that age had never been married in 1975) even though the "ever-married" rate has continued to rise. In addition, more adults are currently divorced. There were 69 divorced persons in 1975 for every 1,000 married persons with intact marriages, as contrasted with 35 per 1,000 in 1960.

The total number of families (a group of two or more persons related by blood, marriage, or adoption and residing together) has increased from 45.1 million in 1960 and 51.6 million in 1970 to 55.7 million in 1975; however, the average family size has decreased from 3.7 and 3.6 in 1960 and 1970 to 3.4 in 1975. In 1976, 90 percent of the U.S. population resided in families. The corresponding 1960 total was 93 percent. Eight percent of Americans lived alone and 0.3 percent were in institutions. Thus, although family and household size may be decreasing and there may be changes in family types, the overwhelmingly dominant living pattern in America remains the same— in families. At most, the various unconventional, new family forms, however much publicized, account for only 1.7 percent of the population.

Although the total number of households has increased during this period, the size of the average household has continued to decline and is now, beginning in 1974, under three persons for the first time in history. Nearly three quarters of all households in 1960 included a head and a spouse, but by 1975 this figure had dropped to two thirds. Between 1960 and 1975 one-person households doubled, so that at present more than one out of every five households consists of a lone individual. The growth of one-person households has been the most significant change in household characteristics in recent years. Although 37 percent of these one-person households consist of elderly persons, the single most rapidly growing group is that of young adults under 35.

Of particular importance is the increased number of female-headed families. One out of every eight families (7.2 million) had a female head in 1975 (no husband living with the family). This family type has increased by an astonishing 30 percent since 1970. Although the increase has occurred for both blacks and whites, it has continued to be larger for blacks (from 28 percent in 1970 to 35 percent in 1975 for blacks, contrasted with 9 percent and 11 percent for whites in those years). The heads of these families are primarily divorced or separated women (48 percent of the families); the percentage of unmarried females has increased, also, while the proportion of widows has declined. Between 1959 and 1972, male-headed families grew by 3 percent; female-headed, by 43 percent.

With regard to population distribution, since 1970 an important change has taken place in one of the most clearly established patterns in the U.S. Metropolitan areas as a whole are growing less rapidly than nonmetropolitan areas and are no longer gaining population through migration from nonmetropolitan areas. In addition, the Southeastern part of the U.S. and the West are clearly the most rapidly growing sections, while the Northeastern industrial states have had relatively stable populations over the last five years.

The civilian labor force is larger than it has ever been. Almost 93 million persons were in the labor force in 1975, which includes over 60 percent of the total civilian noninstitutionalized population aged 16 [17] and over. Women represent over 40 percent of the total labor force. Between 1960 and 1975 women accounted for 13.7 million, or 60 percent, of the labor force growth. The labor force participation rate for women has risen from 37.7 percent in 1960 to 43.4 percent in 1970, 46.3 percent in 1975, and 47.0 percent in 1976. The labor force participation rate for males is approximately 78.0 percent, a continuation of the decline from 83.3 percent in 1960 to 79.7 percent in 1970. For men, the major drop has occurred in males aged 55 and over, reflecting a trend toward earlier retirement. In contrast, labor force participation rates for women have increased in every age group, but especially for those aged 20–44. Over half the women in this age group were in the labor force in 1975. Labor force participation rates of female family heads have increased from 52 percent in 1970 to 54 percent in 1975, while the rate for wives rose from 40.5 percent in 1970 to 44.3 percent in 1975.

Unemployment has increased for all groups over the last few years. Although adult men, household heads (male and female), and married men were particularly hard hit, teen-agers and adult women continue to have higher unemployment rates than adult men, while blacks have higher unemployment rates than whites.

Male blue-collar jobs have decreased in number during recent years; however, professional and service jobs (other than in private households) have increased. Moreover, the increase among professional workers has been much larger for women than for men.

The median income of all families in the U.S. in 1975 was $13,720. This represented a 6 percent increase since 1974 but a 3 percent decrease in constant dollars (taking account of inflation). Median income in constant dollars has risen only slightly since 1970.

Similarly, poverty has shown little change over the last five years. There were about 25.9 million persons with incomes below the poverty level ($5,500 for a nonfarm family of four) in 1975, comprising 12 percent of the

[17] Sixteen is the most common upper limit for compulsory school attendance in the U.S.

total population. Over all, the poverty population was 2.5 million, or 10.7 percent higher than 1974 but only about 2 percent higher than in 1970. In contrast, between 1959 and 1969 the poverty population declined substantially from 39 million to 24 million. Since 1969 there has been little change except that the percentage of aged who are poor has declined considerably as a consequence of increased Social Security benefits in the early 1970s.

Approximately 10 percent of all families were poor in 1975. The average income of families headed by women was the lowest for any type of family. The proportion of poor families headed by women increased from 20 percent in 1959 to 36 percent in 1969, to 46 percent in 1974. Over 11 million children lived in poor families in 1975, and more than half of these were in families with a female head. The poverty rate for children in families headed by females was far higher than for those in families with a male head (52 percent compared to 9 percent).

Median earnings for men working full time in 1975 were $12,760, while comparable women had median earnings of $7,500. The gap between male and female earnings has widened over the past year.

School enrollment has increased recently at all levels except elementary school. In 1975, six out of ten adults aged 25 and over had graduated from high school, while 14 percent had a degree from a four-year college. However, the proportion is growing, and of the group aged 25–34 about 20 percent had completed college. The largest percentage gain in college enrollment has occurred among students older than traditional college age (25 and older) and among females (45 percent of college enrollees in 1975 as compared with 40 percent in 1970).

The major racial and ethnic minorities in the U.S. are the black population and the population of Hispanic origin (Mexico, Puerto Rico, Cuba, Latin America, or Spain). In 1975 the black population numbered 23.8 million and comprised 11 percent of the population. Most blacks are young: 40 percent are under 18 in contrast to 32 percent of the entire population of the U.S. Three quarters of the blacks live in metropolitan areas, most in central cities within these areas. Although most of the black families are two-parent families, 35 percent—more than three times the proportion among the whites—were female-headed in 1975, a percentage which has been rising steadily over the past several years. Forty-three percent of black adults aged 25 and over had completed high school, including 16 percent who had completed at least one year of college. This proportion is enlarging rapidly among the younger blacks: 72 percent of those aged 20–24 had completed high school, including 27 percent who had completed one or more years of college.

Seven and one-half million blacks were below the poverty level in 1974, comprising 31 percent of the black population in the country. Fifteen percent were unemployed in 1975.

A smaller percentage of the population in the U.S. is of Hispanic origin (5 percent).[18] About 44 percent were under 18 while only 4 percent were 65 and older. Hispanic-origin families in 1975 were relatively large, with more than one-third including five or more family members. About three quarters of the families were two-parent, but a significant proportion was female-headed (19 percent). Only 38 percent aged 25 and older had completed high school, although 59 percent of those 20–24 had. Fifteen percent had completed some college education, while 22 percent of the younger group had. Thirteen percent of the adults aged 16 and over were unemployed in 1975, and 2.6 million persons, or 23 percent, were below the poverty level in 1974.

The Sectors

Income-Transfer Programs

Some of the countries in Europe which have developed explicit family policy or policies have begun with population objectives and have sought to advance them by means of income-transfer programs—or have responded to population realities and attempted to meet needs. Often the goal has been redistribution between small and large families, between families without children and those with, or between generations. The uncertainty as to effects has not discouraged the effort. U.S. income-transfer programs (social insurance, assistance, pensions) reflect several types of dynamics: labor market policy, humanitarian concern for the poor, family objectives, social control. It would be difficult in the absence of definitive research to achieve consensus as to the degree to which each group of motives governs in relation to each of the major programs. Obviously, one is here dealing with allegations about implicit policy as well as with what is explicit in statute and regulations.

By way of introduction it might be noted that the U.S. income-transfer

---

[18] If one adds Puerto Ricans in Puerto Rico and estimated illegal aliens, the total may reach 11 percent.

commitment is large: the insurances commanded about 9.1 percent of the gross national product in 1976 and the assistances 3.0 percent. While not at the top of the list, the U.S. expenditure is comparable to that of other countries, particularly (see below) given the lack of family allowances. Public income-transfer programs distributed $156.7 billion in 1976.[19]

Both in the several social insurance programs in the U.S. and in the assistances, a focus on individual applicants and recipients, whose eligibility depended upon labor-force attachment and personal history or status (as individuals who were disabled, unemployed, widowed, orphaned, or in need), has given way, but only in part, to family-oriented considerations. While these latter considerations have been there from the start, they become increasingly significant in the setting of entitlements and benefit levels. However, the unsystematic attention to such variables and the lack of consistency and coherence in the ways in which they have been addressed as between programs documents the absence of an over-all coherent family policy. At the same time, the periodic and now almost constant raising of family-oriented concerns in the hearings and the debates suggests an alertness to family dimensions which certainly affects policy-making.

A historical analysis finds that, in general, over the years 1935 to 1972, Congress paid peripheral, minor attention to family issues and considered family questions as technical details to be determined by other priorities. Yet as Bandler points out,

> . . . [In] social insurance there has been a steady, incremental expansion of family entitlements to remedy hardships and to provide greater equity and social welfare. Since 1939, Congress has extended the range of entitled kin, set some national definitions for family status, permitted entitlement with altered relationships, liberalized the age criteria, and partially modified the gender assumptions on work and family roles.
>
> In the adult categories of public assistance, Congress paid minimal attention to family issues and until the passage of Supplemental Security Income took no action on family definitions, treatment of ineligible family members, or assessment of relatives' support. In Aid to Families with Dependent Children, attitudes on parental duties and state jurisdiction produced idiosyncratic parental definitions, specialized requirements on home standards, and they continue to exclude intact needy families. To date, standardizations of eligibility criteria are a result of judicial and administrative, not legislative, actions. Periodically, the Congress emphasizes parental support, strengthening support requirements and enforcement for absent fathers. It has moved from an avoidance of home standards to a stress on rehabilitative services and regulative provisions, to the current separation of income maintenance and social services. Reversing the long-

---

[19] Data for 1976 are not final as of this writing.

standing policy on the mother's role, Congress mandated work rather than family care.

The overall assessment is that:

In both social insurance and public assistance, the delays, gaps and incongruences indicate the need for a consistent, equitable consideration of family issues throughout the policy-making stages.[20]

The current uneven picture is best summarized in an analysis for a Congressional committee.[21] Writing in the context of the most systematic attention yet assigned in the Congress to the interplay among family policy, poverty, and income-transfer programs, Cox reminds us again that the complexities and inhibition occur at the level of implementation, not in the general rhetoric:

It is generally accepted that a basic purpose of publicly supported social welfare programs is to support, strengthen, enhance, and preserve family life. Public education, housing, health programs, income maintenance, and a variety of other human service programs are essentially concerned with direct, community, or environmental supports for family life and the fulfillment of family responsibilities. Public income transfer programs which distribute more than $100 billion annually have a major role in underpinning the economic well-being of families.[22]

Cox begins with the question of the concept of the family. Noting the census definition ("two or more persons related by blood, marriage, or adoption who reside together"), she comments that in general and in social service usage there is emphasis both on living together and on relationship,

---

[20] Jean Taft Bandler, Abstract, "Family Issues in Social Policy: an Analysis of Social Security" (doctoral dissertation, Columbia University School of Social Work, 1975).

Bandler's historical analysis of Congressional attention to family issues in the income-transfer programs of the Social Security Act, covering Old Age, Survivors, and Disability Insurance, and the adult and children's categories of public assistance, spans the years 1935 to 1972. Her material is drawn from the Congressional documents, hearings, reports, and debates as well as outside studies and personal interviews. Administrative policies, judicial decisions, and state practices also are discussed.

[21] Irene Cox, "Treatment of Families under Income Transfer Programs," in Subcommittee on Fiscal Policy, Joint Economic Committee, Congress of the United States, Studies in Public Welfare, *The Family, Poverty, and Welfare Programs: Household Patterns and Government Policies,* Paper No. 12 (Part II) (Washington, D.C.: U.S. Government Printing Office, 1973), pp. 181–206. This paper, part of a twenty-five-volume series of reports which culminated in recommendations for public assistance reform, is a basic reference work for many aspects of the topic not here reviewed, especially the alleged impact of programs on individual and family behavior.

[22] *Ibid.,* p. 181.

but the term also is employed to describe unrelated persons who live together as an economic or social unit. Income-transfer programs do not contribute to systematic, uniform definition:

> With the possible exception of housing programs, none of the major income transfer programs define a "family" as an eligible unit. Instead, they define eligible individuals. The primary beneficiary is defined by his status relative to a particular program's eligibility criteria: covered wage earner, veteran, unemployed worker, dependent child.[23]

There is considerable attention to relationships in the definition of support obligations and dependency status, not to define a family unit. Cox notes, in fact, that living together is not generally required. And AFDC, with the word "family" in its title ("Aid to *Families* with Dependent Children"), the largest means-tested public assistance program by far, excludes "stable" families by definition (except, perhaps, those with incapacitated fathers or, in some states, unemployed fathers).[24] A major reform proposal to include intact, but poor, families as eligible was defeated in 1971.[25]

The full picture is more complex. While eligibility is usually defined in individual terms, "all types of beneficiary family arrangements are possible . . . . each program has its own rationale for defining eligible persons or units" based on objectives, tradition, legal or moral concepts and so forth. The resulting nonsystem creates a diversity of apparent or alleged (if difficult to measure) incentives and disincentives for family formation and dissolution.[26]

These generalizations are based on a program-by-program overview in the report (here suggested but not fully summarized). Under *social insurance,* particularly Old Age, Survivors, and Disability Insurance, Cox notes the major objective of protecting wage earners's loss of earnings due to retirement because of age or disability. Persons dependent upon the wage earner are protected against income loss should the wage earner suffer one of the covered risks. Dependency is established by recognition of legal responsibility for primary relatives and accepting evidence of certain other assumptions of responsibility as shown in living patterns. However, the stress is on legal relationships, not living arrangements.

Since Social Security was planned as an income-replacement program

---

[23] *Ibid.,* p. 182.   [24] *Ibid.,* pp. 182–83.

[25] Moynihan, *The Politics of a Guaranteed Income.* The issue is once again being discussed as we write.

[26] Cox, "Treatment of Families under Income Transfer Programs," p. 183.

whose premises derive from assumptions about the family and family roles in the 1930s, it is not surprising that many of its features currently inspire debate. Interim reforms have not addressed most outstanding issues. With reference to the survivor-dependency benefits, for example, it is noted that as the two-earner family has become more common than the one-earner "model," there are claims of inequity: working wives gain no added retirement benefits despite their Social Security taxes unless their salaries are high enough to guarantee them benefits larger than what they would receive as dependent spouses of a retired worker (half the husband's entitlement).

For many years divorced wives received no benefits. Now they are vested with rights if married twenty years (subsequently amended to ten), but observers wonder whether there should not be recognition from the very start of the marriage of the nonworking wife's contributions as homemaker and mother. There are proposals that Social Security entitlements be split equally throughout a marriage, whatever each spouse contributes through Social Security taxes. Such policy might retain a work incentive but not overly penalize a homemaker whose husband is in a high salary bracket.

Others, noting that the entitlement structure contains explicit incentives to work or not, and thus explicit incentives for one family pattern over another, go beyond this and wish to have household work and child rearing "credited" to Social Security entitlement (as it is in several of the European countries). Problems of financing arise—as do debates with others who do not wish to perpetuate the image of the woman as homemaker—or who consider this unfair in the light of the "dual role" responsibilities of mothers working outside the home.

Even these proposals are rejected by other observers, for they give benefits to some retirees and dependents on the basis of marriage—yet the Social Security tax is individualized. The single earner is paying the cost of benefits to the married.

Thus the debate begins, and implicit family models and prevalent value systems become more visible. The research must explicate all of this further (and the work is now being done). It requires both an alertness to demographic and structural change, to inequity and to the impossibility of complete neutrality: a benefit scheme has an implicit value structure. Currently, groups within the Congress and HEW are addressing reform options which will particularly consider the divorced spouse, the homemaker, the working mother.[27]

[27] Nancy Gordon, "The Treatment of Women in the Public Pension Systems of Five Countries," working paper 9-5069-01 (Washington, D.C.: Urban Institute, 1978); also "Report of the HEW Task Force on the Treatment of Women under Social Security," April, 1978.

Unemployment insurance replaces a portion of wages for a limited period of unemployment; eleven states add an allowance for dependents.

SSI, a recently federalized public assistance program which offers a "guaranteed income" to the aged, blind, and disabled whose income falls below the set level, provides for individual eligibility. The benefit for a couple is 150 percent of the individual benefit. Where states in the predecessor program covered otherwise ineligible "essential" persons, they too have achieved SSI eligibility. Otherwise, individual eligibility is required; a recognition of relationships which are not technically legal marriages may be interpreted as an economy measure (150 percent rather than 200 percent of a one-person grant) as much as a matter of flexibility about "family."

AFDC, the major assistance program, had an enormous growth between 1960 and 1973. This state-administered program which relies heavily on federal matching funds tripled the number of families covered between 1961 and 1973, apparently due to: (*a*) an increase in eligible family units (due, in turn, to a rise in eligibility levels in states, thus increasing the number of those who might apply, as well as to a growth in female-headed households); and (*b*) a higher participation rate among those who are eligible.[28] The AFDC "legislative objective" is summarized in a Congressional report in family policy terms:

> To encourage the care of dependent children in their own homes or in the homes of relatives by enabling each State to furnish financial assistance, rehabilitation, and other services to needy dependent children and the parents or relatives with whom they are living, to help maintain and strengthen family life, and to help such parents or relatives to attain or retain a capability for self-support.[29]

Children are eligible to age 18 (or to 21 if in school) and must be lacking parental support or care because of a parent's death, continued absence, or physical or mental incapacity (or, at state option, because the father is unemployed), and must be needy (as defined by the state). The child must be living with a relative of a specified relationship or be in court-assigned foster care.[30]

[28] Subcommittee on Fiscal Policy, Joint Economic Committee, Congress of the United States, *Income Security for Americans: Recommendations of the Public Welfare Study* (Washington, D.C.: U.S. Government Printing Office, 1974), p. 92; Barbara Boland, "Participation in the Aid to Families with Dependent Children Program (AFDC)," in *The Family, Poverty, and Welfare Programs*, Paper No. 12 (Part I), pp. 139–79.

[29] Subcommittee on Fiscal Policy, Joint Economic Committee, Congress of the United States, Studies in Public Welfare, *Handbook of Public Income Transfer Programs: 1975*, Paper No. 20 (Washington, D.C.: U.S. Government Printing Office, 1974), p. 140.

[30] *Ibid.*, pp. 140, 143.

When the Social Security Act was originally written, AFDC was seen as continuous with state legislation providing mothers' pensions intended to help widows rear children until they were old enough to work. Since the social insurance program was expected, eventually, to offer coverage to survivors of covered wage earners, a phasing out of most of the AFDC load was expected. No one predicted the growth of divorced and separated households with children and in need of financial aid, or the subsequent explosion in out-of-wedlock births. AFDC continued to grow. In March, 1976, the rolls included 8,133,000 children and 3,353,000 adults. The fathers' status, according to the last published survey (1975) was: divorced, 19.4 percent; separated (with court decree) from the mother, 3.6 percent; deserted or informally separated, 25.0 percent; not married to the mother, 31.0 percent; incapacitated, 7.7 percent; unemployed, 3.7 percent; deceased, 3.7 percent. Only 11.4 percent were at home.

The press and the research literature report extensive opinions as to the alleged incentives built into the structure of the AFDC program for intact families to split so that mothers and their children will be eligible, and for single women to have illegitimate children so as to be covered. While the analyses report mixed results, the most reliable research offers these hypotheses:

1. There is no evidence that recipients have additional children so as to add to their AFDC checks.

2. For women alone who are rearing children, the availability of the AFDC option may decrease the tendency to marry or remarry, since it provides an alternative and secure source of financial support.

3. Perhaps AFDC may encourage or facilitate family break-up in the higher-grant states (a tentative conclusion).

4. The relationship between the AFDC grant level in a community and the salaries for jobs available to minority-group males may be an important element in the equation.[31]

Recent efforts to replace AFDC with programs that offer incentives for families to remain intact involve proposals for a negative income tax which would cover the working poor, as well as other reforms which would assure eligibility of families with employable males and/or would assure work for

[31] See Survey Research Center, Institute for Social Research, University of Michigan, *Five Thousand American Families—Patterns of Economic Progress*, 1974–76 (Ann Arbor, Mich.: the Center, 1976), 4 vols., esp. Vol. IV, Part I; Marjorie Honig, "The Impact of Welfare Payment Levels on Family Stability," in *The Family, Poverty, and Welfare Programs* (Part I), pp. 37–53; Heather L. Ross and Isabel Sawhill, *Time of Transition* (Washington, D.C.: Urban Institute, 1975), esp. chap. 5.

at least one adult member of a family in two-parent families with children. By implication, then, there is widespread feeling that AFDC in some sense represents questionable family policy since it does not offer incentives for traditional family formation and stability. In a long-term perspective, however, a program which makes it possible for female-headed families to achieve some level of assured income for the children and some option for mothers other than immediate remarriage (or remaining in destructive marriages) may also be viewed as a policy that reflects concern for the needs of some types of families.

Some observers have argued that AFDC is a poor substitute for family allowances, the prevalent child-rearing grants in all other major industrial countries. These grants are small in some countries and significant in others. Since they are usually universal, not means-tested, and available where fathers are present (there may be additional modest supports for mother-only families), family allowances are or could be supportive of intact families (or neutral in structural impact).

In any case, the problem with, and feelings about, AFDC in the U.S. is reflective of the inadequate attention paid to family policy in family-related income-transfer programs when they were drawn up and the currently acknowledged need to cope with effects, initially unanticipated and now of concern to significant elements in the electorate.

Food subsidy programs, especially the food stamp program, have expanded in recent years. Cox observes that the eligibility unit "is the household rather than the individual or related family members."[32]

Differences among programs with regard to families or to the treatment of family members create significant problems of coordination between social insurance grants for retirees and their dependents and SSI—but the definitional and eligibility issues are not complex and likely to be corrected. On the other hand, attitudes to a mother's work are different for a widow receiving Social Security survivor benefits as between those benefits and her obligations under AFDC, should she require supplementation. Other technical problems are elaborated by Cox, such as the different treatment of earnings in the several programs.[33] For present purposes it is sufficient to summarize her *general conclusions:* Because of the manner in which programs differ in definition of individuals, family units, or households held eligible there are problems of inequity and conflicting incentives. Each program may have its logic, but the totality defies logic. Inconsistent age definitions, "treatment of

---

[32] Cox, "Treatment of Families under Income Transfer Programs," p. 192.

[33] *Ibid.,* pp. 195–201.

income, work requirements, earnings disregards, recognition of support obligations, benefit levels by category, and circumstances under which individuals are or are not included as family or household members'' add up to an Alice in Wonderland situation. To which are added "differences in accounting periods, assets tests, and treatment of earnings and other income of various family members'' in programs serving the same or similar people.[34]

Again, little more need be said. The social goals of the insurances and the assistance have been different, despite some convergence and a complementary relationship for a significant number of recipients. Social goals of programs enacted at different times are also different. Moreover, there are debates as to the appropriateness and "efficacy of using public programs to influence family structure.'' At the same time, there is general recognition that significant benefit programs are unlikely to be neutral with regard to family life. The case thus develops for redesigning some or all components into a more coherent system and to face the question of goals—whether for the family or for the broader society.

Tax Policy

Tax policy impinges on the family as it does on individuals: through state and local sales and excise taxes; through federal payroll taxes; and through federal and, in some instances, state and city personal income taxes.

Sales and excise taxes take no account of family status. Payroll taxes were originally designed on the assumption that the typical family was a two-person family unit with one earner, the male head of household. The fact that the reality has changed and that this family form is no longer dominant has not yet affected this program. Although there are no explicit family goals related to these two categories of taxation, both are regressive taxes and thus penalize low-income families. Moreover, since payroll and sales taxes have been growing rapidly as a share of government revenues during the last three decades, the burden on low-income families is increasing.

Only in the third category of taxes, personal income taxes, is any real attention paid the family (as contrasted with individuals), and even then no consistent approach is taken in support of the family as a unit, or of family members or family functions. One expert summarizes federal income tax policy in relation to the family, as follows:

> From its inception, the federal income tax law has permitted every taxpayer to file a personal return, embracing his or her own income but excluding the income of the taxpayer's spouse, children and other relatives. On the other hand,

[34] *Ibid.*, pp. 203–6.

married couples may elect to consolidate their income on a joint return, many
exemptions and deductions take account of family links and responsibilities, and
the income or property of one member of a family is sometimes attributed to
another member for a variety of purposes. The Internal Revenue Code, in brief,
is a patchwork, its history being a myriad of compromises fashioned to meet
particular problems.[35]

The result, as Bittker points out, is a continuing tension between rugged individualism and family solidarity which permeates the entire Code.

The major philosophical doctrine underlying federal income tax policy
is that the family should be treated as a unit and taxed accordingly, while individuals who are not members of a family unit should be taxed as individuals. "Tax paying ability is determined by total family income regardless of
the distribution of such income among the members of the family."[36] In
fact, however, the approach taken toward marriage and family responsibility
is clearly inconsistent and contains several anomalies.

There is an incentive for the establishment of traditional marriages in
which there is only one wage earner. "Income splitting" for married couples is viewed increasingly as a tax allowance for family responsibilities.
Furthermore, there is acknowledgment of the family responsibilities of unmarried individuals who may be maintaining a home for a child or another
dependent. Indication of this can be seen in the special tax rate for heads of
households that is somewhat more favorable than the tax rates for single persons although less so than that for married couples filing a joint return.

However, when one turns to the tax treatment of the two-earner family,
an increasingly prevalent family form today, a very different picture
emerges. While married couples with a single earner receive more favorable
treatment than unmarried individuals, even the latter are better off than
married couples with two incomes. There is a "marriage penalty" for persons with relatively equal amounts of income who get married and continue
to have the same amounts of income. Moreover, there are still additional
penalties imposed on two-earner couples:

1. Two-earner couples are taxed as heavily as couples with the same
income but only one wage earner, in spite of the fact that the two-earner
family puts out more effort to obtain that income and, at the same time,
foregoes many of the benefits and free services of an at-home spouse and
may actually have to purchase substitute services, such as child care or other

---

[35] Boris I. Bittker, "Federal Income Taxation and the Family," *Stanford Law Review*, XXVII
(1975), 1391.

[36] *Ibid.*, p. 1392.

household help. Although employed parents are entitled to a tax credit for child care, the amount may not cover the actual costs of such care, and no such credit is provided to cover other expenses incurred as a consequence of both spouses working outside the home.

2. An even more flagrant inequity is that the gross amount of the second salary is taxed at a higher rate than is paid by a single person receiving the same salary. The result is that income tax policy provides either a disincentive for wives to enter paid employment—or an incentive to divorce where both spouses are employed, especially when their salaries are substantial. (It is, of course, not known whether or how much actual behavior is affected.)

If there are inconsistencies in the tax treatment of marriage, there are other kinds of anomalies in the tax treatment of parental responsibilities for children and child rearing. The most obvious illustration is the dependency deduction which by its very nature benefits higher income families more than low-income families. Taxpayers are entitled to a $750 personal exemption for support of dependents (related by blood, marriage, adoption, or co-residence) who receive over half of their support from the taxpayer and who have less than $750 in gross income during the year. Children under nineteen or older children who are full-time students are exempt from this income restriction. However, this uniform deduction actually is worth more to high-income families because the value of the dependency allowance increases as the taxpayer's income (and marginal tax rate) rises.

At present, these tensions, anomalies, and inconsistencies are the subject of growing discussion, and a number of related reforms have been suggested although none has been enacted. Among these, the most important are: legislating a "marriage-neutral" federal income tax so that neither a tax incentive nor a disincentive would exist for marriage (or divorce); providing a modest tax credit for the earnings of the second wage earner in a family, so as not to penalize two-earner families; changing the dependency deduction to a tax credit, so as to treat poor families more equitably.

It is recognized that these policies are more readily stated than implemented for, as indicated, the almost universally accepted ideal of equal taxes for equal-income married couples has not been reconciled with a "marriage-neutral" approach, and both principles appear to be in contradiction with the ideal of truly progressive taxation.[37]

[37] *Ibid.* For a cross-national discussion of some of the issues related to the tax treatment of the family, see Organization for Economic Cooperation and Development, *The Treatment of Family Units in OECD Member Countries under Tax and Transfer Systems* (Paris: OECD, 1977).

Personal Social Services[38]

The domain may be summed up in several relatively clear-cut and not very controversial generalizations:

1. Since the U.S. does not have an organized, coherent system of personal social services, what personal social services are available do not reflect any coherent focus for U.S. family policy.

2. Personal social services in the U.S. are organized by and for problem and age categories; there is no family focus for the most part and—rhetoric aside—none seems to have been intended.

3. Among the age and problem group service clusters, personal social services for families are among the least developed. The U.S. does not have a significant public sector system of family social services, and the voluntary sector services are limited and narrow in scale and scope. In any case, major decisions are left to states and localities, and they have not sought family-related coherence.

4. There are some interesting exceptions, rumblings, and initiatives in several arenas.

What follows elaborates and explains these generalizations briefly and provides essential historical and societal perspective.

It was noted in mid-1975 that a new services title in the Social Security Act (Title XX) did not include among the required service goals any concern with "preserving and strengthening family life."[39] One might have added that, despite relevant rhetoric in earlier amendments and regulations, the situation was not essentially changed. A succession of presidents and legislators has affirmed commitment to the family, in the abstract, while opposing

[38] We here employ the British term for a domain often simply labled "social services" in the U.S. but sometimes confused with education, employment, and health programs. Included in this field, which is only partly developed, if emerging, are: family and child welfare programs; community services for the aging; social services for youth; community centers and day programs of several kinds; meals on wheels and congregate eating arrangements; homemakers; several types of institutional care and residential treatment; vacation camps for families and children; and so forth. We have reported on the U.S. in Sheila B. Kamerman and Alfred J. Kahn, *Social Services in the United States* (Philadelphia: Temple University Press, 1976). An eight-country study is summed up in Alfred J. Kahn and Sheila B. Kamerman, *Social Services in International Perspective* (Washington, D.C.: U.S. Government Printing Office, 1977). The recognition of the domain is not to claim that services are organized in any coherent way or currently planned as one system.

[39] Rev. Msgr. Lawrence J. Corcoran, executive director, National Conference of Catholic Charities, as reported in *Adoption and Foster Care,* 1975, Hearings before the Subcommittee on Children and Youth, U.S. Senate (Washington, D.C.: U.S. Government Printing Office, 1975), p. 486.

program initiatives outside an individualistic-pluralistic tradition and supporting largely categorical, therapeutic, and problem-oriented service programs. There is little that is specifically targeted at the enhancement of the family as an organic unit or which encourages integration around the family at the point of personal social service delivery.

Some of the elements of what we now identify as personal social services developed historically in the U.S. as the domain of church and nonsectarian private charities. When "public" programs started in the nineteenth century, it was because of the involvement of states where voluntary effort was nonexistent or inadequate. The federal role grew slowly and in limited fashion, focusing largely on special "federal impact" circumstances: veterans; for a limited period, post-Civil War freedmen; Indians. The first White House Conference on Children (1909) affirmed the desirability of preserving the family but left action—in the form of mothers' pensions—to the states. Children's Bureau exposés of child labor and child health hazards also led to protective legislation and, eventually, limited—though very important—maternal and child health legislation in the 1920s.

The social service initiatives of the 1935 *Social Security Act* took the form of a limited child welfare services effort for rural areas (later expanded to all areas of high need and then to all counties) and a casework effort in public assistance charged with restoring recipients to self-support and not sharply differentiated until 1956 from administration of cash benefits and investigation to determine financial eligibility. In 1962 federal reimbursement rates for services were raised from 50 to 75 percent, on the assumption that services would restore people to self-support and thus cut assistance rolls. Later in the 1960s the idea emerged that there should be a social service system in public assistance fully separated from eligibility determination. However, by then, public interest was focused almost completely on income-maintenance reform or on the use of child care resources and job training to restore some AFDC mothers to work or prepare them for employment. Moreover, increasingly resources were devoted to purchase of specialized and categorical services from voluntary and public agencies, not to create a coherent delivery system. Other basic social service goals had been assigned to a community mental health system, on the border between medicine and personal social services, with a broad mandate but relatively limited resources for coverage.

In the interim and up to the present, considerable categorical initiatives in the personal social services have responded to public concern with specific social problems, or sensitivity to various types of interest-group advocacy. Recognition is given to the family in statements of concern, but generally not in the program enactments.

Child welfare is a prime example. States are required to assure the availability of child welfare services in all jurisdictions. Since the late 1960s they have had to combine what had been separate (and often better staffed) child welfare programs with the social services to AFDC families, the larger load. There is now no clear picture nationally of the scope, scale, and quality of service. Child welfare authorities at the federal level have a mandate to provide leadership and technical aid for improving foster home and institutional care, facilitating needed adoption, assisting young out-of-wedlock mothers. They state, at the same time, that expansion of child welfare services to carry out such missions is not the same thing as basic promotion of the welfare of children, a goal seen as demanding a family focus.[40] However, initiatives toward a broader conception are limited, as are resources. Major emphasis is placed on assuring adoption and/or more stable foster care for the hard-to-place, but beyond modest experimental initiatives no service design or comprehensive delivery system has been developed and implemented to maximize work with families and children in their own homes so as to prevent breakdown and placement, or generally to enhance family life and the quality of child rearing and socialization. Nor are the administrators derelict in their duty: the mandates and appropriations are limited.

The Title XX services program, in effect in all states since 1975, has apparently not ended the categorical approach to children's services.[41] States which seek federal funds are required to maintain protective services for children and the aged, to offer services both to deinstitutionalize those who could be at home, and to assure good institutional care for those who require it. States and localities are not required to maintain public delivery systems with any specific core services; they have the option of buying services from specialized public or voluntary agencies, and they tend to favor contracts for

---

[40] For detail, see Alfred J. Kahn, "Child Welfare," in *Encyclopedia of Social Work,* Seventeenth Issue (Washington, D.C.: National Association of Social Workers, 1977), I, 100–13; Frank Ferro, Deputy Chief, Children's Bureau, *Children Today,* Vol. V, No. 6 (1976), editorial.

[41] This first, comprehensive service title permits many types of initiative but has thus far not inspired very much local development of comprehensive, family-oriented services. The major claim on its $2.5 billion ceiling is for day care, services to the aged, and foster care. Categorical rather than comprehensive programming prevails.

special and thus fragmented services. The result has not been a comprehensive, family-oriented, integrated service system.

At the very same time, a small yet very visible new "child abuse" program at the federal level, based in the Administration for Children, Youth, and Families (ACYF), has created specialized case registers, case finding, and service experiments for a subcategorical group, further fragmenting efforts in many jurisdictions.

A major effort in recent years to encourage planning, coordination, and, in effect, categorical service delivery to the aged (whether financed under the Older Americans Act or the service titles of the Social Security Act) reinforces such tendencies. The likelihood of a family-oriented personal social service system is lessened and capacity to plan for community care for the aged perhaps diminished as a result. Nor has a structure of policy and funding emerged to facilitate family care, as differentiated from formal service systems, for the aged.

Until 1977 the initiatives for the development of social services at the federal level were divided among: (*a*) the Community Services Administration of the Social and Rehabilitation Service of the Department of Health, Education, and Welfare (HEW), the agency with responsibility for Title XX (the services title in the Social Security Act), and for child welfare funds; (*b*) several subgroups in the Office of Child Development (OCD), part of the Office of Human Development, which took the lead in day care, Head Start, and child abuse programs and sponsored large-scale demonstrations at the junior high school level in family life education; (*c*) the Administration on Aging, the base agency for the Older Americans Act, and also a subunit in the Office of Human Development; (*d*) the Office of Youth Development, also in the Office of Human Development, which administered a program for runaway youth; (*e*) a program for Native Americans; (*f*) numerous categorical programs for the handicapped, the disabled—and rehabilitation services. Each of these units also had, on paper, a broad planning and coordination mandate. The Office of Human Development had a weak coordination mandate. In effect, however, the family was ignored as a social service planning target while problem-categorical service initiatives continued to emerge.

Late in 1977 HEW began a service program reorganization, creating a new Office of Human Development Services (OHDS) which combines five subadministrations: ACYF, Administration on Aging, Administration for Handicapped Individuals, Administration for Public Services (the Title XX funding and the services programs previously tied to the assistances), Administration for Native Americans. The new OHDS is seeking to define a family-oriented personal social services policy. As the reorganization proceeds, however, the difficulty of rising above traditional categorical differentiations (aging, children, youth, each of the major handicapped groups and rehabilitation programs) and of unifying services for the "welfare poor" with other services is apparent. The outcome is quite uncertain. There are few major initiatives to integrate all locally based publicly funded personal social services along family principles.

The experience of recent decades perhaps does create some noncategorical or pro-family pressures. For a variety of reasons, for example, there has been disillusionment with residential institutions; they are costly, often create permanent dependency and harm people in various ways, often interfere with exercise of individual rights, are difficult to staff or operate in accord with good standards, and so on. A campaign for deinstitutionalization of several categories of children, of the aged, of the retarded and mentally ill, however, has been followed by public revulsion at the resultant living conditions for those released. New interest has emerged in support of the family, both to avoid unnecessary placement and to play a postplacement social service role.

As states have expanded public and private family planning programs (in part with federal funds) and as abortion services have become more numerous and accessible (in part as a result of Supreme Court rulings), a parallel interest has emerged in advice services, counseling, and educational efforts related to family life and parenting. This, too, could encourage family-oriented social services which are not only therapeutic and remedial.

In the voluntary sector, two high-standard leadership agencies, the Child Welfare League of America and the Family Service Association of America, thus far have been unsuccessful in efforts to end their organizations' family-child fragmentation, even though some of their member agencies span both fields. The former concentrates on substitute care and adoption services, even though its lobbying arm undertakes broader significant advocacy in relation to day care programs, child health and nutrition, and income maintenance. The latter focuses on case services, especially marital counseling and parent-child relationships, while encouraging what is as yet preliminary and limited work in parent education and parent-effectiveness training. Both systems, but especially voluntary children's agencies, receive substantial funding under public social service legislation. Community mental health centers, which are publicly funded but may be operated as public, quasi-private, or private agencies, are generally in the medical-psychiatric domain although they overlap significantly in all these family and child welfare activities. They also carry out primary and secondary prevention work with a limited population.

Further specification would add to the detail but would not revise the conclusion: personal social services have received public mandate and funding only as social problems have threatened or distressed the larger community: delinquency, the addictions, child abuse and neglect, runaways, developmental disabilities, emotional illness, long-term and intergenerational poverty. The ethos favors individual independence and public nonintervention, while the concerned public also recognizes the need to contain or remedy problems and pathology. Federal social service involvements have been categorical, as has state commitment of their own resources or deployment of federal aid. The focus has been on problem categories and the poor, and the major programs are therefore therapeutic-remedial. Despite frequent affirmations of the importance of prevention, there is great hesitancy about services to the nonpoor and reluctance to interfere with socialization and development—even though there is recognition that preventive programming (also a value) might require this.

This orientation both responds to and encourages proliferation and continuance of categorical interest groups made up of professionals, clients-patients, and other lay supporters of particularistic programs. There is in the U.S. only very limited advocacy of the more general "public interest" in the personal social services field. We lack the family associations, unions, and lobbies of several European countries. The broadest social services advocacy effort of recent years, the failed day care campaign of 1970–71, won support for day care as serving the needs of working mothers, offering a "head start" for the children of the poor, supporting welfare reform, providing a base for local community development, and enhancing the development of children during the preschool years. The supporting coalition was broad, if temporary.[42]

Individualism remains a personal social service theme even where there is evocation of the family and its welfare. Thus, the important 1967 social services amendments to the Social Security Act called for family services as

---

[42] Gilbert Steiner, *The Children's Cause* (Washington, D.C.: Brookings Institution, 1976), chap. 5.

The continued and rapid development of child care programs is fragmented and reflects diverse initiatives and social forces, not one policy or programming effort: Head Start, nursery and prekindergarten programs, day care centers, family day care.

"services to a family, or a member thereof, for the purpose of preserving, rehabilitating, or strengthening the family to attain or retain capability for the maximum self-support or personal independence." The focus remained individualistic. As already noted, even this goal seemed too expansive when the first comprehensive services title in the Social Security Act, Title XX, was enacted late in 1974.

Similarly, the most potent conceptual initiative in child welfare in recent years has involved adding to the protection of children's rights by: (*a*) facilitating termination of parental rights so as to permit long-term foster care or adoption; (*b*) ending the long-term prohibition on changing the foster care status to an adoption status; (*c*) subsidizing adoption and encouraging interstate compacts so as to place hard-to-place children—all in the "best interests of the child." These urgent child welfare reforms have not as yet been paralleled by substantial new efforts in income-maintenance and personal social services, efforts which might increase family capacity to perform its core functions itself.

In the latter category, however, one does note important family supportive initiatives tending toward relatively broad coverage. There has, for example, been a significant expansion of the national school lunch program to a point where (1975 estimate) 25 million children participate and some 9.5 million receive free or reduced-cost meals. Also, more than half of all children aged three to five participate in nursery, day care, kindergarten, or other preschool programs. Public family supportive efforts do expand without explicit decisions formulated in such terms.

Health

The U.S. does not have any large-scale federal or state family-oriented health program offering coverage to most citizens. Its largest public involvements, apart from Indian health services, are in the hospital insurance and supplementary medical insurance for the aged and disabled who are eligible for Social Security benefits (Medicare). Beneficiaries are individual, and the coverage is specific and episodic around illness, disability, and related need for service. Medicare is not a family program.

A state-administered, means-tested Medicaid program, for which there is substantial federal reimbursement, responds to the health service needs of eligible poor families and their children, whether they are below or near the public assistance level. States make full or partial payments on behalf of eligible individuals who receive medical service. While, in theory, a comprehensive family-oriented delivery system could be supported (per capita payments may, for example, be made to health insurance agencies), in effect Medicaid *is* a fee-for-service program and not a delivery system at all, as experienced by most users.[43]

A pattern of tax deductions for part of health insurance premiums and for medical costs above a specified percentage of income helps middle- and upper-income people with high medical costs to some extent; again, the focus is on payment and not delivery. While hospital and surgical coverage is extensive under various insurance plans, the bulk of the population lacks coverage for primary home- and office-based physician services. The family is not the target or concern in most such care.

The U.S. has a history, going back to the 1920s,[44] of federal aid to states for maternal and child health services which concentrated, especially, on causes of infant mortality and achieved considerable early success. The program lapsed and was revived in the 1935 Social Security Act as a grant program to the states. It has suffered considerable political difficulty over the years, has not grown with need, and continues as a program of limited coverage and grants to child health projects in ghetto areas and centers of rural poverty (and, more recently, bloc grants to the states).[45] In some places state and local funds expand the effort. But the U.S. lacks public family-oriented maternal and child health coverage characteristic of many other industrial countries (even though for significant subgroups there is fringe benefit coverage from industry, union, and state-based government employee programs).

In recent years, a mandated early screening program for Medicaid-eligible (poor) children, effective in 1968 but implemented several years later, has called for periodic screening, diagnosis, and treatment. Apart from political delays and uncertainty as to scope and technology of screening, the program has been plagued by the lack of a back-up medical service delivery system to which the screened children would go for treatment. Indeed, the very development of the program may be seen as an effort to compensate for the absence of standard maternal and child health service coverage in the universal system characteristic of many other countries. Thus far, even screening reaches only 8 percent or 9 percent of eligible poor children in large industrial states.

[43] In principle, Medicaid could pay health maintenance service fees, and some of the coverage is or will be of this kind.

[44] Recounted in Steiner, *The Children's Cause*, chap. 9.

[45] These grants assured prenatal and postpartum care in maternity clinics to over 500,000 women in 1975, for example.

In addition to all this, a comprehensive and productive research program in child health problems is carried out or financed through several federal programs.[46]

Health programs, it seems, reflect some commitment to pay for needed service but have not assumed responsibility to mount a medical program of family-oriented service and care. Experiments (which are federally funded) with more comprehensive Health Maintenance Organizations could have other effects, but there is currently no contemplation of coverage. Federal mandating or availability of family planning services for the "welfare" poor and the "medically indigent" clearly are family-oriented but are not universal in coverage. Recent compromises in a legislative and legal battle have precluded the expenditure of federal funds to pay for most abortions. The results of this policy as they affect the birth rates and family situations of the poor are only beginning to become visible.

Housing

Most U.S. housing is a marketplace activity and not guided by explicit governmental programs or policy initiatives. Some governmental programs, nonetheless, have had explicit, and others implicit, family policy components; several programs in particular (mortgage guarantees and favorable tax treatment of home owners) have probably had considerable family impact.

For some forty years a low-rent public housing program has risen, declined, risen, and again declined in popularity. It is largely a state-local effort with federal subsidy; the assistance has taken various forms over the years. The program houses over 2.5 million people, most of them welfare-level poor or near-poor. From time to time federal and local initiatives have assured special provision for large families, the aged, families with young children, ethnic or racial minorities, the handicapped. Special equipment and facilities for families and children or special services have also been mandated or encouraged (day care space, meeting rooms, entertainment rooms, workshops, laundry rooms, and so on). On a small scale some public housing may be said to seek to enhance and support family life as such.

Of greater quantitative impact and visible effect (although hardly a program with explicit objectives corresponding to what occurred) were the post-World War II mortgage insurance and loan guarantee programs (veteran and nonveteran) which facilitated and encouraged the enormous development of American suburbs featuring detached single or two-family homes. Supporting this development has been the legislation permitting local and state taxes

---

[46] Steiner, *The Children's Cause*, pp. 215ff. Also see: Children's Defense Fund, *EPSDT: Does It Spell Health Care for Poor Children?* (Washington, D.C.: Children's Defense Fund, 1977).

and mortgage interest payments to be eligible for federal income tax deductions. The chain of consequent developments has ramified throughout American society. Whereas 2.5 million now live in public housing, some 16 million families, heavily weighted to middle- and upper-income groups, have benefited from these latter provisions.

U.S. housing policy employs a variety of other instruments not central to the present overview.[47] In general, shifts in attitude and negative judgments about many of the efforts of the past have led to a recent concentration on special revenue sharing for housing and community development, an approach which leaves major policy and program initiatives to the state and local levels. The major new federal effort to help low-income families obtain satisfactory housing in recent years has taken the form of: (*a*) assuring reasonable rents for low-income families by paying the difference between what a family can reasonably be expected to spend (varying with family size and other factors) and a fair monthly rental charge on good quality rental and cooperative housing; (*b*) a similar subsidy program to assist low-income families to obtain and pay charges on mortgages (the payment covers certain costs above a reasonable proportion of adjusted income). These programs are attractive and growing, but currently are funded to cover only a small percentage of potentially eligible applicants.[48]

Education
Cremin, in a broad overview, comments as follows:

> Like any educational institution, the family originates some educative efforts, mediates others, and actually insulates its members from still others. What is more, educative efforts within the family involve not only parents teaching children but children teaching parents, parents teaching one another, and children teaching one another.[49]

This perspective poses a programmatic challenge being taken up at several places, and illustrated by the research work of Leichter and her colleagues,[50] or in the efforts to explore possible ways of forging effective link-

---

[47] See Henry J. Aaron, *Shelter and Subsidies* (Washington, D.C.: Brookings Institution, 1972).

[48] See John Palmer and Joseph J. Minarik, "Income Security Policy," in Henry Owen and Charles L. Schultze, eds., *Setting National Priorities: the Next Ten Years* (Washington, D.C.: Brookings Institution, 1976), pp. 515–18.

[49] Lawrence A. Cremin, "The Family as Educator: Some Notes on the Recent Historiography," in Hope Jensen Leichter, ed., *The Family as Educator* (New York: Teachers College Press, 1975), p. 85.

[50] *Ibid.*

ages among communities, schools, and home.[51] It expresses the rationale of those educators, school counselors, and school-community relations personnel who do seek to achieve supportive and cooperative relations between parents and schools. In nursery, prekindergarten, and kindergarten classes in particular, as in day care centers, personnel trained in early childhood education attempt more or less to work with parents—as do social workers—in accord with the pedagogical and philosophical perspectives of the program approaches which they represent.

Much of this, however, is on the level of professional belief and practice. In general, educational programming is a state and local matter. Federal support for programs, especially in poverty areas or where there is the impact of federal establishments, avoids dictating curricular content or educational philosophy. Courts seek to assure racial integration and non-discriminatory or "affirmative action" hiring, not to determine content of school programs. Thus, for the most part, educational programs are not family-oriented or guided by particular family policy goals.

In recent years school systems at all levels have increased the attention devoted to human biology, sex education, and to preparation for family life and parenthood.[52] While several federal agencies have offered encouragement, materials, technical aid, and in some cases project monies, it cannot be said that there is a comprehensive or even far-reaching federal program in this sphere.

Employment

This final human service sector is also one in which government does not seek specifically to develop family-oriented programs and policy. Job-placement services are individually oriented as are minimum wages. No government efforts are made to tie wages to family obligations. Nor are wage earners assisted in meeting their commitments to families by a system of family allowances. A minority of states do provide for supplementary grants for dependents as part of unemployment insurance.

Industry fringe benefit packages, usually the product of collective bargaining, often offer extensive benefits for members or families of members: hospital, surgical, major medical, and dental insurance; maternity leaves; vacation plans; scholarships and camp programs for children; retirement

---

[51] Eugene Litwak and Henry J. Meyer, *School, Family, and Neighborhood: the Theory and Practice of School-Community Relations* (New York: Columbia University Press, 1974).

[52] Personal social service programs in family agencies have also expanded family life education efforts.

facilities; assistance to dependents and survivors of members. As much may be said of some union programs. These are not governmental efforts, and systematic regulation by national government of pension programs has begun only recently.

From time to time special federal public-assistance-related job-training and placement programs have given preference to, or have been designed for, family heads. Currently, the program known as WIN (work incentive) makes a special effort at job training and supportive child care for AFDC mothers whose children are of school age. Ambitious new guaranteed work programs are being debated.

Indicative of a new focus, perhaps, is the recent inauguration by the Bureau of Labor Statistics. U.S. Department of Labor, of a new family statistical series, focusing on employment patterns within the family, the number and percentage of families in which there is no unemployment, some unemployment, or no one in the work force.[53]

Target Groups

Now our perspective shifts from programs to public policy as it is (or is not) oriented to different family members (roles) or age categories rather than to family units as such.

Children

A profile. In mid-1976 there were 65.2 million children in the U.S.[54] under age eighteen of the total population of some 215,118,000.[55] Some 12 percent of these children were under three; 27 percent, under six. In 1976, 97 percent of the children lived with one or two parents, 3 percent with other adults or in institutions. There has been a long-term decline in two-parent orphans, a recent decline in the percentage in two-parent families, but an over-all increase in the proportion of children living with at least one parent. Yet the trend of greatest concern to those interested in child development is the rise in one-parent families. By 1976, 85.2 percent of white children and 49.6 percent of black children lived with both parents (or 80 percent of all children). Of those with one parent, almost all lived only with mothers; 15.8

---

[53] *Monthly Labor Review,* XCIX, No. 12 (1976), 46–48.

[54] The total of children under sixteen was 60 million.

[55] The population early in 1976 was over 214,000,000.

percent of all children under eighteen; 11.8 percent of white children; and 40.1 percent of black children. These one-parent (mother) families, totaling over 5 million and containing over 10.3 million children in 1976, were headed by divorced, separated, widowed, or never-married mothers. Some 20 million children in the U.S. under age eighteen are members of families in which parents are not in intact first marriages. In 1976 alone there were over one million divorces in which approximately 1.25 million children were involved.

The officially stated foster home total is some 250,000 (estimated); there are about 100,000–125,000 children institutionalized as delinquent, dependent, neglected, or in need of supervision; 27,000 psychiatric in-patients; and 95,000 child residents of institutions for the retarded and handicapped.[56] There are official reports, some more rigorous than others, covering counts of retarded and handicapped children, rough estimates of the emotionally disturbed, and totals for those who are victims of serious accidental poisoning or crime. The 1976 infant mortality rate was 15.2 per 1,000 live births; for 1977 it was 14.1 (est.).

These, then, are the data which launch child development and family policy discussions. Such discussions often turn to child care.

Child care. While there has been some U.S. debate in recent years about day care programs and the adequacy of coverage, data about day care and preschool programs are seldom looked at together, and the accelerated trend to some form of preschool participation is not often quoted.

Thus, in 1975, over 90 percent of children age five, over 40 percent of children aged four, and 21 percent of the three-year-olds were in elementary, nursery, and prekindergarten classes, totaling almost 50 percent of the cohort ages three, four, and five and reflecting quite a rapid growth.[57] Of these children one third were in public preschool programs. There were

[56] The need to estimate, the dependence of the federal government on voluntary state reports and reports from voluntary agencies, and the limitation of reports mainly to service-related data (Census apart) are all evidence of our general point about the lack of clear federal mandate. For data sources see Kahn, "Child Welfare"; National Research Council-National Academy of Sciences, *Toward a National Policy for Children and Youth* (Washington, D.C.: the Academy, 1976). Newly published extrapolations from a national sample survey in March, 1977, place the foster care total as 500,000 of whom 395,000 were in foster homes. See Ann W. Shyne and Anita G. Schroeder, *National Study of Social Services to Children and Their Families: Overview* (Rockville, Md.: Westat, Inc., 1978), p. 8.

[57] One quarter of nursery and prekindergarten facilities were all-day. See U.S. Bureau of the Census, *Current Population Reports,* Series P-20, No. 303, "School Enrollment—Social and Economic Characteristics of Students: October, 1975" (Washington, D.C.: U.S. Government Printing Office, 1976), Table 15, p. 48.

some 1.4 million places in licensed day care centers, 61,000 licensed places in family day care homes, and over 2 million unlicensed places of both types also in use. If one adds day care, nursery, and kindergarten totals, some 7.7 to 8 million children out of 20 million under age six are in part-time or all-day care defined as "school" or as "day care" (or 2 million fewer if we discount unlicensed care). However, there is an unknown amount of overlap and duplication in these numbers. Millions of the children in part-time day care or in nursery and kindergarten groups are left to their own devices or in inadequate care after the school day, whatever its length.

Responsibility. Where does responsibility reside? The fact that data are periodically assembled (however imprecisely) and assessed[58] does not signify assignment of a strong, comprehensive, and continuing mandate at the federal level for detailed monitoring, policy development, or program operation for the vast majority of America's children. As indicated, the OCD–U.S. Children's Bureau (now the Administration for Children, Youth, and Families) has carried out funding activities in foster care, adoption, child abuse, and day care generally and administers one major compensatory early childhood program, Head Start (with several related offshoots), serving up to 400,000 children. Its staff and budget have thus far been small and its capacity to plan, coordinate, and advise limited. More ambitious mandates are currently being discussed. Child health and child research projects, and grant programs in several other federal governmental units, most of them elsewhere in HEW, may be individually important but do not represent broad public policy-making for most children. The largest federal impacts are via the AFDC program for over 8,000,000 poor children and through food stamp, school lunch and nutrition programs, Medicaid, and federal leadership in immunization campaigns.

Elementary education, the major public program, is largely a state-local responsibility. The federal governemnt is involved via special funding for poverty and ghetto areas and places where federal facilities or actions impact. Most other educational support is for handicapped and "exceptional" children. At the higher educational (postchildhood) levels even "private" colleges rely heavily on research, library, fellowship, and student loan programs. The U.S. places a larger proportion of its over-eighteen cohort in postsecondary education than any other country.

[58] The 1970 White House Conference on Children, *Profiles of Children* (Washington, D.C.: U.S. Government Printing Office, 1970); Kamerman and Kahn, *Social Services in the United States,* chap. 2; Kurt Snapper et al., *The Status of Children, 1975* (Washington, D.C.: Social Research Group, George Washington University, 1975).

The totality of federal programming for children, then, with a few exceptions, is remedial, thereapeutic, compensatory. It is largely child-, not family-, oriented, does not flow from an over-all policy or debated national objectives. In a recent overview Steiner concluded that the U.S. prefers to undertake categorical-remedial programs rather than comprehensive programming for children and, as yet, has not accepted a family policy responsibility: "The absence of a theory legitimizing a place for family relationships on the public rather than the private agenda discourages grand designs."[59] Children's interests are divided among many legislative jurisdictions, not assigned to one Congressional committee. In Steiner's view, the Senate Subcommittee on Children and Youth has been no more successful than the OCD, several other federal agencies, several voluntary agencies, an abortive "children's lobby," or successive recent White House conferences on children, in grasping the children's policy leadership and achieving ongoing attention and implementation.[60] The basic ethic, Steiner feels, takes as its point of departure Grace Abbott's remark "that all children are dependent but only a relatively small number are dependent on the state."

To Steiner, what has occurred may actually be the better part of wisdom:

> The children's policy most feasible—and most desirable—is one targeted on poor children, handicapped children, and children without permanent homes; unlucky children whose parents cannot provide them a start equal to that provided most children. The commission that makes the most useful contribution is one instructed to inventory that population. The lobbyists most needed are those urging programs targeted to those specific categories. The social altruists performing the most useful service are those who monitor the actual provision of compensatory benefits and services to unlucky children. Ultimately, a far more complex, universal program may be warranted. It may develop that private families really are not equipped to meet most children's needs. Unless and until that case is made more persuasively than it has been, however, a children's policy will be successful enough if it concentrates on ways to compensate demonstrably unlucky children whose bodies or minds are sick or whose families are unstable or in poverty.[61]

Steiner's is not the only view, however. While comprehensive interventive proposals are greeted in some quarters with the cries that public action decreases family responsibility, others—of quite different persuasion—call for more systematic, continual monitoring, policy debates, and planning, variously recommending an official children's commission, a nongovern-

---

[59] Steiner, *The Children's Cause*, p. 240.   [60] *Ibid.*, chap. 10.   [61] *Ibid.*, p. 255.

mental children's commission, a cabinet office for children, one Congressional committee to focus all interests on children, a federal council on children like the Federal Council on Aging. They note the growing public investment on behalf of children via hundreds of programs, but assess the proportion of the budget assigned to be inadequate. Visibility, planning, representation, and advocacy for children are seen as desirable.

Proponents of better organization for child-focused advocacy, planning, and monitoring add the caveat that they wish emphasis to be placed on family-oriented preventive work. The programmatic and organizational impact—judging by past experience—would nonetheless tend to be an increased tendency to focus on family members and roles, not to move toward a family policy or program. The champions of integrated and noncategorical personal social services obviously are in the minority.[62]

Thus far the question of how and whether one can consider the family organically while not ignoring the special needs and problems of children, youth, the aged, working mothers—or any other family member or role—has not been discussed much and has certainly not been dealt with in any major governmental forum.

Youth

If Americans are concerned about any single population group it is about "youth," an unspecified age category often beginning at 11 or 12 (attention being directed to alcoholism, delinquency, and pregnancy), concentrated on ages 14–18 (with attention to many problems), and sometimes defined as also covering older age cohorts. The extensive coverage by the press, journal articles, and sermons devoted to the youth problem refer regularly to high unemployment, drugs, crime, runaways, decline of competence in basic academic skills, teen-age pregnancies, sexual precocity, alienation.

In mid-1976 there were about 45 million in the 14 to 24 age cohort: 16.9 million aged 14 to 17; 16.8 million who were 18 to 21; and 11.4 million who were 22 to 24. Of those 14 through 17, 93.7 percent were in school; the percentage declined to 46.2 for those aged 18 or 19. Only 23.3 percent of the 20 through 24 age cohort were in school. And, of all dependent family members (not family heads) aged 18 to 24 in 1976, 37 percent were in college full time.[63]

[62] Alfred J. Kahn, "New Directions in Social Services," *Public Welfare,* XXXIV, No. 2 (1976), 26–32.

[63] Sources: U.S. Bureau of the Census, *Current Population Reports,* Series P-25, No. 519, "Estimates of the Population of the United States by Age, Sex, and Race: April 1, 1960 to July

Recent work in the "new" social history of the family suggests that despite the extensive twentieth-century writing, adolescence is a relatively recently discovered phenomenon (or, perhaps, institutionalized social category). The research notes that the degree of separatism socially structured for youth, the specific age boundaries which are set, and the roles assigned to youth are obviously connected with basic developments in the economy and in family structure.[64] Whatever the dynamics, there has been no federal-level effort to deal systematically, deliberately, and comprehensively with the "youth problem." If the spotlight is turned on youth at all, it is on their delinquency.

Excellent research in youth behavior and attitudes has been carried out in a number of settings; proposals to take up youth unemployment through one of several forms of youth services or job or training programs have come from several quarters.

The Civilian Conservation Corps and the National Youth Administration offered extensive programs for depression-affected youth in the 1930s. The Army and the Veterans Administration were at the center of the youth program picture in the 1940s and 1950s, as was the Office of Economic Opportunity in the 1960s with training and job efforts. Each program came and went, defined as appropriate and relevant to its emergency, often criticized as inadequate and ineffectual. No continuing policy or responsible governmental structure remained. A 1970 White House Conference on Youth, a split-off from the Conference on Children, attracted press attention but could show little by way of effective follow-up.

At the federal level, the Law Enforcement and Assistance Administration has initiated and supported new efforts to "divert" wayward youth from the system of "juvenile justice" into work and rehabilitative systems. Several Department of Labor and Education programs are concerned with employment training, careers, including a large youth employment measure enacted in the summer of 1977 in response to alarming unemployment rates. Education projects seek to cope with alienation from learning in some segments of the population, as a variety of health and mental health projects

---

1, 1973 (Washington, D.C.: U.S. Government Printing Office, 1974); U.S. Bureau of the Census, *Current Population Reports*, Series P-20, No. 286, "School Enrollment—Social and Economic Characteristics of Students: October, 1974" (Washington, D.C.: U.S. Government Printing Office, 1975).

[64] For example, see John R. Gillis, *Youth and History* (New York: Academic Press, 1974); Joseph F. Kett, *Rites of Passage: Adolescence in America 1790 to the Present* (New York: Basic Books, 1977).

tackle drugs and alcoholism as areas of major concern. The Office of Youth Development in HEW (recently incorporated in the new ACYF) administers funds for a program for runaways and has on paper a broad planning mandate, without sanction or funds to implement it.

In brief, coverage is limited and the impact even less noticeable. Most youth are said to be healthy, bent on careers, entering the system, motivated—despite difficult rites of passage and some dropouts. In any case, the society's attention to youth is not comprehensive, its alarums seldom followed by serious or sustained action, and a locus for governmental concern has not yet been invented. Nor is a strong case for extensive governmental action being made.

In the voluntary sector, there are many interested groups which carry out recreational and character-development programs, but none with a national mandate, a broad constituency, or a mission capable, at this point, of advancing broad proposals for a youth policy.

If and when a youth policy debate begins, it will be necessary and desirable to discuss relative advantages and disadvantages of program separation by age (Are adolescents different from young children in this sense? How different?) and whether adolescents almost by definition do not have concerns and interests in conflict with those of families—in short, whether youth policy is not actually in conflict with family policy. U.S. governmental action and experience do not at this point provide a platform for such a discussion.

The Aged

Some 22.4 million Americans, over 10 percent of the population, are aged 65 and over, and the percentage is increasing steadily. Between 1960 and 1970 the older Americans cohort increased by 21 percent as compared with 13 percent for the under-65 population; between 1970 and 1975 the aged population increased by 12 percent as contrasted with 4.5 percent for the rest of the population. Most aged are female (1.4:1) and most are under 75 (62 percent). Life expectancy is 68.7 for males but close to eight years longer, 76.5 for females. Almost 15 percent of the aged have incomes below the poverty level; however, women and minority aged are heavily over-represented among the poor. The aged become poor because retirement means between a one-half and a two-thirds cut in income from earnings; pensions do not replace an adequate proportion of earnings.

With this statistical picture in view, we turn to policy perspectives.

Public policy in the U.S. does not differentiate between those aged who are family members and those who are not, except that socially isolated aged individuals who have no family are viewed as a vulnerable group and therefore are entitled to priority consideration in receiving certain kinds of services. In contrast, however, there is no public policy designed to enhance or support families in helping or caring for their elderly relatives.

There are several agencies within the government which direct all, most, or some of their attention to the aged, but there is no single center with responsibility for coordinating all of these efforts. HEW contains most of the agencies with primary responsibility, although the Treasury (taxation), Agriculture (food stamps), Transportation, Housing and Urban Development, Defense, Labor, all have programs which impinge directly on the aged. Within HEW, the Social Security Administration, the Administration on Aging, the National Institutes of Health, and the National Institute on Aging all have responsibility for major programs serving the aged.

The Federal Council on Aging was created by law in 1973 to act as an advocate and watchdog agency for the aged. Among its responsibilities are the following:

1. To advise and assist the President on matters relating to the special needs of older Americans
2. To review and evaluate federal policies regarding the aging, assessing their impact on the aged
3. To serve as a spokesman on behalf of older Americans to the President, the Secretary of HEW, and the Congress
4. To inform the public about the problems and needs of the aging.

However, program funding and program administration are not subject to any direct jurisdiction of the Federal Council. There are, also, advocacy and administrative agencies and related efforts directed toward the elderly at state and local levels and in both public and private sectors. Some of the voluntary associations are large and politically quite potent.

Provision for the elderly may be growing, but it is fragmented and haphazard. Regardless of whether or not these multifarious efforts are successful or not, none of the service or benefit programs addresses the older American from the special vantage point of family relationships.

Public policy toward the aged, over all, may represent a somewhat more coherent and comprehensive perspective than public policy toward children or women, but it is certainly not internally consistent in its approach to the elderly as individuals, as spouses, and as family members. For example, Social Security benefits provide a disincentive for marriage between two elderly beneficiaries (subsequently corrected). The marital benefit is often lower than the entitlements of two unmarried individuals. SSI (means-tested, federalized public assistance) provides an incentive for elderly persons to live alone, since the benefit is considerably reduced when the recipient lives with someone (an adult child, for example) whose family income is above the poverty level.

Social Security and SSI have undoubtedly eased the financial burden of families that have aged parents and are concerned with supporting their own young children, as well as easing the burden of the elderly themselves. Adult children no longer have legal responsibility for the financial support of their aged parents. It is worth noting, however, that the lack of comprehensive health insurance or provision for long-term health care at home for all elderly, and the absence of any specific financial assistance ("care" allowance) for families who wish to care for their aged relatives or parents at home (or for spouses who wish to care for their husbands and wives), may pauperize or break up families.

Employing the Census Bureau definition of a family, the overwhelming majority of elderly people live in families (80 percent of the men and 60 percent of the women). Yet except for those who are particularly poor, no special policies exist to support housing—or housing renovations—that might permit longer independent living of the aged with each other or with their families.

Certainly, provision for the aged has increased considerably over the last decade. For example, the percentage of aged who are poor declined from about 35 percent in 1959, to 25 percent in 1969, to 16 percent in 1976. This reduction in the poverty status of the aged is primarily a result of the increase in Social Security benefits in the early 1970s and the passage of SSI. Moreover, benefit levels for the aged SSI recipients, set nationally by the federal government, are higher than what most states provide for children. In addition, there is some form of public provision of health care for all aged (Medicare and Medicaid). Also, there are some special housing subsidies and property tax abatements for the aged and a miscellany of personal social services also, although not in any comprehensive, large-scale program which guarantees coverage for all who need the service.

However, what is equally clear is that the increased concern and attention the aged receive in our society are not directed toward them as family members but as individuals. There are some who say that one consequence is to remove the aged even further from family living. After all, one-person households have been the most rapidly growing household type since 1970, and the aged represent 43 percent of these households. Others suggest that elderly people prefer their independent status—a status which is supported by current public policies.

In summary, as with adolescents, the question arises as to whether a family focus in policy development is desirable: politically, perhaps the aged fare better independently; personally, many do not want old age to signify dependency upon their children. Program developers, however, note the humanity and the economy of the family as a support system and social service agent for the elderly and seek ways of balancing familial and societal responsibility. For some of the aged and for many families, also, such an approach is apparently preferred. The question raised is whether social policy can be sensitive enough to respond to, but not push, the value system in this regard.

In similar fashion, questions are raised about the types of federal governmental structure and local patterns of organization for service delivery which support one or another of the policy options.

Women

Most of the U.S. public policy directed at women treats women as individuals, not as family members, wives, or mothers. Yet despite the paucity of family-focused women policies, some individually oriented policies have implications for the family in so far as they are designed to redress inequities in the legal or economic status of women.[65]

Several governmental bureaus and agencies are concerned with women; however, here, too, none is specifically directed to women as family members. Among these organizations are: the Women's Bureau in the Department of Labor (established in 1920); the Federal Women's Program, directed at assuring equal opportunity to women within the federal government; the Equal Employment Opportunity Commission; and HEW's Office of Civil Rights. All of these have been active in efforts to end sex discrimination in employment; but their effectiveness is still seen as relatively limited.

Two categories of public policies have clear and direct implications for women as family members: income-maintenance programs and family-planning services. As mentioned earlier, Social Security benefits are predicated on the assumption that married women are not employed and are fully supported by their husbands. Benefit entitlements in old age are weighted

---

[65] See also Sheila B. Kamerman, "Public Policy and the Family: a New Strategy for Women as Wives and Mothers," in Jane Roberts Chapman and Margaret Gates, eds., *Women into Wives* (Beverly Hills, Calif.: Sage Publications, 1977), pp. 195–214.

toward women in their roles as dependent spouses, not as independent workers, although in fact, and in contradiction, payroll taxes are paid by each employed marital partner as though each were a single individual. The largest public assistance program, AFDC, is directed at low-income women with minor children (under age eighteen) or with older children who are full-time students. Since this program is not available to intact families, except in those states where families with unemployed fathers may be eligible for assistance, it has become a program for female-headed, single-parent families. As indicated in our discussion of income transfers, given the combination of cash and in-kind benefits available to eligible women under AFDC, some critics have suggested that it is a program which encourages family break-up to obtain benefits, or, at the very least, tends to impede marriage or remarriage where relationships have broken down. It could also be argued, however, as we have noted, that AFDC makes financially viable the female-headed household as a family unit and is thus pro-family, albeit nontraditional family.

Family planning, including sterilization and abortion policies, has obvious implications for the family, even though directed primarily at women. There have been substantial increases in family planning services in the U.S. over the last decade, supplemented further with abortion services once abortion was legalized in the late 1960s. The more effective and sophisticated contraceptive devices (the pill and the IUD), in addition to sterilization (vasectomies for men, laparoscopies and tubal ligations for women), have emerged as the most popular methods of fertility control and appear to have had a significant effect on the birth rate. Most public or publicly supported family planning services are directed, specifically, at low-income women on the assumption that middle- and upper-income women are more knowledgeable and have readier access to contraceptive services and devices.[66] Historically, implicit public policy also has been directed at reducing the birth rate among poor women who are currently or potentially AFDC recipients, and thus economic burdens to the society. Nonetheless, a policy contradiction has emerged recently with legislation passed by Congress which precludes payment for most abortions under Medicaid: family planning is "pushed," abortion made difficult. The courts appear to be backing the legitimacy of the abortion-payment cutback.

As in many other fields, efforts at redressing inequities faced by women, eliminating discrimination, or assuring women of status more

---

[66] Kamerman and Kahn, *Social Services in the United States,* chap. 6.

nearly equal that of men, have tended to focus on the question of legal rights and equality before the law. Such efforts tend to set off a chain of events affecting employment, political participation, family structure, access to assets, which inevitably will have considerable impact on the family, even though such impact is only now beginning to emerge and as yet is only partially understood.

Changes in family law in some states (regarding, for example, ownership of property by marriage partners, entitlements to alimony and child support) have begun to eliminate those discriminatory statutes which still deprive some women of equal status. The Equal Employment Opportunities Act (1972), designed to eliminate sex and minority discrimination in employment, and similar federal anti-sex discrimination legislation, represent efforts to assure women equal economic status with men. A proposed Equal Rights Amendment to the Constitution has not yet been ratified by a sufficient number of states for it to be adopted.

Despite these legal achievements, women continue to have a substantially inferior economic status to men, and this fact has direct consequences for families. Women now are entering the labor force in greater and greater numbers. This trend has accounted for 60 percent of the growth in the work force since 1960. In 1976, over 47 percent of the women aged sixteen and over (and almost 60 percent of those between the ages of 18 and 64) were in the labor force, representing 41.5 percent of the active population. Women with young children are the most rapidly expanding group in the labor force: over 47 percent of women with children aged three to six and over one third of the women with children under age three worked in 1976, and most worked full time.

Yet, in the face of all this, median income and median earnings of women are at most 60 percent of what is earned by men. Moreover, the gap between male and female earnings is widening. Regardless of the reasons for this earning and income inferiority (occupational segregation, seniority obstacles, erratic work histories), continuation of this pattern implies that women in female-headed families and their children are inevitably at great risk of poverty.

Women's roles are clearly changing, but public policy in this country has yet to take full account of these changes or to deal systematically with the question of facilitating multiple roles for women as wives, as mothers, and as workers.

Concluding Note

The U.S. has many federal and state policies, some implicit and some explicit, policies which are concerned with the family and appear to affect its status, role, and well-being. There is no comprehensive, over-all family policy, however, nor is there evidence of either substantial political initiative or allocated organized responsibility for creating such policy.

Nonetheless, our overview has suggested a variety of potential leverage points for those who would advance family policy or, at least, instigate serious discussion of its desirability.

1. Policies are not "harmonized," to use a currently popular formulation. There are substantial instances of contradictions and discrepancies.

2. Incremental, "unharmonized," and often implicit policies have often become significant and potent even though not deliberately undertaken. Policy-making is thus not subject to adequate debate and specific choice.

3. Some of the specific program content and some of the effects on target populations are undesirable or inadequate when assessed on the basis of the broad goals of special interest groups or substantial elements in the electorate. There are, therefore, potent reform initiatives in several domains which are of significance for family policy. These, too, are not for the most part being coordinated from a family policy perspective at present, nor is there agreement that they should be. Nonetheless, the sum total of proposals and initiatives, their costs, and their potential impact is such as to generate a demand that eventual family impact be estimated and discussed.

All of this would appear to offer a platform for public or private initiatives and proposals. In addition, the experience of other industrialized countries which have deliberately formulated and implemented family policies provides evidence that whether or not the U.S. adopts more coherent and explicit family policies, the debate itself can be productive.

⤨15

FAMILY POLICY AS FIELD
AND PERSPECTIVE

NEITHER A CAREFUL reading of the reports from these countries nor the extensive discussion which they generate serves to provide definitive answers to such questions as: What is family policy? What are the costs and benefits of a family policy perspective?

The answers are simply not yet in. Or, perhaps, more accurately, the answers could vary by country, social system, and moment in history! For the functions of social policy and the instruments employed in behalf of such policy are complex and diverse, and our ability to identify and assess consequences is limited.

The Objectives of Family Policy

In terms of the vocabulary employed in our introduction, it was possible to classify the countries on something of a continuum with regard to family policy: explicit or implicit policy, comprehensive or episodic, harmonized to a degree or uncoordinated. However, such classification is in no case completely unambiguous and, in many instances, it is certainly forced. Relatively centralized countries, countries with clearly dominant states, know whether they have explicit policy and are able to cite it. But relatively centralized—if democratic—countries in which diverse political parties contend for power, and even rotate in power, find such parties differing on what the policy is and even on what the attitude toward policy is. Explicit, perhaps, but what is it *exactly?* What does it really *mean?*

Moreover, the picture is often quite mixed. Hilary Land and Roy Parker[1] note, for example, that while an ethic of privacy makes the United Kingdom deny any explicit family policy in most domains (or at least explicit policy across domains), a careful analysis of social security and tax programs reveals a quite coherent, if implicit, policy. The policy runs counter to some widely affirmed values about equality between the sexes and family roles. On the other hand, an explicit housing policy proves under close analysis to lack coherence in several critical senses.

The explicit-implicit dimension clearly is interesting, reflecting as it does whether a society has enough internal homogeneity to announce objectives for this most intimate of institutions, enough power to do something about such objectives, and a value system which supports such action. However, perhaps even more interesting are the questions of what exactly is being attempted (what are the *objectives*) and what *instruments* are being used. These topics would generate very different country classifications, as seen subsequently.

For the family policy discussion focuses variously on labor market policy, population policy, socialization (also protection and control), equality of the sexes, promotion of cultural identity and—in at least one of the countries represented—defense. The orientations are not unexpected, given the forces which generate the interest.[2]

In a sense, some *population policy* is never absent, and any family policy advocate concerned with offering suggestions for enriched and improved child socialization often finds himself accused of pronatalist activity. Some of the countries do have pronatalist goals, whether formulated in terms of concern about a projected unbalanced age-distribution curve which predicts a labor force unable to meet economic production or national defense needs, or an anxiety about payment of social security commitments at a future date when there will be an unfavorable dependency ratio (too few workers to support the retired and the young). A few of these countries define the problem in such terms and act. Other countries have not developed these concerns, while still others are hesitant to articulate them, given the history of pronatalist racism in the 1930s and 1940s.

---

[1] We occasionally cite names by way of attributing sources of ideas and formulations. In so doing we reply upon country papers, discussions at the Arden House Conference of the International Working Party on Family Policy, and similar discussions at a conference subsequently convened in Ottawa by the Canadian Council on Social Development. It should be stressed that the people referred to have not verified the citations and are not responsible for any misunderstandings or inappropriate emphasis on our part. Full names and titles appear in the list of participants.

[2] See our introduction, ''Familier and the Idea of Family Policy.

But *labor market* considerations are substantial and go beyond pronatalist efforts to affect the size of the labor force and the number who pay for social security. In responding to labor force shortages, countries have three additional options: higher productivity, importation of foreign labor, facilitating the entry of women into the out-of-home work force. It is certainly not clear whether the determination of many women to work and thus to achieve fuller societal participation and greater equality is cause or effect here. There are, in this group, countries which had little choice under their particular demographic, political, and economic circumstances after World War II but to assure large-scale female entry into the labor force. Labor supply needs would not otherwise have been met in countries experiencing rapid economic growth, especially countries which had large World War II manpower losses. (The problem may have been particularly acute when, either as part of a policy to assure full employment or because there was no real alternative, productivity remained relatively low in many fields of economic activity.)

In other countries, the economic and political imperatives were quite different, yet the basic long-term trend is similar. There has been dramatic growth in the female labor force in the United States, for example, even during the high unemployment of recent years.

Family policy as labor force policy thus may be cause or effect, or sometimes one and sometimes the other. What it is preoccupied with is facilitating the entry of women into the labor force by means of a package of social welfare benefits and child care programs, benefits and programs sometimes seen by others as instruments of demographic policy. A transition is summarized by Vera Shlakman as follows, commenting on Sweden: first there is concern with the right of mothers to work, then concern with the right of working women to have children.

To the human capital economist, *the family itself is the production unit* with which family policy is concerned. In the words of Carolyn Shaw Bell, ''The family is a producer and it is also a consumer. What the family produces is children, who are future productive resources.'' In this sense, children are, to the economist, investment goods. Since the country as a whole benefits from their productivity it could have reason to make an investment: children are public goods. By contrast, in Dr. Bell's view, a marriage per se produces a form of shared life and perhaps enjoyment which is private. The state has no role in the latter and should support the former—which requires publicly sanctioned redistribution in favor of children—only if it is known that the goal is achieved: do some redistribution schemes produce more and better children? Surprisingly little is firmly known. (Because Bell believes that the individual is the only "entire unit" in society, belonging to more than one family in a lifetime and obviously needing to be a producer, she would favor an individualistic rather than a familial orientation for social policy.)

Harold Watts, another economist, formulates the test differently. He sums up:

> The cardinal fact which warrants society's concern with the family is that human reproduction admits the possibility of immortality for a society, and hence a society's progress or evolution depends critically on the rearing of children: their physical health and development, their intellectual or cognitive training, and their social and cultural indoctrination.

In short, it is a sociological plus an economic perspective.

Watts notes that one might conceivably invent other child-rearing institutions (and some have been tested), but the papers show, as does history,

> a remarkable robustness of that particular institution in that particular role. As a consequence, public policies directed at the ultimate goal of "good outcomes" for upcoming generations of society must work somewhat indirectly through parents and families.

The rationale for family policy leads to questions of *quantity,* as already noted, but also to matters of *quality.* Here Watts meets, but adds to, Bell. Contemporary life is demanding, whether one is in or out of the labor force. The required generalized and specialized capacities are achieved only through collaboration of schools and other formal institutions outside the family with the family. The family role does not decrease as other formal institutions grow. To which we might add that in buttressing this socialization and developmental role of the family the social services can become important instruments of family policy. Insensitively employed, they may weaken the family role and its socialization capacity.

Others might respond to Bell by noting that the state intervenes in marriage and divorce because it has a stake in life styles as well as in production of children. In fact, much of labor policy, too, is currently involved with enriching the experience of the worker, without establishing that this always increases production. Quality questions reach many domains.

Redistribution, services, policy to support the family, are therefore part of an immortality policy. But immortality requires more than a skilled labor force. Some of the countries—or groups and/or regions within the countries reporting—are concerned as well not only with the life style and satisfaction of workers but also with cultural or religious identity, preservation of values, or their distinct nationalisms (the term, while not employed, seems justified). Here they raise memories which create some anxiety too: family policy, after all, also has served racism.

In a sense, family policy as *socialization* overlaps with family policy as labor market policy. However, sociological and economic insights join to note that people become better producers if families are successful consumers. Children need to learn, to identify, to become motivated, and the research concludes that families are the most effective milieu for this. Hence redistribution which compensates for the extra costs of rearing children might be justified by the over-all quality of life thereby assured to families. And those things better achieved via public merit goods, or collective consumption, or societal provision, or social services (the vocabularies vary) are complementary parts of the family-support package. In a narrow economic sense they may be inefficient forms of redistribution. Yet in a societal sense they may be quite effective if targeted at the family types which are of interest.

But some countries now see their family policy essentially as an instrument for achieving *equality between the sexes*. Perhaps this formulation, here represented by Norway and Sweden particularly (even though the goal exists formally in almost all the countries), is an aspect of labor market strategy. Yet the policy components and benefit package become quite different. Indeed, equality policy is one of the newer manifestations of family policy. We begin to note, as we consider the Swedish evolution and debate, for example, that family policy may need to make choices in some instances *between* family members, *among* family roles. Whatever the rationalizations, it is evident that what was viewed as best for father in the past was not always best for mother or child; from the perspective of traditional roles, what is now best for mother may not be best for father or child; what is best for child may not be best for father and mother, and so forth. Here, one goal of family policy could be to ease the tensions that may emerge as a consequence of the changing roles of men and women.

At this point one must note specifically what becomes increasingly obvious as the goals of family policy are explored: family policy often is rationale, rationalization, an instrument of other policies, such as demography, labor market, individual rights, and cultural identity! But the picture is complex, and it can be argued at some times and in some places that the causal pattern runs in the other direction. As much may be said of the final formulation about family policy which emerges in discussion: family policy as quality of life. Is the family a vehicle for achieving life-quality goals formulated on another value base, or is a particular family model a possible criterion for life quality?

This brings us to the broadest and most contemporary formulation: sometimes family policy is addressed explicitly to *quality-of-life* issues that go beyond population, labor force, and political-national objectives. For Watts, the "quality" dimension as part of an "immortality" policy in effect is more than assuring productive and efficient citizens; Bell's recognition of the family as having many "private consumption" preoccupations also may be stated as: the family creates a life quality along motivational principles that do not derive from the market place. Liljeström writes in great detail about societal dynamics which plainly ask that quality-of-life rather than productivity concerns prevail. And Zsuzsa Ferge reminds us that, all other motivations aside, societies do decide to assure their populations of minimum adequate means of living; her own country, Hungary, does not hesitate to assert the significance of the family in nurturing and caring for the young even though labor market dynamics might suggest changing circumstances and a different argument. She is quoted by Magdalena Sokołowska as noting that social policy is employed "to shape social relations so as to serve well-defined values." But elsewhere she also states that family policy is "aimed at influencing the life conditions and attitudes of families in order to assure that the function of the family be in harmony with the requirements of societal development."

So, the family becomes a vehicle for achieving external goals. Similarly, the paper from Czechoslovakia describes family policy as attempting "to influence and regulate the family's behavior according to explicitly stated or silently presumed patterns."

The cynics see only, or largely, demographic and labor market objectives. Some note an interplay among economic, cultural, religious, and humanitarian forces. Others acknowledge that family policy was misused in the past but feel it is possible to turn the family policy instrument generally toward quality-of-life concerns. Still others derive their models from cultural or religions traditions and see a *specific* family type as carrying the essential values for life quality. One should not be surprised, therefore, if family policy continues to be discussed in *all* these terms: population labor market, socialization, social service, ethnic and cultural identity, family patterns, and equality.

The specific banner which is raised is not necessarily the basic dynamic. When a government or a society chooses a policy it selects objectives and constraints, priorities and sacrifices. Some people gain and others pay. One would expect explicit identification of fundamental values to be maximized, at least where there is explicit policy. Societies tend to avoid such identification, however; some do not want to attack an ethic of privacy; others have been built on a rhetoric of individualism; many fear to upset the unification achieved under pluralism. Others hesitate to express their true objectives for still different reasons. Consequently, fundamental values are often not discussed or even recognized. These are the values which may offer the foundation for the population, labor market, socialization, or other policy streams which are either the vehicles for family policy or the more basic dynamics behind such policy. However, it is unlikely that new family policy initiatives will manage to perpetuate such evasion. It is apparent that the level of sophistication rises.

To face issues is not necessarily to emerge with the same answers everywhere. Family policy evolves in the context of ideology about family and about government. It may stress those in need (Finland) or be universal. (While some observers believe that universalism is avoided as more costly, Nicole Questiaux says that there is no substantial evidence to this effect.) Family policy may attract those who seek social change (Hungary) or proponents of the status quo. When social policy cross-cuts child care ideology, the results are often startling: a policy favored by socialists in one country (child-rearing grants) may attract bourgeois parties or church groups in another.

Many political figures, experts, and members of the public are aware of the distinction between family policy as rationale and rationalization and family policy as autonomous domain. Brief consideration will disclose that any deliberately unified family policy has a strong normative foundation. Some normative choices preclude others. The very ''same'' uses of family policy (for population or labor market objectives, for example) may grow out of quite different value sets and thus in reality generate very different policy specifics. Whatever the record of the past, any family policy developments in the future are likely in some of the countries here covered to demand some discussion of fundamental societal goals or objectives—or at least goals for the family (or for the primary living group) in the context of such objectives. In the U.S., as in a good number of other countries, there is discomfort from, or even opposition to, such discussion and choice in the public domain. Family rhetoric is attractive, family policy politically dangerous.

The Specific Instruments

Attitudes toward what is public and what is private, to what is appropriate and what inappropriate for government to do, are deeply embedded in cultural history. The distinctions often seem illogical to outsiders. Yet, one cannot review a series of descriptions of the ways in which implicit and explicit family policy manifests itself in a group of countries without recognizing the large number of shared instruments. This much may be said while also recognizing, as has been implied, that there is no evidence of a universally acceptable theory of family policy. Such theory would appear to require: a theory of the modern family (functions, roles, dynamics); a clear formulation of agreed objectives; a "scientific basis" for utilizing various instruments to achieve such objectives; evidence of effective impact.

Nonetheless, the countries operate in the domains which they choose, employing the instruments which they favor, on the basis of assumptions, hopes, or their own certainties that they know what they wish to achieve and expect the chosen actions to contribute to such achievement. And, if the objectives are not too global (eradicate inequality, end delinquency, assure mental health, and so on), countries are able to see whether intermediate goals are accomplished and then to set new targets for the same or for other instruments.

Historically, *income-transfer* programs have been the most readily identifiable instruments of family policy, whether defined in terms of demographic goals or of broader objectives requiring some degree of income redistribution from those with children to those without, or from those with one or two children to those with several. The Questiaux-Fournier paper from France offers the most extensive illustration of such an approach and also justifies the observation, as do a number of the other papers, especially that of Land and Parker from the U.K., that social security and tax policy must be conceived of as one comprehensive strategy. This has been the case since social insurance, public (social) assistance, means-tested housing allowances, and taxes expanded from marginality to become major factors in individual or familial disposable income at some or all points in the life cycle.

A system of family allowances has been the most direct and efficient income-transfer instrument for these purposes, and it is responsible for small income changes in some of these countries and for large ones in others. Of the countries here represented, only the U.S. lacks family allowances.

Hungary and Czechoslovakia have added to this repertoire a child-rearing grant for women who leave the labor force to care for infants for two or three years. France does something similar, but on a means-tested basis, for all single-earner families or where there are more than three children or one child under age three.

Yet no instrument has precisely the same meaning in any two countries. Only a few years ago, in debate related to proposed income-maintenance reform, the British were reminded that the family allowance check was defined as part of the *mother's* income and that to take it away in order to create a more generous and equitable family benefit scheme involved engineering redistribution within the microeconomy of the family.

Dependency exemptions in the personal *income tax system* express a kind of family policy in some Western countries, but the system has been so structured as to make these exemptions most meaningful at the higher marginal tax rates. A switchover to tax credits which are uniform is thus a means of favoring poor families, especially poor large families.

Not mentioned as often, but of almost equal (in some views, greater) significance as a family policy instrument, is *family law*. Changes in rules and procedures may have enormous impact, affecting as they do marriage, support, divorce, separation, adoption, foster care, division of property, family planning, abortion, guardianship, adolescent independence, treatment of abused children and abusing adults, as well as unruly youth and delinquents. While here highlighted in only three papers (U.S., Israel, Canada), family law has been thus recognized in a major international collaboration.[3] In a sense, the current reform of family law relates to assertion of the equality of the sexes and increased protection of individual rights. Family law would appear to be following, not leading, new trends in family policy.

Child care services are a central family policy vehicle, a necessary response to the entry of women into the labor force, or even a precondition of such entry if the price is not to be too high. Child care services are also a basic response to family change and new family size. Where women do not work outside the home, child care nonetheless becomes a precondition of equality, in some views. Since tax and income-maintenance policies are long established—even if specifics are constantly modified—and family law

---

[3] Maurice Kirk, Massimo Livi Bacci, and Egon Szabady, *Law and Fertility in Europe*, 2 vols. (Dolhain, Belgium: Ordina Editions, 1976). See also Harry D. Krause, *Family Law: Cases and Materials* (St. Paul, Minn.: West Publishing Co., 1976). In the U.S. much of family law is reserved to the states. In Austria, to select a contrasting country, much more of family law is in the "competence" of the federation.

is taken for granted, the child care issue is a central one in the current debate in many countries. There are differences and distinctions, however. Most of continental Europe provides for children from age three, or even a bit younger, to compulsory school age in public preschool programs, most of them associated with the public educational system or publicly subsidized, universal, voluntary, free, and used by practically all the eligible children as soon as there is space.[4] Canada, the U.S., and the U.K. are less committed than this, and less clear as to what constitutes child care for this age group. As a consequence, there is less coverage and considerable overlap and confusion among day care, preschool, nursery school, and playschool.

The uncertain and debated policy on the Continent relates to those under three. Here the countries display a range of policy and provision from an emphasis on social welfare benefits to make it easier for parents (mostly mothers) to care for children at home, to a substantial investment in group or family day care, permitting large numbers of mothers of infants to work. There are splits within Eastern Europe: compare Czechoslovakia and Hungary, on the one hand, with Poland and, especially, the German Democratic Republic on the other. There are countries in the West which do little or nothing (for example, the F.R.G.), leaving care arrangements to the mother (assuming incorrectly that this will keep mothers at home); there are countries that hold both options open (France), or experiment with one or the other (Finland); and those that consider still other alternatives (Norway and Sweden with their proposal of a short work day for parents of young children).[5]

One is fascinated with the intensity of the debate, the effort to bring some degree of empiricism to bear, and the evidence that women continue to enter the labor force and to generate the challenge of child care policy even as inflation and unemployment create problems. Of the papers here presented, only the one from Denmark specifically reports substantial child care cutbacks and a shift toward public reaffirmation of the importance of mothers' care for infants as women are less needed in the labor market. We know that the phenomenon is not isolated, however. In some ways this is ironic, given Jacob Vedel-Petersen's view it is a violation of childhood to define it only as a period of preparation for a productive adulthood. He is a critic of that kind of day care which would stress preparing children for future roles,

---

[4] Coverage ranges from 50 percent to 95 percent of those age three through five and is rapidly reaching the higher figure.

[5] These options are only suggested here and quite incompletely at that. They are the subject of our current comparative research. *The editors.*

preferring to see infancy and childhood as a thing for itself, to be enjoyed in its time. Such day care, when of good quality, would hardly be abandoned because unemployment had brought mothers home again.

The *personal social services* are another instrument of family policy described in a significant number of papers. Even countries which avoid comprehensive measures in the family policy field, and which develop no explicit policy except family law for "average" families, do have services to deal with out-of-wedlock childbirth, family desertion involving children, parent-child difficulties, neglect and abuse, marriage breakdown. Foster care and adoption programs and services to young unwed mothers are almost universal. Perhaps the objective is to buttress the acceptable family variants and to control the deviants—as the minimum, first-level, response.

A more complete appreciation of the family's role in socialization and development takes some countries further. Recognition of the reciprocity between the family and formal institutions creates interest in the social services as support systems for average families[6] as well as for those with "case" problems:[7] giving assistance to the handicapped child or adult while also buttressing the family as a "social service" instrument; providing personal social services to the aged while encouraging adult children in the supportive role and not stereotyping women as home persons or caretakers; offering advice, counseling, education, and information to "average" people about everyday experiences, thus filling gaps created by changes in family and community life and newly emerging norms.

Social services in this sense become resources and amenities in a new age. The policy which encourages and supports them emerges out of charity and humanitarianism in some places, out of very utilitarian impulses in others. It is an acceptable preoccupation in socialist countries, too, where it is noted that economic development does not solve all social problems or eliminate the need for new types of consumer services.

There are still *other policy instruments* that carry family policy objectives, have impact on families, or miss opportunities which, to an analyst at least, seem attractive. Reference is made to housing (the U.K. and Czechoslovakia), education, health. With regard to health, particuarly, George Silver argues that the field can be the core of family policy, but most of the

[6] Alfred J. Kahn and Sheila B. Kamerman, *Not for the Poor Alone* (Philadelphia: Temple University Press, 1975, hardcover; New York: Harper & Row, 1977, paper).

[7] Alfred J. Kahn and Sheila B. Kamerman, *Social Services in International Perspective* (Washington, D.C.: U.S. Government Printing Office, 1977).

papers to not take such a perspective. Despite proposals and examples, it would be difficult to argue that family policy is the major source of guidance for these or other fields of societal action. For one might also list fields such as transportation, commerce, cultural affairs, the military, consumer affairs, which obviously carry their own agendas but which contribute to implicit family policy. They do this, perhaps, by acts of omission and commission, by the implicit models of the family which they assume, by assignments they take on, and by what they leave to the primary group, to the intimacy of the household—extremely important influences even if the full effects of the policy are not articulated.

Housing and education can become arenas in which to observe major family policy departures: witness the Israeli kibbutz (as discussed by Honig and Shamai). One is impressed, however, with the relatively small-scale intervention of education, as an institution, into family policy in so far as there are efforts to absorb change, prepare for new roles, redistribute child care and socialization tasks as mothers work. In the housing field, the first response was to the needs of large families with many children; then the single parent and her child(ren); now, finally, the aged. The solutions offered are largely, but not solely, individualistic.

Where the instruments are used in isolation they may be in conflict and undo intended family effects, but the potency of income-transfer or tax measures alone should not be underestimated. On the other hand, a determined government may harmonize a "package" of measures (Czechoslovakia) for substantial over-all impact. Whether or not the birth rate remains high, the society has been changed.

Harmonization is of course a relative matter; societies are complex and implementation difficult. As much may be said for the distinction between the comprehensive and the episodic. Yet one can identify the countries by the major measures chosen and the degree of harmonization.

One may also ask about the targets of such measures. Obviously, the focus is most commonly on mothers and children and parents and children. Indeed, some of the papers report this as the sense in which family policy is conceived in their countries, and others note it as the operational reality. This should occasion no surprise, given the major concerns to which family policy is directed: population, women in the labor market, redistribution in favor of families with young children, clarification of responsibility for dependents.

However, the discussion sometimes turns as well to the aged *vis à vis* their families. Robert Moroney and Robert Morris[8] have called attention to the need to settle just what incentives and disincentives we wish to offer families to house and assist their elderly. There is little discussion as yet of the young adolescents or of the older adolescents—two groups which may have social-psychological incentives or pressures to separate themselves. The exploration of the functions and dysfunctions of a family policy which considers them is hardly yet visible. Perhaps it is not necessary.

Government Structure and Family Policy

In general, government currently fragments both policy and programmatic interests of the family in many units, bureaus, and departments. This would appear to be even more so in countries with implicit as contrasted with those having broad and explicit family policies. Only a few countries organize administration specifically and comprehensively to deal with a very wide range of family matters. In many places the private sector is the vehicle for implementation of many programs, often on the basis of governmental funding and planning.

In the U.S., advocates of more pro-family or pro-child activity on the part of the government often envision a family department or ministry as an essential and potent vehicle. The reported experience is instructive and relatively unambiguous. Analysis of the country papers and intensive discussion yields undeniable consensus that the European record shows no significant success with family ministries anywhere.

It is not that such ministries have not been tried. Norway, for example, downgraded its family ministry to a subunit within a consumer ministry after some experience. And there are such ministries now: the F.R.G. combines family matters with child and health responsibilities. However, the evidence is plain that the family ministry is always given a limited role and is not powerful. The record suggests that it often is established when the politics of coalition building in a parliamentary system requires an additional portfolio, or (in the past) a cabinet post for a woman.

The inevitability that family ministries will be weak is explained by Friedhelm Neidhardt with reference, first, to issues of substance, and then to questions of power:

---

[8] Robert Moroney, *The Family and the State: Considerations for Social Policy* (London: Longman's, 1976). Personal correspondence with Robert Morris.

. . . the family is a living unit in a place where the private consequences of practically the total output of societal institutions and processes are somewhat manifested and must be integrated with some kind of individual life style. Other policy fields refer to specialized institutions and to specific functional processes: defense, economy, agriculture, justice, housing, labor, and so on. They are differentiated according to special functions that constitute their genuine core problems. . . . Because the family constitutes itself as the private integration of almost the total range of public influences, virtually all family policy problems are genuine problems of other branches of policy. A family ministry, then, can be thought of as a governmental department for everything—or nothing.

. . . the actual responsibilities of a family ministry come out to be very few. There are good reasons for this because of the fact that the societal areas that most heavily influence the family—business, labor market, housing legislation, and so forth—are areas that cannot be monopolized by a purely family policy kind of problem-solving. The family policy view serves for only one aspect among others. And it cannot be held desirable that the policies toward these areas be absorbed by family interests.

Even if it would be desirable, it would not happen. . . . family interest groups—if not heavily supported by population and labor market interests—are not very strong. The point is, on the one hand, that family policy interests are difficult to organize because of their diffusiveness. On the other hand, family interest groups—if organized—do not have strong sanction power.

The shared experience confirms Neidhardt's analysis. Those who nonetheless favor efforts to develop explicit family policy or some governmental monitoring of family interests in a less comprehensive sense are thus left in search of a potent mechanism. Here the evidence is mixed and experimental: a department in a deputy chancellor's office in Austria to assess potential impact on families of proposed laws and regulations; an effort to develop a "systems" analytic approach by a task force in the Labor Ministry in Hungary; a pattern of systematic consultation with voluntary but subsidized family organizations in France and elsewhere, and so forth.

If one accepts the fact that governmental ministries and departments require functional organization, thus leaving child or family departments relatively weak, one arrives at a position much like that taken by Neidhardt. The exact political-governmental mechanism will need to be determined within each country, but his statement of principles may have broad relevance:

What might, then, be a proper organizational unit for acting out family policy? I think this unit must fulfill at least two functional requirements. First, it must be located in a place where the relevant decisions for all ministries regularly come to be coordinated before being executed. Second, it must have power enough to press significant family interests against the particular interests of other areas and to balance them. It is clear that such a unit must lie on the top ranks of the governmental hierarchy. I think that in my country an office within the Chancellor's bureau could meet these requirements—at least, better than a special family ministry.

Such a monitoring function, of course, assumes a readiness to examine family policy objectives and to be explicit about *choices*. This is taken for granted in some countries and feared or strongly opposed in others. The structural question, in short, belongs at this point of the discussion for some and is quite premature or inappropriate for others.

One other very useful insight emerges from the discussion of governmental structure. It is somewhat confirmed by the experience with the U.S. Children's Bureau and the Office of Child Development, but there are also significant illustrations in a number of the country papers: Unable to play a powerful role in harmonizing policy on behalf of family (or child) interests, such a unit may seize the opportunity to operate a new program in need of a home. Then, preoccupied with the political and organizational (and budgetary) fate of its own programs, however marginal they may be on any scale of over-all family and child interests, the unit sacrifices its credentials as an advocate of balanced, harmonized, coherent family (child) policy. It becomes another small bureau with its own interests, claiming a broader role, but unconvincingly.

The solution is a unit properly placed to play its over-all policy advocating or initiating or monitoring role on a level above the operating departments. If the society does not choose to assign such a role, it cannot be "bootlegged" by a departmental operating unit.

Neidhardt also reminds us of another danger: a family ministry with limited programmatic responsibility

> will be inclined to compensate the deficit of material relevance by upgrading the symbolic meaning of its subject. It appears to me that this sort of justification pressure favors the production of family ideologies that I personally do fear . . .

The historical record demonstrates that the subject is serious.

Government structure should not be treated as a simple variable, even though not here looked at in all of its ramifications. The state (*Land*, province) also must be looked at carefully as a family policy arena in all federal systems (three-tier countries), especially the U.S., Canada, and the F.R.G. In some such countries family law varies by state (U.S., Canada), whereas in others large elements are, or become, national in scope (Austria, F.R.G.). The complexity of the subject is suggested by Allen Jensen's observation that in the social field the specific pattern of operational responsibility and policy decision-making as between state and federal government varies with the specifc program.

Can We Know Whether It Works?

The correct sequence for the discussion varies with the perspective on family policy. Were there strong evidence as to whether systematic policy can be formulated and with what effects, such an overview might guide us on governmental structure. However, most of the discussion of policy impact relates only to limited domains, or to proposals, or to a few countries.

The international picture is a very mixed one: some countries appear to justify their policies only by reference to ideology, not through investigation of effects. On the other hand, the great U.S. emphasis on evaluation of all program initiatives, even where poorly elaborated and conceptualized and even before fully mounted, reads like fetishism to many outsiders. Much of the evaluation in most places is *ad hoc* and takes the form of an assessment of social statistics or trends by citizens or politicians, not of formal research. Analysts offer *ex post facto* judgments in many countries as to the efficacy of policies.

The formal evaluative research cannot proceed very far without clarification of values and goals. We are reminded by Vedel-Petersen that the determination to measure effects of day care on cognitive processes is related to the view of child socialization as investment. Given his advocacy of childhood as a stage in its own right, "consumption" to the human capital economist, research that seeks such effects as a basis for assessing day care lacks validity.

But the subject is even more complex. Women work away from home in the search both for more adequate (or higher) living standards and more satisfactory personal roles. The work pattern demands expanded child care arrangements. This, in turn, affects family life and invades familial privacy. How is it to be evaluated? How does one weigh economic standards and consumption, changed relationships, new public-private boundaries, alternative patterns of child socialization? The public discussion has hardly begun to sort out all the value consequences. Evaluation is therefore not a simple matter.

Harry D. Krause and Robert Morris[9] remind us that family policy requires a value dimension to permit choice (or, we add, to evaluate effects). Even a decision to support a variety of life-style options and role alternatives is nonneutral in this sense. (Neutrality might involve deliberate measures to support alternatives favored by groups in the society which differ with one another!)

Given all this, Irwin Garfinkel has offered, in discussion, a cost-benefit perspective on family impact analysis: since it forces specifications of, and agreement on, values, it creates significant strain on the political system. As in all such analyses, such conclusions deter some people but not others!

While it is unclear whether program or policy assessment or prior evaluation from the viewpoint of family interests will be made everywhere, or in relation to all possible major subjects, discussion does disclose considerable opinion to the effect that "impact on the family" is a worthwhile criterion for social policy. The family apparently is "here to stay" (Mary Jo Bane's phrasing), recovering and adapting, whatever the challenges from alternative life styles, new forms like the commune or kibbutz, and new sex roles, especially in the dual-career family. While "family" in this sense needs definition, perspectives on its well-being if translated operationally might yield starting points for ongoing evaluative efforts in the public policy field.

Such assessment could be (but in some views should not be) limited to mothers or parents and children. The family life cycle, conceptualized variously by sociologists and human development psychologists, must not be ignored lest we lose potential insight into the life-cycle price for concentration on one or another stage or objective. On a more immediate level, we note the frequency with which impact on fathers or adolescent children tends to be ignored in family policy assessment. Mention has already been made of the tendency to act as though the aged are not involved: perhaps their interests do call for categorical, not familial, policy-making, but the subject deserves exploration and research.

While the library of completed research using a family well-being perspective is hardly bulging with impressive works, the preparatory work in measurement, surveys, and conceptualization is considerable. There is also agreement that the enterprise is worthwhile, both from those who support the effort out of conviction and those who consider it a practical matter. Lee Rainwater, for example, notes that on the contemporary scene family policy

[9] Personal correspondence.

as a perspective for assessment may become a useful policy tool much as "mental health" and "poverty" were not too long ago.

Conceptually attractive, perhaps. Some work on which to build, certainly. But not easy. Serious efforts to focus on family-relevant effects in assessing social policies will demand, we repeat, an adequate knowledge base, improved measurement capability, value consensus on objectives, and political sanction. The scientific task can be undertaken, and there is a good starting point. The value and political questions yield different answers in different countries.

For researchers the discussion points especially toward important work to be done on the microeconomy of the family, family time budgets, and the results of socialization under various structural arrangements and child-rearing regimes.

In the U.S., experimentation is projected with the development of family impact statements to be submitted in connection with proposed or existing legislative or administrative actions.[10] The assessment, to be useful, should involve attempts at rigorous scientific projection and prediction or evaluation in light of the available knowledge base.

The Austrian Government uses a more informal consultative process, calling in family associations, other interest groups, representatives of ministries, to the Department of Family Affairs, a unit under the Chancellor. An advisory report on potential impact is drawn up on the basis of consensus, after discussion and debate.

While the subject of family impact statements generates interest in an era when environmental impact statements have come into their own, there is recognition that if entered into too early and without caution the flimsy scientific underpinnings will be ignored (the gaps in knowledge and measurement capacity remain considerable) and the value elements in policy choice underplayed or hidden.

The papers and discussions illustrate that there is useful analytic work to be done even if all conceptual and methodological problems are not yet solved. Ferge proposes a modest criterion: that when a program is launched

---

[10] The main U.S. endeavor is currently centered in the Family Impact Seminar, George Washington University, Washington, D.C., under the direction of A. Sidney Johnson III. The obstacles to implementing such impact analyses are discussed in Sheila B. Kamerman, *Developing a Family Impact Statement* (New York: Foundation for Child Development, 1976). The most interesting recently published work is Katherine Bradbury *et al.*, "The Effects of Welfare Reform Alternatives on the Family," Special Report 13 (Madison, Wis.: Institute for Research on Poverty, University of Wisconsin, 1977).

or a policy inaugurated one may observe whether the specific problem tackled actually has been dealt with successfully. It is useful to recognize that any single intervention is always embedded in a broader societal context. The standard cannot be whether anything is "solved," Rather, is there progress against the recognized "evil"?

The record of family policy is mixed, if assessed in this practical way (without control groups) and in accord with the state of the art. In a remarkable illustration of practical, clear-thinking, unpretentious evaluation, Questiaux and Fournier sum up French family policy historically:

1. It did not halt the birth rate decline.

2. It did help stabilize the traditional family.

3. It did, by means of redistribution, help eliminate the special economic burdens carried by familes with several children.

4. It did not successfully motivate families to carry on the care of the sick and the aged.

5. It achieved more in these realms than the F.R.G., a country chosen as offering a legitimate basis for contrast.

This type of macropolicy assessment, growing out of reasonable analysis of available evidence, may not satisfy all rigorous methodologists, but it actually applies a standard which is impressive in the public arena. It also points to targets for specific research work.

Walter Vergeiner's paper uses the birth rate criterion and assesses the results of five years of effort in Czechoslovakia as rewarding. Since the perspective of family policy is as coordinator of the diversity of policies affecting family life and interests, and in view of the large number of measures introduced to "close the fertility gap," it may be possible either to attribute what occurred to a specific measure or particular cluster of measures, or to differentiate calendar effects and long-term changes.

This phase of the discussion ends with repetition: To discuss impacts on the family is to begin to differentiate family types and roles within them (families). To measure effects is to state a standard; to specify objectives is to clarify values; to identify what works means to observe and study over a really long time span, while being willing to experiment and control. Some political systems generate such specificity; others must avoid it.

Perspectives on the Idea of Family Policy

As noted above, Neidhardt has commented that a family ministry (and we might substitute "family policy") can be thought of as everything—or as nothing. All public actions may in some sense impact on individuals and families. Almost all such actions also reside in other functional domains. Everything or nothing? Roy Parker adds that there may be "something." Only if it can be something, something delimited, is family policy a useful preoccupation.

Family policy may be defined as what the state does, by action or inaction, to affect people in their roles as family members or to influence the future of the family ("families"?) as an institution. In this context, the family may be broadly defined in ways going beyond what is recognized in family law, to include primary living groups with elements of continuity.

To define family policy in this way is not to deny that it is at times *rationalization* for actions undertaken for other reasons. It is to recognize that at times the family is the object or the vehicle of direct actions directed to itself, and at times the vehicle for policies with external objectives but is nonetheless affected. The family impact of family policy may be direct or indirect, then.

Nor does this view deny that family policy may be embedded in, or an aspect of, social policy in the broadest sense, or of some of the subdivisions of social policy, especially labor market or population policy. Several papers are explicit on this point, even differentiating social (social sector, social service) from societal policy. However, here the record is complex: in some views, family policy may be subordinate as well as superordinate from time to time.

The family, then, is object and vehicle of social policy. Family policy is rationalization or real intent, an area of autonomous policy. Is family policy never, per se, a *field?* Yes, to a limited or to a substantial degree—varying by country—family policy is also field. Governments may assemble a package of programs which make little sense over all except in their family policy intent and may choose to view and to administer them as a family policy program: perhaps family allowances, maternity or parental benefits, child-rearing allowances, some child care programs for infants, other legislation to help parents of young children, possibly abortion and family planning, family advice and counseling. One could argue that the study of these programs and their effects, and the administration of such benefits, constitutes a family policy field. Undeniably, governments with well-developed explicit family policy do more to develop a family policy field, to recognize it, and to give it organizational outlets than do governments which lack explicit and comprehensive policy.

But family policy as field does not constitute the whole of the interest and does not alone justify the scale of current concern. As field, family policy at most usually covers a modest, if significant, domain. It includes programs to be assessed, improved, dropped, added to. It is likely that the major current interest is aroused by what is probably the central and more ambitious claim of family policy to importance: family policy as *perspective*. We have already noted the considerable interest in impact on family as a criterion for social policy. This translates itself, too, into the notion of structural arrangements in government which assign family policy to a level above cabinet departments and operating units, so as to monitor and report on actual or potential family impact, and/or to advocate and/or to contribute to policy development and planning with family interests in mind. The potential significance of this perspective on family policy merits elaboration.

Harold Watts, it will be recalled, describes family policy as "immortality policy." In seeking good outcomes for the family and for society, he believes, family policy must encompass goals relating to quantity, quality, and equality. The quantity issue (number of children) has already been discussed and the quality question introduced. Much of family policy—if it is more than pronatalism—must be concerned with creating that intrafamilial environment which enhances education, socialization, physical development, and optimum capacity to benefit from what is offered in the more formal extrafamilial institutional system. The quality goals may be defined in terms of the "investment" perspective of the human capital economist who says that there is no other basis for public involvement. Or—in an alternative view—such goals may recognize childhood as a stage in its own right and may see government as justifiably interesting itself in the quality of family life, in parent-child relationships, in happiness ("consumption"). In this latter view, public concern is not limited to production, because there are unavoidable processes at work in complex societies; government action or inaction inevitably affects the quality of family life, for better or for worse. Quality relates to citizenship and productive potential—but also to values, comity, satisfaction, even happiness.

Watts introduced yet another dimension. A policy which sees the family as a major vehicle for "immortality" cannot avoid the issue of the family in relation to equality goals. Family experience is so salient that, no matter what the over-all societal commitment, families (being unequal) inevitably produce inequality among the generations which follow. The phenomenon is reported within all the political systems represented by the papers in this volume. It is documented by substantial research. And in these societies, at least, there is not a strong disposition to solve the problem by doing away with the family—or perhaps there is no conviction that there is a good and feasible substitute. Time and again the resiliency of the institution is referred to.

A number of the societies are committed to lessening inequality of people's real-life situations (statuses). Most of them are pledged to equality of opportunity, assuring a "fair game or contest" by eliminating "preventable handicaps or head starts." Watts sums up his view: This is another area where foresight may enable a society to promote the quality of life for future generations by family policies that "prevent the transmission of unnecessary inequality."

Thus the discussion moves (for some observers) beyond the use of family policy only as a criterion of whether the society is doing all that it might to produce more citizens who will be more productive. Family policy as perspective, as criterion, in this view, becomes a subset of a *quality-of-life dimension*. It is here that we believe it attains its maximum validity and offers its greatest challenge.

In the narrower sense of labor market, population, national, or religious objectives, the family is vehicle, rationale, rationalization. In a slightly broader sense, as noted, family policy is field. But as modern societies depart from economic growth and national power, sources of their real (as contrasted with alleged) criteria for societal action, family policy could be something more. Societies do, increasingly, seek their meaning under the banner of equality, social justice, protection of the environment—perhaps not as a substitute for economic growth but as a constraint upon it or as an object on which the products of growth might be expended. In similar fashion, those objectives which may be summed up as "quality of life" may be thought of as including some goals for the primary living unit's relationships and roles.

Family policy as criterion is an effort to operationalize such perspective. For example, we might consider a shorter workday for parents of young children even if we pay a price in over-all production; we might provide work for everyone, because it is better for families and individuals, even at the possible cost of lower productivity and efficiency; we might assure minimum adequate income to all families even if they cannot earn it, and even if such guarantee undercuts some labor market incentives, because all families have a right to survive and it is a better society that can acknowledge this.

But it is essential to face another aspect of the value conflict that makes the subject difficult. In theory, at least, the equality goals might be better pursued outside, or even contrary to, a family policy outlook. As noted, the family, if left alone, is a vehicle which perpetuates and transmits inequalities. The family undermines much social policy aimed at equalization because families are unequal and are most influential during the early years in which children are socialized.

However, at the same time, the family is highly valued and while changing, does not disappear. What is more, it is the most effective instrument to satisfy the quantity-quality objectives generally. Therefore, the challenge of family policy includes the task of inventing means whereby the family may increasingly participate in the effort to assure "take off" by new generations on a reasonably equal basis. The questions raised are: How may the family become an ally? How may the families of the disadvantaged be mobilized? Failing this, the question is whether one can minimize the transmission (using Watt's phrase) of "unnecessary inequality" through the family while protecting its core and valued functions.

In our view, then, the main case for family policy which emerges is along the quality-of-life dimension. Family life helps specify what that dimension may mean. The Norwegian and Swedish papers illustrate one aspect of the thinking, the Hungarian another. Part of the family policy in this sense is, or could be, whatever will be required institutionally to promote sexual equality, including fuller participation by women in all arenas of work and politics. The implications for changed male roles and new family living patterns are just emerging. Child care and social benefits for families with young children are of major interest. The shaping of a modern family policy perspective could take place around efforts to deal with these urgent contemporary tasks.

To align family policy with quality of life is consonant with an old tradition. The family was long recognized as an island in the midst of a growing industrial system, an island governed by other than market policies and relationships. The family was and is a refuge from definitions and rules that recognize productivity and consumption as the only critical dimensions of life. What social policy does in modern times is to elaborate a sector of other than market policies so as to cover distribution and consumption of rights and benefits (social services, social sector, social welfare, social policy). Family policy is a natural and important component of this domain, variously named but clearly recognizable internationally and expanding everywhere.

Many of the goals which modern societies value are individual goals. Individuals achieve, consume, relate, enjoy. Why, therefore, a family policy and not a "people policy"? Certainly there should be a people policy for some purposes. Family policy is offered as a modest field and as a significant perspective in social policy development, but not as the only perspective. Not *only,* yet *also,* family policy, and significantly so, because whereas many goals are individual many people live and develop in family units; and whereas concern for such units may enhance socialization and enrich daily living, to ignore the families may be to miss major opportunities and to create disastrous contradictions.

Many of the papers note a lack of harmonization or an inadequate harmonization of policy from the perspective of family concerns. The family policy criterion, by definition, asks about coherence and consistency and highlights problems and choices. The policy system falls apart if one wishes to affect children and ignores parents, is concerned with women and ignores the consequences for men, and so forth. A systematic perspective, a criterion, a search for harmonization, does have the potential of raising us above program minutiae and facing us with what we have wrought—or have failed to do. Not, of course, that harmonization requires complete coordination or should allow only one pattern, offer only one option. Good policy may be pluralistic and recognize varied preferences and needs, while still being thoughtful about relationships among components. Taxation should not wipe out social insurance goals; education and health ought not to contradict one another as they affect child care programs; schools and employment ought to be in step, not antagonistic, and so on. But from what perspective, with what decision rules? Family well-being if definable and operationalized might become one of the elements around which harmonization is attempted.

Much of this discussion, as do some of the papers, reads as though policy objectives and policy criteria are always to be arrived at deductively, from state and societal goals. Some of those concerned with the subject offer an alternative: inducing policy from people's lives and initiatives. In this view families themselves are actors, positive forces, not merely objects. Different family types can and should clarify their varied needs and preferences. Some families, some categories of families, have affected family policy substantially at critical points, on subjects of concern. It is important to find ways to encourage such process. The perspective is democratic and attractive. Whether it can be translated into an operating policy system producing coherence is in contention.

Among those who have reviewed the fourteen-country experience and discussed it at length, the over-all assessment varies. Jacques Fournier, working in a country with considerable family policy tradition, comments that some countries have made substantial social policy progress without focusing on family policy ("equality" is an alternative), while others have used family policy successfully as a social policy focus.

There are some who see family policy as a valuable tool, an alternative perspective within social policy, a useful way to focus objectives and push toward a degree of harmonization. They are prepared to discuss hard choices and are encouraged by the record thus far. In this view, to organize around family policy is to achieve goal visibility and coherence, not necessarily to establish one general family ministry to administer all such programs or to advocate a unified, monolithic, mandated policy.

Others, represented in the discussion by Gilbert Steiner, arrive at other conclusions. He sees greater likelihood of success if people organize to achieve specific rights and benefits, not to win support for a concept such as family policy. He reads the experience as suggesting the protection of children as the enduring aspect of government endeavors oriented to the family. The needed responses take the form of specific actions and constraints, not general policies or "resolutions." Government structures are not critical in what happens. To him, what is called family policy is actually population policy, women's policy, employment policy, all filtered through a particular prism. Moreover, privacy is a highly placed value everywhere, so one should give priority to alternative ways of strengthening relationships among the small groups of people who constitute families. If government must act it should do so as a last resort, giving preference to business, unions, churches, and various types of voluntary associations.

Certainly the record may be thus interpreted, but one considers whether the voluntary sector can and does play such a role except as it is protected by public social policy. One may ask whether big churches, big unions, and big business are vehicles for more privacy than big government. One may acknowledge people's preference for narrowly specified "causes," while seeking more comprehensive and effective harmonized policies. It is precisely the effort to apply a series of concerns across many domains, and to protect pluralism while avoiding complete policy sprawl, that makes a family policy orientation in social policy potentially interesting, however difficult to achieve.

Were it possible to protect the quality of life in the modern world merely by affirming the privacy value the issue would be simple. Actually, however, family policy may be needed to create conditions for privacy in the modern world. And it is because people value privacy yet also value other things which are in tension with it (equality; large formal institutions, such as schools and universities; economic growth; fair taxation) that social policy is complex. The voluntary sector, business, churches, and unions are certainly important, but if there is to be social initiative via family policy, there is also need for government.

Certainly the prediction may be correct that pluralistic societies may prefer to focus on specifics, not on over-all policy perspectives. Several papers, especially those from Canada, the U.K., and the U.S., document such practice—at least at the manifest level. A demand for more explicit policy could arise because elements of the implicit policy (as described, for example, by Land and Parker in the social security section of their paper) may be unacceptable, or because some goals need to be approached more directly.

Nonetheless, we are reminded by such debate that the outcome is not easily predicted.

Interested in the possibility of family policy and, therefore, seeking family policy decision rules, Lee Rainwater suggests Rawls's "veil of ignorance."[11] In our terms this might be formulated as follows: Assure for each family the minimum conditions that I would want for my own if I did not know in advance what my family membership would be; or, assure for each family role the minimum necessary prerogatives that I might require if I had to occupy it.

It is not clear whether this version of the Golden Rule is any more acceptable universally than the original, but the value question remains persistent. It is one thing to agree that there are things which cannot and should not be placed on a human investment balance sheet. It is another to acknowledge that such pronouncements do not, of themselves, constitute an alternative, specific scale. Choices must be made. Scarce resources are to be allocated; priorities to be set; outcomes to be pronounced as favorable or unfavorable. Those who would expand and strengthen social policy in general, or would advocate a significant place for family policy in particular, must therefore prepare to deal with specifics. Family policy will not be a usable criterion or perspective, and not an attractive surrogate for "quality of life" in the primary living unit, unless it can be operationalized. This will require being very specific about objectives, desired states, preferred roles, standards. We need more knowledge and we also need more clarity as to our values. We need to learn to assess the states of families and their members

[11] John Rawls, *A Theory of Justice* (Cambridge, Mass.: Harvard University Press, 1971), pp. 136–42.

from identifiable value perspectives. It is far from obvious which societies want to take on this search, and how extensively. It is quite certain that even if they accept the idea of family policy, societies should and will differ in their desired states for families, and thus their policies. None will be exercising wise policy if they ignore their many family forms and types and the consequent need for internal diversity and alternatives.

We are reminded by Vera Shlakman and Mary Jo Bane, among others, that historically it was not the progressive social reformers who raised the banner of family policy. Yet a variety of new issues (how will it be possible for working couples to rear children successfully?) and new values (loosely grouped under the "quality-of-life" rubric) cause countries to put new content into the concept. Whether from Poland and Hungary or from France, Finland, and Israel (to illustrate), there is evidence that what we have here is something different, or at least something that can be different. But it requires thinking and watching.

We conclude that family policy as field is a small sector in countries without explicit family policy and a larger sector where there is explicit family policy. After all, willingness to be explicit is associated with readiness to set goals and to use more of the available instruments quite deliberately.

But whether in countries in which it is a small field or in those where the field is large, the truly interesting potential of family policy is as a source of criteria, as inspiration for decision rules, for social policy. For countries like the U.S., Canada, and the U.K., in any case, where there are few true advocates of a unitary, comprehensive explicit family policy, the issue of impact of action on the family is nonetheless of major interest. Other countries, with explicit policies, are inevitably concerned with policy success and with better organization for the programs and policies that constitute the field for them.

Family policy as perspective is the shared element and probably the most significant for the future. Functional organization of government rather than age-group or interest-group structuring is attractive, but some specifications of decision rules is also essential. However, it should be stressed that family policy is only one source of criteria among several, and it is a source which requires considerable specification and operationalizing if it is to serve in this way. The value dimensions will need to be specified and probed, the knowledge components strengthened. These are no simple tasks, yet they are worth the doing. Family policy assumes considerable interest as the quality-of-life goal attracts increasing public attention and support.

Here one notes the differences between those who focus on the family as a production center (producing children) and those with a more sociological orientation who also see the family as a consumption unit and a source of goal-sets outside the economy.

In any case, whether as a strong or a weak field, *and perhaps primarily as a criterion,* family policy is probably most useful as an organizing principle.

In our view, family policy as criterion has established its identity thus far mainly in relation to families with children. While interesting questions are raised about the aged, the handicapped, and perhaps adolescents, other social policy principles and structures have tended to dominate in relation to other than parent-child structures and roles. Here too, however, the experience of the near future promises to be instructive and significant.

Whether as field or as criterion, in some countries, and certainly in the U.S., family policy will need to protect and encourage diversity and pluralism. Ethnic and racial values cannot be ignored. We also have noted the need to acknowledge diverse family forms and styles as well as geographic variation in values. Pluralism is multidimensional. Henning Friis comments that no one would dream of a single monolithic policy for all of Europe; why, then, consider one for all of the United States? An alternative formulation puts it this way: the policy, if adopted, should encourage diversity, or at the least be neutral among a variety of acceptable alternatives in style, roles, and directions.

American political and cultural diversity thus far has precluded explicit family policy and is behind much current hesitancy. The issue here, as everywhere, will be whether the possible payoff in decreased policy sprawl and coherent public goals will be worth the risks. The decision remains, for this subject as for others, in the realm of politics. Scholars and analysts may define and make proposals about "quantity, quality, and equality"—and for whom. But governmental leaders and citizens must clarify, through the political process, just what it is that people want and how much they want it.

Tables

Table 1 Population and Area

Country	Total Population (thousands) [a]	World Rank by Population/Area [b]	Population Density [b] (per sq. mi.)	Rate of Population Increase [b]	Percent of Population in Urban Areas [c]	Percent of Population 65 and Over [d]	Average Household Size (persons) [e]
Austria	7,545	66	106	234	0.5	53	14.3	2.9 (1972)
Canada	22,479	31	2	5	1.3	78	8.1	3.7 (1967)
Czechoslovakia	14,686	44	91	299	0.6	65	11.3	3.6 (1961)
Denmark	5,045	80	116	304	0.6	82	12.7	2.7 (1970)
Federal Republic of Germany	62,041	10	69	650	0.6	83	13.4	2.7 (1972)
Finland	4,688	84	56	36	0.4	56	9.7	3.0 (1970)
France	52,507	15	44	250	0.8	76	13.1	3.1 (1968)
Hungary	10,478	54	104	296	0.3	48	11.5	3.0 (1973)
Israel	3,299	96	131	413	3.2	84	7.3	3.8 (1971)
Norway	3,985	92	58	31	0.7	45	13.1	2.9 (1970)
Poland	33,691	21	60	281	0.9	57	8.4	3.4 (1970)
Sweden	8,161	64	49	47	0.4	83	14.2	2.6 (1970)
United Kingdom	55,968	13	71	595	0.2	78	13.4	2.9 (1971)
United States	211,909	4	4	60	0.8	75	10.1	3.2 (1970)

[a] *Statistical Yearbook, 1975* (New York: United Nations, 1976). Midyear estimates of 1974 population.
[b] *Statistical Abstract of the United States, 1976* (Washington, D.C.: Government Printing Office, 1977). Figures for 1974.
[c] *World Social Report, 1974* (New York: United Nations, 1975). Estimated figures for 1975.
[d] *Ibid.* Figures for Eastern European countries are based on 1970; for Western Europe, 1972; for North America, 1971; for Israel, 1975.
[e] *Statistical Yearbook, 1974* (New York: United Nations, 1975). United Kingdom includes only England and Wales.

Table 2 Births, Deaths, Fertility, and Life Expectancy

Country	Birth Rate (per 1,000 population)	Fertility (per 1,000 females 10–49)	Death Rate (per 1,000)	Infant Mortality	Life Expectancy at Birth Male	Female
Austria	12.9	48.5	12.5	23.5	67.4	74.7 (1974)
Canada	15.4	51.6	7.5	15.6	69.3	76.4 (1970–72)
Czechoslovakia	19.8	66.3	11.7	20.4	66.8	73.6 (1973)
Denmark	14.1	53.2	10.2	11.5	70.8	76.3 (1972–73)
Federal Republic of Germany	10.1	37.5	11.7	21.1	67.6	74.1 (1971–73)
Finland	13.3	45.3	9.6	10.2	66.6	74.9 (1972)
France	15.2	61.6	10.4	12.1	68.6	74.4 (1972)
Hungary	17.8	62.2	12.0	34.3	66.9	72.6 (1972)
Israel	28.2	95.6	7.3	23.5	70.2	73.2 (1973)
Norway	15.0	58.0	9.9	10.5	71.3	77.6 (1972–73)
Poland	18.4	59.9	8.2	23.5	67.8	74.6 (1974)
Sweden	13.5	52.3	10.6	9.6	72.1	77.7 (1973)
United Kingdom	13.3	50.5	11.9	16.3	67.8	73.8 (1968–70)
United States	15.0	50.8	9.1	16.6	67.4	75.2 (1972)

SOURCE: *Statistical Abstract of the United States, 1976* (Washington, D.C.: Government Printing Office, 1977). All figures are based on 1974 except the life expectancy figures, which are based on the years in parentheses.

Table 3 Economic, Social Conditions, Employment

Country	GNP per capita [a] (dollars)	Education Expenditures as Percent of GNP [b]	Telephones per 100 Population [c]	Labor Force as Percent of Population [d]	Female Workers as Percent of Female Population [e]	Female Workers as Percent of Labor Force [f]	Average Hours Work per Week [g]
Austria	3,510	5.0	26.2	41.5 (1971)	49.0	38.7	34.0
Canada	5,450	8.5	55.0	40.9 (1971)	44.5	35.0	38.4
Czechoslovakia	2,870	4.6	16.8	48.7 (1970)	64.2	44.6	43.4
Denmark	5,210	7.0	42.8	49.0 (1974)	61.9	40.9	34.8
Federal Republic of Germany	5,320	4.0	30.2	43.4 (1975)	48.2	37.2	40.4
Finland	3,600	6.3	35.8	48.1 (1975)	65.1	46.5	38.4
France	4,540	3.6	23.6	41.9 (1976)	44.0	36.1	41.8
Hungary	1,850	4.4	9.6	48.4 (1975)	57.3	44.0	39.3
Israel	3,010	8.2	21.7	32.9 (1974)	33.8	32.0	41.0
Norway	4,660	7.3	33.9	37.7 (1970)	33.1	27.7	33.6
Poland	2,090	5.2	7.1	52.0 (1974)	66.0	46.0	41.5
Sweden	5,910	7.9	63.3	49.7 (1975)	66.5	42.4	35.0
United Kingdom	3,060	5.9	36.6	46.3 (1971)	52.0	37.0	44.0
United States	6,200	6.5	67.7	44.5 (1975)	53.2	39.1	39.4

[a] *World Tables, 1976* (Geneva, Switzerland: World Bank, 1977). In 1973 U.S. dollars.

[b] *UNESCO Statistical Yearbook, 1974.* Public expenditures only. All figures are for 1972 except those for Canada, Finland, Israel, and United Kingdom, which are for 1971.

[c] *Statistical Abstract of the United States, 1976.* Figures are for 1974.

[d] *Yearbook of Labour Statistics, 1976* (Geneva, Switzerland: International Labour Office, 1977). Figures include both employed and unemployed, male and female, all ages.

[e] *Ibid.* Covering ages 15–64 in all but the following: Israel, 14–64; Norway, Sweden, and United States, 16–64. Figures for same year as labor force data except: France, 1968; Hungary and Poland, 1970.

[f] *Ibid.* All ages. Same year as total labor force data.

[g] *Ibid.* In manufacturing. For 1975 except Finland, Norway, Poland, and United Kingdom, which are for 1974, and Sweden, which are for 1973. The figures for Norway and United Kingdom are for male workers only.

PARTICIPANTS, INTERNATIONAL WORKING PARTY ON FAMILY POLICY
April 17–21, 1977

Arden House
Harriman, New York

Dr. Andrew Armitage
Professor,
School of Social Welfare,
University of Calgary,
Calgary, Alberta, Canada

Dr. Mary Jo Bane
Associate Director,
Center for the Study of Women in
  Higher Education and the Professions,
Wellesley College,
Wellesley, Mass., U.S.

Dr. Carolyn Shaw Bell
Department of Economics,
Wellesley College,
Wellesley, Mass., U.S.

Susan Berresford
Program Officer,
Ford Foundation,
New York, New York, U.S.

Dr. Bernice T. Eiduson
Family Styles Project
University of California, Los Angeles,
Los Angeles, Calif., U.S.

Dr. Zsuzsa Ferge
Section Chief and Senior Researcher,
Institute of Sociology,
Hungarian Academy of Sciences,
Budapest, Hungary

Mrs. Barbara Finberg
Program Associate,
Carnegie Corporation,
New York, New York, U.S.

Jacques Fournier
Maître des Requêtes,
Conseil d'Etat,
Paris, France

Dr. Henning Friis
Director,
Danish National Institute of Social Re-
  search,
Copenhagen, Denmark

Dr. Irwin Garfinkel
Director,
Institute for Research on Poverty,
University of Wisconsin,
Madison, Wis., U.S.

Participant affiliations are listed as of the conference dates.

Mitchell I. Ginsberg
Dean,
Columbia University School of Social
 Work,
New York, New York, U.S.

Dr. David Goslin
Executive Director,
Assembly of Behavioral and Social
 Sciences,
National Research Council,
Washington, D.C., U.S.

Mrs. Dona Hamilton[1]
Doctoral candidate,
Columbia University School of Social
 Work,
New York, New York, U.S.

Dr. Hildur Ve Henriksen
Magister of Sociology,
Institute for Social Research,
Oslo, Norway

Robert F. Higgins
Executive Director,
Robert Sterling Clark Foundation, Inc.,
New York, New York, U.S.

Dr. Marjorie Honig
Director, Division of Basic Research,
Bureau of Research and Planning,
National Insurance Institute,
Jerusalem, Israel

Mrs. Joanne Jennings[1]
Doctoral candidate,
Columbia University School of Social
 Work,
New York, New York, U.S.

Allen Jensen
Staff, House Ways and Means Commit-
 tee,
House of Representatives,
Congress of the United States,
Washington, D.C., U.S.

A. Sidney Johnson III
Director,
Family Impact Seminar,
Institute for Educational Leadership,
George Washington University,
Washington, D.C., U.S.

Mary Ann Jones[1]
Doctoral candidate,
Columbia University School of Social
 Work,
New York, New York, U.S.

Dr. Alfred J. Kahn
Co-Director,
Cross-National Studies,
Columbia University School of Social
 Work,
New York, New York, U.S.

Dr. Sheila B. Kamerman
Co-Director,
Cross-National Studies,
Columbia University School of Social
 Work,
New York, New York, U.S.

Dr. Harry Krause
Professor,
College of Law,
University of Illinois,
Champaign, Ill., U.S.

Dr. Edith Krebs
Director,
Women's Section,
Chamber of Labor,
Vienna, Austria

Dr. Dorothy Lally
Chief, Division of International Activi-
 ties,
Office of Human Development, HEW,
Washington, D.C., U.S.

Dr. Hilary Land
Lecturer, Department of Social Adminis-
 tration and Social Work,
University of Bristol,
Bristol, England

---

[1] Recorder at Conference.

Dr. Luis Laosa
Division of Educational Studies,
Educational Testing Service,
Princeton, N.J., U.S.

Dr. Trude Lash
Senior Research Scientist,
Foundation for Child Development,
New York, New York, U.S.

Dr. Rita Liljeström
Professor of Sociology,
Göteborg University,
Göteborg, Sweden

Dr. Jarl Lindgren
Director of Research,
Population Research Institute,
Helsinki, Finland

Norman V. Lourie
Executive Deputy Secretary,
Department of Public Welfare,
Harrisburg, Pa., U.S.

Dr. Brenda McGowan
Assistant Professor,
Columbia University School of Social
  Work,
New York, New York, U.S.

Georgia McMurray
Director,
Department of Public Affairs,
Community Service Society of New
  York,
New York, New York, U.S.

Dr. Rosa Celeste Marin
Dean Emeritus,
School of Social Work,
University of Puerto Rico,
Santurce, Puerto Rico, U.S.

Steven A. Minter
Program Officer,
Cleveland Foundation,
Cleveland, Ohio, U.S.

Dr. Robert Moroney
Professor, Department of City and
  Regional Planning,
University of North Carolina,
Chapel Hill, N.C., U.S.

Dr. Friedhelm Neidhardt
Director and Professor of Sociology,
Sociological Research Institute,
University of Cologne,
Cologne, Federal Republic of Germany

Dr. Arthur J. Norton
Chief,
Marriage and Family Branch,
Bureau of the Census,
Washington, D.C., U.S.

Dr. Janet Norwood
Deputy Commissioner,
Bureau of Labor Statistics,
Washington, D.C., U.S.

T. M. Jim Parham
Office of Intergovernmental Relations,
Office of the President,
Washington, D.C., U.S.

Dr. Roy Parker
Professor, Department of Social Ad-
  ministration and Social Work,
University of Bristol,
Bristol, England

Dr. Robert Perlman
Professor, Florence Heller Graduate
  School,
Brandeis University,
Waltham, Mass., U.S.

Mrs. Martha Phillips
Assistant Minority Council,
House Ways and Means Committee,
House of Representatives,
Congress of the United States,
Washington, D.C., U.S.

Mme. Nicole Questiaux
Maître des Requêtes,
Conseil d'Etat,
Paris, France

Dr. Lee Rainwater
Professor of Sociology,
Harvard University,
Cambridge, Mass., U.S.

Virginia Reno
Social Science Research Analyst,
Office of Research and Statistics,
Social Security Administration, HEW,
Washington, D.C., U.S.

Dr. Halbert B. Robinson
Professor of Psychology,
University of Washington,
Seattle, Wash., U.S.

Dr. Margaret K. Rosenheim
Professor of Social Policy,
School of Social Service Administration,
University of Chicago,
Chicago, Ill., U.S.

Saul Rosoff
Acting Director,
Office of Child Development, HEW,
Washington, D.C., U.S.

Dr. Terry Saario
Program Officer,
Ford Foundation,
New York, New York, U.S.

Rudolfo B. Sanchez
National Director,
National Coalition of Spanish-speaking
  Mental Health Organizations,
Washington, D.C., U.S.

Dr. Isabel V. Sawhill
Director,
Program of Research on Women,
Urban Institute
Washington, D.C., U.S.

Dr. Nira Shamai
Deputy Director for Research Planning,
National Insurance Institute,
Jerusalem, Israel

Dr. Vera Shlakman
Professor,
Columbia University School of Social
  Work,
New York, New York, U.S.

George Silver, M.D.
Director, Health Policy Project,
Yale University School of Medicine,
New Haven, Conn., U.S.

Dr. David B. Smith
Director,
Office of Program Analysis and Evalua-
  tion, HEW,
Washington, D.C., U.S.

Mrs. Virginia Smyth
Acting Deputy Administrator,
Social and Rehabilitation Services,
  HEW,
Washington, D.C., U.S.

Dr. Magdalena Sokołowska
Professor,
Institute of Sociology and Philosophy,
Polish Academy of Sciences,
Warsaw, Poland

Dr. Gilbert Steiner
Senior Fellow,
Brookings Institution,
Washington, D.C., U.S.

Dr. Jacob Vedel-Petersen
Program Director,
Danish National Institute of Social Re-
  search,
Copenhagen, Denmark

Dr. Margaret Watson
Special Assistant,
Office of the Secretary for Human De-
  velopment, HEW,
Washington, D.C., U.S.

Dr. Harold W. Watts
Director,
Center for the Social Sciences,
Columbia University,
New York, New York, U.S.

Peter Weitz
Program Officer,
The German Marshall Fund of the
 United States,
Washington, D.C., U.S.

Index